Communications in Computer and Information Science 1579

More information about this series at https://link.springer.com/bookseries/7899

Somnath Mukhopadhyay · Sunita Sarkar ·
Paramartha Dutta · Jyotsna Kumar Mandal ·
Sudipta Roy (Eds.)

Computational Intelligence in Communications and Business Analytics

4th International Conference, CICBA 2022
Silchar, India, January 7–8, 2022
Revised Selected Papers

 Springer

Editors
Somnath Mukhopadhyay
Assam University
Silchar, India

Sunita Sarkar
Assam University
Silchar, India

Paramartha Dutta
Visva-Bharati University
Santiniketan, West Bengal, India

Jyotsna Kumar Mandal
University of Kalyani
Nadia, India

Sudipta Roy
Assam University
Silchar, India

ISSN 1865-0929   ISSN 1865-0937 (electronic)
Communications in Computer and Information Science
ISBN 978-3-031-10765-8   ISBN 978-3-031-10766-5 (eBook)
https://doi.org/10.1007/978-3-031-10766-5

This Springer imprint is published by the registered company Springer Nature Switzerland AG
The registered company address is: Gewerbestrasse 11, 6330 Cham, Switzerland

Preface

It has always been a source of academic attraction and a challenge to act in the capacity of an editor of a conference proceedings in Springer's CCIS series. The venture of the International Conference on Computational Intelligence in Communications and Business Analytics (CICBA) started in 2017. Being encouraged by the overwhelming response and enthusiasm among the research community, it was felt that it would be an academic injustice if CICBA wasn't converted into a conference series. Accordingly, the second event took place in 2018, with the third in 2021 and the fourth in 2022. Every time an edition of CICBA has ended, the motivation in favor of organizing an even better event has captured the topmost challenge in the agenda. Every time a conference in the series has been a grand success, the endeavour to make the next event in the series more successful, taking into account the lessons learnt from the previous edition, has become imperative. This was especially challenging for the third CICBA conference (2021) as it had to be conducted virtually, in view of the global COVID-19 pandemic.

There was serious apprehension as to whether it would at all be possible to organize the fourth conference in the series (CICBA 2022). It was indeed a matter of relief to all the stakeholders that the Department of Computer Science and Engineering of Assam University, Silchar, India, was able to host an in-person event, leaving behind any apprehension. Now that the entire world is coming out of the shackles of COVID-19, the effort rendered by Assam University deserves kudos. It has been a trying time as we were unsure if an adequate number of good submissions would be received against the backdrop of the prolonged pandemic. It is truly a matter of pleasure, therefore, that there were many meritorious submissions out of which some sailed through peer review to make their appearance in this CCIS proceedings of CICBA 2022.

The peer review policy was extremely stringent for the selection of papers, from initial submission to final acceptance. In the initial stage, we applied our discretion for desk rejection; this was followed by a double-blind peer review process. All papers were subjected to at least three reviews, and a consensus among the reviewers was required to ensure acceptance. Accordingly, out of 107 initial submissions, 13 short papers and 21 full papers were finally accepted for presentation and subsequent publication in the proceedings.

Coming to the composition of the papers appearing in the proceedings, we have categorized them broadly into three domains:

(i) Computational Intelligence (12 contributions),
(ii) Computational Intelligence in Communication (5 contributions), and
(iii) Computational Intelligence in Analytics (17 contributions).

It is needless to mention that all these papers are highly commendable in a technical sense.

We would like to take this opportunity to express our sincere gratitude to Springer, as our publishing partner, for making this effort a success. Moreover, without the impressive submissions made by the authors such an endeavour would not have been possible, not to speak of the active role played by the reviewers who ensured the technical level attained by this proceedings.

In summary, we would like to thank all the stakeholders for their wholehearted cooperation.

Happy reading!!!

Somnath Mukhopadhyay
Sunita Sarkar
Paramartha Dutta
Jyotsna Kumar Mandal
Sudipta Roy

Organization

Chief Patron

Dilip Chandra Nath   Assam University, India

Patron

Laxmi Narayan Sethi   Assam University, India

General Chair

Sushmita Mitra   Indian Statistical Institute Kolkata, India

Organizing Chair

Sudipta Roy   Assam University, India

Program Committee Chairs

Somnath Mukhopadhyay	Assam University, India
Sunita Sarkar	Assam University, India
Paramartha Dutta	Visva-Bharati University, India
J. K. Mandal	Kalyani University, India

International Advisory Board

Amit Konar	Jadavpur University, India
A. Damodaram	Jawaharlal Nehru Technological University, India
Aynur Unal	DigitalMonozukuri, USA
Atal Chowdhury	Jadavpur University, India
Banshidhar Majhi	IIIT Kanchipuram, India
Carlos A. Coello Coello	CINVESTAV-IPN, Mexico
Edward Tsang	University of Essex, UK
Hisao Ishibuchi	Southern University of Science and Technology, China
Kalyanmoy Deb	Michigan State University, USA
L. M. Patnaik	IISc Bangalore, India
PabitraMitra	Indian Institute of Technology Kharagpur, India
Satish Narayana Srirama	University of Tartu, Estonia

Subir Sarkar	Jadavpur University, India
P. N. Suganthan	Nanyang Technological University, Singapore
Umapada Pal	Indian Statistical Institute Kolkata, India

Organizing Committee

Mousum Handique	Assam University, India
Tapodhir Acharjee	Assam University, India
Sourish Dhar	Assam University, India
Abhijit Biswas	Assam University, India
Bhagaban Swain	Assam University, India
Arnab Paul	Assam University, India
Niranjan Wangjam Singh	Assam University, India

Technical Program Committee

Alok Chakraborty	National Institute of Technology Meghalaya, India
Anamitra Roy Chaudhury	IBM Research, New Delhi, India
Angsuman Sarkar	Kalyani Government Engineering College, India
Animesh Biswas	Kalyani University, India
Anirban Chakraborty	IISc Bangalore, India
Anirban Mukhopadhyay	University of Kalyani, India
Arindam Sarkar	Belur Vidyamandir, India
Arnab Majhi	NEHU, India
Arundhati Bagchi Misra	Saginaw Valley State University, USA
Asif Ekbal	Indian Institute of Technology Patna, India
B. B. Pal	University of Kalyani, India
B. K. Panigrahi	Indian Institute of Technology Delhi, India
Basabi Chakraborty	Iwate Prefectural University, Japan
Biswapati Jana	Vidyasagar University, India
Chandreyee Chowdhury	Jadavpur University, India
Debaprasad Das	Assam University, India
Debarka Mukhopadhyay	Christ University, India
Debashis De	Maulana Abul Kalam Azad University of Technology, India
Debasish Chakraborty	ISRO Kolkata, India
Debotosh Bhattacharjee	Jadavpur University, India
Deepsubhra Guha Roy	University of Tartu, Estonia
Dhananjay Bhattacharyya	Saha Institute of Nuclear Physics, India
Dilip Kumar Pratihar	Indian Institute of Technology Kharagpur, India
Ganapati Panda	Indian Institute of Technology Bhubaneswar, India
Girijasankar Mallik	Western Sydney University, Australia

Himadri Dutta	Kalyani Government Engineering College, India
Indrajit Saha	National Institute of Technical Teachers' Training and Research, Kolkata, India
Indranil Ghosh	Calcutta Business School, India
J. K. Singh	Jadavpur University, India
Jyoti Prakash Singh	National Institute of Technology Patna, India
Kakali Dutta	Visva-Bharati University, India
Kamal Sarkar	Jadavpur University, India
Kamrul Alam Khan	Jagannath University, Bangladesh
Kartick Chandra Mondal	Jadavpur University, India
Kaushik Dassharma	Calcutta University, India
Kolin Paul	Indian Institute of Technology Delhi, India
Koushik Dasgupta	Kalyani Government Engineering College, India
Koushik Majumder	Maulana Abul Kalam Azad University of Technology, India
Koushik Mondal	Indian Institute of Technology (ISM) Dhanbad, India
Kousik Roy	West Bengal State University, India
Krishnendu Chakraborty	Government College of Engineering and Ceramic Technology, India
Mili Ghosh	Visva-Bharati University, India
Mita Nasipuri	Jadavpur University, India
Mohammed Hasanuzzaman	Cork Institute of Technology, Ireland
Moirangthem Marjit Singh	NERIST, India
Moutushi Singh	Institute of Engineering & Management, India
Mrinal Kanti Bhowmik	Tripura University, India
Nabendu Chaki	University of Calcutta, India
Nibaran Das	Jadavpur University, India
Nilanjana Dutta Roy	Institute of Engineering and Management, India
Partha Pakray	National Institute of Technology Silchar, India
Partha Pratim Sahu	Tezpur University, India
Parthajit Roy	University of Burdwan, India
Pawan K. Singh	Jadvpur University, India
Prasanta K. Jana	Indian Institute of Technology (ISM) Dhanbad, India
Prashant R. Nair	Amrita Vishwa Vidyapeetham, India
Priya Saha	Lovely Professional University, India
Rajdeep Chakraborty	Netaji Subhas Institute of Technology, India
Ram Sarkar	Jadavpur University, India
Ranjita Das	National Institute of Technology Mizoram, India
Ravi Subban	Pondichery University, India
S. K. Behera	National Institute of Technology Rourkela, India

Samarjit Kar	National Institute of Technology Durgapur, India
Samir Roy	NITTTR, Kolkata, India
Samiran Chattopadhyay	Jadavpur University, India
Sankhayan Choudhury	University of Calcutta, India
Santi P. Maity	Indian Institute of Engineering Science and Technology, Shibpur, India
Sharmistha Neogy	Jadavpur University, India
Siddhartha Bhattacharyya	Rajnagar Mahavidyalaya, India
Sk. Obaidullah	Aliah University, India
Soumya Pandit	University of Calcutta, India
Sriparna Saha	Indian Institute of Technology Patna, India
Subarna Shakya	Tribhuvan University, Nepal
Subhadip Basu	Jadavpur University, India
Subrata Banerjee	National Institute of Technology Durgapur, India
Sudhakar Sahoo	Institute of Mathematics and Applications, Bhubneshwar, India
Sudhakar Tripathi	National Institute of Technology Patna, India
Sujoy Chatterjee	UPES Dehradun, India
Sukumar Nandi	Indian Institute of Technology Guwahati, India
Suman Lata Tripathi	Lovely Professional University, India
Swapan Kumar Mandal	Kalyani Government Engineering College, India
Tamal Datta Chaudhury	Calcutta Business School, India
Tandra Pal	National Institute of Technology Durgapur, India
Tanmoy Chakraborty	IIIT Delhi, India
Tanushyam Chattopadyay	TCS Innovations Kolkata, India
Varun Kumar Ojha	University of Reading, UK

Contents

Computational Intelligence

A Brief Review on Multi-Attribute Decision Making in the Emerging Fields of Computer Science

Satyabrata Nath[1]([✉]) [ID], Purnendu Das[1] [ID], and Pradip Debnath[2] [ID]

[1] Department of Computer Science, Assam University, Silchar, Assam, India
satyabratanath12@gmail.com
[2] Department of Applied Science and Humanities, Assam University, Silchar, Assam, India

Abstract. The decision-making mechanism plays a critical role in assisting experts to estimate and choose the best potential alternatives in this technical age. Multi-Attribute Decision Making (MADM) approaches are commonly utilized in many environments where there are several criteria that need to be evaluated and it is highly challenging to find the best solution. Many MADM innovations have been implemented over the past couple of decades in many fields of computer science that have enabled decision-makers to reach eminent choices. This paper explored the usage of MADM, which is a sub-domain of Multi-Criteria Decision Making, and its applications in 3 emerging and trending computer science fields viz., Cloud Computing, Internet of Things (IoT) and Big Data.

Keywords: Decision-making · MADM · Computer science

1 Introduction

The field of computer science in the 21st century is dominating the globe in every aspect because of its abundant applications in almost every sector providing a simplified, dependable, and resilient process ecosystem. Decision-making is a vital and day-to-day procedure that can be far more challenging for human experts due to the enormous number of criteria that must be considered to produce an effective solution. Most of the real-world problems related to decision-making are vague and their goals and consequences of actions are imprecise [1]. Decision-making strives to find the best solution for an issue. The decision-maker decides to investigate numerous alternatives and choose from a variety of options in order to achieve the desired result [2, 3]. This could be statistical analysis, quantitative or qualitative analysis, or survey to achieve the solution satisfying requirements and reducing the probable conflict on problem definition. Multi-Attribute Decision Making (MADM) takes into account a highly recognized area of organizational analysis that has proved its efficacy in solving various complex real-world decision-making problems containing multiple conflicting attributes [4]. Prioritization is also one of the factors which have to be considered with increasing alternatives [5]. The complexity of the system also rises with the active involvement of the stakeholders in the system design [6].

S. Mukhopadhyay et al. (Eds.): CICBA 2022, CCIS 1579, pp. 3–18, 2022.
https://doi.org/10.1007/978-3-031-10766-5_1

In this paper, a brief six-year (2016–2021) review analysis is carried out on the applications of MADM in three prominent computer science fields consisting of cloud computing, internet of things (IoT) and big data. The motive behind this paper is to examine and classify current trends in MADM applications in different fields of computer science and to address the causes that are taken into account in these areas by the different MADM methods. The study is limited to publications and reputed conferences from authentic and reliable journals from which 60 papers were finalized from the respective areas. This is not an exhaustive analysis, and there would likely be several MADM implementations in unpublished papers.

The paper that remains is structured as follows. We define MADM and its distinct methods briefly in Sect. 2. In Sect. 3, the observation and applications of MADM are described for the respective domains along with tabular and pictorial representations. Section 4 comprises a detailed discussion of the respective MADM methods followed by an overall conclusion in Sect. 5.

2   An Overview of MADM and Its Associated Techniques

MADM methods are one of the two broad categories of Multi-Criteria Decision Making (MCDM) where the number of alternatives is discrete requiring inter and intra attribute comparison where the solution is based on preferences of the alternatives. When the number of choices is infinitely large or continuous, it is solved using another category of MCDM called Multi-Objective Decision Making (MODM) [7]. The MADM methods can further be classified based on decision strategies into outranking methods, ranking methods, fuzzy methods, hybrid methods and other methods [8]. We can see the hierarchical representation of MCDM in Fig. 1. and the key steps of the decision-making process can be observed in Fig. 2.

2.1   Outranking Methods

Outranking approaches are often applied to discrete choice problems since they emphasize pairwise comparisons of alternatives. Most outranking procedures begin with a decision matrix that describes the performance of the alternatives to be assessed in relation to defined criteria [9]. Concordance analysis is used in outranking-based approaches such as ELECTRE [10, 11] and PROMETHEE [12]. It generates an outranking relationship between concordance and discordance matrices and utilizes its indices to select the optimal alternative. Although these approaches are widely used, they are time intensive due to complex calculations. Another famous MADM technique is BWM [13] which utilizes pairwise comparison for decision making.

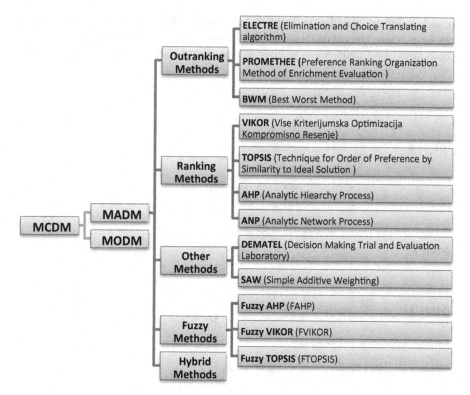

Fig. 1. A representation of MCDM methods.

2.2   Ranking Methods

Ranking based methods perform prioritization of the alternatives after thorough evaluations depending upon the factors that are based on ratio, geometrical mean and different types of distance measures, mainly Euclidean distance. There are various ranking approaches among which AHP [14], TOPSIS [15], ANP [16], VIKOR [17] are more popular.

2.3   Other Methods

Many other methods have been developed with different working principles to efficiently deal with MADM problems. DEMATEL is an effective method for evaluating the interdependence of components and identifying the crucial ones through the use of a visual conceptual framework [18]. Whereas SAW is another effective method based on alternative's weights [19].

2.4   Fuzzy and Hybrid Methods

There may be certain scenarios where the decision-maker faces uncertainties and imprecise data. For these, the implication of fuzzy sets is considered instead of traditional approaches. Fuzzy AHP, Fuzzy TOPSIS and Fuzzy VIKOR are some of the popular fuzzy approaches. Hybrid methods are also gaining popularity for a couple of decades as multiple existing methods can be integrated to achieve better decision-making results.

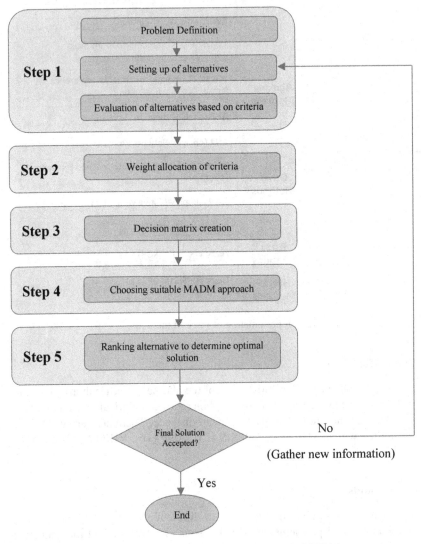

Fig. 2. Key Decision-Making steps in MADM

3   Assessment of MADM Approaches in Different Domains

In this section, we examined the three domains of computer science and portrayed them with tables and charts. The goal of this study is to examine and determine how these

MADM techniques have been used and how useful they are in assisting researchers in decision-making.

3.1 MADM Applications in the Field of Cloud Computing

Cloud computing is a constantly growing industry that offers large-scale storage and resources as cloud services over the internet [20]. Given the allure of cloud computing and its various commercial benefits, many organizations have sought to create cloud apps [21]. As many companies offer services at different cost, performance, and security levels, it becomes difficult for operators to choose the best cloud service, leading to a multi-criteria decision problem, and the usage of MADM approaches plays a part in assisting users. Table 1 summarizes some of the research done in the field of cloud computing using various MADM methodologies and its frequency distribution can be seen in Fig. 3.

Table 1. MADM approaches in Cloud Computing

Year	Aim of the paper	Methods applied
2016	Best cloud model selection [22]	Fuzzy (Delphi + AHP)
	Ranking of services [23]	AHP + PROMETHEE
	Cloud service selection [24]	Fuzzy AHP
	Improving cloud service selection [25]	Fuzzy (AHP + TOPSIS)
	Cloud service performance evaluation [26]	TOPSIS + Choquet integral operator
	Rank cloud service providers [27]	AHP
2017	Task scheduling of cloud resources [28]	ELECTRE III + Differential equation
	Evaluate TOE factors of cloud service [29]	Fuzzy TOPSIS
	Identification of trustworthy cloud service providers [30]	Fuzzy PROMETHEE
	Determining trustworthiness of cloud services [31]	Improved TOPSIS
	Selecting suitable service provider [32]	Fuzzy AHP
	Selection of best node [33]	TOPSIS
2018	Cloud service selection [34]	AHP + TOPSIS
	Selection of cloud computing technology providers [35]	AHP, COPRAS, MULTIMOORA and VIKOR
	Selection of cloud services [36]	BWM
	Estimating quality of cloud services [37]	Neutrosophic AHP

(*continued*)

Table 1. (*continued*)

Year	Aim of the paper	Methods applied
2019	Ranking Smart Data service providers [38]	DEMATEL + ANP
	Selection of cloud services [39]	Grey TOPSIS + AHP
2020	Cloud service selection and ranking [40]	BWM + TOPSIS
	Selecting cloud scheduling solutions [41]	BWM + TOPSIS
	Selection of cloud services using an integrated approach [42]	BWM + TOPSIS
2021	Efficient ranking of cloud services [43]	AHP
2021	Tackling risks in cloud computing [44]	Fuzzy VIKOR

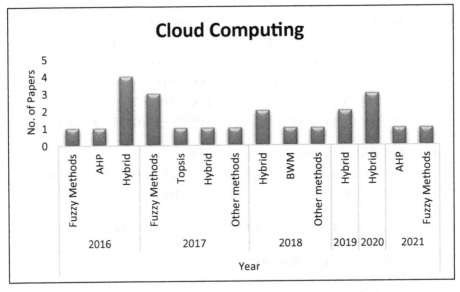

Fig. 3. Frequency distribution of papers in Cloud Computing

3.2 MADM Applications in the Field of IoT

The Internet of Things (IoT) is a framework of numerous products incorporated into sensor systems that generate, send, and analyze data to the cloud to get valuable information for decision making [45]. Many times, analyzing IoT platforms, selecting suitable IoT applications, offering quality services, and other difficulties become complicated decision problems that necessitate the use of MADM solution strategies to overcome the

Table 2. MADM approaches in IoT

Year	Aim of the Paper	Methods applied
2016	Assessment of the viability of IoT applications [46]	AHP
	Assessing the possible contribution to the prevention and control of constrained work in space [47]	AHP
	Selection of flexible IoT services [48]	TOPSIS
2017	Selection of IoT healthcare applications [49]	Fuzzy AHP
	Monitoring industrial energy conservation [50]	AHP
	Analyzing efficient solutions in the IoT systems' design [51]	AHP
2018	Allocation of scarce network resources [52]	AHP
	Evaluation of effective IoT systems for companies [53]	Fuzzy AHP
	Selection of IoT technology [54]	AHP
2019	Assessment of existing edge/cloud IoT databases [55]	AHP
	Exploration and analysis of IoT challenges [56]	MBR + VIKOR
	Investigation of difficulties encountered in the IoT [57]	AHP + ANP
	Determining suitable IoT applications [58]	Fuzzy AHP
	Implementing cloud, fog node, and clients' dynamic resource allotment technique [59]	TOPSIS
2020	Selection of IOT application using recommendation system [60]	AHP + SAW
	Evaluation of the IoT platforms [61]	PLTODIM
	Selection of IoT platforms for smart manufacturing [62]	PROMETHEE II
	Addressing the issue of NFRs management and optimization [63]	Pareto Multi-Criteria optimization
2021	A health security paradigm is designed for security [64]	Fuzzy ANP
	To assist organizations in making sound decisions [65]	HBWM + TOPSIS

choice complications. Table 2 summarizes some of the research done in the field of IoT using various MADM methodologies and its frequency distribution can be seen in Fig. 4.

Table 3. MADM approaches in Big Data.

Year	Aim of the paper	Methods applied
2016	Selection of appropriately qualified applicants [67]	Fuzzy VIKOR
	Selection of suitable cloud platforms for big data project management [68]	Hybrid TOPSIS
	Selecting right cloud services for big data schemes [69]	Hybrid entropy + AHP
2017	Assessing, ranking and choosing the top cloud solutions for projects of big data [70]	Fuzzy (AHP + TOPSIS)
	Analyzing procedures in urban centers for reducing air pollution [71]	Delphi, AHP and fuzzy logic theory
	Analyze big data of long-term heart disorder patients and those who need critical care [72]	BFAWC + TOPSIS
2018	Evaluation of sustainable policy [73]	TOPSIS
	Analyzing public security [66]	PROMETHEE II
	Ranking of important aspects of production companies [74]	DEMATEL + ANFIS
2019	Ranking of alternatives for the right storage ideas to support large-scale analysis [75]	AHP
	Identification of best collection mode for used components in remanufacturing [76]	Hybrid(AHP-EW) and grey MABAC
	Management of supply chain KPIs [77]	Fuzzy ANP + TOPSIS
	Assessment of the generation of electricity with technical, social and environmental factors [78]	Grey TOPSIS
2020	Analyzing the interdependence and influence on company performance of big data analytics abilities [79]	IF-DEMATEL, ANP and SAW
	Assessing the preparedness of organizations for adoption of big data [80]	FBWM
2021	Selection and assessment of Green suppliers [81]	FBWM + FTOPSIS
	Project selection with missing data [82]	Fuzzy TOPSIS

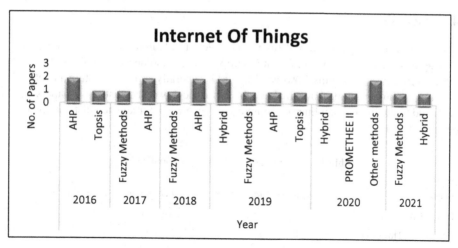

Fig. 4. Frequency d istribution of papers in IoT.

3.3 MADM Applications in the Field of Big Data

In recent years, with the advancement of internet technology, a diverse and massive amount of data has been accumulated and saved in numerical, textual, graphical, audio, and video formats from various data sources like public and commercial agencies, and organizations worldwide. These huge data are generally referred to as Big Data. Evaluating these data has become highly complicated since it requires sophisticated tools and large computational power. The analysis of big data is performed by very strong data management software like Apache Hadoop, HPCC, Apache Storm, MapReduce [66] and MADM can alongside contribute a lot. MADM approaches can be valuable tools to organize and analyze difficult decision-making and can help to make better and more educated choices. Table 3 summarizes some of the research done in the field of Big Data using various MADM methodologies and Fig. 5. represents the frequency distribution of publications.

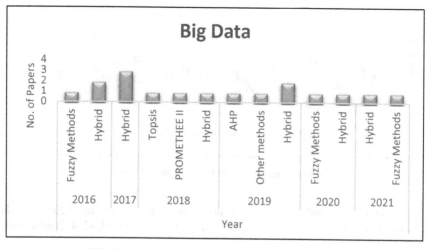

Fig. 5. Frequency distribution of papers in Big Data.

4   Discussion

The decision-making task in real-time is complex and tedious because the decision-making process is subject to conflicting multiple criteria and decision-makers. To solve these multi-criteria problems, however, MADM is generally applied to obtain an optimal solution by numerous decision-makers. In this review, we shortlisted 60 papers that belonged to the three disciplines of computer science whose frequency distribution can be seen in Table 4.

Table 4. Domain-based distribution of publications

Domain	No. of publications	Percentage distribution (%)
Cloud Computing	23	38.33%
Internet of Things (IoT)	20	33.33%
Big Data	17	28.34%
Total	**60**	**100%**

Paper distribution based on the MADM techniques from 2016–2021 can be seen in Fig. 6. It is observed that hybrid methods are mostly used methods. The reason for this is because of their ability to boost efficiency while maintaining consistent results. The majority of the hybrid methods consisted of AHP or TOPSIS or their fuzzified version as an integral part. The AHP and Fuzzy approaches have also been found to be frequently employed. In Fuzzy methods, Fuzzy AHP is the most used technique.

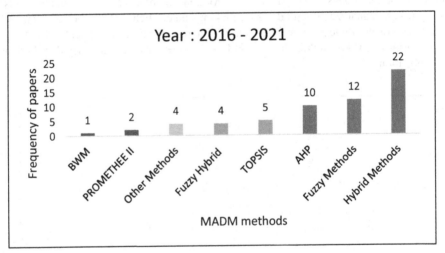

Fig. 6. Frequency of papers based on MADM methods

It has been noted that the maximum papers in cloud computing focused on the selection and ranking of cloud services [23–25, 29, 34, 36, 37, 39, 40, 42, 43] and suitable selection of cloud service providers [27, 30, 32, 35, 38] using the MADM technique depending on the quality of service (QoS) and other characteristics. Application of AHP and TOPSIS, and their fuzzified and hybrid versions are majorly used in most of the papers as these ranking methods are useful in determining weights [23] and efficient in tackling quantitative and qualitative decision factors [24]. The most used criteria in cloud computing include reliability, performance, cost and security.

The IoT and Big data ecosystems are very versatile and widespread. The applications of MADM in both concepts can be extended to different fields like healthcare sectors [49, 72], business environment [53, 54, 57, 65, 80, 82], manufacturing industries [56, 62, 74, 76], cloud platforms [55, 63, 68–70] and many more. Because of their versatility, the researchers were able to incorporate various decision-making techniques to attain the optimal result but in IoT, the AHP method and its variants were the most preferred choice whereas, in Big Data, hybrid methods [68–72, 74, 76, 77, 79, 81] were majorly used. The use of outranking methods is very minimal in these two disciplines because of the vast amount of data and criteria. In both IoT and Big Data, cost and security were the most used criteria.

Despite the fact that Big Data, IoT, and cloud computing are three distinct technologies that originated independently, they are becoming increasingly intertwined over time. The combination of cloud computing, IoT and big data opens great opportunities and leads to better applications in various areas. Researchers have incorporated MADM techniques in these symbiotic integrated approaches which can be seen in [83–86].

From the analysis of the domains, a comparative assessment is done based on the applicability of the methods with respect to usage areas, the data types used and how they are generated, the major MADM methods which are primarily used, and their application in different fields. The assessment can be seen in Table 5.

Table 5. Domain comparisons based on MADM

	Cloud computing	IoT	Big Data
Mainly used for	Ranking of cloud services and providers	1) Selection of IoT services 2) Assessment and evaluations	1) Ordering of Preferences 2) Selection of Big Data analysts
Major MADM approaches used	Hybrid Methods, Fuzzy Methods	AHP, Fuzzy AHP, Hybrid Methods	Hybrid Methods (TOPSIS + Others)
Data Types	Quantitative/ Qualitative	Quantitative/ Qualitative	Quantitative/ Qualitative
Generated Data	Machine and Human Generated	Machine Generated	Human Generated
Usage Areas	Narrow-spectrum	Broad-spectrum	Broad-spectrum

5 Conclusion

The primary goal behind this review is to summarize the application of MADM in some of the most relevant computer science fields of today, which will enable students, researchers and different agencies to advance exploration in the field. This study is restricted to a certain time frame and specific domains of computer science which are considered very significant but there exist many other fields with equal weightage where the application of MADM can be applied to resolve various decision-making issues.

References

1. Bellman, R.E., Zadeh, L.A.: Decision-making in a fuzzy environment. Manage. Sci. **17**(4), B-141 (1970)
2. Power, D.J.: Decision support systems: concepts and resources for managers. Greenwood Publishing Group (2002)
3. Skinner, D.C.: Introduction to decision analysis: a practitioner's guide to improving decision quality. Probabilistic Pub (2009)
4. ur Rehman, Z., Hussain, O.K., Hussain, F.K.: IAAS cloud selection using MCDM methods. In: 2012 IEEE Ninth International Conference on E-Business Engineering, pp. 246–251. IEEE (2012)
5. Saaty, T.L.: Decision making with the analytic hierarchy process. Int. J. Service Sci. **1**(1), 83–98 (2008)
6. Triantaphyllou, E.: Multi-criteria decision making methods. Multi-Criteria Decision Making Methods: A Comparative Study, pp. 5–21. Springer, Boston, MA (2000). https://doi.org/10.1007/978-1-4757-3157-6_2
7. Zanakis, S.H., Solomon, A., Wishart, N., Dublish, S.: Multi-attribute decision making: a simulation comparison of select methods. Eur. J. Oper. Res. **107**(3), 507–529 (1998)
8. Gaur, D., Aggarwal, S.: Selection of software development model using TOPSIS methodology. In: Jain, L., Balas, E., Johri, P. (eds.) Data and Communication Networks. Advances in Intelligent Systems and Computing, vol. 847. Springer, Singapore (2019). https://doi.org/10.1007/978-981-13-2254-9_11
9. Belton, V., Stewart, T.J.: Outranking methods. Multiple Criteria Decision Analysis, pp. 233–259. Springer, Boston, MA (2002)
10. Benayoun, R., Roy, B., Sussman, B.: ELECTRE: Une méthode pour guider le choix en présence de points de vue multiples. Note de travail **49**, 2–120 (1966)
11. Govindan, K., Jepsen, M.B.: ELECTRE: a comprehensive literature review on methodologies and applications. Eur. J. Oper. Res. **250**(1), 1–29 (2016)
12. Brans, J.P., De Smet, Y.: PROMETHEE methods. In: Greco, S., Ehrgott, M., Figueira, J. (eds.) Multiple Criteria Decision Analysis. International Series in Operations Research & Management Science, vol. 233. Springer, New York, NY (2016). https://doi.org/10.1007/978-1-4939-3094-4_6
13. Rezaei, J.: Best-worst multi-criteria decision-making method. Omega **53**, 49–57 (2015)
14. Saaty, R.W.: The analytic hierarchy process—what it is and how it is used. Math. Model. **9**(3–5), 161–176 (1987)
15. Behzadian, M., Otaghsara, S.K., Yazdani, M., Ignatius, J.: A state-of-the-art survey of TOPSIS applications. Expert Syst. Appl. **39**(17), 13051–13069 (2012)
16. Saaty, T.L.: Fundamentals of the Analytic Network Process, ISAHP. Kobe, Japan (1999)
17. Opricovic, S.: Multicriteria optimization of civil engineering systems. Faculty Civil Eng. Belgrade **2**(1), 5–21 (1998)

18. Fontela, E., Gabus, A.: DEMATEL, innovative methods (1974)
19. Zionts, S., Wallenius, J.: An interactive multiple objective linear programming method for a class of underlying nonlinear utility functions. Manage. Sci. **29**(5), 519–529 (1983)
20. Buyya, R., Yeo, C.S., Venugopal, S., Broberg, J., Brandic, I.: Cloud computing and emerging IT platforms: vision, hype, and reality for delivering computing as the 5th utility. Futur. Gener. Comput. Syst. **25**(6), 599–616 (2009)
21. Wang, X.F., Wang, J.Q., Deng, S.Y.: A method to dynamic stochastic multicriteria decision making with log-normally distributed random variables. Sci. World J. 2013 (2013)
22. Lee, S., Seo, K.K.: A hybrid multi-criteria decision-making model for a cloud service selection problem using BSC, fuzzy Delphi method and fuzzy AHP. Wireless Pers. Commun. **86**(1), 57–75 (2016)
23. Bhushan, S.B., Pradeep, R.C.: A network QoS aware service ranking using hybrid AHP-PROMETHEE method in multi-cloud domain. Int. J. Eng. Res. Africa, **24**, 153–164 (2016)
24. Kumar, R.R., Kumar, C.: An evaluation system for cloud service selection using fuzzy AHP. In: 2016 11th International Conference on Industrial and Information Systems (ICIIS), pp. 821–826. IEEE (2016)
25. Sun, L., Ma, J., Zhang, Y., Dong, H., Hussain, F.K.: Cloud-FuSeR: fuzzy ontology and MCDM based cloud service selection. Futur. Gener. Comput. Syst. **57**, 42–55 (2016)
26. Wibowo, S., Deng, H., Xu, W.: Evaluation of cloud services: a fuzzy multi-criteria group decision making method. Algorithms **9**(4), 84 (2016)
27. Chahal, R.K., Singh, S.: Fuzzy logic and AHP-based ranking of cloud service providers. In: Computational Intelligence in Data Mining, vol. 1, pp. 337-346. Springer, New Delhi (2016)
28. Ben Alla, H., Ben Alla, S., Ezzati, A.: A priority based task scheduling in cloud computing using a hybrid MCDM model. In: Sabir, E., García Armada, A., Ghogho, M., Debbah, M. (eds.) Ubiquitous Networking. UNet 2017. Lecture Notes in Computer Science, vol. 10542. Springer, Cham (2017). https://doi.org/10.1007/978-3-319-68179-5_21
29. Sohaib, O., Naderpour, M.: Decision making on adoption of cloud computing in e-commerce using fuzzy TOPSIS. In: 2017 IEEE International Conference on Fuzzy Systems (FUZZ-IEEE), pp. 1–6. IEEE (2017)
30. Kaveri, B.A., Gireesha, O., Somu, N., Raman, M.G., Sriram, V.S.: E-FPROMETHEE: an entropy based fuzzy multi criteria decision making service ranking approach for cloud service selection. In: International Conference on Intelligent Information Technologies, pp. 224–238. Springer, Singapore (2017). https://doi.org/10.1007/978-981-10-7635-0_17
31. Sidhu, J., Singh, S.: Improved topsis method based trust evaluation framework for determining trustworthiness of cloud service providers. J. Grid Comput. **15**(1), 81–105 (2017)
32. Tanoumand, N., Ozdemir, D.Y., Kilic, K., Ahmed, F.: Selecting cloud computing service provider with fuzzy AHP. In: 2017 IEEE International Conference on Fuzzy Systems (FUZZ-IEEE), pp. 1–5. IEEE (2017)
33. Azar, H., Majma, M.R.: Using a multi criteria decision making model for managing computational resources at mobile ad-hoc cloud computing environment. In: 2017 International Conference on Engineering and Technology (ICET), pp. 1–5. IEEE (2017)
34. Kumar, R.R., Mishra, S., Kumar, C.: A novel framework for cloud service evaluation and selection using hybrid MCDM methods. Arab. J. Sci. Eng. **43**(12), 7015–7030 (2018)
35. Büyüközkan, G., Göçer, F., Feyzioğlu, O.: Cloud computing technology selection based on interval-valued intuitionistic fuzzy MCDM methods. Soft. Comput. **22**(15), 5091–5114 (2018). https://doi.org/10.1007/s00500-018-3317-4
36. Nawaz, F., Asadabadi, M.R., Janjua, N.K., Hussain, O.K., Chang, E., Saberi, M.: An MCDM method for cloud service selection using a Markov chain and the best-worst method. Knowl.-Based Syst. **159**, 120–131 (2018)

37. Abdel-Basset, M., Mohamed, M., Chang, V.: NMCDA: a framework for evaluating cloud computing services. Futur. Gener. Comput. Syst. **86**, 12–29 (2018)

38. Al-Faifi, A., Song, B., Hassan, M.M., Alamri, A., Gumaei, A.: A hybrid multi criteria decision method for cloud service selection from Smart data. Futur. Gener. Comput. Syst. **93**, 43–57 (2019)

39. Jatoth, C., Gangadharan, G.R., Fiore, U., Buyya, R.: SELCLOUD: a hybrid multi-criteria decision-making model for selection of cloud services. Soft. Comput. **23**(13), 4701–4715 (2018). https://doi.org/10.1007/s00500-018-3120-2

40. Kumar, R.R., Kumari, B., Kumar, C.: CCS-OSSR: a framework based on Hybrid MCDM for optimal service selection and ranking of cloud computing services. Clust. Comput. **24**(2), 867–883 (2020). https://doi.org/10.1007/s10586-020-03166-3

41. Khorsand, R., Ramezanpour, M.: An energy-efficient task-scheduling algorithm based on a multi-criteria decision-making method in cloud computing. Int. J. Commun. Syst. **33**(9), e4379 (2020)

42. Youssef, A.E.: An integrated MCDM approach for cloud service selection based on TOPSIS and BWM. IEEE Access **8**, 71851–71865 (2020)

43. Nejat, M.H., Motameni, H., Vahdat-Nejad, H., Barzegar, B.: Efficient cloud service ranking based on uncertain user requirements. Clust. Comput. **25**(1), 485–502 (2021). https://doi.org/10.1007/s10586-021-03418-w

44. Taghavifard, M.T., Majidian, S.: Identifying cloud computing risks based on firm's ambidexterity performance using fuzzy VIKOR technique. Glob. J. Flex. Syst. Manag. **23**(1), 113–133 (2021). https://doi.org/10.1007/s40171-021-00292-8

45. Baranwal, G., Singh, M., Vidyarthi, D.P.: A framework for IoT service selection. J. Supercomput. **76**(4), 2777–2814 (2019). https://doi.org/10.1007/s11227-019-03076-1

46. Kim, S., Kim, S.: A multi-criteria approach toward discovering killer IoT application in Korea. Technol. Forecast. Soc. Chang. **102**, 143–155 (2016)

47. Botti, L., Bragatto, P., Duraccio, V., Gnoni, M.G., Mora, C.: Adopting IOT technologies to control risks in confined space: a multi-criteria decision tool. Chem. Eng. Trans. **53**, 127–132 (2016)

48. Ashraf, Q.M., Habaebi, M.H., Islam, M.R.: TOPSIS-based service arbitration for autonomic internet of things. IEEE Access **4**, 1313–1320 (2016)

49. Alansari, Z., Anuar, N.B., Kamsin, A., Soomro, S., Belgaum, M.R.: The Internet of Things adoption in healthcare applications. In: 2017 IEEE 3rd International Conference on Engineering Technologies and Social Sciences (ICETSS), pp. 1–5. IEEE (2017)

50. Li, Y., Sun, Z., Han, L., Mei, N.: Fuzzy comprehensive evaluation method for energy management systems based on an internet of things. IEEE Access **5**, 21312–21322 (2017)

51. Silva, E.M., Agostinho, C., Jardim-Goncalves, R.: A multi-criteria decision model for the selection of a more suitable Internet-of-Things device. In: 2017 International Conference on Engineering, Technology and Innovation (ICE/ITMC), pp. 1268–1276. IEEE (2017)

52. Abedin, S.F., Alam, M.G.R., Kazmi, S.A., Tran, N.H., Niyato, D., Hong, C.S.: Resource allocation for ultra-reliable and enhanced mobile broadband IoT applications in fog network. IEEE Trans. Commun. **67**(1), 489–502 (2018)

53. Ly, P.T.M., Lai, W.H., Hsu, C.W., Shih, F.Y.: Fuzzy AHP analysis of Internet of Things (IoT) in enterprises. Technol. Forecast. Soc. Chang. **136**, 1–13 (2018)

54. Durão, L.F.C., Carvalho, M.M., Takey, S., Cauchick-Miguel, P.A., Zancul, E.: Internet of Things process selection: AHP selection method. Int. J. Adv. Manuf. Technol. **99**(9), 2623-2634 (2018).https://doi.org/10.1007/s00170-018-2617-2

55. Alelaiwi, A.: Evaluating distributed IoT databases for edge/cloud platforms using the analytic hierarchy process. J. Parallel Distrib. Comput. **124**, 41–46 (2019)

56. Kao, Y.S., Nawata, K., Huang, C.Y.: Evaluating the performance of systemic innovation problems of the IoT in manufacturing industries by novel MCDM methods. Sustainability **11**(18), 4970 (2019)

57. Uslu, B., Eren, T., Gür, Ş, Özcan, E.: Evaluation of the difficulties in the internet of things (IoT) with multi-criteria decision-making. Processes **7**(3), 164 (2019)

58. Mashal, I., Alsaryrah, O.: Fuzzy analytic hierarchy process model for multi-criteria analysis of internet of things. Kybernetes (2019)

59. Bashir, H., Lee, S., Kim, K.H.: Resource allocation through logistic regression and multicriteria decision making method in IoT fog computing. Trans. Emerg. Telecommun. Technol. **33**(2), e3824 (2019)

60. Mashal, I., Alsaryrah, O., Chung, T.Y., Yuan, F.C.: A multi-criteria analysis for an internet of things application recommendation system. Technol. Soc. **60**, 101216 (2020)

61. Lin, M., Huang, C., Xu, Z., Chen, R.: Evaluating IoT platforms using integrated probabilistic linguistic MCDM method. IEEE Internet Things J. **7**(11), 11195–11208 (2020)

62. Contreras-Masse, R., Ochoa-Zezzatti, A., Garcia, V., Perez-Dominguez, L., Elizondo-Cortes, M.: Implementing a novel use of multicriteria decision analysis to select IIoT platforms for smart manufacturing. Symmetry **12**(3), 368 (2020)

63. Štefanič, P., Stankovski, V.: Multi-criteria decision-making approach for container-based cloud applications: the SWITCH and ENTICE workbenches. Tehnički vjesnik **27**(3), 1006–1013 (2020)

64. Haghparast, M.B., Berehlia, S., Akbari, M., Sayadi, A.: Developing and evaluating a proposed health security framework in IoT using fuzzy analytic network process method. J. Ambient. Intell. Humaniz. Comput. **12**(2), 3121–3138 (2020). https://doi.org/10.1007/s12652-020-02472-3

65. Zhou, T., Ming, X., Chen, Z., Miao, R.: Selecting industrial IoT Platform for digital servitisation: a framework integrating platform leverage practices and cloud HBWM-TOPSIS approach. Int. J. Prod. Res. 1–23 (2021)

66. Turet, J.G., Costa, A.P.C.S.: Big data analytics to improve the decision-making process in public safety: a case study in Northeast Brazil. In: International Conference on Decision Support System Technology, pp. 76–87. Springer, Cham (2018)

67. Bag, S.: Fuzzy VIKOR approach for selection of big data analyst in procurement management. J. Transp. Supply Chain Manage. **10**(1), 1–6 (2016)

68. Sachdeva, N., Singh, O., Kapur, P.K., Galar, D.: Multi-criteria intuitionistic fuzzy group decision analysis with TOPSIS method for selecting appropriate cloud solution to manage big data projects. Int. J. Syst. Assurance Eng. Manage. **7**(3), 316–324 (2016). https://doi.org/10.1007/s13198-016-0455-x

69. Sachdeva, N., Kapur, P.K., Singh, G.: Selecting appropriate cloud solution for managing big data projects using hybrid AHP-entropy based assessment. In: 2016 International Conference on Innovation and Challenges in Cyber Security (ICICCS-INBUSH), pp. 135–140. IEEE (2016)

70. Boutkhoum, O., Hanine, M., Agouti, T., Tikniouine, A.: A decision-making approach based on fuzzy AHP-TOPSIS methodology for selecting the appropriate cloud solution to manage big data projects. Int. J. Syst. Assurance Eng. Manage. **8**(2), 1237-1253 (2017).https://doi.org/10.1007/s13198-017-0592-x

71. Hsueh, S.L., Cheng, A.C.: Improving air quality in communities by using a multicriteria decision-making model based on big data: a critical review. Appl. Ecol. Environ. Res. **15**(2), 15–31 (2017)

72. Salman, O.H., Zaidan, A.A., Zaidan, B.B., Naserkalid, F., Hashim, M.: Novel methodology for triage and prioritizing using "big data" patients with chronic heart diseases through telemedicine environmental. Int. J. Inf. Technol. Decis. Making, **16**(05), 1211–1245 (2017)

73. Ifaei, P., Farid, A., Yoo, C.: An optimal renewable energy management strategy with and without hydropower using a factor weighted multi-criteria decision making analysis and nation-wide big data-Case study in Iran. Energy **158**, 357–372 (2018)

74. Yadegaridehkordi, E., Hourmand, M., Nilashi, M., Shuib, L., Ahani, A., Ibrahim, O.: Influence of big data adoption on manufacturing companies' performance: an integrated DEMATEL-ANFIS approach. Technol. Forecast. Soc. Chang. **137**, 199–210 (2018)

75. Kachaoui, J., Belangour, A.: An adaptive control approach for performance of big data storage systems. In: Ezziyyani, M. (ed.) AI2SD 2019. AISC, vol. 1105, pp. 89–97. Springer, Cham (2020). https://doi.org/10.1007/978-3-030-36674-2_9

76. Wang, H., Jiang, Z., Zhang, H., Wang, Y., Yang, Y., Li, Y.: An integrated MCDM approach considering demands-matching for reverse logistics. J. Clean. Prod. **208**, 199–210 (2019)

77. Dev, N.K., Shankar, R., Gupta, R., Dong, J.: Multi-criteria evaluation of real-time key performance indicators of supply chain with consideration of big data architecture. Comput. Ind. Eng. **128**, 1076–1087 (2019)

78. Chalvatzis, K.J., Malekpoor, H., Mishra, N., Lettice, F., Choudhary, S.: Sustainable resource allocation for power generation: the role of big data in enabling interindustry architectural innovation. Technol. Forecast. Soc. Chang. **144**, 381–393 (2019)

79. Yasmin, M., Tatoglu, E., Kilic, H.S., Zaim, S., Delen, D.: Big data analytics capabilities and firm performance: an integrated MCDM approach. J. Bus. Res. **114**, 1–15 (2020)

80. Nasrollahi, M., Ramezani, J.: A model to evaluate the organizational readiness for big data adoption. Int. J. Comput. Commun. Control, **15**(3) (2020)

81. Liou, J.J., Chang, M.H., Lo, H.W., Hsu, M.H.: Application of an MCDM model with data mining techniques for green supplier evaluation and selection. Appl. Soft Comput. **109**, 107534 (2021)

82. Mahmoudi, A., Deng, X., Javed, S.A., Yuan, J.: Large-scale multiple criteria decision-making with missing values: project selection through TOPSIS-OPA. J. Ambient. Intell. Humaniz. Comput. **12**(10), 9341–9362 (2020). https://doi.org/10.1007/s12652-020-02649-w

83. Xu, X., et al.: A computation offloading method over big data for IoT-enabled cloud-edge computing. Futur. Gener. Comput. Syst. **95**, 522–533 (2019)

84. Chakraborty, B., Das, S.: Introducing a new supply chain management concept by hybridizing TOPSIS, IoT and cloud computing. J. Inst. Eng. (India): Ser. C **102**(1), 109–119 (2020). https://doi.org/10.1007/s40032-020-00619-x

85. Singla, C., Mahajan, N., Kaushal, S., Verma, A., Sangaiah, A.K.: Modelling and analysis of multi-objective service selection scheme in IoT-cloud environment. In: Cognitive computing for big data systems over IoT, pp. 63–77. Springer, Cham (2018). https://doi.org/10.1007/978-981-10-7635-0_17

86. Albahri, O.S., et al.: Fault-tolerant mHealth framework in the context of IoT-based real-time wearable health data sensors. IEEE Access **7**, 50052–50080 (2019)

Statistical and Syllabification Based Model for Nepali Machine Transliteration

Amit Kumar Roy[1]($\boxtimes$) (ID), Abhijit Paul[2] (ID), and Bipul Syam Purkayastha[1] (ID)

[1] Department of Computer Science, Assam University, Silchar, Assam, India
amitroy.cs@gmail.com
[2] Department of Computer Science, Gurucharan College, Silchar, Assam, India

Abstract. Machine Transliteration is one of the important modules for the development of a correct Machine Translation (MT) system. Machine Translation is the technique of converting sentences in one natural language into another using a machine, whereas Machine Transliteration is the method of converting words in one language into phonetically identical words in another. When Machine Translation is unable to translate the Out-of-Vocabulary (OOV) words, Name Entity words, technical words, abbreviation, etc. then Machine Transliteration transliterates these words phonetically. This paper presents a transliteration system for the English-Nepali language pair using the most widely used statistical method with a linguistic syllabification methodology. A model has been designed based on syllable splitting that splits 19,513 parallel entries which contains person names, place, etc. IRSTLM and GIZA++ are used to build the language model (LM) and translation model (TM) i.e. word alignment respectively over parallel entries. For English-Nepali parallel entries on Syllable based split, an accuracy of 87% has been achieved.

Keywords: NLP · Machine Transliteration · SMT · Syllabification · Nepali language

1 Introduction

The Nepali comes under the Indo-Aryan sub-branch of the Indo-European language family, and it is the primary language of approximately 60% of Nepal's inhabitants [1]. It is the official language of Nepal and India, and it is also spoken in some parts of Bhutan and Myanmar. Nepali is used as the primary language of communication in government affairs, the educational system, television, newspapers, and other organizations in Nepal and some parts of India. The language was known by several names at different periods, such as Khas bhasa (or Khas Kura), Lokabhasa, Gorkhali, and later Nepali, which was inferred from the name of the country itself. Nepali is a Sanskrit-derived language and written in the Devanagari script, which is also used to write Hindi, Konkani, and Marathi. Some dialectal variations of Nepali conform to Hinduism's caste system. Nepali natural language processing is in its infancy, which means it has only recently started its adventure in the field of NLP in India.

S. Mukhopadhyay et al. (Eds.): CICBA 2022, CCIS 1579, pp. 19–27, 2022.
https://doi.org/10.1007/978-3-031-10766-5_2

There are different real world applications of NLP, among them Machine Translation perhaps the ultimate goal of NLP. There has been a lot of research done on machine translation and transliteration for English and Indian languages. However, due to a lack of good grammatical rules and bilingual corpora, little work has been done in the field of machine translation and transliteration for the low resource Nepali language. Machine transliteration is the technique of automatically converting a word phonetically from one language to the other while preserving pronunciation. When the translator is unable to translate the Out-of-Vocabulary (OOV) words, technical words, abbreviations, etc. across languages, the transliteration system converts the words phonetically [10]. The transliteration process is also effective for various NLP jobs viz. information retrieval and extraction, corpus alignment, and so on. As a result, all of these observations motivate the development of an English to Nepali language transliteration system and work for this language.

The transliteration process is further split into three main categories: grapheme-based method, phoneme-based method, and hybrid (phoneme + grapheme) method.

Graphemes are the individual characters of a written language including punctuation marks and numerals. E.g. In the word "akash", there are five graphemes i.e. "a, k, a, s, h", but in the word "आकाश", there are four graphemes "आ, क, ा, श". Grapheme-based transliteration is defined as the procedure of mapping a grapheme sequence from one language to another while neglecting phoneme-level operations [12].

Phonemes are the smallest individual sounding units that express the clear and distinct meaning in a language. E.g. In the words "akash" & "आकाश", there are three phonemes "a, ka, sh" & "आ, का, श". Phoneme-based transliteration does not include orthographic information; instead, the procedure is divided into two stages: conversion from source graphemes to source phoneme/phonetic, and conversion from source phoneme/phonetic to target graphemes [11].

Hybrid based is the combination of both phoneme and grapheme-based approaches.

In this paper, a statistical and syllabification approach is used for the development of the English to Nepali Machine Transliteration system. A set of rules are used for syllabification, which is further explained in this paper. In the next section, different research papers on Machine Transliterations will be discussed.

2 Related Works

Lots of research work has been carried out for the development of the Machine Transliteration system. A few of them are discussed below.

In the paper [2], Odia-English & Odia-Hindi transliteration systems were designed using different statistical tools MOSES, SRILM, and GIZA ++. Two types of parallel corpora (syllable and character spilt based) were prepared to train the model. For syllable-based split, Odia to English and Hindi transliteration systems achieved accuracy 89% and 86% respectively. And for character based split Odia to English and Hindi transliteration systems achieved accuracy 71% and 85% respectively.

In the paper [3] the same approach was used for the English-Hindi language pair. This paper claims an accuracy of 46.3%. Along with phrase based technique, a beam search technique for decoder was used.

A rule based technique with script conversion method was used for the machine transliteration in the paper [4]. According to the paper, script conversion is an important factor in achieving higher accuracy in machine transliteration.

In the paper [5], transliteration in wx-notation and UTF-notation over English-Hindi corpus for Indian names using phrase based statistical machine translation approach was discussed. It claims that wx-notation gives better results than UTF-notation.

The paper [6], presents a transliteration tool for the English-Hindi language pair. This tool can be transliterated bi-direction i.e. from English → Hindi and the other way, from Hindi → English. Syllabification and Statistical approach were used in the paper.

An algorithm was proposed in the paper [7], which transliterates among several Indian languages. The algorithm completely works on the UNICODE format for Indian languages.

3   Preprocessing of Corpus for Transliteration

An English-Nepali parallel corpus of 19,513 entries is prepared manually by the linguistic person. This corpus consists of name entity words (person name, place name, etc.), technical words, abbreviation, etc. UTF-8 notation is used in the corpus. After corpus preparation with the help of a linguistics person, preprocessing steps are applied on parallel corpus for training the system. The flowchart of the preprocessing technique is illustrated in Fig. 1.

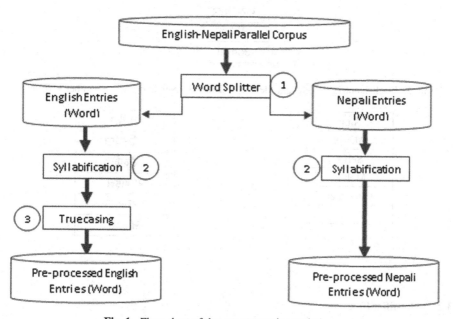

Fig. 1. Flow chart of the pre-processing techniques.

3.1 Word Splitter

The corpus that has been collected from a linguistic person contains 19,513 entries. A small program (word splitter) was written in JAVA which accepts the parallel corpus in such a form where the Nepali translation of an English sentence is given just after the respective sentence as shown in Table 1, as input and generates two different pre-processed text files, one containing English entries and the other containing Nepali entries as shown in Table 2 & 3 respectively.

Table 1. Sample corpus of the parallel entries.

Amit
अमित
Abhijit
अभिजीत
Selfie
सेल्फी
Mobile
मोबाइल
Computer
कमप्यूटर
Akash
आकाश

Table 2. English entries in one text file.

Amit
Abhijit
Selfie
Mobile
Computer
Akash

Table 3. Nepali entries in another text file.

अमित
अभिजीत
सेल्फी
मोबाइल
कमप्यूटर
आकाश

3.2 Syllabification

Before training the system using the IRSTLM language model, the syllabification app-roach is used to split the words into their distinguished phonemes. Because Indian lan-guages are phonetic, breaking a word up to the vowel appears to create the correct sound units. During training, this should be applicable to both the languages and transliterated strings.

Rules for establishing a syllable-based split for English words [2]:
Begin reading the word character by character from left to right.
A single syllable is defined as:

a) A single vowel or a vowel is succeeded by a vowel.
b) Each character group, beginning with a consonant and ends with a vowel.

Rules for establishing a syllable-based split for Nepali words:
Begin reading the word character by character from left to right.
A single syllable is defined as:

a) A single vowel or a vowel is succeeded by ANUSVARA(ं), VISARGA(ः), and CANDRABINDU(ँ).
b) A single consonant or a consonant is succeeded by Matra.
c) In the case of a conjunction, a consonant succeeded by HALANT(्), the characters after HALANT(्) such as a single consonant or a consonant succeeded by a Matra character.

Table 4. English entries after syllabification

A mi t
A bhi ji t
Se lfie
Mo bi le
Co m pu te r
A ka sh

Table 5. Nepali entries after syllabification

अ मि त
अ भि जी त
से ल्फी
मो बाइ ल
क म प्यू ट र
आ का श

3.3 Truecasing

Truecasing relates to the concept that words in the text that is either lowercased or uppercased. It is related to tokenization, where it normalizes the case, i.e. convert uppercase characters to their most likely casing, which is usually lowercase. This aids the system to reduce the sparsity of data. Names usually start with uppercase characters, so you can distinguish between Mr. Stone and a stone. Adopting truecasing process for the Nepali language is pointless because there is no notion of capital and lowercase letters in Nepali. Thus it is exclusively applied to English entries in this system.

Table 6. English entries after truecasing.

a mi t
a bhi ji t
se lfie
mo bi le
co m pu te r
a ka sh

4   Proposed English-Nepali Transliteration System

A statistical approach is used to design the transliteration system. The statistical approach is the widely used approach for the development of machine translation as well as machine transliteration system.

Suppose the (English) source language word $S = S_1 S_2... S_j... S_n$. Where, S_j represents an alphabet or a set of alphabets of the English language.

Similarly, (Nepali) target language word $T = T_1 T_2... T_j... T_n$. Where, T_j represents an alphabet or a set of alphabets of the Nepali language.

If a word is provided in the source language S, it may generate multiple transliterations in the target language. The problem of transliteration can be defined mathematically as

$$T = \text{argmax } P(n) * P\left(\frac{e}{n}\right) \forall t \in T$$

where, $P(n)$ is the prior of Nepali language phoneme & $P\left(\frac{e}{n}\right)$ is the conditional probability of the English language phoneme text given the Nepali phoneme. $P(n)$ is responsible for the fluency of the system and $P\left(\frac{e}{n}\right)$ is responsible for the adequacy of the system. The architecture of the system is shown below.

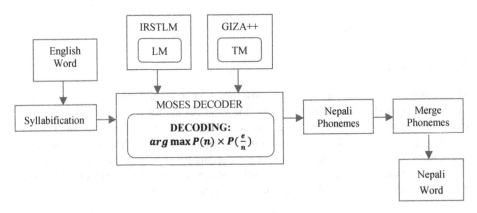

Fig. 2. The proposed system's architecture.

4.1 Implementation

The proposed system has been implemented using phrase based model with the help of different SMT tools, viz. GIZA++ [7] is used for the translation model, IRSTLM [8] is used for the language model, and MOSES [9] is used for decoding.

GIZA++: It is an SMT toolkit that is free to use for research. GIZA++ was developed by Franz Josef Och and Hermann Ney as an expanded version of the GIZA toolkit. The parallel corpus is first bidirectionally aligned. This results in two word alignments that must be balanced. We acquire a high-precision alignment, once we cross the two alignments. When the two alignments are combined, we get a high-recall alignment with more alignment points. The alignments are then utilised to estimate phrase transliteration probability using the scoring function given best t in [14].

IRSTLM: The Ia Ricerca Scientifica e Tecnologica Language Modeling (IRSTLM) Toolkit is a powerful and open access tool for estimating, storing, and accessing large n-gram language models. It is capable of performing with complete integration with the Moses SMT Toolkit.

First, the pre-processed parallel corpus entries of size 19,013 are used to build the translation model (TM). The translation model does the alignment of English pre-processed entries with the Nepali pre-processed entries and prepares the phrase table, which consists of phonemes entries for both languages. Next, another pre-processed Nepali entry file is considered for the preparation of the language model (LM). The language model consists of the probabilities of the phonemes for the target words (Nepali words) & the translation model consists of the conditional probabilities of the English and Nepali words. Then the MOSES is used for finding the best sequence of the phonemes of the target word. Finally, a merger is used to merge the phonemes of the Nepali words i.e. reduce the space in between phonemes.

5 Results and Discussion

Our implemented system has been tested with two test cases. All the tested words are from the general domain. Test case1 gives 100% accuracy as all the words are used from the trained corpus, however, the Test case2 is taken in such a way that it differs from the training corpus. Some of the words in Test case 2 are transliterated incorrectly due to the unavailability of phonemes in the trained corpus. It has also been observed that ambiguous phonemes also create a problem in the transliteration process. The accuracy of the system can be increased by increasing the sizes of the entries in the parallel corpus.

The following formula was used to calculate accuracy.

$$\text{Accuracy} = \frac{\text{No.of correctly transliterated words}}{\text{Total no.of words for transliteration}} \times 100$$

Table 7. Experimental analysis.

	Training	Validation	Testing	Accuracy
Test Case1	19,013	500	100	100%
Test Case2	19,013	500	100	87%

6 Conclusion

We have proposed and implemented a hybrid transliteration system using a statistical and syllabification approach for English to Nepali transliteration in this paper. Different statistical models were developed and implemented, for aligning the characters, freely available tool GIZA++ is used and language models are generated with IRSTLM. A pre-processed parallel corpus of English – Nepali words was used to train the statistical model. The pre-processing steps include word splitting of English-Nepali parallel entries, syllabification of both Nepali and English entries, and true casing of only English entries. The implemented system has achieved an accuracy of 87% with 100 test entries in the English language. The accuracy of the system depends upon the size of parallel corpus i.e., higher accuracy can be obtained by increasing the size of the parallel corpus.

References

1. Arredondo, I.Y., Ballard, H.: Nepali manual: language and culture (2012)
2. Balabantaray, R.C., Sahoo, D.: Odia transliteration engine using moses. In: 2014 2nd International Conference on Business and Information Management (ICBIM), pp. 27–29. IEEE (2014)
3. Rama, T., Gali, K.: Modeling machine transliteration as a phrase based statistical machine translation problem. In: Proceedings of the 2009 Named Entities Workshop: Shared Task on Transliteration (NEWS 2009), pp. 124–127 (2009)
4. Surana, H., Singh, A.K.: A more discerning and adaptable multilingual transliteration mechanism for indian languages. In: Proceedings of the Third International Joint Conference on Natural Language Processing: Volume-I (2008)
5. Sharma, S., Bora, N., Halder, M.: English-hindi transliteration using statistical machine translation in different notation. Training **20000**(297380), 20000 (2012)
6. Diwakar, S., Goyal, P., Gupta, R.: Transliteration among indian languages using wx notation. In: Proceedings of the Conference on Natural Language Processing 2010, No. CONF, pp. 147–150 (2010)
7. GIZA++, https://github.com/moses-smt/giza-pp/tree/master/GIZA++. Accessed 21 July 2021
8. IRSTLM, https://sourceforge.net/projects/irstlm/. Accessed 14 July 2021
9. Statistical Machine Translation System User Manual and Code Guide, http://www.statmt.goes.org/moses/manual/manual.pdf/. Accessed 07 July 2021
10. Younes, J., Achour, H., Souissi, E., Ferchichi, A.: Romanized tunisian dialect transliteration using sequence labelling techniques. J. King Saud Univ. Comput. Inf. Sci. (2020)
11. Sunitha, C., Jaya, A.: A phoneme based model for english to malayalam transliteration. In: International Confernce on Innovation Information in Computing Technologies, pp. 1–4. IEEE (2015)

12. Jia, Y., Zhu, D., Yu, S.: A noisy channel model for grapheme-based machine transliteration. In: Proceedings of the 2009 Named Entities Workshop: Shared Task on Transliteration (NEWS 2009), pp. 88–91 (2009)
13. Och, F.J., Ney, H.: A systematic comparison of various statistical alignment models. Comput. Linguistics, **29**(1), 19–51 (2003)
14. Koehn, P., et al.: Moses: open source toolkit for statistical machine translation. ACL, **45**, 177–180 (2009)

Learning Based Image Classification Techniques

Nayan Kumar Sarkar[1(✉)] ⓘ, Moirangthem Marjit Singh[1] ⓘ, and Utpal Nandi[2] ⓘ

[1] Department of Computer Science and Engineering, North Eastern Regional Institute of Science and Technology, Arunachal Pradesh, India
`nayankrsarkar@gmail.com`
[2] Department of Computer Science, Vidyasagar University, West Bengal, India

Abstract. Although, deep learning approaches have attained remarkable advancements in the application of image classification, they require a large amount of training samples and machines with high computing power. Collecting huge samples against each class for training is a difficult task, sometimes even not possible. To tackle these disadvantages of deep learning-based approach, new paradigms of machine learning, such as Few-Shot Learning (FSL), One-Shot-Learning (OSL), and Zero-Shot-Learning (ZSL) have been developed. The paper presents a survey on various image classification methods which have been developed based on the FSL, OSL, or ZSL paradigm. This paper also highlights a comparative study of the methods and a summary of the methods.

Keywords: Image classification · FSL · OSL · ZSL

1 Introduction

The deep learning (DL) methods have achieved lots of advancements in various application of machine learning like image classification, NLP, robotics, healthcare, and many more. The DL-based image classification approaches are mostly supervised and need lots of samples of each class for training to obtain high performance. Like a human can learn new things from a few training samples or its descriptions, the DL approaches can't learn from less number of labeled samples [1]. The DL-based methods can classify only those instances of any class that were used during the training phase; they cannot classify the untrained instance of any class.

The DL method requires large number of samples for training and the lack of labeled sample is considered as a major problem in DL-based methods [2]. In practical applications, it's a difficult job to collect a large dataset always to train a model. Again, there may not be enough samples available for each class and the model may also need to classify such samples which were not considered during training. These limitations motivated the researches to move towards new paradigms of machine learning like FSL, OSL, and ZSL. These methods take very less number of samples for training and have brought lots of advancements in many applications where it's difficult to find a large dataset. Several methods have been developed based on FSL, OSL and ZSL paradigm.

In this paper, we have surveyed and reviewed some of the FSL, OSL, and ZSL-based image classification methods. The different classification methods covered in this paper are hyperspectral image classification, plant leaf disease detection, multi-label image classification, human disease image classification etc. using different datasets. The performances of most of the methods are evaluated on N-way K-shot settings. It is also found that performance of the methods varies on different datasets and the methods achieved different results with different number of samples considered. The paper is summarized as, Sects. 2-4 highlights the FSL, OSL, and ZSL-based image classification methods respectively. Section 5 shows the result comparison of different methods with different datasets, Sect. 6 consists of a summary of the surveyed approaches and Sect. 7 presents conclusion.

2   Few Shot Learning (FSL)

Few-Shot Learning (FSL) mimics the learning behavior of humans. It can learn from a few numbers of training examples. FSL is a paradigm of machine learning where the classifier learns to classify new instances of a class from a few numbers of training instances of that class. The FSL reduces the burden of huge training data collection and hence reduces training time and computational cost. It brings advancement in many fields such as drug discovery where it is difficult to acquire huge training examples. Application areas of FSL are computer vision, natural language processing, robotics, signal processing, etc.

Some of the FSL based image classification approaches are highlighted in this section. W. Chu et al. [1] proposed a sampling method that combined reinforcement learning and discriminative information extraction. It allows us to detect and extract varying sequences of patches in an image. Omniglot [34] and miniImagenet [35] datasets were used for performance assessment and the proposed method achieved better performance by taking advantage of the extracted features. B. Liu et al. [2] proposed a deep FSL (DFSL) algorithm to classify hyperspectral images with small samples. It achieved its goal by extracting spectral features from a deep neural network. The algorithm was trained to learn a metric space where the samples from similar classes are close to each other. To train the method, Houston, Botswana, KSC, and Chikusei datasets and for the performance evaluation university of Pavia, Pavia Center, Indian pines, and the Salinas datasets were used. The overall performances of the DFSL method with NN and SVM i.e. DFSL + NN and DFSL + SVM were better than several other methods. It is observed that the accuracy of each method increased with the number of samples of each class and the DFSL + NN provides better performance with a minimum number of samples. However, DFSL + SVM delivered the maximum accuracies with the university of Pavia, Indian Pines, and the Salinas dataset. D. Das et al. [3] proposed a two-stage FSL approach for image recognition. The proposed architecture is based on a large dataset of base categories and is applied to only a few samples. The knowledge transfer is carried out in two stages: feature extraction and classification levels. The first step involves introducing the relative feature and the network to the data. In the first training stage, the distance between the mean-class and the Mahalanobis distance is computed. A category-agnostic mapping is then learned to represent the classes and subclasses of the same type. Omniglot, miniImagenet, CUB-200, and CIFAR-100 datasets were used for performance evaluation on N-way-K-shot manner. In comparison, the suggested method achieved the highest classification accuracy with the Omniglot dataset in comparison to the other three datasets. For classifying dermatological images, Prabhu V. et al. [4] suggested an FSL technique called Prototypical Clustering Networks (PCN). The process had two challenges, firstly, long-tailed dataset distribution and large intra-class variability. For the first challenge, they formulated the issue as 'low-shot learning' and for the second challenge, PCN was proposed. They created their dataset from the Dermnet Skin Disease Atlas which contained more than 23,000 images. With a few samples, the PCN technique performed superior in comparison to other techniques. S. Khodadadeh et al. [5] suggested an unsupervised meta-learning algorithm called UMTRA, which stands for Unsupervised Meta-learning with Tasks constructed by Random sampling and Augmentation for the classification of images. On unlabeled datasets, the algorithm performed meta-learning of the classifiers in an unsupervised way. Omniglot and mini-imagenet datasets were used for performance evaluation. The suggested method achieved superior performance in comparison to several other methods. The accuracy of the UMTRA algorithm is also considered better with a lesser number of labels in comparison to MAML algorithm. Again, the algorithm obtained better accuracy with Omniglot than the mini-imagenet dataset. H. Huang et al. [6] proposed a few-shot fine-grained image classification approach named LRPABN, which stands for Low-Rank Pairwise Alignment Bilinear Network. The training of the approach was done in an end-to-end manner. Four popular fine-grained datasets such as CUB birds, DOGS, CARS, and NABirds were considered for performance evaluation. The evaluation was also done on N-way-K shot manner and the results on the data sets demonstrated that the proposed LRPABN approach achieved better performances in comparison to other modern approaches. L. Liu et al. [7] have developed an approach called UTR layer (Universal Representation Transformer) for the classification of few-shot images on meta-dataset. The proposed method achieved the highest performance on seven out of ten Meta- Datasets used for performance assessment. J. Li et al. [8] proposed an unsupervised FSL technique named CSSL-FSL. The CSSL-FSL is comprised of two stages- firstly, the contrastive self-supervised learning stage which obtained transferable feature extractor, and secondly, a classifier training stage. They considered the popular MiniImageNet dataset in their experiment and obtained the best accuracy than other modern FSL methods. In another comparison, though the EGNN method achieved better accuracy with 5-shot and 10-shot, the proposed CSSL-FSL method achieved 9%, 3%, and 8% more accuracies with 1, 20, and 30-shot respectively. They also mentioned that the method could be used in other areas. Z. Xue et al. [9] have developed an attention mechanism-based FSL method called Relative Position Network or RPN for classifying images. Unlike other metric learning-based methods, the RPN method improved distance learning. Results of the method were analyzed using two datasets in a 5-way K-shot manner and obtained the best results in all the cases. To resolve the problem of requirements of a huge training dataset for the deep learning approach, D. Alajaji et al. [10] have developed a deep FSL technique for classifying remote sensing images. The developed technique is a combination of pre-trained SqueezeNet CNN with the prototypical network. They considered 'UC Merced' and 'Optimal31' datasets for experimental analysis. D. Argüeso et al. [11] developed an FSL based approach for classifying different diseases of plant leaves using images. Considering 80 images per class, the proposed method could classify 6 different types of leaf diseases with more than 90% accuracy. C. Zhang et al. [12] have suggested FSL based image classification approach named DeepEMD. It is based on Earth Mover's Distance (EMD) metric. For determining image relevancy, the EMD metric computed the structural distance between the dense images. The performance of the proposed method was evaluated in a 5-way K-shot manner with four image datasets and it obtained higher performance than the other considered methods. For the first time, S. Liu et al. [13] have suggested a multitasking deep learning approach named MDL4OW for classifying hyperspectral images with unlabeled classes in an open world. The performance of the proposed approach was compared with several other approaches including the deep learning-based FSL approaches and both deep learning and non-deep learning-based approaches on three different hyperspectral image datasets. As a result, the MDL4OW method obtained the best accuracies. Recently, Z. Li et al. [14] proposed an FSL based approach called DCFSL, and D. Pal et al. [15] have proposed another approach called SPN for HSI classification. Y. Li et al. [16] developed two FSL based Semi-Supervised (SS) methods called Single SS and Iterative SS for the classification of plant leaf diseases. In comparison to the method of [11], the outputs of the proposed methods are superior. The method in [11] obtained 90% average accuracy with 80-shot. However, the proposed method obtained 90% accuracy with 5-shot, more than 92% accuracy with 10-shot, and 97% accuracy with 80-shot. In the context of meta-learning Y. Tian et al., [38] have developed a simple baseline approach for the classification of few shot image. Although, the approach has not been appreciated highly so far, it performed better on four widely used- miniImageNet [35], tieredImageNet [39], CIFAR-FS [40] and FC-100 [41] datasets in comparison to other modern approaches. In combination with self-distillation, performance of the method further improved by 2–3%. The authors also believe that their findings could be a motivation of rethinking in the few-shot image classification.

3 One Shot Learning (OSL)

In FSL a few supervised sample data is required to train a classifier to classify a new sample. In some situations, like passport checking in airports and borders of countries, it is a challenging task to identify the person correctly whose picture is in the passport. Hence, the concept of One-Shot Learning (OSL) evolved. One-Shot Learning is another paradigm of machine learning where the classifier learns to classify an instance of a class from a single training instance of that class. i.e. the model is trained with a single data instance to classify a new instance of that class. Applications of OSL are face recognition, industrial applications, meta-learning, etc.

This section highlights some of OSL based image classification methods. J. Kozerawski et al. [17] have developed an OSL based approach called Cumulative Learning in short 'CLEAR' for image classification. The algorithm was based on transfer learning and its objective was to guess the decision boundary for image classification relying on a single image only. Five datasets were used for performance analysis and in comparison to 'Threshold', 'Chance', and 'One-class SVM' approaches, the CLEAR approach performed better. Getting inspired by the success of the popular Siamese Networks in OSL,

S.C Hsiao et al. [18] aimed to apply the Siamese Network for classifying malware images. The methodology consisted of three phases as preprocessing, training and testing. In the preprocessing phase, the malware samples were resized and classified. In training, the networks were trained to rank similarity and in the testing phase accuracy was calculated over N-way one-shot manner. For result assessment, the samples were collected from the 'Virus Share'. They mentioned that the approach could be considered as a solution for the early detection of malware. A. Chowdhury et al. [19] proposed the 'meta-meta-classification' approach for OSL classification tasks. The proposed approach learned to examine a learning problem and also combined other learning approaches for solving that problem. Four datasets such as ILSVRC-2012, CUB-2011, Omniglot, and Aircraft were considered for performance evaluation. The proposed approach performed superior to other learning approaches. T. Fechter et al. [20] proposed an OSL based medical image registration approach for tracking periodic motions in multidimensional (3D, 4D) datasets. Intending to extend the human-robot communications based on the signs of sign language S. R. Hosseini et al. [21] have proposed an OSL based 'learning from demonstration' approach to teach new signs of Iranian sign language to the RASA robot. The proposed architecture used the concepts of OSL and CNN for training. It achieved 70% accuracy on test data. C. Liu et al. [42] have proposed an embarrassingly simple baseline approach for one-shot image classification. The approach used MiniImageNet and tieredImageNet datasets for performance assessment and achieved 60.63% and 69.02% accuracy on 5-way 1-shot setting.

4   Zero Shot Learning (ZSL)

Although, FSL and OSL have achieved lots of advancement in ML some applications require classifying instances of a class that were not trained. Zero-shot learning is a solution to such problems. The ZSL is a paradigm of ML that learns to classify an instance of a class that was not trained during training, i.e. in ZSL the train or seen class and test or unseen class are different. The seen and unseen classes are related to each other and the knowledge of the seen class is used to classify an unseen class.

Here, some of the image classification methods which have been developed based on ZSL technique are highlighted. To overcome the demerits of web images and the performance gap of ZSL with outdated supervised methods, L. Niu et al. [22] have developed a hybrid technique for classifying fine-grained images. Three popular ZSL datasets such as, CUB [37], SUN [36], and Dogs were considered for result analysis. The result was compared with several DA, ZSL, and WSL baseline approaches. However, the proposed technique attained the best accuracy with all the used datasets in both ZSL and generalized ZSL settings. Intending to classify samples from both unseen and seen land cover classes R. Gui et al. [23] have suggested a generalized ZSL (GZSL) based framework to classify PolSAR images. In their framework, to relate the seen and unseen classes, semantic attributes were collected first and then establish the semantic relevance among the attributes. Evaluation of the framework was carried out on three RadarSAT-2 datasets and obtained 73% unseen class classification accuracy. The authors are also willing to continue their research to improve the model. Relying on the GCN architecture X. Wang et al. [24] suggested a zero-shot classification method that uses both the knowledge graph and semantic embedding. To overcome the less attention and utilization of modalities in the GZSL approaches, R. Felix et al. [25] have proposed two GZSL approaches which are based on the multi-modal train-test processes. The proposed approaches are called 2ME and 3ME and are the combination of the multi-modal ensemble with classifiers and semantic modalities. The proposed method not only produced optimized balanced seen and unseen classification but also worked in operating points of many GZSL classifications. They considered CUB-200–2011, FLO, SUN, and AWA datasets consisting of seen and unseen classes for performance evaluation. The proposed methods obtained the best accuracy in almost all the cases, but the Cycle-GAN method obtained good accuracy in few cases. However, in the area under the seen and unseen curve (AUSUC) the proposed methods obtained the highest accuracy with all the datasets. J. Li et al. [26] suggested a GANs based ZSL image classification approach named 'Leveraging invariant side GAN' in short 'LisGAN'. In LisGAN, they trained conditional Wasserstein GANs for synthesizing the unreal unseen samples from noises. They also introduced soul samples in the generator of GAN to assure that every generated sample is real. They considered five popular datasets for result evaluation and obtained 43.1%, 70.6%, 58.8%, 69.6%, and 61.7% top-1 ZSL accuracy with the considered aPay, AWA, CUB, FLO, and SUN dataset respectively. In the case of generalized ZSL, the method obtained 62.3%, 51.6%, 68.3%, and 40.2% top-1 mean accuracy with AWA, CUB, FLO, and SUN datasets respectively. However, in comparison to other approaches, the suggested one achieved superior accuracy in both the ZSL and GZSL paradigm. Considering feature generation one step advanced E. Schönfeld et al. [27] have proposed a cross-modal embedding approach called 'Cross-and Distribution Alignment- variational Autoencoder' in short 'CADA-VAE' for the GZSL and FSL. In the approach, a variational autoencoder is trained for both semantic and visual modalities. The objective of the method was the alignment of learned distributions from images and construction of latent features from side information which contained the important multi-modal information of unseen class. The method was evaluated on four datasets and performed better than the other 11 methods. Using the coupled dictionary learning, M. Rostami et al. [28] developed a ZSL technique called 'Transductive AAw'. The primary concept of the approach was to share the same sparse representation of semantic attributes and visual features of an image. To learn sparse dictionaries, they considered semantic attributes from unseen and seen classes, and images from the seen classes. D. Huynh and E. Elhamifar [29] have proposed a multi-attention technique for predicting multiple labels in an image called 'Learning by Sharing Attentions', LESA in short. As it is a non-trivial task to design an attention mechanism for recognizing multiple unseen and seen labels in an image, therefore, despite generating attention for the unseen labels, they allowed them to select from shared attentions. They also proposed a loss function consisting of three components. The assessment of the method was performed on the NUS-WIDE dataset and it performed superior in comparison to other modern methods. V. Khare et al. [30] addressed the domain shift issue among the unseen and seen classes distribution and proposed the Adversarial Domain Adaptation (ADA) method. The proposed method was based on the class distribution of seen and unseen classes. They parameterized the class distributions to make the method capable of learning unseen class distributions. Though the proposed method was very similar to VAE or GAN-based methods, it performed superior to other state-of-the-art methods in the zero-shot-learning setting. This method also used the SUN, CUB, and AWA2 datasets for performance evaluation and attained 63.3%, 70.9%, and 70.4% accuracy respectively. K. Demertzis et al. [31] developed a ZSL approach called 'MAME-ZSL' for classifying hyperspectral images. The proposed model is considered as the first model in the domain with some advancements like –intermediate learning, avoids overfitting and reduction of training time and computational costs, etc. The model also improved classification accuracy, training stability, and overall performance. For the first time in GZSL, A. Gupta et al., [32] proposed a multi-label feature synthesis approach. They introduced the ALF, FLF, and CLF fusion approaches for synthesizing multi-label features. MS-COCO, Open Images, and NUS-WIDE datasets were used for performance evaluation. For the first time, [32] used the MS-COCO dataset for the evaluation of the ZSL approach. With a goal to solve the problem of sample shortage of many diseases, D. Mahapatra et al. [43] have suggested a generalized ZSL method for the classification of medical images. The proposed method have used self-supervised learning (SSL) techniques to synthesize the feature vector of unseen classes and to train the feature generator. The method's performance was evaluated on both natural and medical images. The considered natural datasets are CUB [37], AwA1 [44], AwA2 [45], SUN [36] and FLO [46] and medical image datasets are CAMELYON17 [47], NIH Chest Xray [48], CheXpert [49], Kaggle Diabetic Retinopathy [50] and Gleason Grading Challenge [51].

5   Result Comparison of Different Methods with Different Datasets

In this section, performance comparison of the image classification methods reviewed in the paper are presented. Table 1, 2, 3, 4 and 5 depicts the classification accuracy of the methods using various datasets where different numbers of training samples are considered. The graphical plots corresponding to Tables 1, 2, 3, 4, and 5 are shown in Fig. 1, 2, 3, 4, and 5 respectively. Methods using same datasets have been compared in the paper.

Table 1. Result comparison of Hyperspectral Image (HSI) classification methods with 5 samples per class.

Methods	OA in % on Indian Pines	OA in % on Salinas
DCFSL [14]	66.81	89.34
SPN [15]	99.49	97.95

Table 1 consists of the performance of hyperspectral image classification methods and it is found that the SPN method with 5 samples obtained 99.49% overall accuracy on Indian Pines (IP) dataset. Table 2 shows the comparative results of HSI classification methods on Pavia University, IP and Salinas dataset considering 20 samples per class. However, the DFSL + SVM method obtained the best accuracy on Salinas dataset. Performance of the method is poor on the IP dataset. The performance of 5-way 5-shot

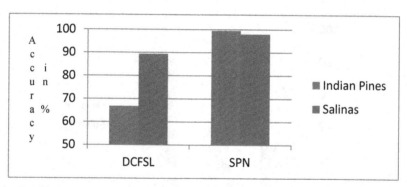

Fig. 1. Graphical plot for the result comparison of HSI classification methods considering 5 samples per class.

Table 2. Result comparison of Hyperspectral Image (HSI) classification methods with 20 samples per class.

Methods	OA in % on Pavia University	OA in % on Indian Pines	OA in % on Salinas
DFSL + SVM [2]	90.69	83.01	93.42
MDL4OW [13]	85.07	68.92	87.40

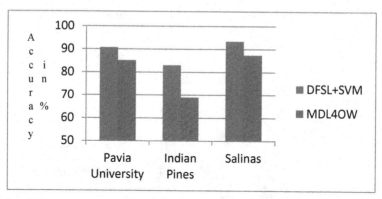

Fig. 2. Graphical plot for the result comparison of HSI classification methods considering 20 samples per class.

Table 3. Result comparison of the image classification methods on Omniglot and MiniImagenet dataset in 5-way 5-shot setting.

Methods	Omniglot	MiniImagenet
CS [1]	99.65	67.96
2S [3]	99.50	70.91
UMTRA [5]	95.43	50.73

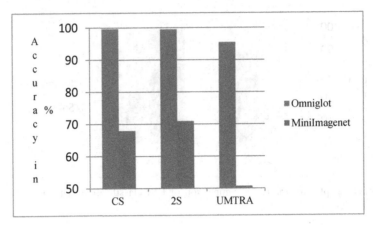

Fig. 3. Graphical plot for the result comparison of the methods in 5-way 5-shot setting.

Table 4. Result comparison of the image classification methods on Omniglot and MiniImagenet datasets in 5-way 1-shot setting.

Methods	Omniglot	MiniImagenet
CS [1]	97.56	51.03
2S [3]	99.20	52.68
UMTRA [5]	83.80	39.93

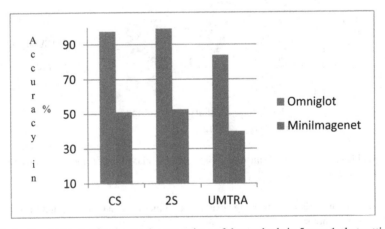

Fig. 4. Graphical plot for the result comparison of the methods in 5-way 1-shot setting.

and 5-way 1-shot classification methods are shown in Table 3 and 4 respectively. All the methods achieved outstanding result on the Omniglot dataset. However, their performance is poor on the MiniImagenet dataset. In 5-way 5-shot setting the CS method obtained the best performance, and in 5-way-1-shot setting the 2S method obtained the

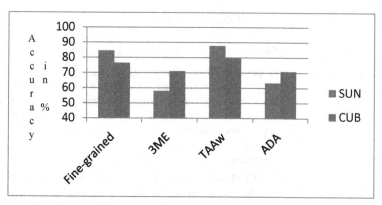

Fig. 5. Graphical plot for the result comparison of ZSL image clasification methods on SUN and CUB dataset

Table 5. Result comparison of ZSL methods on SUN and CUB dataset

Methods	SUN	CUB
Fine-grained [22]	84.50	76.47
3ME [25]	58.10	71.10
TAAw [28]	87.72	79.63
ADA [30]	63.30	70.90

best performance on the Omniglot dataset respectively. Finally, the Table 5 shows the performance comparison of ZSL methods on the SUN and CUB dataset. The TAAw method achieved the highest accuracy on both the datasets. From the performance analysis, it is observed that the methods considered more samples for training achieved better accuracy and performance of the same method varies on different dataset.

6   Summary

This section consists of a summary of the above discussed FSL, OSL and ZSL based image classification methods which are summarized in Table 6.

Table 6. Summary

Method	Findings	Limitations
FC and CS [1]	Proposed FC (Fully Connected) and CS (Cosine Similarity) frameworks are more effective and superior than many FSL approaches. Considered hyper-parameter is number of fine tuning iterations	Though the methods obtained more than 99% accuracy with the Omniglot dataset but it was not outstanding with the miniImagenet dataset
DFSL [2]	The DFSL method achieved superior classification accuracy than several semisupervised methods with a few training samples. UP, PC, IP and Salinas datasets were considered for performance evaluation and the DFSL with SVM obtained the highest accuracy with 25 samples	Performance of the method can be improved considering large –scale datasets
2S [3]	The approach obtained outstanding result on the Omniglot dataset but not on the miniImagenet, CUB-200 and CIFA-100 dataset	Performances of the approach on the other datasets need to be improved
PCN [4]	The method was developed for analyzing dermatological diseases. Performance of PCN is better than PN method	
UMTRA [5]	UMTRA can be applied to both image and video classification. On the Omniglot dataset it performed better than MAML comparatively with number of samples. The hyperparameters used in the method are meta-batch size and number of updates	Performance was better on the Omniglot than Mini-Imagenet dataset. However, overall performance can be improved
LRPABN [6]	LRPABN was trained in an end-to-end manner. Four popular fine- grained datasets- CUB Birds, DOGS, CARS and NABirds were used for result analysis	Although, the method achieved better result in 5-way setting, still the performance can be improved

(continued)

Table 6. (*continued*)

Method	Findings	Limitations
CSSL-FSL [8]	CSSL-FSL is a two phased unsupervised FSL paradigm. It achieved almost 69% accuracy on the miniImageNet dataset in 5-way-5-shot manner	
RPN [9]	It is developed based on attention mechanism. To improve metric learning the approach considered finer information from the feature maps	The method achieved 73.17% average accuracy on 5-way 10-shot setting. However, further improvement can takes place
Distance-metric FSL[11]	The method is based on Inception V3 and linear SVM. It classified leaf disease considering only 80 images per class and achieved more than 90% accuracy. Complexity of the method is less	
DCFSL [14]	Propose approach consists of two types of FSL one is for source domain and other is for the target domain. Considering four HSI datasets, effectiveness of the method was compared with several supervised, semi-supervised and unsupervised methods	Though the DCFSL method achieved very good classification accuracy, its training time is long
SPN [15]	Based on Prototypical Networks, SPN model was developed to classify HSI with less number of training samples. It achieved very good result on Indian Pines and Salinas dataset considering 25 training samples	However, the method achieved only 76.33% overall accuracy on the Houston dataset
Single SS and Iterative SS [16]	Semi-supervised FSL approaches to classify leaf diseases. In comparison, both the methods achieved 2.8% and 4.6% average improvement respectively	

(*continued*)

Table 6. (*continued*)

Method	Findings	Limitations
Siamese CNN [18]	The method is a solution to early detection of malware appearance based on OSL approach. Different hyper-parameters used in the method are mini-batch size, learning rate, total number of iterations, number of classes chosen for testing and number of one-shot task	Accuracy can be improved
LfD [21]	The LfD teaches sign languages to RASA robot. The method used OSL and CNN techniques and achieved 70% accuracy	Small sized with little variety dataset was considered for performance evaluation
Hybrid [22]	The method was built with a goal to reduce the noise in web images and performance gap between the traditional-supervised and ZSL approach while classifying fine grained images	Performance was good on CUB dataset in comparison to the SUN and Dogs datasets. However, performance can be improved
2ME, 3ME [25]	These are Generalized ZSL approach and are based on the multi-modal train-test process. Performance varies with the seen and unseen classes	
TAAw [28]	The method shares semantic attribute and visual features of an image. Semantic attributes were considered from unseen and seen classes, and images from the seen classes	Accuracy of the TAAw method was poor on the CUB dataset comparatively
ADA [30]	Addressed the domain shift problem between the unseen and seen classes in ZSL	Accuracy was better on AWA2 dataset in comparison to SUN and CUB dataset
MAME-ZSL [31]	The method classifies HSI with less training time and computational costs. It also avoids overfitting. In future it may be implemented with other complex architectures	

(*continued*)

Table 6. (*continued*)

Method	Findings	Limitations
Simple [38]	The approach has been developed in the context of meta-learning. Though, the method is unsung it has achieved outstanding performance	
Baseline [42]	It is an embarrassingly simple approach for one-shot image classification. Without any complex structure features were pruned for the recognition task	The approach performed superior on the tiered-ImageNet dataset in comparison to miniImageNet
SCGZSL [43]	The GZSL method uses self-supervised learning for synthesizing feature vector and to train feature generator. It's performance was analysed on both natural and medical images	

7 Conclusion

To overcome the demerits of deep learning-based image classification methods, new paradigms of machine learning like, FSL, OSL, and ZSL have been developed. Unlike deep learning-based methods, these methods can classify images like a human with less number of training samples. ZSL methods can also classify images that were not considered during training. It is found that the surveyed methods achieved various classification accuracies with different datasets. It is also found that the performance of the methods varies with the different number of samples considered during training. Though, some methods obtained very good accuracy with the Omniglot dataset their performance is poor on the MiniImageNet dataset. Again, in case of ZSL methods, performances of the methods are varies on the SUN and CUB datasets. Hence, in future further research and investigation is essential to carry out on the development of efficient methods.

References

1. Chu, W., Li, Y., Chang, J., Wang Y.F.: Spot and learn: a maximum-entropy patch sampler for few-shot image classification. In: IEEE/CVF Conference on Computer Vision and Pattern Recognition (CVPR), pp. 6244–6253 (2019). https://doi.org/10.1109/CVPR.2019.00641
2. Liu, B., Yu, X., Yu, A., Zhang, P., Wan, G., Wang, R.: Deep few-shot learning for hyperspectral image classification. IEEE Trans. Geosci. Remote Sens. **57**(4), 2290–2304 (2019). https://doi.org/10.1109/TGRS.2018.2872830
3. Debasmit, D., George Lee, C.S.: A Two-Stage Approach to Few-Shot Learning for Image Recognition. https://doi.org/10.1109/TIP.2019.2959254

4. Prabhu, V., Kannan, A., et al.: Few-shot learning for dermatological disease diagnosis. In: Proceedings of the 4th Machine Learning for Healthcare Conference, in Proceedings of Machine Learning Research, vol. 106, pp. 532–552 (2019). https://proceed-ings.mlr.press/v106/prabhu 19a.html

5. Khodadadeh, S., et al.: Unsupervised Meta-Learning for Few-Shot Image Classification. arXiv:1811.11819

6. Huaxi, H., Junjie, Z., et al.: Low-Rank Pairwise Alignment Bilinear Network for Few-Shot Fine-Grained Image Classification. https://doi.org/10.1109/TMM.2020.3001510

7. Lu, L., Will, H., Guodong, L., Jing, J., Hugo, L.: A Universal Representation Transformer Layer for Few-Shot Image Classification. arXiv:2006.11702 (2020)

8. Jianyi, L., Guizhong, L.: Few-Shot Image Classification via Contrastive Self-Supervised Learning (2020)

9. Xue, Z., Xie, Z., et al.: Relative position and map networks in few-shot learning for image classification. In: IEEE/CVF Conference on Computer Vision and Pattern Recognition Workshops (CVPRW), pp. 4032–4036, (2020). https://doi.org/10.1109/CVPRW50498.2020.00474

10. Alajaji, D., Alhichri, H.S., Ammour, N., Alajlan N.: Few-shot learning for remote sensing scene classification. In: Mediterranean and Middle-East Geoscience and Remote Sensing Symposium (M2GARSS), pp. 81–84 (2020). https://doi.org/10.1109/M2GARSS47143.2020. 9105154

11. David, A., et al.: Few-shot learning approach for plant disease classification using images taken in the field. Comput. Electron. Agriculture, **175**, 105542 (2020). https://doi.org/10. 1016/j.compag.2020.105542

12. Chi, Z., Yujun, C., Guosheng, L., Chunhua, S.: DeepEMD: few-shot image classification with differentiable earth mover's distance and structured classifiers. In: Proceedings of the IEEE/CVF Conference on Computer Vision and Pattern Recognition (CVPR), pp. 12203–12213 (2020)

13. Liu, S., Shi, Q., Zhang, L.: Few-shot hyperspectral image classification with unknown classes using multitask deep learning. IEEE Trans. Geosci. Remote Sens. **59**(6), 5085–5102 (2021). https://doi.org/10.1109/TGRS.2020.3018879

14. Li, Z., Liu, M., Chen, Y., et al.: Deep cross-domain few-shot learning for hyperspectral image classification. IEEE Trans. Geosci. Remote Sens. **60**, 1–18 (2021)https://doi.org/10.1109/ TGRS.2021.3057066

15. Pal, D., Bundele, V., Banerjee, B., Jeppu, Y.: SPN stable prototypical network for few-shot learning-based hyperspectral image classification. IEEE Geosci. Remote Sens. Lett. **19**, 1–5 (2021). https://doi.org/10.1109/LGRS.2021.3085522

16. Li, Y., Chao, X.: Semi-supervised few-shot learning approach for plant diseases recognition. Plant Methods **17**, 68 (2021). https://doi.org/10.1186/s13007-021-00770-1

17. Kozerawski, J., Turk, M.: CLEAR cumulative LEARning for One-Shot One-Class Image recognition. In: IEEE/CVF Conference on Computer Vision and Pattern Recognition, pp. 3446–3455 (2018). https://doi.org/10.1109/CVPR.2018.00363

18. Shou-Ching, H., Da-Yu, K., Zi-Yuan, L., Raylin, T.: Malware image classification using one-shot learning with siamese networks. Procedia Comput. Sci. **159**, 1863–1871 (2019). https:// doi.org/10.1016/j.procs.2019.09.358

19. Arkabandhu, C., Dipak, C., Swarat, C., Chris, J.: Meta-Meta-Classification for One-Shot Learning (2020). arXiv:2004.08083

20. Tobias, F., Dimos, B.: One Shot Learning for Deformable Medical Image Registration and Periodic Motion Tracking (2020), arXiv:1907.04641

21. Hosseini, S.R., Taheri, A., et al.: One-shot learning from demonstration approach toward a reciprocal sign language-based HRI. Int. J. Soc. Robot. **10**, 1–13 (2021).https://doi.org/10. 1007/s12369-021-00818-1

22. Niu, L., Veeraraghavan, A., Sabharwal, A.: Webly supervised learning meets zero-shot learning: a hybrid approach for fine-grained classification. In: IEEE/CVF Conference on Computer Vision and Pattern Recognition, pp. 7171–7180 (2018). https://doi.org/10.1109/CVPR.2018.00749

23. Rong, G., Xin, X., et al.: A generalized zero-shot learning framework for PolSAR land cover classification. Remote Sens. **10**(8), 1307 (2018). https://doi.org/10.3390/rs10081307

24. Xiaolong, W., Yufei, Y., Abhinav, G.: Zero-shot recognition via semantic embeddings and knowledge graphs. In: IEEE/CVF Conference on Computer Vision and Pattern Recognition (CVPR) (2018). https://doi.org/10.1109/CVPR.2018.00717

25. Rafael, F., Michele, S., et al.: Multi-modal Ensemble Classification for Generalized Zero Shot Learning (2019), arXiv:1901.04623

26. Jingjing, L., Mengmeng, J., et al.: Leveraging the invariant side of generative zero-shot learning. In: IEEE/CVF Conference on Computer Vision and Pattern Recognition (CVPR), pp. 7394–7403 (2019). https://doi.org/10.1109/CVPR.2019.00758

27. Edgar, S., Sayna, E., et al.: Generalized Zero- and Few-Shot Learning via Aligned Variational Autoencoders (2018), arXiv:1812.01784

28. Mohammad, R., Soheil, K., et al.: Zero-Shot Image Classification Using Coupled Dictionary Embedding. In: AAAI (2019). arXiv:1906.10509

29. Dat, H., Ehsan, E.: A shared multi-attention framework for multi-label zero-shot learning. In: IEEE/CVF Conference on Computer Vision and Pattern Recognition (CVPR) (2020). https://doi.org/10.1109/CVPR42600.2020.00880

30. Varun, K., Divyat, M., et al.: A generative framework for zero-shot learning with adversarial domain adaptation. In: Proceedings of the IEEE/CVF Winter Conference on Applications of Computer Vision, pp. 3101–3110 (2020)

31. Konstantinos, D., Lazaros, I.: GeoAI: a model-agnostic meta-ensemble zero-shot learning method for hyperspectral image analysis and classification. MDPI (2020).https://doi.org/10.3390/a13030061www

32. Akshita, G., et al.: Generative multi-label zero-shot learning (2021). arXiv preprint arXiv:2101.11606

33. Wei, W., et al.: A survey of zero-shot learning: settings, methods, and applications. ACM Trans. Intell. Syst. Technol. **10**, 1–37 (2019). https://doi.org/10.1145/3293318

34. Lake, B., Salakhutdinov, R., Gross, J., Tenenbaum, J.: One shot learning of simple visual concepts. In: Proceeding of the Annual Meeting of the Cognitive Science Society, vol. 3 (2011)

35. Vinyals, O., Blundell, C., Lillicrap, T., Kavukcuoglu, K., Wierstra, D.: Matching networks for one shot learning. In: Advances in Neural Information Processing Systems (NIPS) (2016)

36. Xiao, J., Hays, J., Ehinger, K.A., Oliva, A., Torralba, A.: Sun database: large-scale scene recognition from abbey to zoo. In: CVPR (2010)

37. Wah, C., Branson, S., Welinder, P., Perona, P., Belongie, S.: The Caltech-UCSD Birds-200–2011 Dataset. Technical Report CNS-TR-2011–001, California Institute of Technology (2011)

38. Tian, Y., Wang, Y., Krishnan, D., Tenenbaum, J.B., Isola, P.: Rethinking few-shot image classification: a good embedding is all you need? In: Vedaldi, A., Bischof, H., Brox, T., Frahm, J.-M. (eds.) ECCV 2020. LNCS, vol. 12359, pp. 266–282. Springer, Cham (2020). https://doi.org/10.1007/978-3-030-58568-6_16

39. Ren, M., et al.: Meta-learning for semi-supervised fewshot classification. In: ICLR (2018)

40. Luca, B., Joao, F.H., Philip, H.S.T., Andrea, V.: Meta-learning with differentiable closed-form solvers. arXiv preprint arXiv:1805.08136 (2018)

41. Boris, O., Pau, R.L., Alexandre, L.T.: Task dependent adaptive metric for improved few-shot learning. In: NIPS (2018)

42. Liu, C., Xu, C., Wang, Y., Zhang, L., Fu, Y.: An embarrassingly simple baseline to one-shot learning. IEEE/CVF Conference on Computer Vision and Pattern Recognition Workshops (CVPRW) **2020**, 4005–4009 (2020). https://doi.org/10.1109/CVPRW50498.2020.00469

43. Mahapatra, D., Bozorgtabar, B., Ge, Z.: Medical image classification using generalized zero shot learning. In: Proceedings of the IEEE/CVF International Conference on Computer Vision, pp. 3344–3353 (2021)

44. Lampert, C.H., Nickisch, H., Harmeling, S.: Attribute-based classification for zero-shot visual object categorization. IEEE Trans. Pattern Anal. Mach. Intell. **36**(3), 453–465 (2013)

45. Xian, Y., Lampert, C.H., Schiele, B., Akata, Z.: Zero-shot learning a comprehensive evaluation of the good, the bad and the ugly. IEEE Trans. Pattern Anal. Mach. Intell. **41**(9), 2251–2265 (2018)

46. Nilsback, M., Zisserman, A.: Automated flower classification over a large number of classes. In: 2008 Sixth Indian Conference on Computer Vision, Graphics Image, pp. 722–729 (2008)

47. Bandi, P., et al.: From detection of individual metastases to classification of lymph node status at the patient level: the CAMELYON17 challenge. IEEE Trans. Med. Imag. **38**(2), 550–560 (2019)

48. Wang, X., Peng, Y., Lu, L., Lu, Z., Bagheri, M., Summers, R.M.: Chestx-ray8: hospital-scale chest x-ray database and bench-marks on weakly-supervised classification and localization of common thorax diseases. In: Proceeding CVPR (2017)

49. Jeremy, I., Pranav, R., Michael, K., et al.: CheXpert: a large chest radiograph dataset with uncertainty labels and expert comparison. arXiv preprint arXiv:1901.07031 (2017)

50. Kaggle and EyePacs. Kaggle diabetic retinopathy detection. https://www.kaggle.com/c/diabetic-retinopathydetection/data, July 2015

51. Karimi, D., Nir, G., et al.: Deep learning-based gleason grading of prostate cancer from histopathology images-role of multiscale decision aggregation and data augmentation. IEEE J. Biomed. Health Inform. **24**(5), 1413–1426 (2020)

eXtreme Gradient Boosting Scheme for Fundus Vessels Separation

Shirsendu Dhar[1], Sumit Mukherjee[2(✉)], Ranjit Ghoshal[1],
and Bibhas Chandra Dhara[3]

[1] St. Thomas' College of Engineering and Technology, Kolkata 700023, India
[2] Tata Consultancy Services, Kolkata 700156, India
`sum.mukherjee@gmail.com`
[3] Jadavpur University, Kolkata 700098, India

Abstract. Glaucoma, diabetic retinopathy, hypertension, and other ophthalmologic illnesses can easily be detected by examining the vascular structures in the retina. This makes vessel extraction in retinal fundus images extremely important when it comes to detect and diagnosis of any eye relater disorders. It is a challenging feat, especially given the many noises and the diverse structure of the thin vessels. An innovative approach is coined in this article for extraction vascular structure for detection and diagnosis of a variety of eye illnesses. First, different image processing techniques are applied to aid required features extraction. In next step, a model is constructed using the stated features for each image for which input and ground truth exists. All these models are tested on the other sets of the images and accuracy scores are computed. Based on the accuracy score final model is chosen. Model outcomes are analysed using standard evaluation parameters and found to be one of the best in class.

Keywords: Retinal image · Vessel separation · Extreme gradient boosting · Machine learning · Feature extraction

1 Introduction

The ocular fundus, which is the inner lining of the eye, is made up of the Sensory Retina, Retinal Pigment Epithelium, Bruch's Membrane, and Choroid. Ophthalmoscopy (Fig. 1), also known as funduscopy, is an imaging technique that uses a highly sophisticated ophthalmoscope to allow a medical practitioner to see within the eye's fundus and other components for analysing eye related problems. The structural orientation of retinal blood vessels is an important diagnostic indicator for diabetic retinopathy, hypertension, and glaucoma, among other eye problems. Therefore, extracting vessels from retinal fundus images is highly recommended to obtain relevant information about the eye related illness.

The presence of various noises inside the narrow vessels, which also display a diversity of structures, complicates the technique of retinal vascular extraction.

© The Author(s), under exclusive license to Springer Nature Switzerland AG 2022
S. Mukhopadhyay et al. (Eds.): CICBA 2022, CCIS 1579, pp. 45–58, 2022.
https://doi.org/10.1007/978-3-031-10766-5_4

The purpose of this article is to solve such a complex issues. Morphological techniques are utilised in traditional approaches to eliminate noise from pictures, but this destroys the granular characteristics of the vessels and even affects the vascular structures. Hence morphological techniques may inject additional errors and not recommended when it comes to take critical decision. Here, an attempt has been made to extract the vessels without affecting the granular structures so that critical decision can be made based on the output.

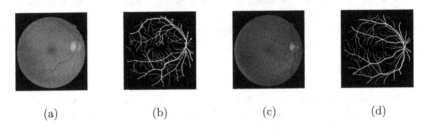

(a)   (b)   (c)   (d)

Fig. 1. (a) and (c) Retinal RGB images, (b) and (d) Corresponding ground truths

Several techniques [1,2] have been proposed, including matching filters, to boost contrast and separability of blood vessels from the background and to facilitate sequential vessel detection. Marin et al. [3] proposed deep learning to categorise features based on grey levels and moment invariants. To train the support vector machine (SVM), Ricci et al. [4] suggested utilising two orthogonal line operators as feature vectors and pixels were categorized into vessel and non-vessel pixels using SVM. Similar works can be found in the following literature [5–7]. In a recent study by Frucci et al. [8], some direction map-based approaches were used. Morphological processing was utilized to extract vessels from retinal fundus image by Imani et al. [10] and Zana et al. [9]. Roychowdhury et al. [11] and Franklin et al. [12] used some machine learning techniques for this purpose also. Mendonca et al. [13] devised a new approach based on centre line detection and mathematical morphology. Oliveira et al. [14] employed a fully convolutional neural network (CNN) capable of attaining the state-of-the-art outcomes. Guo et al. [15] proposed a multi-scale and multi-level deeply trained CNN with short connections for vessel segmentation to convey semantic information between side-output layers, short connections were used. A new formulation of patch-based completely CNNs was also given in the article, resulting in more precise segmentation of the retinal blood vessels. Feng et al. [16] introduced a patch-based completely CNNs that permits accurate segmentation of the retinal blood vessels. By using local entropy sampling and a skip CNN architecture with class-balancing loss, the patch-based completely CNN training was improved and speeded up the whole process. Liskowski et al. [17] used a deep neural network trained on a huge sample of examples preprocessed with global contrast normalisation, zero-phase whitening, and enhanced with geometric modifications and gamma corrections in a recent supervised segmentation technique. However, most of these deep learning models necessitate a high-performance system setup as well as a large dataset collection, and they are exceedingly computationally expensive to train. In the proposed method the images are processed through 41 different filters (32 Gabor Filter variation, Canny Edge, Roberts Edge, Sobel Edge, Scharr Edge, Prewill Edge, Gaussian with sigma 3 and 7, Median with sigma 3 and Variance with sigma 3). Then, along with the above 41 filtered images, the original image and the ground truth image are unwrapped into a single dimension and a data-frame is formed from that. Now, N models, each of the those N images are trained on their respective data-frames, are applied on the rest of the $(N-1)$ images and the corresponding accuracy of each model is being calculated. On the basis of these accuracy results, the top 15 images, whose models scored the highest were selected, and the final model was built on the by using the XGBoost classification on the combined data-frames of these images. This proposed method was carried out on the DRIVE data [5]. The following is a breakdown of how this article is structured. Image extraction by 41 methods is demonstrated in Sect. 2. The working of XGBoost is described in Sect. 3. Section 4 explains the selecting and merging process of the best 15 images. Section 5 examines the proposed method's performance. Section 6 brings the article to a conclusion.

2   Feature Extraction

The proposed vessel extraction approach may be broken down into a few basic steps. To extract vessels from a retinal fundus image, first transform the image from RGB to green channels, which provides the best contrast for blood vessels (Fig. 2). The idea behind this method is that the original image will go through a series of filters and processing steps that will result in a final output that is close to the ground truth image. Weights will be assigned to the filters or processing that will allow this advised strategy to achieve the intended goal. Filers have been used in the proposed work listed below.

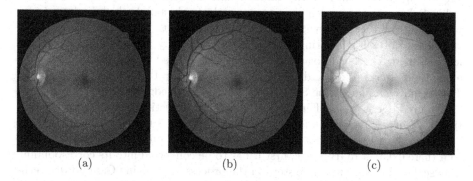

(a)   (b)   (c)

Fig. 2. (a), (b) and (c) are the red, green and blue channels of the RGB image (Color figure online)

2.1   32 Gabor Filters

Gabor Filters, in the context of image processing can be used in texture analysis, edge detection, feature extraction which can be used by machine learning algorithm for training purposes. The Gabor Filters are band pass filters, i.e. they will allow certain band of frequencies and reject others. The Gabor function can be mathematically represented in the following Eq. 1, where x, y defines the kernel size, σ is standard deviation of the gaussian envelope, θ represents orientation of the normal to the parallel stripes of a Gabor function, λ for wavelength of the sinusoidal factor, γ for spatial aspect ratio and ψ is phase offset. The few kernel filters used in the model are in Fig. 3.

$$g(x, y, \sigma, \theta, \lambda, \gamma, \psi) = \frac{-(x^2 + \gamma^2 y^2)}{(2\sigma^2)} exp[i(2\pi(\frac{x}{y}) + \psi)] \tag{1}$$

2.2   The Different Edge Detectors

Edge Detectors are simply used to locate areas in an image where there is an abrupt change in intensity or colour. A high value indicates a steep change and low indicates shallow. The following figure represents PoI or Pixel of Interest, that would give idea about neighbourhood, collection of pixels in matrix form.

Roberts Masks are used to detect the diagonals, which an improvement to the ordinary masks which detects only the horizontal and vertical masks. The masks representation are in Fig. 4. Being an even mask and having less neighbourhood and small size (2×2), it carries a slight disadvantage.

To counter these disadvantages, Sobel and Prewitt masks comes (Fig. 5). The Sobel mask has two kernels $(3 \times 3$ matrix), corresponding to horizontal and vertical direction. These two kernels are convoluted with the original image through which the edge points are calculated. This approach works through calculation of the gradient of the image intensity at every pixel within the image.

The Prewitt mask is similar to the Sobel but with minor difference. The Prewitt operator shall give the values which are symmetric around the centre, unlike Sobel operator which gives more weight to the point which is closer to (x, y). The fig represents Prewitt x and y operator values.

Scharr Filter is a filtering method used to identify and highlight edges and features using the 1st derivative. Typically this is used to identify the gradients along the $x - axis$ (dx = 1, dy = 0) and $y - axis$ (dx = 0, dy = 1) independently. This is quite similar to the Sobel filter. Fig. 6 shows edge filter effects.

Canny Edge is a bit different than other edge detection technique, with additional features. One of its many advantages is that it suppresses the noise while detecting the edges flawlessly. This technique works only in gray scale images, so if there exists a RGB image, first it has to be converted into its corresponding gray scale. There are multiple steps in the process of applying Canny Edge technique. In the beginning the image is processed by Gaussian Blur, which helps in removing the noise in the input image, making it smooth and enabling further process to be flawless. The second step is Intensity Gradient Calculation. The Canny Edge transformation in Fig. 7.

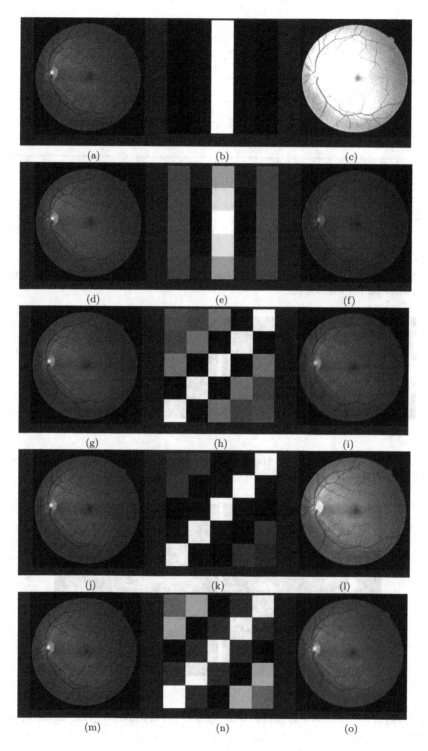

Fig. 3. (a), (d), (g), (j) and (m) are the Green channel of the Retinal Fundus images, (b), (e), (h), (k) and (n) are the Gabor kernels, (c), (f), (i), (l) and (o) are corresponding images after using gabour kernels. (Color figure online)

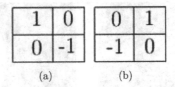

1	0
0	-1

(a)

0	1
-1	0

(b)

Fig. 4. (a) and (b) are the 2 Robert Mask to detect the 2 diagonals

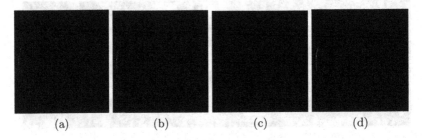

-1	0	1
-2	0	2
-1	0	1

(a)

1	2	1
0	0	0
-1	-2	-1

(b)

-1	0	1
-1	0	1
-1	0	1

(c)

1	1	1
0	0	0
-1	-1	-1

(d)

Fig. 5. (a) & (b) are the vertical and horizontal Sobel masks, (c) & (d) are the vertical and horizontal Prewitt masks.

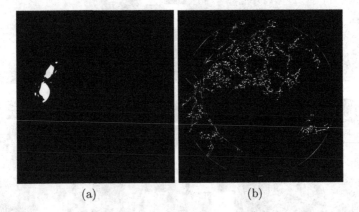

(a) (b) (c) (d)

Fig. 6. (a), (b), (c) and (d) are the edge detected images by Prewitt, Sobel, Roberts and Scharr Masks respectively.

(a) (b)

Fig. 7. (a) is the Retinal Fundus RGB image and (b) is the corresponding canny edge image.

2.3   Blurring Methods

Blur Filters, soften a selection of pixels or an image and are useful for retouching. They smooth the transition by averaging the color values. Gaussian Blur or smoothing is the result of blurring an image by a Gaussian function. The visual effect of this technique is a smooth blur resembling that of viewing through a translucent screen. It is represented in the following way.

$$y[m,n] = median x[i,j], (i,j) \epsilon w \tag{2}$$

The median filter is a type of non-linear digital filter that is commonly used to remove noise. This noise reduction is a separate pre-treatment step that will boost the outcomes of future approaches. It's used to remove salt and pepper noise from images and smooth them out. Neighbourhood averaging can suppress isolated out-of-range noise, but the side effect is that it also blurs sudden changes such as line features, sharp edges, and image details all corresponding to high spatial frequency. The median filter is an effective method that can, to some extent, distinguish out-of-range isolated noise from legitimate image features such as edge lines.

3   XGBoost

XGBoost or "eXtreme Gradient Boosting" is a Supervised Tree based algorithm, where the use of training data(with multiple features) x_i is used to predict a target variable y_i. XGBoost is built on Decision Trees concept.

3.1   Decision Trees

The decision tree ensembles models consists of a set of classification and regression trees(CART), where each leaf or node represents a test. Suppose decision tree has to be built to find the perfect fit for a job. We classify the already existing pool into different leaves and assign them the score on the corespondent leaf. In CART, which is a bit different decision trees, the leaves contain the real score associated with it, which gives us a richer interpretation that goes beyond classification. This also helps us in optimization purposes also.

Usually, a single tree is not found to be that effective in practice. So, instead of that, an ensemble model is used which sums the prediction of multiple trees together. Here is an example of a tree ensemble of two trees. The prediction scores of each individual tree are summed to get the final result. Here, both the trees are trying to complement each other to make the model work better. Mathematically the model can be represented as

$$y_i = \sum_{k=1}^{K} f_k(x_i), f_k \epsilon F \tag{3}$$

where F is set of all possible CARTs and K,f are the number of trees and functional space in F respectively. The optimized objective function can be written as

$$obj(\theta) = \sum_{i}^{n} l(y_i, \hat{y}_i) + \sum_{k=1}^{K} \Omega(f_t) \tag{4}$$

3.2 Tree Boosting

Both Random Forest and XGBoost shares Tree ensembles as their common feature. They differ in the manner in which they are trained. Boosting builds models from individual decision trees or "weak learners" in an iterative way. But unlike Random Forest, individual models are not completely built on random subsets of data or features. Instead, in boosting, more weight is put on individual models in a sequential way, in another words, learns from past mistakes. The name Gradient comes from Gradient Boosting, the same algorithm deep learning uses to find the minima in the loss function.

3.3 XGBoost

The XGBoost (eXtreme Gradient Boosting) is an advanced, or an optimized version of boosting which was developed very recently in 2016, by University of Washington and won numerous Kaggle competition through it. Due to its high performance, in addition to less training time and size, its used as an alternative to deep learning algorithms. To optimize the normal boosting, it uses tricks like computation of 2nd order gradients to figure out the direction of gradients. It also uses L1 and L2 regularization to prevent over-fitting. Parallel computing makes this super fast.

4 Algorithm: Way of Working

As there are only 20 images in the DRIVE dataset, which is considerably low to train any model, so dataset is needed to be handled carefully. So at first 41 different filters or extraction techniques are defined. Each image is then processed through and then flattened out. Then for every image, a model was trained based on the cross-sectional data of that image. After creating 20 such models, each model was tested on the total set of images (20).

On the basis of the mean accuracy in Table 1, the top 15 images (75 of the total set) was taking for the training set and rest 5 was for testing. With this approach the effects of outliers have been muted as much as possible. The algorithmic steps are detailed out below:

1. Images are processed through 41 different filters as described in Sect. 2.
2. Then, output of the 41 filters, the original image and the ground truth image are unwrapped into a single dimension data-frame.
3. Now, N models, each of the those N images are trained on their respective data-frames.
4. Each model is fed with the rest of the $(N-1)$ images and the corresponding accuracy is considered as score.
5. On the basis of scores, the top 15 images, whose models scored the highest are selected, and the final model is built on by using the XGBoost classification on the combined data-frames of these images.

Table 1. Mean of variance of the each model (sorted in descending order of Mean accuracy)

Rank	Model name	Mean accuracy	Mean variance
01	35trainingModel	0.801	0.0039
02	25trainingModel	0.784	0.005
03	32trainingModel	0.764	0.0124
04	22trainingModel	0.763	0.0183
05	39trainingModel	0.757	0.011
06	37trainingModel	0.756	0.011
07	34trainingModel	0.754	0.002
08	23trainingModel	0.748	0.02
09	27trainingModel	0.746	0.0137
10	36trainingModel	0.741	0.0171
11	40trainingModel	0.720	0.008
12	31trainingModel	0.719	0.014
13	28trainingModel	0.714	0.0248
14	30trainingModel	0.713	0.0103
15	24trainingModel	0.711	0.0215
16	29trainingModel	0.708	0.0134
17	26trainingModel	0.688	0.0082
18	21trainingModel	0.678	0.0254
19	33trainingModel	0.668	0.0214
20	38trainingModel	0.586	0.0236

5 Analysis and Evaluation of Results

This experiment is conducted on globally available DRIVE dataset[1] of retinal fundus images. It includes 20 train and test images, as well as the ground truth result. The images were captured as part of a Dutch diabetic retinopathy screening programme. It includes photos from 400 diabetic people ranging in age from 25 to 90 years old. Out of which 40 photographs have been randomly selected, 7 showing signs of mild early diabetic retinopathy, and the rest 33 do not show any sign of it. This 40-image set is broken into two sets, each with 20 images: test and training.

Output of the proposed method on some of the test images are shown in Fig. 8 with their corresponding RGB and ground truth images. To test the performance of the proposed method, following parameters have been considered: sensitivity, specificity and accuracy. The pixel classes are defined as follows:

T : The pixel is *white* on ground truth as well as on the model output
$\hat{T}$: The pixel is *black* on ground truth as well as on the model output
F : The pixel is *black* on ground truth and *white* on the model output
$\hat{F}$: The pixel is *white* on ground truth and *black* on the model output

Based on the pixel distribution among classes T, $\hat{T}$, F, $\hat{F}$ the attributes sensitivity, specificity and accuracy are determined as:

$$Sensitivity = \frac{T}{T + \hat{F}}$$

$$Specificity = \frac{\hat{T}}{\hat{T} + F}$$

$$Accuracy = \frac{T + \hat{T}}{T + \hat{T} + F + \hat{F}}$$

These proposed attributes are formulated to measure the similarity between ground-truth map and a vessel probability map. Table 2 gives the detailed results of experiment on test images of the dataset. The results of the experiments were compared with those of other works. On comparing, it shows that we have developed a method to extract vessel from retinal fundus image that has superior accuracy and specificity to other methods. The comparison study of these attributes have been presented in Table 3.

---

[1] DRIVE dataset is available at http://www.isi.uu.nl/Research/Databases/DRIVE/download.php.

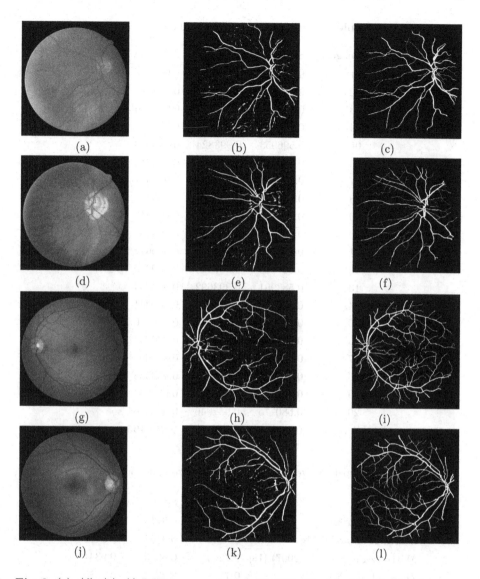

Fig. 8. (a), (d), (g), (j) RGB image set from DRIVE. (b), (e), (h), (k) Model output for (a), (d), (g), (j) respectively. (c), (f), (i), (l) Ground truth image for (a), (d), (g), (j) respectively.

Table 2. Outcome of model on DRIVE dataset

Image #	Sensitivity	Specificity	Accuracy
01	0.724083	0.985099	0.961811
02	0.746937	0.988892	0.964114
03	0.556471	0.991615	0.948236
04	0.702115	0.989867	0.963396
05	0.596953	0.993824	0.956643
06	0.572051	0.993762	0.952715
07	0.652660	0.989337	0.958571
08	0.554123	0.987529	0.950239
09	0.471448	0.996824	0.954246
10	0.638017	0.988947	0.960065
11	0.713768	0.984961	0.960683
12	0.667813	0.987853	0.960219
13	0.583961	0.993692	0.953634
14	0.730292	0.981664	0.961341
15	0.758491	0.969942	0.954810
16	0.645128	0.991518	0.960244
17	0.509156	0.993923	0.953003
18	0.632344	0.987693	0.959538
19	0.791787	0.988360	0.972054
20	0.680775	0.987946	0.965356
Average	**0.64642**	**0.98866**	**0.957495**

Table 3. Vessel separation result comparison

References	Sensitivity	Specificity	Accuracy
Staal et al. (2004) [5]	0.7194	0.9773	0.9442
Soares et al. (2006) [6]	0.7332	0.9782	0.9466
Martinez-Perez et al. (2007) [18]	0.7246	0.9655	0.9344
Zhang et al. (2010) [19]	0.7125	0.9725	0.9385
Martin et al. (2011) [3]	0.7067	0.9801	0.9452
Miri et al. (2011) [20]	0.7155	0.9765	0.9435
Singh et al. (2014) [21]	0.7138	0.9801	0.9460
Fu et al. (2016) [22]	0.7603	N.A	0.9523
Oliveira et al. (2017) [14]	0.7810	0.9800	0.9543
Guo et al. (FS-DSN) (2018) [15]	0.7756	0.9802	0.9542
Guo et al. (S-DSN) (2018) [15]	**0.7893**	0.9789	0.9547
Proposed method	0.6445	**0.9872**	**0.9574**

6   Future Prospects and Conclusion

In this article, proposed scheme uses 41 image filters and eXtreme Gradient Boosting for the extraction of retinal vessels. The method is effective in deleting the majority of noises with high precision. The beauty of this technique is that it uses the combined dataset to build the model by selecting the best images. The model provides an accuracy of 95%, also it is pretty fast. For its efficacy, strength, and convenience of use, the proposed method is a good candidate for implementation in a pre-screening programme for clinical prediction of ophthalmological illnesses.

References

1. Hoover, A., Kouznetsova, V., Goldbaum, M.: Locating blood vessels in retinal images by piecewise threshold probing of a matched filter response. IEEE Trans. Med. Imaging **19**, 203–210 (2000)
2. Cinsdikici, M., Aydin, D.: Detection of blood vessels in ophthalmoscope images using MF/ant (matched filter/ant colony) algorithm. Comput. Methods Programs Biomed. **96**, 85–95 (2009)
3. Marin, D., Aquino, A., Gegndez-Arias, M.E., Bravo, J.M.: A new unsupervised method for blood vessel segmentation in retinal images by using gray-level and moment invariants-based features. IEEE Trans. Med. Imaging **30**(1), 146–158 (2011)
4. Ricci, E., Perfetti, R.: Retinal blood vessel segmentation using line operators and support vector classification. IEEE Trans. Med. Imaging **26**(10), 1357–1365 (2007)
5. Staal, J.J., Abramoff, M.D., Niemeijer, M., Viergever, M.A., van Ginneken, B.: Ridge based vessel segmentation in color images of the retina. IEEE Trans. Med. Imaging **23**, 501–509 (2004)
6. Soares, J.V.B., Leandro, J.J., et al.: Retinal vessel segmentation using the 2-D Gabor wavelet and supervised classification. IEEE Trans. Med. Imaging **25**(9), 1214–1222 (2006)
7. Niemeijer, M., Staal, J.J., van Ginneken, B., Loog, M., Abramoff, M.D.: Comparative study of retinal vessel segmentation methods on a new publicly available dataset. SPIE Med. Imaging **5370**, 648–656 (2004)
8. Frucci, M., Riccio, D., Sanniti di Baja, G., Serino, L.: SEVERE, segmenting vessels in retina images. Pattern Recogn. Lett. **82**, 162–169 (2016)
9. Zana, F., Klein, J.C.: Segmentation of vessel-like patterns using mathematical morphology and curvature evaluation. IEEE Trans. Image Process. **10**, 1010–1019 (2001)
10. Imani, E., Javidi, M., Pourreza, H.R.: Improvement of retinal blood vessel detection using morphological component analysis. Comput. Methods Programs Biomed. **118**–3, 263–279 (2015)
11. Roychowdhury, S., Koozekanani, D., et al.: Blood vessel segmentation of fundus images by major vessel extraction and subimage classification. IEEE J. Biomed. Health Inform. **19**(3), 1118–1128 (2014)
12. Franklin, S.W., Rajan, S.E.: Computerized screening of diabetic retinopathy employing blood vessel segmentation in retinal images. Biocybern. Biomed. Eng. **34**(2), 117–124 (2014)

13. Mendonca, A.M., Campilho, A.: Segmentation of retinal blood vessels by combining the detection of center lines and morphological reconstruction. IEEE Trans. Med. Imaging **25**(9), 1200–1213 (2006)

14. Oliveira, A., Pereira, S., Silva, C.A.: Augmenting data when training a CNN for retinal vessel segmentation: how to warp? In: IEEE 5th Portuguese Meeting on Bioengineering (ENBENG), Coimbra, pp. 1–4 (2017). https://doi.org/10.1109/ENBENG.2017.7889443

15. Guo, S., Gao, Y., Wang, K., Li, T.: Deeply supervised neural network with short connections for retinal vessel segmentation, arXiv:1803.03963v1, 11 March 2018

16. Feng, Z., Yang, J., Yao, L.: Patch-based fully convolutional neural network with skip connections for retinal blood vessel segmentation. In: 2017 IEEE International Conference on Image Processing (ICIP), Beijing, pp. 1742–1746 (2017). https://doi.org/10.1109/ICIP.2017.8296580

17. Liskowski, P., Krawiec, K.: Segmenting retinal blood vessels with deep neural networks. IEEE Trans. Med. Imaging **35**(11), 2369–2380 (2016). https://doi.org/10.1109/TMI.2016.2546227

18. Martinez-Perez, M.E., Hughes, A.D., Thom, S.A., Bharath, A.A., Parker, K.H.: Segmentation of blood vessels from red-free and fluorescein retinal images. Med. Image Anal. **11**(1), 47–61 (2007)

19. Zhang, B., Zhang, L., Zhang, L., Karray, F.: Retinal vessel extraction by matched filter with first-order derivative of Gaussian. Comput. Biol. Med. **40**–4, 438–445 (2010)

20. Miri, M.S., Mahloojifar, A.: Retinal image analysis using curvelet transform and multistructure elements morphology by reconstruction. IEEE Trans. Biomed. Eng. **58**(5), 1183–1192 (2011)

21. Singh, D., Singh, B.: A new morphology based approach for blood vessel segmentation in retinal images. In: 2014 Annual IEEE India Conference (INDICON), pp. 1–6, December 2014

22. Fu, H., Xu, Y., Lin, S., Wong, D.W.K., Liu, J.: Deepvessel: retinal vessel segmentation via deep learning and conditional random field. In: International Conference on Medical Image Computing and Computer-Assisted Intervention, pp. 132–139 (2016)

Deep-learning Based Autoencoder Model for Label Distribution Learning

Mainak Biswas[1]([✉]) and Jasjit S. Suri[2]

[1] Vignan's Foundation for Science, Technology and Research
(Deemed to be University), Guntur, Andhra Pradesh 522002, India
mainakmani@gmail.com
[2] AtheroPoint LLC, Roseville, CA, USA
https://sites.google.com/view/mainak-biswas/home

Abstract. Label ambiguity in data is one of the serious challenges in Machine Learning. In such cases, the significance of each label matters. Label Distribution Learning (LDL) is a new way to deal with label ambiguity. In LDL, instances are defined through the degree to which it is represented by its labels or classes. In this paper, deep learning using autoencoders has been proposed for a computing this degree of labels. The autoencoder consists two parts i.e., encoder and decoder. The encoder compresses the input whereas the decoder decompresses it. The idea of compression is to learn relationship between patterns of data which remains unchanged. The idea of decompression is to recover the original input from the compressed input. Since autoencoders are semi-supervised we have appended a fully connected network for computing degree for each labels. Our results show that DLDL shows the least mean-square error among the contemporary methods.

Keywords: Machine learning · Deep learning · Label distribution learning

1 Introduction

Supervised algorithms are needed to be re-seen for label ambiguity in era of Big Data. Label Distribution Learning [1–3] is a new way to view supervised algorithms. In supervised learning, the classification is always been mutually exclusive. In the case of label distribution learning (LDL) [4,5], a more natural way is to classify an instance a is to assign a real number d_a^b to each possible label b, representing the degree to which b describes a. Data mining algorithms can be adapted to LDL in various ways. Geng has proposed that there are three ways in which older and newer problems can be resolved through LDL, which are:

1. Problem Transformation Convert single-label examples into weighted single-label examples, i.e., each of n single-label instance is transformed to L single-label examples such that it forms a $c \times n$ matrix, where each value represents

the degree d_a^b, a varies from $i = 1 \cdots n$ instances, and b varies from $j = 1 \cdots L$, for L labels. A machine learning algorithm must be able to predict the degree of belonging $d_{a_i}^{b_j}$ for each label b_j

2. Algorithm Adaptation Some of the prevalent algorithms can be naturally extended to deal with label distributions. The Angular Label Distribution Learning (ALDL) [4] is one such algorithm that can be adapted for LDL. Given a new instance a, its nearest neighbors are first found in the set. Then, based on angular distribution of test instance with highest label trained instance and k-nearest neighbor, new label distributions are computed. This approach is also called 'Algorithm Adaptation'.

3. Specialized Algorithm Certain algorithms meet criteria of LDL exquisitely. Geng et al. proposed two algorithms CPNN and IIS-LLD [1] for facial age estimation, which had datasets meeting all criteria of LDL dataset.

In this work, we have applied deep learning [6] for the purpose of label distribution learning (DLDL) using algorithm adaptation. We have used autoencoder, [6,7] a deep learning model for this purpose. The outline of the paper is as follows: Sect. 2 describes methodology, experimental results are given in Sect. 3, and finally conclusion is given in Sect. 4.

2   Methodology

Deep learning algorithms are a broad class of machine learning tools capable of high level abstractions from input data using multiple non-linear transformations using model architectures. Autoencoder is a class of semi-supervised deep learning techniques for data compression for learning of interesting inter-relationships of features within the data. Autoencoders [8] are called semi-supervised as they have specific targets i.e. the input itself and employment of loss function. Originally, the autoencoders produce lossy representation of the input data while training and testing.

2.1   Autoencoder

An autoencoder consists of two parts i.e., encoder and decoder. The encoder is used for compressing the data while decoder is used for decompressing the encoded data and reconstruct the input. The block diagram model of an autoencoder is shown in Fig. 1. It's seen that input data is sent into the encoder to produce compressed data which is again decompressed to get a representation of the original input data.

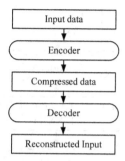

Fig. 1. Autoencoder block diagram.

3 DL-based LDL Model

In this work, autoencoder model architecture has been deployed for LDL. The DL-based LDL model is shown in Fig. 2. There are two stages in the process. Each stage applies a different algorithm. The first stage is an DL-based autoencoder whose purpose is to reconstruct the input. Once done, the reconstructed input is fed into the second stage fully connected network for getting degree of belongingness for each label. There are three encoding layers for compression and three decoding layers for decompression. However, unlike a general autoencoder we have employed a fully connected network at the end of autoencoder where we have applied mean-square error loss function. In an autoencoder loss functions and learning parameters are applied in the last decoding layer. The DL-based LDL model works as follows: at first the input data is inserted into the encoder, the first layer encoder compresses the input data into a compressed (128 × 1) sized file (E.Layer1: Compressed O/p shown in Fig. 2) which are further compressed into compressed (64 × 1) sized file (E.Layer2: Compressed O/p shown in Fig. 2) by second encoder and finally compressed (32 × 1) sized file (E.Layer3: Compressed O/p shown in Fig. 2) which is fed into the decoder and entire process is reversed by the three decoder layers. Finally, the reconstructed input is fed into the fully connected layer (FCN) with outputs equaling number of labels. Mean-square error loss function is applied to the FCN which is given by:

$$MSE = \frac{1}{L} \sum_{i=1}^{L} (b - b')^2 \tag{1}$$

where, MSE denotes mean-square error, L represents the number of labels, b implies the observed LDL values and b' indicates predicted LDL values. The results discussed in the next section shows that the DL-based model outperforms other conventional models by a huge margin.

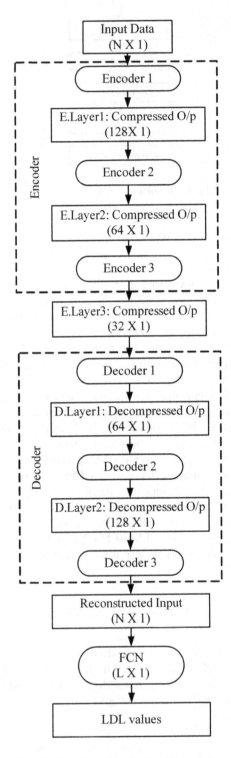

Fig. 2. Deep learning LDL architecture.

4   Experimental Datasets, Results and Analysis

In this section, we discuss the results from the implementation of various methodologies including the DL-based model on various datasets. The training protocol, datasets and experimental results are discussed in the next sub-sections.

4.1   Training Protocol

The training protocol used is K10 cross validation protocol. In here, the training dataset is randomly divided into mutually exclusive ten parts. Ten combinations are formed from these ten parts. Each combination consists of nine parts for training and one part for testing. Each of these combinations are fed for training/testing by the given methodologies including our DL-based model.

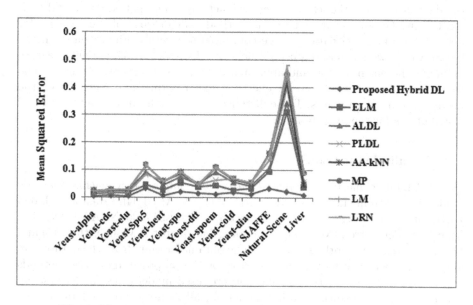

Fig. 3. Mean-square error chart for LDL using different techniques.

4.2   Datasets

Yeast Dataset and its Varients. Yeast dataset [9] are collected from biological experiments on the yeast Saccharomyces Cerevisiae. In each dataset, the labels correspond to the discrete times during one biological experiment. The gene expression level at each time point is recorded.

SJAFFE Dataset. The dataset 11 is extension facial expression image databases, i.e., [10]. The JAFFE database contains 213 grayscale expression images by 10 Japanese female models. 300 features were extracted from each grayscale expression using local binary pattern.

Natural Scene Dataset. The twelfth dataset Natural Scene [1] results from the inconsistent multi-label rankings of 2000 natural scene images.

Liver Dataset. Sixty three patients (36 abnormal and 27 normal) were collected after IRB approval by Instituto Superior Tecnico (IST), University of Lisbon, Portugal and written informed consent provided by all the patients [11]. The images were retrospectively analyzed. Using pathological tests in the lab 36 patients were found to be abnormal and 26 were found normal. To modify the dataset for LDL the features were extracted from 63 patients using GLCM, GLRM and Gabor feature extraction methods. Mean value of each feature for normal and abnormal patients were computed separately. Finally, label distribution values were computed using Euclidean distance of each patients' feature points to the mean normal and abnormal feature points computed earlier. The computation gives two distances, one from mean normal and second from the mean abnormal data points. These distances are normalized to give rise to label distributions for the liver dataset.

4.3   Result Comparisons

The DLDL model has been compared with seven contemporary machine learning models i.e., Extreme Learning Machine (ELM) [12], ALDL [4], Probabistic Label Distribution Learning (PLDL) [5], Algorithm Adaptation-kNN (AA-kNN) [13], Multilayer Perceptron (MP) [14], Levenberg-Marquardt (LM)algorithm [15] and Layer Recurrent Network (LRN) [16]. The obtained results from the dataset are given in Table 1. The mean squared error for the proposed and other methods is given dataset wise. It is seen that the proposed model gives the least mean squared error with respect to other models for all datasets. For all datasets, the average performance improvement is approximately 83.30% for ELM, 89.15% with respect to ALDL, 88.34 % for PLDL, 90.96 % for AA-kNN, 91.37 % for MP, 91.39% for LM and 91.31% for LRN. The performance improvement data is given in Table 2. The line plot shown in Fig. 3, also shows visually the performance of DLDL is better than others. We see that the mean-squared error line for DLDL is almost negligible with respect to other methods for all datasets.

Table 1. Comparison table of various methods for LDL.

SN	Datasets	Proposed	ELM	ALDL	PLDL	AA-kNN	MP	LM	LRN
01	Yeast-alpha	**0.0048**	0.0117	0.0179	0.0152	0.0232	0.023	0.0231	0.0230
02	Yeast-cdc	**0.0063**	0.0153	0.0218	0.0184	0.0278	0.0277	0.0277	0.0276
03	Yeast-elu	**0.0061**	0.0152	0.0232	0.0173	0.028	0.0279	0.0279	0.0279
04	Yeast-Spo5	**0.0329**	0.0451	0.0917	0.0843	0.1161	0.1184	0.1185	0.1181
05	Yeast-heat	**0.0084**	0.0273	0.0457	0.0593	0.0585	0.0591	0.0587	0.0588
06	Yeast-spo	**0.0205**	0.0539	0.0739	0.0833	0.0915	0.0923	0.0924	0.0927
07	Yeast-dtt	**0.0148**	0.0392	0.0467	0.0480	0.0475	0.0482	0.0481	0.0479
08	Yeast-spoem	**0.0121**	0.0429	0.092	0.0634	0.1082	0.1108	0.1096	0.1105
09	Yeast-cold	**0.0191**	0.0257	0.0562	0.0680	0.0680	0.069	0.0691	0.0690
10	Yeast-diau	**0.0127**	0.0324	0.0424	0.0542	0.0539	0.0545	0.0543	0.0543
11	SJAFFE	**0.0324**	0.0937	0.1065	0.1357	0.1602	0.1612	0.1582	0.1384
12	Natural Scene	**0.0219**	0.3118	0.3446	0.4030	0.4232	0.45	0.4434	0.4809
13	Liver	**0.0093**	0.0386	0.0595	0.0575	0.0471	0.0898	0.0975	0.0870

Table 2. Percentage improvement of performance of DLDL over other methods.

	ELM	ALDL	PLDL	AA-kNN	MP	LM	LRN
Yeast-alpha	58.97	73.18	68.42	79.31	79.13	79.22	79.13
Yeast-cdc	68.63	77.98	73.91	82.73	82.67	82.67	82.61
Yeast-elu	68.42	79.31	72.25	82.86	82.8	82.8	82.8
Yeast-Spo5	89.36	94.77	94.31	95.87	95.95	95.95	95.94
Yeast-heat	82.42	89.50	91.91	91.79	91.88	91.82	91.84
Yeast-spo	91.09	93.50	94.24	94.75	94.8	94.81	94.82
Yeast-dtt	87.76	89.72	90.00	89.89	90.04	90.02	89.98
Yeast-spoem	88.81	94.78	92.43	95.56	95.67	95.62	95.66
Yeast-cold	81.32	91.46	92.94	92.94	93.04	93.05	93.04
Yeast-diau	85.19	88.68	91.14	91.09	91.19	91.16	91.16
SJAFFE	94.88	95.49	96.46	97.00	97.02	96.97	96.53
Natural-Scene	98.46	98.61	98.81	98.87	98.93	98.92	99.00
Liver	87.56	91.93	91.65	89.81	94.65	95.08	94.48
Average	**83.30**	**89.15**	**88.34**	**90.96**	**91.37**	**91.39**	**91.31**

5   Conclusion

We have presented a novel deep-learning based methodology for label distribution learning. Our methodology clearly shows better results than previous methods. We need to apply our model of deep learning.

References

1. Geng, X., Smith-Miles, K., Zhou, Z.-H.: Facial age estimation by learning from label distributions. In: Proceedings of 24th AAAI Conference Artificial Intelligence, Atlanta, GA, pp. 451–456 (2010)
2. Geng, X., Yin, C., Zhou, Z.-H.: Facial age estimation by learning from label distributions. IEEE Trans. Pattern Anal. Mach. Intell. 35(10), 2401–2412 (2013)
3. Geng, X.: Label distribution learning. IEEE Trans. Knowl. Data Eng. 28(7), 1734–1748 (2016)
4. Biswas, M., Kuppili, V., Edla, D.: ALDL: a novel method for label distribution learning. Sādhanā 44(3), 53 (2019)
5. Kuppili, V., Biswas, M., Reddy, D.: PLDL: a novel method for label distribution learning. Sādhanā 16, 1021–1027 (2019)
6. Biswas, M., et al.: State-of-the-art review on deep learning in medical imaging. Front. Biosci. (Landmark edition) 24, 392–426 (2019)
7. Saba, L., et al.: The present and future of deep learning in radiology. Eur. J. Radiol. 114, 14–24 (2019)
8. Hinton, G.E., Krizhevsky, A., Wang, S.D.: Transforming auto-encoders. In: Honkela, T., Duch, W., Girolami, M., Kaski, S. (eds.) ICANN 2011. LNCS, vol. 6791, pp. 44–51. Springer, Heidelberg (2011). https://doi.org/10.1007/978-3-642-21735-7_6
9. Eisen, M.B., Spellman, P.T., Brown, P.O., Botstein, D.: Cluster analysis and display of genome-wide expression patterns. Proc. Natl. Acad. Sci. 95(25), 14863–14868 (1998)
10. Lyons, M.J., Akamatsu, S., Kamachi, M., Gyoba, J., Budynek, J.: The Japanese female facial expression (JAFFE) database. In: Proceedings of Third International Conference on Automatic Face and Gesture Recognition, pp. 14–16 (1998)
11. Biswas, M., et al.: Symtosis: a liver ultrasound tissue characterization and risk stratification in optimized deep learning paradigm. Comput. Methods Prog. Biomed. 155, 165–177 (2018)
12. Huang, G.B., Zhu, Q.Y., Siew, C.K.: Extreme learning machine: theory and applications. Neurocomputing 70, 489–501 (2006)
13. Hou, P., Geng, X., Huo, Z. W., Lv, J.Q.: In: Thirty-First AAAI Conference on Artificial Intelligence (2017)
14. Taud, H., Mas, J.F.: Geomatic approaches for modeling land change scenarios, pp. 451–455 (2018)
15. Moré, J.J.: The Levenberg-Marquardt algorithm: implementation and theory. In: Watson, G.A. (ed.) Numerical Analysis. LNM, vol. 630, pp. 105–116. Springer, Heidelberg (1978). https://doi.org/10.1007/BFb0067700
16. Goudreau, M.W., Giles, C.L., Chakradhar, S.T., Chen, D.: First-order versus second-order single-layer recurrent neural networks. IEEE Trans. Neural Netw. 5, 511–513 (1994)

A Secure Image Watermarking Technique Using Chinese Remainder Theorem in Integer Wavelet Transformation Domain

Santa Singh[1], Partha Chowdhuri[1(✉)], Pabitra Pal[2], Prabhash Kumar Singh[1], and Biswapati Jana[1]

[1] Department of Computer Science, Vidyasagar University, West Midnapore, India
prc.email@gmail.com
[2] BSTTM, IIT DELHI, New Delhi, Delhi 110016, India

Abstract. In this research work, a secured watermarking method has been proposed using Chinese Remainder Theorem (CRT) in combination with Integer Wavelet Transform (IWT). The CRT is applied for embedding watermark information by modifying IWT coefficient. The scheme uses the SHA-512 hash algorithm which encrypts the original watermark bit before embedding. The secret informations are embedded into the IWT coefficients of the LH, HL and HH subbands as calculated by the CRT method. The combination of CRT and IWT are produce a high imperceptible image without compromising the robustness of the proposed method. The metrics like PSNR, SSIM are used to analyse the imperceptibility and NCC, BER are used to analyse the robustness of the scheme. After that, the outcomes are evaluated with a number of other relevant schemes in order to validate the superiority.

Keywords: Watermarking · Integer Wavelet Transform · SHA-512 · Chinese Remainder theorem · Image encryption

1 Introduction

In this era of digital communication, the Internet has become one of the most important channels of communication. Almost half of the global population is now active internet users. The easy sharing of information and diffusion of digital material are facilitated by a huge number of internet users. When digital information is secured by the intellectual property rights, however, the ease of information sharing causes challenges. The researchers are developing different strategies, methodologies, and algorithms to protect digital content and to secure intellectual property rights. The technique of hiding information is one such strategy that can be applied. Watermarking has evolved from an information-hiding technology to a solution for copyright protection. Watermarking is a technique for embedding data into a medium in such a way that it is undetectable to the human visual system (HVS) to protect copyright and information authentication. The Least Significant Bit (LSB), Singular Value Decomposition (SVD), Fourier Transform (FT), Discrete Cosine Transform (DCT), and Discrete Wavelet Transform (DWT) etc. are all common watermarking algorithms. Integer Wavelet Transform (IWT) wavelet transform is better than Discrete Wavelet Transform (DWT) as it uses integers as the coefficients, which makes the embedding process very simple and fast. The Chinese Remainder Theorem (CRT) algorithm is another watermarking approach. This technique is not only used for data security, but also for picture encoding, image sharing, and authentication. CRT has a faster processing time and gives less distortion to the image. With the increase of cloud technology, the transmission of a higher amount of data becomes easier. But personal privacy becomes an important issue. So, to protect privacy, designing a hybrid scheme by combining encryption and transformation is the need of the current research scenario. Transformation of the image makes the procedure complex to extract the original watermark image whereas encryption makes the scheme secure from the third party user.

The remaining part of the manuscript is rearranged as: Sect. 2 described the survey of some literature work. In Sect. 3, some preliminary methodologies are discussed. The proposed scheme is introduced in Sect. 4. Section 5 depicts the achieved result and comparative analysis. Finally, the conclusion and scope of further works are given in Sect. 6.

2   Literature Review

In 2004, Luo et al. [10] proposed a watermarking technique using CRT in the DCT domain. In this technique, the watermark information is embedded into the DCT coefficients followed by the application of CRT. In 2010, Patra et al. [16] proposed a watermarking scheme with the help of CRT in DCT domain. In their scheme, the 8×8 DCT coefficient block is chosen randomly depending on the value of Z of CRT. In 2013, Keyvanpour et al. [9] proposed a DWT domain based watermarking scheme that implements chaotic maps for information hiding. They used Haar filter to get three-level DWT coefficients. The chaotic map is used for encrypting the watermark information before embedding process. Chaturvedi et al. [5] proposed a watermarking scheme in the DWT domain. The algorithm uses LL subband of the DWT to embed secret information. The scheme exhibits better PSNR for lower scaling factor and vice versa. In 2014, Moniruzzaman et al. [11] proposed a DWT based watermakring scheme that divides LL Subband coefficients into 3×3 sub-blocks before embedding secret information with the help of XOR operation on logistic map. Esgandari et al. [6] proposed a chaotic map based watermarking technique in the DWT domain. The watermarking scheme developed by Sudibyo et al. [19] uses CRT method to embed watermark information in the DWT domain using the Haar Wavelet Transform. In 2017, Adi et al. [2] proposed a watermarking scheme with the help of CRT. Their scheme uses Canny edge detection algorithm to embed the watermark information on the edges of the cover image. The method also utilized pair-wise co-prime integers to embed the watermark. A dual-band IWT based watermarking scheme was propose by Adi et al. [4] that maintains a good trade-off between visual quality and robustness.

3   Chinese Remainder Theorem (CRT) and Integer Wavelet Transform (IWT)

Both the CRT and the IWT will be discussed in this part of the article.

3.1   Chinese Remainder Theorem (CRT)

According to CRT, for any given positive integers x & y; where $x < n_1$ & $y > n_2$, there exists a unique integer Z, where $Z < M$. Here, n_1 and n_2 are two co-prime numbers. The values of a_1, a_2, b_1, b_2 can be determined by:

$$a_1 = M/n_1 = n_2$$
$$a_2 = M/n_2 = n_1$$
$$(a_1 b_1) \; mod \; n_1 = 1$$
$$(a_2 b_2) \; mod \; n_2 = 1$$

(1)

Then, the unique integer Z can be found using the following equation:

$$Z = (x.a_1 b_1 + y.a_2 b_2) \; mod \; M \tag{2}$$

The co-prime numbers x and y are used to calculate the value of Z using inverse CRT. M is the product of co-prime numbers n_1 and n_2. The values of x and y can be calculated using n_1 and n_2 where $x < n_1$ and $y < n_2$. The following equation gives the relationship between the said numbers.

$$x = Z \; mod \; n_1$$
$$y = Z \; mod \; n_2$$

(3)

3.2   Integer Wavelet Transform (IWT)

Some important signals in the real-world are encoded as integers. An IWT, applied to implement the developed scheme, might be very efficient for integer-encoded signals. The IWT is a fully reversible integer-to-integer analysis algorithm for wavelets. Compared with the DWT and CWT, the IWT is not only more memory-efficient and computationally faster but also completely reversible. The IWT is able to reconstruct the integer signal perfectly from the IWT integer coefficients.

The IWT approach utilises two distinct varieties of wavelet filters. The first one is a high pass filter, while the second one is a low pass filter; together, they split signals into four sub-bands [8] namely LL, HL, LH, HH. The LL sub-band provides a low-frequency value, the LH sub-band provides vertical details, the HL sub-band furnishes horizontal details and the HH sub-band represents the diagonal details [20]. The lowest sub-band, LL contains the most important values [17]. The Integer Wavelet Transform (IWT), which uses only integer values, is actually a variation of Discrete Wavelet Transform (DWT) which used floating point values. This property ensures reversibility of the IWT based schemes. Haar and Daubechies are among the most widely used filter methods in wavelet transforms. The IWT is very fast, simple and memory efficient [3].

4   Proposed Scheme

The embedding and extraction processes have each been broken down into their respective steps here.

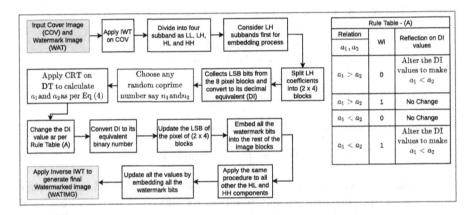

Fig. 1. Embedding procedure of the proposed scheme

4.1   Embedding Procedure

Figure 1 presents a diagrammatic representation of the process of watermark embedding. At first a cover image (COV) is taken into the account and then IWT is applied.We use IWT to achieve four sub-bands LL, LH, HL and HH. Then, watermark bits are generated from the watermark image. A shared secret key is taken and SHA-512 hashing algorithm is applied to the secret key to get a 512 bit secret key. This 512 bit secret key is XOR-ed with the original watermark bits to get the watermark bits to be embedded. Next, the LH sub-band is considered first for the embedding process. The LH coefficients are split into (2×4) blocks and from each block the LSBs from the 8 coefficient are collected and converted to its decimal equivalent (DI). Two co-prime numbers say n_1 and n_2 are chosen. Then CRT is applied on DT to calculate a_1 and a_2 as per Eq. 4. After this step is done, the DI value is changed according to the Rule Table (A) in Fig 1 and After that, DI is changed into the corresponding eight-bit binary number (B). The LSBs of the coefficients of the 2×4 block are updated using B. All of the bits that constitute the watermark are included into the remaining coefficient blocks. We apply the same procedure to HL and HH sub-bands for embedding rest of the watermark bits. The final watermarked image is reconstructed using inverse IWT. The step-by-step embedding procedure is described in the schematic diagram in Fig 1.

$$DT \equiv a_1(mod\ n_1),$$
$$DT \equiv a_2(mod\ n_2), \tag{4}$$

$$where\ n_1\ and\ n_2\ are\ two\ co-prime\ numbers.$$

4.2 Extraction Process

The extraction scheme is just the reverse method of embedding procedure. At the time of extraction we need the same shared secret key to get the sequence of the data embedded.

5 Experiment and Comparative Evaluation

In this section, the performance of the proposed model has been evaluated using some standard performance metrics and the experimental results are analysed. The experiments are performed using Java 8 with Windows 10 environment. The performance metrics such as MSE, PSNR, SSIM, Q-Index are used to evaluate

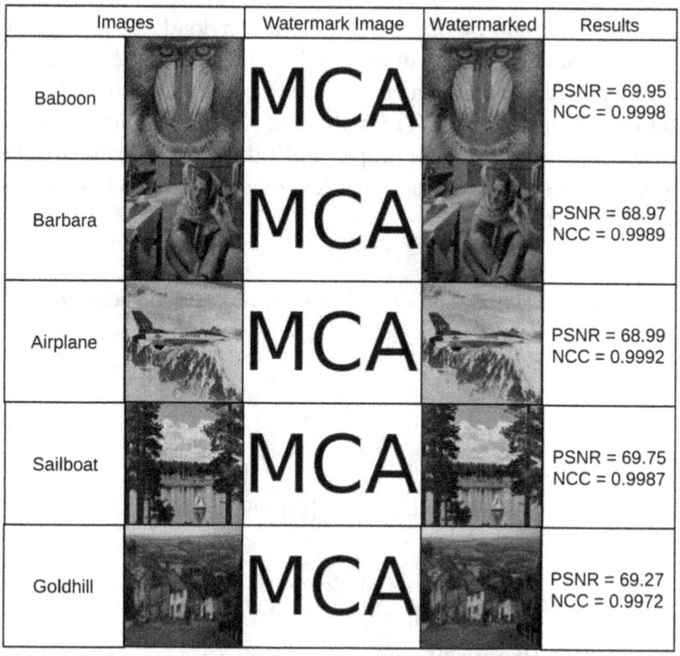

Images		Watermark Image	Watermarked	Results
Baboon		MCA		PSNR = 69.95 NCC = 0.9998
Barbara		MCA		PSNR = 68.97 NCC = 0.9989
Airplane		MCA		PSNR = 68.99 NCC = 0.9992
Sailboat		MCA		PSNR = 69.75 NCC = 0.9987
Goldhill		MCA		PSNR = 69.27 NCC = 0.9972

Fig. 2. Experimental results of some sample images collected from [1]

the imperceptibility of the developed and NCC, BER are used to check the robustness of the scheme. Some images of size 512×512 from three standard image databases [1,7,12] have been considered for the experimental purpose. The output findings for various sample images are shown in Fig. 2.

5.1 Imperceptibility Analysis

Mean Square Error (MSE) [13], Peak Signal to Noise Ratio ($PSNR$) [13], Structural Similarity Index Measurement ($SSIM$) [18] and Quality Index ($Q-Index$) [13] are calculated precisely to evaluate the imperceptibility of the watermarked image. The experimental findings are presented in terms of MSE, PSNR, Q-Index, and SSIM are given in the Table 1.

Table 1. Imperceptibility analysis

Images	Capacity	MSE	PSNR (dB)	Q-Index	SSIM
Baboon	24576	0.021	69.95	0.9997	0.9998
Barbara	24576	0.022	68.97	0.9998	0.9999
Airplane	24576	0.023	68.99	0.9996	0.9997
Sailboat	24576	0.019	69.75	0.9997	0.9999
Goldhill	24576	0.020	69.27	0.9998	0.9998

From the Table 1, it can be observed that the payload of the suggested procedure is 24576 bits for a grayscale image with the size of (512×512). The visual quality of the watermarked image is also very good in terms of PSNR which is around 69.75 dB on average. The values of Q-Index, and SSIM are almost near to 1 which proves the better imperceptibility of the watermarked image. The developed process is compared with few existing research schemes which is represented in the Table 2.

Table 2. Comparison of PSNR with the existing schemes

Schemes	PSNR(dB)
Esgandari et al. [6]	40.1
Parah et al. [14]	40.58
Patra et al. [15]	41
Moniruzzaman et al. [11]	49
Zhang [10]	52.46
Keyvanpour et al. [9]	56.88
Usman et al. [19]	63.55
Proposed scheme	**69.75**

The Table 2 demonstrates that the suggested procedure outperforms the other current investigated systems in terms of PSNR which is 42.50%, 41.82%, 41.21%, 29.75%, 24.79%, 18.45%, and 8.89% increase over the existing schemes [6,9–11,14,15], and [19] respectively.

5.2   Robustness Analysis

The Bit Error Rate (BER) [14], Normalized Co-relation Coefficient (NCC) [21], Standard Deviation (SD) [14], and Corelation Coefficient (CC) [14] are computed to assess the robustness of the proposed scheme. The results in terms of SD, CC, BER, and NCC are given in the Table 3.

Table 3. Robustness analysis of the proposed scheme

Images	SD of		CC of	NCC	BER
	Cover	Watermarked	Cover and Watermarked		
Baboon	21.461	21.571	0.9888	0.9998	0.0012
Airplane	22.252	22.462	0.9886	0.9992	0.0017
Goldhill	22.267	22.291	0.9984	0.9972	0.0013
Sailboat	21.569	21.687	0.9896	0.9987	0.0016
Barbara	21.362	21.397	0.9985	0.9989	0.0014

The Table 3 shows that the NCC value is near to 1 and the BER value is 0.0015 on an average which is near to 0. The SD and CC values also proves that their is minimum difference between the original image and the particular watermarked image. All these values prove the robustness of the presented method.

6   Conclusion

In this thorough research study, an IWT based watermarking scheme has been brought forward. The scheme uses SHA-512 hashing algorithm for better security. The embedding algorithm modifies a minimum number of pixels in a block of pixel to embed watermark bits using the CRT method. This ensures the excellent imperceptibility of the generated watermarked image. Modifying the original watermark bits using the SHA-512 hashing algorithm adds extra security to the proposed scheme. The use of IWT instead of DWT ensures extraction of the watermark precisely from the watermarked image. The proposed work has been analysed using various standard metrics to show the superiority of the scheme over the existing schemes. So it has been clearly declared that the embedding capacity is 24576 bits with an average PSNR of 69.75 dB which is much above the satisfactory level for a watermarking process. From the experimented results, it has also been noted that the scheme provides better robustness against various malicious attacks. However, the suggested process still has some limitations when a trade-off is observed between capacity, imperceptibility and robustness. In the future, there is a chance to improve the embedding capacity range of the presented scheme without compromising the imperceptibly of the watermarked image.

References

1. University of Southern California (2021). http://sipi.usc.edu/database/database. php/, Accessed 27 Oct 2021
2. Adi, P.W., Astuti, Y.P., Subhiyakto, E.R.: Imperceptible image watermarking based on chinese remainder theorem over the edges. In: 2017 4th International Conference on Electrical Engineering, Computer Science and Informatics (EECSI), pp. 1–5. IEEE (2017)
3. Adi, P.W., Rahmanti, F.Z., Abu, N.A.: High quality image steganography on integer haar wavelet transform using modulus function. In: 2015 International Conference on Science in Information Technology (ICSITech), pp. 79–84. IEEE (2015)
4. Adi, P.W., Rahmanti, F.Z., Winarno, E.: Robust watermarking through dual band IWT and Chinese remainder theorem. Bull. Electr. Eng. Inf. $7(4)$, 561–569 (2018)
5. Chaturvedi, N., Basha, S.J.: Analysis of image watermarking by dwt and performance under attacks. Int. J. Comput. Technol. Electron. Eng. (IJCTEE) 2 (2012)
6. Esgandari, R., Khalili, M.: A robust image watermarking scheme based on discrete wavelet transforms. In: 2015 2nd International Conference on Knowledge-Based Engineering and Innovation (KBEI), pp. 988–992. IEEE (2015)
7. Funt, et al.: HDR Dataset Computational Vision Lab Computing Science, Simon Fraser University, Burnaby, BC, Canada (2021). http://www.cs.sfu.ca/$~$colour/ data/funt_hdr/, Accessed 27 Oct 2021
8. Gupta, D., Choubey, S.: Discrete wavelet transform for image processing. Int. J. Emerg. Technol. Adv. Eng. $4(3)$, 598–602 (2015)
9. MohammadReza Keyvanpour and Farnoosh Merrikh Bayat: Blind image watermarking method based on chaotic key and dynamic coefficient quantization in the dwt domain. Math. Comput. Model. $58(1–2)$, 56–67 (2013)
10. Luo, X.F., Xu, Q., Zhang, J.: A digital watermarking algorithm based on Chinese remainder theorem. In: 2014 10th International Conference on Communications (COMM), pp. 1–4. IEEE (2014)
11. Moniruzzaman, M., Hawlader, M.A.K., Hossain, M.F.: Wavelet based watermarking approach of hiding patient information in medical image for medical image authentication. In: 2014 17th International Conference on Computer and Information Technology (ICCIT), pp. 374–378. IEEE (2014)
12. UK Nottingham Trent University. UCID Image Database (2021). http:// jasoncantarella.com/downloads/ucid.v2.tar.gz, Accessed 27 Oct 2021
13. Pal, P., Chowdhuri, P., Jana, B.: Weighted matrix based reversible watermarking scheme using color image. Multimedia Tools Appl. $77(18)$, 23073–23098 (2018). https://doi.org/10.1007/s11042-017-5568-y
14. Parah, S.A., Sheikh, J.A., Loan, N.A., Bhat, G.M.: A robust and computationally efficient digital watermarking technique using inter block pixel differencing. In: Hassanien, A.E., Fouad, M.M., Manaf, A.A., Zamani, M., Ahmad, R., Kacprzyk, J. (eds.) Multimedia Forensics and Security. ISRL, vol. 115, pp. 223–252. Springer, Cham (2017). https://doi.org/10.1007/978-3-319-44270-9_10

15. Patra, J.C., Phua, J.E., Bornand, C.: A novel dct domain crt-based watermarking scheme for image authentication surviving jpeg compression. Digital Signal Process. **20**(6), 1597–1611 (2010)
16. Patra, J.C., Phua, J.E., Rajan, D.: DCT domain watermarking scheme using Chinese remainder theorem for image authentication. In: 2010 IEEE International Conference on Multimedia and Expo, pp. 111–116. IEEE (2010)
17. Sathik, M.M., Sujatha, S.S.: A novel dwt based invisible watermarking technique for digital images. Int. Arab. J. e Technol. **2**(3), 167–173 (2012)
18. Qingtang, S., Niu, Y., Wang, Q., Sheng, G.: A blind color image watermarking based on dc component in the spatial domain. Optik **124**(23), 6255–6260 (2013)
19. Sudibyo, U., Eranisa, F., Rachmawanto, E.H., Sari, C.A., et al.: A secure image watermarking using Chinese remainder theorem based on haar wavelet transform. In: 2017 4th International Conference on Information Technology, Computer, and Electrical Engineering (ICITACEE), pp. 208–212. IEEE (2017)
20. Susanto, A., Sari, C.A., Rachmawanto, E.H., et al.: Hybrid method using hwt-dct for image watermarking. In: 2017 5th International Conference on Cyber and IT Service Management (CITSM), pp. 1–5. IEEE (2017)
21. Zhang, W., Shih, F.Y.: Semi-fragile spatial watermarking based on local binary pattern operators. Optics Commun. **284**(16–17), 3904–3912 (2011)

A Dual Image Based Data Hiding Scheme Based on Difference of Pixel Values in Integer Wavelet Transform Domain

Sweta Midya[1], Partha Chowdhuri[1(✉)], Pabitra Pal[2], Prabhash Kumar Singh[1], and Biswapati Jana[1]

[1] Department of Computer Science, Vidyasagar University, West Midnapore, India
prc.email@gmail.com
[2] BSTTM, IIT DELHI, Delhi 110016, New Delhi, India

Abstract. In this paper, a dual image-based data hiding scheme has been proposed in Integer Wavelet Transform (IWT) domain. The proposed method can embed secret data utilizing the differences between the values of the adjacent pixels. Here, the cover image is converted to integer coefficients after applying IWT. The coefficients of the IWT subbands are divided into a number of non-overlapping blocks. The maximum difference of a particular coefficient from another coefficient inside a block is calculated. The number of secret bits to be embedded in a single coefficient inside a block depends on the amount of this maximum difference value. The decimal equivalent of the secret bits is split to embed in the dual images. The secret data is folded to minimize the modification of the original pixel in both of the dual images. Using the Integer Wavelet Transform (IWT) domain instead of spatial domain minimizes the distortion in pixel values in both the stego images. Moreover, different subbands of the IWT coefficients are used efficiently to solve the problems regarding the center folding strategy. The experimental results show the superiority of the proposed scheme over some existing schemes in terms of imperceptibility and robustness. The proposed scheme embeds secret bits depending on the characteristics of the image. It also maintains a minimum difference between the same pixel values in both the stego images and retains good visual quality of the stego images.

Keywords: Data hiding · Dual images · Integer Wavelet Transform · Pixel difference · Center folding strategy

1 Introduction

In this era of digitalization, the digital information traverses the cyber world using the most convenient medium for information exchange, the Internet. As the Internet is accessed by everybody, important digital information passes through it can be stolen or altered by any malicious user. Therefore, many data hiding schemes have been proposed to secure the digital information before sending it

S. Mukhopadhyay et al. (Eds.): CICBA 2022, CCIS 1579, pp. 76–84, 2022.
https://doi.org/10.1007/978-3-031-10766-5_7

over the Internet. A data hiding scheme actually embeds some secret information into a cover media to generate a stego media. The data hiding can be done in any of the domains like spatial domain and transform domain. Data hiding in each domain has their advantages and disadvantages. In spatial domain, a number of data hiding schemes have been proposed based on least significant bits (LSB) replacement and pixel-value differing (PVD). On the other hand, the Singular Value Decomposition (SVD), Discrete Wavelet Transform (DWT), and Discrete Cosine Transform (DCT) are commonly used in the transform domain. The proposed scheme uses the advantage of both spatial domain and transform domain. The scheme uses IWT to get the transform domain coefficients and LSB method is used to embed the information inside the coefficients instead of directly in the pixels. Use of LSB replacement in the IWT domain makes the whole embedding process of the proposed scheme very simple and fast.

The rest of the paper is organized as: Literature Review is discussed in Sect. 2. In Sect. 3, some preliminary methodologies are discussed. The proposed method is introduced in Sect. 4. Section 5 depicts the experimental results and comparative analysis. Finally, the conclusion and scope of further works are given in Sect. 6.

2   Literature Review

Many researchers have proposed data hiding schemes using Pixel Value Difference (PVD) method after it was first proposed by Wu and Tsai [1]. The PVD method has the ability to embed huge amount of data in a cover image without compromising the imperceptibility of the stego image. But one major limitation of PVD method is that the data hiding scheme cannot be made reversible. Reversibility has very important aspect in military and medical applications. So, some reversible data hiding schemes using PVD method have been proposed to overcome this issue [2,3]. The dual image based data hiding schemes are one of the very popular techniques for implementing reversibility in a PVD based methods. Chang et al. [4] in 2007 first proposed a dual image based reversible data hiding scheme. This scheme also uses exploiting modification direction (EMD) scheme [5] to increase the payload. Lee et al. [6] proposed a dual image based reversible data hiding scheme in 2009 using the concept of central point. This scheme checks whether data embedding is possible by using the relationship between two images. Qin et al. [7] proposed a scheme that uses EMD scheme to embed data based on some rules. Lu et al. [8] proposed a dual image based data hiding scheme based on center folding strategy (CFS) method. The CFS method minimizes the distortion in the image pixels by adjusting secret data range. In this scheme, secret data are embedded in two stego-images by using the ceil and floor function. Yao et al. [9] proposed a dual image based reversible data hiding scheme that improved the Lu et al.'s scheme using some selection strategy to classify secret data into even and odd numbers. Shastri and Thanikaiselvan's [10] scheme improved the image quality of Yao et al.'s scheme by shiftable pixel coordinate selection strategy method, and lookup table along with the CFS method. Jose et al. [17] proposed a RDH scheme using encrypted images which hides secret data as ciphertext. Sahu et al. [18] developed an image steganographic communication method that maintains a fair trade-off among capacity, visual quality, and attack survival ability. An interpolation based reversible data hiding scheme proposed by Kim et al. [19] prevents malicious attacks by third parties.

In this paper, a dual image based data hiding scheme has been proposed using the pixel value difference and CFS method in order to minimize the dissimilarity between the dual stego images as well as to increase the imperceptibility of the stego images. Moreover, the limitation of the CFS method is controlled by using the Integer Wavelet Transform (IWT) domain and utilizing the subbands of the IWT coefficients.

3   Integer Wavelet Transform and Center Folding Strategy

3.1   Integer Wavelet Transform (IWT)

The Integer Wavelet Transform (IWT) is one of the methods used in transform domain for data hiding. Unlike Discrete Wavelet Transform (DWT) which generates floating point coefficients, IWT generates integer coefficients. It helps in designing a data hiding scheme which can extract exact secret data from the stego image. The IWT method uses low pass and high pass wavelet filters. It decomposes the image signals into LL, HL, LH, HH subbands. Among these, the LL sub-band represents the original image. For further level of decomposition, this LL subband is used. The vertical details subband (LH), the horizontal detail subband (HL) and the diagonal details subband (HH) contains comparatively less important information regarding an image. Haar wavelet filter, used in the proposed scheme, is one of the most commonly used filters which is very simple and efficient for generating integer coefficients using Integer Wavelet Transform.

3.2   Center Folding Strategy

Lu et al. [8] proposed a scheme that uses Centre Folding Strategy (CFS) to reduce the distortion in an image after secret data embedding. In the scheme, k bits of binary secret data is converted to its decimal equivalent (d). The value of k is calculated by the Eq. 1. The Eq. 4.1 is used to calculate $\bar{d}$ which is the folded value of d.

$$k = \lfloor log_2 s \rfloor \tag{1}$$

$$\bar{d} = d - 2^{k-1} \tag{2}$$

If the range of d is $R = \{0, 1, 2, ..., 2^{k-1}\}$, then the range of folded value $\bar{d}$ will be $\bar{R} = \{-2^{k-1}, 2^{k-1}+1, ..., -1, 0, 1, 2, ...2^{k-1}-2, 2^{k-1}-1\}$. The $\bar{d}$ is split into two values $\bar{d}_1$ and $\bar{d}_2$ using the Eq. 3.

$$\bar{d}_1 = \left\lfloor \frac{\bar{d}}{2} \right\rfloor, \bar{d}_2 = \left\lceil \frac{\bar{d}}{2} \right\rceil \tag{3}$$

The $\bar{d}_1$ is added and the $\bar{d}_2$ is subtracted from a pixel in two stego images.

4   The Proposed Scheme

In this section, the embedding and extraction process of the proposed scheme has been discussed in detail.

4.1   Embedding Procedure

The schematic diagram of the data hiding procedure is given in Fig. 1. At first, Integer Wavelet Transform (IWT) is applied to the input cover image (C). The

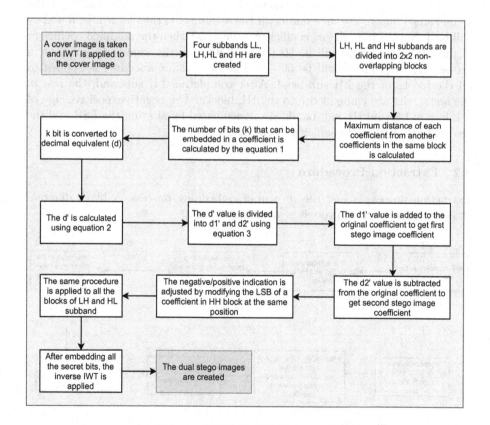

Fig. 1. Embedding procedure of the proposed scheme

four sub-bands generated are LL, LH, HL, and HH. Then, the secret bits are generated from the secret image (W). The secret data is inserted into the LH, HL, and HH sub-bands only. The LL sub-band is left untouched through the embedding process. Because, data embedding in LL sub-band affects image quality greatly as it contains most vital information of the entire image. The integer coefficients of the LH, HL, and HH sub-bands are divided into a number of 2×2 non-overlapping blocks. The LH sub-band is first taken into account for the embedding purpose. After this, the maximum difference of each coefficient from another coefficients in the same block is calculated. The number of secret bits (k) that can be embedded in a coefficient (f) is calculated by $k = \lfloor log_2 s \rfloor$, where s is the maximum difference of a coefficient from another coefficient in the same block. Then, k number of secret bits are taken and converted to its decimal equivalent (d). According to the Center Folding Strategy (Sect. 3.2), the folded value $\bar{d}$ of d is calculated using the equation . This decreases the d value to significant amount. One limitation with CFS is that it can generate negative $\bar{d}$ value also. In order to overcome this limitation, the negative or positive value of the $\bar{d}$ is marked by changing the LSB of the coefficient at the same position in the HH sub-band. After this, the $\bar{d}$ value is divided into two values $\bar{d}_1$ and $\bar{d}_2$ using the Eq. 3. The $\bar{d}_1$ value is added to the original coefficient f for the first stego image and $\bar{d}_2$ value is subtracted from the original coefficient f for the second stego image. For an example, if the $\bar{d}$ value is 7, then $\bar{d}_1$ will be 3 and $\bar{d}_2$ will be 4. Now, if the original coefficient value is 50, then the modified coefficient in the first stego image will be $50 + 3 = 53$ whereas the modified coefficient in the second stego image will be $50 - 4 = 46$. The same procedure is applied to all the blocks of the LH sub-band. After completing LH subband, the rest of the secret bits are embedded into the HL blocks. The negative/positive sign of $\bar{d}$ values in LH and HL sub-bands are remembered by altering the LSB and the second LSB of the HH coefficient respectively.

4.2   Extraction Procedure

Extraction process is just the reverse of embedding process. A block diagram showing the extraction process is given in the Fig. 2.

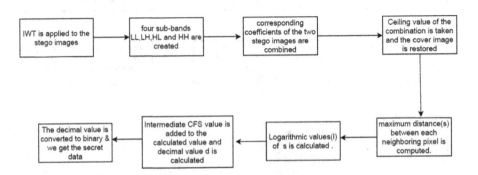

Fig. 2. Extraction procedure of the proposed scheme

5 Experiment Results and Analysis

In this section, the proposed scheme is tested and analysed using some standard performance metrics. All the experiments have been performed on Windows 10 environment using Java 8 as the development tool. The imperceptibility of the proposed scheme is measured by the metrics like Mean Square Error (MSE) [11], Peak Signal to Noise Ratio ($PSNR$) [11], Structural Similarity Index Measurement ($SSIM$) [12] and Quality Index ($Q - Index$) [11] whereas the robustness of the scheme are checked by the metrics like Bit Error Rate (BER) [13], Normalized Co-relation Coefficient (NCC) [14], Standard Deviation (SD) [13], and Corelation Coefficient (CC) [13]. Some 512×512 images from the $SIPI$ image database [15] have been used for the experiments. The results of the experiments on some images are shown in Fig. 3

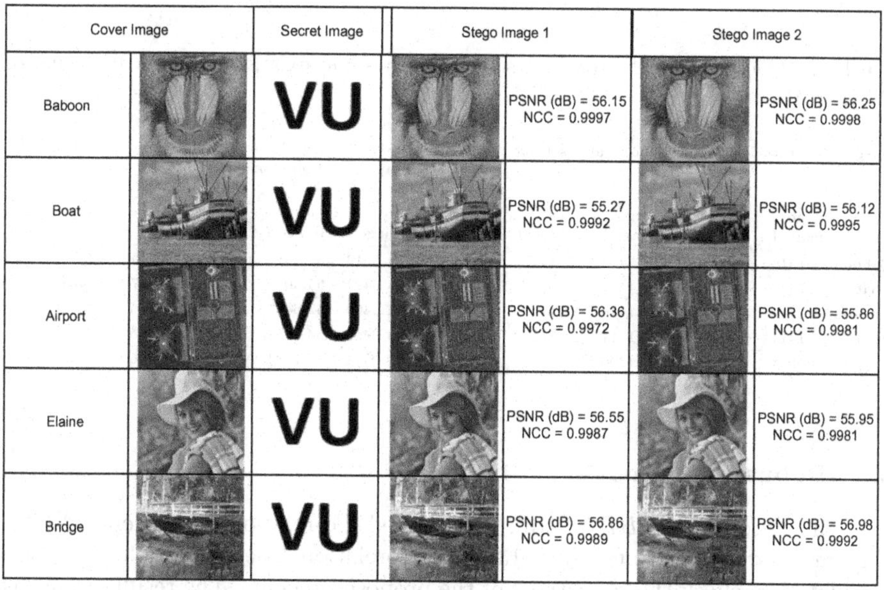

Cover Image		Secret Image	Stego Image 1		Stego Image 2	
Baboon		VU		PSNR (dB) = 56.15 NCC = 0.9997		PSNR (dB) = 56.25 NCC = 0.9998
Boat		VU		PSNR (dB) = 55.27 NCC = 0.9992		PSNR (dB) = 56.12 NCC = 0.9995
Airport		VU		PSNR (dB) = 56.36 NCC = 0.9972		PSNR (dB) = 55.86 NCC = 0.9981
Elaine		VU		PSNR (dB) = 56.55 NCC = 0.9987		PSNR (dB) = 55.95 NCC = 0.9981
Bridge		VU		PSNR (dB) = 56.86 NCC = 0.9989		PSNR (dB) = 56.98 NCC = 0.9992

Fig. 3. Experimental results of some sample images collected from SIPI image database

5.1 Imperceptibility Analysis

The MSE, $PSNR$, $SSIM$, and $Q - Index$ are computed to check the imperceptibility of the dual stego images. The corresponding results are tabulated in the Table 1. It can be observed from the Table 1 that visual quality of the stego images are very good in terms of PSNR (dB) which is around 56.25 dB on average. The values of $Q - Index$, and $SSIM$ near to 1 implies satisfactory level of imperceptibility of the stego images. A comparative study of the proposed scheme with some well known schemes have been carried out and the results are given in the Table 2. From the results shown in the Table 2, it can be concluded that the proposed scheme is superior to the schemes [8–10], and [16] in terms of PSNR.

Table 1. Imperceptibility analysis

Image	Capacity	MSE	PSNR(dB)	Q-Index	SSIM
Baboon	524108	0.027	56.15	0.9998	0.9987
Boat	524296	0.029	55.27	0.9996	0.9989
Airport	524288	0.025	56.36	0.9997	0.9979
Elaine	524112	0.026	56.55	0.9997	0.9991
Bridge	524186	0.029	56.86	0.9995	0.9988

Table 2. Comparison of proposed scheme with some existing schemes in terms of PSNR (dB)

Image	Lu et al.'s scheme [8]		Yao et al.'s scheme [9]		Shastri and Thaniksekvan's scheme [10]		Kim ,Ryu & Jung's scheme [16]		Proposed scheme	
	Stego image I	Stego image II	Stego image I	Stego image II	Stego image I	Stego image II	Stego Image I	Stego image II	Stego image I	Stego Image II
Baboon	51.1410	51.1410	51.1410	51.1411	54.6650	51.6514	54.3882	49.0005	56.15	56.25
Boat	51.1411	48.1477	51.1412	51.1411	54.6392	51.6491	53.9046	49.1195	55.27	56.12
Airport	51.1410	51.1411	51.1410	51.1411	54.6863	51.6466	52.6487	48.2680	56.36	55.86
Elaine	51.1411	51.1411	51.1411	51.1411	54.6863	51.6495	54.1089	49.1711	56.55	55.95
Bridge	28.0364	28.0364	51.1606	51.1606	54.3411	51.0411	52.7151	48.3978	56.86	56.98

5.2 Robustness Analysis

The Bit Error Rate (BER) [13], Normalized Co-relation Coefficient (NCC) [14], Standard Deviation (SD) [13], and Corelation Coefficient (CC) [13] are calculated to check the robustness of the proposed scheme. The results in terms of BER, NCC, SD, and CC are shown in the Table 3.

Table 3. Robustness analysis of the proposed scheme

Image	SD of		CC of	NCC	BER
	Cover	Stego	Cover and Stego		
Baboon	21.461	21.571	0.9888	0.9998	0.0012
Boat	22.252	22.462	0.9886	0.9992	0.0017
Airport	22.267	22.291	0.9984	0.9972	0.0013
Elaine	21.569	21.687	0.9896	0.9987	0.0016
Bridge	21.362	21.397	0.9985	0.9989	0.0014

From the Table 3 it is clear that the BER value is 0.0015 on an average which implies that minimum distortion is there in the stego images. Also, the NCC value near to 1 proves better correlation between the stego image pixels. The SD and CC values also proves that their is minimum difference between the original cover image and the stego images. All these values prove better robustness of the proposed scheme. So, the proposed scheme is secured from the security threats to some extent.

6 Conclusion

In this article, a dual image based data hiding scheme using pixel value difference has been proposed. The proposed scheme uses center folding strategy in the Integer Wavelet Transform (IWT) domain. The secret data is embedded into the LH, HL, and HH coefficients instead of the pixel values. Use of center folding strategy in the scheme minimizes the difference between the coefficients of two stego images. This not only maintain similarity between two stego images but also increases the imperceptibility of the stego images. Moreover, the HH subband is utilized to mark negative or positive values generated during center folding strategy which has a limitation of generating negative values also. Experimental results shows that the proposed scheme maintains good embedding capacity and better image quality with less distortion in the stego images. Also, the proposed scheme has different embedding capacity for different images as the payload depends on the characteristics of the cover image. This makes the proposed scheme very robust against some attacks. However, the proposed scheme has a limitation of good trade-off between capacity and imperceptibility. In future, there is a scope to improve the data hiding capacity of the proposed scheme using any interpolation technique without compromising the imperceptibly of the stego images.

References

1. Wu, N.I., Wu, K.C., Wang, C.M.: Exploring pixel-value differencing and base decomposition for low distortion data embedding. Appl. Soft Comput. **12**(2), 942–960 (2012)
2. Tian, J.: Reversible data embedding using a difference expansion. IEEE Trans. Circ. Syst. Video Technol. **13**(8), 890–896 (2003)
3. Zhang, R., Lu, C., Liu, J.: A high capacity reversible data hiding scheme for encrypted covers based on histogram shifting. J. Inf. Secur. Appl. **47**, 199–207 (2019)
4. Chang, C.C., Kieu, T.D., Chou, Y.C.: Reversible data hiding scheme using two steganographic images. In: TENCON 2007–2007 IEEE Region 10 Conference, pp. 1–4. IEEE (2007)
5. Zhang, X., Wang, S.: Efficient steganographic embedding by exploiting modification direction. IEEE Commun. Lett. **10**(11), 781–783 (2006)

6. Lee, C.F., Wang, K.H., Chang, C.C., Huang, Y.L.: A reversible data hiding scheme based on dual steganographic images. In: Proceedings of the 3rd International Conference on Ubiquitous Information Management and Communication, pp. 228–237 (2009)

7. Qin, C., Chang, C.-C., Hsu, T.-J.: Reversible data hiding scheme based on exploiting modification direction with two steganographic images. Multimedia Tools Appl. **74**(15), 5861–5872 (2014). https://doi.org/10.1007/s11042-014-1894-5

8. Lu, T.C., Wu, J.H., Huang, C.C.: Dual-image-based reversible data hiding method using center folding strategy. Signal Process. **115**, 195–213 (2015)

9. Yao, H., Qin, C., Tang, Z., Tian, Y.: Improved dual-image reversible data hiding method using the selection strategy of shiftable pixels' coordinates with minimum distortion. Signal Process. **135**, 26–35 (2017)

10. Shastri, S., Thanikaiselvan, V.: Dual image reversible data hiding using trinary assignment and centre folding strategy with low distortion. J. Visual Commun. Image Represent. **61**, 130–140 (2019)

11. Pal, P., Chowdhuri, P., Jana, B.: Weighted matrix based reversible watermarking scheme using color image. Multimedia Tools Appl. **77**(18), 23073–23098 (2018). https://doi.org/10.1007/s11042-017-5568-y

12. Su, Q., Niu, Y., Wang, Q., Sheng, G.: A blind color image watermarking based on DC component in the spatial domain. Optik **124**(23), 6255–6260 (2013)

13. Parah, S.A., Sheikh, J.A., Loan, N.A., Bhat, G.M.: A robust and computationally efficient digital watermarking technique using inter block pixel differencing. In: Hassanien, A.E., Fouad, M.M., Manaf, A.A., Zamani, M., Ahmad, R., Kacprzyk, J. (eds.) Multimedia Forensics and Security. ISRL, vol. 115, pp. 223–252. Springer, Cham (2017). https://doi.org/10.1007/978-3-319-44270-9_10

14. Wenyin, Z., Shih, F.Y.: Semi-fragile spatial watermarking based on local binary pattern operators. Optics Commun. **284**(16–17), 3904–3912 (2011)

15. SIPI Image Database. http://sipi.usc.edu/database/database.php/, Accessed 27 Oct 2021

16. Kim, P.H., Ryu, K.W., Jung, K.H.: Reversible data hiding scheme based on pixel-value differencing in dual images. Int. J. Distrib. Sensor Netw. **16**(7), 1550147720911006 (2020)

17. Jose, A., Subramanian, K.: High-capacity reversible data hiding using quotient multi pixel value differencing scheme in encrypted images by fuzzy based encryption. Multimedia Tools Appl. **80**(19), 29453–29479 (2021). https://doi.org/10.1007/s11042-021-11122-5

18. Sahu, M., Padhy, N., Gantayat, S.S., Sahu, A.K.: Shadow image based reversible data hiding using addition and subtraction logic on the LSB planes. Sens. Imaging **22**(1), 1–31 (2021). https://doi.org/10.1007/s11220-020-00328-w

19. Kim, P.H., Jung, K.H., Yoon, E.J., Ryu, K.W.: An improved interpolation method using pixel difference values for effective reversible data hiding. J. Korea Multimedia Soc. **24**(6), 768–788 (2021)

An IWT Based Reversible Watermarking Scheme Using Lagrange Interpolation Polynomial

Ashis Dey[1] , Pabitra Pal[2] , Partha Chowdhuri[3]($\boxtimes$) ,
Prabhas Kumar Singh[3], and Biswapati Jana[3]

[1] Department of Computer Science, Silda Chandra Sekhar College,
721515 Silda, India
[2] BSTTM, IIT Delhi, Delhi 110016, New Delhi, India
[3] Department of Computer Science, Vidyasagar University,
Midnapore 721102, West Bengal, India
prc.email@gmail.com

Abstract. Sharing the secret among the partners is an interesting technique that distributes the secret information in several shares for enhancing security. Nowadays, the reversible watermarking scheme becomes very popular due to increasing privacy and security issues in the day to day life. Here, a new watermarking scheme has been proposed using Integer Wavelet Transform (IWT) and Lagrange Interpolation Polynomial (LIP). The reversibility can meet with the help of the IWT scheme and LIP provides the flavor of secret sharing. Moreover, experimental results with comparison have been drawn at the end of the paper. The experimental shows that the proposed scheme can achieve 58.9 dB PSNR with a high payload of 1.5 bpp. From the experimental results, it can be concluded that the proposed scheme outperforms the other existing scheme.

Keywords: Watermarking · Lagrange Interpolation Polynomial
(LIP) · Integer Wavelet Transform (IWT) · Reversibility

1 Introduction

With the rapid growth of internet technology the security becomes the paramount feature for digital communication. In this digital era, the information can be downloaded without authorization form the legitimate owner of the documents which leads to issues such as copyright protection and authentication, data integrity violation. To resolve these problem, researcher were investigating various data concealing strategies like data hiding, watermarking, steganography and cryptography.

Watermarking basically used for providing the authentication and copyright protection of a scheme. In a watermarking scheme sender embeds the secret information inside within the cover and sends the watermarked cover over the network. At the receiver end, receiver extract the watermark information from the

S. Mukhopadhyay et al. (Eds.): CICBA 2022, CCIS 1579, pp. 85–99, 2022.
https://doi.org/10.1007/978-3-031-10766-5_8

watermarked cover and check the authentication of the user. There are various watermarking techniques based on the research domain such as spatial domain watermarking and transform domain watermarking. The spatial domain watermarking is generally used for the less computational complexity than the transform domain watermarking. Some of the major requirements of digital image watermarking are

- **Imperceptibility**: The visual quality of the watermarked image will not be degraded too much after embedding the watermark image into the cover image.
- **Robustness**: The watermarking as much as robust such that it can sustain various types of geometric attacks.
- **Embedding Capacity:** The embedding information should be as large as possible.

But there is problem if anybody wants to increase any one of the three parameters then other should be decrease. So to maintain a good trade-off among these three parameter is a challenging task in the current research scenario.

Moreover designing a scheme reversible is the another important research challenge. Many reversible data hiding schemes have been suggested e.g. lossless compression [20], least significant bit matching [15], difference expansion, histogram shifting, prediction error expansion [23], adaptive prediction-error labeling [21] etc. to solve the above mentioned problem. But they also have various limitation which are discussed in the literature review section.

Currently, various reversible data hiding schemes based on Secret Sharing (SS) have been developed [3,8,14,25] to minimized the encryption method's computational cost. One secret is partitioned into n shares in (k, n)-threshold SS. The basic secrets message can be recovered using k-out-of-n distributed shares.

In this scheme, a new secure reversible watermarking scheme has been proposed for the shared images using lagrange interpolation polynomial (LIP) and integer wavelet transform (IWT). At first, IWT has been applied to the cover image to get the four subbands. Then the watermark image is distributed into four shared images using LIP. At the receiver end, the watermark image and the original image can successfully recovered without loosing any information.

Contributions: The main contributions in this paper are

1. **Reversibility:** Reversibility is an important issue for any watermarking scheme.The proposed scheme ensures that original cover image and watermark image can fully recovered from the watermarked image.
2. **Fault-tolerance:** In the (k, n) threshold scheme, using k marked shared images original cover image and watermark bits can be fully recovered, even if (n-k) marked shared images are damaged during data transmission.

Organization of the Paper: The rest of this paper is organized as follows. Section 2 describes the literature review. The basic methodologies are presented in Sect. 3. In Sect. 4, the main embedding and extraction scheme has been proposed. Experiments and discussion are described in Sect. 5. Finally, conclusion is drawn in Sect. 6.

2   Related Works

Wang et al. [20] proposed a new high capacity reversible data hiding scheme using intra-block lossless compression. But they achieve very low embedding rate i.e., 0.00625 bpp. Singh [17] presented a survey on various data hiding techniques. WU et al. [21] suggested a new high capacity and secure reversible data hiding scheme where adaptive prediction error have been used. They achieved 869880 bit embedding capacity. To enhance the hiding capacity, Li et al. [9] developed a reversible data hiding (RDH) technique which is used Sudoku and Arnold transformation for image encryption. They used random bits and scanned documents as secret bits to achieve the embedding rate 7.714 bpp when scanned document used as secret bit. A Reversible Information hiding (RIH) method has been introduced by Sahu et al. [15] based on Dual-Layer LSB matching. To enhanced the embedding efficiency the used dual layer LSB matching technique. They have achieved average PSNR 47.64 dB and embedded capacity 1,572,864 bit. Xiong et al. [23] developed a RDH scheme for encrypted images with a SHE new encryption technique. They used sorting block-level prediction-error expansion (SBPEE) technique to embedded data into encrypted image. They have achieved good PSNR value 73 dB and 0.005 bpp embedding rate in their scheme. To enhance the embedding capacity, Ke et al. [8] proposed a RDH scheme in Fully Homomorphic Encrypted Domain based on key-switching and bootstrapping technique where they have achieved average PSNR value of 41.6308 dB and maximum embedding capacity of 103120 bit. Chen et al. [1] suggested a SS-based reversible data hiding scheme with multiple information hiders. To enhance the security of shared image, Hua et al. [5] invented a high security RDHEI based on multiple data hiders using CFSS polynomial. Chen et al. [2] proposed a another new RDH scheme using Paillier Cryptosystem. This scheme allow to send encrypted image and data to data processor separately without any information. Pal et al. [13] proposed a modern dual image-based reversible watermarking scheme for authentication and tamper detection. The tamper detection bits are created in the embedding process by using the LBP operator in the colored cover image. They used dual image based scheme to achieve the reversibility and security. They have achieved good quality PSNR 53 dB and payload 6,93,600 bit. Chowdhuri et al. [4] proposed a dual image based data hiding technique using weighted matrix. This scheme is used for image authentication and tampered detection. They have achieved better PSNR value more than 53 dB with embedding capacity 2,24,256 bits. Qin et al. [14] invented two modern RDHEI scheme of multiple data hiders using secret sharing over GF(p) and GF(2^8). They used difference preservation technique for embedding secret information. This scheme not fault-tolerant if shared image is distorted or damaged. They have achieved high embedding capacity and low computational complexity. Jana et al. [6] suggested a partial reversible data hiding technique where they have been used (7,4) hamming code. They have achieved good PSNR value 57 dB and 37,376 bit embedding capacity. Ke et al. [8] invented a new RDH technique in Encrypted Domain. They have been used CRT method for shared the Secret Image. Their scheme mainly used in one to one communication technique. The embedding capacity of their scheme is more than 0.9 bpp and computational complexity is low compared to the state-of-art schemes. Wu et al. [21] suggested a partial RDH scheme based on minimal square error and hamming code. Chen et al. [3] proposed a RDHEI technique using Lightweight Cryptography and Multiple SS scheme. They used only one data hider. They achieved maximum payload capacity 0.498 bpp. Mata Mendoza et al. [11] suggested a RDHI method to protect the patient information using encrypted key. Their scheme achieved more than 57 dB PSNR value and 0.5 bpp embedding capacity. Wang et al. [20] invented a new RDHEI technique using prediction error and block classification. They achieved 0.5641 bpp embedding rate which is better some existing scheme. Their scheme recovered total secret data and original image with out any loss. Wang et al. [19] suggested a new RDHEI model for minimize the error using block based encrypted image technique. They achieved 2.83 bpp embedding rate with full PSNR value. Wang et al. [18] proposed a high capacity PBTL-RDHEI scheme using parametric binary tree labeling. They have achieved 1.827 bpp embedding rate with higher PSNR value 57 dB. Xu et al. [24] invented a RDHEI technique using vector quantization prediction and parametric binary tree labeling. They achieved more than 3 bpp embedding rate. Mata Mendoza et al. [10] proposed a new hybrid watermarking technique combine with visible and robust imperceptible to prevent the medical documents from detachment and authentication. They have achieved more than 54 dB PSNR value and payload capacity 0.23 bpp.

3   Preliminaries

In this section, the concepts secret sharing (SS) technique has been discussed.

3.1   Secret Sharing

Secret Sharing can divide the secret into multiple shares. The original secrets can be reconstructed with the specified number of shares. Shamir [16] proposed a scheme using the polynomial to share a secret integer. In a (k, n)-threshold SIS scheme, a (k-1)-degree polynomial is selected in the sharing phase.

$$f(x) = (a_0 + a_1 x + a_2 x^2 + \ldots\ldots + a_{k-1} x^{k-1}) mod\ p$$

where p is a prime number, and the secret will be substituted into the coefficient a_0. Since the pixel values in a gray scale image vary from 0 to 255, and f(x) should not exceed this range, p is set to 251.

The size of the obtained shares is $1/k$ of the secret image. With any k out of n shares, all the coefficients of $f(x)$ can be retrieved by

$$f(x) = f(x_1)(\frac{(x-x_2)(x-x_3)....(x-x_k)}{(x_1-x_2)(x_1-x_3)....(x_1-x_k)}) + f(x_2)(\frac{(x-x_1)(x-x_3)....(x-x_k)}{(x_2-x_1)(x_2-x_3)....(x_2-x_k)}) +$$
$$......... + f(x_k)(\frac{(x-x_1)(x-x_2)....(x-x_{k-1})}{(x_k-x_1)(x_k-x_2)....(x_k-x_{k-1})})mod(p)$$

Thus, the k pixels of the secret image are retrieved. However, since the prime number p is set to 251, the pixel values lager than 250 need to be preprocessed additionally. To address this issue, Galois Field $GF(2^8)$ is utilized.

4   Proposed Scheme

The proposed watermarking scheme has been described in the following way.

4.1   Embedding Process

In this paper, a new reversible watermarking scheme has been proposed using lagrange interpolation polynomial (LIP) and integer wavelet transform (IWT). At first, input a cover image (CV) and it is decomposed into four sub-bands (LL, HL, LH and HH) using IWT. Then consider LH sub-bands for the embedding process. Split the coefficients of LH sub-band into (2×2) blocks. Collect 8 bits i.e., 2-LSB bits of each of four pixels and convert into its decimal equivalent (DI) value. Then watermark image (WT) is considered each pixel of the watermark is considered for the embedding process. Now these DI and WT values are stored into the two variable say P and Q. These P and Q are considered as the polynomial coefficient. The numerical example of proposed embedding procedure has been describe in Fig. 2.

$$f_i(x) = (Q + P_ix + x^2) \quad (\mod m(x)) \tag{1}$$

where $m(x)$ is GF(2^8) which is Galois Field polynomial.

Hence the private key $(x = 1, 2, 3, 4)$ has been applied using Eq. (1) to get the shared shadow images. Apply same procedure for HL and HH sub-bands all block of an image. After embedding watermark bits into cover image update all pixel values and inverse IWT is applied to generate watermarked image (Fig. 1).

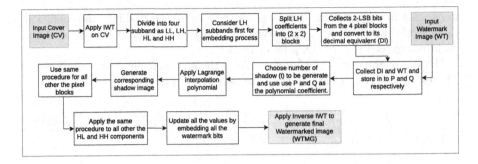

Fig. 1. Block diagram of the proposed watermarking scheme

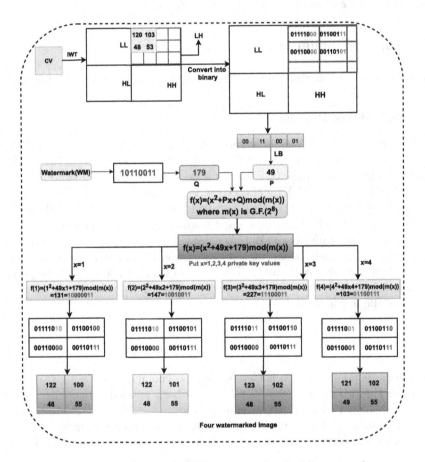

Fig. 2. Numerical example of the proposed embedding procedure

The algorithmic description has been depicted in Algorithm 1.

Algorithm 1: Embedding Algorithm

Input : Input Cover Image (CV) and Watermark image (WT)
Output: Shared Watermarked Images (WTMG)

Algorithm Embedding():

    Step 1: A cover image (CV) is considered for the embedding process.
    Step 2: IWT is applied into (CV) to generate four sub-bands (say, LL, LH, HL and HH).
    Step 3: LH sub-band is now considered for further process.
    Step 4: The coefficients of LH has been chosen and divided into (2×2) blocks.
    Step 5: Four pixel values are taken into the account.
    Step 6: 2-LSB bits are extracted from each of the four pixels and stored into LB.
    Step 7: LB is converted to its decimal equivalent (DI)
    Step 8: P − > DI The (DI) value is stored into P.
    Step 9: An image pixel from the watermark image is considered and stored into Q.
    Step 10: Construct a polynomial using P and Q as polynomial coefficient.
    Step 11: The shadow (t) value is set to 4.
    Step 12: The private key ($x = 1, 2, 3, 4$) applied into this polynomial for creating four shadow images.
    Step 13: Step 4 to Step 12 are used for all other pixel blocks.
    Step 14: The same procedure is applied for all HL and HH sub bands components.
    Step 15: Update all pixel value after embedding watermark pixels.
    Step 16: Inverse IWT is applied.
    Step 17: The final watermarked image ($WTMG$) is generated.

4.2 Extraction Process

In this section, a detail extraction procedure has been described. The basic secret sharing mechanism has been used to extracted the original watermark and the cover image even if some of the shared image has been lost. Here also lagrange interpolation polynomial formula has been used to extract the watermark image from the shared watermarked image. At first, all the shared watermarked image blocks are converted into equivalent decimal form. Then extract all the embedded information from watermarked images using the lagrange interpolation polynomial (LIP). The numerical example of proposed extraction procedure has been describe in Fig. 3.

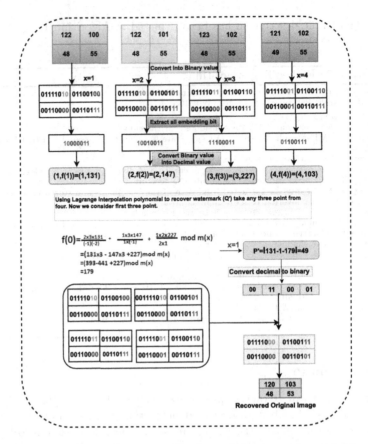

Fig. 3. Numerical example of the proposed extraction procedure

5   Experimental Analysis and Discussion

In this section the experimental result of proposed scheme are discussed using various metrics like PSNR [12], SSIM [14], VIF. For the experiment, some images of size (512×512) has been chosen from a standard image database (USC-SIPI Image Database). The Fig. 4 depicts the standard color cover images of (512×512) pixels collected form USC-SIPI image database. The proposed scheme used JAVA 8 and Windows 10 operating system for experiment.

5.1   Imperceptibility Analysis

The imperceptibility of the scheme has been analyzed using some standard metric such PSNR, MSE, VIF and SSIM.

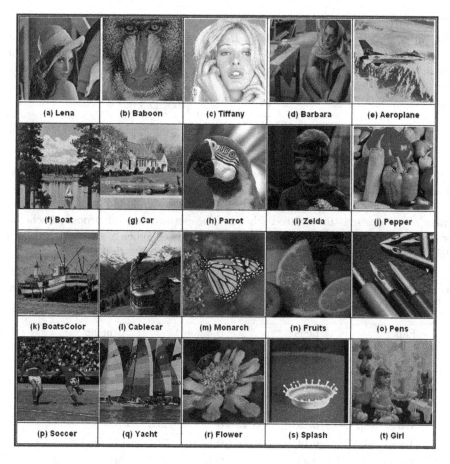

Fig. 4. Standard color cover images of (512×512) pixels collected form USC-SIPI image database.

Peak Signal to Noise Ratio (PSNR): The PSNR has been calculated using Eq. (2).

$$PSNR = 10 \log_{10} \frac{255^2}{MSE},$$ (2)

Practically, PSNR value of a image higher than 31 dB is consider as better quality image according to the human visual system and higher PSNR is expected for better algorithm.

Structured Similarity Index Measure (SSIM): SSIM is used to measure the similarity between two images. The value of SSIM lies between $(-1, 1)$. The SSIM value is near about 1 indicates that the two images are identical.

Visual Information Fidelity(VIF): VIF quantify overall quality of images. The value of VIF lies between (0,1). If VIF = 0 denotes that all information about marked images are lost to distortion and VIF = 1 denotes that visual quality of marked images are good. The VIF of an image can be evaluated using Eq. (3).

$$VIF = \frac{\sum_{k \in subbands} I(\bar{\alpha}^{n,k}; \bar{\beta}^{n,k} \mid x^{n,k})}{\sum_{k \in subbands} I(\bar{\alpha}^{n,k}; \bar{\gamma}^{n,k} \mid x^{n,k})} \tag{3}$$

where, $\bar{\alpha}^{n,k}, \bar{\beta}^{n,k}, \bar{\gamma}^{n,k}$ denote the vector of n blocks in subband k and $x^{n,k}$ is the maximum likelihood of $X^{n,k}$ in subband k.

From Table 1 shows that the comparison between embedding rate and PSNR value of various existing related scheme. The performance of proposed scheme is better than some other existing scheme. Proposed scheme can achieved 58.9 dB PSNR and 1.5 bpp embedding rate.

Table 1. Comparison of the payload and visual quality with respect to the other existing scheme

Paper	Lena		Baboon		Airplane	
	ER(bpp)	PSNR	ER(bpp)	PSNR	ER(bpp)	PSNR
Chen et al. [1]	0.48	35.7	0.44	25.3	0.49	32.5
Wang et al. [20]	2.26	57	1.025	57	2.37	57
Hua et al. [5]	2.91	Inf	1.25	Inf	3.24	Inf
Wu et al. [21]	0.43	53.4	0.43	53.3	0.43	53.3
Jana et al. [6]	0.14	52.1	0.14	52.1	0.14	52.1
Yang et al. [26]	0.43	53.3	0.43	53.3	0.43	53.3
Wu et al. [22]	1.50	36.9	1.50	36.9	1.50	36.8
Proposed scheme	1.50	58.9	1.50	58.6	1.50	59.1

The Fig. 5 depicts the comparison graph interms of ER. From the graph it is clearly seen that the proposed scheme provides 1.5 bpp in terms PSNR.

The Fig. 6 depicts the comparison graph interms of PSNR. From the graph it is clearly seen that the proposed scheme provides better results with respect to the other schemes.

Table 2 shows experimental results in terms of PSNR, SSIM, and VIF to evaluate the visual quality of watermarked image. From this table it is noted that proposed scheme achieved high PSNR value of 58.9 dB with near unity value of SSIM and VIF.

The Fig. 7 depicts the Graphical representation of VIF results for various images. It is seen that lena images outperforms than others.

The Fig. 8 depicts the Graphical representation of PSNR results for various images. It is seen that lena images outperforms than others.

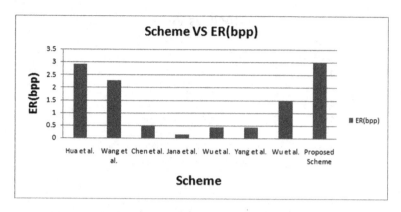

Fig. 5. Graph for Scheme VS ER(bpp)

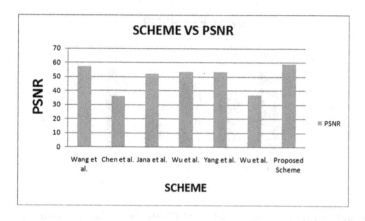

Fig. 6. Graph for Scheme VS PSNR

Table 2. Embedding rate and visual quality of different images

IMAGE	ER(bpp)	PSNR	SSIM	VIF
Lena	1.50	58.9	0.999	0.985
Baboon	1.50	58.6	0.998	0.981
Tiffany	1.50	58.7	0.997	0.983
Peppers	1.50	58.8	0.999	0.983
Boat	1.50	59.1	0.998	0.983

The Fig. 9 depicts the Graphical representation of SSIM results for various images. It is seen that lena and pepper images outperform than others.

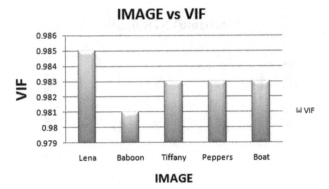

Fig. 7. Graphical representation of VIF results for various images

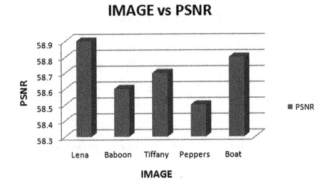

Fig. 8. Graphical representation of PSNR results for various images

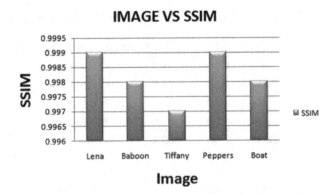

Fig. 9. Graphical representation of SSIM results for various images

Table 3. Comparison with respect to other existing medical image scheme

Paper	ER(bpp)	PSNR	SSIM	VIF
MataMendoza et al. [10]	0.23	54.91	0.995	0.983
MataMendoza et al. [11]	0.5	57.56	0.981	0.973
Proposed scheme	1.50	59.1	0.998	0.985

The comparison also done between some medical image based scheme which is shown in Table 3 in terms of ER(bpp), PSNR, SSIM and VIF. From Table 3, it is observe that proposed scheme is also better than some existing medical image based scheme.

Table 4. Comparison with respect to other existing scheme

Method	Reversibility	Privacy preserving	Encryption complexity	Decryption complexity	Multi-party data embedding	Independence between the data hiders
Chen et al. [1]	Yes	Yes	O(n)	$O(nlog^2 n)$	Yes	No
Wu et al. [22]	Partial	No	–	–	No	–
Ke et al. [7]	Yes	Yes	$O(n^2)$	$O(n^2)$	No	–
Chen et al. [2]	Yes	Yes	O(n)	$O(nlog^2 n)$	No	–
Wang et al. [20]	Yes	Yes	$O(n^2)$	$O(n^2)$	Yes	–
Yang et al. [26]	Partial	No	–	–	No	–
Jana et al. [6]	Partial	No	–	–	No	–
Proposed Scheme	Yes	Yes	O(n)	$O(n)$	Yes	Yes

The comparison between various existing and proposed watermarked schemes are shown in Table 4 in terms of Reversibility, Encryption complexity, Decryption complexity, Privacy etc. From the Table 4, it is clear that the proposed scheme outperforms than the existing scheme in terms of said parameters.

5.2 Complexity

The study of computational complexity of a system increasingly required for model integration. In the proposed model the computational complexity has been measured by the various parameters. From the embedding algorithm one can easily conclude that the computational complexity for the embedding procedure will be $O(n)$. Again from the extraction algorithm it can be finalized that the computational complexity will be $O(n)$ for the extraction procedure.

6 Conclusion

In this scheme, a new watermarking technique has been proposed using IWT and Lagrange Interpolation polynomial (LIP) to enhance the security and privacy issue. The IWT is used to achieve the reversibility of the scheme whereas the LIP is used to leverage the shared secret flavor. The receiver can extract the watermarked image and original image without any distortion, which means reversibility can be preserved. The proposed scheme can achieve 58.9 dB PSNR and with a high embedding capacity 1.5 bpp. In future, polynomial based secret sharing have to used to reduced the data expansion and enhanced the security of shared data. Furthermore, the encryption technique would be the great extent of the proposed scheme.

References

1. Chen, B., Lu, W., Huang, J., Weng, J., Zhou, Y.: Secret sharing based reversible data hiding in encrypted images with multiple data-hiders. IEEE Trans. Depend. Secure Comput. **19**, 978–991 (2020)
2. Chen, H., Chang, C.C., Chen, K.: Reversible data hiding schemes in encrypted images based on the paillier cryptosystem. Int. J. Netw. Secur. **22**, 521–531 (2020)
3. Chen, Y.C., Hung, T.H., Hsieh, S.H., Shiu, C.W.: A new reversible data hiding in encrypted image based on multi-secret sharing and lightweight cryptographic algorithms. IEEE Trans. Inf. Forensics Secur. **14**, 3332–3343 (2019)
4. Chowdhuri, P., Pal, P., Jana, B.: A new dual image-based steganographic scheme for authentication and tampered detection using (7, 4) hamming code, pp. 163–174 (2019)
5. Hua, Z., Wang, Y., Yi, S., Zhou, Y., Jia, X.: Secure reversible data hiding in encrypted images using cipher-feedback secret sharing. ArXiv abs/2106.14139 (2021)
6. Jana, B., Giri, D., Mondal, S.K.: Partial reversible data hiding scheme using (7, 4) hamming code. Multimedia Tools Appl. **76**(20), 21691–21706 (2016). https://doi.org/10.1007/s11042-016-3990-1
7. Ke, Y., Zhang, M., Liu, J., Su, T., Yang, X.: Fully homomorphic encryption encapsulated difference expansion for reversible data hiding in encrypted domain. IEEE Trans. Circ. Syst. Video Technol. **30**, 2353–2365 (2020)
8. Ke, Y., Zhang, M., Zhang, X., Liu, J., Su, T., Yang, X.: A reversible data hiding scheme in encrypted domain for secret image sharing based on Chinese remainder theorem. ArXiv abs/2010.08502 (2020)
9. Li, X.Y., Zhou, X., Zhou, Q.L., Han, S., Liu, Z.: High-capacity reversible data hiding in encrypted images by information preprocessing. Complexity **2020**, 6989452:1–6989452:12 (2020)
10. Mata-Mendoza, D., et al.: Secured telemedicine of medical imaging based on dual robust watermarking. Visual Comput. **38**, 2073–2090 (2021)
11. Mata-Mendoza, D., Nuñez-Ramirez, D., Cedillo-Hernández, M., Nakano-Miyatake, M.: An improved ROI-based reversible data hiding scheme completely separable applied to encrypted medical images. Health Technol. **11**, 1–16 (2021)
12. Pal, P., Chowdhuri, P., Jana, B.: Weighted matrix based reversible watermarking scheme using color image. Multimedia Tools Appl. **77**(18), 23073–23098 (2018). https://doi.org/10.1007/s11042-017-5568-y
13. Pal, P., Jana, B., Bhaumik, J.: Watermarking scheme using local binary pattern for image authentication and tamper detection through dual image. Secur. Priv. **2**(2), e59 (2019)

14. Qin, C., Jiang, C., Mo, Q., Yao, H., Chang, C.C.: Reversible data hiding in encrypted image via secret sharing based on gf(p) and gf(28). IEEE Trans. Circ. Syst. Video Technol. **32**, 1928–1941 (2021)
15. Sahu, A.K., Swain, G.: Reversible image steganography using dual-layer LSB matching (2019)
16. Shamir, A.: How to share a secret. Commun. ACM **22**, 612–613 (1979)
17. Singh, A.K.: Data hiding: current trends, innovation and potential challenges. ACM Trans. Multimedia Comput. Commun. Appl. **16**(3s) (2020). https://doi.org/10.1145/3382772
18. Wang, P., Cai, B., Xu, S., Chen, B.: Reversible data hiding scheme based on adjusting pixel modulation and block-wise compression for encrypted images. IEEE Access **8**, 28902–28914 (2020)
19. Wang, X., Yao Li, L., Chang, C.C., Chen, C.C.: High-capacity reversible data hiding in encrypted images based on prediction error compression and block selection. Secur. Commun. Netw. **2021**, 9606116:1–9606116:12 (2021)
20. Wang, Y., Cai, Z., He, W.: High capacity reversible data hiding in encrypted image based on intra-block lossless compression. IEEE Trans. Multimedia **23**, 1466–1473 (2021)
21. Wu, X., Qiao, T., Xu, M., Zheng, N.: Secure reversible data hiding in encrypted images based on adaptive prediction-error labeling. Signal Process. **188**, 108200 (2021). https://doi.org/10.1016/j.sigpro.2021.108200, https://www.sciencedirect.com/science/article/pii/S0165168421002383
22. Wu, X., Yang, C.N., Liu, Y.W.: A general framework for partial reversible data hiding using hamming code. Signal Process. **175**, 107657 (2020)
23. Xiong, L., Dong, D.: Reversible data hiding in encrypted images with somewhat homomorphic encryption based on sorting block-level prediction-error expansion. J. Inf. Secur. Appl. **47**, 78–85 (2019)
24. Xu, S., Horng, J.H., Chang, C.C.: Reversible data hiding scheme based on VQ prediction and adaptive parametric binary tree labeling for encrypted images. IEEE Access **9**, 55191–55204 (2021)
25. Yan, X., Lu, Y., Liu, L., Song, X.: Reversible image secret sharing. IEEE Trans. Inf. Forensics Secur. **15**, 3848–3858 (2020)
26. Yang, H.Y., Qi, S.R., Niu, P.P., Wang, X.Y.: Color image zero-watermarking based on fast quaternion generic polar complex exponential transform. Signal Process. Image Commun. **82**, 115747 (2020)

A New Image Encryption Based on Two Chaotic Maps and Affine Transform

Supriyo De[1(✉)], Jaydeb Bhaumik[2], and Debasis Giri[3]

[1] Department of Electronics and Communication Engineering, Techno Engineering College Banipur, Habra 743 233, India
supriyo.tech@gmail.com
[2] Department of Electronics and Telecommunication Engineering, Jadavpur University, Kolkata 700 032, India
jaydeb.bhaumik@jadavpuruniversity.in
[3] Department of Information Technology, Maulana Abul Kalam Azad University of Technology, Nadia, Kolkata 741 249, India

Abstract. In the present era, the non-linear and dynamic phenomenon of chaos play a vital role in image encryption. In this paper, we proposes a new image encryption method based on cubic map and Hénon map. The cubic map is employed and combined with affine transformation in substitution phase. The key expansion technique is built up with the Hénon map. Finally, the encryption process incorporates the Nonlinear key mixing (Nmix) function which enables to propagate the bit-pattern from n^{th} ciphered pixel to $(n + 1)^{th}$ ciphered pixel. The performance of the scheme has been successfully verified by several well known statistical attacks, differential attacks, and brute force search. Moreover, in comparative studies the proposed scheme has confirmed its potential with respect to related existing schemes.

Keywords: Image encryption · Multi-dimensional chaos · Affine transform · Nmix · Randomness test · Differential attack

1 Introduction

A sharp growth has been observed in the area of digital communication since last two decades. This technical advancement enhances the usage of multimedia data, such as digital image transfer through the public network. Consequently, confidentiality, data integrity and authentication play major role for transferring the digital image through the public network. In this scenario, image encryption is an effective technique which can protect the images from unauthorized access. Designing of a good image encryption scheme becomes a challenge due to its high correlation and large data size. There is a scope for the researchers to design high speed, less complex image encryption algorithm. Nowadays, chaos based scheme plays a significant role in image encryption because of its non-linear and dynamic characteristics.

© The Author(s), under exclusive license to Springer Nature Switzerland AG 2022
S. Mukhopadhyay et al. (Eds.): CICBA 2022, CCIS 1579, pp. 100–114, 2022.
https://doi.org/10.1007/978-3-031-10766-5_9

In [3], the modification is incorporated in Hénon map for betterment the performance of image encryption scheme. Moreover, a hybrid chaotic shift transformation (HCST), and a sine map have been introduced here for confusion and diffusion process respectively. The scheme has ensured satisfactory security level with respect to different cryptographic analyses. Tong et al. have introduced a new high dimensional chaotic system for image encryption in [5]. Here, permutation process has built up by a new separated Cat map which ensures better security. Further, different security analysis parameters evaluate the performance of the scheme. In [6], quantum chaotic-based diffusion and spatial permutation have been incorporated in an image encryption technique. The robustness of the scheme has tested and validated by several common statistical and differential attacks.

Zhang et al. [7] have introduced multiple dynamic s-boxes in image encryption using piecewise linear chaotic map and Chen chaotic map. In [8], an image encryption scheme has been developed by substitution and diffusion. The authors have employed piecewise linear chaotic map along with logistic map for generating the random sequence. Apart from various common statistical and differential attacks, both the scheme [7,8] have been successfully verified χ^2-test for histograms of the obtained cipher images.

Chaos based partial encryption technique has been reported in [12]. It associates with SPIHT compressed bit stream and stream cipher encryption. The scheme ensures good balance in between computational overhead and confidentiality. Taneja et al. have introduced a logistic map and Arnold's cat map based image encryption scheme in [10]. Here, the plain images have been separated in significant and insignificant part by gradient based edge detection technique. Further, two distinct parts are encrypted individually in spatial domain and transform domain. in [11], permutation and substitution based image encryption technique has been reported. Here, Arnold's cat map is used for performing the permutation operation. On the other hand, the substitution process has been implemented using the Hénon map.

In this paper, we proposes a substitution-diffusion based image encryption method. In substitution, cubic map based expanded sequence combines with affine ciphering technique. On the other hand, Hénon map is applied to generate the pseudo random sequence. From the details analysis of cubic map and Hénon map, we have set the range of controlling parameters for both maps. In encryption, Nmix function has been employed along with the exclusive-OR operation. The proposed scheme has examined with different cryptanalysis tests which confirm the resistance against several well-known attacks. Moreover, multifarious statistical analyses ensure the random behavior of the expanded key stream and cipher images.

The rest of the paper is organized as follows: A brief overview of two chaotic maps, affine transform and nonlinear Boolean function Nmix is provided in Sect. 2 which are employed to design our scheme. We describes our image encryption method in Sect. 3. Section 4 shows the experimental results and comparative analyses with related existing schemes and finally Sect. 5 concludes the paper.

2   Preliminaries

The article incorporates cubic map, Hénon map, affine ciphering technique and Nmix function for designing an image encryption scheme. A brief analysis of cubic map, Hénon map, affine ciphering technique and Nmix function have been described in this section.

2.1   Cubic Map

It is a one dimensional bimodal map. Cubic map can be presented in discrete time. The general expression for this map is defined as

$$x_{n+1} = mx_n(1 - x_n^2) \tag{1}$$

where m is the controlling parameter.

The cubic map deals with two critical points and it can be implemented to describe the population dynamics of certain genetic groups. From the above expression it is clearly observed that the range of f(x) varies from $[-1, 1]$ to $[-2/(\sqrt{3}), 2/(\sqrt{3})]$ where $m \in [0, 3]$. On the other hand, in discrete form, the lyapunov exponent of the cubic map can be obtained from [17] and the corresponding characteristic is depicted in Fig. 1(b). Simultaneously, the bifurcation diagram for the said map has been shown in Fig. 1(a). Figure 1(a) and (b), ensure that the cubic map shows chaotic behaviour for $2.59 < m < 3$.

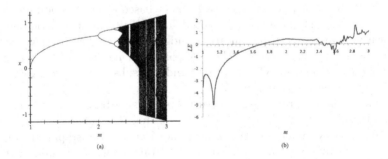

Fig. 1. Cubic map (a) Bifurcation diagram (b) Lyapunov exponent plot

2.2   Hénon Map

The Hénon map is a two dimensional chaotic model proposed in [18]. It carries the basic properties of Lorenz system. It plays a significant role in the field of chaos theory due to its complex and dynamic phenomenon. It is presented as

$$p_{n+1} = q_n + 1 - ap_n^2$$
$$q_{n+1} = bp_n \tag{2}$$

where (p_i, q_i) represents the two dimensional state of the system and a, b are the two controlling parameters.

The bifurcation diagram has been analyzed for the two control parameters a and b respectively and the obtained responses are plotted in Fig. 2(a) and (b). On the other hand, lyapunov exponents are obtained to determine the perfect operating area for the Hénon map. Figure 2(c) shows the lyapunov exponents (LE1 and LE2) of the Hénon map. Here, we have limited the analysis to obtain the lyapunov exponents for variation of controlling parameter b only (for $a = 1.4$) and obtained a wide range of b ($0.1 < b < 0.2$ and $0.25 < b < 0.3$), which ensures good chaotic nature of the Hénon map as marked in Fig. 2(c).

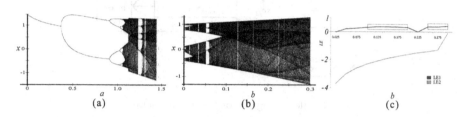

Fig. 2. Hénon map (a) Bifurcation diagram for $b = 0.3$ (b) Bifurcation diagram for $a = 1.4$ (c) Lyapunov exponent plot for $a = 1.4$

2.3 Affine Ciphering Technique

It is a well known mono-alphabetic substitution cipher technique. The encoding and decoding techniques are as follows

$$y = (P \times x + N) mod Q$$
$$x = P^{-1}(y - N) mod Q \tag{3}$$

where x: plain text; y: cipher or substituted text; P & Q are relatively prime integer; N: integer; $P.P^{-1} \bmod Q = 1$;

2.4 Nonlinear Key Mixing (Nmix)

In [14], Bhaumik et al. have proposed an ideal candidate for key mixing known as Nmix. The function Nmix is reversible, balanced and has significant non-linearity. It operates on two n-bit inputs $A = (a_{n-1}\ a_{n-2}\ ...\ a_0)$ and $K = (k_{n-1}\ k_{n-2}\ ...\ k_0)$. It produces the output $B = (b_{n-1}\ b_{n-2}\ ...\ b_0)$ as follows

$$b_i = a_i \oplus k_i \oplus d_{i-1}$$
$$d_i = \bigoplus_{j=0}^{i} a_j.k_j \oplus a_{i-1}a_i \oplus k_{i-1}k_i; \text{for } i = 0 \text{ to } n-1 \tag{4}$$

where d_i is the carry term propagating from i^{th} bit position to $(i + 1)^{th}$ bit position and the output (d_{n-1}) is discarded to make size n bits, the input carry $d_{-1} = 0$ and input bits $a_{-1} = 0$, and $k_{-1} = 0$.

3 Proposed Scheme

In this section, proposed image encryption scheme has been elaborately described. The proposed scheme associates with image substitution, key expansion and image encryption as shown in Fig. 3. The operation of each part is presented as follows.

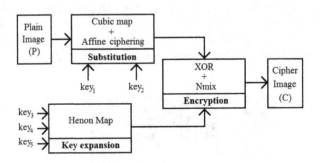

Fig. 3. Block diagram of proposed scheme

3.1 Image Substitution

Image substitution technique is designed with the help of affine ciphering technique and the cubic map. Here, a unique coupling technique has been introduced for image substitution which ensures good resistivity against plain text attack.

At first, key_1 and key_2 have been used to set the initial value and control parameter value of the cubic map respectively (x_0, m). From the previous analysis shown in Fig. 1, we have selected a suitable range of key_1 and key_2 for obtaining good chaotic responses from the cubic map. The range of key_1 is $[-2/(\sqrt{3}), 2/(\sqrt{3})]$ and the range of key_2 is $[2.59, 3]$. To overcome the inertia of the said map, first few values $(buffer)$ obtained from the system are discarded for further processing. Here, affine ciphering technique has been employed, but the value of A, B are updated each time from the generated random sequence obtained from the cubic map. The value of N is chosen 251, which is nearest prime number of $(2^8 - 1)$. Algorithm 1 illustrates the detail operation of image substitution. In first round, the substitution process operates from top to bottom direction of the plain image and in second round, it follows the reverse direction. Finally, the substituted image obtained in PI.

Input: key_1, key_2, P;
Output: PI;

Algorithm for image substitution

$x_0 = key_1, m = key_2$;
for $(i = 0; i < buffer; i++)$ **do**
   $x_1 = mx_0(1 - x_0^2)$;
   $x_0 = x_1$;
end
for $(i = 0; i < r; i++)$ **do**
   for $(j = 0; j < c; j++)$ **do**
      for $(k = 0; k < p; k++)$ **do**
         while 1 **do**
            $x_1 = mx_0(1 - x_0^2)$;
            $A = round(x_1 \times 10^{15}) \bmod 256$;
            $x_0 = x_1$;
            if $gcd(A, N) == 1$ **then**
               $x_1 = mx_0(1 - x_0^2)$;
               $B = round(x_1 \times 10^{15}) \bmod 256$;
               $x_0 = x_1$;
               $break$;   //break from while(1)
            end
         end
         $PI(i, j, k) = [A \times P(i, j, k) + B] \bmod N$;
      end
   end
end
for $(i = r - 1; i \geq 0; i--)$ **do**
   for $(j = c - 1; j \geq 0; j--)$ **do**
      for $(k = p - 1; k \geq 0; k--)$ **do**
         while 1 **do**
            $x_1 = mx_0(1 - x_0^2)$;
            $A = round(x_1 \times 10^{15}) \bmod 256$;
            $x_0 = x_1$;
            if $gcd(A, N) == 1$ **then**
               $x_1 = mx_0(1 - x_0^2)$;
               $B = round(x_1 \times 10^{15}) \bmod 256$;
               $x_0 = x_1$;
               $break$;   //break from while(1)
            end
         end
         $PI(i, j, k) = [A \times PI(i, j, k) + B] \bmod N$;
      end
   end
end
return PI;

Algorithm 1: Image substitution

3.2 Key Expansion

In this section, the key expansion technique has been elaborated for the proposed scheme. The scheme accepts a set of keys (key_3, key_4 and key_5) for the key expansion. Here, the Hénon map has been employed and key_3, key_4 are used to set the initial value of the system variables x_0, y_0 respectively. On the contrary, the control parameter b is assigned by the key_5. From the previous analysis of lyapunov exponents in Fig. 2(c), we have chosen the range of control parameter b as $(0.1 < b < 0.2$ and $0.25 < b < 0.3)$ and initial value x_0, y_0 as $[-1, 1]$ which ensures good chaotic nature. In this regard, the value of another control parameter a is set to 1.4. Here also, few initial iteration $(buffer)$ has been discarded to overcome the inertia as already stated earlier. The entire key expansion technique described as follows.

Input: $key_3, key_4, key_5, r, c, p;$
Output: $KEY;$

Algorithm for key expansion

$x_0 = key_3, y_0 = key_4, b = key_5, a = 1.4;$
for $(i = 0; i < buffer; i++)$ **do**
    $x_1 = y_0 + 1 - ax_0^2;$
    $y_1 = bx_0;$
    $x_0 = x_1;$
    $y_0 = y_1;$
end
$L = r.c.p;$ //dimension of plain image
for $(i = 0; i < L; i++)$ **do**
    $x_1 = y_0 + 1 - ax_0^2;$
    $y_1 = bx_0;$
    $x_0 = x_1;$
    $y_0 = y_1;$
    $KEY(i) = round[(x_1 \times 10^{16} + y_1 \times 10^{16}) \bmod 256];$
end
return $KEY;$

Algorithm 2: Key expansion

3.3   Image Encryption

An image encryption technique operates on substituted image (PI) and expanded key (KEY). Here, the non-linear function Nmix [14] has been employed with the linear operator xor for performing the key diffusion. Both, xor and Nmix operate on the 8-bit integer. The algorithm carries the bit pattern of first pixel of plain image and key throughout the cipher image which makes the scheme robust against differential attack. The entire technique described in Algorithm 3.

The trajectory and return map for the expanded key for 100 samples are presented in Fig. 4(a) and (b) respectively. In addition, we have examined the auto-correlation of the expanded key to verify its random property. Figure 5 depicts the obtained auto-correlation of the expanded key (100 samples). The above analyses describe good random behavior of the expanded key stream.

Input: PI, KEY;
Output: C;
___
Algorithm for image encryption
___
$n = 0$;
$[r, c, p] = size(PI)$;   //dimension of plain image/permuted image
for $(i = 0; i < r; i + +)$ **do**
    for $(j = 0; j < c; j + +)$ **do**
        for $(k = 0; k < p; k + +)$ **do**
            if $n > 0$ **then**
                $C(i, j, k) = PI(i, j, k)$ **xor** $KEY(n + +)$ **Nmix** $Temp$;
                $Temp = C(i, j, k)$;
            end
            else
                $C(i, j, k) = PI(i, j, k)$ **xor** $KEY(n + +)$;
                $Temp = C(i, j, k)$;
            end
        end
    end
end
return C;

Algorithm 3: Image encryption

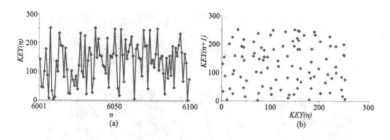

Fig. 4. (a) Trajectory of generated key (b) Return map of generated key

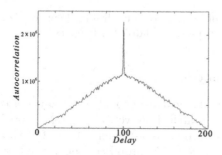

Fig. 5. Auto-correlation of generated key (100 samples)

4   Experimental Results, Security Analysis and Comparative Analysis

In this section, we have presented the experimental outcomes of the proposed scheme. Moreover, the scheme has been verified by several well known security analysis parameters. Here, selected sample images from the several image databases such as, STARE Image Database [19], UCID Image Database [20], The USC SIPI Image Database [21] and Funt et al.'s HDR Dataset Computational Vision Lab Computing Science [22] are used for the experimental studies. All the experiments have been performed using MATLAB 7.1 and run under CPU INTEL CORE I3 at 1.7 GHz in Microsoft Windows 7 environment. The default key values $key_1 = 0.6$, $key_2 = 2.6$, $key_3 = 0.54$, $key_4 = 0.45$ and $key_5 = 0.29$ are chosen for the entire experimental setup.

4.1 Encryption Decryption Test

The proposed image encryption method has been tested with several images and obtained outcomes for ciphered images and corresponding deciphered images are shown in Fig. 6(a)–(e) and Fig. 6(f)–(j) respectively. The obtained cipher images presented in Fig. 6(a)–(e) are appeared as noisy images which ensure the effectiveness of the image encryption scheme.

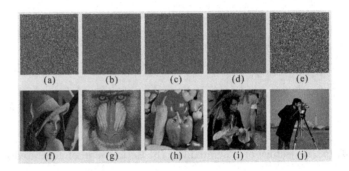

Fig. 6. Ciphered image of (a) Lena (b) Mandrill (c) Peppers (d) Man (e) Cameraman; Deciphered image of (f) Lena (g) Mandrill (h) Peppers (i) Man (j) Cameraman

4.2 Key Space Analysis

A good crypto system should have enough large key space which can able to prevent the brute force search. However, in [15,16], it has been found that an encryption scheme is said to be robust against brute force attack if and only if it has key space larger than 2^{104}. The proposed scheme used total five keys namely, key_1, key_2, key_3, key_4 and key_5. Each key has 10^{15} effective key variation. So, the total key space for the scheme becomes $10^{15} \times 10^{15} \times 10^{15} \times 10^{15} \times 10^{15} = 10^{75}$ which is more than enough to inhibit the brute force attack.

4.3 Resistance Against Differential Attack

Differential attack is another significant basis of analysis for a crypto system. Here, the performance evaluation has been carried out for 1) plaintext sensitivity and 2) avalanche effect. Number of Pixel Change Rate (NPCR) and Unified

Average Changing Intensity (UACI) have been measured to verify the performance of the proposed scheme for plaintext sensitivity. The obtained outcomes are presented in Table 1. In hypothesis test [13], we have chosen the level of significance $\alpha = 0.05/0.01/0.001$. On the other hand, the proposed scheme secures average avalanche effect 49.9999957% for several test images.

Table 1. NPCR and UACI test for plaintext sensitivity

Test images	NPCR(%)/UACI(%)	NPCR(N_α^*)/ UACI(U_α^{*-},U_α^{*+}) critical value		
Dimension 256 × 256		$N_{0.05}^* = 99.5693\%$	$N_{0.01}^* = 99.5527\%$	$N_{0.001}^* = 99.5341\%$
		$U_{0.05}^{*-} = 33.2824\%$	$U_{0.01}^{*-} = 33.2255\%$	$U_{0.001}^{*-} = 33.1594\%$
		$U_{0.05}^{*+} = 33.6447\%$	$U_{0.01}^{*+} = 33.7016\%$	$U_{0.001}^{*+} = 33.7677\%$
Cameraman	99.5884/33.3929	Pass/Pass	Pass/Pass	Pass/Pass
Lena	99.6051/33.4711	Pass/Pass	Pass/Pass	Pass/Pass
Dimension 512 × 512		$N_{0.05}^* = 99.5893\%$	$N_{0.01}^* = 99.5810\%$	$N_{0.001}^* = 99.5717\%$
		$U_{0.05}^{*-} = 33.3730\%$	$U_{0.01}^{*-} = 33.3445\%$	$U_{0.001}^{*-} = 33.3115\%$
		$U_{0.05}^{*+} = 33.5541\%$	$U_{0.01}^{*+} = 33.5826\%$	$U_{0.001}^{*+} = 33.6156\%$
Mandrill	99.6101/33.4055	Pass/Pass	Pass/Pass	Pass/Pass
Peppers	99.6077/33.4660	Pass/Pass	Pass/Pass	Pass/Pass
Dimension 1024 × 1024		$N_{0.05}^* = 99.5994\%$	$N_{0.01}^* = 99.5952\%$	$N_{0.001}^* = 99.5906\%$
		$U_{0.05}^{*-} = 33.4183\%$	$U_{0.01}^{*-} = 33.4040\%$	$U_{0.001}^{*-} = 33.3875\%$
		$U_{0.05}^{*+} = 33.5088\%$	$U_{0.01}^{*+} = 33.5231\%$	$U_{0.001}^{*+} = 33.5396\%$
Airport	99.6187/33.4585	Pass/Pass	Pass/Pass	Pass/Pass
Man	99.6202/33.4600	Pass/Pass	Pass/Pass	Pass/Pass

4.4   Key Sensitivity

Here, key sensitivities are examined for five keys separately. For assessing a selective key sensitivity, one key is differed and rest of four keys are unchanged. In this measurement, a minor variation (10^{-15}) in each selected key shows excellent impact on key sensitivity. On average, the proposed scheme has secured NPCR and UACI values 99.6118% and 33.4558% respectively for key sensitivity analysis.

Further, the proposed image encryption scheme has been tested for wrong key decryption. Here, decryption process has been performed for minor variation (10^{-15}) in each key_i independently and the obtained results are shown in Fig. 7.

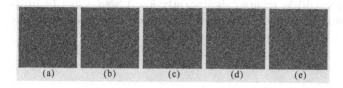

Fig. 7. (a) Deciphered Lena image obtained using slightly different key_1 (10^{-15}) (b) Deciphered Lena image obtained using slightly different key_2 (10^{-15}) (c) Deciphered Lena image obtained using slightly different key_3 (10^{-15}) (d) Deciphered Lena image obtained using slightly different key_4 (10^{-15}) (e) Deciphered Lena image obtained using slightly different key_5 (10^{-15})

4.5 Histogram Analysis

A good crypto-system should have equally distributed histogram for the key and the cipher. Here, we have shown histogram of expanded key stream, histogram of plain image and corresponding cipher image of Lena in Fig. 8.

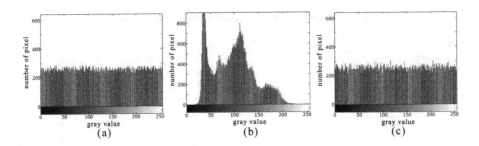

Fig. 8. Histogram of (a) expanded key (b) plain image Lena (c) cipher image Lena

Further, we have evaluated the χ^2 value for the expanded key stream with different dimension such as, (256×256), (512×512), (1024×1024), $(256 \times 256 \times 3)$, $(512 \times 512 \times 3)$ and $(1024 \times 1024 \times 3)$ and obtained the χ^2 value 224.92, 231.55, 252.03, 247.20, 242.47 and 237.40 respectively. All the outcomes satisfy the null hypothesis with level of significance $\alpha = 0.05/0.01/0.001$.

4.6 Correlation, Entropy and PSNR Analyses

Correlation used to identify how the adjacent pixel of an image is correlated. In cipher image, poor correlation has been observed for adjacent pixels. Further, Fig. 9 depicts the co-occurrence matrix obtained from the plain image (Lena) and cipher image (Lena). The obtained outcomes in cipher end indicate that the cipher image has uniformly distributed co-occurrence matrix. Next, the uncertain nature of cipher images is measured by global and local entropy. Here, obtained results of local entropy [9] for the proposed scheme satisfy the null hypothesis for the level of significance $\alpha = 0.05$, 0.01 and 0.001. On the other hand, the proposed scheme has secured significantly low PSNR value ($<10\,\text{dB}$) for several encrypted images. The obtained results referring to correlation coefficient, entropy and PSNR are presented in Table 2.

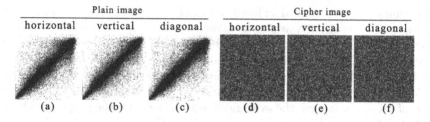

Fig. 9. Pixel distribution of Lena plain image for (a) horizontal direction (b) vertical direction (c) diagonal direction; Pixel distribution of Lena cipher image for (d) horizontal direction (e) vertical direction (f) diagonal direction

Table 2. Correlation, entropy and PSNR analysis

Test cipher image	Correlation coefficient - Direction				Entropy		PSNR
	Horizontal	Vertical	Diagonal	Anti-diagonal	Global	Local	(dB)
Cameraman	0.00062	−0.00043	0.00074	0.00050	7.9992	7.9022	8.23
Lena	−0.00074	0.00035	−0.00012	0.00028	7.9993	7.9025	8.46
Mandrill	−0.00091	−0.00044	0.00027	0.00090	7.9991	7.9021	8.62
Peppers	0.00049	0.00034	−0.00063	0.00047	7.9994	7.9027	8.02
Airport	0.00097	0.00090	−0.00068	−0.00082	7.9995	7.9024	8.42
Man	0.00029	0.00074	−0.00024	−0.00042	7.9994	7.9022	8.27

4.7   Test of Randomness

We have examined random behavior of the expanded key stream using both DIEHARD and NIST SP 800-22 test suites. In DIEHARD test suite, the expanded key stream successfully satisfies the null hypothesis (level of significance 0.05) by securing the P values in between [0.397, 0.712] for all 18 tests. Further, all the 16 tests in NIST SP 800-22 test suite have successfully verified the random nature of the expanded key stream with level of significance 0.01. Here, the range of obtained P value is [0.231, 0.739].

4.8   Time Complexity of Encryption and Key Generation Schemes

From the above explained algorithm, it has been found that the proposed image encryption scheme along with key expansion procedure have the time complexity in $\mathcal{O}(r \times c \times p)$; where r, c and p are dimension of plain image. So, for $p = 1$ (gray image) and for $N = r = c$, the complexity of the algorithm becomes $\mathcal{O}(N^2)$. In terms of processing speed, the proposed scheme takes average encryption time 0.9831 s for the plain image dimension (256×256).

4.9   Comparative Analysis

In comparison, the performance of the proposed scheme has been verified with respect to related existing schemes. In Table 3, the evaluated responses have

been compared with related existing schemes [3,5–8] in terms of plain text
sensitivity, key sensitivity, avalanche effect, correlation coefficient and entropy.
Apart from the previous comparisons, the proposed scheme has secured PSNR
value 8.4624 dB for the cipher image Lena, whereas, related existing schemes
[3,4,10–12] and [1] have shown the PSNR value 11.25 dB, 9.3008 dB, 9.2281 dB,
8.3655 dB, 9.2335 dB and 8.2896 dB respectively for the same cipher image. In
terms of processing speed, the average encryption time for the proposed scheme
is 0.9831 s for the plain image dimension (256 × 256), whereas, related existing
schemes [2–4] and [1] have shown the average encryption time 2.42 s, 25.334485 s,
1.215625 s and 1.0698929 s respectively.

Table 3. Comparative analysis on plain text sensitivity, key sensitivity, avalanche
effect, correlation coefficient and entropy

Scheme	Test item: Lena								
	Plain text sensitivity		Key sensitivity		Avalanche effect (%)	Correlation coefficient			Entropy
	NPCR(%)	UACI(%)	NPCR(%)	UACI(%)		Horizontal	Vertical	Diagonal	
Ref. [8]	99.6083	33.4554	99.61	33.45	–	0.0017	−0.0021	−0.0008	7.9993
Ref. [7]	99.6057	33.4733	99.61	33.46	–	0.0032	−0.0002	0.0011	7.9993
Ref. [6]	99.6012	33.5376	99.60	33.55	49.9978	0.0011	0.0007	0.0008	–
Ref. [5]	99.6273	33.3506	99.40	33.28	49.7954	0.0038	0.0058	0.0133	7.9999
Ref. [4]	99.66	33.62	–	–	–	0.0026	−0.0038	0.0062	7.9832
Ref. [3]	99.5865	28.6372	–	–	–	−0.0020	0.0001	0.0001	7.9990
Ref. [2]	99.6834	33.6163	–	–	–	−0.0093	−0.0006	0.0016	7.9992
Ref. [1]	99.6368	33.4924	99.61	33.49	50.000009	−0.0008	0.0003	−0.0001	7.9993
Proposed scheme	99.6201	33.4525	99.62	33.47	49.9999	−0.0007	0.0003	−0.0001	7.9993

5 Conclusion

In this paper, cubic map, Hénon map and affine transform based a new image
encryption scheme has been proposed. Here, a deep study has been done for
choosing the effective operating area of each chaotic map. In encryption, Nmix
function introduces a non-linear closed loop arrangement which makes the
scheme more sensitive relating to differential attacks and key sensitivity analysis. The proficiency of our method has been successfully verified by different
well known security analysis techniques. The random nature of the proposed key
expansion technique has been successfully validated by the DIEHARD and NIST
randomness test suites. In addition, the scheme shows good robustness against
differential attack and it has large key space to prevent brute force attack. Moreover, in comparison section, the proposed scheme shows enough potential with
respect to related existing schemes. So, the simulated results, and comparative
analyses establish that our method is effective and relevant for secure image
encryption.

References

1. De, S., Bhaumik, J., Giri, D.: A secure image encryption scheme based on three different chaotic maps. Multimedia Tools Appl. **81**, 5485–5514 (2021). https://doi.org/10.1007/s11042-021-11696-0

2. Musanna, F., Dangwal, D., Kumar, S., Malik, V.: A chaos-based image encryption algorithm based on multiresolution singular value decomposition and a symmetric attractor. Imaging Sci. J. **68**(1), 24–40 (2020)

3. Sheela, S.J., Suresh, K.V., Tandur, D.: Image encryption based on modified Henon map using hybrid chaotic shift transform. Multimedia Tools Appl. **77**(19), 25223–25251 (2018). https://doi.org/10.1007/s11042-018-5782-2

4. Ahmad, J., Hwang, S.O.: A secure image encryption scheme based on chaotic maps and affine transformation. Multimedia Tools Appl. **75**(21), 13951–13976 (2015). https://doi.org/10.1007/s11042-015-2973-y

5. Tong, X.J., Wang, Z., Zhang, M., Liu, Y., Xu, H., Ma, J.: An image encryption algorithm based on the perturbed high-dimensional chaotic map. Nonlinear Dyn. **80**(3), 1493–1508 (2015). https://doi.org/10.1007/s11071-015-1957-9

6. Seyedzadeh, S.M., Norouzi, B., Mosavi, M.R., Mirzakuchaki, S.: A novel color image encryption algorithm based on spatial permutation and quantum chaotic map. Nonlinear Dyn. **81**(3), 511–529 (2015). https://doi.org/10.1007/s11071-015-2008-2

7. Zhang, X., Mao, Y., Zhao, Z.: An efficient chaotic image encryption based on alternate circular S-boxes. Nonlinear Dyn. **78**(1), 359–369 (2014). https://doi.org/10.1007/s11071-014-1445-7

8. Zhang, X., Zhao, Z., Wang, J.: Chaotic image encryption based on circular substitution box and key stream buffer. Signal Process. Image Commun. **29**(8), 902–913 (2014)

9. Wu, Y., Zhou, Y., Saveriades, G., Agaian, S., Noonan, J.P., Natarajan, P.: Local Shannon entropy measure with statistical tests for image randomness. Inf. Sci. **222**, 323–342 (2013)

10. Taneja, N., Raman, B., Gupta, I.: Combinational domain encryption for still visual data. Multimed Tools Appl. **59**, 775–793 (2012)

11. Taneja, N., Raman, B., Gupta, I.: Chaos based cryptosystem for still visual data. Multimed Tools Appl. **61**, 281–298 (2012)

12. Taneja, N., Raman, B., Gupta, I.: Chaos based partial encryption of SPIHT compressed images. Int. J. Wavelets Multiresolut. Inf. Process. **9**(2), 317–331 (2011)

13. Wu, Y., Noonan, J.P., Agaian, S.: NPCR and UACI randomness tests for image encryption. Cyber J. Multidisc. J. Sci. Technol. J. Sel. Areas Telecommun. (JSAT) **1**, 31–38 (2011)

14. Bhaumik, J., Chowdhury, D.R.: Nmix: an ideal candidate for key mixing. In: Proceedings of International Conference on Security and Cryptography (SECRYPT), Milan, Italy, pp. 285–288 (2009)

15. Alvarez, G., Li, S.: Some basic cryptographic requirements for chaos-based cryptosystems. Int. J. Bifurcation Chaos **16**(8), 2129–2151 (2006)

16. Stinson, D.: Cryptography: Theory and Practice, 2nd edn. CRC/C&H, Boca Raton (2002)

17. Rogers, T.D., Whitley, D.C.: Chaos in the cubic mapping. Math. Model. **4**(1), 9–25 (1983)

18. Hénon, M.: A two-dimensional mapping with a strange attractor. Commun. Math. Phys. **50**(1), 69–77 (1976)

19. University of California, San Diego, "STARE Image Database". https://cecas. clemson.edu/ahoover/stare/, Accessed 02 May 2018
20. Nottingham Trent University, UK, "UCID Image Database". http:// jasoncantarella.com/downloads/ucid.v2.tar.gz, Accessed 02 May 2018
21. University of Southern California, "The USC-SIPI Image Database". http://sipi. usc.edu/database/database.php, Accessed 02 May 2018
22. Funt, et al.: HDR Dataset Computational Vision Lab Computing Science, Simon Fraser University, Burnaby, BC, Canada. http://www.cs.sfu.ca/colour/data/funt_ hdr/, Accessed 02 May 2017

miRNA and mRNA Expression Analysis of Human Breast Cancer Subtypes to Identify New Markers

Shib Sankar Bhowmick[1]([✉]) and Debotosh Bhattacharjee[2]

[1] Electronics and Communication Engineering Department, Heritage Institute of Technology,
Kolkata, West Bengal, India
shibsankar.bhowmick@heritageit.edu
[2] Department of Computer Science and Engineering,
Jadavpur University, Kolkata, West Bengal, India

Abstract. MicroRNAs (miRNAs) play a key role in the regulation of gene expression. Perfect or in-perfect complementarity of binding between miRNAs and a messenger RNA (mRNA) may lead to mRNA degradation or translational inhibition. In this regard, we have explored the role of miRNA and their target mRNAs in tumorous and normal tissues of molecular breast cancer subtypes such as Basal, human epidermal growth factor receptor 2, luminal A, and luminal B. Thus, we have carried out this research using the expression profile of 825 patient samples. For this analysis, a comparative analysis between the tumorous and adjacent normal groups of samples is conducted. The major finding of this research is the identification of the most significant miRNAs and their corresponding significant target mRNAs associated with the breast cancer subtypes. The biological significance of the identified miRNAs and their target mRNAs are validated by KEGG pathway analysis, gene ontology enrichment analysis, and survival analysis. Moreover, we report a comparison of our method with the panel selection strategies of DESeq and edgeR based on differentially expressed miRNAs.

Keywords: Bio-marke · Breast cancer subtype · MicroRNA · messenger RNA · Statistical analysis

1 Introduction

MicroRNAs (miRNAs) are short, non-coding RNAs that play essential roles in gene expression regulation by binding to the $3'$ UTR of target messenger RNAs (mRNAs), causing a block of translation and/or mRNA degradation [13]. Experimental result reveals that miRNAs operate as oncogenes or tumor suppressors in carcinogenesis [9]. As a consequence, identification of abnormal miRNAs, a ranking of significant miRNAs, and detection of miRNA-mRNA pair become an essential research direction. In this regards studies like [23] integrate miRNA and mRNA expression profiles to understand miRNA-control on a whole genome. The report suggests miRNA plays a decisive role in the biology of many cancers including breast cancer [14].

S. Mukhopadhyay et al. (Eds.): CICBA 2022, CCIS 1579, pp. 115–128, 2022.
https://doi.org/10.1007/978-3-031-10766-5_10

Cancer cases and cancer-related fatalities are increasing globally every year. Breast cancer alone is liable for 23% of all cancer cases, worldwide [8]. The research studies found that every year approximately 12% of women are affected by breast cancer [8]. Breast cancer is classified into four distinct molecular subtypes named Basal, human epidermal growth factor receptor 2 (Her2), luminal A (LumA), and luminal B (LumB). The experimental report found levels of specific miRNAs/mRNAs differ between tumorous and non-tumorous breast tissue [1]. Furthermore, miRNAs/mRNAs are differentially expressed between molecular breast cancer subclasses such as Basal, Her2, LumA, and LumB [7]. The identification of miRNAs/mRNAs [27] specific to the breast cancer subclasses presents a unique opportunity for the early detection of breast cancer. In different molecular subtypes of breast cancer, miRNAs play a predominant role as master regulators of differentiation. To date, the investigation of miRNAs and their target mRNAs in breast cancer is an important research direction [19]. The advent of Next-generation sequencing (NGS) [12] technologies and the availability of public repositories (i.e. The Cancer Genome Atlas [29]) for miRNA and mRNA expression data have opened a new opportunity for whole miRNOme research. In this regard, a method like DIANAmirExTra [2], mirAct [16], miTEA [26], cWords [22], and [6] analyzed miRNA expression data to find their effects over target mRNAs. However, many of these methods are complicated in nature.

In this study, we have tried to explore the role of miRNA/mRNA in different breast cancer subtypes. For this analysis, miRNAs, and mRNAs expression profiles in tumorous and adjacent non-tumorous tissues are considered. The integrated analysis identified dys-regulated miRNAs and their target mRNAs that may lead to tumorigenesis. This is further been justified by in-silico miRNA target prediction algorithms. According to the proposed method, the comparative analysis of the tumor and adjacent non-tumorous group of samples is carried out using FDR and fold change (FC), to segregate differentially expressed miRNAs. Significantly differentially expressed miRNAs and mRNAs in each subtype of Breast cancer are identified using Spearman's Correlation analysis. Additionally, pathways enriched in significantly differentially expressed miRNA targets, Gene Ontology enrichment analysis, and Kaplan-Meier (KM) survival analysis of the investigated miRNA/mRNA markers are discussed, with emphasis on their roles in cancer diagnosis. Major findings of this paper are:

- Identification of significantly differentially expressed 20, 13, 27, and 23 number of up-regulated and 6, 9, 3, and 8 number of down-regulated miRNAs in Basal, Her2, LumA, and LumB subtypes of breast cancer, respectively (Sect. 4.1).
- Statistical analysis indicates, these miRNAs regulate a significant proportion (1095, 230, 1487, and 1059 number of predicted targets in Basal, Her2, LumA, and LumB subtypes, respectively) of their in-silico method identified target mRNAs. (Sect. 4.1)
- The identified significantly differentially expressed miRNA targets are primarily connected with Signal Transduction and Cancers pathway groups (Sect. 4.2).
- Gene set enrichment analysis on the identified miRNA targets denote most active biological processes are involved in the cellular process like transcription whereas cellular components, and molecular functions are related to cellular structures, including whole cells or cell parts (Sect. 4.3).
- During survival analysis, we found evidence of significantly differentially expressed miRNAs role in clinical characteristics, such as time-to-death (Sect. 4.4).

2 Literature Review

Emerging evidence reveals that miRNA profiles vary between normal and tumor tissues and different clinico-biological features are found to be attached with a specific set of miRNAs [17]. Breast cancer research by [11] identified 12 miRNA among these 4 are prognostic. According to the study of Blenkiron and his colleagues, several miR-NAs are linked with the Basal, Her2, LumA and, LumB breast cancer subtype [7]. Furthermore, recent research identified that distinct molecular breast cancer subtypes such as Basal, Her2, LumA, and LumB have a completely different set of mRNA profiles [25]. Subsequently, a growing number of investigations have suggested that miRNAs are closely attached to the breast cancer subtypes [5, 28]. Nonetheless, through this research, we have tried to investigate the unknown role of miRNA and mRNA in breast cancer subtypes.

3 Materials and Methods

3.1 Dataset

We have collected the tumorous and non-tumorous tissue samples of 825 breast cancer patients from The Cancer Genome Atlas (TCGA) [29]. For this analysis, *Breast Invasive Carcinoma, TCGA, Nature 2012* data is considered from the repository (http://www.cbioportal.org/). According to the repository information, the expression values are recorded as reads per million count (RPMC), consisting of 517 miRNAs, and 12659 mRNAs. Although we have collected 825 patient samples, the choice of common sample among miRNA and mRNA reduces the number of tissue samples corresponding to Basal, Her2, LumA, LumB subtypes, and adjacent non-tumorous tissue to 41, 24, 86, 39, and 41, respectively. Clinical data information is also collected for the mentioned sample from TCGA. The summary of miRNA, mRNA, and clinical data is depicted in Table 1.

Table 1. Data description for breast cancer and its subtypes involved in our study

		miRNA expression data	mRNA expression data	Clinical data
Patient information		825	825	825
Tumorous Subtypes	Basal	41		
	Her2	24		
	LumA	86		
	LumB	39		
Normal samples		41		

3.2 Pre-processing of miRNA Expression Profiles to Find Differentially Expressed miRNAs for Each Subtype

At first, we have normalized the miRNA raw expression data using log transformation. The general reason behind log transformation is to make the expression data similar across orders of magnitude. Thereafter, differential expression analysis is done on the normalized miRNA expression data. By this process, differentially expressed miRNAs corresponding to each subtype of breast cancer are identified. For this analysis, Benjamini-Hochberg False Discovery Rate (FDR) [4] is used. As accordingly [30], differentially expressed miRNAs among the tumorous and adjacent non-tumorous tissues are chosen with fold change > 1.5 or < -1.5 [10] and FDR < 0.05, respectively.

3.3 Integrated Analysis of miRNA and mRNA Expressions Data to Select Relevant miRNA Targets

For this analysis, common samples among miRNA and mRNA expression data corresponding to Basal, Her2, LumA, and LumB subtypes are considered. Here, Spearman's correlation coefficient between every differentially expressed miRNA and all mRNAs expression of common samples is computed. Spearman's correlation is selected for the non-parametric distribution of expression data in each sample. miRNAs are known for causing a block of translation and/or mRNA degradation. In reality, miRNA make a negative relationship with the mRNA samples. This is known as miRNA-mRNA interaction [20]. Hence, mRNAs having negative Spearman's correlation coefficient with the miRNAs are identified by this process (correlation coefficients < 0.0001). Next, miRSystem [18] target prediction algorithm is used to determine in-silico targets of the differentially expressed miRNAs. Only mRNAs, with negative Spearman's correlation coefficient and predicted by miRSystem target prediction algorithm, are considered to be relevant targets of the selected miRNAs in each tumor subtype.

3.4 Identify Significantly Differentially Expressed miRNAs and Target mRNAs in Each Subtype of Breast Cancer

We have computed the negative correlation between every differentially expressed miRNA and all mRNAs expression of common samples by Spearman's correlation analysis. Only miRNAs with FDR < 0.05 and having average negative Spearman's correlation coefficient, are considered significantly differentially expressed. Next, differentially expressed mRNAs from the relevant mRNAs are identified with fold change >1.5 or < -1.5 and FDR <0.05 [30] among the tumorous and normal samples. Furthermore, the negative correlation is computed between every differentially expressed mRNA and all significantly differentially expressed miRNAs expression of common samples using Spearman's correlation analysis. By this process, an mRNA with FDR <0.05 and average Spearman's correlation coefficient < 0.0001 is considered significantly differentially expressed. The FDR value is used here as a ranking metric of the identified miRNAs/mRNAs. According to this ranking metric, mRNA/miRNA with the smallest FDR value is ranked one and we have rearranged the significantly differentially expressed miRNAs/mRNAs according to this ranking. The recognized significantly differentially expressed miRNAs/mRNAs specific to the breast cancer subtypes are considered to be the new bio-markers.

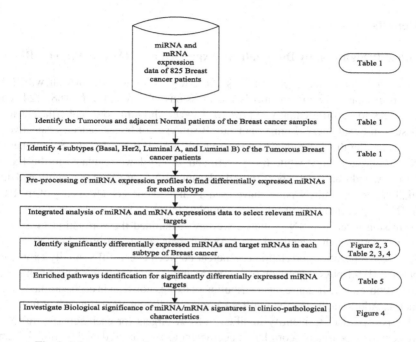

Fig. 1. Schematic overview of the proposed method to identify new markers

3.5   Enriched Pathways Identification for Significantly Differentially Expressed miRNA Targets

Enriched pathways for significantly differentially expressed miRNA targets among four different tumor subtypes are identified by this investigation. Here, Enrichr [15] tool is employed to do the KEGG pathway enrichment analysis. The enrichment results are summarized by classifying the pathways into different pathway groups and pathway categories. A ranking metric is considered for these pathway groups according to the underlying pathway numbers. In this regards, a higher number of pathways in a group signifies a higher rank. In case of a tie, the pathway group having a more significant *p-value* is considered highly ranked. This process is carried out separately for up and down-regulated miRNA targets. Moreover, pathway categories are also rearranged according to the pathway ranking.

3.6   Investigate the Biological Significance of miRNA/mRNA Signatures in Clinico-Pathological Characteristics

The biological significance of these informative miRNA/mRNA bio-markers is examined in terms of Gene Ontology (GO) analysis. Here GO taxonomy categories like biological processes (BP), molecular functions (MF), and cellular components (CC) are analyzed to see their association with the significantly differentially expressed miRNA targets. Additionally, survival analysis of the identified signature miRNAs is carried out using Kaplan-Meier (KM) plots [21]. A schematic overview of the proposed method for miRNA/mRNA expression analysis is summarized in Fig. 1.

4   Results

4.1   Identify Significantly Differentially Expressed miRNAs and Target mRNAs

We have used Benjamini-Hochberg False Discovery Rate in combination with fold change to evaluate 517 mature miRNA expressions. We found 196, 188, 124, and 160 miRNAs to be differentially expressed between the tumorous and adjacent normal tissues in Basal, Her2, LumA, and LumB subtypes of breast cancer, respectively. Moreover, among the differentially expressed miRNAs 130, 99, 54, and 86 number of miRNAs are up-regulated while 66, 89, 70, and 74 are down-regulated in the Basal, Her2, LumA, and LumB subtypes. To find relevant mRNA targets of the mentioned differentially expressed miRNAs, we have used a unified approach consisting of miRNA and mRNA expression data of the same samples. miRNAs are known for suppressing the expression level of mRNAs, hence we have examined the correlation in expression values between the identified miRNAs and their targets mRNAs. For this analysis, Spearman's negative correlation coefficient between every differentially expressed miRNA and all mRNAs expression of common samples are computed. Spearman's correlation is chosen here because the distribution of expression data in each sample is nonparametric. Additionally, in-silico miRNA targets prediction algorithm called miRSystem [18] is used here to identify in-silico miRNA targets for each subtype. mRNAs having negative Spearman's correlation coefficient as well as predicted by miRSystem, are considered to be relevant targets of the identified differentially expressed miRNAs in each tumor subtype of our experiment.

Among the differentially expressed up-regulated miRNAs, we found 20, 13, 27, and 23 miRNAs in Basal, Her2, LumA, and LumB subtypes are significantly enriched (FDR < 0.05, Table 2 and 3) with the predicted mRNA targets. Our method selected significantly differentially expressed up and down-regulated miRNAs are also compared with the sets predicted by in-silico algorithms DESeq [3] and edgeR [24]. In this regard, we report a comparison of our method with the panel selection strategies of DESeq and edgeR based on differentially expressed miRNAs. The result indicates, most of our selected miRNAs are statistically significant (FDR < 0.05) in both DESeq and edgeR elected panels. According to the analysis, DESeq select 59.63% of our selected miRNAs, edgeR chooses 71.55% of our selected miRNAs, while both DESeq and edgeR jointly elect 57.79% of our method selected miRNAs. Moreover, some of our method-selected miRNAs are found to be significant by DESeq and not identified by edgeR. Although few dissimilarities are observed especially in the case of down-regulated miRNAs, still our selected panel of miRNAs is mostly elected by DESeq and edgeR. Therefore, the identified significantly differentially expressed miRNAs of our method are being justified by the most popular in-silico algorithms.

Significantly enriched differentially expressed up and down-regulated miRNAs count for the breast cancer subtypes is given in Fig. 2. The figure suggests only *two* common down-regulated miRNAs among the Basal, Her2, LumA, and LumB subtypes while for up-regulated miRNAs this count is *six*. Suggesting that most of the method-selected miRNAs are autonomous to the breast cancer subtypes. Up and down-regulated common miRNAs among Basal, Her2, LumA, and LumB subtypes are shown in Table 4.

Table 2. Significantly enriched differentially expressed miRNAs of Breast cancer subtypes (Basal, Her2)

Basal					
Up-regulated			Down-regulated		
miRNA	Tumor vs. Non-tumorous tissue	Spearman correlation	miRNA	Tumor non-tumorous tissue	Spearman correlation
	FDR			FDR	
hsa-miR-196a	7.55e–08	1.19e–08	hsa-miR-193a	7.02e–09	1.68e–07
hsa-miR-200b	2.85e–10	1.50e–08	hsa-miR-452	8.70e–04	1.68e–07
hsa-miR-200c	5.92e–09	1.20e–07	hsa-miR-378a	7.48e–05	1.30e–06
hsa-miR-200a	7.60e–13	3.55e–07	hsa-miR-365a	4.90e–09	1.30e–06
hsa-miR-210	7.42e–22	5.40e–07	hsa-miR-205	6.13e–03	1.35e–06
hsa-miR-203a	7.55e–08	5.68e–07	hsa-miR-195	4.62e–13	3.15e–04
hsa-miR-106b	4.92e–21	5.68e–07			
hsa-miR-182	2.36e–14	5.89e–07			
hsa-miR-141	2.36e–14	5.89e–07			
hsa-miR-183	6.62e–21	7.73e–07			
hsa-miR-96	1.55e–21	1.04e–06			
hsa-miR-21	1.67e–15	2.90e–06			
hsa-miR-3613	3.69e–11	2.90e–06			
hsa-miR-191	8.53e–07	4.78e–06			
hsa-miR-181b	3.69e–11	2.63e–05			
hsa-miR-425	3.69e–14	2.64e–05			
hsa-miR-148b	1.34e–15	2.83e–05			
hsa-miR-192	5.62e–15	4.06e–05			
hsa-miR-3065	6.39e–06	4.06e–05			
hsa-miR-130b	9.97e–18	2.87e–04			
Her2					
Up-regulated			Down-regulated		
miRNA	Tumor vs. non-tumorous tissue	Spearman correlation	miRNA	Tumor non-tumorous tissue	Spearman correlation
	FDR			FDR	
hsa-miR-181a	3.63e–10	4.72e–06	hsa-miR-99a	1.01e–12	7.93e–05
hsa-miR-200c	2.72e–07	4.72e–06	hsa-miR-675	3.79e–05	7.93e–05
hsa-miR-20b	1.60e–05	5.17e–06	hsa-miR-378a	3.99e–08	8.01e–05
hsa-miR-21	1.11e–20	7.79e–06	hsa-miR-193a	1.46e–04	9.23e–05
hsa-miR-210	1.48e–13	8.42e–06	hsa-miR-199b	4.76e–09	9.81e–05
hsa-miR-141	1.14e–08	8.42e–06	hsa-miR-125b-2	1.41e–13	9.81e–05
hsa-miR-148b	9.15e–10	8.42e–06	hsa-miR-365a	1.56e–07	1.09e–04
hsa-miR-130b	1.65e–11	1.03e–05	hsa-miR-125b	1.41e–13	1.64e–04
hsa-miR-192	7.99e–12	4.87e–05	hsa-miR-195	1.41e–13	1.83e–04
hsa-miR-196a	2.63e–09	5.04e–05			
hsa-miR-203a	1.94e–07	8.28e–05			
hsa-miR-92b	5.02e–07	8.28e–05			
hsa-miR-3065	1.20e–04	8.28e–05			

To justify the relation among shortlisted miRNAs in different subtypes, we have checked the correlation among the selected miRNAs using Spearman's correlation coefficient. For this analysis, identified common miRNAs among breast cancer subtypes are called. According to Table 4, up-regulated miRNAs pair hsa-miR-141 and hsa-miR-200c and down-regulated miRNAs pair hsa-miR-193a and hsa-miR-365a among the breast cancer subtypes are found to be correlated. Correlation values of the correlated miRNAs are indicated in the bold font in that table. Hence it is proved that a majority of the shortlisted significantly differentially expressed common miRNAs are autonomous to the breast cancer subtypes.

Table 3. Significantly enriched differentially expressed miRNAs of Breast cancer subtypes (LumA, LumB)

LumA

Up-regulated			Down-regulated		
miRNA	Tumor vs. non-tumorous tissue FDR	Spearman correlation	miRNA	Tumor non-tumorous tissue FDR	Spearman correlation
hsa-miR-615	1.60e–05	1.70e–14	hsa-miR-205	0.002662	0.000000
hsa-miR-210	2.31e–18	1.41e–09	hsa-miR-193a	0.000000	0.000017
hsa-miR-200c	2.83e–06	1.41e–09	hsa-miR-365a	0.000000	0.000059
hsa-miR-92b	1.86e–13	1.41e–09			
hsa-miR-141	1.86e–10	1.72e–09			
hsa-miR-106b	6.88e–08	2.73e–09			
hsa-miR-183	8.25e–23	6.18e–09			
hsa-miR-342	9.91e–16	6.18e–09			
hsa-miR-96	8.25e–23	8.73e–09			
hsa-miR-20b	2.04e–04	1.44e–07			
hsa-miR-425	3.04e–06	2.04e–07			
hsa-miR-182	4.25e–22	4.11e–07			
hsa-miR-200a	3.18e–09	4.46e–07			
hsa-miR-200b	1.40e–07	6.71e–07			
hsa-miR-191	6.88e–08	9.73e–07			
hsa-miR-203a	3.03e–07	1.01e–06			
hsa-miR-130b	6.06e–06	1.49e–06			
hsa-miR-106a	2.04e–04	1.56e–06			
hsa-miR-345	1.48e–04	4.11e–06			
hsa-miR-3613	1.40e–05	4.11e–06			
hsa-miR-1301	5.90e–13	4.11e–06			
hsa-miR-32	3.44e–09	7.85e–06			
hsa-let-7g	1.15e–07	1.27e–05			
hsa-miR-3065	1.31e–06	1.27e–05			
hsa-miR-148b	1.17e–12	1.90e–05			
hsa-miR-331	5.91e–09	2.67e–05			
hsa-miR-192	3.36e–10	4.71e–05			

LumB

Up-regulated			Down-regulated		
miRNA	Tumor vs. non-tumorous tissue FDR	Spearman correlation	miRNA	Tumor non-tumorous tissue FDR	Spearman correlation
hsa-miR-106b	7.55e–12	4.72e–07	hsa-miR-193a	0.000112	0.000009
hsa-miR-342	6.17e–11	4.72e–07	hsa-miR-126	0.000001	0.000015
hsa-miR-15b	9.84e–08	2.16e–06	hsa-miR-365a	0.000060	0.000015
hsa-miR-200c	6.80e–08	2.16e–06	hsa-miR-486	0.000000	0.000015
hsa-miR-141	9.96e–13	2.92e–06	hsa-miR-144	0.000000	0.000016
hsa-miR-192	9.37e–12	8.19e–06	hsa-miR-26a	0.000001	0.000047
hsa-miR-182	8.91e–16	8.19e–06	hsa-miR-215	0.002316	0.000048
hsa-miR-628	5.67e–03	1.27e–05	hsa-miR-451a	0.000000	0.000070
hsa-miR-210	1.71e–18	1.42e–05			
hsa-miR-3607	3.80e–05	1.42e–05			
hsa-miR-345	3.22e–05	2.79e–05			
hsa-miR-200a	9.84e–10	4.29e–05			
hsa-miR-425	6.80e–08	4.29e–05			
hsa-miR-3613	5.64e–07	4.29e–05			
hsa-miR-191	5.49e–09	4.38e–05			
hsa-miR-200b	5.83e–07	4.80e–05			
hsa-miR-183	4.15e–19	6.09e–05			
hsa-miR-148b	7.83e–13	7.19e–05			
hsa-miR-331	3.54e–11	8.54e–05			
hsa-miR-32	4.93e–07	1.20e–04			
hsa-miR-106a	1.72e–06	1.21e–e–04			
hsa-miR-3065	1.88e–04	2.06e–04			
hsa-miR-96	1.71e–18	3.15e–04			

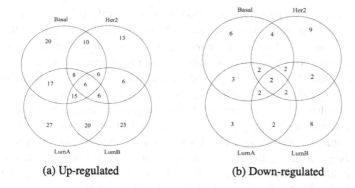

(a) Up-regulated   (b) Down-regulated

Fig. 2. Number of significantly enriched differentially expressed miRNAs with negatively correlated predicted targets

Table 4. Correlation between selected common miRNAs across tumorous and adjacent normal tissues of breast cancer subtypes. MIRNAs represented in bold are the down-regulated miRNAs

	hsa-miR-141	hsa-miR-148b	hsa-miR-192	hsa-miR-200c	hsa-miR-210	hsa-miR-3065	hsa-miR-193a	hsa-miR-365a
hsa-miR-141	–	−0.08	−0.01	**0.68**	−0.16	−0.03	−0.02	−0.31
hsa-miR-148b	−0.08	–	0.20	−0.03	0.10	−0.10	−0.15	0.31
hsa-miR-192	−0.01	0.20	–	−0.01	−0.21	0.11	−0.25	0.09
hsa-miR-200c	**0.68**	−0.03	−0.01	–	−0.07	0.15	−0.01	−0.25
hsa-miR-210	−0.16	0.10	−0.21	−0.07	–	0.25	0.44	0.09
hsa-miR-3065	−0.03	−0.10	0.11	0.15	0.25	–	0.06	0.09
hsa-miR-193a	−0.02	−0.15	−0.25	−0.01	0.44	0.06	–	**0.39**
hsa-miR-365a	−0.31	0.31	0.09	−0.25	0.09	0.09	**0.39**	–

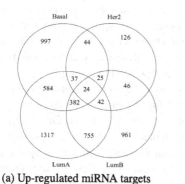

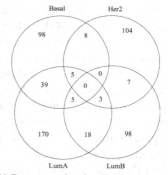

(a) Up-regulated miRNA targets   (b) Down-regulated miRNA targets

Fig. 3. Number of significantly differentially expressed mRNAs targets of the differentially expressed miRNAs in breast cancer subtypes

Furthermore, differentially expressed mRNA targets of the differentially expressed miRNAs are distinguished using absolute fold change (FC) > 1.5 and FDR < 0.05 between the tumorous and adjacent normal samples. Thereafter, significantly differentially expressed mRNA targets are identified by average negative Spearman's correlation coefficient and FDR values. Experimental outcome reveals for up-regulated miRNAs, the number of significantly differentially expressed mRNA targets in all four subtypes are higher than the down-regulated miRNA targets. In the case of down-regulated miRNA, no common mRNA targets are found among the four subtypes. Hence, a majority of the identified down-regulated miRNA targets are unique. However, few similar targets are observed among the cancer subtypes, especially for up-regulated miRNAs. Significantly differentially expressed mRNA target information of up-regulated and down-regulated miRNAs are given in Fig. 3 a and b, respectively.

Notably, the significantly differentially expressed miRNAs in Basal, Her2, LumA, and LumB subtypes, highlight several dys-regulated target mRNAs. In the case of up-regulated miRNAs, the highest percentage of common mRNA targets are found between the LumA, and LumB subtypes (33%). For down-regulated miRNAs, Basal and LumA subtypes have the highest percentage of common targets (14%). This perhaps signifies the influence of up-regulated miRNAs in governing target mRNAs. The identified new significantly differentially expressed miRNAs and their targets in the molecular breast cancer subtypes could be considered as a possible marker for early detection of breast cancer.

4.2 KEGG Pathways Associated with Significantly Differentially Expressed miRNA Targets

KEGG pathway enrichment analysis helps us to locate the pathways associated with significant targets of the differentially expressed miRNAs. For this analysis Enrich-Net[1] [15] tool is called to determine the associated pathways. In this connection, the KEGG pathways enriched in significantly differentially expressed up and down-regulated miRNA targets of the selected breast cancer subtypes are shown in Table 5. According to that table, a pathway group is formed by several significant pathways, and their significance is represented by *p-values* ranges. Interestingly, both up and down-regulated miRNA targets have a distinct set of pathways. For example, up-regulated miRNA targets are associated with *Cellular Processes and Organismal Systems pathways*, particularly *Cell Growth and Death, Cellular community, Circulatory System, Endocrine System, Nervous System, and Immune System pathways*. On the contrary, down-regulated miRNA targets mainly govern *Genetic Information Processing pathways*, especially, *Translation, Folding, Sorting and Degradation, Transcription pathways*. Only the *Cancers pathway groups* and *Signal Transduction* groups are commonly enriched by up and down-regulated miRNA targets in all four subtypes.

---

[1] http://www.enrichnet.org/.

Table 5. Pathways enriched in significantly differentially expressed miRNA targets

Category	Pathway group	Up-regulated miRNA				Rank
		Basal	Her2	Lum A	Lum B	
Environmental information processing	**Signal transduction**	18 (<0.01–0.037)	9 (<0.01–0.040)	22 (<0.01)	20 (<0.01–0.045)	1
	Signaling molecules and interaction	–	1 (<0.01)	1 (<0.01)	3 (<0.01)	11
	Membrane transport	–	–	–	–	–
Human diseases	**Cancers**	11 (<0.01–0.045)	5 (<0.01–0.039)	19 (<0.01–0.011)	20 (<0.01–0.048)	2
	Substance dependence	1 (<0.048)	–	3 (<0.01–0.036)	2 (<0.01)	10
	Neurodegenerative diseases	–	1 (<0.041)	1 (<0.01)	1 (<0.01)	14
	Immune diseases	–	–	–	–	–
Organismal systems	Endocrine system	11 (<0.01–0.022)	4 (<0.014–0.039)	14 (<0.01–0.019)	15 (<0.01–0.020)	3
	Nervous system	6 (<0.01–0.016)	1 (<0.01)	8 (<0.01–0.032)	5 (<0.01–0.023)	4
	Immune system	1 (<0.01)	1 (<0.018)	4 (<0.01–0.018)	5 (<0.01–0.04)	6
	Development	1 (<0.01)	2 (<0.01–0.046)	3 (<0.01)	3 (<0.01)	7
	Circulatory system	2 (<0.01–0.033)	1 (<0.014)	2 (<0.01)	2 (<0.01)	8
Cellular processes	Cellular community	5 (<0.01–0.021)	2 (<0.01–0.012)	4 (<0.01)	5 (<0.01)	5
	Transport and catabolism	1 (<0.01)	2 (<0.016–0.024)	1 (<0.01)	1 (<0.01)	12
	Cell growth and death	2 (<0.019–0.047)	–	2 (<0.016–0.031)	–	13
Metabolism (M.)	Glycan biosynthesis & M	–	1 (<0.011)	2 (<0.018–0.025)	3 (<0.01–0.034)	9
	Carbohydrate M	–	–	1 (<0.01)	–	15
	Amino acid M	–	–	–	–	–
	Lipid M	–	–	–	–	–
	M. of Cofactors & Vitamins	–	–	–	–	–
Genetic information processing	Translation	–	1 (<0.019)	–	–	16
	Folding, sorting and degradation	–	–	–	–	–
	Transcription	–	–	–	–	–
Category	Pathway group	Down-regulated miRNA				Rank
		Basal	Her2	Lum A	Lum B	
Environmental information processing	**Signal transduction**	1 (<0.026)	5 (<0.01)	8 (<0.01–0.057)	3 (<0.01–0.036)	2
	Signaling molecules and interaction	–	–	–	–	–
	Membrane transport	–	–	1 (<0.053)	–	15
Human diseases	**Cancers**	5 (<0.01–0.045)	14 (<0.01–0.035)	10 (<0.01–0.040)	6 (<0.01–0.058)	1
	Substance dependence	–	–	–	–	–
	Neurodegenerative diseases	–	–	–	–	–
	Immune diseases	–	1 (<0.015)	–	–	11
Organismal systems	Endocrine system	–	2 (<0.023–0.035)	5 (<0.01–0.054)	3 (<0.012–0.048)	3
	Nervous system	–	1 (<0.024)	–	–	12
	Immune System	–	–	1 (<0.059)	–	16
	Development	–	–	–	–	–
	Circulatory system	–	–	–	–	–
Cellular processes	Cellular community	–	1 (<0.037)	1 (<0.01)	1 (<0.051)	7
	Transport and catabolism	–	–	–	1 (<0.01)	8
	Cell growth and death	1 (<0.01)	1 (<0.026)	1 (<0.021)	1 (<0.01)	6
Metabolism (M.)	Glycan biosynthesis & M	–	–	–	–	–
	Carbohydrate M	–	–	–	–	–
	Amino acid M	–	–	–	1 (<0.026)	14
	Lipid M	–	–	1 (<0.012)	–	10
	M. of Cofactors & Vitamins	–	–	–	1 (<0.01)	9
Genetic information processing	Translation	2 (<0.010–0.052)	2 (<0.01)	1 (<0.059)	–	5
	Folding, sorting and degradation	1 (<0.01)	2 (<0.034–0.058)	3 (<0.01–0.0148)	–	4
	Transcription	1 (<0.028)	–	–	–	13

4.3 Gene Ontology Analysis

Gene enrichment analysis helps us to understand the GO taxonomy categories like biological processes (BP), molecular functions (MF), and cellular components (CC) association with the significantly differentially expressed miRNA targets. In our study, GO enrichment analysis of the target mRNAs in different subtypes has been carried out using Enrichr [15] tool. According to the investigation, a lower *p-value* represents a significant GO term. The result shows *positive regulation of transcription from RNA polymerase II promoter (GO:0045944), negative regulation of centri-*

ole elongation (GO:1903723), and ubiquitin-dependent SMAD protein catabolic process (GO:0030579) are the most active biological processes, which are involved in one of the important cellular processes like transcription. Among the cellular component and molecular function taxonomies, *focal adhesion (GO:0005925), actin filament (GO:0005884), rhabdomere microvillus membrane (GO:0035997),* and *nuclear chromatin (GO:0000790)* are mainly deal with cellular network.

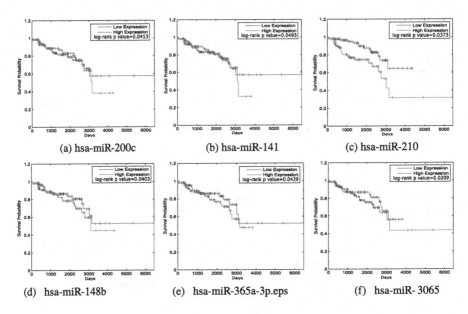

(a) hsa-miR-200c   (b) hsa-miR-141   (c) hsa-miR-210

(d) hsa-miR-148b   (e) hsa-miR-365a-3p.eps   (f) hsa-miR- 3065

Fig. 4. Kaplan-Meier plots of the selected *six* common miRNAs across tumorous and normal tissues of Breast cancer subtypes

4.4 Survival Analysis

We next evaluated the significantly differentially expressed common miRNAs by Kaplan-Meier survival analysis [21]. For this purpose, clinical characteristics, such as time-to-death information for selected patients are considered. In this regard, the ability of selected miRNAs is checked by dividing the corresponding patients into high and low expression subgroups using a median split. Accordingly, the log-rank test is accomplished to collect the *p-values*. Figure 4 depicts the survival plots of the selected *six* common miRNAs across tumor subtypes. The log-rank *p-values* of the plots suggest that low and high-expression subgroups have different survival probabilities. It is evident from Fig. 4 (a)–(f) that high-expression subgroup patients have a lower survival probability.

5   Conclusions

In this research, integrated analysis is performed to identify the informative miRNAs and their target mRNAs associated with different breast cancer subtypes. For this analysis, first differentially expressed miRNAs are identified followed by integrated analysis of miRNA and mRNA. Finally, significantly differentially expressed miRNAs and target mRNAs in each subtype of breast cancer are determined. In this regard machine learning based statistical analysis is performed. Subsequently, different biological significance tests like KEGG pathway analysis, gene ontology enrichment analysis, and Kaplan-Meier survival analysis are performed to justify the selection of miRNA and mRNA. The finding of these analyses suggests that the selected miRNAs have different survival probabilities in the low and high-risk group samples. Moreover, gene ontology analysis has also unveiled the biological processes, molecular functions, and cellular components of the selected miRNA targets related to breast cancer subtypes. KEGG pathway analysis reveals that the selected miRNA targets are related to a few common pathway groups. Besides this, a majority of the significantly differentially expressed mRNA targets of the informative miRNAs are found to be unique. Although, 33% upregulated common miRNA targets are found between Basal and LumA subtypes. Overall, this investigation has identified the informative miRNAs and their target mRNAs as probable biomarkers for different breast cancer subtypes.

References

1. Adhami, M., Haghdoost, A.A., Sadeghi, B., Malekpour Afshar, R.: Candidate miRNAs in human breast cancer biomarkers: a systematic review. Breast Cancer **25**(2), 198–205 (2017). https://doi.org/10.1007/s12282-017-0814-8
2. Alexiou, P., Maragkakis, M., Papadopoulos, G.L., Simmosis, V.A., Zhang, L., Hatzigeorgiou, A.G.: The DIANA-mirExTra web server: from gene expression data to microRNA function. PloS one **5**(2), e9171 (2010)
3. Anders, S., Huber, W.: Differential expression analysis for sequence count data. Genome Biol. **11**(10), R106 (2010)
4. Benjamini, Y., Hochberg, Y.: Controlling the false discovery rate: a practical and powerful approach to multiple testing. J. Royal Stat. Society Ser. B (Methodological) **57**, 289–300 (1995)
5. Bhowmick, S.S., Bhattacharjee, D., Rato, L.: In silico markers: an evolutionary and statistical approach to select informative genes of human breast cancer subtypes. Genes Genom. **41**(12), 1371–1382 (2019)
6. Bhowmick, S.S., Bhattacharjee, D., Rato, L.: Integrated analysis of the miRNA-mRNA next-generation sequencing data for finding their associations in different cancer types. Comput. Biol. Chem. **84**, 107152 (2020)
7. Blenkiron, C., et al.: MicroRNA expression profiling of human breast cancer identifies new markers of tumor subtype. Genome Biol. **8**(10), 1–16 (2007)
8. Bray, F., Ferlay, J., Soerjomataram, I., Siegel, R.L., Torre, L.A., Jemal, A.: Global cancer statistics 2018: GLOBOCAN estimates of incidence and mortality worldwide for 36 cancers in 185 countries. CA Cancer J. Clin. **68**(6), 394–424 (2018)
9. Calin, G.A., Croce, C.M.: MicroRNA signatures in human cancers. Nat. Rev. Cancer **6**(11), 857–866 (2006)

10. Dalman, M.R., Deeter, A., Nimishakavi, G., Duan, Z.H.: Fold change and p-value cutoffs significantly alter microarray interpretations. BMC Bioinf. **13**(2), 1 (2012)

11. Foekens, J.A., et al.: Four miRNAs associated with aggressiveness of lymph node-negative, estrogen receptor-positive human breast cancer. Proc. Natl. Acad. Sci. **105**(35), 13021–13026 (2008)

12. Grada, A., Weinbrecht, K.: Next-generation sequencing: methodology and application. J. Invest. Dermatol. **133**(8), e11 (2013)

13. He, L., Hannon, G.J.: MicroRNAs: small RNAs with a big role in gene regulation. Nat. Rev. Genet. **5**(7), 522–531 (2004)

14. Iorio, M.V., et al.: MicroRNA gene expression deregulation in human breast cancer. Cancer Res. **65**(16), 7065–7070 (2005)

15. Kuleshov, M.V., et al.: Enrichr: a comprehensive gene set enrichment analysis web server 2016 update. Nucleic Acids Res., gkw377 (2016)

16. Liang, Z., Zhou, H., He, Z., Zheng, H., Wu, J.: mirAct: a web tool for evaluating microRNA activity based on gene expression data. Nucleic Acids Res. **39**(suppl_2), W139–W144 (2011)

17. Lu, J., et al.: MicroRNA expression profiles classify human cancers. Nature **435**(7043), 834–838 (2005)

18. Lu, T.P., Lee, C.Y., Tsai, M.H., Chiu, Y.C., Hsiao, C.K., Lai, L.C., Chuang, E.Y.: miRSystem: an integrated system for characterizing enriched functions and pathways of microRNA targets. PloS one **7**(8), e42390 (2012)

19. Mattie, M.D.: Optimized high-throughput microRNA expression profiling provides novel biomarker assessment of clinical prostate and breast cancer biopsies. Molec. Cancer **5**(1), 1–14 (2006)

20. Oh, M., et al.: Literature-based condition-specific miRNA-mRNA target prediction. PloS one **12**(3), e0174999 (2017)

21. Pepe, M.S., Mori, M.: Kaplan-meier, marginal or conditional probability curves in summarizing competing risks failure time data? Stat. Med. **12**(8), 737–751 (1993)

22. Rasmussen, S.H., Jacobsen, A., Krogh, A.: cWords-systematic microRNA regulatory motif discovery from mRNA expression data. Silence **4**(1), 2 (2013)

23. de Rinaldis, E., et al.: Integrated genomic analysis of triple-negative breast cancers reveals novel microRNAs associated with clinical and molecular phenotypes and sheds light on the pathways they control. BMC Genom. **14**(1), 643 (2013)

24. Robinson, M.D., McCarthy, D.J., Smyth, G.K.: edgeR: a bioconductor package for differential expression analysis of digital gene expression data. Bioinformatics **26**(1), 139–140 (2010)

25. Sørlie, T., et al.: Gene expression patterns of breast carcinomas distinguish tumor subclasses with clinical implications. Proc. Natl. Acad. Sci. **98**(19), 10869–10874 (2001)

26. Steinfeld, I., Navon, R., Ach, R., Yakhini, Z.: miRNA target enrichment analysis reveals directly active miRNAs in health and disease. Nucleic Acids Res. **41**(3), e45–e45 (2012)

27. Vikram, R., Ramachandran, R., Abdul, K.S.M.: Functional significance of long non-coding RNAs in breast cancer. Breast Cancer **21**(5), 515–521 (2014). https://doi.org/10.1007/s12282-014-0554-y

28. Volinia, S., Croce, C.M.: Prognostic microrna/mrna signature from the integrated analysis of patients with invasive breast cancer. Proc. Natl. Acad. Sci. **110**(18), 7413–7417 (2013)

29. Weinstein, J.N., et al.: The cancer genome atlas pan-cancer analysis project. Nat. Genet. **45**(10), 1113–1120 (2013)

30. Zhuang, X., et al.: Integrated miRNA and mRNA expression profiling to identify mRNA targets of dysregulated miRNAs in non-obstructive azoospermia. Sci. Rep. **5**, 1–9 (2015)

A Survey on Computational Intelligence Techniques in Learning and Memory

Anuj Singh[(✉)] and Arvind Kumar Tiwari

Kamla Nehru Institute of Technology, Sultanpur, Sultanpur, India
{anuj.2295,arvind}@knit.ac.in

Abstract. Learning and Memory is a branch of artificial intelligence that studies the critical brain functions in order to create novel computational intelligence techniques and methods focused on learning and memory. As a consequence, human intelligence demands a review on computational intelligence techniques in learning and memory. This paper explains why without learning, the goal of achieving human intelligence is still a long bit away. This paper discusses hippocampus learning, human learning and memory, hidden markov model, behavioral plasticity in learning and memory, PET and fMRI, as well as the neurological illnesses. Here, we outline the important work done in the domain of learning as well as memory. This paper examines the evolution of learning and memory during several decades. This study also discusses the merits and limitations of several learning and memory models and techniques.

Keywords: Learning and memory · Cognitive learning · Hippocampus learning · Behavioral plasticity · Episodic memory · Hidden Markov model

1 Introduction

Learning is the action of collecting new, revising and enlarging, actual knowledge, nature, art, values and may concern synthesizing distinct types of information. Learning capability is possessed by humans being, animals also some types of machines. Learning is not mandatory but it is depending upon a set of circumstances. Learning builds upon and frame by what we earlier know. Learning may be considered as a process, instead of a set of procedural knowledge. It generates modification in the organism and it is permanent. Learning may take place as a part of human education, training, schooling. It may be goal-oriented aided by motivation. Learning may happen as an outcome of habituation, classical conditioning or as an outcome of other complicated activities such as play. It may take place-responsive or unresponsive experience. Learning that an unconcerned case cannot be avoided and also not escaped is named learned helplessness. Play approached by many philosophers as the initial learning. Children study with the real world, acquire the basic rules and communicate through play. Near about 85% of the human brain, growth takes place during five years of a baby child's life. Learning is a very essential activity in which human beings engage. It is the core of our educational system even though most of what a human being learns exists outside of school. In early

S. Mukhopadhyay et al. (Eds.): CICBA 2022, CCIS 1579, pp. 129–153, 2022.
https://doi.org/10.1007/978-3-031-10766-5_11

times philosophers have a desire to discover the spirits of the human learning how it occurs, how a person can affect the learning process of some another person by teaching and similar type of other activities [1].

A very huge amount of theories for learning have been proposed. There are various types of learning such as:

Perceptual Learning: It occurs through sensory system communication with the environment and through practice in doing particular sensory tasks. It is the capability to study to identify stimuli that have been spotted previously. The main function is to recognize and classify objects [2].

Stimulus-response Learning: It is the capability to study to carry out a specific behavior when a particular stimulus is present network formation between motor and sensory systems [3].

Motor Learning: It is a change that happens from experience or practice in the ability to respond. Motor learning is the formation of changes within the motor system. Motor learning includes bettering the accuracy of movements. It is essential for complicated movements like climbing trees, playing cards and running [4].

Relational Learning: Ability to identify and reply to the relationship between the objects regardless of the nature of the objects has been identified as a symbol of human reasoning [5].

Spatial Learning: It is complicated from associative learning by which the human or animal wants to obtain the association between loosely related bits together with a piece of information [6].

Episodic Learning: It is the method of storing experiences in the episodic memory as well as retrieving that facts or information and using it to upgrade behavior. Episodic memory is a long term memory used to keep episodes from past experiences [7].

Observational Learning: It happens through observing the activity, nature and the attitude of others. Observational learning is the type of social learning that holds numerous forms based on different processes [8].

2 Computational Intelligence Techniques

Here, we present about important computational intelligence techniques that are used for learning and memory like Recurrent Neural Network, Convolutional Neural Network as well as Long Short Term Memory.

2.1 Recurrent Neural Network

One of the deep learning algorithms for sentiment analysis that is focused on sequential data is the recurrent neural network. It uses sequential information to generate the outcome depending on earlier computations. It can accept multiple input vectors and create multiple output vectors. Formerly, conventional neural networks used separate inputs that were unsuitable for various Natural Language Processing tasks. Recurrent neural network utilizes memory cells that are capable of storing data about extensive sequences. Sequential data is data that is organized in such a way that comparable items follow one another. Recurrent neural networks often do analysis using short-term memory. It can learn more recent words than older terms, resulting in the vanishing gradient issue. To tackle the vanishing gradient problem RNN employs LSTM.

2.2 Long Short Term Memory

Sepp Hochreiter and Juergen Schmidhuber developed the long short term memory model which is employed for sequential information. The long short term memory architecture is a kind of recurrent neural network that remembers information across arbitrary time periods. It is employed in the solution of the vanishing gradient issue. It has the ability to learn long-term dependence. At evaluation time t, recurrent neural network has only two gates: an input gate as well as an output gate from last hidden state, and there is no knowledge about the past to remember. Recurrent neural networks can remember their inputs for a long time due to long short term memory. Long short term memory does this by storing knowledge in their memory for a long period of time. This memory cell is called a gated cell because it determines to choose whether or not retain or remove data based on the relevance of the data.

2.3 Convolutional Neural Network

The neural network image processing group was the first to design the convolutional neural network. As feature extractors, a convolutional neural network uses two processes called convolution and pooling. Like the Multi-layer perceptron, the result of this series of operations is linked to a fully connected layer. Max-pooling and average-pooling are the two types of pooling that are employed.

3 Related Work

In the literature review, researchers proposed various computational intelligence techniques for learning and memory. In paper [9], the author presented a model that proposed a key functional role of neurogenesis on learning as well as memory. Many new neurons are developing every day in the hippocampus over working life. Based on a few factors like age, exercise, they are merged into the neuronal circuits. Computational hippocampal function reproduction provides for examination of the outcome of neurogenesis. The number of granular cells in a phase subsequent is increased by 30% concerning their original number. In paper [10], the authors presented a Hierarchical Context HMM for behavior realization with the help of video streams for application in the nursing center. Hierarchical Context Hidden Markov Model figure out old behaviors by spatial, temporal and activities context. The model was used in the nursing center for the recognition of behaviors. They exactly illustrate 85% of the elderly behaviors and for abnormal detection 90% accuracy with 0% false alarm. In paper [11], authors proposed a hidden markov models based approach to recognize what two video sequences, build upon equivalent type of activity. If sequence is very small the EM algorithm gives inaccurate measures. An attainable approach to the above type of problem is a strong EM algorithm that gives an interval-evaluated measurement of the probabilities of the hidden markov model. In paper [12], the authors proposed the genes as well as signaling pathways that are change in mutants with intensify memory and also their job in the synaptic plasticity. Eventually, they talk about how the information of memory enhancing procedure will be utilized to grow analysis of cognitive disorders which are combined with impaired plasticity. In paper [13], the authors illustrated two principles to implement individual leveled machine learning: continuity and glocality. They also introduced a multimodal memory game to learned cognitive learning and algorithms. In this memory game two human players and one machine learner query and give answered the scenes and dialogs to watch the movies afterward. Experimental results were discussed to explain the utility of the game for considering learning and intelligence at the human level. In paper [14], the authors presented a general model for the learning of imitation to outline spatio-temporal demonstrations using their emotional and working nature. They used HMM to prototype identical demonstrations. The efficiency of the model is calculated in two tasks. One is the imitation of a few body languages through communication with teachers. This type of job the idea from other type modalities like vision and motor are used in a large number of experiments. The second is to research a set of surgery by describing its psychological consequences. In the paper [15], authors generated a technique that was used to spontaneously make a distinction among baseline, plan, and epochs of neural movement. They used an innovative model for catching how neural activity changed among these epochs. They were working on hmm in which the state correlates to epoch and connects with the poisson firing model. Using a hidden markov model, they determine transition time from baseline to epochs a transition changes and recognized using outset on analytical hidden Markov model state probabilities. Also, they demonstrate that there hidden markov model that discovers transitions analogous to targets not present in the training data set. In paper [16], the author considered many distant jobs for neuronal gene function in learning. The different roles in the care of the neural functioning, replenishment of cellular elements, maintenance of the plastically identify neuronal connections, the unification of information at transcription factor-promoter interaction. They actively advocated that only cautious scrutiny of learning gene expression phenomena aid in the understanding of the complicated learning process. In paper [17], the authors presented a short review of experimental research which shows many transcription factors families. Results recommend that transcription pattern regulation illustrated the signatures of molecular synaptic changes for a long period and memory formation. Last few years main attentiveness of molecular neuroscience recognition of transcription factors. It is extremely regulated processes that include consolidating interaction and some other type proteins.

In paper [18], the authors presented a model of episodic memory and it is based on the concept synchronization of the neural system. Episodic memory is necessary for interpretation of the system of human intelligence. The hippocampus plays a key in the encoding along with retrieval of episodic memory. This model gives benefit for selective retrieval memory search as well as instantaneous memory formation and can forecast memory recall process using integrating eye movement data set at encoding. In paper [19], authors presented a review of physiological data constructed models of hippocampal along with self-localization to set up or organize what is well known for the brain's navigational networks from a computational aspect. In the last few years, the physiological design of neural substrates for navigation has grown very quickly. But how the different parts of the circuit interconnect to execute the all calculation for the navigational skill of mammals remain unsolved. In paper [20], authors proposed a skeleton in what way the hippocampus neocortex, as well as basal ganglia, work simultaneously to hold up cognitive as well as behavioral activity in the brain of a mammal. This is established on a theory of computational tradeoffs to reach a goal one learning activity needs distinct parameters against those essential to reach a goal other forms of learning. In paper [21], the author discussed the hidden markov model to analyze motifs in ordinary nature in a specific birdsong as well as to draw out and matching single-neuron activity trends in multi-neuron recordings. Hidden markov model is a very beneficial tool for the model-based summary of complicated behavioral as well as neurophysiological data. The abundance of data created in this type of experiment creates a bigger problem in data analysis. The problem addressed not entirely using hidden markov model the experimenter will describe the variance in few behaviors as well as encrypted in the neural recordings. In this work recent hidden markov model function to clarify how the hidden markov model improves the exploratory read out and give perception into neural population coding. In paper [22], authors presented a short review of the synaptic ion channels in learning as well as episodic memory and they tell implications of this figure out the molecular biology of human learning along with memory systems. The human central nervous system receives a huge quantity of information in the environment through sensory routes. In paper [23], the author illustrated a different approach that is mainly focused on the semi-supervised approach to training partially hidden discriminative models like CRF and MEMM. They show his models allow incorporating labeled and unlabeled data for learning and parallel providing flexibility and accuracy. Results in this domain indicate these models much superior to their counterparts. In paper [24], the author illustrated an algorithm that depends on a graph regularization method to diagnose cancer. They carry out the functional enrichment of gene network need for learning. Improvement in efficiency for cancer diagnosis was 24.9% with other existing methods. In paper [25], the author illustrated the way a development process may outcome framework that learn. The outcome of the choices along with genetic linkage uses many types of successful learning mechanisms. In paper [26], the author thinks about the issue of learning ideas from a small number of examples which humans do routinely and computers are rarely efficient. They give theoretical analysis as well as empirical learning with the human for the task of learning to be consistent with axis-aligned rectangles in feature space. In paper [27], the authors proposed a parallel approach to enhance the quality of the network. This method takes as input a combined network and builds up this network to superior illustrate co-functionality relationships among gene pairs. A learning algorithm is the Soul of the method. The algorithm learns functional similarity among genes that reconstruct the input network. This method produces better results than approaches. In paper [28], advancement in the field of genomics, as well as proteomics, makes it able to catch the biological networks at the systems level. They elaborated on a computational model of learning and memory which was motivated by the bimolecular networks. They studied the learning and memory system by using hyper-networks and observe that a system consisting of a huge number of the miscellaneous low-dimensional element has an impartially competitive possibility of short term efficiency as well as long-term survival. In paper [29], authors illustrated a consolidative synthesis across animal studies, concentrating on latest cluster of proof indicating an important task for the genes managing dopaminergic function in the front striatal circuitry which includes DARPP-32, COMT, DAT1, DRD2, along with DRD4. A large number of individual differences in learning and cognition as well as the disturbance of processes in the neurological circumstances are affected by individual genetic factors. These genetic findings are clarified in theoretical substructure established under broader cognitive circumstances. In paper [30], authors illustrated the role of the hippocampus going back numerous decades to report many new concepts that seem to analyze on a role for the hippocampus in emotion together with a stress response. Self-consciousness of adult neurogenesis outcomes with few differences in the behavioral and offer a critical job for newly developed neurons in learning as well as memory and other changes in the behavioral occur inconsistently with this function. In paper [31], authors illustrated the consequence of chronic hippocampal-dependent stress, the study of young, adult male rodents as well as spatial navigation tasks. Chronic stress affects spatial capability depended on upon class of job, the dependent variable determined as well as how the task was accomplished, the type along with period of stressors, animal living conditions affecting food accessibility and cage mates. Chronic stress affects any region of the brain therefore, how chronic stress changes the hippocampal spatial capability is likely to rely on many other brain structures being involved in behavioral training and testing.

The review of ERP mapping studies illustrated that there is an excellent correlation among brain imaging studies that plot hemodynamic changes along with ERP results. It enlarged total amount of recording they have to acquire additionally perception into electrical activity in the neural network's basic explicit memory. This agreement is very significant because the union of high temporal ERP resolution, will give considerably boost the intelligence of spatiotemporal dynamics of the individual brain networks [32]. In paper [33], the authors presented the olfactory memory and find the differences and similarities between visual-verbal memory and odor memory. They determined whether the olfactory memory system can be review to be distinct. Olfactory memory has good distinguishing characteristics, but huge data is essential to consult this distinction. They give methods for the work of an olfactory memory system that should build a rising on the separate memory system hypothesis. In the paper [34], the author illustrated an experimental based framework that combines temporal evolution of the motor memory processes along with delayed retention frequently as well as the time course of practice used in the field of the behavioral motor learning model. Behavioral research gives justification for the difference between a fast performance that goes to long-term performance and practice. In paper [35], authors presented a short review along with meta-analyses to the whole outcome from rodent survey examining the influence of the chronic stress over learning. Outcome tells the main consequence of stress on universal ability to learn. Stressed rodents granted bad incorporation of memories; however, analogy among groups at the stage of the acquisition was found. Effects were autonomous of age as well as the type of stress. Stress yields an extra harmful consequence on spatial navigation test results. They have suggested a set of principles termed for the Behavioral Experiments to help enough documenting of behavioral experiments.

Mitogen activated protein kinase is a major and extremely sustained family of the enzymes correlated with the regulative targets along with cell membrane receptors. Throughout the individual's brain, there is nearly fully developed neuronal proliferation as well as differentiation however regulation of mitogen-activated protein kinase and thus its upstream along with downstream molecular pathways is extensive with extracellular signal-regulated kinase signaling pathway are highest explored signal transduction pathways [36]. In paper [37], authors illustrated the dissimilarity between declarative, explicit and conscious memory system. Research in the area of memory system has generally illustrated the distinct long-term memory in central nervous system as implicit against explicit or declarative against non-declarative. In this model implicit memory system will not occur as a coherent memory system on some other way will alternatively be displayed as a principle of development from the experience from on a large scale mechanism of cortical plasticity [38]. The main objective of instruction should be to encourage lifelong learning to produce permanent changes in understanding along with skills that will help lifelong retention. In training, process performance is calculated and it is an undependable index of lifelong changes. They illustrated literature in verbal-learning domains that involve the difference among performance and learning as well as look at work in metacognition that recommends that individuals frequently incorrectly spell out their performance in the time of acquisition as an authentic guide to long-term learning [39]. The amnestic consequences of benzodiazepines have attracted a lot of people interested in this field of research. This returns clinical suggestion of memory failure for individuals advised these drugs as well as the potential of BZs as mechanisms in modeling organic memory concerns. An unrealizable bone of contention is the scope to which the amnestic consequences of BZs are distinct from their anxiolytic effects as well as sedative effects. In paper [40], authors illustrated the issue for analyzing the interrelationship among the many effects of BZs along with summarizing volunteer as well as patient research appropriate to separating amnestic from another effect. Insulin is the top familiar for act on the peripheral insulin target tissues like muscle to control glucose homeostasis. In the brain of human insulin and insulin receptor are establish in distinct regions of the human brain. While insulin or insulin receptor correlated with hypothalamus is very essential in the control of energy homeostasis. The current advancement in this field has indicated that insulin signaling plays a key role in the field of synaptic plasticity by modulating inhibitory and excitatory receptor activities and activating the most significant signal transduction cascades to alter gene expression for the long-term retention of memory [41]. The capability to unobtrusively monitor mental workload along with levels of task engagement in a working environment could be productive in finding additional efficient methods to interact with technology. This information could be used to optimize the blueprint of effective working environments. The capability to unobtrusively monitor mental workload in the operational environment could help recognize accurate as well as efficient and more productive methods for humans to interconnect with technology [42]. Several researchers have shown that people with memory impairment can learn relatively less complex information both in the laboratory and in everyday life. In paper [43], authors presented whether patients may acquire nuanced knowledge of the domain-specific skills required to communicate with a microcomputer along with memory disorders. The result illustrated that patients with changing severity memory disorders could study how to handle computer screen information, edit, run simple programs, write and recovery operations [43]. Destruction of the hippocampal network destroys present memory but leaves remote memory intact. Such models come across the structure of element sets when learning about each item is interwoven with learning about another item. The neocortex is constantly learning how to find the structure in experiences [44]. Using a place-navigation task, the anterior, as well as posterior cingulate cortical areas, were examined in four examinations. Rats together with absolute bilateral cingulate cortex aspiration as well as single aspiration of the posterior cingulate cortex could not directly dip into an invisible platform placed in a stable location. When animals were tested for forty in a position that changed their jobs in which they received sixteen-day trials every day with platforms placed in a newly discovered area, they did not appear to be reliable in the place of navigation [45]. To layout the desired associations, an associative memory does not need a teacher. It performs a search for output pattern that corrects the reinforcement signal for each input key. An associative search network merges pattern recognition abilities effectively and easily.

In paper [46], the author illustrates the associative search problem and address the conditions for which the problem is efficient of fixing it along with giving outcome from computer simulations. There are many ways to address the question about how neurological networks are changed in reaction to an individual's engagement with his or her surroundings. These enhancements are the subject of either learning or memory systems in rat along with their fundamental biochemical mechanisms, an effort which has contributed significantly to the general view of the behavioral neural basis. Such techniques have expanded our knowledge of cognitive operations, which include combining a large number of sensory stimuli to create the most complicated adaptive responses [47]. It is a very well-known exercise that is capable of improving cognitive function, but it is not clear what exactly these effects will be applied to further exercise. The effect of non-compulsory cognitive function exercise along with neuron trophic factor protein levels is an important player in mechanisms that regulate memory formation dynamics as well as storage assessed here immediately after a three-week running cycle or after a week or two-week post-exercise interval Exercised mice showed better efficiency compared to sedentary animals on the radial arm water maze. Several errors happened in animal training after a time delay of one week, but maximum memory function was seen in those trained instantly after an exercise cycle. This method of estimating temporal endurance of biochemical as well as a cognitive consequence of exercise reveals new ideas in the field of exercise learning along with the present that the useful effect of exercise on brain plasticity continues to progress even though exercise has been completed [48]. In the paper [49], authors focused to evaluate data of studies in which contribution of acetylcholine in cognitive functions was examined and studies from 3 fields of research behavioral pharmacology, behavioral neuroscience and dementia are considered. In the area of behavioral neuroscience clearly defined cholinergic toxin has been generated. More clear the cholinergic damage the very less amount of effects can be observed at the behavioral level. With the help of data on the market acetylcholine better involved in the attention processes then in learning [49]. Nonverbal imagery, as well as verbal symbolic processes, is thinking about correlation to associative learning as well as memory. These hypothesized processes are effectively well-known in stimulus attributes along with experimental procedures. The availability of imagery is direct with image-evoking value or item concreteness. Stimulus characteristics interact with presentation rates, type of memory task as well as mediation instructions. Subjective-report data along with Performance from the experimental outcome of the model so that imagery-concreteness is a very strong attribute yet point out among the relevant items. The findings give proof of the explanatory as well as the heuristic value of imagery concept [50].

In paper [51], the authors illustrated memory theory in prototypical schemas. This theory undertakes the selection, abstraction, interpretation and integration encoding-processes. The article estimates both critical as well as supporting evidence for these processes, taking into account the need for memory theory to account for three observations: incompleteness, accuracy, and distortion. The evidence seems to so that representation of memory is very accurate as the schema theory would imply. In paper [52], the author demonstrated hippocampal reflection of endothelial in vascular development is increased through an enriched environment as well as output in a spatial maze. An enhance environment is related to hippocampal plasticity. Hippocampal gene release of the endothelial vascular growth factor in adult rats resulted in 2-fold greater neurogenesis related to increased and enhanced learning. Expression of a mutant kinase which is dominant-negative insert domain protein receptors inhibited basal neurogenesis as well as impaired learning. Co-expression of mutant kinase insert domain protein receptors antagonized vascular endothelial growth factor improved neurogenesis as well as learning without impairing endothelial cell proliferation. Besides, RNA interference inhibition of vascular endothelial growth factor expression blocked neurogenesis environmental induction. These facts help a paradigm where the vascular endothelial growth factor, acting through kinase inserts domain protein receptors, mediates the neurogenesis and cognition effects of the environment.

In paper [53], the authors presented a demonstration of a strong memory system for a visual environment that occurs to control spatial observation. Half of the layouts were repeated over blocks for the duration entire session along with targets that appeared within the fixed position in these arrays. This search facilitation is called by contextual cueing and guided by the incidentally established association between destination locations as well as spatial configurations. The outcomes illustrated how implicit learning, as well as the memory of visual context, can convoy spatial attention in the direction of the task-relevant point of a scene. In paper [54], authors wanted to recognize the pioneer of mathematics learning at the starting phase of primary school. Very less number of experimental reports presents in this area and mostly uses correlation analysis or between-subjects designs. This work examined longitudinal data to explore the correlation between mathematics learning and basic abilities explainable. This data is built on a survey of 170 primary school children at the starting as well as ending of the first year. Causally interpreted and linear structural relations were employed for the analysis of the correlations among mathematics achievement and cognitive abilities. The model illustrated that tests of counting ability along with working memory are efficient as a pioneer of mathematics learning in early stages.

The field of many types of memory is examined from the biological stance. Fact-and-event memory is special with a variety of oblivious memory capabilities like simple conditioning, skills, and habits. Current evidence so that declarative, as well as non-declarative memory, has non-identical operating properties. A human brain substructure for understanding memory circumstance is established in studies including monkeys, humans, rats and current studies along with normal humans with the help of event-related potentials [55]. In paper [56], the authors presented the latest development in this field, move forward based on the way of behaving as well as insights hand over by computational modeling. Evidence recommends that newly born neurons could be sophisticated in the hippocampal functions that are secondary on dentate gyrus. Computational research suggests that previous newborn neurons should be fully grown and could function as a pattern integrator. The merger of adult-born neurons and wiring of a fully grown hippocampus recommend a key task for fully grown hippocampal neurogenesis in the area of learning and memory [56]. Functional neuroimaging of language that allows cerebellar participation in a cognitive assignment, PET and fMRI learning has carried on giving proof that the duty of the cerebellum enlarges far off that of motor control along with that this structure gives in cognitive operations. In this paper author illustrate neuroimaging evidence as cerebellar participation in implicit learning and memory, working memory as well as language, they discuss few of the key issue as well as circumstance lookout by researchers who use the neuroimaging to explore the cerebellar function [57]. Cyclophilin D is a key part of mitochondrial transition pore, the opening of which leads to cell death. CypD's interaction with the amyloid-b mitochondrial protein potentiates neuronal, synaptic, and mitochondrial stress. The CypD cortical mitochondria play as a resistant to A b- as well as Ca2+ induced mitochondrial inflammation too permeability transition. CypDhave a greater calcium buffering capability also generates a small number of mitochondrial reactive oxygen species. The absence of CypD prevents neurons against cell death caused by b-or oxidative stress. CypD greatly improves both learning and memory, including synaptic activity in an Alzheimer's disease, in addition to alleviating a b-mediated loss of long-term potential. CypD mediated mitochondrial transfer pore is specifically correlated with the synaptic or cellular disorders observed in Alzheimer's disease pathogenesis [58]. In paper [59], the author proposed a recent situation of genetic studies of learning as well as memory in the fruit fly and Drosophila melanogaster. Two main trends are backed by new results. First is the discovery in genetically accessible systems together with the manipulation of genes with behavioral plasticity. The second is that the core cellular mechanism of straightforward forms of learning is evolutionarily preserved as well as biological pathways must also be preserved in invertebrates [59]. In paper [60], the author proposed a new idea for work on anxiety along with memory. Anxious subjects capture in inappropriate processing which prevents processing resources. It follows the premise that anxiety will have a differential consequence on the quality of performance. Anxiety will reduce processing effectiveness on every occasion. Dependencies on the estimate of the efficiency will frequently unknown harmful effects of anxiety on handling effectiveness. Neurodegenerative disorders of the nervous system are usually correlated with impaired learning along with memory after some time leading to dementia. A key point in pre-clinical research is to investigate approaches to improve cognitive ability. Using a mouse model that permits temporally as well as spatially limited generalization of neuronal loss, this work so that environmental enrichment reinstated learning along with behavior as well as restored access to long-term memories following severe neuronal loss [61]. A large number of proof points to the fact that learning and memory formation is controlled by cholinergic mechanisms. This research provides support for cholinergic regulation of the different memory systems, provided that regulation of cholinergic specific neural system functions can affect memory for such work that is usually associated with those neural systems. By merging lesions with designed tasks, identify parallel memory structures, almost all activities require a combinatorial involvement of the various neural systems. In paper [62], the authors highlighted the idea that the intensity of the release of acetylcholine in multiple neural systems will affect comparative contributions to learning and memory of such systems. New studies of magnitude of acetylcholine release access with during vivo micro-break data sets during training and injection of cholinergic drugs directly into various neural synapses give evidence disclosing the magnitude of acetylcholine is crucial involving those systems throughout duration of learning.

In paper [63], the author used deep learning approaches as well as 3D convolutional neural networks along with in particular sparse auto encoders to construct a general procedure or algorithm that might forecast disorder status of any individual using a MRI scan of brain. Pattern recognition employing neuroimaging data for diagnose of Alzheimer's disease is a major area of the current time. In this experiment, the ADNI data set is used that involves 2265 scans. The 3D convolutional neural networks exceed many other classifiers identified in the production of state-of-art as well as literature results [63]. A lot of potential diseases changing drugs for Alzheimer's disorder have sat down to reveal consequences on the progression of the disease in treatment because the Alzheimer's disease is too sophisticated to get clinical profit from diagnosis. Low concentrations of amyloid-b peptide in the cerebrospinal fluid highly predictive biomarkers of Alzheimer's disease dementia development in patients with mild cognitive impairment are associated with relatively high tau and phosphorylated tau. Inter-laboratory alterations in outcome presently accessible immunoassays are of study. Present global quality control along with improvement efforts the systems includes the generic pre-analytical operating approach as well as analytical procedures [64]. In paper [65], the author estimated the highest prediction effectiveness for the chance in Alzheimer's disease that is based on genetic factors of liability along with disease prevalence. They disclose that the latter recorded AUC for Alzheimer's diagnosis using polygenic scores reach around 90% of the accuracy. In paper [66], the author's integrated approach for grading of medial temporal lobe systems with estimated high cortical thicknesses to predict between individuals with mild cognitive impairment from a unit T1-weighted magnetic resonance imaging scan. Optimized biomarkers of Alzheimer's disease depending on magnetic resonance imaging can enable refined prediction of disease. They could also work for important tools if plotting clinical analyses of the person living with Alzheimer's disease. Alzheimer's disease along with cognitively normal individuals they produce a set of the property effectively discriminating among mild cognitive impairment subject areas who transform to the Alzheimer's disease as well as those that remain stable over three years. They recognized five features optimizing the classification of mild cognitive impairment converters and highlight that these characteristics are very robust in cross-validation as well as allow a forecasting efficiency of 72% [66]. Negative age stereotypes were encountered to forecast unfavorable results between older individuals; it was not known even if impacts of stereotypes expand to cerebral changes attributed to Alzheimer's disease (AD). Drawing on dementia-free participants in this study, Aging's Baltimore Longitudinal Training, whose age assumptions were tested decades before annual MRI was conducted along with brain autopsies. These reserves had a substantially steeper hippocampal-volume loss as well as significantly larger neurofibrillary tangles aggregation behind amyloid plaques, accounting for essential covariates before long in life. Such findings argue for a new way of identifying pathways linked to AD pathology [67].

In 2011, the National Institute on Aging collaborated with the Alzheimer's Association to produce precise clinical criteria for the mild cognitive impairment, preclinical, and dementia phases of Alzheimer's disease (AD). Scientific advancements prompted the National Institute on Aging and the Alzheimer's Association to work together to update the 2011 recommendation. This enhancement is a research framework. The Alzheimer's Association Research Framework, in collaboration with the National Institute on Aging, outlines fundamental pathologic approaches that may be documented in vivo using biomarkers. The diagnosis in this study is not based on the clinical result of the illness framework. The clinical paradigm based on human biomarker diagnosis of Alzheimer's disease [68]. In paper [69], a polygenic hazard score developed by the author that forecasted above and beyond the age of Alzheimer's disease onset. Better estimation of the development of Alzheimer's between adults with mild cognitive impairment is of practical significance. This work discussed the predictive value of PHS alone as well as the basic structural MRI performance data on the Mini-Mental State Exam. PHS predicted a substantial progression span of 120 months from mild cognitive impairment to Alzheimer's disease ($p = 1.07e-5$) along with PHS were more predictive than APOE alone ($p = 0.015$). The combination of baseline brain atrophy score with PHS along with MMSE score significantly enhanced estimation over non-PHS models. Including PHS in the model has also increased the sensitivities of the prediction model, the region under the curve and precision. In paper [70], the author presented a strategy for locating and detecting unusual behaviors in crowd videos using the model of the Social Force. A grid of particles is put over the image in this work along with it being advertised with the optical flow space-time average. While using operating particles as an individual, their forces of interconnection are predicted using the model of social force. The interaction force is outlined in the image plane to find Flow of force for every pixel in each frame and arrange the frames as abnormal and normal with the help of a bag of words approach. This work is used a dataset from the University of Minnesota for the field of escape panic scenarios together with a dataset of crowd videos grab from the web. This work illustrates that the proposed method takes over the dynamics of crowd behavior successfully. In paper [71], the authors illustrated the fundamentals of video tracking as well as presented major works in the area of accurate tracking in 2D or 3D space of a group of peoples. In the present time, video monitoring capabilities of different biological species have been mostly improved. Behavioral video-based surveillance has become a very common tool for risk assessment to collect quantified behavioral data. Rapidly improved machine learning has boosted the exploration of behavioral responses under environmental conditions along with chemical stress Mostly used computational methods are analyzed in conjunction with the detection of aquatic toxicity.

The quick improvement in technology together with the progress of infotainment systems very important is being given to occupant safety. In the current time vehicles are assembled with a large number of sensors together with Embedded Control Units Controller Area System plays a pivotal part in controlling whole communication among Embedded Control Units, sensors, and actuators. Nearly all mechanical connections were substituted by smart processing units that accept impulses from sensors as input and provide measurements for appropriate engine functioning as well as vehicle functionality in conjunction with many active safety mechanisms like ABS and ESP. The conventional engine used a short time window of CAN-bus to run and implement driver adaptive systems [72]. In paper [73], the author illustrated discriminative approaches and appropriate work on behavior variability as well as pattern clustering. With full growth of pervasive and sensing computing techniques, more research is being accomplished in using various sensing techniques for learning human behavior. Started with key modalities of pervasive sensing and then highlighted behavior modeling. The impact of interacting with individuals or objects in our environment is considered as well as new research opportunities and challenges are spotlighted. In paper [74], the authors illustrated a method to identity verification that is entirely focused on a detailed examination of the face video streams. This approach used behavioral and physiological features. Through asking subjects to vocalize a given word or sentence, behavioral characteristics are acquired as well as physical characteristics are acquired from the face looks of the subject.

In paper [75], the author illustrated how hardware together with software can be put into a unit to find the answer for surveillance problem and outline developments as well as methods of stages associated in the video surveillance along with examining the problems for behavior analysis, motion analysis as well as standoff biometrics for the recognition of prior recognized suspects together with behavior understanding. Surveillance cameras are affordable, low price and everywhere but human resources need to analyze and monitor them is costly. Surveillance cameras can be a very important and convenient tool when they can be used to locate or identify events requiring exposure together to take action on time. In paper [76], the authors illustrated a new approach to recognize driver activities using a multi-modal and multi-perspective video-based system for real-time as well as strong monitoring of major human parts. The multi-perspective feature gives unnecessary trajectories of the human parts and multi-modal features provide hardiness of feature detection. The combination of an operation triplet together with an HMM centered classifier gives a semantic-level examination of the human activity. Intelligent vehicle systems and driver assistance systems are the framework for this project. In paper [77], the authors illustrated a learning mechanism to traces the video browsing response of users. Video streaming has become a prominent advertisement and entertainment platform. With the help of this information, fast video previews are generated. This working model the state transitions of a user when browsing to be an HMM's hidden state. Predict Hidden Markov model parameters with aid of maximum likelihood estimation for every measurement the user sequence interconnection with video clips. Video previews are then created the video's interesting component inferred from a careful examination of the video viewers browsing states. Audio coherence is preserved by picking the videos with full clauses, including the relevant phrases. In paper [78], the authors presented activity analysis by the LJ tracking system over many conditions in VIRAT data. Growth in the field of video tracking has direct many characteristics such as tracking accuracy, algorithm comparison, and target detection as well as implementation methods. There are some other characteristics of full-motion video monitoring that need more research to understand the detection of action and event. The main characteristic of behavioral analysis involves control in the environment between people, groups, and objects. Analysis of behavior extends the identification of events from monitoring accuracy to characterizing number, types of relationships and in analyzing human activities among actors. The relationship includes the relationship between actors and other individuals, artifacts, vehicles and facilities in time and space. The detection of events is more mature while active analysis needs innovative techniques for relationship understanding [78]. In the working memory study of the functional imaging demonstrate cerebellar involvement gives a cognitive task of the cerebellum. Cognitive inputs are explained primarily as part of the WM's Baddeley model's phonological loop Underlying inquiries are performed under visual-verbal WM conditions. In paper [79], the author raised the issue of if a cerebellum in the environment of higher degree cognitive functions supports some other important aspects of WM. In 17 young participants, a direct comparison of conceptual and abstract visual worlds was rendered with a 2-back pattern, by extracting percentage change from the fMRI information in the BOLD message [79]. It is possible to acquire functional characterization of next-level motor systems by modulating the demands on motor circuits. In this study, researchers conducted whole-brain fMRI together with parametric statistical analysis in eight healthy participants to learn about task-related motor circuit registration associated with the unilateral movement of fingers pattern to increase both length and complexity. For this type of analysis, the statistical parametric mapping technology has been applied. Categorical analysis of the main motor action effect has allowed brain activation in both the proven cortical and subcortical motor networks [80]. Positron emission tomography neuroimaging studies along with fMRI have started to clarify the human emotion's functional neuroanatomy. Together with fMRI activation studies, they reviewed 55 PETs. In this study, the researcher divided the brain into 20 sections that are not overlapping and defined every region through its sensitivity through individual emotions to different methods of induction and in emotional tasks with no cognitive demand [81].

In paper [82], the author showed the MYC network a very well-preserved superfamily of basic-helix-loop-helix-zipper proteins charged to integrating extracellular along with intracellular signals as well as modulating global gene expression. This work outlined biological properties along with molecular characteristics of modules for networking with significance on functional relationships between members of the network. Recommend that these types of network interactions also help to modulate the development of transcriptional metabolism to equalize nutrient demand with supply to keep the homeostasis of growth in addition to influencing cell destiny [82]. The majority of transcription factors may be linked to a population of optimal site-related sequences. Some transcription factors may bind to two separate sequences in DG representing two local optima. To determine the molecular mechanism work out the Human HOXB13 Structures along with CDX2 bound to CAATAAA and TCGTAAA [83]. Genome sequence assemblies are at present able to be used for seven different animals, containing mice, humans and nematode worms. The study of the genome shows a startling reality about genetic material. Vertebrate genomes have about twice as many genes as invertebrate genomes have [84]. In paper [85], author illustrated first higher-order behavioral experiment together with the organism monitor used for the Critical Assessment of Functional Annotation Assessments and previously laid out functions of multiple genes, as information regulators for neuronal plasticity processing borderline as well as memory formation. The very genuine forms of identification can be offered by traditional genetic and molecular testing but low-throughput. The Functional Annotation Critical Evaluation attempts to measure the effectiveness of the computational methods. In Critical Assessment of Functional Annotation 3, authors performed on the selected screens. They used homology and past Critical Assessment of Functional Annotation Predictions in this work to identify 29 primary Drosophila genes and find 11 new genes involved in long-term memory production.

Two main honeybee species are the eastern also known as Apis cerana cerana (Acc) as well as western also known as Apis mellifera ligustica (Aml) honeybee. In the present time, almost nothing is known regarding the current molecular neurobiology of central nervous system sub organs of Apis cerana cerana (Acc) and Apis mellifera ligustica (Aml). This research characterizes and tests the similarity or dissimilarity in the species' brain between the proteomes of mushroom bodies (MBs), optical lobes (OLs) and antennal lobes (ALs). Apis cerana cerana and Apis mellifera ligustica have developed similar proteome signatures in mushroom bodies and optical lobes to perform the neural activities unique to the domain. In the species' mushroom bodies, enriched functional groups associated with protein metabolism and Ca2transport relative to antennal lobes and optical lobes indicate that Ca2 and proteins are important for consolidating learning with memory through signal transduction modulation and synaptic structure. Besides enhanced ribonucleoside metabolism in the species, optical lobes suggest his function as the second phototransduction messenger healing. Separate proteome settings have formed the species' antennal lobes to the prime olfactory. This is assisted by the cytoskeleton organization in the antennal lobes of Apis cerana cerana to maintain olfactory. The functional groups involved in the transport of hydrogen ions in the antennal lobes of Apis mellifera ligustica suggest their important capacity in olfactory processes [86]. Long-term memory development in Drosophila melanogaster is very significant. Based on past experiences, it allows a person to change behaviors. In this study, RNA sequencing was used to recognize differentially expressed genes, together with transcript isoforms between males and naïve males, through court conditioning regulations that are adequate to suppress long-term courtship. Transcriptome inspection after 24 h training commends disclose transcripts isoforms and genes with familiar functions in transcriptional regulation, translation, cytoskeletal dynamics, and nervous system development. A huge amount of differentially expressed transcript isoforms were recognized. The consequence is the biological complexity underlying this behavioral plasticity and the discovery of many new potential research fields for future learning [87]. Changes in the plastic cerebral that assess learning and memory have been linked to sleep. Symptoms that sleep include the detection of fresh memory comes from a broad experimental scale. Reactivations in the sleep time of neuronal assemblies have been illustrated in numerous experimental designs in recent times threatened by some new environmental situation. Neuronal assemblies are proposed to assist in the retrieval of fragments of memory during sleep time. Sleep's fundamental role in memory and learning is still to be adequately described [88]. Drosophila has strong behavioral plasticity to support the odor that predicts food reward or punishment. Two types of plasticity are a step in by the mushroom body neurons. In the mushroom body (MB) many signaling molecules play important roles. D1 dopamine receptor dDA1 is extremely enriched in mushroom body neuropil. As well as an important receptor that mediates appetitive learning and aversive in pavlovian olfactory conditioning. The findings discussed here clearly illustrate the important roles of the aversive D1 dopamine receptor along with appetite for pavlovian conditioning [89]. The feature of epigenetic control as well as the potential for enduring, stable effects on the gene expression which survive a starting transient signal, might be of remarkable significance for the post-mitotic neurons, that are likely to updates on the activity along with connectivity. Continuous changes in the structure of chromatin are expected to result in epigenetic inheritance processes. Current work in chromatin biology provides new opportunities for the introduction of regulatory mechanisms based on long-term neuronal modifications with inferences for brain function learning, diseases and behavior [90]. Life in soil is a cognitive as well as real challenges that nematode Caenorhabditis elegans masters by using 302 neurons. By these 302 neurons, the nervous system fits together can perform a range of behaviors. In paper [91], the author illustrated many behavioral plasticity models in C. elegans along with underlying neuronal circuits with the forward genetic analysis. It also illustrates how genomic approaches and reverse genetics can lead to the analyzing function of genes in behavior [91]. Addiction is a situation of uncontrollable use of the drug. Laboratory observations have met on the conclusion that addiction means the pathological annexation of neural processes that generally work for reward-related learning. The important substrates of constant uncontrollable use of the drug are hypothesized to be cellular mechanisms and molecular mechanisms that fundamental long-term associative memory in many forebrain circuits [92]. Animal behavioral characteristics frequently cover with gene expression denoting a genomic constraint. This design outlines a space in our perception of the time course of environmentally reactive gene expression. Move forward in behavioral genomics take a look at how gene expression dynamics have a mutual connection with behavioral traits that scope from fixed to labile. This work illustrated that certain genomic regulatory mechanisms may forecast the timescale of an environmental consequence on behavior [93]. In paper [94], the authors presented age-related transfer from work by adult honey bees is linked to small change within messenger abundance of RNA in the human brain for 39% points of 5,500 genes studied. This finding brings to light the use of a widely replicated experimental of 72 microarrays that shows a large amount of substantial Genomic plasticity in the brain of human adults as shown so far. Experimental manipulations that unbundle human behavior and age have shown that changes in messenger RNA are primarily associated with conduct. Brain messenger RNA profiles accurately predicted the behavior of 57 out of 60 bees, establishing a strong link between individual and naturally occurring human brain gene expressions [94]. The purpose of artificial intelligence is to imitate human cognitive functions. It brings a fundamental shift to healthcare, driven by the easy availability of data on healthcare. In paper [95], the authors investigated the present situation of medical AI implementations and discussing their future. Cancer, neurology, and cardiology are the core areas of disease that use AI tools. The AI implementations in stroke are then reviewed in even more information in the three important fields of diagnosis, treatment [95]. Neurotransmitters are chemical substances that function as messengers in the process of synaptic transmission. They are important for people's health as well as any disruption in their behaviors can lead to serious psychological disorders like Parkinson's disease, Alzheimer's disease. For research and treat these mental disorders, tracking the concentrations of several neurotransmitters is of major significance. Several researchers have currently addressed the use of specific substances to build biosensors for recognition of neurotransmitters both in vivo as well as ex vivo. In paper [96], the author discussed the important materials used to build up neurotransmitter sensors and many approaches to the alteration of the sensor surface are analyzed to improve sensing efficiency [96]. Due to the greater significance of discovering simple, reliable methods for evaluating fresh genetic factors associated with genetic diseases, signaling proteins are a key subject in drug research. The sophistication of protein structure impedes the direct link between the molecular structure and signaling activity. The suggested solution requires the need for protein star graphs to encode the peptide sequence details into different topological indices measured with the help of the S2SNet tool. The method of identification of the quantitative structure-activity bond acquired using machine learning techniques is capable of predicting unique peptides of signaling. Testing several 3114 unidentified function proteins from the PDB repository evaluated the model's predictive efficiency. There are significant signaling pathways of three UniprotIDs via a signaling forecast higher than 98% [97].

There are no objective laboratory-based tests available for Major depressive disorder. While disruptions in several neurotransmitter mechanisms were involved in major depressive disorder, the biochemical alterations affecting the condition remain unclear and a systematic universal neurotransmitter assessment in Major depressive disorder has still not been conducted. Using a GC-MS combined with a selected metabolomics approach based on LC-MS/MS, they quantified levels of 19 plasma metabolites associated in GABAergic neurotransmitter, catecholaminergic neurotransmitter, as well as serotonergic neurotransmitter mechanisms in 50 first-episode subjects, antidepressant drugnaïve major depressive disorder as well as 50 healthy volunteers to find possible metabolite biomarkers for major depressive disorder. An autonomous sample cohort consisting of 49 individuals with major depressive disorder, 30 patients with BD as well as 40 healthy tests were used to verify the specificity of individual biomarkers. There was the stronger diagnostic significance of GABAergic as well as catecholaminergic than a serotonergic pathway. A board of four candidate plasma metabolite biomarkers could identify major depressive disorder topics of interest with an AUC of 0.968 and 0.953 between in training as well as test set [98]. In paper [99], authors described a quick overview of electrochemical biosensors, along with a detailed explanation of current trends throughout the implementation as well as evaluation of CP-based electrochemical neurotransmitter sensors as well as their components. They discussed the primary neurotransmitter sensing principle, such as histamine, glutamate, nitrogen monoxide, aspartate, tyrosine, epinephrine, etc. Besides, they have illustrated the integration with several other analytical techniques. Detection issues, as well as the future outlook of the neurotransmitter sensors for the construction of biomedical as well as healthcare implementations, were discussed. Neurotransmitters are natural chemical messengers that play a significant role in most of the cognitive processes, with irregular rates associated with physical, psychiatric, as well as neurodegenerative disorders like Alzheimer's Huntington's, etc. The quick and reliable identification is therefore of major medical importance. In recent years, electrochemical techniques have been used efficiently for the identification of neurotransmitters, outclassing more complex analytical techniques like chromatography, flow injections, etc. This work most effective as well as encouraging electrochemical enzyme-free as well as enzymatic sensors for detecting neurotransmitters. Concentrating on the operation of global researchers primarily over the past ten years, without claiming to have become comprehensive, they provide a summary of the progress that has been made throughout this period in sensing strategies. Special emphasis is given to nanostructured-based sensors that show a significant enhancement in analytical efficiency [100]. Microglia are the brain's endogenous immune cells, expressing chemokine as well as cytokine receptors communicating with peripheral immune cells. New research has shown that microglia still react to neurotransmitters, the traditional signaling substances of the human brain. In paper [93], the authors presented the evidence for neurotransmitter receptor activity on microglia as well as the impact of that kind of receptor activation on microglial behavior. Neurotransmitters advise microglia to conduct different kinds of reactions, like initiating an inflammatory cascade or possessing a neuroprotective phenotype. Knowing how microglia react to various neurotransmitters will, therefore, have major consequences for regulating these cells reactivity in acute injury and managing chronic neurodegenerative diseases [101].

Voltage-sensor domains are functional transmembrane regions of voltage-gated ion channels that reflect changes in membrane susceptibility by inducing final confirmation changes combined with the ion-conducting pore gating. Many other spider-venom peptides operate as gating modifications through connecting as well as trapping the voltage-gated channels to VSDs inside an open or closed region. They were using nuclear magnetic resonance to define the molecular key information of the activity among the VSD of the voltage-gated potassium channel KvAP as well as spider-venom peptide VSTx1 to know molecular foundation underlying the above mechanism of action. The subsequent association network raises the energy resistance to conformation changes needed for channel gating as well as they believe that it is the process through which gating regulator substances prevent voltage-gated ion channels [102]. Voltage-gated ion channels are top choices for the drug industry, however, drug identification on Voltage-gated ion channels is difficult, as drug associations are limited to different transcriptional channel states mediated by transmembrane potential changes. They have integrated numerous optogenetic tools for developing complex drug profiling assays to established light-step procedures to confront VGC states on time scale. They illustrate that light-induced electrophysiology yields medicinal relevant information of top quality with outstanding examination windows for medicines that operate on big cardiac VGCs, such as hKv1.5, hERG, etc. LiEp-based testing stayed reliable if some optogenetic actuators, as well as various kinds of organic or genetic voltage sensors, were used [103]. Voltage-gated ion channels have become an essential category of drug goals as well as arbitrate electrical dynamics throughout excitable tissues. Mechanical ion channel research often includes sophisticated voltage-clamp protocols that are implemented by manual and perhaps even automated electrophysiology. In paper [104], design all-optical electrophysiology strategies for analyze ion channel regulation based on operation, in a design consistent with high-throughput screening have been presented [104]. Pain signaling is analytically based on voltage-gated ion channels. The neurogenic function of such crucial ion channels after nerve injury as well as modifications in channels linked with mutations in reaction to inflammation as well as gain-of-function causes' hyper excitability that underlies pain. A key theme of translational pain study has become the search for ion channel pharmacological modulators, with even a strong emphasis on the advancement of peripheral channel modulators which do not play important tasks in the CNS. This work outlines recent developments in sodium, calcium, as well as potassium-gated voltage channels which are being examined as biochemical goals for treating pain [105]. Work in the field of physiology is becoming molecular through the implementation of technological progress in processes of structural analysis, recombinant DNA techniques the subject of study was shifting away from traditional physiology to become more and more focused on drug mechanisms. This study, a beautiful example of that kind of growth in the field of ion channel studies that would not be nearly as robust if it was not clarified for individuals illnesses. For the above purpose, structure-function relationships, as well as electrophysiology of ion channel, can never be isolated from it's genetic as well as a clinical description of channelopathies of ions. Different between the publications of such a subject is that all known human genetic disorders of voltage-gated ion channels are listed including different fields of pharmacy, like cardiology, neurology, nephrology, myology as well as fascinating similarities in disease mechanisms underlined. Almost all forms of voltage-gated ion channels for cations as well as anions are defined in conjunction with knowledge regarding structure, isoforms, and gene encoding [106]. Like several proteins, ion channels have moving particle performing key functions. The channel proteins include the soluble, ion-selective pore which passes plasma membrane, and they also have a set of unique' gating' processes to open as well as close such pore in reaction towards molecular stimuli like ligand binding or maybe a transmembrane voltage shift [107]. In paper [108], the author evaluated current advancements in the disciplines of neurology and AI about the functional roles of replay. Complementary research implies that replay might aid learning processes such as generalisation and continuous learning, allowing for information transfer across the two domains and furthering our knowledge of biological as well as artificial learning and memory.

4   Conclusion

Learning and Memory is a branch of artificial intelligence that studies the critical brain functions in order to create novel computational intelligence techniques and methods focused on learning and memory. As a consequence, human intelligence demands a review on computational intelligence techniques in learning and memory. This paper explained why without learning, the goal of achieving human intelligence is still a long bit away. Here, we discussed hippocampus learning, human learning and memory, hidden markov model, behavioral plasticity in learning and memory, PET and fMRI, as well as the neurological diseases. Here, we also outlined the important work done in the domain of learning as well as memory. This paper examined the evolution of learning and memory during several decades. This study also discussed the merits and limitations of several learning and memory models and techniques.

References

1. Botkin, J.W., Elmandjra, M., Malitza, M.: No Limits to Learning: Bridging the Human Gap: The Report to the Club of Rome. Elsevier (2014)
2. Goldstone, R.L.: Perceptual learning. Annu. Rev. Psychol. **49**(1), 585–612 (1998)
3. Schwabe, L., et al.: Stress modulates the use of spatial versus stimulus-response learning strategies in humans. Learn. Mem. **14**(1–2), 109–116 (2007)
4. Singer, R.N.: Motor Learning and Human Performance: An Application to Motor Skills and Movement Behaviors. Macmillan, New York (1980)
5. Koller, D., et al.: Introduction to Statistical Relational Learning. MIT Press (2007)
6. Tolman, E.C., Ritchie, B.F., Kalish, D.: Studies in spatial learning. II. Place learning versus response learning. J. Exp. Psychol. **36**(3), 221 (1946)
7. Tyre, M.J., Orlikowski, W.J.: The episodic process of learning by using. Int. J. Technol. Manag. **11**(7–8), 790–798 (1996)
8. Bandura, A.: Observational learning. In: The International Encyclopedia of Communication (2008)
9. Weisz, V.I., Argibay, P.F.: A putative role for neurogenesis in neurocomputational terms: inferences from a hippocampal model. Cognition **112**(2), 229–240 (2009)
10. Chung, P.C., Liu, C.D.: A daily behavior enabled hidden Markov model for human behavior understanding. Pattern Recogn. **41**(5), 1572–1580 (2008)
11. Antonucci, A., De Rosa, R., Giusti, A.: Action recognition by imprecise hidden Markov models. In: Proceedings of the International Conference on Image Processing, Computer Vision, and Pattern Recognition (IPCV), p. 1. The Steering Committee of The World Congress in Computer Science, Computer Engineering and Applied Computing (WorldComp) (2011)
12. Zhang, B.T.: Hypernetworks: a molecular evolutionary architecture for cognitive learning and memory. IEEE Comput. Intell. Mag. **3**(3) (2008)
13. Zhang, B.T.: Cognitive learning and the multimodal memory game: toward human-level machine learning. In: IEEE International Joint Conference on Neural Networks, IJCNN 2008. IEEE World Congress on Computational Intelligence, pp. 3261–3267, June 2008
14. Hajimirsadeghi, H., Ahmadabadi, M.N., Araabi, B.N.: Conceptual imitation learning based on perceptual and functional characteristics of action. IEEE Trans. Auton. Ment. Dev. **5**(4), 311–325 (2013)
15. Kemere, C., et al.: Detecting neural-state transitions using hidden Markov models for motor cortical prostheses. J. Neurophysiol. **100**(4), 2441–2452 (2008)
16. Kaczmarek, L.: Gene expression in learning processes. Acta Neurobiol. Exp. **60**(3), 419–424 (2000)
17. Alberini, C.M.: Transcription factors in long-term memory and synaptic plasticity. Physiol. Rev. **89**(1), 121–145 (2009)
18. Sato, N., Yamaguchi, Y.: Simulation of human episodic memory by using a computational model of the hippocampus. In: Advances in Artificial Intelligence 2010 (2010)
19. Widloski, J., Fiete, I.: How does the brain solve the computational problems of spatial navigation? In: Derdikman, D., Knierim, J.J. (eds.) Space, Time and Memory in the Hippocampal Formation, pp. 373–407. Springer, Vienna (2014). https://doi.org/10.1007/978-3-7091-1292-2_14

20. Atallah, H.E., Frank, M.J., O'Reilly, R.C.: Hippocampus, cortex, and basal ganglia: insights from computational models of complementary learning systems. Neurobiol. Learn. Mem. **82**(3), 253–267 (2004)

21. Florian, B., Sepp, K., Joshua, H., Richard, H.: Hidden Markov models in the neurosciences. In: Hidden Markov Models, Theory and Applications (2011)

22. Lee, Y.S.: Genes and signaling pathways involved in memory enhancement in mutant mice. Mol. Brain **7**(1), 43 (2014)

23. Tran, T., Bui, H., Venkatesh, S.: Human activity learning and segmentation using partially hidden discriminative models. arXiv preprint arXiv:1408.3081 (2014)

24. Park, C., Ahn, J., Kim, H., Park, S.: Integrative gene network construction to analyze cancer recurrence using semi-supervised learning. PLoS ONE **9**(1), e86309 (2014)

25. Chalmers, D.J.: The evolution of learning: an experiment in genetic connectionism. In: Connectionist Models, pp. 81–90 (1991)

26. Lake, B.M., Salakhutdinov, R., Tenenbaum, J.B.: Human-level concept learning through probabilistic program induction. Science **350**(6266), 1332–1338 (2015)

27. Phuong, T.M., Nhung, N.P.: Predicting gene function using similarity learning. BMC Genomics **14**(4), S4 (2013)

28. Kello, C.T., Rodny, J., Warlaumont, A.S., Noelle, D.C.: Plasticity, learning, and complexity in spiking networks. Crit. Rev.™ Biomed. Eng. **40**(6) (2012)

29. Frank, M.J., Fossella, J.A.: Neurogenetics and pharmacology of learning, motivation, and cognition. Neuropsychopharmacology **36**(1), 133 (2011)

30. Cameron, H.A., Glover, L.R.: Adult neurogenesis: beyond learning and memory. Annu. Rev. Psychol. **66**, 53–81 (2015)

31. Conrad, C.D.: A critical review of chronic stress effects on spatial learning and memory. Prog. Neuropsychopharmacol. Biol. Psychiatry **34**(5), 742–755 (2010)

32. Friedman, D., Johnson Jr, R.: Event-related potential (ERP) studies of memory encoding and retrieval: a selective review. Microsc. Res. Tech. **51**(1), 6–28 (2000)

33. Herz, R.S., Engen, T.: Odor memory: review and analysis. Psychon. Bull. Rev. **3**(3), 300–313 (1996)

34. Kantak, S.S., Winstein, C.J.: Learning–performance distinction and memory processes for motor skills: a focused review and perspective. Behav. Brain Res. **228**(1), 219–231 (2012)

35. Moreira, P.S., Almeida, P.R., Leite-Almeida, H., Sousa, N., Costa, P.: Impact of chronic stress protocols in learning and memory in rodents: systematic review and meta-analysis. PLoS ONE **11**(9), e0163245 (2016)

36. Peng, S., Zhang, Y., Zhang, J., Wang, H., Ren, B.: ERK in learning and memory: a review of recent research. Int. J. Mol. Sci. **1**, 222–232 (2010)

37. Reber, P.J.: The neural basis of implicit learning and memory: a review of neuropsychological and neuroimaging research. Neuropsychologia **51**(10), 2026–2042 (2013)

38. Soderstrom, N.C., Bjork, R.A.: Learning versus performance: an integrative review. Perspect. Psychol. Sci. **10**(2), 176–199 (2015)

39. Curran, H.V.: Benzodiazepines, memory and mood: a review. Psychopharmacology **105**(1), 1–8 (1991)

40. Zhao, W.Q., Chen, H., Quon, M.J., Alkon, D.L.: Insulin and the insulin receptor in experimental models of learning and memory. Eur. J. Pharmacol. **490**(1–3), 71–81 (2004)

41. Berka, C., et al.: EEG correlates of task engagement and mental workload in vigilance, learning, and memory tasks. Aviat. Space Environ. Med. **78**(5), B231–B244 (2007)

42. Glisky, E.L., Schacter, D.L., Tulving, E.: Computer learning by memory-impaired patients: acquisition and retention of complex knowledge. Neuropsychologia **24**(3), 313–328 (1986)

43. McClelland, J.L., McNaughton, B.L., O'reilly, R.C.: Why there are complementary learning systems in the hippocampus and neocortex: insights from the successes and failures of connectionist models of learning and memory. Psychol. Rev. **102**(3), 419 (1995)

44. Sutherland, R.J., Whishaw, I.Q., Kolb, B.: Contributions of cingulate cortex to two forms of spatial learning and memory. J. Neurosci. **8**(6), 1863–1872 (1988)

45. Barto, A.G., Sutton, R.S., Brouwer, P.S.: A reinforcement learning associative memory. Biol. Cybern **40**(20), 2 (1981)

46. Barnes, C.A.: Spatial learning and memory processes: the search for their neurobiological mechanisms in the rat. Trends Neurosci. **11**(4), 163–169 (1988)

47. Berchtold, N.C., Castello, N., Cotman, C.W.: Exercise and time-dependent benefits to learning and memory. Neuroscience **167**(3), 588–597 (2010)

48. Blokland, A.: Acetylcholine: a neurotransmitter for learning and memory? Brain Res. Rev. **21**(3), 285–300 (1995)

49. Paivio, A.: Mental imagery in associative learning and memory. Psychol. Rev. **76**(3), 241 (1969)

50. Alba, J.W., Hasher, L.: Is memory schematic? Psychol. Bull. **93**(2), 203 (1983)

51. Cao, L., et al.: VEGF links hippocampal activity with neurogenesis, learning and memory. Nat. Genet. **36**(8), 827–835 (2004)

52. Chun, M.M., Jiang, Y.: Contextual cueing: implicit learning and memory of visual context guides spatial attention. Cogn. Psychol. **36**(1), 28–71 (1998)

53. Passolunghi, M.C., Vercelloni, B., Schadee, H.: The precursors of mathematics learning: working memory, phonological ability and numerical competence. Cogn. Dev. **22**(2), 165–184 (2007)

54. Squire, L.R.: Declarative and nondeclarative memory: multiple brain systems supporting learning and memory. J. Cogn. Neurosci. **4**(3), 232–243 (1992)

55. Deng, W., Aimone, J.B., Gage, F.H.: New neurons and new memories: how does adult hippocampal neurogenesis affect learning and memory? Nat. Rev. Neurosci. **11**(5), 339–350 (2010)

56. Desmond, J.E., Fiez, J.A.: Neuroimaging studies of the cerebellum: language, learning and memory. Trends Cogn. Sci. **2**(9), 355–362 (1998)

57. Du, H., et al.: Cyclophilin D deficiency attenuates mitochondrial and neuronal perturbation and ameliorates learning and memory in Alzheimer's disease. Nat. Med. **10**, 1097–1105 (2008)

58. Dubnau, J., Tully, T.: Gene discovery in Drosophila: new insights for learning and memory. Annu. Rev. Neurosci. **21**(1), 407–444 (1998)

59. Eysenck, M.W.: Anxiety, learning, and memory: a reconceptualization. J. Res. Pers. **13**(4), 363–385 (1979)

60. Morris, G.P., Clark, I.A., Zinn, R., Vissel, B.: Microglia: a new frontier for synaptic plasticity, learning and memory, and neurodegenerative disease research. Neurobiol. Learn. Mem. **105**, 40–53 (2013)

61. Gold, P.E.: Acetylcholine modulation of neural systems involved in learning and memory. Neurobiol. Learn. Mem. **80**(3), 194–210 (2003)

62. Payan, A., Montana, G.: Predicting Alzheimer's disease: a neuroimaging study with 3D convolutional neural networks. arXiv preprint arXiv:1502.02506 (2015)

63. Blennow, K., Dubois, B., Fagan, A.M., Lewczuk, P., de Leon, M.J., Hampel, H.: Clinical utility of cerebrospinal fluid biomarkers in the diagnosis of early Alzheimer's disease. Alzheimer's Dement. **11**(1), 58–69 (2015)

64. Escott-Price, V., Shoai, M., Pither, R., Williams, J., Hardy, J.: Polygenic score prediction captures nearly all common genetic risk for Alzheimer's disease. Neurobiol. Aging **49**, 214-e7 (2017)

65. Eskildsen, S.F., Coupé, P., Fonov, V.S., Pruessner, J.C., Collins, D.L., Alzheimer's Disease Neuroimaging Initiative: Structural imaging biomarkers of Alzheimer's disease: predicting disease progression. Neurobiol. Aging **36**, S23-31 (2015)

66. Levy, B.R., Ferrucci, L., Zonderman, A.B., Slade, M.D., Troncoso, J., Resnick, S.M.: A culture–brain link: negative age stereotypes predict Alzheimer's disease biomarkers. Psychol. Aging **31**(1), 82 (2016)

67. Jack, C.R., Jr., et al.: NIA-AA research framework: toward a biological definition of Alzheimer's disease. Alzheimer's Dement. **14**(4), 535–562 (2018)

68. Kauppi, K., et al.: Combining polygenic hazard score with volumetric MRI and cognitive measures improves prediction of progression from mild cognitive impairment to Alzheimer's disease. Front. Neurosci. **12**, 260 (2018)

69. Mehran, R., Oyama, A., Shah, M.: Abnormal crowd behavior detection using social force model. In: 2009 IEEE Conference on Computer Vision and Pattern Recognition, pp. 935–942 (2009)

70. Xia, C., Fu, L., Liu, Z., Liu, H., Chen, L., Liu, Y.: Aquatic toxic analysis by monitoring fish behavior using computer vision: a recent progress. J. Toxicol. (2018)

71. Sathyanarayana, A., Boyraz, P., Purohit, Z., Lubag, R., Hansen, J.H.: Driver adaptive and context aware active safety systems using CAN-bus signals. In: 2010 IEEE Intelligent Vehicles Symposium, pp. 1236–1241 (2010)

72. Atallah, L., Yang, G.Z.: The use of pervasive sensing for behaviour profiling—A survey. Pervasive Mob. Comput. **5**(5), 447–464 (2009)

73. Bicego, M., Grosso, E., Tistarelli, M.: Person authentication from video of faces: a behavioral and physiological approach using pseudo hierarchical hidden Markov models. In: Zhang, D., Jain, A.K. (eds.) ICB 2006. LNCS, vol. 3832, pp. 113–120. Springer, Heidelberg (2005). https://doi.org/10.1007/11608288_16

74. Ko, T.: A survey on behavior analysis in video surveillance for homeland security applications. In: 2008 37th IEEE Applied Imagery Pattern Recognition Workshop, pp. 1–8. IEEE (2008)

75. Cheng, S.Y., Park, S., Trivedi, M.M.: Multi-spectral and multi-perspective video arrays for driver body tracking and activity analysis. Comput. Vis. Image Underst. **106**(2–3), 245–257 (2007)

76. Syeda-Mahmood, T., Ponceleon, D.: Learning video browsing behavior and its application in the generation of video previews. In: Proceedings of the Ninth ACM International Conference on Multimedia, pp. 119–128 (2009)

77. Blasch, E., et al.: Video-based activity analysis using the L1 tracker on VIRAT data. In: 2013 IEEE Applied Imagery Pattern Recognition Workshop (AIPR), pp. 1–8. IEEE (2013)

78. Hautzel, H., Mottaghy, F.M., Specht, K., Müller, H.W., Krause, B.J.: Evidence of a modality-dependent role of the cerebellum in working memory? An fMRI study comparing verbal and abstract n-back tasks. Neuroimage **47**(4), 2073–2082 (2009)

79. Haslinger, B., et al.: The role of lateral premotor–cerebellar–parietal circuits in motor sequence control: a parametric fMRI study. Cogn. Brain Res. **13**(2), 159–168 (2002)

80. Phan, K.L., Wager, T., Taylor, S.F., Liberzon, I.: Functional neuroanatomy of emotion: a meta-analysis of emotion activation studies in PET and fMRI. Neuroimage **16**(2), 331–348 (2002)

81. Carroll, P.A., Freie, B.W., Mathsyaraja, H., Eisenman, R.N.: The MYC transcription factor network: balancing metabolism, proliferation and oncogenesis. Front. Med. **12**(4), 412–425 (2018)

82. Morgunova, E., et al.: Two distinct DNA sequences recognized by transcription factors represent enthalpy and entropy optima. Elife **7**, e32963 (2018)

83. Levine, M., Tjian, R.: Transcription regulation and animal diversity. Nature **424**(6945), 147 (2003)

84. Tanimizu, T., Kono, K., Kida, S.: Brain networks activated to form object recognition memory. Brain Res. Bull. **141**, 27–34 (2018)

85. Kacsoh, B.Z., et al.: New Drosophila long-term memory genes revealed by assessing computational function prediction methods. G3: Genes Genomes Genet. **9**(1), 251–267 (2019)
86. Meng, L., et al.: Proteomics reveals the molecular underpinnings of stronger learning and memory in eastern compared to western bees. Mol. Cell. Proteomics **17**(2), 255–269 (2018)
87. Winbush, A., Reed, D., Chang, P.L., Nuzhdin, S.V., Lyons, L.C., Arbeitman, M.N.: Identification of gene expression changes associated with long-term memory of courtship rejection in Drosophila males. G3: Genes Genomes Genet. **2**(11), 1437–1445 (2012)
88. Maquet, P.: The role of sleep in learning and memory. Science **294**(5544), 1048–1052 (2001)
89. Kim, Y.C., Lee, H.G., Han, K.A.: D1 dopamine receptor dDA1 is required in the mushroom body neurons for aversive and appetitive learning in Drosophila. J. Neurosci. **27**(29), 7640–7647 (2007)
90. Dulac, C.: Brain function and chromatin plasticity. Nature **465**(7299), 728 (2010)
91. Hobert, O.: Behavioral plasticity in C. elegans: paradigms, circuits, genes. J. Neurobiol. **54**(1), 203–223 (2003)
92. Hyman, S.E., Malenka, R.C., Nestler, E.J.: Neural mechanisms of addiction: the role of reward-related learning and memory. Annu. Rev. Neurosci. **29**, 565–598 (2006)
93. Rittschof, C.C., Hughes, K.A.: Advancing behavioural genomics by considering timescale. Nat. Commun. **9**(1), 489 (2018)
94. Whitfield, C.W., Cziko, A.M., Robinson, G.E.: Gene expression profiles in the brain predict behavior in individual honey bees. Science **302**(5643), 296–299 (2003)
95. Jiang, F., et al.: Artificial intelligence in healthcare: past, present and future. Stroke Vasc. Neurol. **2**(4), 230–243 (2017)
96. Si, B., Song, E.: Recent advances in the detection of neurotransmitters. Chemosensors **6**(1), 1 (2018)
97. Fernandez-Lozano, C., Cuinas, R.F., Seoane, J.A., Fernandez-Blanco, E., Dorado, J., Munteanu, C.R.: Classification of signaling proteins based on molecular star graph descriptors using Machine Learning models. J. Theor. Biol. **384**, 50–58 (2015)
98. Pan, J.X., et al.: Diagnosis of major depressive disorder based on changes in multiple plasma neurotransmitters: a targeted metabolomics study. Transl. Psychiatry **8**(1), 1 (2018)
99. Moon, J.M., Thapliyal, N., Hussain, K.K., Goyal, R.N., Shim, Y.B.: Conducting polymer-based electrochemical biosensors for neurotransmitters: a review. Biosens. Bioelectron. **102**, 540–552 (2018)
100. Tavakolian-Ardakani, Z., Hosu, O., Cristea, C., Mazloum-Ardakani, M., Marrazza, G.: Latest trends in electrochemical sensors for neurotransmitters: a review. Sensors **19**(9), 2037 (2019)
101. Pocock, J.M., Kettenmann, H.: Neurotransmitter receptors on microglia. Trends Neurosci. **30**(10), 527–535 (2007)
102. Lau, C.H., King, G.F., Mobli, M.: Molecular basis of the interaction between gating modifier spider toxins and the voltage sensor of voltage-gated ion channels. Sci. Rep. **6**, 34333 (2016)
103. Streit, J., Kleinlogel, S.: Dynamic all-optical drug screening on cardiac voltage-gated ion channels. Sci. Rep. **8**(1), 1153 (2018)
104. Zhang, H., Reichert, E., Cohen, A.E.: Optical electrophysiology for probing function and pharmacology of voltage-gated ion channels. Elife **5**, e15202 (2016)
105. Zamponi, G.W., Han, C., Waxman, S.G.: Voltage-gated ion channels as molecular targets for pain. In: Tuszynski, M.H. (ed.) Translational Neuroscience, pp. 415–436. Springer, Boston, MA (2016). https://doi.org/10.1007/978-1-4899-7654-3_22

106. Lehmann-Horn, F., Jurkat-Rott, K.: Voltage-gated ion channels and hereditary disease. Physiol. Rev. **79**(4), 1317–1372 (1999)
107. Yellen, G.: The moving parts of voltage-gated ion channels. Q. Rev. Biophys. **31**(3), 239–295 (1998)
108. Roscow, E.L., Chua, R., Costa, R.P., Jones, M.W., Lepora, N.: Learning offline: memory replay in biological and artificial reinforcement learning. Trends Neurosci. **44**(10), 808–821 (2021)

Enhanced Marker-Controlled Watershed Segmentation Algorithm for Brain Tumor Segmentation

J. Pearline Sheba Grace$^{(\boxtimes)}$ (iD) and P. Ezhilarasi (iD)

Department of Electronics and Communication Engineering,
St. Joseph's College of Engineering, OMR, Chennai, India
pearljoshua23@gmail.com, ezhilarasip@stjosephs.ac.in

Abstract. Image processing has always been a vivid area of research that helps mankind unveil the wondrous works. In this paper, the proposed image segmentation algorithm is used to segment the region of interest (ROI) from the MR images. The ultimate idea behind the process of segmentation is to segregate tumor region from the homogenous anatomical structures. The paper proposes an enhanced marker controlled watershed segmentation algorithm which will help in the precise segmentation of the region of interest (ROI) from the provided input image. The Enhanced Marker-Controlled Watershed Segmentation Algorithm helps in identifying the tumor region and segment it such that the tumor can be analyzed for further diagnosis. The proposed method provides a precise accuracy of 99.14% which determines the fact that the tumor region is being segmented accurately with few false positive rate.

Keywords: Tumor · Magnetic resonance imaging · Image segmentation · Gradient magnitude · Watershed segmentation

1 Introduction

In a healthy human, old cells are being replaced with new cells within every particular period of time and when this process fails it leads to an unnecessary mass growth of tissues which is referred to as tumor. Thus the abnormal mass of tissues in the brain is known as brain tumor. They are also called as lesion or neoplasia. Brain tumors are further classified as Primary and Metastatic tumors. Primary tumors also known as benign or non-cancerous, are the ones that originate from brain tissues and its surrounding. Metastatic brain tumor also called as cancerous or malignant, are the ones that originate from other parts of the body and migrated to the brain through the bloodstream. Early detection of brain tumor can increase the survival rate up to 90% [13]. There is no specified reason for the cause of brain tumor has been proved yet.

MRI is a scanning technique for creating detailed images of the human body. It uses large magnets that produces strong magnetic field and radio waves that will help in generating images of the internal parts of the body. MRI scan is one among the most

S. Mukhopadhyay et al. (Eds.): CICBA 2022, CCIS 1579, pp. 154–166, 2022.
https://doi.org/10.1007/978-3-031-10766-5_12

popular methods used, benefits in visualizing the anatomy in various planes that include Axial, Sagittal and Coronal planes [14]. MRI is much more effective than CT since it has low radiation and high contrast features. The main advantage of the usage of MRI when to other imaging techniques is that there is absolutely no risk of ionizing radiation.

A MRI image of the brain is a way of transferring the anatomical information about the internal structures and also helps in the detection of various brain conditions. The MRI image needs to be analyzed in order to diagnose the abnormality that is present in the brain [15]. The first step to analyze the image is to understand the information that is being conveyed by the image. It is often clear that the entire image is not required for analysis, but only certain areas that contains the same characteristics. In order to segregate the areas with similar characteristics, segmentation is performed to the image as the primary step in image processing. Image segmentation is the process of segregating the set of pixels on the basis of their similarities. In other words, it is the process of identifying, grouping and isolating of the regions and surfaces of the image which often is referred to as structural units or segments, in order to extract and the relevant information that is required for the diagnosis of brain tumor [16]. Segmentation is often carried out based on features like color, intensity or even texture. Early diagnosis of the tumor helps in increasing the survival rate by reducing the critical issues. Segmenting the image according to the similarities help in identifying tumor region in a much efficient way.

The process of segmenting an image is an essential procedure when it comes to extracting relevant information from the grey or RGB images. It helps in the conversion of complex image into a simple image, in order to locate boundaries and identify tumoral region in the image. Figure 1 denotes the basic process of segmentation. Based on the basic properties such as discontinuity and similarity, segmentation algorithms are being developed to segment the images. The motive behind the process of segmentation is to analyze homogenous criteria and to understand the image complexity.

The segmentation process characterized based on discontinuity is referred to as edge-based segmentation whereas the segmentation based on similarity is the one referred to as region-based segmentation. Segmentation technique can be done in various ways, that include manual, semi-automatic and fully-automatic [17]. Manual segmentation methods are usually performed by expert radiologist or specialized clinicians. Manual segmentation performed are considered and accepted widely as ground truth. The major advantage of using manual segmentation techniques is that we can utilise the knowledge of an expert in the field, whereas the disadvantages of this segmentation is that it is extremely time consuming and is prone to intra and inter-observer variability. Since the segmentation process is carried out slice-by-slice [19], there is quite a chance of larger variability.

The disadvantages in the manual segmentation technique has led to the discovery of future advancements referred to as the semi-automatic segmentation technique. It reduces the time consumption in the process of segmentation, since the user intervention in the process is being replaced by various algorithms either at the beginning or the final stages of the segmentation process. Though it aims in solving some of the major disadvantages including intra-observer variability and time consumption, it still contains inter-observer variability since the manual user intervention and the algorithm equally influences the result [20]. Automatic segmentation techniques are the ones that does

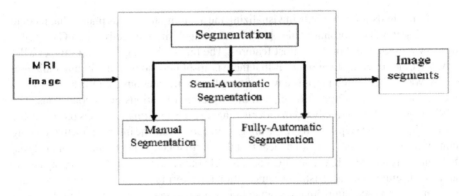

Fig. 1. Process of segmentation

not rely on any user interaction and the segmentation can be done by two methods: learning and non-learning. Deep learning methods are one among the recently popular learning methods, where the segmentation is performed by a neural network that is being trained with labelled examples. The major advantage of automatic segmentation is that it drastically reduces the time consumption once the method is being trained. Depending on the size of image that needs to be segmented, it ranges from seconds to a few minutes, but usually faster and efficient when compared to that of the methods with user interaction. The disadvantage of automatic segmentation is that it requires large amount of labelled data in order to train an accurate model and it also requires long training time and specialized software like GPU to train the model efficiently. The errors in automatic segmentation are systematic errors whereas the errors in the case of manual and semi-automatic segmentation are incidental errors.

The drawbacks of watershed algorithm is the segmented image is further being segmented into small segments and is uniform in size. Over-segmentation extracts important boundaries but may create insignificant boundaries. The presence of noise affects the quality of the output of the segmentation process. Watershed segmentation suffers from the major drawback of over segmentation and this drawback is being controlled with the help of markers. The concept of markers helps in controlling over-segmentation. This algorithm is affected by noise and irregularities in the edges. The advantages of enhanced marker controlled watershed segmentation that will overcome the disadvantages of marker controlled watershed segmentation are the use of internal foreground and external background markers that'll help in overcoming the limitations of over-segmentation.

2   Literature Survey

In recent years, the research in the field of image segmentation has grown enormously leading to various segmentation algorithms. In this section, the related works of image segmentation techniques by various authors are being studied.

Sujatha Saini and Komal Arora [1] explained about the basic idea of image segmentation and the classification of image segmentation techniques. It discusses about various segmentation algorithms that can be used in a variety of segmentation techniques.

Song Yuheng and Yan Hao [2] have discussed about various segmentation techniques, analyses the algorithms of image segmentation techniques and compares their advantages and disadvantages. It is finally being accepted that it may be cynical to find an image segmentation technique that adapts with all the images. In near future, algorithms that tend to adapt with various images will be proposed.

Vairaprakash Gurusamy and Subbu Kannan [3] explained how segmenting an image is a major step when it comes to analysing an image. The review paper mainly focuses on the basic properties of an image including discontinuity and similarity and speaks about various techniques that are used for image segmentation. Image segmentation by using threshold technique is proven to provide much better results. It has been concluded that region-growing and threshold techniques are much better and efficient than clustering and edge detection techniques.

Sindhu Devanooru et al. [4] talks about introducing a taxonomy that consists of Data, Image Segmentation Processing and View (DIV), which is being demonstrated by state-of-the-art publications on deep neural networks. With the help of this detailed analysis, they have proven that Modified FCM produces brain segmentation results much accurately. The proposed solution has a wider view on the three major factors namely, Data, Image Segmentation Processing and View respectively. The future work on this field focusses on improving the quality of image segmentation and also in the processing of large amount of MRI data accurately and simultaneously.

N. Arun Kumar et al. [5] speaks about fully-automatic model-based segmentation using Artificial Neural Networks in identifying brain tumor identification and classification. The pre-processing stage of the segmentation method is to perform Fourier transform such that to improve or return the required data from Fourier domain to its original domain without losing any data during the inverse process. The ROI of the enhanced image is obscure thus to extract the required borders, they have performed feature extraction with the feature descriptor called as Histogram of Oriented Gradients (HOG). The non-brain region is being filtered with the use of histogram thresholding. The main challenge is to understand the homogenous nature of the brain. The performance measures of the segmentation are 92.14% accuracy, 89% sensitivity and 94% specificity.

Steven Lawrence Fernandes et al. [6] proposed a tool and associated methodology that will help in exploring a clinical brain image with much better accuracy thus providing a clearer insight on early and ideal treatment methods. This tool gives all the probable methods in which the treatment of brain tumors can be easily diagnosed and can be treated preventing permanent disability or even death.

S. U. Aswathy et al. [7] proposed an enhanced segmentation algorithm that is based on support vector machine and genetic algorithm. For FLAIR images, the algorithm shows better tumor detection that helps in determining boundary region more accurately. The accuracy and precision achieved through the proposed algorithm is about 99.65 respectively. The error rate in this algorithm is quite low when compared to other algorithms. The major advantage is that it drastically reduces the need for any pre-processing methods.

Suresha. D et al. [8] introduced a hybrid algorithm with a combination of K-means Clustering technique and Support Vector Machine (SVM) to detect whether tumor is present or not. This algorithm uses Machine Learning and requires less time for training sets, predicts accurately the region of tumors.

Hyunseok Seo et al. [9] speaks briefly on comparing around 40 different segmentation techniques and provides a new segmentation method under a specific network referred to as the Graph Neural Networks (GNN) and Generative Adversarial Network (GAN) which are implemented as powerful tools for the segmentation of non-Euclidean domain structures (medical images). GNNs are mainly used in the segmentation process of biomedical images since graph-structured images is bound to be more efficient since medical images do not have a constrained boundary. Deep learning methods requires many hyper parameters which means that minor deviations in these parameters will lead to major disproportionate changes that will affect the results at a greater extent.

Prabhjot Kaur and Tamalika Chaira [10] focuses that CT/MRI images are not clear and introduces a novel clustering approach based on fuzzy concept which enhances the vague image before the segmentation process. The enhanced image will be then segmented by Gaussian kernel-based Fuzzy C-means clustering. The proposed method has efficiently even amidst of noise.

V. Sivakumar and N. Janakiraman [11] proposes a modified watershed segmentation algorithm for segmenting the ROI from the MRI images. In this pre-processing stage, the input MR image is being pre-processed by high pass filter and then enhanced by the use of Enhanced Canny Edge Detection approach. Then modified watershed segmentation algorithm is performed such that to segment the required ROI. The proposed method is being implemented with Xilinx Virtex-5 FPGA. The proposed method is executed in three phases namely pre-processing, edge detection and segmentation. The authors have compared various methods of k-means clustering and fuzzy-means clustering.

V. Rajinikanth and M. S. Couceiro [12] introduces an optimal multi-level image segmentation using firefly algorithm. The new optimal multi-level image segmentation approach introduced is based on RGB Histogram using Brownian search-based Firefly Algorithm (BFA), Levy search-based Firefly Algorithm (LFA) and Conventional Firefly Algorithm (CFA). The obtained results prove that LFA and FA has faster convergence than BFA.

3   Enhanced Marker-Controlled Watershed Segmentation Algorithm

In this paper, an Enhanced Marker-Controlled watershed algorithm is introduced to segment MRI of the brain and detect its tumor region. In this algorithm, we use gradient magnitude which is used to pre-process the grayscale image before using the Enhanced Marker-Controlled Watershed Segmentation. The gradient is usually high at the borders and low at the inside which means that it'll help in analysing the region of tumor. Markers are used in order to modify the gradient magnitude. The proposed algorithm is mainly used in segmenting MRI images of the brain since the segmentation of cerebral ventricles can also be done with minimal interaction. The major criterion of this proposed algorithm is to locate the region of tumor by using the homogeneity of the grayscale image. The

Enhanced Marker-Controlled Watershed Segmentation algorithm is a region-based and contour detection algorithm which will be implemented based on region-growing in order to avoid over-segmentation. The number of markers used denotes the final number of watershed regions. The markers used in this proposed algorithm employ automatically in order to save human time. The segmentation process is done in six major steps.

The proposed algorithm performs morphological operations such as erosion-based and dilation-based reconstruction in order to mark the regions required for segmentation. The foreground and background markers are super-imposed with the original image. Application of the proposed algorithm helps in segmenting the region of interest.

Original Watershed Segmentation Algorithm uses grayscale images in either 2D or 3D form to proceed with the technique. The enhanced algorithm requires two or more images in order to perform the segmentation. This includes an input image and a mask image. The input image is usually a grayscale image in 2D or 3D form and the mask is the one referred to as the ground truth which is used as a template for the segmentation of the image. The initial step is to Read the Image. It includes RGB to grayscale conversion. It converts the true color RGB into grayscale image. The next step is to use the gradient magnitude as the segmentation function or mask. The gradient is often high at the borders and low at the objects. This mask will be the ground truth for the segmentation to take place. The mask is a binary image of the same dimensions of that of the input image. It performs watershed transform to the gradient magnitude. Once it performs the transform, the next step is to mark the foreground objects. This step includes morphological operations like opening which is an erosion followed by a dilation while opening by reconstruction is an erosion followed by a morphological reconstruction.

These steps are being explained followed by the results and discussion. For the segmentation process, FLAIR images are opted because to supress the cerebrospinal fluid effect on the MR image. Figure 2 denotes the work-flow of the Enhanced Marker-Controlled Watershed Segmentation. Segmentation using Enhanced Marker-Controlled Watershed Segmentation performs much better than the original Watershed Segmentation as it helps in identifying and marking the region of interest (ROI).

Once the foreground objects are being marked, the next step is to compute background markers. It includes the marking of background of the cleaned-up image. Dark pixels in the image belong to the background of the image. The markers used to mark the background are the ones that select to specify markers as binary and needs to be labelled. Once the dark pixels are marked, it is now time to start the process of thresholding operation. Now, it is time to compute the watershed transform of the segmentation function. Watershed Transform is the process of separating different objects based on the brightness of the grayscale image.

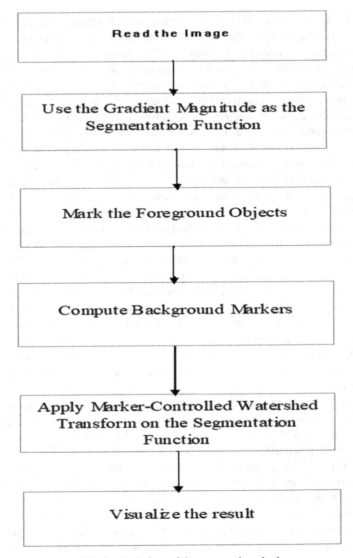

Fig. 2. Work flow of the proposed method

In this proposed algorithm, we introduce Binary markers and the pixel values in this algorithm are treated as elevation points. In this the original or input image is being super-imposed along with the mask or ground truth which will help in obtaining the ROI with greater accuracy. The images in Fig. 4 and its sub-ordinates represent the watershed transform of and the morphological operations that are performed on the gradient magnitude. The final step is to visualize the result which means that to display the label matrix as a color image. It can use transparency to superimpose the pseudo-color label matrix on top of the original intensity image.

The evaluation metrics considered are with the help of parameters like TP, TN, FP and FN where, TP – True Positive, TN – True Negative, FP – False Positive, FN – False Negative.

The evaluation metrics are Accuracy, Precision, Specificity and Sensitivity where each of these metrics are calculated with the help of formulae,

$$Accuracy = \frac{(TP + TN)}{(TP + FP + FN + TN)} \tag{1}$$

$$Precision = \frac{(TP)}{(TP + FP)} \tag{2}$$

$$Specificity = \frac{(TN)}{(TN + FP)} \tag{3}$$

$$Sensitivity = \frac{(TP)}{(TP + FN)} \tag{4}$$

Equation (1–4) denotes the formulae used for evaluating the metrics. The proposed method of enhanced marker-controlled watershed segmentation provides much better and enhanced results compared to that of the original watershed segmentation.

4 Results and Discussion

It has been proven that the Enhanced Marker-controlled Watershed Segmentation provides much better and improved results with an accuracy of about 99.14%, precision of 97.80% and sensitivity and specificity of 88.11% and 99.87% respectively. The watershed transform of the gradient magnitude in order to locate the light and dark pixels as high and low respectively before performing morphological operations. Once an operation is performed, then the result is being reconstructed and super-imposed with the original input image and ground truth in order to provide better and improved accuracy. The technique is used in image processing and segmentation and the software used is MATLAB R2019.

The images in Fig. 3 includes the original MR image and the gradient magnitude of the image. This proposed algorithm can't be directly applied to the gradient magnitude since it leads to over-segmentation. In order to avoid false segmentation, the concept of markers is used to mark the regions that ought to be segmented.

In this algorithm, we use morphological image reconstruction in order to create foreground and background markers. Figure 4 denotes the morphological operations that are performed in order to compute foreground markers that help in tumor region with higher accuracy and better clarity.

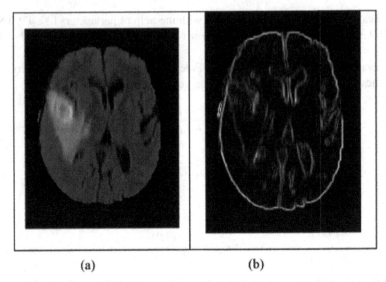

Fig. 3. (a) Original MR image of the brain, (b) Gradient magnitude

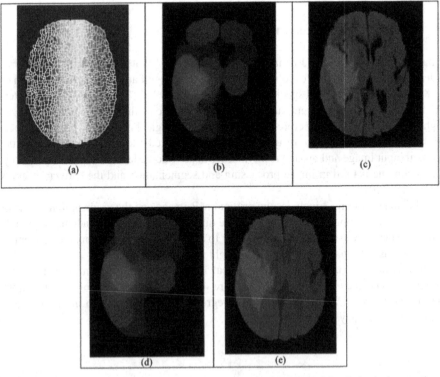

Fig. 4. (a) Watershed transform of the gradient magnitude, (b)–(e) Morphological operations performed on the gradient magnitude

The below Fig. 5 denotes the results of the parametric metrics which will in compare the output of all the given images. Considering various features of an MRI image, it proves that the accuracy of the segmented image is much better when compared to the original segmentation methods. Figure 6 shows the background markers and object boundaries super-imposed on original image that are performed in order to segment the ROI of the MRI image. The metrics of this algorithm is obtained with the help of comparing the image with the ground truth or the provided mask image which is of the same dimension of that of the input image.

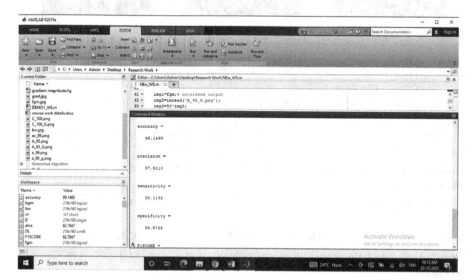

Fig. 5. Screenshot of the output

The below figures display the images where the background of the image is being marked such that it becomes easier to mark the boundaries of the image. Once the background of the image is being marked with the help of markers and then the image is being super-imposed on the original image. The super-imposed image helps in segmenting the tumor region with much accuracy and more clarity.

The below given Table 1 denotes the comparison of evaluated metrics with the previous techniques and algorithms that has been used in image segmentation process. The proposed algorithm provides higher accuracy in predicting the region of tumor and also has much better clarity than the related algorithms.

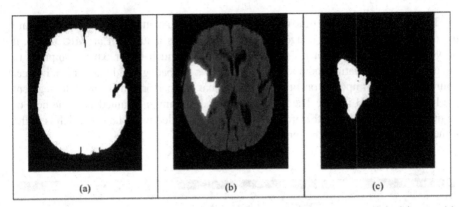

(a)   (b)   (c)

Fig. 6. (a) Background markers, (b) Object boundaries super-imposed on original image, (c) Segmented image

Table 1. Comparison of performance metrics with existing techniques

Methods	Accuracy (%)	Precision (%)	Specificity (%)	Sensitivity (%)
Enhanced Marker-Controlled Watershed Segmentation	*99.14*	*97.80*	88.11	*99.87*
Fully-Automatic Segmentation with ANN [5]	91.48	92.14	94	89
Deep Learning using CNN and RNN [9]	97.31	91.4	92.48	86
Modified Watershed Algorithm with FPGA [11]	98.21	95	84.04	98.82

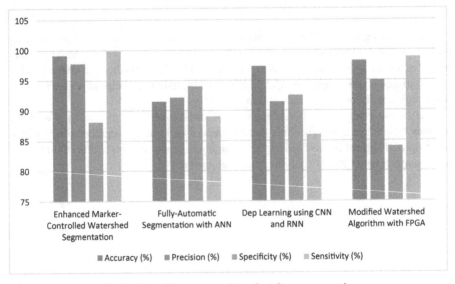

Fig. 7. Pictorial representation of performance metrics

The above Fig. 7 denotes the pictorial representation of performance metrics. This figure helps in comparing the performance metrics of various existing approaches. The concept that sensitivity and specificity are inversely proportional to that of each other, which means that as sensitivity increases, specificity decreases and vice versa. High specificity values means that the output has got few false positive results. If the value of specificity keeps on decreasing, it could result in high number of false positives. Even when tumor is not present, it shows that it is present. Hence, increase in specificity is expected in future work. This automatic watershed segmentation has completed segmenting the tumor region with an accuracy of 99%.

5   Conclusion

Image segmentation is all about segmenting the ROI with better clarity and accuracy of the segmented image. This area has a promising future, since parameters such as precision, specificity and sensitivity needs to be improved each time. The proposed method of Enhanced Marker-Controlled Watershed Algorithm has been studied and has been proven to provide much better results when compared to that of the original Segmentation technique. The evaluation metrics such as accuracy, precision and sensitivity has been shown a drastic increase, thus providing better clarity and accuracy in segmenting the region of tumor. The accuracy of Enhanced Marker-Controlled Watershed Segmentation Algorithm is said to be 99.14% which plays a major role in defining the tumor region in the image.

References

1. Saini, S., Arora, K.: A study analysis on the different image segmentation techniques. Int. J. Inf. Comput. Technol. 4(14), 1445–1452 (2014). ISSN 0974-2239
2. Kannan, S., Gurusamy, V., Nalini, G.: Review on image segmentation techniques. In: National Conference on. Recent Trends and Research. Issues in Computer Science (2014)
3. Rajinikanth, V., Couceiro, M.S.: RGB histogram based color image segmentation using firefly algorithm. In: International Conference on Information and Communication Technologies (ICICT 2014). Elsevier (2014)
4. Kumar, M.J., Kumar, D.G.R., Reddy, R.V.K.: Review on image segmentation techniques. Int. J. Sci. Res. Eng. Technol. (IJSRET) 3(6), 993–997 (2014). ISSN 2278-0882
5. Taneja, A., Ranjan, P., Ujjlayan, A.: A performance study of image segmentation techniques. In: 2015 4th International Conference on Reliability, Infocom Technologies and Optimization (ICRITO) (Trends and Future Directions), pp. 1–6 (2015). https://doi.org/10.1109/ICRITO. 2015.7359305
6. Parihar, A.S.: A study on brain tumor segmentation using convolution neural network. In: 2017 International Conference on Inventive Computing and Informatics (ICICI), pp. 198–201 (2017). https://doi.org/10.1109/ICICI.2017.8365336
7. Angulakshmi, M., Lakshmi Priya, G.G.: Automated brain tumor segmentation techniques. Int. J. Imaging Syst. Technol. **27**, 66–77 (2017)
8. Song, Y., Yan, H.: Image segmentation techniques overview. In: 2017 Asia Modelling Symposium (2017). ISSN 2376-1172, 17990043

9. Arunkumar, N., et al.: Fully automatic model-based segmentation and classification approach for MRI brain tumor using artificial neural networks. Concurr. Comput.: Pract. Exp. **32**(1), e4962 (2018). https://onlinelibrary.wiley.com/toc/15320634/2020/32/1

10. Thivya Roopini, I., Vasanthi, M., Rajinikanth, V., Rekha, M., Sangeetha, M.: Segmentation of tumor from brain MRI using fuzzy entropy and distance regularised level set. In: Nandi, A., Sujatha, N., Menaka, R., Alex, J. (eds.) Computational Signal Processing and Analysis. Lecture Notes in Electrical Engineering, vol. 490. Springer, Singapore (2018). https://doi.org/10.1007/978-981-10-8354-9_27

11. Fernandes, S.L., et al.: A reliable framework for accurate brain image examination and treatment planning based on early diagnosis support for clinicians. Neural Comput. Appl. **32**(20), 15897–15908 (2019)

12. Seo, H., Badiei Khuzani, M., et al.: Machine learning techniques for biomedical image segmentation: An overview of technical aspects and introduction to state-of-art applications. Med. Phys. **47**(5), e148–e167 (2020). ISSN 0094-2405

13. Suresh Manic, K., Hasoon, F.N., Shibli, N.A., Satapathy, S.C., Rajinikanth, V.: An approach to examine brain tumor based on Kapur's Entropy and Chan–Vese algorithm. In: Yang, X.S., Sherratt, S., Dey, N., Joshi, A. (eds.) Third International Congress on Information and Communication Technology. Advances in Intelligent Systems and Computing, vol. 797. Springer, Singapore (2019). https://doi.org/10.1007/978-981-13-1165-9_81

14. Aswathy, S.U., Devadhas, G.G., Kumar, S.S.: A tumour segmentation approach from FLAIR MRI brain images using SVM and genetic algorithm. Int. J. Biomed. Eng. Technol. **33**(4), 386–397 (2020)

15. Devunooru, S., et al.: Deep learning neural networks for medical image segmentation of brain tumours for diagnosis: a recent review and taxonomy. J. Ambient Intell. Humaniz. Comput. **12**(1), 455–483 (2020)

16. Suresha, D., Jagadisha, N., Shrisha, H.S., Kaushik, K.S.: Detection of brain tumor using image processing. In: Proceedings of the Fourth International Conference on Computing Methodologies and Communication (ICCMC 2020). IEEE Xplore (2020). Part Number: CFP20K25-ART; ISBN: 978-1-7281-4889-2

17. Kaur, P., Chaira, T.: A novel fuzzy approach for segmenting medical images. Soft Comput. **25**(5), 3565–3575 (2021)

18. Sivakumar, V., Janakiraman, N.: A novel method for segmenting brain tumor using modified watershed algorithm in MRI image with FPGA. BioSystems **198**, 104226 (2020)

19. Arunmozhi, S., Sivagurunathan, G., et al.: A study on brain tumor extraction using various segmentation techniques. In: 2020 International Conference on System, Computation, Automation and Networking (ICSCAN), 20200194 (2020)

20. Rajinikanth, V., Kadry, S., Nam, Y.: Convolutional-neural-network assisted segmentation and SVM classification of brain tumor in clinical MRI slices. Inf. Technol. Control **50**(2), 342–356 (2021)

Computational Intelligence
in Communication

GSA Based FOPID Controller Tuning in NSOF Domain for a Class of Nonlinear Systems

Debasish Biswas[1]([✉])[iD], Kaushik Das Sharma[2][iD], and Gautam Sarkar[2]

[1] Department of Electrical Engineering, Techno International New Town, Kolkata 700156, India
debasish.biswas@tict.edu.in
[2] Department of Applied Physics, University of Calcutta, Kolkata 700009, India
kdsaphy@caluniv.ac.in

Abstract. The objective of this paper is to reveal the implementation technique of fractional order proportional, integral and derivative (FOPID) controller for the class of nonlinear systems and its tuning method via the gravitation search algorithm (GSA) in a tracking control. The proposed method utilizes the continuous surface of the FOPID controller to deal with the effect of nonlinearities in the plant. The class of non-linear integer order plant with FOPID controller results in a fractional-order dynamic system. The fractional-order dynamics are transformed into an algebraic vector-matrix equation using the non-sinusoidal orthogonal function (NSOF) set. The FOPID controller is tuned via GSA in the NSOF domain for a benchmark simulation case study to validate the proposed scheme.

Keywords: FOPID controller · Gravitation search algorithm (GSA) · Non-linear dynamics · Non-sinusoidal orthogonal function (NSOF)

1 Introduction

PID controllers are the most successful controller to meet the performance specification, but their performance degrades due to discontinuity in phase lead or lag [1–10]. The FOPID controller can meet the performance specification as fractional order derivative, and integral controller provides continuous phase lag and phase lead respectively [11,12]. But in the presence of fractional order controller, the overall system dynamics of any output feedback-based system becomes fractional-order. This paper proposes a FOPID controller tuning technique in an output feedback-based tracking control system for a class of nonlinear plants to minimize the tracking error.

The fractional order PID controller may be a good choice in comparison to the PID controller, but the implementation method of fractional order derivative (D) and integral (I) controller includes non-causal convolution integral and thus increases the complexity [13–15] in calculation. The generalized form of PID

S. Mukhopadhyay et al. (Eds.): CICBA 2022, CCIS 1579, pp. 169–182, 2022.
https://doi.org/10.1007/978-3-031-10766-5_13

controller is the $PI^{\lambda}D^{\beta}$ controller and $\lambda < 0$ and $\beta > 0$. The PID controller has four distinct points of operation: P, PI, PD, PID, and FOPID controller can have any value in the plane. So, the degree of freedom increases for the designer as there are two additional parameters (λ, β) are involved for fine-tuning [16]. Many analytic rules are available for tuning the FOPID controller, like tuning by phase margin, gain margin, iso-damping, method of dominant poles, internal model control etc. [16]. Specifications integral absolute error-IAE, like integral squared error-ISE, integral time multiplied absolute error-ITAE are considered as the cost functions for tuning the FOPID controller to provide better performance [16]. In output feedback based tracking control with fractional order PID controller for the nonlinear plants, the swarm-based optimization techniques are most suitable to tune parameter of the fractional order PID controller efficiently [17]. These intelligent techniques do not guarantee convergence but include wide search space [17]. So, they can find a solution which is best among the least. Moreover, the members of the NSOF domain like Sample and Hold Function-SHF, Triangular Function-TF, Hybrid Function (HF) [18–20] can be used to implement the FOPID controller.

The novelty of the proposed strategy is the formulation and tuning of the NSOF domain based fractional order PID controller using GSA for a class of nonlinear plants. The NSOF domain transformation technique is used to solve the dynamics numerically and derive the stability condition. The parameters of the FOPID controller are tuned for an inverted pendulum on the cart system.

The major contributions of this paper are:

- the plant dynamics along with the FOPID controller is transformed to HF domain and it becomes algebraic vector-matrix equation.
- The GSA is implemented to tune the parameters of fractional order PID controller to minimize the tracking error.

The rest of the paper is arranged as follows: For a class of non-linear plants, the problem of minimization of tracking error with FOPID controller is formulated in Sect. 2. The description of NSOF domain-based FOPID controller and closed-loop dynamics is discussed in Sect. 3. The tuning technique of HF domain based FOPID controller using GSA is discussed in Sect. 4. In Sect. 5, proposed controller design technique is validated using simulations studies, and finally the conclusion is presented in Sect. 6.

2   Problem Formulation

Let control objective is to design a FOPID control law for a nth order nonlinear plants given as [17]

$$\left.\begin{array}{l} \boldsymbol{x}^{(n)}(t) = f(\boldsymbol{x}(t)) + bu(t) \\ y(t) = x(t) \end{array}\right\} \tag{1}$$

where, the non-linearity in system defines in $f(.)$ is an function of $\boldsymbol{x}(t) \in \mathbb{R}^{n \times 1}$, $u(t) \in \mathbb{R}$ is the control signal, and $y(t) \in \mathbb{R}$ output of the plant, and $b(> 0)$

is an unknown constant. The state vector for the nth order plant is $\boldsymbol{x}(t) = \left[x_1(t), x_2(t), \cdots, x_n(t)\right]^T = \left[x(t), \dot{x}(t), \cdots, x^n(t)\right]^T \in \mathbb{R}^{n \times 1}$.

Here, $u(t)$ - the control signal should be such that, output of the plant $y(t)$ will follow a bounded reference signal $r(t)$. To guarantee the closed-loop stability of the system all other closed-loop variables are bounded. So that, $e(t) = y(t) - r(t)$ - the tracking error is minimum and the dynamics is asymptotically stable.

The control law to fulfil the above said control objective with a fractional order PID controller for the plant in (1) is the following:

$$u(t) = \frac{1}{b}[-f(\boldsymbol{x}(t)) + u_{FOPID}(t)] \tag{2}$$

where, $u_{FOPID}(t)$ is the control signal to take care of the transient and steady state performance of the dynamics. Now, assuming proportional controller gain is K_P, integral controller gain is K_I and derivative controller gain is K_D, ideal control is given as:

$$u^*(t) = \frac{1}{b}[-f(\boldsymbol{x}(t)) + K_p^* e(t) + K_I^* \mathscr{D}^{\lambda^*} e(t) + K_D^* \mathscr{D}^{\beta^*} e(t)] \tag{3}$$

where, $\lambda < 0$, $\beta > 0$ and $\mathscr{D}^{\lambda^*}$ is the integration operator with order λ^* and $\mathscr{D}^{\beta^*}$ is the derivative operator of order β^*, and $K_P^*, K_I^*, K_D^*, \lambda^*, \beta^*$ are known.

The ideal control law of (3) guarantees the perfect tracking, i.e., if $\lim_{t \to \infty} e(t) = 0$. The closed-loop dynamic system in (1) can be written as:

$$\dot{\boldsymbol{X}}(t) = \boldsymbol{A}\boldsymbol{X}(t) + \boldsymbol{B}[f(\boldsymbol{x}) + bu^*(t)] \tag{4}$$

where,

$$\boldsymbol{A} = \begin{bmatrix} 0 & 1 & 0 & \cdots & 0 \\ 0 & 0 & 1 & \cdots & 0 \\ \vdots & \vdots & \vdots & \ddots & \vdots \\ 0 & 0 & 0 & \cdots & 1 \\ 0 & 0 & 0 & \cdots & 0 \end{bmatrix}_{[n \times n]}, \boldsymbol{B} = \begin{bmatrix} 0 \\ 0 \\ 0 \\ \vdots \\ 1 \end{bmatrix}_{[n \times 1]}$$

The closed loop system are globally asymptotically stable when the tracking error $e(t)$ tends to zero, all closed-loop variable are uniformly bounded and $u_{FOPID}(t) \leq M_u < \infty$, where M_u is set by the designer. The objective is to tune the parameters of the fractional order PID controller for the dynamics in (1). For plant in (1), $f(.)$, b are not known in many practical situations.

3   Operators of Non-Sinusoidal Orthogonal Function Domain

A complete set of non-sinusoidal orthogonal function (NSOF) can represent a time function to a tolerable degree of accuracy. Let $S_n(t)$ is a complete set of non-sinusoidal orthogonal function. Then in a time interval $[0, T)$, the time function $f(t) = \sum_{j=0}^{\infty} f_j S_j(t)$ where, f_j s are the coefficients to the jth member of the orthogonal function. Now, with a large value of m for practical realization, $f(t) = \sum_{j=0}^{m} f_j S_j(t)$. The coefficients f_j are calculated so that the mean integral squared error (MISE) is minimum.

3.1 Hybrid Function Set

One of the member of NSOF domain is the hybrid function (HF) set. The hybrid function set is a combination of SHF set and TF set. A set of SHF function, with m number of component functions, can be defined as [19]

$$
S_j(t) = \begin{cases} 1, & jh \le t < (j+1)h \\ \\ 0, & \text{otherwise} \end{cases} \tag{5}
$$

where, $j = 0, 1, \cdots, (m-1)$.

A set of TF, with m number of component functions, can be defined as [19]

$$
T_j(t) = \begin{cases} \frac{(t-jh)}{h}, & jh \le t < (j+1)h \\ \\ 0, & \text{otherwise} \end{cases} \tag{6}
$$

where, $i = 0, 1, \cdots, (m-1)$.

Now, using the SHF and TF function sets, the definition of HF set is as follows:

A square integrable function $f(t)$ of the Lebesgue measure can be represented into hybrid function HF($m$term) series with the help of SHF and TF set [18]. In time interval $[0, T)$, the HF series of $f(t)$ is as follows:

$$
f(t) \approx \begin{bmatrix} d_0 & d_1 & \cdots & d_i & \cdots & d_{(m-1)} \end{bmatrix} \boldsymbol{S}_{(m)}(t) + \begin{bmatrix} b_0 & b_1 & \cdots & b_i & \cdots & b_{(m-1)} \end{bmatrix} \boldsymbol{T}_{(m)}(t) \tag{7}
$$

where, $d_i \triangleq f(ih)$, $b_i \triangleq f[(i+1)h] - f(ih)$, $b_i = d_{(i+1)} - d_i$. In vector matrix form of, the hybrid function series of $f(t)$ in (7) is given below:

$$
f(t) = \boldsymbol{F}_S^T \boldsymbol{S}_{(m)}(t) + \boldsymbol{F}_T^T \boldsymbol{T}_{(m)}(t) \tag{8}
$$

where, $\boldsymbol{F}_S \in \mathbb{R}^{m \times 1}$ is weighting coefficient of $f(t)$ in SHF domain and $\boldsymbol{F}_T \in \mathbb{R}^{m \times 1}$ is weighting coefficient of $f(t)$ in TF domain.

3.2 Operational Matrix in HF Domain

Integer or fractional order integration or differentiation can be evaluated using the Grunwarld-Letnikov (GL) method based on the backward difference technique [13]. Whereas fractional integration using Reimann-Louville (RL) technique and fractional derivative using the Caputo method are based on casual convolution [13]. These above said numerical techniques could be inserted time delay in system dynamics and increase the processing time. Besides this, using the definition of integration or derivative, we can find a FO-operational matrix for integration or differentiation in the hybrid function domain to avoid complicating conventional fractional-order techniques. The nth order derivative of the function $f(t)$ using forward difference method is the following:

$$_a\mathscr{D}_t^n \triangleq \lim_{h\to 0} h^{-n} \sum_{k=0}^{m} (-1)^{-k} \frac{\Gamma(n+1)}{\Gamma(n-k+1)\Gamma(k+1)} f\left(t + (m-k)h\right) \qquad (9)$$

where, n is positive integer, with a lower limit a and an upper limit T, we have, $\Gamma(.)$, is the gamma function and $\left(\frac{T-a}{m}\right) = h$.

Considering α is arbitrary number, differintegral of the function $f(t)$ is

$$_a\mathscr{D}_T^\alpha f(t) \approx \lim_{h\to 0} h^{-\alpha} \sum_{k=0}^{m} (-1)^k p_j f\left(t + (\alpha - j)h\right]) \qquad (10)$$

where,

$$\zeta_k = \begin{cases} \dfrac{\Gamma(\alpha+k)}{\Gamma(\alpha)\Gamma(k+1)}, & \alpha \text{ is negative} \\[3mm] (-1)^{-k}\dfrac{\Gamma(\alpha+1)}{\Gamma(\alpha-k+1)\Gamma(k+1)}, & \alpha \text{ is positive} \end{cases}$$

here, $\infty \le \alpha \le \infty$. with $(m+1)$ number of samples in the interval $[a, T)$, differintegral of $f(t)$ in matrix form is given below:

$$_a\mathscr{D}_T^\alpha f(t) = h^{-\alpha} \begin{bmatrix} d_0 \\ d_1 \\ \vdots \\ d_{(m-1)} \end{bmatrix}^T \begin{bmatrix} \zeta_0 & \zeta_1 & \zeta_2 & \cdots & \zeta_{m-2} & \zeta_{m-1} \\ 0 & \zeta_0 & \zeta_1 & \cdots & \zeta_{m-3} & \zeta_{m-2} \\ 0 & 0 & p_0 & \cdots & p_{m-3} & p_{m-4} \\ \vdots & \vdots & \vdots & \ddots & \vdots & \vdots \\ 0 & 0 & 0 & \cdots & \zeta_0 & \zeta_1 \\ 0 & 0 & 0 & \cdots & 0 & \zeta_0 \end{bmatrix}$$

$$+ h^{-\alpha} \begin{bmatrix} b_0 \\ b_1 \\ \vdots \\ b_{(m-1)} \end{bmatrix}^T \begin{bmatrix} \zeta_{10} & \zeta_{21} & \zeta_{32} & \cdots & \zeta_{(m-1)(m-2)} & \zeta_{(m)(m-1)} \\ 0 & \zeta_{10} & \zeta_{21} & \cdots & \zeta_{(m-2)(m-3)} & \zeta_{(m-1)(m-2)} \\ 0 & 0 & \zeta_{10} & \cdots & \zeta_{(m-2)(m-3)} & \zeta_{(m-3)(m-4)} \\ \vdots & \vdots & \vdots & \ddots & \vdots & \vdots \\ 0 & 0 & 0 & \cdots & \zeta_{10} & \zeta_{21} \\ 0 & 0 & 0 & \cdots & 0 & \zeta_{10} \end{bmatrix} \qquad (11)$$

where, $\zeta_{ji} = \zeta_j - \zeta_i, i = 0,1,2,3,\cdots,(m-1)$ and $j = 1,2,3,\cdots,m$. Now, the expression of differintegral of the $f(t)$ in hybrid function domain in-terms of operational matrix operator is

$$_a\mathscr{D}_T^\alpha f(t) \approx \boldsymbol{F}_S^T \mathscr{D}_S^\alpha \boldsymbol{S}_{(m)}(t) + \boldsymbol{F}_T^T \mathscr{D}_T^\alpha \boldsymbol{T}_{(m)}(t) \qquad (12)$$

where $\mathscr{D}_S^\alpha$ and $\mathscr{D}_T^\alpha$ are the differintegral operational matrices of an order α, in SHF and TF domain respectively.

4   Design of FOPID Controller

PID controller is widely used to achieved desire transient specification and reduce
the steady-state error. Intelligent tuning techniques of PID parameters provide
a minimum error if the integral and derivative operators of the PID controller
are realized efficiently. Here, the FOPID controller is expressed in NSOF domain
using integral and derivative operational matrices. The accuracy of the controller
is high if the number of the component in NSOF domain is large. After incorporating the FOPID controller in the closed-loop dynamics, the overall system
dynamics in the NSOF domain is simulated to find the parameters of the FOPID
controller.

4.1   FOPID Controller in NSOF Domain

In the tracking control system, FOPID controller in the feedforward path is
used to stabilize the system and minimize the tracking error in terms of IAE.
The bounded input and output signal of the generalized controller are $e(t)$, $u(t)$,
respectively. The control law from the fractional order PID controller is

$$u_{FOPID}(t) = u_P(t) + u_I(t) + u_D(t) \tag{13}$$

where, $u_P(t)$ represents the proportional controller, $u_I(t)$ represents integral controller, and $u_D(t)$ represents derivative controller. Now, generalised form of the
fractional order PID controller from (13) is given as:

$$u_{FOPID}(t) = K_P e(t) + K_I \mathscr{D}_t^\lambda e(t) + K_D \mathscr{D}_t^\beta e(t) \tag{14}$$

The hybrid function domain representation of the fractional order PID controller
in (14) is given as:

$$\boldsymbol{U}_S^T \boldsymbol{S}(t) + \boldsymbol{U}_T^T \boldsymbol{T}(t) = (\boldsymbol{U}_{PS}^T + \boldsymbol{U}_{IS}^T + \boldsymbol{U}_{DS}^T)\boldsymbol{S}(t) + (\boldsymbol{U}_{PT}^T + \boldsymbol{U}_{IT}^T + \boldsymbol{U}_{DT}^T)\boldsymbol{T}(t)$$
$$= \boldsymbol{E}_S^T(K_P I + K_I \mathscr{D}_S^\alpha + K_D \mathscr{D}_S^\beta)\boldsymbol{S}(t) + \boldsymbol{E}_T^T(K_P I + K_I \mathscr{D}_T^\alpha + K_D \mathscr{D}_T^\beta)\boldsymbol{T}(t) \tag{15}$$

where, $\boldsymbol{U}_S \in \mathbb{R}^{(m \times 1)}$ is SHF term and $\boldsymbol{U}_T \in \mathbb{R}^{(m \times 1)}$ TF term of $u_{FOPID}(t)$,
respectively. $\boldsymbol{E}_S \in \mathbb{R}^{(m \times 1)}$ is SHF term and $\boldsymbol{E}_T \in \mathbb{R}^{(m \times 1)}$ TF term of $e(t)$,
respectively. $\boldsymbol{U}_{PS} \in \mathbb{R}^{(m \times 1)}, \boldsymbol{U}_{IS} \in \mathbb{R}^{(m \times 1)}, \boldsymbol{U}_{DS} \in \mathbb{R}^{(m \times 1)}$ is SHF term and
$\boldsymbol{U}_{PT} \in \mathbb{R}^{(m \times 1)}, \boldsymbol{U}_{IT} \in \mathbb{R}^{(m \times 1)}, \boldsymbol{U}_{DT} \in \mathbb{R}^{(m \times 1)}$ TF term of proportional, integral
and derivative controller respectively.

Now, assuming $m = 2$, the internal structure of the FOPID controller can be
written using (15) and it becomes:

$$\boldsymbol{U}_{S_{(2)}}^T \boldsymbol{S}_{(2)}(t) + \boldsymbol{U}_{T_{(2)}}^T \boldsymbol{T}_{(2)}(t)$$
$$= \begin{bmatrix} e_{S0} \\ e_{S1} \end{bmatrix}^T \begin{bmatrix} K_p + \zeta_{\alpha 0} K_I h_F^\alpha + \zeta_{\beta 0} K_D h_F^\beta & \zeta_{\alpha 1} K_I h_F^\alpha + \zeta_{\beta 1} K_D h_F^\beta \\ 0 & K_p + \zeta_{\alpha 0} K_I h_F^\alpha + \zeta_{\beta 0} K_D h_F^\beta \end{bmatrix}$$
$$+ \begin{bmatrix} e_{T0} \\ e_{T1} \end{bmatrix}^T \begin{bmatrix} K_p + \zeta_{\alpha 10} K_I h_F^\alpha + \zeta_{\beta 10} K_D h_F^\beta & p_{\alpha 21} K_I h_F^\alpha + \zeta_{\beta 21} K_D h_F^\beta \\ 0 & K_p + \zeta_{\alpha 10} K_I h_F^\alpha + \zeta_{\beta 10} K_D h_F^\beta \end{bmatrix} \tag{16}$$

where, $\zeta_{\alpha i}$ with $i = 0, 1$ are components of integral controller operational matrix in SHF domain, $\zeta_{\beta i}$ with $i = 0, 1$ are components of derivative controller operational matrix in TF domain, $\zeta_{\alpha j i}$ with $i = 0, 1$, and $j = 1, 2$ are components of integral controller operational matrix in TF domain, and $\zeta_{\beta j i}$ with $i = 0, 1$, and $j = 1, 2$ are components of derivative controller operational matrix in TF domain. Then, the expression of control signal in HF domain is as follows:

$$\boldsymbol{U}_{S_{(2)}}^T \boldsymbol{S}_{(2)}(t) + \boldsymbol{U}_{T_{(2)}}^T \boldsymbol{T}_{(2)}(t) = \boldsymbol{E}_{S_{(2)}}^T \boldsymbol{W}_{S(2\times2)} \boldsymbol{S}_{(2)}(t) + \boldsymbol{E}_{T_{(2)}}^T \boldsymbol{W}_{T(2\times2)} \boldsymbol{T}_{(2)}(t) \quad (17)$$

where, $\boldsymbol{W}_{S(2\times2)}$ is fractional order PID controller operational matrix in SHF domain, and $\boldsymbol{W}_{T(2\times2)}$ is fractional order PID controller operational matrix in TF domain.

Now, when HF domain component functions is m, SHF and TF component of the control signal in (13) can be written as:

$$\left. \begin{array}{l} U_S = \boldsymbol{E}_S^T \boldsymbol{W}_{S_{(m)}} \\ U_T = \boldsymbol{E}_T^T \boldsymbol{W}_{T_{(m)}} \end{array} \right\} \quad (18)$$

where, $\boldsymbol{W}_{S_{(m)}}$ and $\boldsymbol{W}_{T_{(m)}}$ are the mth column of $\boldsymbol{W}_{S_{(m\times m)}}$ and $\boldsymbol{W}_{T_{(m\times m)}}$ respectively.

In the next subsection, we will represent the error dynamics in HF domain.

4.2   System Dynamics in NSOF Domain

The error dynamics of the closed-loop system for a special class of nonlinear plants in (1) with fractional order PID controller is the following:

$$\dot{e}(t) = \boldsymbol{A}e(t) + \boldsymbol{B}(u^*(t) - u_{FOPID}(t)) \quad (19)$$

The time domain dynamics of (19) in NSOF domain can be written as:

$$\begin{aligned} &\boldsymbol{G}_S \boldsymbol{S}(t) + \boldsymbol{G}_S \boldsymbol{T}(t) \\ =&\boldsymbol{A}(\boldsymbol{E}_S \boldsymbol{S}(t) + \boldsymbol{E}_T \boldsymbol{T}(t)) + \boldsymbol{B}(\boldsymbol{U}_S^* \boldsymbol{S}(t) + \boldsymbol{U}_T^* \boldsymbol{T}(t))(\boldsymbol{U}_{FOPID_S} \boldsymbol{S}(t) + \boldsymbol{U}_{FOPID_T} \boldsymbol{T}(t)) \end{aligned} \quad (20)$$

where, $\boldsymbol{G}_S, \boldsymbol{G}_T, \boldsymbol{E}_S, \boldsymbol{E}_T, \boldsymbol{U}_{FOPID_S}, \boldsymbol{U}_{FOPID_T} \in \mathbb{R}^{m\times1}$ are the weighting coefficient of the rate vector, state vector, the control vector, in the NSOHF domain, respectively.

Now, equating the error dynamics coefficient from SHF and TF domain

$$\left. \begin{array}{l} \boldsymbol{G}_S = \boldsymbol{E}_S \mathscr{D}_S^1 = \boldsymbol{A}\boldsymbol{E}_S \boldsymbol{S}(t) + \boldsymbol{B}\boldsymbol{E}_{1S}(\boldsymbol{W}_S^* - \boldsymbol{W}_{FOPID_S})\boldsymbol{S}(t) \\ \boldsymbol{G}_T = \boldsymbol{E}_T \mathscr{D}_T^1 = \boldsymbol{A}\boldsymbol{E}_T \boldsymbol{T}(t) + \boldsymbol{B}\boldsymbol{E}_{1T}(\boldsymbol{W}_T^* - \boldsymbol{W}_{FOPID_T})\boldsymbol{T}(t) \end{array} \right\} \quad (21)$$

where, $\boldsymbol{W}_S^* \in \mathbb{R}^{(m\times m)}$, $\boldsymbol{W}_T^* \in \mathbb{R}^{(m\times m)}$, $\boldsymbol{W}_{FOPID_S} \in \mathbb{R}^{(m\times m)}$, $\boldsymbol{W}_{FOPID_T} \in \mathbb{R}^{(m\times m)}$.

In the following subsection, we will apply Lyapunov stability analysis technique in HF domain to derive the asymptotic stability condition of the closed loop system.

4.3 Stability Analysis

Let us define the Lyapunov function for the system in (19) [21] as:

$$V_e(t) = \frac{1}{2} e^T P e \qquad (22)$$

where, the Lyapunov equation is $PA + A^T P = -Q$ with a positive definite matrix P. Here Q is a positive definite or semi-definite matrix. in hybrid function domain, the Lyapunov function is as follows:

$$V_{eS} S(t) + V_{eT} T(t) = \frac{1}{2} [E_S^T S(t) + E_T^T T(t)]^T P [E_S^T S(t) + E_T^T T(t)] \qquad (23)$$

Applying the lemma 2 from [20], we can write:

$$V_{eS} S(t) + V_{eT} T(t) = diag(E_S^T P E_S) S(t) + diag(E_T^T P E_S) T(t)$$
$$+ diag(E_S^T P E_T) T(t) + diag(E_T^T P E_T) T(t) \qquad (24)$$

where, weighting coefficients of the Lyapunov function are V_{eS} and V_{eT} in the SHF and TF domain. In the hybrid function domain, the rate of change of Lyapunov function is as follows:

$$V_{eS} \mathscr{D}_S^1 S(t) + V_{eT} \mathscr{D}_T^1 T(t)$$
$$= 0.5 (E_S \mathscr{D}_S^1 S(t) + E_T \mathscr{D}_T^1 T(t))^T P (E_S S(t) + E_T T(t))$$
$$+ 0.5 (E_S S(t) + E_T T(t))^T P (E_S \mathscr{D}_S^1 S(t) + E_T \mathscr{D}_T^1 T(t)) \qquad (25)$$

Now, putting the value from Eq. (21), we get following expression [21]:

$$V_{eS} \mathscr{D}_S^1 S(t) + V_{eT} \mathscr{D}_T^1 T(t)$$
$$= diag(E_S^T (A^T P + P A) E_S) S(t) + diag(E_S P B (U_S^* - U_{FOPIDs})) S(t)$$
$$+ diag(E_T^T (A^T P + P A) E_S) T(t) + diag(E_T P B (U_S^* - U_{FOPIDs})) T(t)$$
$$+ diag(E_S^T (A^T P + P A) E_T) T(t) + diag(E_S P B (U_T^* - U_{FOPID_T})) T(t)$$
$$+ diag(E_T^T (A^T P + P A) E_T) T(t) + diag(E_T P B (U_T^* - U_{FOPID_T})) T(t) \qquad (26)$$

The rate of change of Lyapunov function in terms of FOPID controller operational matrix is as follows:

$$V_{eS} \mathscr{D}_S^1 S(t) + V_{eT} \mathscr{D}_T^1 T(t)$$
$$= diag(E_S^T (-Q) E_S) S(t) + diag(E_S P B E_{1S} (W_S^* - W_{FOPIDs})) S(t)$$
$$+ diag(E_T^T (-Q) E_S) T(t) + diag(E_T P B E_{1S} (W_S^* - W_{FOPIDs})) T(t)$$
$$+ diag(E_S^T (-Q) E_T) T(t) + diag(E_S P B E_{1T} (W_T^* - W_{FOPID_T})) T(t)$$
$$+ diag(E_T^T (-Q) E_T) T(t) + diag(E_T P B E_{1T} (W_T^* - W_{FOPID_T})) T(t) \qquad (27)$$

The continuous-time representation of (27) in terms of quasi-continuous equation is the following:

$$\frac{dV_e(t)}{dt} = -0.5e^T(t)\boldsymbol{Q}e(t) + e^T(t)\boldsymbol{PB}e(t)(w^*(t) - w_{FOPID}(t)) \qquad (28)$$

With a proper choice of $K_P, K_I, K_D, \lambda,$ and β, the term $w^*(t) - w_{FOPID}(t)$ becomes zero and thus, resulting $\dot{V}_e(t) < 0$. It implies that the tracking error $e(t) \approx 0$. Then the Eq. (28) becomes

$$\frac{dV_e(t)}{dt} = -0.5e^T(t)\boldsymbol{Q}e(t) \leq 0 \qquad (29)$$

Now, applying the Barbalat's lemma, the overall closed-loop systems become asymptotically stable.

5   Tuning of FOPID Controller via GSA

5.1   Gravitational Search Algorithm

Rashedi, Nezamabadi-pour and Saryazdi [22] introduced the GSA algorithm. This technique is based on the law of gravitation. In this population-based search algorithm, search agents are a collection of masses. Using the gravitational forces, the isolated masses are transferring information among them to find optimal fitness values. GSA follows the two common aspects of meta-heuristic techniques: exploration and exploitation. A trade-off between these two aspects is the indication of high performance of search algorithm.

In this algorithm, the masses are considered as objects. They are communicating each other by the law of gravity through the gravitational force considering the exploitation. After defining the position of the masses, the gravitation forces and accelerations are calculated using active and passive masses. The forces on each object are modified by incorporating some stochastic characteristics, and the accelerations are re-calculated based on updated force and inertial mass. The velocity and positions are now updated to find the IAE of fitness function and continued based stopping criterion. See [22,23] for a detailed iteration scheme and formulae.

5.2   PID Controller Tuning

Due to this simple logical algorithm, GSA is selected to tune the fractional order PID controller parameters to minimize the IAE for a tracking control system with a special class of nonlinear plants. In GSA algorithm, the proportional gain (K_P), the derivative gain (K_D) and the integral gain (K_I), the order of the integral controller (λ) and the order of the derivative controller (β) of the fractional order PID controller are considered as agents of the algorithm. The characteristics of the individual gain take the value of the fitness function towards the optimal value. The calculated forces among the agents of FOPID parameters

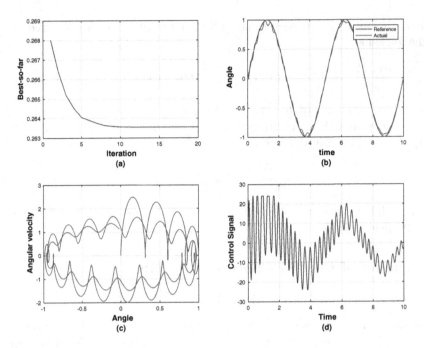

Fig. 1. A Graphical analysis of GSA based tuning of conventional FOPID controller for inverted pendulum (a) Evaluation curve of IAE using GSA (b) Phase response (c) Phase portrait between position of the pendulum and its velocity (d) Control signal.

is considered as information sharing among the agents, and the parameters are updated based on the performance of the agents.

Tuning of the FOPID controller parameters using GSA involves the following steps:

a. Define the search space for fractional order PID parameters.
b. Randomly initialize FOPID parameters (agent) inside the search space considering exploration.
c. Find the IAE (fitness evaluation of agents) for that tracking control system.
d. Calculate the best and worst parameters of the FOPID controller based on their fitness value.
e. Transfer the information (calculation of forces among the agents) between the FOPID parameters.
f. Update the parameters of the FOPID controller (position, acceleration and velocity).
g. Repeat the step c to f until stop criteria is reached.

In the following section, implementation of different variant of the FOPID controller for inverted pendulum system and the analysis are discussed.

6   Simulation Results

We have implemented the conventional FOPID and NSOHF domain-based
FOPID control law for an inverted pendulum. The dynamics of the plant is
described as:

$$\dot{x}_1(t) = x_2(t)$$
$$\dot{x}_2(t) = \frac{(M+m)g sinx_1 - mlx_2(t)sinx_1cosx_1}{mlcos^2x_1 - \frac{4l}{3}(M+m)} - \frac{cosx_1}{mlcos^2x_1 - \frac{4l}{3}(M+m)}u(t)$$

$$(30)$$

where $x_1(t)$ is measure of angle from vertical axis, $x_2(t)$ is the angular velocity of
pendulum, $u(t)$ is the input voltage applied to the motor. The system parameters
are: m is the mass of pendulum, M is the mass of the cart, $2l$ is the length of
pendulum. g is the acceleration due to gravity. In this case study, the system
parameters are $M = 1$ Kg, $m = 0.1$ Kg. The reference signal is $r(t) = sin(2\pi t/5)$.

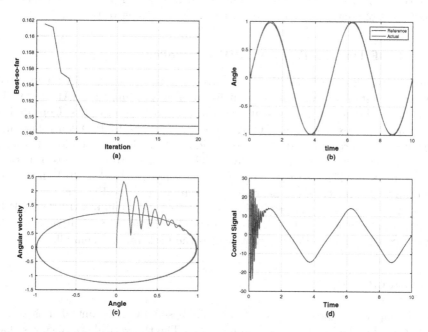

Fig. 2. Graphical analysis of GSA based tuning of NSOHF domain-based FOPID
controller for inverted pendulum (a) Evaluation curve of IAE using GSA (b) Phase
response (c) Phase portrait between position of the pendulum and its velocity (d)
Control signal.

Table 1. Performance of different variants of the FOPID controller using GSA.

Sl. no.	Controller	IAE
1	Conventional PID	2.9874
2	Conventional FOPID	0.2687
3	NSOF domain based PID	2.5439
4	NSOF domain based FOPID	0.1490

6.1   Conventional FOPID Controller

The inverted pendulum in (30) is subjected to track the reference signal using a conventional FOPID controller. GSA based tuning techniques with 10 agents and 20 iterations for 10 s provides a minimum tracking error of 0.2687. The evaluation of IAE using GSA is shown in Fig. 1(a). The Fig. 1(b) is showing the tracking performance of the pendulum. Although, the tracking performance is giving IAE value is equal to 0.2687 but the velocity profile $(x_2(t))$ is oscillatory in nature which evident from the phase portrait in Fig. 1(c). As a result the smoothness of control signal is not satisfactory according to the Fig. 1(d).

6.2   NSOF Domain-Based FOPID Controller

Here, the HF domain based FOPID controller is tuned using GSA for inverted pendulum system in (30) with output feedback to minimize the IAE for tracking a sinusoidal signal, $r(t) = sin(2\pi t/5)$ in time interval of 0–10 s. Considering exploration and exploitation of GSA is used to tune the FOPID controller, and the number of iteration is 20. Figure 2(a) and Fig. 2(d) shows closed-loop tracking response and control signal, respectively. The tracking error in terms of performance index in this case is 0.1490. The phase portrait of Fig. 2(a) shows the uniformity of velocity of the pendulum as compared to the Fig. 1(c).

GSA based conventional PID/FOPID and NSOF domain based PID/FOPID tuning results in terms of IAE are listed in Table 1 for comparative study. It shows NSOHF domain FOPID controller is the best among them all.

7   Conclusion

In this paper, the proposed NSOF domain based FOPID controller is tuned using GSA for the inverted pendulum system. The theoretical study shows that proper selection of NSOF domain component function with GSA algorithm can provide bounded signal for asymptotic stability. The evaluation of IAE using other variants of PID controller also studied here for the for inverted pendulum on cart, and NSOF domain based FOPID controller substantiates its superiority.

References

1. Hagglund, T., Astrom, K.J.: PID controllers: theory, design, and tuning. ISA-The Instrumentation, Systems, and Automation Society (1995)
2. Kiong, T.K., Qing-Guo, W., Chieh, H.C., Hägglund, T.J.: Advances in PID Control. Springer, London (1999). https://doi.org/10.1007/978-1-4471-0861-0
3. Åström, K.J., Hägglund, T.: The future of PID control. Control. Eng. Pract. **9**(11), 1163–1175 (2001)
4. Åström, K.J.: Autonomous controllers. Control. Eng. Pract. **1**(2), 227–232 (1993)
5. Åström, K.J., Hang, C.C., Persson, P., Ho, W.K.: Towards intelligent PID control. Automatica **28**(1), 1–9 (1992)
6. Viola, J., Angel, L.: Delta parallel robotic manipulator tracking control using fractional order controllers. IEEE Lat. Am. Trans. **17**(03), 393–400 (2019)
7. Bertsias, P., et al.: Design of operational amplifier based fractional-order controller for a maglev system. In: 2020 43rd International Conference on Telecommunications and Signal Processing (TSP), pp. 221–224. IEEE (2020)
8. Dimeas, I., Petras, I., Psychalinos, C.: New analog implementation technique for fractional-order controller: a DC motor control. AEU-Int. J. Electron. Commun. **78**, 192–200 (2017)
9. Pappas, G., Alimisis, V., Dimas, C., Sotiriadis, P.P.: Analogue realization of a fully tunable fractional-order PID controller for a DC motor. In: 2020 32nd International Conference on Microelectronics (ICM), pp. 1–4. IEEE (2020)
10. Yaghi, M., Efe, M.Ö.: H2/hinfinty-neural-based FOPID controller applied for radar-guided missile. IEEE Trans. Industr. Electron. **67**(6), 4806–4814 (2019)
11. Podlubny, I.: Fractional-order systems and PI/sup/spl lambda//D/sup/spl mu//-controllers. IEEE Trans. Autom. Control **44**(1), 208–214 (1999)
12. Yeroglu, C., Tan, N.: Note on fractional-order proportional-integral-differential controller design. IET Control Theory Appl. **5**(17), 1978–1989 (2011)
13. Oldham, K., Spanier, J.: The fractional calculus theory and applications of differentiation and integration to arbitrary order. Elsevier (1974)
14. Sabatier, O.P., Machado, J.A.T.: Advances in fractional calculus: the-oretical developments and applications in physics and engineering. SIAM J. Appl. Math. **63**, 612 (2003)
15. Baleanu, D., Machado, J.A.T., Luo, A.C.J.: Fractional Dynamics and Control. Springer, New York (2011). https://doi.org/10.1007/978-1-4614-0457-6
16. Pan, I., Das, S.: Intelligent Fractional Order Systems and Control: An Introduction, vol. 438. Springer, Heidelberg (2012). https://doi.org/10.1007/978-3-642-31549-7
17. Sharma, K.D., Chatterjee, A., Rakshit, A.: A hybrid approach for design of stable adaptive fuzzy controllers employing Lyapunov theory and particle swarm optimization. IEEE Trans. Fuzzy Syst. **17**(2), 329–342 (2009)
18. Deb, A., Sarkar, G., Mandal, P., Biswas, A., Ganguly, A., Biswas, D.: Transfer function identification from impulse response via a new set of orthogonal hybrid functions (HF). Appl. Math. Comput. **218**(9), 4760–4787 (2012)
19. Deb, A., Sarkar, G., Sengupta, A.: Triangular Orthogonal Functions for the Analysis of Continuous Time Systems. Anthem Press, London (2011)
20. Biswas, D., Sharma, K.D., Sarkar, G.: Stable adaptive NSOF domain FOPID controller for a class of non-linear systems. IET Control Theory Appl. **12**(10), 1402–1413 (2018)
21. Khalil, H.K.: Nonlinear systems (2002)

22. Rashedi, E., Nezamabadi-Pour, H., Saryazdi, S.: GSA: a gravitational search algorithm. Inf. Sci. **179**(13), 2232–2248 (2009)
23. Chakraborti, T., Sharma, K.D., Chatterjee, A.: A novel local extrema based gravitational search algorithm and its application in face recognition using one training image per class. Eng. Appl. Artif. Intell. **34**, 13–22 (2014)

Artificial Neural Network for Fault Diagnosis in Active Distribution Network

Syamasree Biswas Raha$^{(\boxtimes)}$ ⓘ and Debasish Biswas ⓘ

Department of Electrical Engineering, Techno International New Town, Kolkata, WB, India
syamasree@gmail.com, debasish.biswas@tict.edu.in

Abstract. In present power scenario, the active distribution networks (ADN) are frequently suffering with severe faults due to uncertain penetration of renewable energy in the network which needs appropriate protection measures for smooth functionalities. In this regard fault diagnosis can provide optimum solution which is extremely limited for ADN. In this work, a modified IEEE 9 bus network is formulated in Power World Simulator where three microgrid (MG) models are incorporated to run in the generating (PV) mode. In the proposed model, LG and LLG fault signals are injected and corresponding fault parameters as phase voltages, phase angles and phase currents are noted for the three phases. Now, by observing different fault parameters in an ADN, it is quite difficult to identify exact faults quickly which causes delay to procure appropriate protections. To resolve the problem, the fault parameter data sets are further diagnosed by formulating an artificial neural network (ANN) for identifying the exact faults using MATLAB 7.1. platform. The training, testing and validation of the input data sets are performed utilizing multilayer perceptron feed forward neural network with back propagation algorithm. To verify the performance of the ANN classifier, supervised learning is procured to determine Mean Square Error (MSE). The result shows $2.7311e-10$ at epoch 403 as the validation performance for the fault detector and the regression factor is 1. Further, the gradient, momentum parameter (mu) and validation checks are also determined in respect of fault diagnosis in the ADN which are presenting satisfactory response in the domain.

Keywords: Active distribution network (ADN) · LG and LLG fault diagnosis · Artificial neural network (ANN)

1 Introduction

Fault diagnosis is a very challenging aspects of present smart grid involving active distribution network (ADN) [1]. Due to uncertain penetration of renewable energy in the ADN network, faults are observed to occur frequently [2–4]. As a results, load shedding in the main grid, islanding operations of the microgrids, damages to the different electrical components are found to occur resulting to poor mechanical, electrical and economic performances [5]. Further, Single-Phase Arc Grounding Fault in the Distribution Network [6] also causes major damage including life risks in the network. These problems are seriously treated by several researchers however optimum solutions are

S. Mukhopadhyay et al. (Eds.): CICBA 2022, CCIS 1579, pp. 183–196, 2022.
https://doi.org/10.1007/978-3-031-10766-5_14

yet to receive in respect of determining exact fault parameters and identification of exact faults while diagnosing these parameters.

In this direction, many case studies on fault analysis are performed by many researchers. A novel current differential protection scheme for active distribution networks was presented by Guo et al. where faults due to DG penetrations are solved utilizing the d-axis component of the current at both ends of the feeder. This further helped to distinguish internal fault from the external fault by comparing differential current with restraining current [7]. Further, Zaabi et al. considered fault analysis of induction machine using finite element method (FEM) [8]. In that work, the authors proposed Fast Fourier Transform (FFT) analysis on stator current and electromagnetic torque to detect the faults of broken rotor bar which obtained successful results of fault detections. In this direction, few researchers applied Artificial Neural Network (ANN) based fault location determination in high voltage transmission line was considered using voltage and current signals [9, 10]. Further, fuzzy logic-based fault detection and classification in Unified Power Quality Conditioner (UPQC)-compensated distribution line was also demonstrated by Das et al. elsewhere [11]. Chine et al. applied ANN-based fault diagnosis technique for photovoltaic stings [12] also. In this discussion of fault analysis, few advanced technologies like augmented complex Kalman Filter for fault detection in LV distribution networks [13], supervised learning in active distribution networks [14] and hybrid machine learning classifier-based digital differential protection scheme for intertie zone of large-scale centralized DFIG-based wind farms [15] are also studied.

The above case studies majorly focused on fault analysis either by incorporating a new solution strategy or by analyzing data sets for fault identifications. The majority case studies are applied in the distribution network, transmission lines or any motor connected loops [16]. In this connection, case studies on all type of major faults likely LG and LLG considering multiple microgrids connected in the active distribution network (ADN) where DGs are injecting power in an uncontrolled way, are rarely available. Hence, in this work fault diagnosis of LG and LLG typed faults are considered in different way.

Here, a grid-connected multiple microgrids with DG based IEEE 9-bus networks are developed in Power World Simulator. Since, DG based power injections can cause severe faults like LG and LLG, these faults are injected in the proposed network [17]. Here, nine fault parameters such as three phase voltages, phase angles and phase currents are noted. Since, these fault parameters are very close to each other, sometimes it is difficult to identify the exact fault. Hence, the determination of fault parameters are sufficient for fault analysis, but fault diagnosis require the verification of faults to take quick and proper action to mitigate it. For this purpose, with the recorded fault parameters as input vectors, artificial neural network (ANN) is formulated in MATLAB 7.1 platform where these data sets are trained, tested and validated utilizing multilayer perceptron feed forward neural network with a target vector sets for each input to identify the exact fault. The fault diagnosis process is finally solved by obtaining validation performance, regression, gradient, mu factors. Hence, before going to the detailed working process, fault diagnosis in active distribution network (ADN) is discussed a priory.

2 Fault Diagnosis in Active Distribution Network (ADN)

In present power scenario, due to uncertain power injections by the DG units cause severe faults. These faults cause abrupt variations in the voltage or current values which can further damage the different sensitive components attached in the smart grid ADN with loadshedding, microgrid islanding etc. Amongst the various ADN faults, the line to ground (LG) or double line to ground (LLG) faults are mostly found to occur which are showing different variations in respect of their fault parameters. In this situation, for quick protection implementation of the network without any disaster, fault diagnosis is very much essential to procure. Fault diagnosis is the procedure to study fault parameters and to identify fault types from these parameters [16, 17]. Hence, fault diagnosis is implemented here by injecting these two fault signals simultaneously to the proposed network. Here, artificial neural network (ANN) played an important role in the fault diagnosing study which needs to explain a priory in the next section [18].

3 Artificial Neural Network

An artificial neural network (ANN) is being inspired from the structure of the biological neural network. An ANN works on the principle of human brain working with interconnected processing units which are comprising of an input part, summing part and the output part. The summing part receives input data, weights each data, and generates a weighted sum [18]. The weighted sum is called the activation function from which signals go to the output part. In neural network, realization of a nonlinear mapping is procured between the inputs and outputs depending upon the activation function [19].

Now in this work, fault diagnosis is procured by the supervised learning where multilayer perceptron feedforward neural network (FFNN) helps to identify fault type for bettor working. The working steps of the ANN based fault diagnosis are given below:

3.1 ANN Based Fault Diagnosis

For fault diagnosis, fault parameters as inputs to be provided in the ANN network. Here, the input vectors are presented as given below:

3.1.1 Input Vectors

In the proposed model, the ANN receives total nine input vectors as given by Eq. (1).

$$z = (V_a, V_b, V_c, Ph\_angle_a, Ph\_angle_b, Ph\_angle_c, I_a, I_b, I_c) \tag{1}$$

In the Eq. (1), three phase voltage are V_a, V_b, V_c respectively, three phase angles are Ph_angle_a, Ph_angle_b, Ph_angle_c and three phase currents are I_a, I_b, I_c respectively. The ANN model layout for fault diagnosis is shown in the Fig. 1.

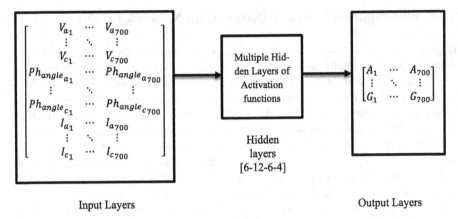

$$\begin{bmatrix} V_{a_1} & \cdots & V_{a700} \\ \vdots & \ddots & \vdots \\ V_{c_1} & \cdots & V_{c700} \\ Ph_{angle_{a_1}} & \cdots & Ph_{angle_{a700}} \\ \vdots & \ddots & \vdots \\ Ph_{angle_{c_1}} & \cdots & Ph_{angle_{c700}} \\ I_{a_1} & \cdots & I_{a700} \\ \vdots & \ddots & \vdots \\ I_{c_1} & \cdots & I_{c700} \end{bmatrix}$$

Multiple Hidden Layers of Activation functions

Hidden layers [6-12-6-4]

$$\begin{bmatrix} A_1 & \cdots & A_{700} \\ \vdots & \ddots & \vdots \\ G_1 & \cdots & G_{700} \end{bmatrix}$$

Input Layers   Output Layers

Fig. 1. Feed-forward neural network model layout developed for fault diagnosis

Now, the inputs are passing through the hidden layers where the network training function updates weight and bias values according to Levenberg-Marquardt optimization. Here four hidden layers are considered as shown in Fig. 1. For better performances and accuracy number of hidden layers are increased.

3.1.2 Activation Function

Here, sigmoid function is used as an activation function which is a continuous version of ramp function after several trial runs. Hence, by following the mentioned steps, fault diagnosis is performed here in the proposed work. For performance analysis of the ANN, mean squared error (mse) which is a network performance function, is determined. In addition to these, regression, the gradient, momentum parameter (mu) and validation checks are also determined.

3.1.3 Target Vectors

Here, three phases and the ground terminal is chosen as the output or the target vectors corresponding to each input fault parameter sets.

Now, by training, testing and validating the input vectors corresponding to the given output vectors, validation performance of the proposed ANN model is obtained. In addition to this, the gradient, momentum parameter (mu), validation checks, and regression are also determined to demonstrate the proficiency of the proposed model. Thus, the ANN is formulated and utilized to diagnosis fault in ADN.

4   Proposed Model and Case Studies

In this work a modified IEEE 9 bus system is considered as an active distribution network (ADN) which is developed using Power World Simulator [17]. In the network, there are three generator buses at the voltage level of 16.5 kV (bus 1), 18 kV (bus 2), and 13.80 kV (bus 3) and the other six buses are maintained at the voltage of 230 kV [20]. These buses are connected among themselves by three transformers and six transmission lines as shown in the Fig. 2. Now, as a modification to the IEEE 9 bus system, three microgrids are incorporated in three low voltage buses (bus no. 1, 2, and 3) of the network. The microgrids (MG) are working in the PV mode where distributed generators (DG) are injecting power to the grid. The active and the reactive load demand of the bus no. 1 is 75 MW and 25 MVar where DG is injecting 36 MW and 18 MVar power to the bus. In the bus no. 2, the load demand in terms of active and reactive power of the MG model is 80 MW and 30 MVar respectively where DG is supplying 46 MW and 19 MVar power to the grid. Finally, the load demand of the MG available to bus no. 3 in terms of active and reactive power is 40 MW and 10 MVar respectively where DG is injecting 16 MW and 6 MVar power here.

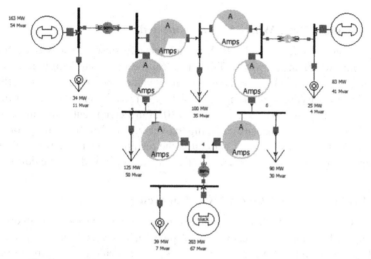

Fig. 2. Modified IEEE-9 bus network using power world simulator

Now, the presence of microgrid models transform the distribution network into active distribution network (ADN) where rapid power injections by the DG units cause severe faults. Since, LG and LLG faults are found most common in the ADN network, these fault signals are injected to the proposed network as case study-I which is performed in the Power World Simulator. From the case study I, the fault parameters in terms of three phase voltages, phase currents and phase angles are noted. Now, for effective fault diagnosing the data sets from the case study-I as normalized inputs are trained, tested, and validated utilizing multilayer perceptron feed forward neural network for identifying the exact fault as case study-II. The supervised learning-based ANN model is developed in MATLAB 7.1. platform. Now, the results for fault diagnosis are required to explain.

5 Result Analysis

In this work, two case studies on fault diagnosis are considered utilizing Power World Simulator and MATLAB 7.1 Platform. Initially, a modified IEEE 9 bus [20] network is prepared in Power World Simulator to obtain fault parameters for LG and LLG faults as case study I. Thereafter, the results from the simulation are trained, tested, and validated by considering artificial neural network (ANN) in the MATLAB 7.1. platform as case study II. The different case studies for fault diagnosis are illustrated here one by one.

5.1   Case Study-I

In the presented work, initially LG faults are simulated to bus 1 where microgrid is connected in PV mode. After fault initiation, fault parameters in terms of three phase voltages, three phase angles and three phase currents are noted for L-G and LLG both the types. Hence, the findings of different fault parameters are described simultaneously below:

5.1.1   LG Fault at Bus 1 Where MG-1 Connected

After inception of A-G fault, the fault parameters are observed to violate from the standard value which are shown in Table 1. It can be observed from the Table 1 that V_a becomes zero and V_b, V_c are changing to high value when A-G occurs. Further, the phase angles are varying in the range of 144.13°, −138.22° and 150.92° for the three phases where it supposed to be within −10° to 10°. Further, current values are also noted for the three phases which also are changing to over current flow in the range of 1.28 pu, 1.74 pu and 0.7190 pu respectively. Similarly, the results are stored in the Table 1 while considering B-G and C-G faults where similar data are observed to have during fault.

5.1.2   LLG Fault at Bus 1 Where MG-1 Connected

Alike the LG fault, LLG fault signals are also injected in the proposed network. While considering A-B-G fault, V_a becomes 1.42 pu which is very high compared to the standard operating value of 0.9–1.10 pu where V_b, V_c are changing to zero. Further, the phase angles are varying in the range of 2.79°, 167.09° and 171.62° for the three phases where it supposed to be within −10° to 10° Further, the phase current values are also noted as 1.23 pu, 3.04 pu and 3.97 pu respectively for the three phases which also are indicating very high compared to the normal operating ranges (Table 2).

Table 1. LG fault parameters for bus 1 (Microgrid-1)

Sl no.	Bus under fault	Phase Volt A	Phase Volt B	Phase Volt C	Phase Ang A	Phase Ang B	Phase Ang C	Phase Cur A	Phase Cur B	Phase Cur C
1.	1 (A-G)	0.00	1.60	1.37	144.13	−138.22	150.92	1.288	1.74	0.71
2.	1 (B-G)	1.40	0.00	1.70	151.29	146.16	−138.23	0.81	1.45	1.63
3.	1 (C-G)	1.66	1.37	0.00	−139.23	153.11	145.35	1.74	0.76	1.32

Table 2. LLG fault parameters for bus 1 (Microgrid-1)

Sl no.	Bus under fault	Phase Volt A	Phase Volt B	Phase Volt C	Phase Ang A	Phase Ang B	Phase Ang C	Phase Cur A	Phase Cur B	Phase Cur C
1.	1 (A-B-G)	1.42	0.00	0.00	2.79	167.09	171.62	1.23	3.048	3.98
2.	1 (B-C-G)	0.00	1.44	0.00	173.23	2.77	167.07	3.36	1.21	3.77
3.	1 (C-A-G)	0.00	0.00	1.51	168.22	171.02	2.76	3.99	3.24	1.25

5.1.3 LG Fault at Bus 2 Where MG-2 Connected

Alike the last case, here A-G fault is injected in the bus 2 where microgrid-2 is connected. After fault initiation, the different fault parameters are observed to violate from the standard value which are shown in Table 3. Alike the previous case, V_a becomes zero and V_b, V_c are showing very high values as 1.60 pu and 1.36 pu respectively when A-G occurs. Further, the phase angles are varying in the range of 178.54°, −138.24° and 150.94° for the three phases where it supposed to be within −10° to 10°. Further, the phase current values are also changing for the three phases while causing either over current flow such as 1.28 pu, 1.75 pu and 0.73 pu respectively. Similarly, the fault parameters for the B-G and C-G faults are also presented in the Table 3 where similar observations are found during these faults.

5.1.4 LLG Fault at Bus 2 Where MG-2 Connected

Now, LLG faults are also one observed rapidly to occur in the ADN network which is also considered here in the bus 2 in presence of microgrid-2. Hence, the LLG fault signals are injected in the proposed network and fault parameters are noted. While considering A-B-G fault, V_a becomes 1.42pu which is very high compared to the standard operating

Table 3. LG fault parameters for bus 2 (Microgrid-2)

Sl no.	Bus under fault	Phase Volt A	Phase Volt B	Phase Volt C	Phase Ang A	Phase Ang B	Phase Ang C	Phase Cur A	Phase Cur B	Phase Cur C
1.	2 (A-G)	0.00	1.60	1.37	178.54	−138.24	150.94	1.28	1.74	0.73
2.	2 (B-G)	1.39	0.00	1.67	149.29	176.16	−139.23	0.77	1.22	1.73
3.	2 (C-G)	1.65	1.40	0.00	−138.23	150.25	179.33	1.79	0.70	1.29

voltage value of 0.9–1.10 pu where V_b, V_c are changing to zero. Further, the phase angles are varying in the range of 2.78°, 55.42° and 42.12° for the three phases where it supposed to be within −10° to 10°. Further, the phase current values are also noted as 1.25 pu, 2.99 pu and 3.93 pu respectively for the three phases which also are indicating unusual readings compared to the normal operating ranges (Table 4).

Table 4. LLG fault parameters for bus 2 (Microgrid-2)

Sl no.	Bus under Fault	Phase Volt A	Phase Volt B	Phase Volt C	Phase Ang A	Phase Ang B	Phase Ang C	Phase Cur A	Phase Cur B	Phase Cur C
1.	2 (A-B-G)	1.42	0.00	0.00	2.78	55.42	42.12	1.24	2.99	3.92
2.	2 (B-C-G)	0.00	1.44	0.00	43.32	2.79	57.87	3.86	1.20	2.95
3.	2 (C-A-G)	0.00	0.00	1.48	58.33	41.45	2.80	2.96	4.33	1.22

5.1.5   LG Fault at Bus 3 Where MG-3 Connected

Alike the last two case studies, LG fault signals are also injected in the bus 3 where microgrid-3 is connected. After A-G fault signal initiation, the different fault parameters are observed to violate from the standard value which are shown in Table 5. Alike the previous cases, V_a becomes zero and V_b, V_c are presenting very high values as 1.59 pu and 1.37 pu respectively. Further, the phase angles are varying in the range of 174.41°, −138.95° and 150.00° for the three phases where it supposed to be within −10° to 10°. Further, the phase current values are also changing for the three phases while causing either poor current flow or over current flow such as 0.97 pu, 1.07 pu and 0.20 pu respectively. Similarly, the fault parameters for the B-G and C-G faults are also demonstrated in the Table 3 which provides similar observations like these faults.

5.1.6   LLG Fault at Bus 3 Where MG-3 Connected

Similar to the previous cases, LLG faults are also initiated in the proposed ADN network while injecting fault signals in the bus 3 in presence of microgrid-3. While considering A-B-G fault, V_a becomes 1.41pu which is very high compared to the standard operating voltage value of 0.9–1.10 pu where V_b, V_c are falling to zero. Further, the phase angles are observed to vary in the range of 2.02°, −132.07° and −126.70° for the three phases where it supposed to be within −10° to 10°. Further, the phase current values are also noted as 0.53 pu, 3.99 pu and 4.37 pu respectively for the three phases which also are indicating either very poor current flow or over current flow compared to the normal operating ranges (Table 6).

Table 5. LG fault parameters for bus 3 (Microgrid-3)

Sl no.	Bus under fault	Phase Volt A	Phase Volt B	Phase Volt C	Phase Ang A	Phase Ang B	Phase Ang C	Phase Cur A	Phase Cur B	Phase Cur C
1.	3 (A-G)	0.00	1.60	1.37	174.41	−138.95	150.00	0.966	1.073	0.201
2.	3 (B-G)	1.35	0.00	1.58	152.34	179.24	−134.22	0.206	0.967	1.065
3.	3 (C-G)	1.62	1.39	0.00	−140.23	149.25	177.21	1.087	0.207	0.929

Table 6. LLG fault parameters for bus 3 (Microgrid-1)

Sl no.	Bus under Fault	Phase Volt A	Phase Volt B	Phase Volt C	Phase Ang A	Phase Ang B	Phase Ang C	Phase Cur A	Phase Cur B	Phase Cur C
1.	3 (A-B-G)	1.42	0.00	0.00	2.02	−132.07	−126.70	0.53	3.98	4.38
2.	3 (B-C-G)	0.00	1.43	0.00	−126.52	2.06	−130.54	4.28	0.59	3.95
3.	3 (C-A-G)	0.00	0.00	1.44	−133.53	−128.42	2.04	3.99	4.47	0.55

From the above data analysis, it can be understood that for any types of faults, a rapid variation to the different parameters of the three-phase power network occurs. Amongst these parameters, total nine parameters such as three phase voltages, three phase angles and three phase currents are considered to note for fault analysis. These parameters show significant variations from the schedule value during faults. Hence, by analyzing these data it is quite difficult to conclude which type of faults are occurring in the network for taking corrective measurements. Further, DG penetrations in the ADN are sometime becoming much rapid and uncontrolled, immediate preventions are desirable. Hence, the quick identification of the exact fault types are essentially required for the ADN. In this regards, fault diagnosis is required to procure which is considered here as case study II utilizing ANN.

5.2   Case Study II

As explained in Sect. 3.1, ANN based fault diagnosis is procured by the following steps.

5.2.1   Step 1

While procuring fault diagnosis, fault parameters such as three phase voltages, three phase angles and three phase currents are considered as input vectors of the ANN as nine fault parameters for the six set of faults such as A-G, B-G, C-G, A-B-G, B-C-G and C-A-G where four parameters are considered as output or target vectors (three phases and ground). Considering 100 data sets to each faults, total 600 faults parameter data are generated. Further, 100 data on without any fault are also collected to get total 700 data sets by which input vector matrix of (9 * 700) is formulated. Now, for every input data sets, target vector matrix of (4 * 700) are considered.

5.2.2 Step 2

After extensive practices by varying the number of neurons and number of hidden layers and different activation functions the structure of 6–12–6–4 finally chosen for the ANN detector/classifier with transfer functions (sigmoid) is found optimum to achieve best validation performance of $2.7311e-10$ at epoch 403 which is very satisfactory compared to the work available elsewhere [21]. The best validation performance is shown in Fig. 3. The error histogram with 20 bins are also noticed and shown in Fig. 4. The regression factor is one of the important criteria of performance evaluation of the proposed ANN which is also presented in Fig. 5. Finally, the gradient, momentum parameter (mu) and validation checks are also noticed to demonstrate the performance of the ANN in Fig. 6. From the Fig. 6, it can be noticed that gradient is obtained as $9.9714 * 10-8$ at epoch 403, mu- $1e-08$ at epoch 403 which shows quite satisfactory output in respect of fault diagnosis.

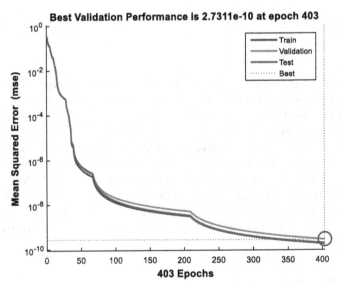

Fig. 3. Performance analysis graph for Mean Squared Error (mse)

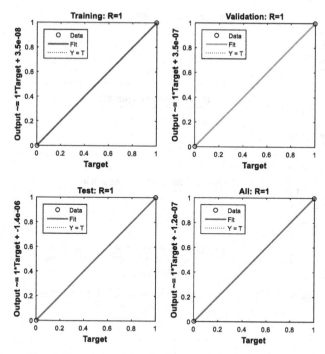

Fig. 4. Regression determination graph for fault diagnosis

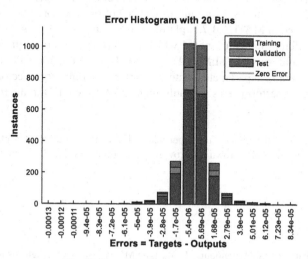

Fig. 5. Error histogram analysis graph

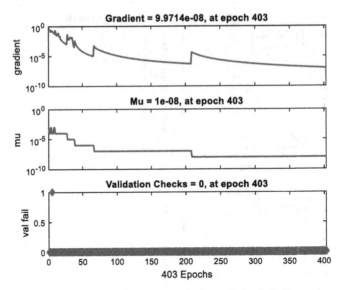

Fig. 6. Validation performance analysis graph for fault diagnosis

6 Conclusion

In this work, a modified IEEE-9 bus active distribution network is considered for fault diagnosis study. While procuring this, the proposed network is developed in Power World Simulator where two frequently occurring faults likely LG or LLG fault signals are injected in the network and vital fault parameters such three phase voltages, phase angles and phase currents are noted. Further, to identify the exact fault types for initiating fast preventive measures a multilayer perceptron feed forward neural network model is developed in MATLAB 7.1. platform. Here, the variations of the fault parameters for the different faults are noted which are further scrutinized through artificial feed forward neural network (FFNN). Here, ANN helps to diagnose different faults by processing the input fault parameter vectors and corresponding target vectors while indicating satisfactory performances for fault diagnosis for the ADN in the present power scenario.

Acknowledgement. The authors of the paper acknowledge the department of electrical engineering, Techno International New Town for providing smooth research environment to work in this area.

References

1. Wang, C., Pang, K., Shahidehpour, M., Wen, F.: MILP-based fault diagnosis model in active power distribution networks. IEEE Trans. Smart Grid. **12**(5), 99–107 (2021)

2. Das, T.K., Chattopadhyay, S., Das, A.: Harmonics assessment based symmetrical fault diagnosis in PV array based microgrid system. In: Chattopadhyay, S., Roy, T., Sengupta, S., Berger-Vachon, C. (eds.) Modelling and Simulation in Science, Technology and Engineering Mathematics. MS-17 2017. Advances in Intelligent Systems and Computing, vol. 749. Springer, Cham (2019). https://doi.org/10.1007/978-3-319-74808-5_9
3. Bangash, K.N., Farrag, M.E.A., Osman, A.H.: Manage reverse power flow and fault current level in LV network with high penetration of small scale solar and wind power generation. In: International Universities Power Engineering Conference (UPEC). IEEE Proceedings (2018)
4. Hadjidemetriou, L., Kyriakides, E., Blaabjerg, F.: A new hybrid PLL for interconnecting renewable energy systems to the grid. IEEE Trans. Ind. Appl. **49**(6), 115–123 (2013)
5. Long, B., Liao, Y., Chong, K.T., Rodríguez, J., Guerrero, J.M.: MPC-controlled virtual synchronous generator to enhance frequency and voltage dynamic performance in islanded microgrids. IEEE Trans. Smart Grid **12**(2), 953–964 (2021)
6. Liu, B., Tang, J., Wu, X., Wang, J., Yang, C.: Analysis of Arc model and its application in single-phase grounding fault simulation in distribution networks. In: China International Conference on Electricity Distribution. IEEE (2018)
7. Guo, X., et al.: A novel current differential protection scheme for active distribution networks. In: IEEE 3rd Student Conference on Electrical Machines and Systems (SCEMS) (2020)
8. Zaabi, W., Bensalem, Y., Trabelsi, H.: Fault analysis of induction machine using finite element method (FEM). In: 15th International Conference on Sciences and Techniques of Automatic Control and Computer Engineering (STA) (2014)
9. Coban, M., Tezcan, S.S.: Artificial neural network based fault location on 230 kV transmission line using voltage and current signals. In: 4th International Symposium on Multidisciplinary Studies and Innovative Technologies (ISMSIT) (2020)
10. Hagh, M.T., Razi, K., Taghizadeh, H.: Fault classification and location of power transmission lines using artificial neural network. In: IEEE International Power Engineering Conference (2007)
11. Das, S., Adhikari, S.: Fuzzy logic based fault detection and classification in Unified Power Quality Conditioner (UPQC)-compensated distribution line. In: IEEE International Conference on Power Electronics, Drives and Energy Systems (PEDES) (2020)
12. Chine, W., Mellit, A.: ANN-based fault diagnosis technique for photovoltaic stings. In: 5th International Conference on Electrical Engineering - Boumerdes (ICEE-B) (2017)
13. Shafiei, M., Pezeshki, H., Ledwich, G., Nourbakhsh, G.: Fault detection in LV distribution networks based on augmented complex Kalman filter. In: Australasian Universities Power Engineering Conference (AUPEC) (2019)
14. Sun, B., Zhang, H., Shi, F.: Machine learning based fault type identification in the active distribution network. In: IEEE 3rd Information Technology, Networking, Electronic and Automation Control Conference (ITNEC) (2019)
15. Rezaei, N., Uddin, M.N., Amin, I.K., Othman, M.L., Marsadek, M.B., Hasan, M.D.: A novel hybrid machine learning classifier-based digital differential protection scheme for intertie zone of large-scale centralized DFIG-based wind farms. IEEE Trans. Ind. Appl. **56**(4), 56–67 (2020)
16. Chen, T.: Fault Diagnosis and Fault Tolerance. Springer, Heidelberg (1992). https://doi.org/10.1007/978-3-642-77179-8
17. Glover, J.D., Sarma, M.S., Overbye, T.J.: Power System Analysis and Design, 5th edn. Cengage Learning Publishers, USA (2002)
18. Engelbrecht, A.P.: Computational Intelligence: An Introduction, 2nd edn. Wiley, Hoboken (2007)
19. Oliva, D., Houssein, E.H., Hinojosa, S. (eds.): Metaheuristics in Machine Learning: Theory and Applications. SCI, vol. 967. Springer, Cham (2021). https://doi.org/10.1007/978-3-030-70542-8

20. Shoaib, A.S., Kundan, K., Asif, R.S., Shubash, K., Aizaz, A.S.: IEEE-9 short circuit analysis & over current relaying coordination of IEEE 9-bus system. In: International Multi-Topic ICT Conference (IMTIC). IEEE (2018)
21. Ahmed, E., Khairy, S., Mohamed, B.: Artificial neural network based fault classification and location for transmission lines. In: Conference on Power Electronics and Renewable Energy (CPERE). IEEE (2019)

A Secure Communication Gateway with Parity Generator Implementation in QCA Platform

Suparba Tapna[1], Kisalaya Chakrabarti[2], and Debarka Mukhopadhyay[3]([✉])

[1] Durgapur Institute of Advanced Technology and Management, Durgapur, India
[2] Haldia Institute of Technology, Haldia, India
[3] Christ (Deemed to be University), Bengaluru, India
debarka.mukhopadhyay@gmail.com

Abstract. Quantum-Dot Cellular Automata (QCA) has arisen as a potential option in contrast to CMOS in the late time of nanotechnology. Some appealing highlights of QCA incorporate incredibly low force utilization and dissemination, high gadget pressing thickness, high velocity (arranged by THz). QCA based plans of normal advanced modules were concentrated broadly in the ongoing past. Equality generator and equality checker circuits assume a significant part in blunder discovery and subsequently, go about as fundamental segments in correspondence circuits. In any case, not very many endeavors were made for an efficient plan of QCA based equality generator as well as equality checker circuits up until now. In addition, these current plans need functional feasibility as they bargain a ton with normally acknowledged plan measurements like territory, postponement, intricacy, and manufacture cost. This article depicts new plans of equality generator and equality checker circuits in QCA which beat every one of the current plans as far as previously mentioned measurements. The proposed plans can likewise be effortlessly reached out to deal with an enormous number of contributions with a straight expansion in territory and inactivity.

Keywords: Parity generator · Quantum-Dot Cellular Automata · Pseudorandom Binary Sequence (PRBS) · Exclusive-OR (XOR) gate · Security · Quantum enhancement logic

1 Introduction

The most recent sixty years have seen colossal development in CMOS-based coordinated circuits. Be that as it may, compromised by numerous physical limitations, further chip size down-scaling is by all accounts arriving at its breaking point. Subsequently, the indications of chip deviation creation from the anticipated evolution of "Moore's Law" have begun to demonstrate [1]. Thus, the center is moving to novel arising nano-technologies that may make more down-scaling of coordinated circuits conceivable. QCA is among the emerging nanotechnologies that can supplant CMOS in impending nano-innovation time [2].

S. Mukhopadhyay et al. (Eds.): CICBA 2022, CCIS 1579, pp. 197–209, 2022.
https://doi.org/10.1007/978-3-031-10766-5_15

Perhaps the most fascinating element of QCA is incredibly low force scattering and utilization. This is accomplished by the way that data ows in QCA gadgets with no ow of current [2]. Low force utilization and dissemination, high gadget pressing thickness, high velocity (arranged by THz) empower acknowledgment of more thick circuits with quick exchanging speed, accomplishing room temperature activities [3–5] by QCA. Plan and reproduction of basic registering modules such as multiplexers, adders, and multipliers [6–8] were concentrated colossally. Be that as it may, lesser exertion has been seen toward planning correspondence circuits. The equality-based technique is quite possibly the most generally utilized mistake discovery technique for information transmission [9]. In advanced frameworks, twofold information being communicated and prepared might be exposed to the commotion that may adjust information bits from 0s to 1s and the other way around. During transmission from the transmitter, equality chomped is added to the first information word to show if the number of 1s contained in the information word is odd or even. At the less than desirable end, the equality piece of the got word is tallied by including the quantity of 1s within it and is contrasted with the communicated one with recognizing the existence of a mistake in the information. An equality generator is a combinational rationale circuit that produces the equality bits in the transmitter end [9]. Then again, a circuit that verifies the equality in the recipient is termed equality checker [9]. A joined circuit or gadget comprising of equality generator & equality checker is ordinarily utilized in computerized frameworks to recognize the single piece blunders in the communicated information word. Even equality bit plots show the equality bit as 0 and 1 when the data stream has an even (odd) number of 1s. In odd equality, bit plot shows that equality bit is set to 1(0) if the data stream comprises an even (odd) number of 1s. The equality checker at the collector could be odd or even rely upon the kind of equality generator utilized at the transmitter. For an even equality checker, a mistake is demonstrated with yield 1 (such as the quantity of 1s in its info is discovered to be odd rather than even). Likewise, for an odd equality checker, a mistake is shown by the yield 1 (such as the quantity of 1s in its information is discovered to be even rather than odd). A couple of plans of equality generator, as well as equality checker circuits in QCA, were introduced in the writing [13–15]. In any case, existing plans need reasonable feasibility as they bargain a great deal with normally acknowledged plan measurements like region, deferral, intricacy, and cost of creation. It could be noticed that the fundamental guideline associated with the execution of equality circuits is that amount of the odd number of 1s is consistently 1 and the amount of many numbers of 1s is consistently zero. Thus, XOR work, which creates 0 and 1 yield when the information sources have an even (odd) number of 1s, has an essential part in executing such circuits. As needs are, the general efficiency of such circuits relies a great deal upon the execution of XOR capacities. A cautious investigation of the current plans of equality generator as well as checker circuits uncovers that every one of these plans utilizes fell 2-input XOR entryways (without investing a lot of energy in streamlining the individual XOR doors) for executing the ideal XOR work. In this article, we have utilized a mix of two info and three input XOR doors to execute the ideal XOR work for acknowledging equality generator& equality checker circuits in QCA. We have viably used the way that execution of an n-digit XOR work in QCA may be enhanced by utilizing a blend of two information and three input XOR doors utilizing ESOP based changes [16] as opposed to utilizing 2-input XOR entry-ways as it were. It likewise helps in acknowledging bigger equality generator & checker circuits utilizing the more modest forms in a precise way. Reproduction tests performed to look at the proposed plans of QCA equality generator as well as checker circuits with the current ones likewise exhibit the normal bene t. The proposed ones are observed to beat every one of the current plans regarding generally acknowledged plan measurements. The remainder of the article is coordinated as follows: Sect. 2 presents the essentials of QCA innovation. Area III surveys the related earlier work. The suggested plans are represented in Sect. 4. Synopsis of similar investigation between the recommended plan with the current ones is shown in Sects. 5 and 6 of this work.

1.1   Basics of QCA

The idea of QCA was exhibited by the "Metal-Island" execution [17]. Other conceivable execution systems incorporate semiconductor, atomic and attractive [17]. In this paper, we have deemed the semiconductor execution of QCA. The fundamental activity of QCA gadgets depends on the quantum mechanical impacts and Coulombic charge quantization [2]. The essential component, frequently alluded to as QCA cell, is a square-formed compartment-like design to hold the charge. Every QCA cell has 4 possible wells (dabs), one at every side of the phone and 2 free electrons that are equipped for burrowing quantum precisely, starting with one quantum speck then onto the next. At harmony, the 2 electrons within a cell consistently involve the antipodal locales because of Coulombic shock. This oers approach to two vivaciously comparable plans. These two plans, as demonstrated in Fig. 1, are indicated as two distinct polarizations p = −1 and p = +1 which address rationale 1 and rationale 0, separately. Data ow in QCA is accomplished by Coulombic cooperations between electrons existing in adjoining cells without ow of electrons which prompts incredibly low force dispersal. In a progression of QCA cell, each cell simply

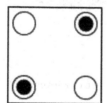
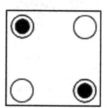

Fig. 1. Binary depiction of QCA cells

Modifies their spellbound state as indicated by the neighboring cell to make the flow of data conceivable. Dominant part entryway or lion's share elector (M) and inverter gate (I) [6] are the 2 essential structure squares of QCA circuits. Figure 2 indicates its plan format in QCA. The all-inclusive nature of the blend of these two doors works with the execution of any rationale circuit utilizing them.

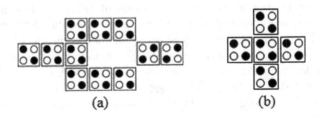

(a)   (b)

Fig. 2. QCA design layout fundamental building blocks (a) Inverter (b) Majority voter

QCA permits 2 wires to cross one another in a similar layer with no meddling one another. As demonstrated in Fig. 3(a), such coplanar hybrid [6] is acknowledged utilizing two distinct kinds of wires: a double wire (comprising of a progression of typical QCA cells) and an altered chain (comprising of cells pivoted 45 from its ordinary direction). Wire intersections executed utilizing numerous layers (like metal wire hybrids in CMOS) are likewise conceivable in QCA (Fig. 3(b)). A semi-adiabatic timing component is likewise utilized in QCA for data synchronization and to satisfy the forced necessity of the QCA gadget. A 4-stage clock zone framework, presented by Lent et al. [3], with a 90-stage shift starting with 1 clock zone then onto the next is regularly utilized (Fig. 4). The 4-stages (zones) are termed as a switch, hold, relax & release individually. The directions or condition of electrons in a QCA cell is shifted during the switch or delivery stage as it were.

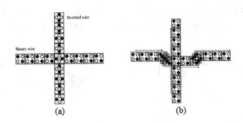

(a)   (b)

Fig. 3. (a) Coplanar & (b) Multilayer crossover in QCA

2   Related Prior Work

An important part of the exploration on QCA so far has zeroed in on the plan and reenactment of fundamental rationale gates [6] and different advanced modules such as multipliers [7], multiplexers [8], and adders [18,19]. Be that as it may, as referenced in Sect. 1, not very many such endeavors may be observed in the writing in planning correspondence circuits and its segments like equality generators as well as checkers. A 4-cycle even equality checker comprising of three two-input XOR doors with coplanar and multi-facet hybrids was first suggested by Lent et al., [3]. Generally speaking, the plan devours an enormous number of QCA cells ("299 QCA cells") and causes high inertness (8 clock zones). With an expectation of enhancing the plan regarding the region, Navi and Navin [16] suggested a 4-bit odd equality checker that burns through 145 QCA cells. Be that as it may, this plan is found to cause restrictively enormous inactivity (12 clock zones). In [16], Navi and Navin likewise introduced a 3-digit even equality generator that burns through 99 QCA cells and causes the inactivity of 8 clock zones. Afterward, Ottavi et al. [12] presented plans of four input even & odd equality checkers the two of which devour 94 QCA cells and bring about the inactivity of 7 clock zones. Ottavi et al. [12] additionally presented a 3-cycle even equality as well as a 3-digit odd equality generator which burns through 64 & 66 QCA cells, separately, and causes a dormancy of 7 and 11 clock zones, individually. A region effectual even equality generator, as well as checker circuit, were subsequently suggested by Navi [15] in which the 3-cycle even equality generator devours just 60 QCA cells and 4-bit even equality checker burns-through QCA cells of 117. In any case, the inactivity brought about by 8 and 9 clock zones, individually. A three-bit odd equality generator, as well as a 4 four-bit odd equality checker, have been suggested by Frost & Kogge in [11], utilizing revocable rationale for nano-correspondence. The plan of equality generator burns through 72 QCA cells which causes idleness of seven-clock zones though the plan of the equality checker (utilizes a "2-2 Feynman gate structure" [20]) burns through 126 QCA cells along with idleness of eight-clock zones. This is proven that such current plans bargain a great deal with at least one normally acknowledged plan measurements like territory, deferral, intricacy, and cost of creation. Besides, a large portion of these plans present more modest estimated equality generators & checkers (3-bit/4-cycle) and scarcely gives any insight with the goal that they may be reached out to acknowledge these circuits with greater size (15-piece/16-digit or significantly greater). As previously specified disadvantages go about as significant hindrances against the pragmatic feasibility of these plans. In like manner, efficient and for all intents and purposes, feasible plans of equality generators and equality checkers have gotten a lot of fundamental.

3   Proposed QCA Parity Generator Circuit

For the considerations stated in Sect. 1, XOR work, which yields zero (1) yield when the number of 1s in the sources of information is even (odd), is essential in the execution of equality generator and checker circuits. An n-input XOR work was generally executed by joining a few two-input XOR doors. More diminished, utilization of present plans of QCA two-input XOR gate [15, 21], which utilize countless dominant part entryways, lead to significant bargain with the space just as dormancy. For example, execution of a 4-cycle XOR work utilizing three two-input XOR entryways [15] considers any rate 9 larger part doors. Notwithstanding, it has been observed that more proficient n-input XOR work's execution is conceivable by utilizing mixes of two info as well as three-input XOR entryways under ESOP-based change [16]. In like manner, we have utilized the blend of two info and three input XOR gates to execute n-digit XOR work as opposed to depending entirely on two-input XOR entryways which was the situation in present executions. We have likewise utilized greater part rationale decrease [13–15] to additionally advance the plans of individual XOR gates (two information and three input). The coherent articulation (AB + AB), addressing two-input XOR capacity may be re-composed equally as M [M(A, B, 1), M(A, B, 0), 0] utilizing dominant part rationale decrease, here M (X, Y, Z) addresses a three-input lion's share door [6] having X, Y, Z inputs. The given Boolean articulation may be executed utilizing three-input larger part entryways and Fig. 5(a) demonstrate one inverter. Essentially, the coherent articulation (A'B'C'+ A'BC' + AB'C' + ABC), addressing a three-input XOR capacity may be re-composed as M [M (A', B', C'),C,M(A, B, C')] utilizing larger part rationale decrease, here M (X, Y, Z) addresses a three-input lion's share entryway having X, Y, Z inputs. Figure 5(b) indicates the diagram representation of gate level execution of the aforementioned articulation. The legitimate articulation for the yield of a three-bit even equality generator is A xor B xor C, consequently, it tends to be carried out just by utilizing the three-input XOR entryway of Fig. 5(b).

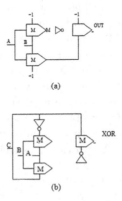

(a)

(b)

Fig. 4. Implementation of (a) two-input XOR and (b) three-input XOR at Gate level

The legitimate articulation for the yield of 3-cycle odd equality generator (i.e., A xor B xor C) plan measurements as a component of the quantity of data sources (n), we can be re-composed as (A'B'C'+ A'BC + AB'C + ABC') have figured the overall articulations for the region, idleness, such as M [M (A, B, C), C', M (A', B', C)] utilizing majority gate decrease.

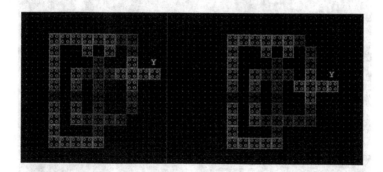

Fig. 5. Layout of introduced 3-bit parity generator (a) even (b) odd

The above articulation shows that a 3-digit odd equality generator can likewise be executed by utilizing three majority gates. Figures 6(a) and 6(b) indicate the designs of the suggested three-digit even & odd equality generators, individually. As clear from the figures, the plans comprise 49 QCA cells with no hybrid and cause 0.75 clock cycle (three clock zones) inactivity. Expecting 18 nm 18 nm QCA cell size with a hole of 2 nm between two sequential cells, every one of the formats burns through a space of $0.04\,\mu\mathrm{m}^2$.

4   Proposed Work for Secure Network Channel

The proposed circuit is relevant for prediction of nature in cryptographic architecture for QCA based secure nano communication framework has proposed the secure communication cryptographic framework by exploiting the proposed circuit in this work. Thus, it may be reproducing the more enhanced the suitable prediction for the architecture of the proposed and authenticated symmetric cryptographic model in this proposed work. Actually, in this work, we have to implement such kind of circuit that is also utilized for secure communication. For parity generator, we have already considered the several Inputs and output, and mainly consider for checking any error in bitstream but the major consideration is been depicted the realization of Pseudorandom Binary Sequence (PRBS) which is used as a keystream for the nano communication and act the suitable one for bit changes for every interval of time. This work is being considered for a secure way to predict a large number of cells is consist of the majority gate in the inverter. In Table six majority gate and four inverters, we have to consider. But to a large extent that is to utilize the channel coding application, it is required only one parity generator and the complexity is 14 majority gates and four inverters. Thus, we proposed a secure way to require a more efficient channel coding application in Quantum Dot Cellular Automata (QCA) framework.

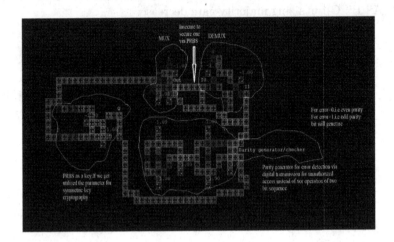

Fig. 6. QCA nanocommunication with parity generator

Thus, the Nano communication is more secure so we have to propose a nano network with parity generator Pseudo random binary Sequence generator for Crypto network in model prediction.

5   Result and Discussion

The circuit is executed as well as mimicked utilizing Bi-stable recreation motor QCA Designer-2.0.3 [10], the yield comes after second check beat as demonstrated represents the end of encoder when in Fig. 13 along with confirmed utilizing unique truth table. Figure 13 represents the end of encoder when Si = 0, Xi = 1 then Xi = 0 and Yi = 1, Si = 1 then Yi = 1 and so on as demonstrates by green bolt. At the end of the decoder when Si = 0, Yi = 1 then Xi = 1 and Si = 1, Yi = 1, then Xi = 0, and so on as shown by the blue bolt. The accompanying boundaries are utilized for a Bi-stable estimate: 65.00 nm impact Radius, 9.8×10^{-22} J Clock high, 1000 Maximum Iterations, 12800 No. of tests, 12.900 Relative permittivities, 5 nm Dot distance, 20 nm Cell structure, and 20 nm Cell width (Figs. 7, 8 and Tables 1, 2).

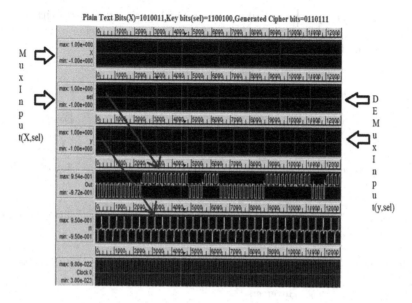

Fig. 7. Simulation result of QCA encoder and decoder with parity generator circuit

2.0000 is set as amplitude factor of Clock, 11.50000 nm set as Layer separation, 0.001000 Convergence tolerance, and 3.8×10^{-23} J Clock low. We have

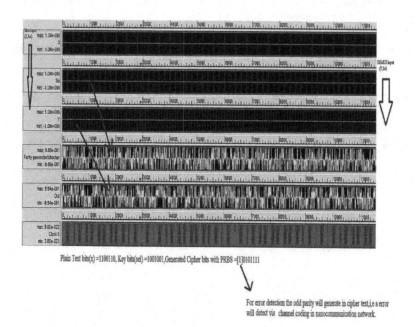

Fig. 8. Simulation result of QCA nano communication with parity generator

to consider the comparative study between QCA parity generator with encoder and decoder and QCA nano communication with parity generator which the depicted in the following figures (Fig. 9 and Fig. 10).

Table 1. QCA encoder and decoder with parity generator

QCA parity generator	No. of majority gate used	No. of cells	Area (nm^2)	Delay
One [Proposed]	Six majority gate and three inverters	40	324	3 clock cycles
Sixteen [11]	Nine majority gate and five inverters	48	410	4 clock cycles
Eleven [8]	Eight majority gate and four inverters	52	385	4 clock cycles

Table 2. QCA Nano communication circuit with parity generator

Parity generator	No.of majority gate used	No. of cells	Area (nm^2)	Delay
One [Proposed]	Fourteen majority gate and four inverters	221	0.42	2 clock cycles
Four [20]	Twenty majority gate and five inverters	209	0.68	3 clock cycles
Two [19]	Nineteen majority gate and two inverters	253	0.72	4 clock cycles
Three [18]	Fifteen majority gate and five inverters	201	0.44	4 clock cycles

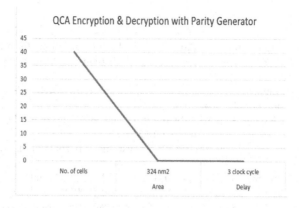

Fig. 9. QCA encryption and decryption with parity generator

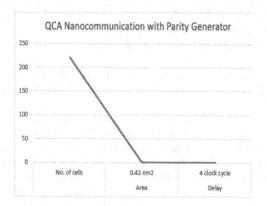

Fig. 10. QCA nano communication with parity generator

6   Conclusion

Because of the creation of side-channel assaults, the cryptographic gadget may be exploited as far as to force and electromagnetic investigation assaults. Along these lines, Since QCA has an extremely low force use and extraordinarily fast pace of time, the proposed circuit may be the guiding principle for producing a safe QCA encryption module instead of a conventional frame. The encryption as well as unscrambling are carried out on 7-bits message utilizing 7-bits key however this very well may be done on any message bits length also key pieces utilizing the proposed circuit. Now, the circuit needed just 3 MVs, 42 cells, 3 clock zones, 2 inverters, along with 36000 nm zones for both decoders as well as the encoder. Future cryptographic calculations execution for QCA-based secure nano correspondence framework may be accomplished utilizing this proposed circuit.

References

1. Compano, R., Molenkamp, L., Paul, D.J.: Technology roadmap for nanoelectronics. In: European Commission IST Programme, Future and Emerging Technologies, pp. 1–104 (2000)
2. Lent, C.S., Tougaw, P.D., Porod, W., Bernestein, G.H.: Quantum cellular automata. Nanotechnology **4**, 49–57 (1993)
3. Niemer, M.T., Kogge, P.M.: Problems in designing with QCAs: layout = timing. Int. J. Circuit Theory Appl. **29**, 49–62 (2001)
4. Bernstein, G.H., et al.: Magnetic QCA systems. Microelectron. J. **36**, 619–624 (2005)
5. Huang, J., Lombardi, F.: Design and Test of Digital Circuits by Quantum-dot Cellular Automata. Artech House Inc., Norwood (2007)
6. Lee, S., Cho, K., Choi, S., Kang, S.: A new logic topology-based scan chain stitching for test-power reduction. IEEE Trans. Circuits Syst. II **67**(12), 1–5 (2020)
7. Pomeranz, I.: Extended transparent-scan. IEEE Trans. Very Large Scale Integr. VLSI Syst. **27**(9), 2096–2104 (2019)
8. Navi, K., Sayedsalehi, S., Farazkish, R., Azghadi, M.R.: Five-input majority gate, a new device for quantum-dot cellular automata. J. Comput. Theor. Nanosci. **7**, 1546–1553 (2010)
9. Karmakar, R., Chattopadhyay, S., Kapur, R.: A scan obfuscation guided design for-security approach for sequential circuits. IEEE Trans. Circuits Syst. II Express Briefs **67**(3), 1–5 (2020)
10. Walus, K., Jullien, G.A., Dimitrov, V.S.: RAM design using quantum-dot cellular automata. Nanotechnol. Conf. Trade Show **2**, 160–163 (2003)
11. Kanda, M., Hashizume, M., Ashikin Binti Ali, F., Yotsuyanagi, H., Lu, S.-K.: Open defect detection not utilizing boundary scan flip-flops in assembled circuit boards. IEEE Trans. Compon. Packag. Manuf. Technol. **10**(5), 895–907 (2020)
12. Mukherjee, N., et al.: Time and area optimized testing of automotive ICs. IEEE Trans. Very Large Scale Integr. VLSI Syst. **29**(1), 1–13 (2021)
13. Debnath, B., Das, J.C., De, D., Ghaemi, F., Ahmadian, A., Senu, N.: Reversible palm vein authenticator design with quantum dot cellular automata for information security in nanocommunication network. IEEE Access **8**, 174821–174832 (2020)
14. Kim, J., Lee, S., Kang, S.: Test-friendly data-selectable self- gating (DSSG). IEEE Trans. Very Large Scale Integr. VLSI Syst. **27**(8), 1972–1976 (2019)
15. Walus, K., Dysart, T.J., Jullien, G.A., Budiman, R.A.: QCADesigner: a rapid design and simulation tool for quantum-dot cellular automata. IEEE Trans. Nanotechnol. **3**(1), 26–31 (2004)
16. Mukhopadhyay, D., Dutta, P.: A study on energy optimized 4 dot 2 electron two dimensional quantum dot cellular automata logical reversible flip-flops. Microelectron. J. **46**, 519–530 (2015)
17. Kim, K., Ibtesam, M., Kim, D., Jung, J., Park, S.: CAN-based aging monitoring technique for automotive ASICs with efficient soft error resilience. IEEE Access **8**, 22400–22410 (2020)
18. Ottavi, M., Vankamamidi, V., Lombardi, F., Pontarelli, S.: Novel memory designs for QCA implementation. In: The fifth IEEE Conference on Nanotechnology, pp. 545–548 (2005)
19. Debnath, B., et al.: Security analysis with novel image masking based quantum-dot cellular automata information security model. IEEE Access **8**, 1–4 (2020)

20. Datta, K., Mukhopadhyay, D., Dutta, P.: Comprehensive study on the performance comparison of logically reversible and irreversible parity generator and checker designs using two-dimensional two-dot one-electron QCA. Microsyst. Technol. **25**(5), 1659–1667 (2017). https://doi.org/10.1007/s00542-017-3445-2
21. Datta, K., Mukhopadhyay, D., Dutta, P.: Comprehensive design and analysis of Gray code counters using 2-dimensional 2-dot 1-electron QCA. Microsyst. Technol. **28**, 1–19 (2018). https://doi.org/10.1007/s00542-018-3818-1
22. Ghosh, M., Mukhopadhyay, D., Dutta, P.: A novel parallel memory design using 2 dot 1 electron QCA. In: IEEE 2nd International Conference on Recent Trends in Information Systems, pp. 485–490 (2015)

VCI Construction and Shifting Strategy Based Steganography for 3D Images

Subhadip Mukherjee[✉], Sunita Sarkar, and Somnath Mukhopadhyay

Department of Computer Science and Engineering, Assam University,
Silchar 788011, India
itissubhadip@gmail.com

Abstract. The prime goal of any steganography technique is to establish a digital covert communication, whereas, the hiding capacity is the big point of concern. The majority of the existing techniques and approaches investigates the trade-off between the hiding capacity and distortion. In this paper, we propose a novel information hiding technique in which we have explored a shifting strategy preceded by the vertex component interval or VCI construction mechanism to embed the confidential data within a 3-dimensional (3D) image effectively. Instead of using critical geometric way, we have used truncated space to decrease the hiding distortion and increase visual quality. Moreover, in this proposed method, the embedding capacity does not depend upon the shape of images that is why it can prevent the vertex reordering attack. Here, the truncation length is used to adjust the quality of the stego-image. Our innovative approach's versatility and great performance have been proved in a variety of experiments.

Keywords: 3d image steganography · Vertex component interval · PSNR · Information security

1 Introduction

Data hiding intends to hide a private message in a media files and only the authentic receiver can extract the private message with the help of a shared keys [2]. The sender tries to conceal as much data as possible within the cover media, whereas the receiver focuses on the hidden data's resilience at the price of hiding capacity. Generally, data hiding [13,15] is of two types, one is watermarking [16] and other is steganography [14]. The watermarking is the process of concealing digital data within a media file, mainly for copyright protection. There exist many 3D watermarking methods [12] but with limited data hiding capacity, because, they were not developed for this outcome to begin with. Whereas 3D image steganography [8,19] is the process of hiding data within a 3D image for developing a covert communication. In our proposed technique, a truncated space of information is generated. The components x, y, and z are decomposed in intervals of same size within the constructed truncated space. The

S. Mukhopadhyay et al. (Eds.): CICBA 2022, CCIS 1579, pp. 210–219, 2022.
https://doi.org/10.1007/978-3-031-10766-5_16

private data can then be integrated inside the component values by moving them across intervals. Because each value's alteration is constrained to the shortened space, the stego model's distortion might be minimal. We may also change the truncation length to keep the distortion within a certain range. The suggested technique can survive similarity transformation assaults because we pre-process models with uniform-scale, rotation, and normalisation. Our contributions are:

- We propose a new 3D steganography technique on the basis of the strategy of bit shifting, which hides the private data within a 3D image model.
- The proposed algorithm provides the efficiency of adjustable embedding capacity and visual quality.
- Instead of utilizing cover image's vertices directly, we construct the VCI, which produces a remarkable property that the distortion in the proposed steganography technique may be adjusted by changing the length of truncation.

2 Related Works

Several 3D data hiding schemes have been proposed in both spatial [9,10] and transform [6,11,21] domain. Hiding data in the spatial domain results larger amount of capacity in compare to transform domain, but at the cost of stego image's quality. Though in general, in transformed domains the steganography schemes results better robustness. But our intention is to embed private message in spatial domain because we want to maximise capacity. Instead of modifying the model vertices directly, we use a truncated space to improve the visual quality. In the year 2003, a bit substitution-based image steganography scheme was suggested by Cayre et al. [4], which could combat against similarity-transformation and vertex-reordering attacks. However, the biggest downsides are the limited embedding capacity and inefficient triangle traversal. After that, Wang et al. [18] suggested a steganography where they used a multilevel hiding and jump technique and obtained 3 three bits per vertex (bpv). Chao et al. [5] proposed a multilayer hiding procedure to achieve higher capacity of $3 \times l$, where l is the layer numbers. However, because to the fast-rising distortion, the number of embedded layers is restricted. Yang et al. [20] calculated a suitable quantization level for the model vertices and applied watermark bits to Least Significant Bits should be replaced if they aren't being used. It had a good capacity and minimal distortion, but when the quantity of embedded noise rises, the inaccuracy increases considerably, and it can not survive attacks various steganalysis. Tsai [17] suggested an adaptive data hiding technique that took hiding capacity and complexity estimation into account. Bogomjakov et al. [3] presented a new 3D steganography scheme using permutation for changing the polygon and vertex ordering. However, they obtained capacity of less than one bpv. Lin et al. [11] used vertex representation orders, triangle representation orders, and connection information to develop a distortion-free steganography technique in the representation domain. To increase embedding capacity, the approach might be used with other spatial-based steganography algorithms. However, the 3D steganography methods currently available have a very limited embedding capability. Despite the advancement of the aforementioned studies, it still warrants much further inquiry on lower distortion, robustness and higher hiding capacity.

3   Proposed Scheme

We propose a new 3D image steganography technique by constructing vertex component intervals with shifting strategy (see Fig. 1). The three components are x, y, and z of a vertex of a given 3D image I with the vertex set V. To achieve a standard mesh for data embedding with the translation, rotation, and uniform scaling, a pre-processing of the image is needed Initially.

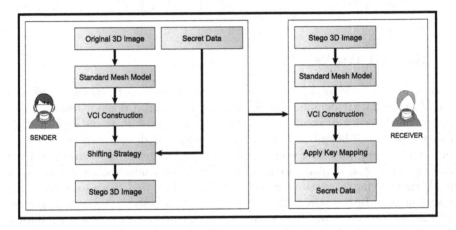

Fig. 1. Flowchart of the proposed method.

3.1   VCI Construction and Shifting Strategy

The vertex set V is basically a set of real numbers, in which some vertex belongs to the truncated space T_s and the remaining vertices are belongs to the residual space R_s. The set V of the original image is expressed in Eq. (1)

$$V = a \times (T_s(k) + T_r(k)) \tag{1}$$

where, a is the sign variable which represents positive or negative sign, $T_s(k)$ and $R_s(k)$ are the unsigned truncated and residual data, and k is the truncation length in decimal.

After the successful construction of the truncated space $T_s(k)$, take the component x_s and divide its range $[min\{x_s\}, max\{x_s\}]$ into equal-sized 2^m number of intervals $\{x_{s0}, x_{s1}, x_{s2}, ..., x_{s2^m-1}\}$, where m is an integer and the range of m in our experiment is $0 \leq m < \log_2 10^{15-k} + 1$ due to the digit limitation of Matlab. Several values that correspond to the vertices may be found in each interval. All the values within the intervals are used in the data embedding process except $min\{x_s\}$ and $max\{x_s\}$ and m bits of secret information can be concealed within each value. We have to avoid $min\{x_s\}$ and $max\{x_s\}$ to construct the same VCI in the extraction process which is very essential to extract the hidden data.

Each component's (z, y or x) absolute value is represented as $0.**...***$, where $0 < * < 9$, and it consists of fifteen decimal places in our experiment. Hence, for the range of k, $0 < k < 15$, the stego image is represented using the Eq. (2)

$$V' = a \times (T'_s(k) + T_r(k)) \tag{2}$$

where, V' represents the set of vertices of the stego image and $T'_s(k)$ is the stego vertex belongs to the truncated space.

For security purpose, we have applied a shifting strategy through a key mapping mechanism for embedding secret data within the original 3D image. The key mapping uses both k and m for the intervals of each vertex component. For shifting the cover values into the embeddable places in the mapping intervals, the embedded process simply employs the Key mapping (see Table 1).

Table 1. Key mapping for truncation length = 31.

Interval	31-bit data
0	0...00
1	0...01
2	0...10
3	0...11
...	...
31	1...11

3.2 Embedding Procedure

Entire embedding procedure of the proposed scheme is described step by step in Algorithm 1. This procedure takes an original 3D image and hides the secret data within the image using the Algorithm 1 and generates the stego 3D image.

3.3   Extraction Procedure

Entire embedding procedure of the proposed scheme is described step by step in Algorithm 2. This procedure takes the stego 3D image and extracts the hidden secret data from the image using the Algorithm 2.

Algorithm 1. Embedding Procedure

Step 1: Obtain a standard model from the original image I.

Step 2: Generate the space of truncation $T_s(k)$ using equation 1.

Step 3: For the component x_s in $T_s(k)$, split $[min\{x_s\}, max\{x_s\}]$ into 2^m equal sized intervals and obtain the set $\{x_{s0}, x_{s1}, x_{s2}, ..., x_{s2^m-1}\}$.

Step 4: Generate the equal sized intervals for the components y_s and z_s in the same way as described in Step 3.

Step 5: For each embeddable value, embed m bits of secret message within the value using the key mapping by performing a shift to another interval. Do not embed any secret data within $min\{x_s\}$ and $max\{x_s\}$.

Step 6: Repeat Step 4 and 5 until the entire private bits are concealed.

Step 7: Generate the stego-image I' using V' in Eq. 2.

Algorithm 2. Extraction Procedure

Step 1: Preprocess the stego image I' and generate the space of truncation as described in Subsection 3.1.

Step 2: Generate the equal sized intervals for all the components using the received key m which was used in the data embedding process.

Step 3: Since $max\{x_s\}$, $min\{x_s\}$, $max\{y_s\}$, $min\{y_s\}$, $max\{z_s\}$, and $min\{z_s\}$ are remained unchanged in the stego image, so for components x, y and z, the interval stego value belongs to $T'_s(k)$ can be easily identified.

Step 4: Now determine the stego values as well as their corresponding stego intervals. After that, according to the key mapping, extract m bits private message from the stego value.

Step 5: After extracting all the secret bits, combine the bits and get the private message.

---

4   Experimental Results

Various 3D images are taken from [1] (see Fig. 2) for showing the efficiency of our scheme in terms of visual quality and embedding capacity, where each component of a single vertex of an image contains 15 decimal places. The experiments are performed in Matlab 7.6.0 software. The visual quality of the stego-image is justified using measurement of peak-signal to noise-ratio (PSNR), which is calculated using Eq. 3.

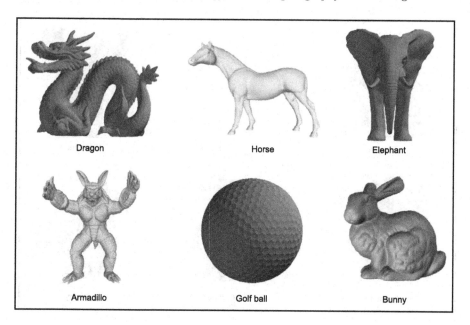

Fig. 2. Test images.

$$PSNR = 20 \log_{10} \frac{D_d}{\sqrt{\frac{1}{V_n} \sum_{x=1}^{V_n} \|w_x - w'_x\|^2}} \tag{3}$$

where, the total number of vertices is represented by V_n, D_d is the bounding box's diagonally distance of the original 3D model, W'_x and W_x are the vertices of stego and original images, respectively. Embedding capacity (EC) is basically measures the number of secret bits hidden in an image and it is calculated using Eq. 4, where T is the total number of hidden bits.

$$EC = \frac{T}{V_n} \tag{4}$$

In Table 2, the maximum value of m for different truncation lengths $k = \{0, 1, ..., 14\}$ is displayed. With correspondence to Table 2, the PSNR and EC, for different k and m, of the proposed scheme is shown in Table 3, where, NA means not applicable. We discovered that the truncation length k has significant impact on the PSNR, whereas the m has very little impact. The stego-images are shown in Fig. 3.

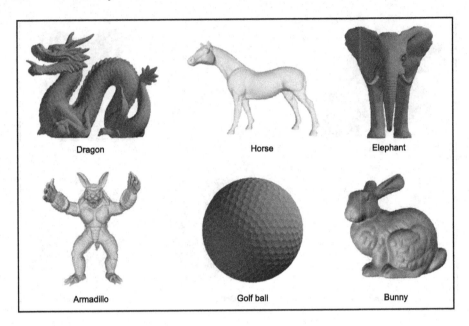

Fig. 3. Stego images.

Table 2. The maximum value of m for each value of k.

Maximum value of m	4	7	11	14	17	21	24	27	31	34	37	41	44	47	50
Length of truncation k	14	13	12	11	10	9	8	7	6	5	4	3	2	1	0

Table 3. PSNR and EC for different values of k and corresponding m.

k	Metrices	m					
		50	40	25	15	10	1
14	PSNR	NA	NA	NA	NA	NA	290.77
	EC	NA	NA	NA	NA	NA	2.99
10	PSNR	NA	NA	NA	210.29	210.26	210.30
	EC	NA	NA	NA	44.98	29.98	2.99
8	PSNR	NA	NA	NA	170.31	170.32	170.55
	EC	NA	NA	NA	44.98	29.98	2.99
6	PSNR	NA	NA	130.28	130.25	130.28	130.42
	EC	NA	NA	74.96	44.98	29.98	2.99
4	PSNR	NA	NA	90.26	90.22	90.28	90.30
	EC	NA	NA	74.96	44.98	29.98	2.99
0	PSNR	13.90	13.94	13.93	13.89	13.92	13.95
	EC	149.93	119.94	74.96	44.98	29.98	2.99

In Table 4, PSNR values of different images for $m = \{1, 5, 10, 15, 25, 30, 35\}$ and k = 4 are shown. The results in this table shows the consistency of the proposed scheme. As stated in Table 2, for k = 4, we can use the maximum value of m i.e., 37; that is why in Table 4, we have shown the PSNR values for maximum m = 37. The PSNR value of each image is very close for different values of m. In Table 5, comparison with other existing schemes is shown. Here, n is the number of layers in [5] and [11], whereas α is a constant in [11]. We can see that our proposed method provides larger EC than other methods. For k = 6 and m = 31, proposed method can embed 90 bpv, it could be larger i.e., 150 bpv, if we set k = 0. Here, the relationship of PSNR and EC is adjustable which makes the proposed scheme more flexible and effective. Moreover, the computational complexity of the proposed method is $O(n^2)$.

Table 4. The PSNR values of different images (k = 4) for different values of m.

m	Images					
	Golf ball	Elephant	Horse	Armadillo	Bunny	Dragon
1	133.14	129.09	130.42	133.18	133.67	131.32
5	132.77	128.77	130.26	133.14	133.24	131.39
10	132.96	128.90	130.28	133.22	133.12	131.42
15	133.01	128.58	130.25	133.49	133.38	131.25
25	133.01	128.96	130.28	133.39	133.14	131.26
30	132.96	128.83	130.35	133.08	133.15	131.12
37	132.82	128.84	130.29	133.38	133.15	131.24

Table 5. Comparison with other existing schemes.

Schemes	Domain	Capacity	Distortion	Vertex reordering	Uniform scaling
[4]	Spatial	V_n	Incremental	Yes	Average
[6]	Spatial and representation	$9V_n$	Incremental	No	Average
[5]	Spatial	$3nV_n$	Incremental	Yes	Average
[11]	Spatial and representation	$\alpha + 3nV_n$	Incremental	Yes	Average
[20]	Spatial	$70V_n$	Adjustable	Yes	Average
[7]	Geometric	$6V_n$	Incremental	Yes	Average
Proposed	Spatial	$90V_n$	Adjustable	Yes	Yes

5 Conclusion

In this paper, we have proposed a new 3D image steganography scheme using VCI construction and bit shifting strategy. The proposed scheme has the capability of adjusting the EC with better visual quality. The advantages of our scheme are: higher EC, adjustable distortion, efficiency and robustness. Our method can survive from different attacks like vertex reordering, rotation, uniform scaling. Our proposed method provides larger EC i.e., for truncation length k = 6, the proposed method can embed 90 bpv and it could be larger i.e., 150 bpv, if we set k = 0. Our exhaustive tests and comparisons with existing state-of-the-art methods have shown that our scheme has a high hiding capacity, customizable stego image visual, and adequate security.

References

1. Stanford 3D Scanning Repository. http://graphics.stanford.edu/data/3Dscanrep/
2. Anusha, M., Bhanu, K., Divyashree, D.: Secured communication of text and audio using image steganography. In: 2020 International Conference on Electronics and Sustainable Communication Systems (ICESC), pp. 284–288. IEEE (2020)
3. Bogomjakov, A., Gotsman, C., Isenburg, M.: Distortion-free steganography for polygonal meshes. In: Computer Graphics Forum, vol. 27, pp. 637–642. Wiley Online Library (2008)
4. Cayre, F., Macq, B.: Data hiding on 3-d triangle meshes. IEEE Trans. Signal Process. **51**(4), 939–949 (2003)
5. Chao, M.W., Lin, C.h., Yu, C.W., Lee, T.Y.: A high capacity 3d steganography algorithm. IEEE Trans. Vis. Comput. Graph. **15**(2), 274–284 (2008)
6. Cheng, Y.M., Wang, C.M.: A high-capacity steganographic approach for 3d polygonal meshes. Vis. Comput. **22**(9), 845–855 (2006)
7. Farrag, S., Alexan, W.: A high capacity geometrical domain based 3d image steganography scheme. In: 2019 International Conference on Advanced Communication Technologies and Networking (CommNet), pp. 1–7. IEEE (2019)
8. Farrag, S., Alexan, W.: Secure 3d data hiding technique based on a mesh traversal algorithm. Multimedia Tools Appl. **79**(39), 29289–29303 (2020)
9. Girdhar, A., Kumar, V.: A reversible and affine invariant 3d data hiding technique based on difference shifting and logistic map. J. Ambient. Intell. Humaniz. Comput. **10**(12), 4947–4961 (2019)
10. Jiang, R., Zhang, W., Hou, D., Wang, H., Yu, N.: Reversible data hiding for 3d mesh models with three-dimensional prediction-error histogram modification. Multimedia Tools Appl. **77**(5), 5263–5280 (2018)
11. Lin, C.H., Chao, M.W., Chen, J.Y., Yu, C.W., Hsu, W.Y.: A high-capacity distortion-free information hiding algorithm for 3d polygon models. Int. J. Innov. Comput. Inf. Control **9**(3), 1321–1335 (2013)
12. Liu, G., Wang, Q., Wu, L., Pan, R., Wan, B., Tian, Y.: Zero-watermarking method for resisting rotation attacks in 3d models. Neurocomputing **421**, 39–50 (2021)
13. Mukherjee, S., Jana, B.: A novel method for high capacity reversible data hiding scheme using difference expansion. Int. J. Nat. Comput. Res. (IJNCR) **8**(4), 13–27 (2019)
14. Mukherjee, S., Sarkar, S., Mukhopadhyay, S.: A LSB substitution-based steganography technique using DNA computing for colour images. In: Mandal, J.K., Mukhopadhyay, S., Unal, A., Sen, S.K. (eds.) Proceedings of International Conference on Innovations in Software Architecture and Computational Systems. SADIC, pp. 109–117. Springer, Singapore (2021). https://doi.org/10.1007/978-981-16-4301-9_9
15. Mukherjee, S., Sarkar, S., Mukhopadhyay, S.: Pencil shell matrix based image steganography with elevated embedding capacity. J. Inf. Secur. Appl. **62**, 102955 (2021)

16. Singh, R., Ashok, A.: An optimized robust watermarking technique using CKGSA in frequency domain. J. Inf. Secur. Appl. **58**, 102734 (2021)
17. Tsai, Y.Y.: An adaptive steganographic algorithm for 3d polygonal models using vertex decimation. Multimedia Tools Appl. **69**(3), 859–876 (2014)
18. Wang, C.M., Cheng, Y.M.: An efficient information hiding algorithm for polygon models. In: Computer Graphics Forum, vol. 24, pp. 591–600. Citeseer (2005)
19. Xiang, X., Liu, Q., Qin, J., Tan, Y.: 3D coverless image steganography scheme based on 3D slice technology. In: Sun, X., Zhang, X., Xia, Z., Bertino, E. (eds.) ICAIS 2021. CCIS, vol. 1424, pp. 291–300. Springer, Cham (2021). https://doi.org/10.1007/978-3-030-78621-2_23
20. Yang, Y., Peyerimhoff, N., Ivrissimtzis, I.: Linear correlations between spatial and normal noise in triangle meshes. IEEE Trans. Visual Comput. Graphics **19**(1), 45–55 (2012)
21. Zhou, H., Zhang, W., Chen, K., Li, W., Yu, N.: Three-dimensional mesh steganography and steganalysis: a review. IEEE Trans. Vis. Comput. Graph. (2021)

Optimal MAC Scheduling Algorithm for Time-Sensitive Applications in Multi-UE Scenarios in 5G NR MmWave

Sudipta Majumder[1](✉) and Abhijit Biswas[2]

[1] Department of CSE, DUIET, Dibrugarh University, Dibrugarh, Assam, India
`sudipta2020@dibru.ac.in`
[2] Department of CSE, Assam University, Silchar, Assam, India
`abhijit.biswas@aus.ac.in`

Abstract. 5G Millimetre-wave (mmWave) utilizes frequencies ranging from 24 GHz to 100 GHz. There are various scheduling techniques in 5G mmWave, which work distinctly for different applications. Time-sensitive applications are very sensitive to the response time of resource allocation requests. We have compared the performance of various media access control (MAC) schedulers in scarce resources and the high demand of resources in the 5G mmWave network to find the optimal scheduler for the scenarios. We have used Netsim version 12.02 for the simulation.

We have created the simulation test-bed with user equipment (UEs) placed at different locations with different constant bit rate (CBR) applications in the 5G mmWave network and recorded the necessary observations. We have considered network metrics like throughput, delay, jitter, and a few other parameters to evaluate network performance. After analyzing data, we have found that max throughput is best suited for time-sensitive applications when UEs are placed near the next-generation base station (gNB). We arrived at this conclusion because throughput is approximately 33% and 6% higher than round-robin and Fair Scheduling algorithms. The delay of round-robin and Fair Scheduling is 192% and 231% higher than the max throughput. Also, jitter is almost 300% higher for the same. Similarly, The fair Scheduling algorithm is best suited for time-sensitive applications, placed far away from gNB, compared to round-robin, max throughput, and proportional fair Scheduling algorithms. Our findings will help service providers with limited resources and critical and time-sensitive applications.

Keywords: 5g mmWave · Round robin · Proportional fair · Fair scheduling · Max throughput · Throughput · Jitter · Delay

1 Introduction

As the name implies, 5G is the fifth generation standard used in cellular networks. Early 2019 has seen an increased inclination towards 5G mobile technology, which was evident from many companies' testing and deployment of 5G

S. Mukhopadhyay et al. (Eds.): CICBA 2022, CCIS 1579, pp. 220–236, 2022.
https://doi.org/10.1007/978-3-031-10766-5_17

technology. The geographical area of this network is divided into small sections known as cells. All devices in a cell, are connected to the internet via a network of smaller antennas. Radio waves are used to communicate between antennas and devices.

The 5G network employs two types of bands. They are low band frequencies that use 602 to 850 MHz sequences and high band frequencies that use 20 to 100 GHz. It should be noted that 5G low band cell towers have nearly identical coverage area and range as 4G towers. However, the coverage area for high band 5G (also known as mmWave or mmW) is very limited. The internet speed in the high band 5G coverage area is much faster than in the low band 5G coverage area.

Quality of Service (QoS) is a critical 5G parameter. The 5G network thrives on increasing spectral efficiency. Latency reduction is essential for this. 5G necessitates handling various types of traffic and a diverse set of devices. The QoS requirements for these devices are distinct. Implementing a scheduling technique based on the channel access mechanism and radio resources allocation is difficult. Various parameters, such as channel conditions, number of users, graphics type, and so on, play essential roles in the design of scheduling algorithms [8,20].

In this research article, we investigated finding the optimal scheduling algorithm for UEs placed at different locations in w.r.t to gNBs in 5g mmWave network at scarce resources supply and high resource demand situations. The motivation of this research is that all scheduling algorithms react differently in different situations and it all may not be best suited for extreme conditions like scarce resources and high demand. By carrying out this research, we will predict the optimal scheduling for gNBs when UEs are placed near, far, and medium distance in scarce resources and high demand situations in a 5g mmWave network. Our findings will help gNBs make the best decision regarding selecting MAC schedulers.

In this section, we provided a brief introduction to the research problem. The rest of the article is divided into the methodology, results, discussion, conclusion, and reference sections. The methodology section gives the details of the methods of experiments and justification of the approach. The result and discussion section offers all the findings in tabular and graphical form and discusses our findings and their impacts. We summarized the important finding and related future work in the conclusion and future work section. Finally, we mentioned all the referred research articles in the reference section.

2   Literature Review

In this section, we have summarized all the research articles that give a theoretical base for the research and help us determine the nature of our research. We studied various MAC scheduling algorithms in the 5G mmWave network. The core of wireless communication networks in 5G is radio resource management (RRM). Its objective is to guarantee the QoS required by the devices and the users [15,16]. The RRM tries its best to optimally utilises the available radio frequency spectrum and the infrastructure for the radio network [2,4,12]. The function of RRM can be divided into two groups, namely scheduling and resource allocation [1,5]. Thus, we may call it a scheduler and a resource allocator. The primary function of the scheduler is to determine which user must be served first. The Schedulers are located in base stations [21].

It also decides the required number of packets to be scheduled at any instance of time and allocation of resource blocks (RBs) to the current user. It also determines what number of RBs will be required to maintain the QoS requirement of each user and device. It is the scheduler's responsibility to maintain the overall system performance even if there is high traffic volume. The cellular mobile network should, to the greatest extent possible, meet the service requirements of UE applications via RRM mechanisms [22]. The RRM is responsible for various jobs for the management of QoS for all the users and devices. These include cell search, radio link monitoring, power control, cell reselection, radio admission control(RAC), handover of UEs, self-organising networks(SONs), intercell interference control(ICIC) and last but not least, scheduling [7,18]. [10] proposed a unified scheduler for maximizing instantaneous throughput and fairness over each RB. The responsibility of RAC is to check and manage if a new bearer, with a guaranteed bit rate (GBR), can be established or not, depending upon the current network load [13].

Also, there is another entity called channel quality indicator (CQI). Its function is to receive CQI information from the UEs and to report the current QoS between the UEs and eNB. The scheduler makes critical decisions on scheduling based on the information provided by the CQI manager. Thus, the scheduler decides where the next packet will be sent using the current CQI report of all users in the cell. Now, let's discuss the scheduling algorithms used by the scheduler of RRM.

2.1 Round-robin Scheduling

Round robin scheduling is one of the simplest schedulers available. It does not consider the current radio channel condition while deciding which user equipment to serve next. It equally shares available resources with all the UE on a first-come, first-serve (FCFS) basis [9]. The main drawback of round-robin scheduling is that it does not do fair scheduling with all the user equipment in terms of offering the same quality of service.

In order to do justice to the required QoS to UE, it will need to prioritize user equipment with low radio channel conditions by increasing the frequency of the service. It is because it serves all the user equipment irrespective of their channel condition. As a result, the overall throughput is lower.

2.2 Fair Scheduling

This scheduler is also called the UE-based maximum rate scheduler. The functioning of the scheduler is very much similar to that of the proportional fair scheduler, with the exception that Packets are always sent through the link which has the best conditions.

The best-case scenario for this algorithm is when the system has the lowest value of CQIs; then, it will transmit over the available RBs. All the traffics in the RB queue are regrouped into four traffic classes. Each traffic class has priorities of packet transmission, which may vary from one another. This scheduling algorithm maximizes the throughput for each UE based on the QCI value of different RBs

2.3   Proportional Fair Scheduler

The proportional fair scheduling algorithm is sometimes referred to as single carrier proportional fair scheduling or multi-carrier proportional fair depending upon which environment is used. The LTE-Advanced network or 5G network is a multi-carrier network. Hence, proportional fair scheduling is referred to as a multi-carrier proportional fair algorithm in our case.

The proportional fair algorithm is relatively more complex than the round-robin and max throughput algorithm. The objective of the proportional fair scheduling algorithm is to improve overall network throughput by considering current radio channel condition [14]. Still, at the same time, it has to ensure the same average or minimum throughput is maintained.

This algorithm will result in less starvation of UEs with low radio channel conditions. The PF essentially shares spectral resources to UE with related best radio channel conditions. The algorithm can be expressed as

$$k = arg\ max_i \frac{R_i}{\underline{R_i}} \qquad (1)$$

where

k is the selected UE; R_i is the to data rate for UE_i; $\underline{R_i}$ is the average data rate of UE_i.

The average data rate is needed to be calculated over some specific period of time. The period is generally kept short so that the average data rate is not influenced by the long-term difference of radio channel conditions. Also, the period is not kept too short so that it does not get influenced by extreme variation of the short-term variation.

2.4   Max Throughput Scheduler

This algorithm is also known as the maximum rate scheduler [11]. The MT schedules the user with the currently available best radio channel condition by considering the current radio channel condition and radio link quality.

The objective of the scheduler is to maximize the throughput of the system and serve the UEs with the best available channel conditions. We can mathematically express the algorithm for the scheduler as follows:

$$k = arg\ max_i R_i \qquad (2)$$

where

R_i is the to current data rate for UE_i

The drawback of the algorithm is that it is not fair every time. If a UE is near eNB, it will be getting better radio channel conditions, whereas the far-away UEs are more likely to have poor channel conditions for a longer period of time . It is possible for the far-away UEs never to get good channel condition leading to "starvation" [13].

Perdana, Doan, et al. have assessed the performance of round-robin and proportional fair scheduling algorithms in 5G mmWave in terms of delay throughput and fairness in [17]. They studied and measured voice traffic performance. Firyaguna, Fadhil et al. have investigated the scheduling in 5G mmWave under human blocking and in [6]. The performance of 5G mmWave networks with physical-layer and capacity-limited blocking was investigated by Wu, Jingjin, and their colleagues in [23]. Saikia and Majumder have studied the effect of DoS attack in the performance of various MAC schedulers in 5g mmWave [19]. Similarly, Arnab Roy, Pachuau, and colleagues surveyed queuing delay, its effects, and management on various models such as the little theorem, M/M/1, and M/M/m in 5g in [3].

The primary goal of this research is to contribute to the efforts made by scholars to build efficiently performing MAC schedulers, selection of appropriate schedulers for the 5G NR mmWave network and fill in the gaps left by them. To achieve the goal, we have studied and analyzed the host to host layer, internet layer, and network access layer of the TCP/IP reference model of the 5G NR mmWave and MAC scheduling algorithms and found that the appropriate selection of MAC scheduling algorithm is very much essential for optimal performance of the network.

3   Methodology

A typical 5G NR nnWave setup includes a number of devices. Wireless nodes, wired nodes, access points, routers, EPC (Evolved Packet Core), gNB (equivalent to eNB in LTE), and user equipment are examples of such devices (UE). We have used Netsim 12.2 for the simulation of 5G NR mmWave. Our experiment setup used the following tools for the simulation of devices specific to the NetSim 5G NR library.

- UE (mmWave UE): People use user equipment, also known as UEs, for communication. The UE could be a cellular phone.
- gNB(mmWave eNB): This device is equivalent to eNB in LTE. It has got an LTE interface for wireless connection to UEs. It also has LTE S1 for wired connection to evolved packet Core. It has unlimited buffer capacity.
- EPC (evolved packet Core): The purpose of EPC is to connect gNB and new generation Core (NG). Packet gateway (PGW), mobility management entity (MME), and secure web gateways comprise the evolved packet core (SWG). The EPC is similar to the LTE EPC. The EPC can connect to all

of the routers in the NG core, and the NG core can connect to assess points, switches, servers, and so on.

The flow chart in Fig. 1 depicts how we did our research for MAC-based scheduling algorithm assessment. As the Fig. 1 shows, we have designed and set environments in a module for a 5G mmWave network. Then, we have designed simulation scenarios for our investigation. Once the test-bed was ready, we implemented a round-robin scheduler, fair scheduler, proportional fair scheduler, and max throughput scheduler to create multiple simulation scenarios. We have collected sufficient data through multiple executions of the simulation scenarios for various performance metrics. In this research article, we investigated finding the optimal scheduling algorithm for UEs placed at different locations in w.r.t to gNBs in 5g mmWave network at scarce resources supply and high resource demand situations. The motivation of this research is that all scheduling algorithms react differently in different situations. They all may not be best suited for extreme conditions like scarce resources and high demand. This research will predict the optimal scheduling for gNBs when UEs are placed near, far, and medium in scarce resources and high-demand situations in the 5g mmWave network. Our findings will help gNBs make the best decision regarding selecting MAC schedulers. First and foremost, the 5g mmWave module was created in Netsim version 12.2. After that, we created the simulation scenarios. Precaution and care are taken to ensure that most performance evaluation expectations are met.

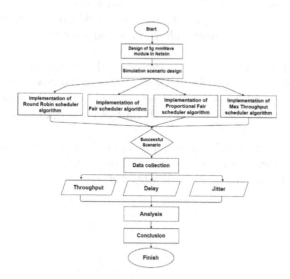

Fig. 1. Research method flow chart

After that, simulations were run for each scheduling algorithm, such as round robin, max throughput, proportional fair and fair scheduling algorithms. We made the required arrangements to collect the data during the process.

Data were gathered once the simulation was successful. We took three sets of parameters into account when evaluating the network's performance. They were throughput, latency, and jitter. After the relevant data was available, we calculated those parameters and then analyzed them. The pace at which a message is successfully delivered via a communication link is known as network throughput. It can be expressed as:

$$\alpha = \frac{\beta}{\gamma} \tag{3}$$

where

α = The throughput per user (Mbps); β = The sum of throughputs (Mbps); γ = The numbers of user.

Network latency is a design and performance property of a telecommunications network. It is the amount of time it takes for a piece of data to travel from one communication endpoint to the next over a network. It is commonly expressed in tenths or fractions of a second. It can be expressed as:

$$D_{nodal} = D_{proc} + D_{queue} + D_{trans} + D_{prop} \tag{4}$$

where

D_{nodal} = Nodal delay, D_{proc}= Processing delay, D_{queue}= Queuing delay, D_{trans}= Transmission delay, D_{prop}= Propagation delay.

Jitter happens when data packets are transferred with a temporal delay over your network connections. Route alterations and network congestion are both common causes for it.

The Fig. 2 shows that three UEs were used. Furthermore, we used only one gNB, EPC, and wired node. The UEs were placed 400, 800, and 1200 m apart from the gNB. The UEs were deliberately placed in those locations so that the effect of distance between UE and gNB on the performance of the scheduling algorithm could be measured.

The performance of MAC scheduling algorithms such as round robin, fair scheduling, max throughput scheduling, and proportional fair scheduling would be evaluated with the help of the following network.

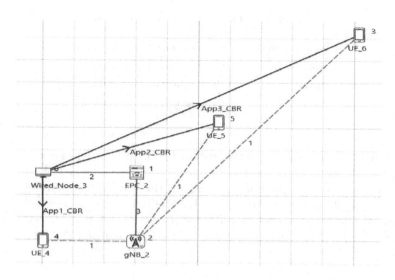

Fig. 2. Network test-bed for 5g NR mmWave

Table 1. gNB data link layer properties

Parameter	Value
Scheduler	Round robin
	Proportional fair
	Max throughput
	Fair scheduling

Table 2. Properties of Aplication used

Parameter	App 1	App 2	App 3
Application type	CBR	CBR	CBR
Source id	3	3	3
Destination id	4	5	6
QoS	UGS	UGS	UGS
Transport protocol	UDP	UDP	UDP
Packet size (Bytes)	1460	1460	1460
Inter arrival time	$10\,\mu s$	$10\,\mu s$	$10\,\mu s$
Start time	1	1	1

Table 3. gNB Physical layer properties

Parameter	Value
CA configuration	CA_2DL_1UL_n39_n41
CA numerology	2
Channel bandwidth	100 MHz
LOS probabillity	0
LOS mode	USER DEFINED
Outdoor scenario	URBAN MACRO

Table 4. Wired link properties

Link Type	Speed
Down link speed	5000 Mbps
Up link Speed	5000 Mbps

Table 5. Application and UE placements

Application Name	Device connections	Distance
App1	UE 4 to gNB 1	400 m
App2	UE 5 to gNB 1	800 m
App3	UE 6 to gNB 1	1200 m

The following are the simulation parameters used in the network.

Table 1 shows properties at the data link layer of gNB. Scheduler parameter can be any one of the routing protocols at any time. Table 2 explains the various properties of all three applications at UEs. Similarly, Table 3 and Table 4 show the physical layer properties of gNB and wired link properties, respectively. Finally, Table 5 shows the connection between devices and distances among them.

4   Results and Discussions

Instantaneous throughput and cumulative moving average are calculated and shown in Fig. 3 to 11 for multiple applications and scheduling algorithms.

We are measuring instantaneous throughput over a very short time interval. We can see from the Figs. 3, 4 and 5 that the throughput has decreased significantly for each application, and as a result, the cumulative moving average has also decreased. The figures given are for the round-robin scheduling algorithm.

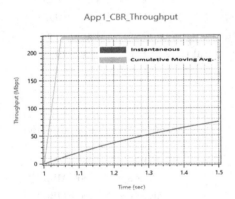

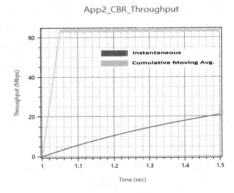

Fig. 3. Instantaneous throughput & cumulative moving average for App1 for round robin Scheduling

Fig. 4. Instantaneous throughput & cumulative moving average for App2 for round robin Scheduling.

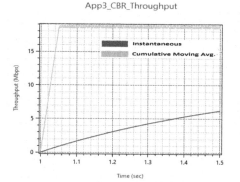

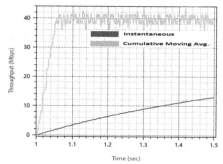

Fig. 5. Instantaneous throughput & cumulative moving average for App-3 for round robin Scheduling.

Fig. 6. Instantaneous throughput & cumulative moving average for App-1 for fair scheduling.

We measure the instantaneous throughput if the measurement is taken over a very short time interval. If the measurement is taken over a long time interval, for example, the transfer of a whole group of files, we are measuring the average throughput. Average throughput is usually more consistent than instantaneous throughput. In statistics, a moving average (rolling average or running average) is a calculation to analyze data points by creating a series of averages of different subsets of the full data set. It is also called a moving mean or rolling mean.

In a cumulative moving average, the data arrive in an ordered datum stream, and we take the average of all of the data up until the current datum. The cumulative moving average in the Figs. 3, 4 and 5 are in the range of 230 to 240 Mbps, 60 to 65 Mbps and 19 to 20 Mbps range respectively for each applications in round-robin algorithms. The variations are because of the distance of placement of UEs from the gNB.

The instantaneous and cumulative moving averages for fair scheduling algorithms are shown in Fig. 6, 7 and 8. The cumulative moving averages for applications with fair scheduler are moving around 40 Mbps, as shown in Figs. 6, 7 and 8, because all the UEs, irrespective of their distance, are fairly scheduled by fair scheduling algorithm. It should be noted that the distance between user equipment (UE) and gNB has almost no effect on the algorithm's performance, as observed from the graphs. The Fig. 9 shows that the throughput is incredibly high for App1 as compared to that of App2 in Fig. 10. As a result, the cumulative moving average is high as well.

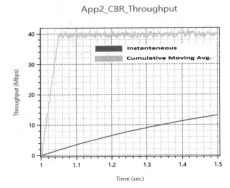

Fig. 7. Instantaneous throughput & cumulative moving average for App2 for fair scheduling.

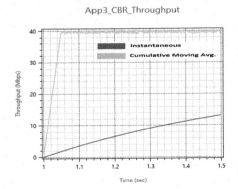

Fig. 8. Instantaneous throughput & cumulative moving average for App3 for fair scheduling.

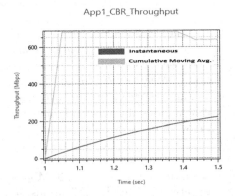

Fig. 9. Instantaneous throughput & cumulative moving average for App1 for proportional fair scheduling.

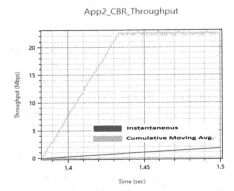

Fig. 10. Instantaneous throughput & cumulative moving average for App2 for propertional fair scheduling.

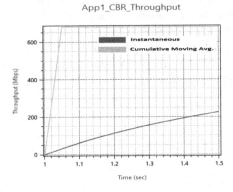

Fig. 11. Instantaneous throughput & cumulative moving average for App1 for max throughput Scheduling.

As shown in Fig. 10, the network's performance has deteriorated significantly for App1. In addition, the throughput is reduced to zero in the case of App3, which is located 1200 m away. As a result, we haven't included the graph here.

Figure 11 shows that the instantaneous throughput and cumulative moving average are extremely high for App1 with max throughput algorithms. However, for UE 5 and UE 6, the instantaneous throughput and cumulative average are both zero. As a result, we have omitted both graphs. The throughputs are calculated based on Eq. 3.

The Table 6 shows us the throughputs of various applications in various scheduling algorithms. App1 is the application used to connect the wired node to UE 4. Similarly, App2 and App3 are the applications for communication between wired nodes and UE 5 and UE 6, respectively.

It should be noted that the throughput for App3 in the proportional fair and max throughput algorithms is zero. App3 is connected to UE 6, which is located at the furthest position as compared to UE 4 and UE 5. Physical layer (PHY) rate is the maximum speed that data can move across a wireless link between a wireless client and a wireless router. The PHY rate is decided based on the signal-to-noise ratio (SNR). A UE closer to the gNB will get a higher PHY rate than a UE further away. In the given scenario, the distances from the gNB are such that UE6-Distance > UE5-Distance > UE4-Distance. Hence, the throughput for App2 and App3 for the max throughput scheduler is zero. Similarly, the throughput of App3 for the proportional fair scheduler is zero.

Table 6. Throughputs for different applications in different scheduling algorithms

	Round robin	Fair scheduler	Proportional fair	Max throughput
App1	225.330	39.314	666.764	676.435
App2	62.791	39.478	5.232	0
App3	18.594	39.641	0	0

The Table 7 displays the system's average throughputs for various applications and scheduling algorithms. Even though Apps 2 and 3 have zero throughput, we find that the max throughput algorithm has the highest throughput. It has happened because the algorithm is unjust and causes UEs to starvation.

Table 7. Average throughputs for different applications in different scheduling algorithms

Round robin	Fair scheduler	Proportional fair	Max throughput
102.238	39.478	223.999	225.478

The Table 8 and 9 show the delays and average delays for all the applications in different scheduling algorithm simulation scenarios. The delays are calculated based on Eq. 4.

Table 8. Delays for different applications in different scheduling algorithms

	Round robin	Fair scheduling	Proportional fair	Max throughput
App1	201878	243516.8	104386.29	105089
App2	236809.8	242473.03	440723.28	0
App3	246538.7	241485.39	0	0

Table 9. Average delays for different applications in different scheduling algorithms

Round robin	Fair scheduler	Proportional fair	Max throughput
228408.8	242491.74	181703.192	35029.693

The jitters and average jitters for all applications in different scheduling algorithm simulation scenarios can be seen in the Tables 10 and 11

Table 10. Jitters for different applications in different scheduling algorithms

	Round robin	Fair scheduler	Proportional fair	Max throughput
App1	59.689	302.503	26.120	25.890
App2	190.588	297.425	525.337	0
App3	623.925	288.526	0	0

Table 11. Average jitters for different applications in different scheduling algorithms

Round robin	Fair scheduler	Proportional fair	Max throughput
291.401	296.151	183.819	8.630

Interestingly, we can see in Table 9 that even though the max throughput has the maximum throughput, the average delay is very high. The fair scheduling algorithm has the most amount of average jitter as shown in Fig. 11. The round-robin and fair scheduling algorithms have 192% and 231% higher delay (refer Fig. 15) than max throughput and proportional fair algorithms, respectively. Jitter is over 300 percent higher for the same (refer Fig. 16).

The throughputs for App1 for proportional fair and max throughput is substantially higher than round-robin and fair scheduling algorithms, as shown in Figs. 12. This is useful for applications that must be completed within a certain amount of time. The throughput is around 33% and 6% higher than that of round-robin and fair scheduling methods, respectively.

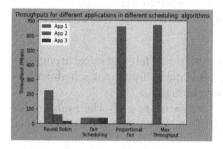

Fig. 12. Comparison of throughputs for applications for scheduling algorithms

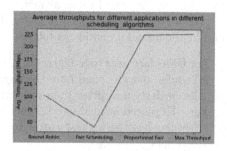

Fig. 13. Applications' avg .throughputs for scheduling algorithms

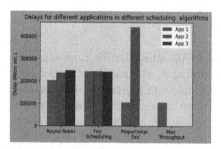

Fig. 14. Comparison of delay for applications for scheduling algorithms

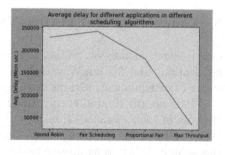

Fig. 15. Applications' avg. delay for scheduling algorithms

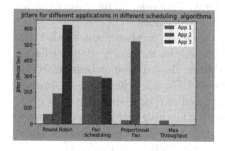

Fig. 16. Comparison of jitters for applications for scheduling algorithms

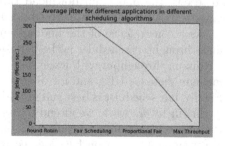

Fig. 17. Applications' avg. jitters for scheduling algorithms

The Figs. 12 and 13 show that for UE placed in a remote location, i.e. for App3, the fair scheduling method outperforms App3 of round-robin, proportional fair, and max throughput algorithms in terms of throughput.

In Fig. 14 and 15, though the delay for App3 in fair scheduling and round-robin are comparable but the jitter performs better in fair scheduling than round-robin algorithm. That is, the jitter in fair scheduling is approximately 216% lesser than that of the round-robin algorithm, as we can see in Fig. 16 and 17.

We can summarize our findings for the optimal scheduler for scarce resources and high demand scenarios as follows:

– For UEs place near (0 to 600 m) to gNB, proportional fair and max throughput scheduler give the maximum throughput. But max throughput scheduler has a lesser delay and jitter than proportional throughput.
– For UEs placed at medium distance (600 to 1000 m) to gNB, the round-robin scheduler has the highest throughput and lower delay and jitter than other schedulers.
– For UEs placed over a large distance (1000 m and above) to gNB, fair scheduler has the highest throughput than other schedulers. Throughput of fair scheduler and round-robin are comparable, but fair scheduler has lower jitter than round-robin.

5   Conclusion and Future Work

Our research focuses on finding the optimal MAC scheduler for time-sensitive applications in a 5G mmWave network. According to the results obtained, the choice of scheduling algorithms has a significant impact on network performance.

PRBs are distributed evenly among the three nodes (UEs) by round-robin. Because of their distances from the gNB, throughputs are in the order UE1 > UE2 > UE3. Each UE's individual throughput is exactly one-third of the total throughput. When using proportional fair scheduling, resource allocation is made in such a way that closer UEs receive a proportionally higher allocation (based on CQI) than UEs further away. PRBs are allotted in max throughput scheduling to receive the maximum download throughput. Fair scheduling ensures strict fairness, resulting in equal throughput for all applications.

As a consequence of the findings and its analysis, we can propose that the max throughput scheduler is the best-suited scheduler for nearly placed UEs for maximum throughput with lesser delay and jitter. Round robin is best suited for medium distance UEs, and for distantly placed UEs, fair scheduling is optimal. Finally, fair scheduler is best suited for UEs placed at a large distance from gNB.

In our future work, we intend to use machine learning techniques to improve the performance of the round-robin and fair scheduling algorithms for time-sensitive applications on UEs located far from the gNB in 5g mmWave.

References

1. Ahmad, A., Ahmad, S., Rehmani, M.H., Hassan, N.U.: A survey on radio resource allocation in cognitive radio sensor networks. IEEE Commun. Surv. Tutor. **17**(2), 888–917 (2015)
2. Akyildiz, I.F., Lee, W.Y., Vuran, M.C., Mohanty, S.: Next generation/dynamic spectrum access/cognitive radio wireless networks: a survey. Comput. Netw. **50**(13), 2127–2159 (2006). https://doi.org/10.1016/j.comnet.2006.05.001
3. Roy, A., Pachuau, J.L., Saha, A.K.: An overview of queuing delay and various delay based algorithms in networks. Computing **103**(10), 2361–2399 (2021). https://doi.org/10.1007/s00607-021-00973-3
4. Castaneda, E., Silva, A., Gameiro, A., Kountouris, M.: An overview on resource allocation techniques for multi-user mimo systems. IEEE Communications Surveys & Tutorials **19**(1), 239–284 (2016). https://doi.org/10.1109/COMST.2016.2618870
5. Clerckx, B., Joudeh, H., Hao, C., Dai, M., Rassouli, B.: Rate splitting for mimo wireless networks: a promising phy-layer strategy for lte evolution. IEEE Commun. Mag. **54**(5), 98–105 (2016). https://doi.org/10.1109/MCOM.2016.7470942
6. Firyaguna, F., Bonfante, A., Kibiłda, J., Marchetti, N.: Performance evaluation of scheduling in 5g-mmwave networks under human blockage. arXiv preprint arXiv:2007.13112 (2020)
7. Fodor, G., Rácz, A., Reider, N., Temesváry, A.: Architecture and protocol support for radio resource management (rrm). In: Long Term Evolution, pp. 113–168. Auerbach Publications (2016)
8. Héliot, F., Imran, M.A., Tafazolli, R.: Low-complexity energy-efficient resource allocation for the downlink of cellular systems. IEEE Trans. Commun. **61**(6), 2271–2281 (2013). https://doi.org/10.1109/TCOMM.2013.042313.120516
9. Hyytiä, E., Aalto, S.: On round-robin routing with fcfs and lcfs scheduling. Perf. Eval. **97**, 83–103 (2016). https://doi.org/10.1016/j.peva.2016.01.002
10. Jabeen, S., Haque, A.: An ici-aware scheduler for nb-iot devices in co-existence with 5g nr. In: 2021 IEEE 4th 5G World Forum (5GWF), pp. 236–240 (2021). https://doi.org/10.1109/5GWF52925.2021.00048
11. Jang, J., Lee, K.B.: Transmit power adaptation for multiuser of dm systems. IEEE J. Sel. Areas Commun. **21**(2), 171–178 (2003). https://doi.org/10.1109/JSAC.2002.807348
12. Mehaseb, M.A., Gadallah, Y., Elhamy, A., Elhennawy, H.: Classification of lte uplink scheduling techniques: an m2m perspective. IEEE Commun. Surv. Tutor. **18**(2), 1310–1335 (2015). https://doi.org/10.1109/COMST.2015.2504182
13. Müller, C.F., Galaviz, G., Andrade, Á.G., Kaiser, I., Fengler, W.: Evaluation of scheduling algorithms for 5G mobile systems. In: Sanchez, M.A., Aguilar, L., Castañón-Puga, M., Rodríguez-Díaz, A. (eds.) Computer Science and Engineering—Theory and Applications. SSDC, vol. 143, pp. 213–233. Springer, Cham (2018). https://doi.org/10.1007/978-3-319-74060-7_12
14. Nilsson, P., Pióro, M.: Solving dimensioning tasks for proportionally fair networks carrying elastic traffic. Perf. Eval. **49**(1–4), 371–386 (2002). https://doi.org/10.1016/S0166-5316.02.00114-1
15. Olwal, T.O., Djouani, K., Kurien, A.M.: A survey of resource management toward 5G radio access networks. IEEE Commun. Surv. Tutor. **18**(3), 1656–1686 (2016). https://doi.org/10.1109/COMST.2016.2550765

16. Pedersen, K.I., Kolding, T.E., Frederiksen, F., Kovacs, I.Z., Laselva, D., Mogensen, P.E.: An overview of downlink radio resource management for utran long-term evolution. IEEE Commun. Mag. **47**(7), 86–93 (2009). https://doi.org/10.1109/MCOM.2009.5183477

17. Perdana, D., Sanyoto, A.N., Bisono, Y.G.: Performance evaluation and comparison of scheduling algorithms on 5g networks using network simulator. Int. J. Comput. Commun. Control **14**(4), 530–539 (2019). https://doi.org/10.15837/ijccc.2019.4.3570

18. Sesia, S., Toufik, I., Baker, M.: LTE-the UMTS Long Term Evolution: From Theory to Practice. John Wiley & Sons, Hoboken (2011)

19. Sudipta Majumder, B.S.: Analysis of performance vulnerability of mac scheduling algorithms due to syn flood attack in 5g nr mmwave. Int. J. Adv. Technol. Eng. Explor. (2021). https://doi.org/10.19101/IJATEE.2021.874340

20. Suganya, S., Maheshwari, S., Latha, Y.S., Ramesh, C.: Resource scheduling algorithms for lte using weights. In: 2016 2nd International Conference on Applied and Theoretical Computing and Communication Technology (iCATccT), pp. 264–269. IEEE (2016). https://doi.org/10.1109/ICATCCT.2016.7912005

21. Taboada, I., Liberal, F., Fajardo, J.O., Blanco, B.: An index rule proposal for scheduling in mobile broadband networks with limited channel feedback. Perf. Eval. **117**, 130–142 (2017). https://doi.org/10.1016/j.peva.2017.09.007

22. Wang, S., Xi, B., Zhang, Z., Deng, B.: A downlink scheduling algorithm based on network slicing for 5G. In: Gao, H., Fan, P., Wun, J., Xiaoping, X., Yu, J., Wang, Y. (eds.) ChinaCom 2020. LNICST, vol. 352, pp. 212–225. Springer, Cham (2021). https://doi.org/10.1007/978-3-030-67720-6_15

23. Wu, J., Wang, M., Chan, Y.C., Wong, E.W., Kim, T.: Performance evaluation of 5g mmwave networks with physical-layer and capacity-limited blocking. In: 2020 IEEE 21st International Conference on High Performance Switching and Routing (HPSR), pp. 1–6. IEEE (2020). https://doi.org/10.1109/HPSR48589.2020.9098993

Computational Intelligence in Analytics

N-Gram Feature Based Resume Classification Using Machine Learning

Pradeep Kumar Roy[1(✉)] and Shivam Chahar[2]

[1] Department of Computer Science and Engineering,
Indian Institute of Information Technology, Surat, India
pkroynitp@gmail.com
[2] School of Computer Science and Engineering, Vellore Institute of Technology,
Vellore, India

Abstract. Shortlisting the right resume for the job is a tedious task for a job recruiter. For each post, thousands of applicants send their resumes; among all, very few resumes fit for the published job recruitment. Finding suitable resumes from a huge pool of resumes manually is a time-consuming process. This research addresses the above issue by suggesting a machine learning-based automated resume classification model. The automated resume classification model helps to classify the resume into different categories. Many classification models are used during the model development and found that the random forest classifier provides the most promising outcomes. The random forest classifier achieved the highest micro precision, recall, F1-score, and an accuracy value of 0.99 for the best case with the combination of uni- and bi-gram features.

Keywords: Resume classification · Supervised learning · Machine learning · Job recommendation

1 Introduction

Online job portals have begun to accept an overwhelming number of resumes in various types and formats from job seekers of various academic qualifications, work histories, and expertise in recent years. Finding and recruiting the best applicants from a diverse pool of recruits remains one of the HR department's most critical and difficult activities. According to LinkedIn, India has the largest number of workers who are "actively looking for a new job" [1]. To meet these challenges, many businesses have turned to e-recruiting systems. To solve the problems of sampling, matching, and classifying applicant resumes, these systems use a variety of tools and approaches. One of the approaches used, for example, discusses the automated pairing of employee resumes with their corresponding work offers [2].

The most difficult aspect is the lack of a standardized resume framework and structure, which makes shortlisting preferred profiles for appropriate positions very time-consuming and repetitive [3,4]. It's not straightforward to extract

S. Mukhopadhyay et al. (Eds.): CICBA 2022, CCIS 1579, pp. 239–251, 2022.
https://doi.org/10.1007/978-3-031-10766-5_18

details from resumes with high accuracy and recall. Even though resumes are a restricted space, they can be written in a variety of formats (e.g. in tables or plain texts), languages (e.g., English or in any native language), and file forms (e.g., Word, PDF, Text etc.). Furthermore, writing styles can be extremely varied. If non-relevant profiles can be eliminated in the process as early as possible, costs are saved in both time and resources [5].

One of the biggest challenges that are faced by the industry is the high volume of resumes received and filtering them to find the best match for the job. Recruiters are confronted with heightened demand to demonstrate recruit consistency, but they don't have the tools to correlate resume processing to post-hire metrics. Without the proper tools, it becomes very hard for recruiters to map the curriculum vitae (CV) to the job description. The word resume and CV carry the same meaning in this article. It is also difficult to determine whether the applicant is suitable/qualified for the position for which they are being recruited. Many researchers have attempted to address this issue using machine learning algorithms to identify work postings and resumes in relevant occupational groups. While these methods have shown to be more effective in terms of less time consumption, they have high error rates, and poor classification precision [6,7].

This paper presents an automated Machine Learning-based model to address the above problems in the resume shortlisting process. The model uses the attributes derived from the candidate's resume as feedback to classify them. Existing machine learning-based models are used to classify the incoming resume into different categories. We have compared the outcomes of the different models to select the best working model for the said task.

The rest of the paper is organized as follows: Sect. 2 discusses the existing research on a similar domain. In Sect. 3, we have explained the working steps of the proposed model. Section 4 discusses the outcomes of different classification models, and finally Sect. 5 concludes the work.

2   Literature Review

The number of work applicants is growing all the time; any job posting attracts many applications, many of which are important to the position being advertised. It poses a significant challenge for work recruiters, as they must choose the most qualified profile/resume from a large list of applicants [8–10]. To solve the e-recruitment issues, various methods and strategies have been suggested. In this sense, some methods solve problems with the matching process between employee resumes and work offers. In contrast, others try to distinguish resumes and job postings before beginning the matching process [11–15]. Martinez-Gil et al. [13] have suggested a method for comparing and querying knowledge in the human resources domain automatically. Standard approaches that merely search for similar keywords in the material of job postings and the applicant's resume, missing the implicit textual aspects in the text of both documents, are outperformed by the new method.

Lu et al. [16] proposed a detailed survey that covered the various methods that the researcher had used with the recommendation system in the previous few years. They talked about how recommendation systems are commonly used in real-time applications. Collaborative filtering, Content-based filtering, Knowledge-based filtering, and Hybrid methods are the four major categories of recommendation services [17]. Fazel-Zarandi and Fox [18], suggested a hybrid approach that uses a commonality-based approach to rate candidates to balance job seekers and job advertising. To boost the matching process, the proposed framework uses semantic technologies. However, the key disadvantage of this solution is the high cost of the matching method (due to its run-time complexity). Malinowski et al. [19] used an Expectation-Maximization (EM) algorithm for a job recommendation, which took into account both the candidate resume and the job description of the organization.

Golec and Kahya [20] used a fuzzy-based approach to assess candidate relevance with the listed job description. Paparrizos et al. [21] suggested another model that uses a hybrid classifier. They used knowledge extraction, manual attributes, and other methods for the job recommendation. Other methods employed machine learning algorithms to mark resume segments with the relevant category, taking advantage of the resume's semantic layout, which places related knowledge units in the same textual segments [11,12].

Even though resume classification is one of the major issues for the industry, it has received very little attention from the research community in recent years. The number of resumes for each job post is more than a thousand, and finding the relevant one manually from it is not an easy task. Conducting face-to-face interviews to select the candidate from the pool is also a time-consuming process [15]. To overcome this issue, a model that can do initial filters and classify the resume based on the job keywords may help recruiters save time and get the most desirable candidates for the post.

3   Research Methodology

As described in Sect. 1, the major issue faced by the industry is to filter suitable resumes from the pool of resumes that make sense of the candidate's resume and segregate qualified candidates into the talent pipeline right at the beginning of the recruitment process. We provide a machine learning based model to classify the resumes. The solution would assist in identifying the suitable CV from the pool of CVs.

3.1   Proposed Method

This research aims to classify the candidates' resumes into different categories. We designed a machine learning-based approach to accomplish this goal. The proposed model consisted of two steps: i) prepare the input for the model and ii) deploy an inference. Figure 1 depicts the entire architecture for the proposed model.

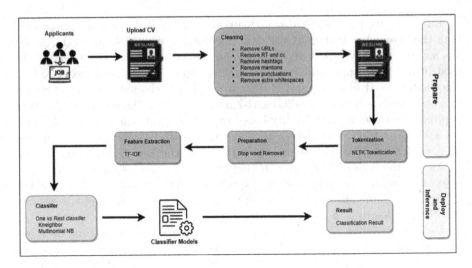

Fig. 1. Proposed framework to classify the resumes

Dataset Description: The data is in .csv format with two columns i) Category - What industry segment does the resume belong to and ii) Resume - The complete resume of the candidate containing the details of the candidates, such as Age, Qualification, Gender, etc. Figure 2 displays the total number of instances for each domain, and Fig. 3 shows category distribution in percentage.

Data Preprocessing: The CVs given as data will be cleansed -in this process, special or invalid characters are deleted. Cleaning consisted of removing URLs, Punctuation, Extra whitespace and other irrelevant information from the resume field of the imported raw CV file. After these moves, we had a clean dataset with no special characters, numbers, etc. NLTK tokenizers are used to separate the dataset into tokens. After this stop words were filtered, stop words like and, the, was, and others often appear in the text and are not useful in the prediction process, so they are removed. Steps involved in filtering stop words:

1. The input words were tokenized into individual tokens and stored in an array.
2. Every word now matches the list of Stop Words in the NLTK library
3. If the words appear in the oneSetOfStopWords list, they are removed from the main sentence array.
4. The procedure was replicated until the tokenized array's last element was not matched.
5. Now, there are no stop words in the resultant array.

The extraction of features is the next step. We used the Tf-Idf to extract features from a preprocessed dataset. The cleansed data was imported, and Tf-Idf was used to extract features. To process a machine learning-based classification model or learning algorithms, they require a fixed-size numerical vector as

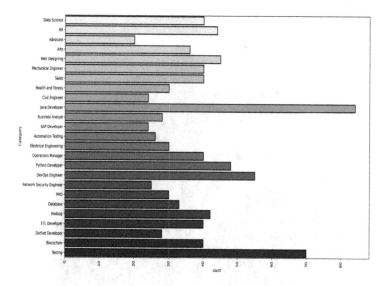

Fig. 2. Category distribution of resume

input. The texts are translated to a specified equal length vector form during the preprocessing steps. There are many methods for extracting features, including BoW (Bag of Words), tf-idf (Term Frequency, Inverse Document Frequency), and others. The appearance (and frequency) of words is taken into account in the BoW model. For each word in our dataset, we measured tf-idf (term frequency and inverse document frequency) using the scikit learn library function: sklearn.feature_extraction.text.TfidfVectorizer to measure a tf-idf vector. Sublinear df is set to True to use a logarithmic form for frequency. Stop word is set to "english" to remove all generic pronouns ("a", "an", "the", "there", etc.), reducing non-informative elements.

To develop the model, we have used the following classifiers.

1. K Nearest Neighbour (KNN) [22] - KNN is based on the idea that instances in a dataset can always be found in close proximity to those with identical characteristics. If each instance has a classification label, the value of an unclassified instance's label can be calculated by looking at the class of its closest Neighbours. The KNN finds the K nearest instances to the query instance and classifies them by finding the single most common class name. Several algorithms use weighting schemes to change each instance's distance measurements and voting influence for more precise results. The power of KNN has been seen in many real areas; however, there are some concerns about the usefulness of KNN, such as: (i) they are sensitive to the similarity function used to compare instances, (ii) they need a lot of storage, and (iii) they lack a principled way to choose K, unless you use cross-validation or other computationally expensive techniques.

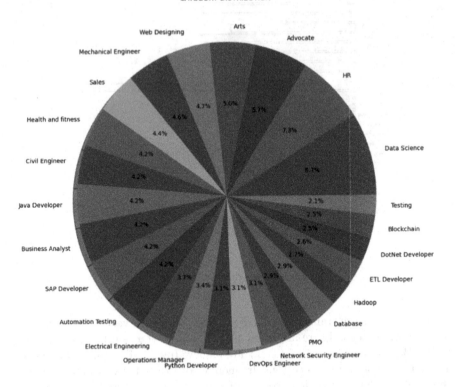

Fig. 3. Category distribution of resume in percentage

2. Naive Bayes (NB) [23]- The NB classifier is simple Bayesian networks made up of DAGs with only one parent (representing the unobserved node) and multiple children (representing observed nodes), with a firm expectation of child node independence in the form of their parent. The conditional probability is used in the fundamental architecture of Naive Bayes.

3. Random Forest (RF) [24] - The RF classifier is an ensemble classifier that makes a prediction using a series of CARTs [25]. The trees are constructed by replacing a subset of training samples (a bagging approach). This approach ensures that the same sample may be chosen several times, while others can go unselected at all. Additional RF features, such as using variable importance to optimize feature space and calculating the association between high-dimensional datasets using internal proximity matrix measurements, have sparked interest in recent years.

4. Gradient Boosting (GB) [26] - GB creates additive regression models by iteratively fitting a basic parameterized function (base learner) to existing "pseudo"-residuals using the least squares. The pseudo-residuals are the gradient of the loss functional being reduced concerning the model values at each training data point tested at the current level. By integrating random-

ization into the technique, the approximation precision and execution speed of gradient boosting can be significantly enhanced.

5. Support Vector Machine (SVM) [27] - The concept of a "margin"-either side of a hyperplane that divides two data classes-is central to SVMs. It has been shown that increasing the margin and thereby having the maximum possible difference between the dividing hyperplane and the instances on either side of it reduces the predicted generalization error. SVM is a well-known cutting-edge machine learning technique.

6. Logistic Regression (LR) [28]- The logistic function, which is at the heart of the system, is called logistic regression. The logistic function, also known as the sigmoid function, was created by statisticians to explain the properties of population growth in nature, such as how it rises rapidly and eventually reaches the environment's carrying capacity. It's an S-shaped curve that can map any real-valued number to a value between 0 and 1, but never exactly between those two points.

7. Decision Tree (DT) [29] - To beginners and professionals in the field of machine learning, Murthy [30] gave an outline of decision tree research and a sample of their utility. Decision trees are classification trees that sort instances based on feature values. Each branch of a decision tree represents a value that the node may assume, and each node represents a function in an instance to be categorized. Starting at the root node, instances are grouped and sorted based on their function values. Since a decision tree is a hierarchy of evaluations, dealing with an unknown feature value during classification normally entails moving the example down all branches of the node where the unknown feature value was found, with each branch producing a class distribution.

The classifiers mentioned above are used to classify the model. The outcomes of these models are discussed in Sect. 4.

4   Experimental Results

This research uses the supervised model to classify the resume in their respective category. Precision, recall, F1-score, and accuracy are used to evaluate the model. Mathematically, the precision, recall, F1-score and accuracy is defined as follows: Precision: it is the fraction of truly identified resumes among retrieved resumes. The recall is the fraction of truly predicted resumes among all resumes. F1-score is the harmonic mean of precision and recall. Accuracy is the number of resumes truly predicted in each class among the total dataset [31–34].

Various n-gram features were extracted using the Tf-Idf vectorizer from the processed resume. The results obtained using different n-gram features with DT classifier is shown in Table 1. The n-gram ranges 1,1 means only uni-gram features is selected, 2, 2 means only bi-gram, 1, 2 means both the uni and bi-grams and 1,3 means from uni to tri-gram features are considered. The best results were obtained using uni-gram and bi-gram features where the precision, recall, F1-score and Accuracy values are 0.97 for all cases.

Table 1. Results obtained with DT classifier on different settings

n-gram	Precision	Recall	F1-score	Accuracy
1,1	0.91	0.90	0.89	0.91
2,2	0.92	0.90	0.89	0.91
1,2	0.97	0.97	0.97	0.97
1,3	0.92	0.90	0.90	0.93
1,4	0.89	0.86	0.86	0.89
1,5	0.92	0.91	0.90	0.94

The KNN classifier yielded the best performance with the combination of uni-, bi-, and tri-gram features. The average macro precision, recall, F1-score, and accuracy obtained by the model is 0.97 (Table 2), which is similar to the performance of DT. As shown in Table 3, the performance of the model improved compared to the DT and KNN by achieving the macro average precision, recall, F1-score, and an accuracy value of 0.99, 0.98, 0.98 and 0.98, respectively. Next, we have used NB, SVM, and GB classifier, the outcomes of NB, SVM, and GB classifiers are shown in Table 4, 5, 6, respectively. The performance of these models is also similar to the previous models. Finally, we have used another ensemble learning-based classifier, namely RF, to check the prediction accuracy. The RF classifier achieves better performance as compared to DT, KNN, LR, NB, SVM, and GB by achieving the macro average precision, recall, F1-score, an accuracy value of 0.99, 0.99, 0.99, 0.99, respectively with the combination of uni- and bi-gram features (Table 7).

Table 2. Results obtained with KNN classifier on different settings

n-gram	Precision	Recall	F1-score	Accuracy
1,1	0.99	0.98	0.98	0.98
2,2	0.94	0.93	0.92	0.94
1,2	0.98	0.95	0.95	0.97
1,3	0.97	0.97	0.97	0.97
1,4	0.82	0.81	0.80	0.83
1,5	0.89	0.86	0.86	0.89

The best outcomes of the individual classifiers with their n-gram settings are present in Table 8. DT yielded the best performance with the combination of uni- and bi-gram features. KNN classifier achieved the best performance with uni-gram features, LR classifier used uni- to five-gram feature to achieve the best performance. The NB classifier gives the best outcome with the combination of uni- and bi-gram features. SVM uses only bi-gram feature for the best outcomes,

Table 3. Results obtained with LR classifier on different settings

n-gram	Precision	Recall	F1-score	Accuracy
1,1	0.99	0.98	0.98	0.98
2,2	0.94	0.93	0.92	0.94
1,2	0.98	0.95	0.95	0.97
1,3	0.97	0.97	0.97	0.97
1,4	0.82	0.81	0.80	0.83
1,5	0.89	0.86	0.86	0.89

Table 4. Results obtained with NB classifier on different settings

n-gram	Precision	Recall	F1-score	Accuracy
1,1	0.98	0.95	0.96	0.95
2,2	0.94	0.92	0.92	0.95
1,2	0.98	0.95	0.95	0.97
1,3	0.86	0.83	0.80	0.88
1,4	0.95	0.94	0.93	0.95
1,5	0.92	0.90	0.90	0.93

Table 5. Results obtained with SVM classifier on different settings

n-gram	Precision	Recall	F1-score	Accuracy
1,1	0.92	0.90	0.90	0.93
2,2	0.94	0.94	0.94	0.95
1,2	0.83	0.80	0.78	0.84
1,3	0.85	0.72	0.71	0.80
1,4	0.86	0.83	0.80	0.88
1,5	0.91	0.90	0.89	0.91

Table 6. Results obtained with GB classifier on different settings

n-gram	Precision	Recall	F1-score	Accuracy
1,1	0.94	0.91	0.92	0.93
2,2	0.92	0.9	0.90	0.93
1,2	0.99	0.98	0.98	0.98
1,3	0.89	0.89	0.87	0.92
1,4	0.98	0.95	0.95	0.97
1,5	0.92	0.91	0.90	0.91

Table 7. Results obtained with RF classifier on different settings

n-gram	Precision	Recall	F1-score	Accuracy
1,1	0.95	0.94	0.93	0.95
2,2	0.89	0.89	0.87	0.92
1,2	0.99	0.99	0.99	0.99
1,3	0.92	0.91	0.90	0.94
1,4	0.92	0.91	0.90	0.94
1,5	0.92	0.90	0.90	0.93

and the GB classifier used tri-gram to five-gram features for the best outcomes. Finally, the RF classifier uses the combination of uni- and bi-gram features for the best outcomes.

Table 8. The best performing model of individual classifier

Classifier	Best n-gram	Precision	Recall	F1-score	Accuracy
DT	1,2	0.97	0.97	0.97	0.97
KNN	1,1	0.99	0.98	0.98	0.98
LR	1,5	0.97	0.99	0.98	0.98
MNB	1,2	0.98	0.95	0.95	0.97
SVM	2,2	0.94	0.94	0.94	0.95
GB	3,5	0.99	0.98	0.98	0.98
RF	1,2	0.99	0.99	0.99	0.99

5   Conclusion

This research suggested a machine learning model to classify the candidate's resume into different categories. For each job post, thousands of resumes are received by the recruiter. However, all resumes are not suitable. Many filtering processes are applied to shortlist candidate resumes, like skill, age, educational background, etc., which leads to many misclassifications. The suggested machine learning framework helps to save the recruiter's time by classifying the candidate resume into different categories in the beginning. Many machine learning-based models are used in this research to find the best model for the said task. The model's outcomes confirmed that among the selected classifiers, the random forest classifiers achieved the highest prediction accuracy with the highest precision and recall values. In the future, with a job description, the classified resume may be mapped to rank the resume based on their predicted similarity score. This helps the recruiter call for an interview - a limited number of candidates ranked at the top of the predicted list. Deep learning techniques such as Convolutional Neural Network (CNN), Long-Short Term Memory (LSTM), and similar ones can also be used for resume classification by considering the resume content.

References

1. Howard, J.L., Ferris, G.R.: The employment interview context: social and situational influences on interviewer decisions 1. J. Appl. Soc. Psychol. **26**(2), 112–136 (1996)
2. Kmail, A.B., Maree, M., Belkhatir, M.: MatchingSem: online recruitment system based on multiple semantic resources. In: 2015 12th International Conference on Fuzzy Systems and Knowledge Discovery (FSKD), pp. 2654–2659. IEEE (2015)
3. Lin, Y., Lei, H., Addo, P.C., Li, X.: Machine learned resume-job matching solution. arXiv preprint arXiv:1607.07657 (2016)
4. Roy, P.K., Singh, J.P., Nag, A.: Finding active expert users for question routing in community question answering sites. In: Perner, P. (ed.) MLDM 2018. LNCS (LNAI), vol. 10935, pp. 440–451. Springer, Cham (2018). https://doi.org/10.1007/978-3-319-96133-0_33
5. Yi, X., Allan, J., Croft, W.B.: Matching resumes and jobs based on relevance models. In: Proceedings of the 30th Annual International ACM SIGIR Conference on Research and Development in Information Retrieval, pp. 809–810 (2007)
6. Javed, F., Luo, Q., McNair, M., Jacob, F., Zhao, M., Kang, T.S.: Carotene: a job title classification system for the online recruitment domain. In: 2015 IEEE First International Conference on Big Data Computing Service and Applications, pp. 286–293. IEEE (2015)
7. Kessler, R., Béchet, N., Roche, M., Torres-Moreno, J.-M., El-Bèze, M.: A hybrid approach to managing job offers and candidates. Inf. Process. Manag. **48**(6), 1124–1135 (2012)
8. Zhang, L., Fei, W., Wang, L.: PJ matching model of knowledge workers. Procedia Comput. Sci. **60**, 1128–1137 (2015)
9. Breaugh, J.A.: The use of biodata for employee selection: past research and future directions. Hum. Resour. Manag. Rev. **19**(3), 219–231 (2009)
10. Roy, P.K., Singh, J.P., Baabdullah, A.M., Kizgin, H., Rana, N.P.: Identifying reputation collectors in community question answering (CQA) sites: exploring the dark side of social media. Int. J. Inf. Manag. **42**, 25–35 (2018)
11. Kessler, R., Torres-Moreno, J.M., El-Bèze, M.: E-Gen: automatic job offer processing system for human resources. In: Gelbukh, A., Kuri Morales, Á.F. (eds.) MICAI 2007. LNCS (LNAI), vol. 4827, pp. 985–995. Springer, Heidelberg (2007). https://doi.org/10.1007/978-3-540-76631-5_94
12. Yu, K., Guan, G., Zhou, M.: Resume information extraction with cascaded hybrid model. In: Proceedings of the 43rd Annual Meeting of the Association for Computational Linguistics (ACL 2005), pp. 499–506 (2005)
13. Martinez-Gil, J., Paoletti, A.L., Schewe, K.-D.: A smart approach for matching, learning and querying information from the human resources domain. In: Ivanović, M., et al. (eds.) ADBIS 2016. CCIS, vol. 637, pp. 157–167. Springer, Cham (2016). https://doi.org/10.1007/978-3-319-44066-8_17
14. Clyde, S., Zhang, J., Yao, C.-C.: An object-oriented implementation of an adaptive classification of job openings. In: Proceedings the 11th Conference on Artificial Intelligence for Applications, pp. 9–16. IEEE (1995)

15. Roy, P.K., Chowdhary, S.S., Bhatia, R.: A machine learning approach for automation of resume recommendation system. Procedia Comput. Sci. **167**, 2318–2327 (2020)

16. Lu, J., Wu, D., Mao, M., Wang, W., Zhang, G.: Recommender system application developments: a survey. Decis. Support Syst. **74**, 12–32 (2015)

17. Wei, K., Huang, J., Fu, S.: A survey of e-commerce recommender systems. In: 2007 International Conference on Service Systems and Service Management, pp. 1–5. IEEE (2007)

18. Fazel-Zarandi, M., Fox, M.S.: Semantic matchmaking for job recruitment: an ontology-based hybrid approach. In: Proceedings of the 8th International Semantic Web Conference, vol. 525, no. 01, p. 2009 (2009)

19. Malinowski, J., Keim, T., Wendt, O., Weitzel, T.: Matching people and jobs: a bilateral recommendation approach. In: Proceedings of the 39th Annual Hawaii International Conference on System Sciences (HICSS 2006), vol. 6, pp. 137c–137c. IEEE (2006)

20. Golec, A., Kahya, E.: A fuzzy model for competency-based employee evaluation and selection. Comput. Ind. Eng. **52**(1), 143–161 (2007)

21. Paparrizos, I., Cambazoglu, B.B., Gionis, A.: Machine learned job recommendation. In: Proceedings of the Fifth ACM Conference on Recommender Systems, pp. 325–328 (2011)

22. Horton, P., Nakai, K.: Better prediction of protein cellular localization sites with the it k nearest neighbors classifier. In: Ismb, vol. 5, pp. 147–152 (1997)

23. Rish, I., et al.: An empirical study of the Naive Bayes classifier. In: IJCAI 2001 Workshop on Empirical Methods in Artificial Intelligence, vol. 3, no. 22, pp. 41–46 (2001)

24. Belgiu, M., Drăguţ, L.: Random forest in remote sensing: a review of applications and future directions. ISPRS J. Photogramm. Remote Sens. **114**, 24–31 (2016)

25. Breiman, L.: Random forests. Mach. Learn. **45**(1), 5–32 (2001)

26. Friedman, J.H.: Stochastic gradient boosting. Comput. Stat. Data Anal. **38**(4), 367–378 (2002)

27. Kowsari, K., Jafari Meimandi, K., Heidarysafa, M., Mendu, S., Barnes, L., Brown, D.: Text classification algorithms: a survey. Information **10**(4), 150 (2019)

28. Menard, S.: Applied Logistic Regression Analysis, vol. 106. Sage (2002). https://books.google.co.in/books?hl=en&lr=&id=EAI1QmUUsbUC&oi=fnd&pg=PP7&dq=Applied+Logistic+Regression+Analysis&ots=4VGQI-qVJP&sig=4m7ea9FOnr2GKmpEje65WwfQ1PI&redir_esc=y#v=onepage&q=Applied%20Logistic%20Regression%20Analysis&f=false

29. Kotsiantis, S.B., Zaharakis, I.D., Pintelas, P.E.: Machine learning: a review of classification and combining techniques. Artif. Intell. Rev. **26**(3), 159–190 (2006)

30. Murthy, S.K.: Automatic construction of decision trees from data: a multidisciplinary survey. Data Min. Knowl. Disc. **2**(4), 345–389 (1998)

31. Roy, P.K., Singh, J.P., Banerjee, S.: Deep learning to filter SMS spam. Future Gener. Comput. Syst. **102**, 524–533 (2020)

32. Roy, P.K., Jain, A., Ahmad, Z., Singh, J.P.: Identifying expert users on question answering sites. In: Goyal, D., Bălaş, V.E., Mukherjee, A., Hugo C. de Albuquerque, V., Gupta, A.K. (eds.) ICIMMI 2019. AIS, pp. 285–291. Springer, Singapore (2021). https://doi.org/10.1007/978-981-15-4936-6_32

33. Tripathi, D., Reddy, B.R., Shukla, A.K.: CFR: collaborative feature ranking for improving the performance of credit scoring data classification. Computing, **104**, 893–923 (2021)

34. Tripathi, D., Edla, D.R., Bablani, A., Shukla, A.K., Reddy, B.R.: Experimental analysis of machine learning methods for credit score classification. Prog. Artif. Intell. **10**(3), 217–243 (2021). https://doi.org/10.1007/s13748-021-00238-2

Generating Equations from Math Word Problem Using Deep Learning Approach

Sandip Sarkar[1]([✉]), Dipankar Das[2], Partha Pakray[3], and David Pinto[4]

[1] Computer Science and Application, Hijli College, Kharagpur, India
sandipsarkar.ju@gmail.com
[2] Computer Science and Engineering, Jadavpur University, Kolkata, India
[3] Computer Science and Engineering, NIT Silchar, Silchar, India
[4] Facultad de Ciencias de la Computacion, Benemerita Universidad Autonoma de Puebla, Puebla, Mexico

Abstract. Building an automatic system to solve Math word problem is very interesting in AI domain. From last four decades Math word problem takes more attention of the researchers. Automatic system of math word problem can increase the effectiveness of e-learning system which is often used in current days. Many research claimed promising result but most of them has worked on small dataset or similar types of problems. It is really difficult to build a system which can work on huge dataset as well as different types of math word problem In this paper, we are trying to build a hybrid deep learning system which can work on large dataset as well as different forms of math word problem. We have done our experiments on Math23K dataset. Our proposed model gives better result than statistical learning and rule based approach. For our experiments we have used Bahdanau attention mechanism which gives better result than traditional methods for math word problem. The accuracy of our proposed mechanism is 0.58 in BLEU score.

Keywords: Math word problem · Deep learning · Seq-to-seq models

1 Introduction

Current teaching-learning systems like e-learning system, intelligent tutoring system (ITS) and computer-based training system have been using different types of artificial intelligence(AI) and natural language processing (NLP) techniques for conducting examination and evaluation using online assignments and quizzes. The main aim of these teaching-learning systems is to enhance the teaching quality and make the learning process more effective. AI based techniques with the help of NLP minimize the role of human teacher. It is very helpful for the student of middle school to solve math word problem. Student of non-native English can not understand the math word problem when it contains complex words or may in complex form. Automatic Math solver can help those students to understand the problem and solve them. On the other hand, computer enhances the speed and accuracy of mathematical calculation to minimize manual work. However it is very challenging to design a system to solve math word problem

S. Mukhopadhyay et al. (Eds.): CICBA 2022, CCIS 1579, pp. 252–259, 2022.
https://doi.org/10.1007/978-3-031-10766-5_19

[19]. Since 1960 researchers are trying to build automatic system to solve math word problem. Researchers had worked on other language like Arabic in the field of math word problem [18].

Table 1. Problem definition

Problem: Jack has 8 cats and 2 dogs. Jill has 7 cats and 4 dogs. How many dogs are there in all?
Equation: x = 2+4
Solution: 6
Problem: Rachel has 17 apples. She gives 9 to Sarah. How many apples does Rachel have now?
Equation: x = 17 − 9
Solution: 8

In arithmetic word problems, there are four basic mathematical operations i.e. $+$, $-$, $*$, $/$ and one unknown variable. On the other hand algebraic word problem contains complex operations like square root, exponential with multiple unknown variables. Our proposed method is to solve arithmetic word problem. Arithmetic word problem can be represented using the form of a sequence of k words $(w_0, w_1, ..., w_{ki})$. There are n quantities $q_1, q_2, ..., q_n$ mentioned in the text and an unknown variable x whose value is to be resolved.

Table 1 shows the simple example of Math word problem. In this example we have to find total number of dogs. Our aim is to generate the equation of that question using deep learning approach. If we can generate the equation then it helps us to find the answer. If we consider the first example of Table 1, we generate the equation "$x = 2 + 4$" from the math word problem and solve it using basic math operation.

In this paper we are trying to build a Sequence-to-Sequence model which is popular in the field of NLP to solve the Math word problem. Naturally a math word problem can be solved using different types of equations. We also consider this types of situation using equation normalization to convert all duplicate equation into a common equation. We have done our experiments on Math23K dataset. For experiments, we have used Bahdanau attention mechanism which learns to align and translate jointly [2]. It is also known as Additive attention because it performs a linear combination of encoder states and the decoder states.

The remainder of the paper is organized as follows. We first discuss about related work in Sect. 2, followed by dataset description in Sect. 3. The details description of our proposed model is given in Sect. 4. Experimental setup is given in Sect. 5. Section 6 contains the experimental result of our proposed model. Observation is given in Sect. 7. Finally we conclude our paper and discuss about future work in Sect. 8.

2   Related Works

Most of the researchers used statistical method to solve the math word problem [7, 8, 25]. On the other hand, some of the researchers have used a hybrid model which consists of several sub-module. DeepMind [8] used semantic parsing and built a system similar to the latent system to capture the mathematical logic. But the accuracy of those method gives poor result with compared to deep learning approach.

Researcher used many methods like template based [6, 22], tree based [20, 24], Rule based approach [1, 5, 10], parsing based [17] and deep learning [9, 21, 23, 23] based approach for math word problems. But most of the methods give high accuracy on limited math word problem.

Bobrow in the year 1964 proposed and implemented a rule based approach STUDENT to extract the equations and numbers using pattern matching techniques [3]. In 1985, Fletcher designed and implemented a solver for math word problem [4]. The main disadvantage of rule based approaches are that these can not capture all the variations of the datasets because these are based on hand-crafted logic.

On the other hand, most of the researcher capture patterns in the math word problem using statistical methods. Hosseini built a system, ARIS that observes all sentences in the math word problem and finds the relevant variables and their values [5]. ARIS then maps this problem into an equation that represents the problem, and solves this problem.

Mitra has built a system which produces equation templates to solve a specific domain problem [10]. This system worked only for addition and subtraction operations.

Wang proposed template based approach to solve math word problem [22]. To solve math word problem it requires a corpus which contains a set of templates with math problem. The main aim of this approach is to find a suitable template for each math problem. The main disadvantage of this approach is that it is not suitable for math problems having complex sentences and works on small dataset.

Some researchers has solved math word problem using tree-based solution [20, 24]. In tree-based solution arithmetic expression is represent by using binary tree structure and highest priority operators present in lower Laval and lowest priority operators present in root of the tree.

In recent time seq2seq model is used in many fields like machine translation, text simplification [16], Question Answering [14, 15] and many other fields of NLP [11] . In our approach we have used sequence-2-sequence model to generate math equations which gives better result than traditional methods [13].

3   Dataset

Most of the dataset which are used for math word problem are small and do not contain different types of math problems. For our experiments we have used Math23K dataset. We observed that Math23K is most promising dataset for math word problem. Math23K dataset is crawled from mainly different types of online education websites [22]. If we consider deep learning approach, then it requires large dataset for training. Math23K is suitable for our experiments as it contains highest number of math word problem (i.e. 23,161 math word problems) and the unknown variable of this problem is one.

Table 2. Description of dataset

Dataset	Problem statement	Equations	Solutions
Math23K	**Original Text:** 打字员打一部书稿，每小时打3.6千字，5小时完成，如果每小时打4.5千字，几小时能打完这部书稿？ **Translated Text:** A typist typed a manuscript, and he typed 3.6 thousand words per hour and finished it in 5 h If he typed 4.5 thousand words per hour, how many hours would he be able to finish the manuscript?	x = 3.6 * 5/4.5	x = 4

Table 3. Statistics of Math23K dataset

Dataset	Problems	Sentences	Words	Vocabulary size	Question length	Equation length
Math23K	23162	70125	822k	11k	70.76	13.944

Those problems are mainly for elementary school students. Using rule-based extraction mechanism, they extracted mathematical problems and answers from solutions. Using one linear algebra expression we can solve math word problem of Math23K dataset (Table 2).

The size of previously used dataset for math word problem are small and the diversity of those dataset is low. Table 3 shows that Math23K dataset contains 70,125 number of sentences with 822k words. The average length of Questions and equations are 70.76 and 13.94 respectively.

4 Proposed Method

Our proposed model deals with math word problems with one unknown variable. This Model is divided into three modules: (1) pre-processing module, (2) Training module and (3) output module. At first we simplify the sentences which contain complex form or consisted of complex word. As already discussed, our method is mainly based on sequence-to-sequence model. For encoding and decoding Bi-directional GRU and LSTM cells are used respectively. Figure 1 shows the overall architecture of our system.

First we add a space between every character in the equation string. For math statement, every character is converted into lowercase, then spaces around all punctuations are added. And finally digits and extra spaces are removed.

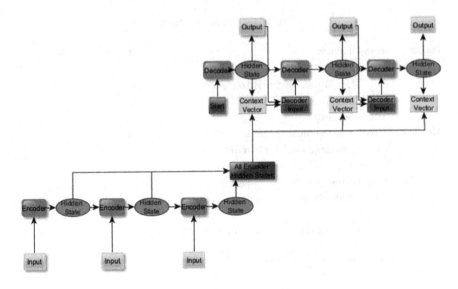

Fig. 1. System architecture

Equation Normalization is very important in math word problem. The equation $X = 67 - 8 + 5$ and $X = 67 - (8 - 5)$ are similar and produce same output. To reduce the variety of equation, we have used equation normalization approach.

5   Training

Google Colaboratory (also known as Colab) is a well known cloud based platform for deep learning which requires huge processing power [12]. It is based on Jupyter notebook which is open-source and browser based tool. Google Colab contains freely accessible robust GPU.

As of August 20, 2019, Google Colab provided 12 GB Nvidia Tesla K80 GPU and an Intel Xeon processor with two cores @2.3 GHz and 13 GB RAM. Recently, Colab has started offering free TPU.

Our system is based on encoder-decoder model. We use one Bi-LSTM for encoder with 256 hidden units, 32 embedding dimension, 32 batch size and one LSTM cells with same parameter. In addition, we use Adam optimizer with learning rate 0.001. The epochs, batch size, and dropout rate are set to 10, 100, and 0.5, respectively.

6   Result

Our proposed model works on Math23K dataset. We use 80% of dataset for training and 20% of dataset for testing. The accuracy of our proposed model is 0.58 in BLEU score. Our model performs well on Math23K dataset. More information about the output is given in the observation section.

7   Observation

Our proposed seq2seq model achieved promising result if we consider it with other statistical methods. As we already discussed that our model only works for math word problems containing one unknown variable. On the other hand, our model performs well on large complex dataset consists of complex sentences. It can also generate different types of equations. Figure 2 shows the output of our model.

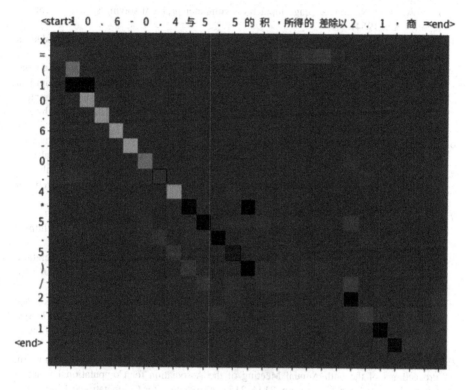

Fig. 2. System output

8   Conclusion and Future Work

We have proposed a seq2seq model with Bahdanau attention mechanism. It can generate equations from math word problem. Experimental result shows that proposed model gives promising result than sate-of-art statistical model on math word problem dataset. In future, we will try to work on math word problem dataset which contains more problems [26] and on the dataset which consists of more than one unknown variable which is more complex in the field of math word problem. There are still some portion in which we can improve the accuracy of the system. We want to extend this work to generate non linear equations. Besides we want to implement this techniques in different domains like physics, chemistry and others to word problem.

References

1. Amnueypornsakul, B., Bhat, S.: Machine-guided solution to mathematical word problems. In: Proceedings of the 28th Pacific Asia Conference on Language, Information and Computing, pp. 111–119, Department of Linguistics, Chulalongkorn University, Phuket, Thailand, December 2014. https://www.aclweb.org/anthology/Y14-1015
2. Bahdanau, D., Cho, K., Bengio, Y.: Neural machine translation by jointly learning to align and translate (2016)
3. Bobrow, D.G.: Natural language input for a computer problem solving system. Technical report, USA (1964)
4. Fletcher, C.: Understanding and solving arithmetic word problems: a computer simulation. Behav. Res. Methods Instrum. Comput. **17**, 565–571 (1985)
5. Hosseini, M.J., Hajishirzi, H., Etzioni, O., Kushman, N.: Learning to solve arithmetic word problems with verb categorization. In: Proceedings of the 2014 Conference on Empirical Methods in Natural Language Processing (EMNLP), pp. 523–533. Association for Computational Linguistics, Doha, Qatar, October 2014. https://doi.org/10.3115/v1/D14-1058, https://www.aclweb.org/anthology/D14-1058
6. Huang, D., Shi, S., Lin, C.Y., Yin, J.: Learning fine-grained expressions to solve math word problems. In: Proceedings of the 2017 Conference on Empirical Methods in Natural Language Processing, pp. 805–814. Association for Computational Linguistics, Copenhagen, Denmark, September 2017. https://doi.org/10.18653/v1/D17-1084, https://www.aclweb.org/anthology/D17-1084
7. Ilany, B.S.: Language and mathematics: bridging between natural language and mathematical language in solving problems in mathematics. Creat. Educ. **01**, 138–148 (2010). https://doi.org/10.4236/ce.2010.13022
8. Ling, W., Yogatama, D., Dyer, C., Blunsom, P.: Program induction by rationale generation: learning to solve and explain algebraic word problems. abs/1705.04146 (2017). http://arxiv.org/abs/1705.04146
9. Mehta, P., Mishra, P., Athavale, V., Shrivastava, M., Sharma, D.: Deep neural network based system for solving arithmetic word problems. In: Proceedings of the IJCNLP 2017, System Demonstrations, pp. 65–68. Association for Computational Linguistics, Tapei, Taiwan, November 2017. https://www.aclweb.org/anthology/I17-3017
10. Mitra, A., Baral, C.: Learning to use formulas to solve simple arithmetic problems. In: Proceedings of the 54th Annual Meeting of the Association for Computational Linguistics (Volume 1: Long Papers), pp. 2144–2153. Association for Computational Linguistics, Berlin, Germany, August 2016. https://doi.org/10.18653/v1/P16-1202, https://www.aclweb.org/anthology/P16-1202
11. Pathak, A., Pakray, P., Sarkar, S., Das, D., Gelbukh, A.F.: Mathirs: retrieval system for scientific documents. Computación y Sistemas **21**(2) (2017). http://www.cys.cic.ipn.mx/ojs/index.php/CyS/article/view/2743
12. Pessoa, T., Medeiros, R., Nepomuceno, T., Bian, G.B., Albuquerque, V., Filho, P.P.: Performance analysis of google colaboratory as a tool for accelerating deep learning applications. IEEE Access 1 (2018). https://doi.org/10.1109/ACCESS.2018.2874767
13. Robaidek, B., Koncel-Kedziorski, R., Hajishirzi, H.: Data-driven methods for solving algebra word problems. CoRR abs/1804.10718 (2018). http://arxiv.org/abs/1804.10718
14. Sarkar, S., Das, D., Pakray, P.: JU NITM at IJCNLP-2017 task 5: a classification approach for answer selection in multi-choice question answering system. In: Proceedings of the IJCNLP 2017, Shared Tasks, pp. 213–216. Asian Federation of Natural Language Processing, Taipei, Taiwan, December 2017. https://aclanthology.org/I17-4036

15. Sarkar, S., Das, D., Pakray, P., Avendaño, D.E.P.: Developing MCQA framework for basic science subjects using distributed similarity model and classification based approaches. Int. J. Asian Lang. Process. **30**(3), 2050015:1–2050015:18 (2020). https://doi.org/10.1142/S2717554520500150, https://doi.org/10.1142/S2717554520500150

16. Sarkar, S., Das, D., Pakray, P., Pinto, D.: A hybrid sequential model for text simplification. In: Priyadarshi, N., Padmanaban, S., Ghadai, R.K., Panda, A.R., Patel, R. (eds.) ETAEERE 2020. LNEE, vol. 690, pp. 33–42. Springer, Singapore (2021). https://doi.org/10.1007/978-981-15-7504-4_4

17. Shi, S., Wang, Y., Lin, C.Y., Liu, X., Rui, Y.: Automatically solving number word problems by semantic parsing and reasoning. In: Proceedings of the 2015 Conference on Empirical Methods in Natural Language Processing, pp. 1132–1142. Association for Computational Linguistics, Lisbon, Portugal, September 2015. https://doi.org/10.18653/v1/D15-1135, https://www.aclweb.org/anthology/D15-1135

18. Siyam, Bilal, Saa, A.A., Alqaryouti, O., Shaalan, K.: Arabic arithmetic word problems solver. In: Procedia Computer Science, abs/1808.07290 (2017)

19. Sundaram, S.S., Khemani, D.: Natural language processing for solving simple word problems. In: Proceedings of the 12th International Conference on Natural Language Processing, pp. 394–402. NLP Association of India, Trivandrum, India, December 2015. https://www.aclweb.org/anthology/W15-5955

20. Wang, L., Wang, Y., Cai, D., Zhang, D., Liu, X.: Translating a math word problem to a expression tree. In: Proceedings of the 2018 Conference on Empirical Methods in Natural Language Processing, pp. 1064–1069. Association for Computational Linguistics, Brussels, Belgium, October–November 2018. https://doi.org/10.18653/v1/D18-1132, https://www.aclweb.org/anthology/D18-1132

21. Wang, L., Zhang, D., Gao, L., Song, J., Guo, L., Shen, H.T.: MathDQN: solving arithmetic word problems via deep reinforcement learning. In: AAAI (2018)

22. Wang, L., et al.: Template-based math word problem solvers with recursive neural networks. In: Proceedings of the AAAI Conference on Artificial Intelligence, vol. 33, pp. 7144–7151 (07 2019). https://doi.org/10.1609/aaai.v33i01.33017144

23. Wang, Y., Liu, X., Shi, S.: Deep neural solver for math word problems. In: Proceedings of the 2017 Conference on Empirical Methods in Natural Language Processing, pp. 845–854. Association for Computational Linguistics, Copenhagen, Denmark, September 2017. https://doi.org/10.18653/v1/D17-1088, https://www.aclweb.org/anthology/D17-1088

24. Xie, Z., Sun, S.: A goal-driven tree-structured neural model for math word problems. In: Proceedings of the Twenty-Eighth International Joint Conference on Artificial Intelligence, IJCAI-19, pp. 5299–5305. International Joint Conferences on Artificial Intelligence Organization, July 2019. https://doi.org/10.24963/ijcai.2019/736, https://doi.org/10.24963/ijcai.2019/736

25. Zhang, D., Wang, L., Xu, N., Dai, B.T., Shen, H.T.: The gap of semantic parsing: a survey on automatic math word problem solvers. CoRR abs/1808.07290 (2018). http://arxiv.org/abs/1808.07290

26. Zhao, W., Shang, M., Liu, Y., Wang, L., Liu, J.: Ape210k: a large-scale and template-rich dataset of math word problems. CoRR abs/2009.11506 (2020). https://arxiv.org/abs/2009.11506

Clustering-Based Semi-supervised Technique for Credit Card Fraud Detection

Sagnik Lahiri[1], Sumit Misra[2(✉)], Sanjoy Kumar Saha[3],
and Chandan Mazumdar[3]

[1] Department of Computer Science and Engineering, Jadavpur University,
Kolkata, India
[2] RS Software (India) Limited, Kolkata, India
sumitmisra65@gmail.com
[3] Centre for Distributed Computing, Department of Computer Science and
Engineering, Jadavpur University, Kolkata, India

Abstract. Among the high volume and frequency of credit card transactions in today's world, the fraudulent ones must be flagged instantaneously. To establish its credibility the algorithm must do so with high sensitivity and minimum false alerts. We propose a light weight and easily re-trainable two stage semi-supervised approach to handle the problem. In the first phase we eliminate noisy data points (outliers) and extract core data points through a clustering technique. The extracted core points form the basis of training data. Set of core points are enhanced further to address the challenge of class imbalance (as fraudulent data is very less). Training set is used in the second phase to model the final classifier using k-D Tree. Experimental results on bench-marked dataset establish that the proposed model is well suited for real-time prediction of fraud transactions with high specificity.

Keywords: Credit card fraud detection · Clustering based outlier removal · k-D tree based classification

1 Introduction

Globalization and rapid growth of the eCommerce industry has resulted in a considerable proliferation of credit card transactions throughout the world. The rapid growth in the number of credit card transactions has also led to a substantial rise in fraudulent activities. A credit card fraud is defined as a criminal deception with the primary purpose of acquiring financial gains by illegal means. Real world data of financial transactions lacks proper background information due to confidentiality issues. This is also one of the major challenges.

Fraud detection mechanisms have become an essential part of banking systems to prevent loss through cybercrimes. These systems deal with huge amounts of data. The systems need to be well equipped with super scalable architecture

S. Mukhopadhyay et al. (Eds.): CICBA 2022, CCIS 1579, pp. 260–268, 2022.
https://doi.org/10.1007/978-3-031-10766-5_20

which could stream such volumes of data. Along with these the system must use lightning fast machine learning models to detect fraud transactions. Commonly used fraud detection includes methods [1,6] that are based on Neural Network (NN), association rules, fuzzy system, decision trees, Support Vector Machines (SVM), Artificial Immune System (AIS) and genetic algorithms.

Fraud detection methods can be broadly classified into supervised and unsupervised methods. In the context of a supervised approach, fraud detection task is basically a binary (fraud or non-fraud) classification problem. Popular supervised methods for credit card fraud detection are Artificial Neural Networks [17] and Support Vector Machines [20].

One of the earliest works used neural networks for fraud detection [14]. In this approach the neural network was trained with huge volumes of labeled credit card transactions. The work of Awoyemi et al. [3] presents a comparative analysis of other popular classifiers like Naive Bayes, K-nearest Neighbours, and Logistic Regression. Data mining techniques have also been combined with supervised learning models to obtain better results. Another approach by Brause et al. [8] achieved a low false alarm rate by combining advanced data mining techniques with neural networks. Syeda et al. [21] proposed a parallel granular neural network (GNN) to speed up data mining and the knowledge discovery process for credit card fraud detection. Aleskerovet al. [2] developed a neural network based data mining system for credit card fraud detection popularly known as CARDWATCH. Convolutional Neural Networks (CNN) have been used by Fut et al. [13] to learn hidden intrinsic patterns associated with fraudulent behavior. Pumsirirat et al. [18] proposed the use of Autoencoders with Restricted Boltzmann Machines (RBMs) for fraud detection. In another work [16] Autoencoder has been used to transform the transaction attributes into a lower dimensional feature vector. This feature vector was then fed to classifiers to obtain fast results.

A survey [7] shows that there has been huge emphasis on supervised learning techniques. However, unsupervised approach has not received much attention. Most existing unsupervised approaches are based on an outlier detection system, assuming outlier transactions as potential fraudulent transactions. Bolton and Hand [7] relied on behavioral outlier detection techniques. Optimization approaches have also been used by the researchers. RamaKalyani and UmaDevi [19] utilized Genetic Algorithm (GA) based optimization parameters and those are considered in rule based detection. Migrating birds optimization has also been used for fraud detection [11]. Many graph based semi-supervised techniques [4,15,22] also have been tried.

Study reveals that there are many challenges associated with credit card fraud detection. Very often fraud transactions are indistinguishable from the legitimate ones. As a result achieving the goal of high fraud detection with low false alarm becomes difficult. The frequency of a fraud transaction will be much less when compared to non-fraud ones. This makes credit card transaction datasets highly skewed and that poses a challenge in learning. It has also been observed that clustering based semi-supervised learning techniques [6] have not been considered for detecting the fraudulent credit card transactions. Keeping all these aspects in mind, we propose a two stage clustering based semi-supervised learning model that can classify transactions as fraud or non-fraud in real time. Proposed methodology is elaborated in Sect. 2. Experimental results are presented in Sect. 3 followed by the concluding remarks in Sect. 4.

2 Proposed Methodology

Fraud detection is a complicated problem as illegitimate transactions are hidden within the legitimate transactions. It becomes very difficult to differentiate them with the limited information available in financial datasets. There exist transactions which are inherently different from the regular day to day transactions. These may be fraud or non-fraud transactions. But they create hindrances in forming generalized rule or partitioning technique that can be applied to categorize the data in general. The proposed method inculcates the concept of separating out these samples as outliers or noise. It must be noted that unlike many works the proposed methodology does not consider outliers as the fraudulent ones. Rather it filters out these noisy samples for building the model.

It is also very important to identify fraud transactions in real time. Hence, the model should be lightweight and easily re-trainable to cope up with the change in the trends. The model should should have false positive rate. Considering all these issues we propose a **two stage semi-supervised** approach for building the classifier. The first stage is used for preparing the training set. It takes care of selecting the right data points from the initial training-set to avoid over-fitting or under-fitting. The second stage uses a k-D Tree based model, which once trained, can classify a transaction very fast by computing the nearness to the labelled data points. The stages are detailed in the following sections.

2.1 Preparation of Training Dataset

A subset of labelled data points corresponding to both fraudulent and non-fraudulent transactions are taken as the initial training dataset. It is refined by eliminating the outliers or noisy data points and thereby core points are extracted. After refinement, the dataset is enhanced to address the class imbalance problem. Thus, the training dataset is formed. The steps are detailed as follows.

Selection of Core Points for Training: Real world data contains many irregularities like arbitrary shape of clusters and the presence of noise. Simple clustering algorithms like K-Means cannot handle such irregular data. Density Based Spatial Clustering of Applications with Noise (DBSCAN) [12] is one such algorithm that addresses these challenges. DBSCAN uses two parameters to execute (a) epsilon (*eps*) which specifies be the radius of neighborhood with respect to some point, and (b) minimum number of points (*minPoints*) that is needed to form a dense region. If a point has more than *minPoints* within a radius of *eps*, it is labelled as **core** point. If a point has less than *minPoints* within *eps* radius but is within *eps* radius of a core point, it is labelled as **border point**. A point that is neither core or border point are labelled as **outlier point**. The worst case run-time complexity is $O(n^2)$, however, as this step is offline, it does not have impact on the fraud detection performance.

In our work, $p\%$ (empirically taken as 70%) of fraud and non-fraud transactions are taken as initial training dataset. The DBSCAN algorithm identifies each sample as one of **core, border** or **outlier** points. As the fraud samples are quite less in number, core points are determined only from the non-fraud samples. All fraud samples are forcibly considered as core points. This is done to ensure the inclusion of fraud samples in the set of core points.

Addressing Class Imbalance Issue: It has been discussed that the fraud transactions are relatively very few in numbers. Hence it is important to address the issue of class imbalance . In the real-world scenario non-fraud samples heavily outnumbers the fraud samples. The common strategies for dealing with such a challenge include under-sampling the data of majority class and/or oversampling the data of the minority class. However, the ratio of fraud samples to non-fraud samples is generally very low. Hence, to maintain the balance it is required to carry out drastic under-sampling of the non-fraud class. Then it may lead to loss of relevant information. On the other hand, random replication of fraud samples leads to over-fitting. Further, it may result into increase in the false positive rate.

At first, Synthetic Minority Oversampling Technique (SMOTE) [9] has been applied on the fraud samples and it is followed by Random Under-Sampling (RUS) of the non-fraud samples. The total number of fraud samples used were 10% (empirically decided) of the number of non-fraud samples. This approach was taken to preserve the inherent nature of the data and also to reduce the class bias significantly.

2.2   Formation of K-D Tree Based Model

As discussed in the last section, DBSCAN algorithm returns a set of noise free core points. This set is further augmented using SMOTE and RUS to resolve the issue of class imbalance. The final dataset thus obtained is used as the search space for the k-D Tree based classification model.

For multi-dimensional data, one of the best light-weight models that can help in rapid classification is k-D Tree [5]. It is a multi-dimensional binary search tree with k as the dimension of search space. k-D Tree helps to organize and partition the data points based on specific conditions which efficiently prunes the search space. As a result there is no need to visit every single data point. Bently [5], introduced the k-D Tree data structure and many associative search algorithms. In our work, we have used two of the search algorithms - (a) *Region − Search*: It identifies whether or not a transaction lies within any region under a node (of a k-D Tree) being searched in $O(n^{1-1/k})$ time where n is the number of points in the tree and k is the dimension as defined before, and (b) *Nearest − Neighbor − Search*: For a given point it identifies the nearest point(s) from a set of points in $O(log(n))$. Both the algorithms are very fast and hence the classification of the online transaction can be achieved with very low latency.

Overall methodology for training dataset preparation and model generation can be summarized as follows.

1. Preparation of training dataset
   (a) Randomly select $p\%$ of fraud and non-fraud data points as initial set (IS)
   (b) Apply DBSCAN on the non-fraud points of IS to extract core points.
   (c) Include fraud samples from IS set into the set of core points (CS)
   (d) Use SMOTE on the fraud samples in CS to obtain the augmented set of fraud samples (FS)
   (e) Use Random Under Sampling on the non-fraud samples in CS to obtain the set of sampled points (NFS)
   (f) Obtain training set, $TS = FS \cup NFS$
2. Use TS to prepare the k-D Tree

Classification: To detect whether an unknown transaction is a fraudulent one or not, it has to be compared with the training data points. This comparison is done with the help of k-D Tree formed using the training data points. The transaction to be tested is described by the a feature vector (V) as in case of a training data point. $Region - Search$ algorithm on k-D Trees is used to find match for V. It identifies the set of core points (CP) in the tree within the R neighborhood of V. If $\#\{CP\} = 0$ then V is taken as outlier. Otherwise, V is labelled as the category of the majority core points. In case number of fraud and non-fraud core points in CP is same then $Nearest - Neighbor$ algorithm is applied to find the nearest core point and corresponding category is taken as the prediction. It may be noted that $Region - Search$ is less costly in comparison to $Nearest - Neighbor$ search and $Nearest - Neighbor$ is required only for a special case. Hence,the classification process is of low cost.

3 Experiment and Results

Experiments are performed on the credit card transaction dataset of ULB Machine Learning Group [10]. This dataset contains 284, 807 transactions spanning over two days and out of those only 492 are frauds. Due to the privacy issue original attributes of the transactions are not provided and 28 principal components obtained after Principal Component Analysis (PCA) on original attributes are made available. Hereafter, a transaction will be referred as sample or data point and each of corresponding 28 PCA will be termed as feature.

Exploratory Data Analysis: In order to get the feel of the data we have carried with various analysis prior to devising the methodology. Exploratory analysis of the dataset [10] showed insignificant correlation (both positive and negative) between any two features. Further analysis of data points are done by considering a pair of features and the data points are plotted in two-dimensional feature space. It is observed that the data points are mostly forming the clusters and also has outliers. This observation has motivated us to consider clustering based refinement of training data. During such exploration it is also noted that

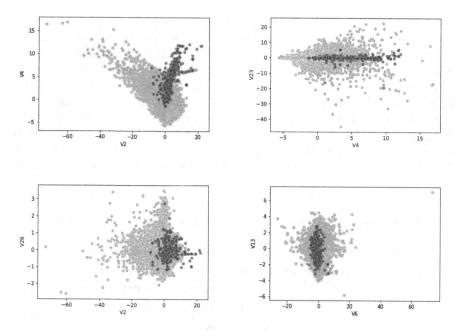

Fig. 1. Data Visualization (Red and Cyan denote fraud and non-fraud respectively) (Color figure online)

with respect to a pair of features, significant overlap may exist between the clusters of fraud and non-fraud data points. In some cases, a majority class (non-fraud) cluster completely envelops a cluster of the minority (fraud) class. Few such plots from the exploratory analysis are shown in Fig. 1. Only Using such overlapped labelled clusters categorization can not be accomplished in real time. That has acted as the driving force for k-D Tree based detection.

Results: From the given dataset, a subset consisting of 70% of fraud and non-fraud data points are taken for generating the model. Remaining 30% data points form the test set. Fraud is taken as positive. Based on True Positive (TP), False Positive (FP), True Negative (TN) and False Negative (FN) following metrics are used to measure the performance.

$$Accuracy = \frac{TP + TN}{TP + FP + TN + FN}$$

$$Precsion(P) = \frac{TP}{TP + FP}$$

$$Recall(R) = \frac{TP}{TP + FN}$$

$$F1 - Score = \frac{2 \times P \times R}{P + R}$$

The performance of the proposed methodology is compared with the outcome of three other popular classification techniques applied on the same dataset. The considered classifiers are Multi-Layer Perceptron (MLP), K-Nearest Neighbour (KNN) and Logistic Regression (LR). It may be noted that partitioning of the dataset into test set and set for generating the training data has been carried out randomly. The whole process is repeated ten times and average performance values are shown in Table 1. The accuracy and the F1-score are the highest for the proposed model. The recall is highest for the MLP classifier (M2) but it has the lowest precision. The LR classifier (M3) has the lowest recall. The KNN classifier performs closest to the proposed methodology. However, KNN is time consuming.

Table 1. Comparison of performance of different models in identifying fraud

Methodology	Accuracy	Precision	Recall	F1-Score
Proposed methodology	**0.9995**	0.8971	0.7578	**0.8215**
MLP	0.9993	0.7794	**0.7794**	0.7794
LR	0.9991	0.8452	0.5221	0.6455
KNN	0.9994	**0.9100**	0.7426	0.8178

F1-score takes care of both miss in fraud detection and false alarm rate and in this metric proposed methodology outperforms all the other three models. It is to be noted that proposed methodology categorizes a test data as outlier, fraud and non-fraud. For a fraud (non-fraud) data, if it is classified as outlier then in measuring the performance it has been treated as false negative (false positive). Thus it has penalized the system most. Despite of that it maintains significant level of precision and recall. The response is also quite fast for the proposed methodology. The test dataset contains 85, 443 sample transactions which are classified using the k-D Tree. On an average, the classification process is executed at a rate of 300 μs per transaction on a machine with CPU clock frequency of 2.20 GHz and 4 GB of RAM. Thus it is well suited for real time application.

4   Conclusion

In this work, a semi-supervised model has been proposed to detect the fraud transactions using credit cards. The first stage refines and enhances the training dataset. DBSCAN based refinement has been done to get rid of outliers. With refined dataset enhancement is done to address the issue of class imbalance. Fraud data is over sampled using SMOTE and non-fraud data is under sampled using RUS. At the next stage a k-D Tree is formed with the training data. A test data is categorized by finding the match with the data points in the k-D Tree. Thus, the k-D Tree serves as the fast and lightweight model for classification.

Experimental results establish that the proposed model is well suited for making accurate prediction of fraud transactions in real-time and it does so with a smaller number of false positives. The methodology should be able to handle the change in trend of the transaction profile. Once the drift in the trend is noted the training dataset and tree formation can be made as an offline process. In future, efforts may be driven towards detecting the drift and to device efficient re-training techniques.

References

1. Abdallah, A., Maarof, M.A., Zainal, A.: Fraud detection system: a survey. J. Netw. Comput. Appl. **68**, 90–113 (2016)
2. Aleskerov, E., Freisleben, B., Rao, B.: CARDWATCH: a neural network based database mining system for credit card fraud detection. In: Proceedings of the IEEE/IAFE 1997 Computational Intelligence for Financial Engineering (CIFEr), pp. 220–226. IEEE (1997)
3. Awoyemi, J.O., Adetunmbi, A.O., Oluwadare, S.A.: Credit card fraud detection using machine learning techniques: a comparative analysis. In: 2017 International Conference on Computing Networking and Informatics (ICCNI), pp. 1–9. IEEE (2017)
4. Bangcharoensap, P., Kobayashi, H., Shimizu, N., Yamauchi, S., Murata, T.: Two step graph-based semi-supervised learning for online auction fraud detection. In: Joint European Conference on Machine Learning and Knowledge Discovery in Databases, pp. 165–179. Springer (2015). https://doi.org/10.1007/978-3-319-23461-8_11
5. Bentley, J.L.: Multidimensional binary search trees used for associative searching. Commun. ACM **18**(9), 509–517 (1975)
6. Bolton, R.J., Hand, D.J.: Statistical fraud detection: a review. Stat. Sci. **17**, 235–249 (2002)
7. Bolton, R.J., Hand, D.J., et al.: Unsupervised profiling methods for fraud detection. Credit scoring and credit control VII, pp. 235–255 (2001)
8. Brause, R., Langsdorf, T., Hepp, M.: Neural data mining for credit card fraud detection. In: Proceedings 11th International Conference on Tools with Artificial Intelligence, pp. 103–106. IEEE (1999)
9. Chawla, N.V., Bowyer, K.W., Hall, L.O., Kegelmeyer, W.P.: SMOTE: synthetic minority over-sampling technique. J. Artif. Intell. Res. **16**, 321–357 (2002)
10. Pozzolo, A.D.: Adaptive machine learning for credit card fraud detection (2015)
11. Duman, E., Elikucuk, I.: Solving credit card fraud detection problem by the new metaheuristics migrating birds optimization. In: International Work-Conference on Artificial Neural Networks, pp. 62–71. Springer (2013). https://doi.org/10.1007/978-3-642-38682-4_8
12. Ester, M., Kriegel, H.P., Sander, J., Xu, X., et al.: A density-based algorithm for discovering clusters in large spatial databases with noise. In: KDD, vol. 96, pp. 226–231 (1996)
13. Fu, K., Cheng, D., Tu, Y., Zhang, L.: Credit card fraud detection using convolutional neural networks. In: International Conference on Neural Information Processing, pp. 483–490. Springer (2016). https://doi.org/10.1007/978-3-319-46675-0_53

14. Ghosh, S., Reilly, D.L.: Credit card fraud detection with a neural-network. In: Proceedings of the Twenty-Seventh Hawaii International Conference on System Sciences, vol. 3, pp. 621–630. IEEE (1994)
15. Lebichot, B., Braun, F., Caelen, O., Saerens, M.: A graph-based, semi-supervised, credit card fraud detection system. In: International Workshop on Complex Networks and their Applications, pp. 721–733. Springer (2016). https://doi.org/10.1007/978-3-319-50901-3_57
16. Misra, S., Thakur, S., Ghosh, M., Saha, S.K.: An autoencoder based model for detecting fraudulent credit card transaction. Procedia Comput. Sci. **167**, 254–262 (2020)
17. Ogwueleka, F.N.: Data mining application in credit card fraud detection system. J. Eng. Sci. Technol. **6**(3), 311–322 (2011)
18. Pumsirirat, A., Yan, L.: Credit card fraud detection using deep learning based on auto-encoder and restricted Boltzmann machine. Int. J. Adv. Comput. Sci. Appl. **9**(1), 18–25 (2018)
19. RamaKalyani, K., UmaDevi, D.: Fraud detection of credit card payment system by genetic algorithm. Int. J. Sci. Eng. Res. **3**(7), 1–6 (2012)
20. Singh, G., Gupta, R., Rastogi, A., Chandel, M.D., Ahmad, R.: A machine learning approach for detection of fraud based on SVM. Int. J. Sci. Eng. Technol. **1**(3), 192–196 (2012)
21. Syeda, M., Zhang, Y.Q., Pan, Y.: Parallel granular neural networks for fast credit card fraud detection. In: 2002 IEEE World Congress on Computational Intelligence. 2002 IEEE International Conference on Fuzzy Systems. FUZZ-IEEE 2002. Proceedings (Cat. No. 02CH37291), vol. 1, pp. 572–577. IEEE (2002)
22. Zhu, X., Lafferty, J., Rosenfeld, R.: Semi-supervised learning with graphs. Ph.D. thesis, Carnegie Mellon University, language technologies institute, school of ... (2005)

Fake News Identification Through Natural Language Processing and Machine Learning Approach

Debasish Patra[✉] and Biswapati Jana

Department of Computer Science, Vidyasagar University, West Midnapore, Midnapore 721102, West Bengal, India
logicaldebasish@gmail.com

Abstract. With the rapid advancement of technology and ease of access to the Internet our daily life is changing day by day. Within a few years, now we are heavily dependent on Internet and social media. In social media and online news platform, it is very easy to circulate news. With the ease of accessing and sharing news on the Internet and social media platforms, some major concerns are growing in the background. The most severe problem that has been on the core of these concerns is the fake news. For the last few years fake news detection has become the most emerging problem area among the researchers. In this paper, the goal is to use Natural Language Processing (NLP) techniques for text analytics and train different machine learning models to detect fake news based on the text of the news. The solution described in this study can be implemented in real-world social media to reduce the negative impact of fake news or false information from an untrustworthy source. Text preparation is done with tokenization, lemmatization, and stop word techniques. Vectorization is done by N-gram, Terms Frequency Inverse Document Frequency (TF-IDF) or one-hot encoding. Different machine learning algorithms trained and tested in this work out of which Naïve Bayes has given best results with an accuracy of 95.2% .

Keywords: Fake news detection · Machine learning · TF-IDF · Natural Language Processing · Naïve Bayes

1 Introduction

Image, text, audio, and video make up the majority of our digital environment. All of these contents can be used to make news, or any one of these contents can be used to make news. As of now most of the fake news are circulating in the form of text articles. The widespread availability of the internet is fueling this demand. The first platform that springs to mind when we think about social media is Facebook. This platform has grown in popularity tremendously since its launch, that claims that by 2020, it has reached 2.8 billion monthly active users, accounting for about a third of the world's population. This social media network has been seriously harmed by fake news as time has passed. Despite the fact that Facebook's algorithm has been updated numerous

S. Mukhopadhyay et al. (Eds.): CICBA 2022, CCIS 1579, pp. 269–279, 2022.
https://doi.org/10.1007/978-3-031-10766-5_21

times to filter out fraudulent and misleading content, it remains one of the most popular social media platforms for dissipating incorrect news. Twitter is the second social media network that comes up in the context of fake news because of its way to transfer and recopy any news. Twitter has 330 million active users as of February 2019. Since its inception, this platform has steadily been impacted by fake news and misinformation. Nevertheless, in March 2020, Twitter said that it would begin flagging tweets that may include fake news or misinformation, as well as providing fact-checking website links in some circumstances. However, this procedure will not solve the problem. In this sense, the third platform is Instagram, which is one of the most popular. This platform is used for photo and video sharing. As of May 2019, Instagram had one billion users.

While social media has had many positive effects on our society, it has also revealed certain unpleasant realities that are a source of concern in our society. The most powerful influence of social media on our culture is the spread of fake news or misinformation. On social media platforms, there is a lack of regulation and fact checking, which is a huge source of concern for both the platforms and our society. Fake news appears in a variety of forms on social media. Because news can take many different forms, such as text, image, video, or a combination of these, it is difficult to categorize it. As a result, the researchers have found it more difficult to develop a practical method for detecting fake news and misinformation. Though it is a difficult undertaking, some excellent research work on the identification of fake news has been done in recent years.

Another factor that has added to the misery of the false news situation is the use of social bots. A social bot is a self-contained agent capable of simulating human interaction on social media without the need for human involvement. Since the 2016 US presidential election, when at least 4 lakh bots posted nearly 38 lakh tweets, this problem has grown increasingly apparent. According to estimates, social bots make for 9–15% of active Twitter accounts nowadays. Many social media networks, including Facebook, are victims of social bots. Social bots are to blame for a lot of the fake news we see on social media platforms.

It is a reality that fake news spreads faster on social media than accurate news. When it comes to political news, the travel speed increases significantly. According to statistics, political and celebrity news make up the majority of fake news on social media. Human conduct also plays a significant influence, as the majority of users forward posts or news stories without verifying whether they are factual or not.

For these reasons we have done this work where combination of machine learning models and NLP can detect fake news to some extent. We are quite successful as this model is classifying text articles as real or fake with more than 95% accuracy.

2   Literature Review

For the last few years fake news detection has been a great attraction for the researchers. There are some already published work on fake news detection.

Jain et al. [1] presented a work by using machine learning and NLP. In machine learning they used support vector machine (SVM). The model consists of three modules which are Aggregator, News Authenticator and News Suggestion/Recommender system. The strategy was a mix of Naïve Bayes and Support Vector Machine. With the combination of Naïve Bayes, Support Vector Machine and NLP the model achieved 93.50% accuracy.

Shlok Gilda [2] had done a work on fake news detection by using Term Frequency-Inverse Document Frequency (TF-IDF) of bi-grams with probabilistic context free grammar (PCFG). The dataset consists of 11000 articles where several classification algorithms such as Support Vector Machine Stochastic Gradient Descent, Gradient Boosting, Decision Trees, and Random Forests used. When all of these models were compared it shows that, among them Support Vector Machine gained highest accuracy with 76.2%.

Granik and Mesyura [3] presented a work on Facebook news (Buzzfeed) posts using Naïve Bayes classifier. The work uses a simple machine learning algorithm. The work achieved 74% accuracy on the test set.

Han and Mehta [4] did a work on fake news detection where different traditional machine learning approaches and deep learning approaches are discussed and compared with respect to their performance. Among the models, it was concluded that deep learning techniques CNN and LSTM achieved the highest accuracy close to 80%.

Kong et al. [5] used NLP for text analytics and deep learning techniques for fake news detection. The dataset is collected from Kaggle. Text preprocessing techniques such as regular expression, tokenization, lemmatization, and stop words removal are employed in NLP approaches after vectorization into N-gram vectors or sequence vectors using terms frequency inverse document frequency (TF-IDF) or one-hot encoding. The Keras Deep Learning technique achieved a highest accuracy of 90.3%.

In [6, 7], a full discussion on several methodologies is presented, along with comparisons to false knowledge and the pattern of spread with author credibility. The work in [8] explore many forms of fake news, such as satire, propaganda, clickbait, and hoaxes. The authors cover various aspects of fake news [10–15], but there is minimal comparison between machine learning and deep learning methodologies. It described standard tools and datasets including LIAR, FEVER, and CREDBANK. [9] conducted a systematic survey that included a quick comparison of terminologies and their references.

Our proposed work can detect fake news with better accuracy. The work is structured as: The dataset used and data preprocessing is explained in Sect. 3; the feature extraction process is described in Sect. 4; the proposed methodology and result obtained from the work is illustrated in Sect. 5 and finally the conclusion is discussed in Sect. 6.

3   Dataset and Pre-processing

3.1   Dataset Used

There are many sources from where we can obtain different news dataset. Our work is mainly focused on the accuracy of the news classification not on the dataset. If a model can perform well on any dataset, then we can say that the model is not dependent on the dataset or on the source of the dataset. The model can be generalized on any social media platform for the detection of fake and real news.

In this work we have selected Kaggle fake news dataset. The training dataset consists of 20800 labelled news articles collected from different sources. The true articles are labelled as 1 whereas the false news articles are labelled as 0. The test dataset contains 6035 news articles.

3.2 Data Preprocessing

The raw dataset cannot be used for the training of the model. That is why we need to clean the dataset in order to implement the model using this dataset. For the cleaning purpose Scikit-Learn, Numpy and Pandas has been used in our model.

First, we have obtained the independent features by dropping the label column. Then the dependent feature 'label' is stored in another variable. After that the cleaned and processed dataset has been obtained.

The dataset has been divided into training dataset, test dataset and validation dataset. Out of the total dataset 60% is used for training dataset, 20% for test dataset and remaining 20% for validation.

4 Feature Extraction

We used feature extraction and selection algorithms from the Sci-kit learn python library in our investigation. We used approaches like bag-of-words, n-grams to extract features, and then TF-IDF (Term Frequency- Inverse Document Frequency). To extract the features, we utilized Word2vec and POS tagging.

TF-IDF: It is an information retrieval strategy in which the value of a token rises if it appears frequently in the document and lowers if it appears less frequently in the corpus, resulting in an accurate metric value. It calculates a word frequency score that attempts to highlight the most intriguing terms.

N-gram: Any consecutive sequence of n tokens or words is called an n-gram. Because they collect more context on each word, a bag of n-grams can be more useful than a bag of words.

Bag of Words: It's a basic approach of representing text data and extracting features from it. We do this by tokenizing words for each observation and calculating their occurrence.

Word2vec: It [16] converts words into embeddings, which are numerical vectors in which semantically comparable words are close in distance.

POS Tagging: The technique of assigning certain parts of speech relating to a word based on its context and meaning is known as part-of-speech (POS) tagging. It can be used to remove grammatical ambiguity or to disambiguate word meanings in order to gain a feeling of the news' veracity.

Linguistic elements are very efficient in finding deceptive content as to how it is written is to disguise the genuine content by highlighting or using specific inaccurate words to entice visitors to fake news. The linguistic elements provide a set of certain words that are typically found in fake news on social media. After processing we get a vector matrix of these news articles. The words that are frequently used in these fake articles will help the model to predict fake news. The methodology of our work is presented in Fig. 1.

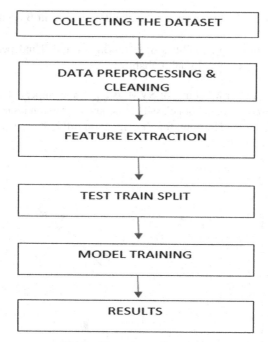

Fig. 1. Flow chart of the model

5 Result and Discussion

To classify the news articles, we have used Support Vector Machine, K - nearest neighbors, Random Forest and Naive Bayes classification algorithm. The entire program was developed in Python using Jupiter Notebook on Anaconda Navigator. To perform the tests, our source code makes use of python libraries such as Keras, NLTK, Numpy, Pandas, Sci-kit. The major criteria used to performance of various algorithms were accuracy, precision, recall, and F-score. To develop the model the algorithms which are used in our work are described as follows:

Naïve Bayes: The Naive Bayes algorithm is a supervised learning algorithm for addressing classification issues that is based on the Bayes theorem. It is mostly utilized in text classification tasks that require a large training dataset. The Nave Bayes Classifier is a simple and effective classification method that helps in the development of fast machine learning models capable of making quick predictions. It's a probabilistic classifier, which means it makes predictions based on an object's probability. The equation of Bayes theorem is given as:

$$P(A|B) = \frac{P(B|A)\, P(A)}{P(B)} \tag{1}$$

where A and B are events and $P(B) \neq 0$.

P(A|B) is the conditional probability: the likelihood of event A occurring given that B is true.

P(B|A) is the conditional probability: the likelihood of event B occurring given that A is true.

P(A) and P(B) are the probabilities of observing A and B independently of each other, which is known as the marginal probability.

SVM: The Support Vector Machine, or SVM, is a popular Supervised Learning technique that may be used to solve both classification and regression issues. However, it is mostly utilized in Machine Learning for Classification difficulties. The working of the SVM algorithm is shown in Fig. 2.

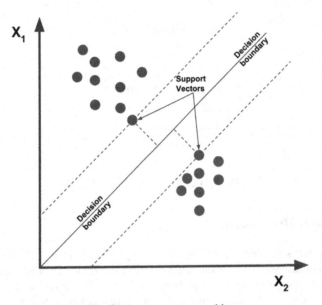

Fig. 2. Support vector machine

The SVM algorithm's purpose is to find the optimum line or decision boundary for categorizing n-dimensional space into classes so that additional data points can be readily placed in the correct category in the future. A hyperplane is the name for the best decision boundary.

K-Nearest Neighbor: The K-Nearest Neighbor algorithm is based on the Supervised Learning technique and is one of the most basic Machine Learning algorithms. The K-NN method assumes that the new case/data and existing cases are similar and places the new case in the category that is most similar to the existing categories.

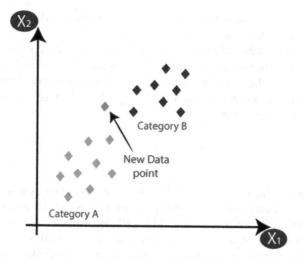

Fig. 3. K-nearest neighbor

The K-NN method stores all available data and evaluates a new data point based on its similarity to the existing data. This means that new data can be quickly sorted into a well-defined category using the K-NN method. The K-NN approach can be used for both regression and classification, but it is more commonly utilized for classification tasks. The working of KNN algorithm with the value of k = 2, is shown in Fig. 3.

Random Forest: The Random Forest is a well-known machine learning method that uses the supervised learning technique. In machine learning, it can be utilized for both classification and regression issues. It is based on ensemble learning, which is a method

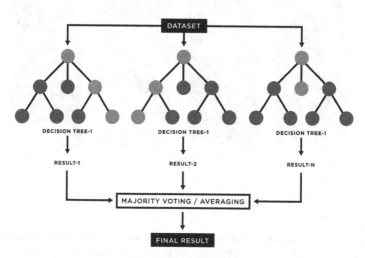

Fig. 4. Random forest

of integrating several classifiers to solve a complex problem and increase the model's performance. The working model is shown in Fig. 4.

"Random Forest is a classifier that incorporates a number of decision trees on various subsets of a given dataset and takes the average to enhance the predicted accuracy of that dataset," according to the name. Instead of relying on a single decision tree, the random forest collects the prediction from each tree and predicts the final output based on the majority of votes of predictions.

5.1 Results

The model is first trained using random forest algorithm using the extracted feature set of Kaggle fake news dataset. It has given a prediction with 74% accuracy. Then we have experimented with KNN algorithm. The KNN algorithm gives better performance than random forest algorithm with an accuracy of 77%. After this SVM algorithm is performed on the feature set to observe if there is any enhancement on performance over the previous algorithms and we got an accuracy of 82%. Lastly, Multinomial Naïve Bayes algorithm is tested which has given highest accuracy among all algorithms that is 95.2%. The comparison of accuracy between the algorithms are given in Fig. 5.

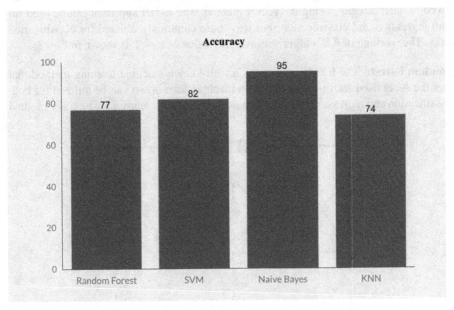

Fig. 5. Accuracy comparison of different algorithms

For each method, we calculated precision, recall, and F-1 score, the results of which are listed in Table 1. In terms of precision, recall, and F-1 score, it was discovered that Naive Bayes outperforms all other algorithms. The simulation of our fake news detection system is done in Jupyter Notebook on Anaconda Navigator.

Table 1. Table for various metrics

Model	Accuracy	Precision	Recall	F1-score
Random forest	77%	0.78	0.76	0.789
SVM	82.6%	0.83	0.84	0.837
Naïve Bayes	95.2%	0.94	0.96	0.958
KNN	74.3%	0.76	0.75	0.76

6 Conclusion

In our research work, the best machine learning model trained is Naïve Bayes that has achieved up to 95.2% accuracy with 96% precision. Previously there are some models that have used news title in training models. But instead of using news title we have used news text and from our work it is evident that it has given better accuracy.

Here we have trained four different models and compared different measurement metrics between them. We have to test these models on more available datasets to observe how system performs on those datasets (Fig. 6).

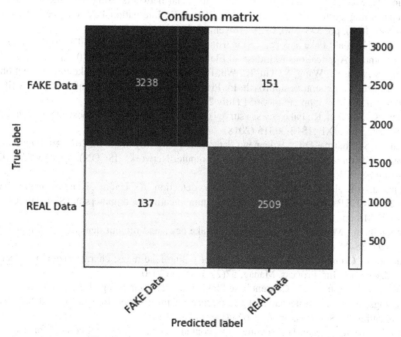

Fig. 6. Confusion matrix of Naïve Bayes model

In our future work we will try to combine different algorithms to make an ensemble learning model which could give more accuracy with respect to the current model. We also try to use some deep learning algorithm like LSTM (Long-Short Term Memory) for the fake news detection purpose.

Acknowledgements. This study is **funded** by the **Department of Science and Technology – Science and Engineering Research Board (DST-SERB), Govt. of India** under the research project entitled "Fake Image and News Detection on Social Media Through Trustware Based Community Portal" **(No-EEQ/2019/000317)**. The authors are thankful to Vidyasagar University for providing infrastructural facilities required for carrying out the project.

References

1. Jain, A., Shakya, A., Khatter, H., Gupta, A.K.: A smart system for fake news detection using machine learning. In: 2019 International Conference on Issues and Challenges in Intelligent Computing Techniques (ICICT), vol. 1, pp. 1–4. IEEE (September 2019)
2. Gilda, S.: Evaluating machine learning algorithms for fake news detection. In: 2017 IEEE 15th Student Conference on Research and Development (SCOReD), pp. 110–115. IEEE (December 2017)
3. Granik, M., Mesyura, V.: Fake news detection using naive Bayes classifier. In: 2017 IEEE First Ukraine Conference on Electrical and Computer Engineering (UKRCON), pp. 900–903. IEEE (May 2017)
4. Han, W., Mehta, V.: Fake news detection in social networks using machine learning and deep learning: performance evaluation. In: 2019 IEEE International Conference on Industrial Internet (ICII), pp. 375–380. IEEE (November 2019)
5. Kong, S.H., et al.: Fake news detection using deep learning. In: 2020 IEEE 10th Symposium on Computer Applications & Industrial Electronics (ISCAIE). IEEE (2020)
6. Yang, S., Shu, K., Wang, S., Gu, R., Wu, F., Liu, H.: Unsupervised fake news detection on social media: a generative approach. In: Proceedings of the AAAI Conference on Artificial Intelligence, vol. 33, pp. 5644–5651 (July 2019)
7. Zhou, X., Zafarani, R.: Fake news: a survey of research, detection methods, and opportunities. arXiv preprint arXiv:1812.00315 (2018)
8. Sharma, S., Sharma, D.K.: Fake news detection: a long way to go. In: 2019 4th International Conference on Information Systems and Computer Networks (ISCON), pp. 816–821. IEEE (November 2019)
9. Elhadad, M.K., Li, K.F., Gebali, F.: Fake news detection on social media: a systematic survey. In: 2019 IEEE Pacific Rim Conference on Communications, Computers and Signal Processing (PACRIM), pp. 1–8. IEEE (August 2019)
10. Bondielli, A., Marcelloni, F.: A survey on fake news and rumour detection techniques. Inf. Sci. **497**, 38–55 (2019)
11. Zhang, X., Ghorbani, A.A.: An overview of online fake news: characterization, detection, and discussion. Inf. Process. Manag. **57**(2), 102025 (2020)
12. Wynne, H.E., Wint, Z.Z.: Content based fake news detection using N-gram models. In: Proceedings of the 21st International Conference on Information Integration and Web-based Applications & Services, pp. 669–673 (December 2019)
13. Shu, K., Wang, S., Liu, H.: Beyond news contents: the role of social context for fake news detection. In: Proceedings of the Twelfth ACM International Conference on Web Search and Data Mining, pp. 312–320 (January 2019)
14. Liu, H.: A location independent machine learning approach for early fake news detection. In: 2019 IEEE International Conference on Big Data (Big Data), pp. 4740–4746. IEEE (December 2019)

15. Sabeeh, V., Zohdy, M., Al Bashaireh, R.: Enhancing the fake news detection by applying effective feature selection based on semantic sources. In: 2019 International Conference on Computational Science and Computational Intelligence (CSCI), pp. 1365–1370. IEEE (December 2019)
16. Mikolov, T., et al.: Efficient estimation of word representations in vector space. arXiv preprint arXiv:1301.3781 (2013)

An Empirical Analysis on Abstractive Text Summarization

Tawmo, Prottay Kumar Adhikary, Pankaj Dadure, and Partha Pakray[✉]

Department of Computer Science and Engineering, National Institute of Technology,
Silchar, India
parthapakray@gmail.com

Abstract. With the massive growth of blogs, news stories, and reports, extracting useful information from such a large quantity of textual documents has become a difficult task. Automatic text summarization is an excellent approach for summarising these documents. Text summarization aims to condense large documents into concise summaries while preserving essential information and meaning. A variety of fascinating summarising models have been developed to achieve state-of-the-art performance in terms of fluency, human readability, and semantically meaningful summaries. In this paper, we have investigated the OpenNMT tool for task text summarization. The OpenNMT is the encoder-decoder-based neural machine translation model which has been fine-tuned for the task of abstractive text summarization. The proposed OpenNMT based text summarization approach has been tested on freely available dataset such as CNNDM & MSMO dataset and depicts their proficiency in terms of ROUGE and BLEU score.

Keywords: Text summarization · Abstractive summary · News articles · OpenNMT

1 Introduction

The advent of the Internet has enabled individuals to contribute to the increasing sea of text data available online such as magazine articles, blog posts, or news articles. Articles need to be concise for the users viewing as it saves both effort and time. Therefore automatic text summarization is implemented in generating a storyline of events with compressed sentences while retaining essential information from the original story or any article, saving time to read through the whole article. Text summarization [9] is defined as creating a shortened version of a text document that captures the salient meaning of the original text. Text summarization is broadly categorized into two types based on the output type, extractive and abstractive summarization. Extractive summarization is a technique that simply creates a summary of the original document by extracting the crucial sentences verbatim. Extractive text summary only includes sentences that are present in the original text. Abstractive text summary is a type of summarization similar to how a human would generally produce a summary of a

S. Mukhopadhyay et al. (Eds.): CICBA 2022, CCIS 1579, pp. 280–287, 2022.
https://doi.org/10.1007/978-3-031-10766-5_22

piece of text. Abstract text summarization generates new sentences which are not present in the original text to create the summary.

Applications of automatic text summarization range from generic summarization to summarizing webpages, reports, tweets and emails. Even with remarkable advancement in the field of automatic text summarization, it still remains a challenging task. Issues such as redundancy, ordering of the sentence, coreference contribute to the complexity of the task [3] and another factor also adding to the complexity is evaluating the quality of the automatically generated summary. Evaluation metrics such as BLEU, ROUGE and METEOR are deployed to measure the generated summary's quality, but there is no absolute measurement for assessing the generated summary's quality.

The main contribution of this paper is to investigate the performance of the OpenNMT tool for the task of abstractive text summarization. To validate the proficiency of the designed approach, CNNDM and MSMO datasets have been used, and experimental results have been shown in terms of ROUGE and BLEU. The manuscript discusses the related works in Sect. 2. It describes the dataset used in the proposed model in Sect. 3. In Sect. 4, it discusses about the system architecture and Sect. 5 describes the experimental results. Section 6 is about the conclusion and future research direction.

2 Related Work

Numerous research works have been carried out in extractive summarization as early as fifty years ago. One of the pioneering works was by Luhn's [15] statistical technique; sentences consisting of highest frequency and lowest frequency words were not considered essential and less likely to be included in the summary. Some notable work contributed by Edmunson [7,8] includes scoring a sentence's importance by considering a linear combination of features such as the position, word frequency, cue words and the structure of the document, sentences which has the highest weight were to be included in the summary. Abstractive text summarization is more complex than the extractive method because the abstraction-based summarization task involves language generation to form a coherent synopsis. One of the first deep learning technique for abstractive text summarization was proposed by Rush et al. [19] in 2015 based on the encoder-decoder architecture. The RNN Encoder-Decoder architecture was proposed by Cho et al. [4], which can learn from the mapping sequence of a variable length to another sequence of a variable length. Similarly, Sutskever et al. [21] used multilayered Long Short-term Memory (LSTM) to map the source sequence to a fixed dimensionality vector and then from the vector decode the target sequence with another deep LSTM. The model proposed by [4] and [21] was further extended on by Bahdanau et al. [1]. They pointed out that compressing all the information of the source sequence into a fixed-length vector may lead to the neural network having difficulty coping as the source sequence length increases. They addressed this potential issue by letting a model search for a set of input words when generating each target word. Abstractive summarization requires more computational power than extractive summarization and is more complex. Abstractive summarization produces more fluent summaries but requires more computational power than extractive summarization and is more complex. Graham et al.'s. [10] bottom-up attention restrains abstractive summarizers capacity to copy words from the source. Their proposed model employs the combination of extractive and abstractive approaches that is during decoding, a content selector selects which phrases in the source document should be included in the summary, and a copy mechanism is applied solely to those phrases. In recent years, transformer architecture [5,13,24] has led to significant advancements in various NLP tasks. Zhang et al. [26] showed that Pegasus outperformed the state of the art models. Pegasus creates a pseudo-summary by selecting and masking entire sentences from texts, then concatenating the gap sentences. To accomplish abstractive summarising, pre-training leverages extracted gap sentences and sequence-to-sequence. ProphetNet [18] is based on the Transformer [22] encoder-decoder architecture which demonstrated state-of-the-art results for abstractive summary experimented on CNNDM and Gigaword corpus. Another transformer based model by Zaheer et al. [25] combines global and local attention methods, followed by the usage of global nodes to collect tokens in a sequential order which reduces the complexity of the long sequence by compressing it into a small number of elements. More recently, Du et al. [6] proposed GLM (General Language Model) to address the challenge of models not performing well on all main categories of natural language understanding, conditional generation, and unconditional generation at the same time also achieving model produced State-of-the-art results.

To evaluate the quality of the system produced summary, various evaluation methods are employed, such as Rouge [14], BLEU [17] and many more [2]. It is vital to have a reliable metric for the summary to evaluate the algorithms for automatic summarization.

3   Dataset

The CNN/Daily-mail (CNNDM) and MSMO datasets have been used to test, train and validate the proposed model. The CNNDM dataset has been collected from the website of Huggingface[1]. The CNNDM dataset contains 2,86,817 news articles that have been used for training the model. For frequent evaluation, 13,368 documents have been used as validation data, and finally, 11,490 documents have been used for testing. Each document of the dataset contains approximately 28 sentences pair. In addition to this, we have used the MSMO dataset, which has been collected from the website of NLPR[2]. The MSMO dataset contains news articles that have a body, title, and summaries in it. We have used the body as our source data and the title as summary data. The MSMO dataset contains 2,93,625 article bodies and titles as a source and target data that has been used for training. For testing, 10,295 articles have been used, and for val-

---

[1] https://huggingface.co/datasets/cnn_dailymail.
[2] http://www.nlpr.ia.ac.cn/cip/dataset.htm.

idation, we have used 10,339 articles. The dataset statistics has presented in Table 1.

Table 1. Dataset description

Data	CNNDM	MSMO
Train	2,86,817	2,93,625
Validation	13,368	10,339
Test	11,490	10,295

4   System Architecture

We have used the open-source framework for Neural Machine Translation(NMT) called OpenNMT [12]. NMT is a methodology for machine translation that has led to exceptional advances in human evaluation than rule-based and statistical machine translation (SMT) systems [23]. It comprises of vanilla NMT models as well as attention, gating, stacking, input feeding, regularisation, beam search, and all other features required for state-of-the-art performance [12]. OpenNMT provides simple interfaces preprocess, train and translate, which requires parallel source and target files as input. A schematic overview of data structures in OpenNMT is shown in Fig. 1.

4.1   Encoder-Decoder Architecture

An encoder is constituted of a stack of several recurrent units (LSTM or GRU). The encoder we have used is a bidirectional encoder that consists of two one encoding the normal sequence and another for the reversed sequence. The two encoders are independent. The decoder is a unidirectional LSTM that computes the next hidden states based on word embedding, target words, given the previous states. The data input consists of a parallel source (src) and target (tgt) data containing one sentence per line with tokens separated by a space. A YAML configuration file is built to specify the path of the input, the output text and the training parameters. From the configuration file, vocabs are built which is essential for training the model. The default configuration of OpenNMT consists of a two-layer LSTM with 500 hidden units for the encoder as well as the decoder. Finally, the inference is generated by running a beam search. We use 128-dimensional word-embedding, and 512-dimensional 1 layer LSTM to replicate the bottom-up Abstractive summarization by Gehrmann et al. [10]. The encoder side has bidirectional LSTM meaning that the 512 dimensions are split into 256 dimensions per direction. Also, the maximum norm of the gradient was set to 2, and renormalized if the gradient norm exceeds this value and do not use any dropout. The major steps in OpenNMT are preprocessing, training and translation and it implements the attention encoder-decoder architecture.

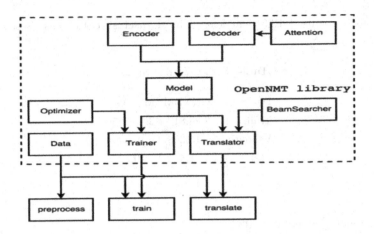

Fig. 1. Schematic overview of OpenNMT [11]

5   Experimental Results

The first model has been trained on the CNNDM dataset, we selected 50000 unique words from the source and target vocabulary. The model has been trained on 200000 epochs (train_steps) with a batch size of 8. Model weights were saved for every 5000 epochs. Another model has been trained on the MSMO dataset. We selected 230000 unique words from the source vocabulary and 85000 unique words from the target vocabulary. The model has been trained on 9000 epochs (train_steps) which has a batch size of 32. The generated summary from the two models is evaluated on the BLEU metric and ROUGE metric. Table 2 & 3 shows the ROUGE score and BLEU score of each model respectively. A comparative table on the source summary and the model generated summary is shown in Fig. 2. The document level BLEU score analysis on the CNNDM and MSMO dataset are shown in Fig. 3 and 4 respectively.

- The model trained on CNNDM dataset yielded a more coherent summary than the model trained on MSMO dataset, having a better score on both the ROUGE and the BLEU metric.
- When the dataset samples are too small in abstractive summarization, the content becomes more abstract. The summary tokens aren't always present in the source. It makes prediction extremely difficult, and as a result, our summarizer systems do not provide appropriate performance measurements. The MSMO dataset, for example, is a smaller dataset as compared to CNNDM thus, yielding a lower ROUGE and BLEU score than the CNNDM dataset. Figure 3 & 4 shows the document level BLEU score analysis of the CNNDM and MSMO dataset respectively.

Table 2. Comparison of ROUGE score of CNNDM dataset for proposed work with Abstractive model [16] and Pointer generator model [20]

Metric	Proposed work		Sequence-to-Sequence RNN [16]	Pointer generator [20]
	CNNDM	MSMO	CNNDM	CNNDM
ROUGE-1	37.728	37.000	35.46	36.44
ROUGE-2	15.737	16.561	13.30	15.66
ROUGE-L	25.010	28.389	32.65	33.42

Table 3. Obtained BLEU score for CNNDM and MSMO dataset

Metric	CNNDM	MSMO
BLEU-1	33.9	28.9
BLEU-2	14.3	12.8
BLEU-3	8.2	6.6
BLEU-4	5.5	4.0
BLEU	12.18	9.94

Source Summary	Predicted Summary
spanish researchers say climate change impacted human migration until 1 4 million years ago it was too cold to inhabit southeast spain but then the climate warmed to 13 c lrb 55 f rrb and became more humid this enabled hominins our distant ancestors to move to new regions.	climate change impacted human migration until 1 4 million years ago it was too cold to inhabit southeast spain but then the climate warmed to 13 c lrb 55 f rrb our distant ancestors to move to new regions.
jayden wingler of arizona was interviewed by fox news earlier this week about a theme park accident which left him with severe burns on his legs while on camera the youngster eloquently recalled what happened with arm actions and wide eyed facial expressions to match his emotions.	jayden wingler of phoenix arizona was interviewed by fox news earlier this week about a theme park accident which left him with severe burns on his legs while on camera the youngster eloquently recalled what happened with arm actions and wide eyed facial expressions to match his emotions.
faith myers 14 from nebraska was filmed by her mother as she woke in bed still high from the procedure anesthesia footage shows her being quizzed about what she would like to eat with the thought of a shake clearly filling her with dread i do not want all the boys in my yard she mumbles after sausages are also given a thumbs down faith and her mother finally settle on jell o.	myers 14 from nebraska was filmed by her mother as she woke in bed still high from the procedure anesthesia footage shows her being quizzed about what she would like to eat with the thought of a shake clearly filling her with dread.

Fig. 2. Comparative analysis of source and system generated summary

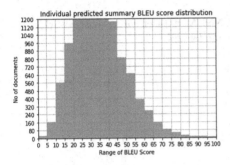

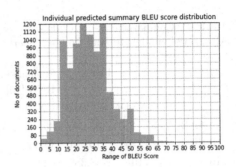

Fig. 3. BLEU score analysis on document level of CNNDM dataset

Fig. 4. BLEU score analysis on document level of MSMO dataset

6   Conclusions and Future Scope

In this work, we have presented the OpenNMT based abstractive summarization with very promising results. The experimental results showed that the OpenNMT model produces more conceptual, comprehensible and abstractive summaries. To evaluate the quality of the generated summaries, ROUGE and BLEU scores have taken into the consideration. The experimental results achieved the highest values of BLEU score (12.18 for CNNDM, and 9.94 for MSMO, respectively). A precise evaluation metric to direct the training process is a critical prerequisite for a summarizer model. This work mainly focused on generation of the concise and coherent summary. In the future, new state-of-the-art deep learning model will be used to handle out-of-vocabulary words.

Acknowledgement. The work presented here falls under the Research Project Grant No. IFC/4130/DST-CNRS/2018-19/IT25 (DST-CNRS targeted program). The authors would like to express gratitude to the Centre for Natural Language Processing and Artificial Intelligence Lab, Department of Computer Science and Engineering, National Institute of Technology Silchar, India for providing infrastructural facilities and support.

References

1. Bahdanau, D., Cho, K., Bengio, Y.: Neural machine translation by jointly learning to align and translate. arXiv preprint arXiv:1409.0473 (2014)
2. Banerjee, S., Lavie, A.: METEOR: an automatic metric for MT evaluation with improved correlation with human judgments. In: Proceedings of the ACL Workshop on Intrinsic and Extrinsic Evaluation Measures for Machine Translation and/or Summarization, pp. 65–72 (2005)
3. Carbonell, J., Goldstein, J.: The use of MMR, diversity-based reranking for reordering documents and producing summaries. In: Proceedings of the 21st Annual International ACM SIGIR Conference on Research and Development in Information Retrieval, pp. 335–336 (1998)

4. Cho, K., et al.: Learning phrase representations using RNN encoder-decoder for statistical machine translation. arXiv preprint arXiv:1406.1078 (2014)
5. Devlin, J., Chang, M.W., Lee, K., Toutanova, K.: BERT: pre-training of deep bidirectional transformers for language understanding. arXiv preprint arXiv:1810.04805 (2018)
6. Du, Z., et al.: All NLP tasks are generation tasks: a general pretraining framework. arXiv preprint arXiv:2103.10360 (2021)
7. Edmundson, H.P.: New methods in automatic extracting. J. ACM (JACM) **16**(2), 264–285 (1969)
8. Edmundson, H.P., Wyllys, R.E.: Automatic abstracting and indexing-survey and recommendations. Commun. ACM **4**(5), 226–234 (1961)
9. Fattah, M.A., Ren, F.: Automatic text summarization. World Acad. Sci. Eng. Technol. **37**(2), 192 (2008)
10. Gehrmann, S., Deng, Y., Rush, A.M.: Bottom-up abstractive summarization. arXiv preprint arXiv:1808.10792 (2018)
11. Klein, G., Kim, Y., Deng, Y., Nguyen, V., Senellart, J., Rush, A.M.: OpenNMT: neural machine translation toolkit. arXiv preprint arXiv:1805.11462 (2018)
12. Klein, G., Kim, Y., Deng, Y., Senellart, J., Rush, A.M.: OpenNmt: open-source toolkit for neural machine translation. arXiv preprint arXiv:1701.02810 (2017)
13. Lewis, M., et al.: BART: denoising sequence-to-sequence pre-training for natural language generation, translation, and comprehension. arXiv preprint arXiv:1910.13461 (2019)
14. Lin, C.Y.: Rouge: a package for automatic evaluation of summaries. In: Text Summarization Branches Out, pp. 74–81 (2004)
15. Luhn, H.P.: The automatic creation of literature abstracts. IBM J. Res. Dev. **2**(2), 159–165 (1958)
16. Nallapati, R., Zhou, B., Gulcehre, C., Xiang, B., et al.: Abstractive text summarization using sequence-to-sequence RNNs and beyond. arXiv preprint arXiv:1602.06023 (2016)
17. Papineni, K., Roukos, S., Ward, T., Zhu, W.J.: BLEU: a method for automatic evaluation of machine translation. In: Proceedings of the 40th Annual Meeting of the Association for Computational Linguistics, pp. 311–318 (2002)
18. Qi, W., et al.: ProphetNet: predicting future n-gram for sequence-to-sequence pre-training. arXiv preprint arXiv:2001.04063 (2020)
19. Rush, A.M., Chopra, S., Weston, J.: A neural attention model for abstractive sentence summarization. arXiv preprint arXiv:1509.00685 (2015)
20. See, A., Liu, P.J., Manning, C.D.: Get to the point: summarization with pointer-generator networks. arXiv preprint arXiv:1704.04368 (2017)
21. Sutskever, I., Vinyals, O., Le, Q.V.: Sequence to sequence learning with neural networks. In: Advances in Neural Information Processing Systems, pp. 3104–3112 (2014)
22. Vaswani, A., et al.: Attention is all you need. In: Advances in Neural Information Processing Systems, pp. 5998–6008 (2017)
23. Wu, Y., et al.: Google's neural machine translation system: bridging the gap between human and machine translation. arXiv preprint arXiv:1609.08144 (2016)
24. Xue, L., et al.: mT5: a massively multilingual pre-trained text-to-text transformer. arXiv preprint arXiv:2010.11934 (2020)
25. Zaheer, M., et al.: Big bird: transformers for longer sequences. In: NeurIPS (2020)
26. Zhang, J., Zhao, Y., Saleh, M., Liu, P.: PEGASUS: pre-training with extracted gap-sentences for abstractive summarization. In: International Conference on Machine Learning, pp. 11328–11339. PMLR (2020)

Facial Emotion Recognition in Static and Live Streaming Image Dataset Using CNN

Aishani Seal, Ranita Saha, Rishav Kumar, Subham Goenka, and Lopamudra Dey[✉]

Department of Computer Science and Engineering, Heritage Institute of Technology, Kolkata,
India
aishani.seal.cse21@heritageit.edu.in,
lopamudra.dey@heritageit.edu

Abstract. Human communication relies heavily on facial expressions. Although detecting emotion from facial expression has always been a simple task for humans, doing so with a computer technique is rather difficult. It is now possible to discern emotions from images because of recent advances in computer vision and machine learning. They frequently disclose people's true emotional situations beyond their spoken language. Furthermore, visual pattern-based understanding of human effect is a critical component of any human-machine interaction system, which is why the task of Facial Expression Recognition (FER) attracts both scientific and corporate interest. Deep Learning (DL) approaches have recently achieved very high performance on FER by utilizing several architectures and learning paradigms. We have considered two types of images here, mainly static and live streaming datasets, and compared their performance using a convolution neural networks (CNN) strategy.

Keywords: CNN · Facial emotion recognition · Accuracy · Live streaming dataset

1 Introduction

Several approaches based on diverse techniques have been proposed in the last decades to solve different FER tasks. Although each method had its advantages, the Deep Learning-based techniques consistently outperformed the others [1, 7, 12]. FER aims to help identify the state of human emotions using particular facial images [6]. The purpose of research on FER is to recognize facial emotion states with high accuracy automatically. Sometimes it is challenging to find the similarity of the same emotional state between different people since they may state the same emotional state in various ways. For example, the expression may vary in other situations, such as the individual's mood, skin color, age, and environmental surroundings. Some facial expression recognition approaches divide the face into categories such as happiness, sadness, and rage [13] or try to identify the different powerful motions that the face can make [14]. In paper [8], the authors proposed a deep learning model called *IRFacExNet* (Infrared facial expression

S. Mukhopadhyay et al. (Eds.): CICBA 2022, CCIS 1579, pp. 288–297, 2022.
https://doi.org/10.1007/978-3-031-10766-5_23

network) that produces 88.43% recognition accuracy. They had compared the performance of the algorithm with other existing algorithms on an openly available dataset, namely *IRDatabase*. In [11] the authors suggested a Deep Pain DL-based architecture for autonomously detecting pain by classifying facial terms. Rather than physically extracting facial traits, the authors sent the facial images straight into a CNN coupled to Long Short-Term Memory to increase accuracy. Based on the Hill-Climbing algorithm, Manosij Ghosh et al. suggested a new feature selection (FS) technique in [10]. The technique is then tested using feature vectors generated from facial photographs from two major FER datasets: RaFD and JAFFE. Saha et al. generated an optimal set of features using Pearson's Correlation Coefficient in [9] using filter harmony technique on images.

The existing methodologies mostly focus on face investigation while maintaining the background and adding a slew of unneeded and misleading features that muddle the CNN training process [3]. The FER using CNN (FERC) algorithm presented in this paper proposes expressional analysis and characterizes the given image into different emotion classes. We have taken the database of normal images and live streaming images from Kaggle [2] by Jonathan Oheix and Github respectively to analyze the models and compare the results in terms of accuracy. We anticipate that the FERC emotion finding technique will be useful in a variety of fields, including learner prediction, education, criminal investigation, lie detectors, and so on.

2 Proposed Work

This paper proposes an advanced technique called FER using CNN. To conduct the research, we have taken the testing dataset of normal static images and live streaming datasets from the Kaggle and GitHub websites [2] and compared their accuracy.

2.1 Datasets

(a) Facial Emotion Recognition of Testing Dataset of Normal Images
The more our data replicates the real world, the more our model behaves as if it does in the real world and executes well. As a result, data is also required for this FER operation. We will use that to train our model, and then we will put it to the investigation with records of live video data.

Data Pre-processing
The images taken from Kaggle are pre-processed to get equal-sized data. All images must be assigned to one of seven categories that represent various facial expressions. 0 = Anger, 1 = Disgust, 2 = Fear, 3 = Happiness, 4 = Sadness, 5 = Surprise, and 6 = Neutral have been assigned to these facial expressions. After converting all images into data frame, the number of emotion categories and the number of images in each of those categories are checked and mentioned in Table 1.

Table 1. Number of images under each category of emotion

Emotion label	Emotion	Number of images
0	Anger	4953
1	Disgust	547
2	Fear	5121
3	Happiness	8989
4	Sadness	6077
5	Surprise	4002
6	Neutral	6198

A graph has been plotted to visualize the number of images under each label.

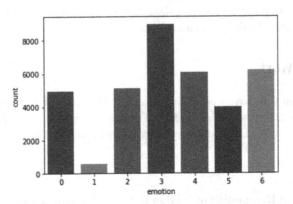

Fig. 1. Graph to visualise number of data under each category of emotion

The graph (Fig. 1) depicts the number of images under each of the categories of emotions in this dataset. Since the majority of data belongs to 3: happy, 4: Sad, 6: Neutral classes, we will train our CNN model on the top three classes only (since these three classes have the maximum number of data) [4].

(b) Facial Emotion Recognition (FER) of testing dataset using Live Streaming:-
The live streaming dataset is taken from GitHub for training and mentioned in the drive URL (https://drive.google.com/u/1/open?id=1iQ3BgBx031F0QsumgeAzwbN x1GY4gzEQ). We have considered five classes from the live streaming dataset because we have five expressions namely happy, sad, neutral, angry, and surprise (mentioned in Table 2). We have taken an image size of 48, 48, and batch size of 8. Then we provide a path of the training set and validation set. For training, we will scale down an image by dividing it by 255.

Table 2. Number of Images under each category of emotion in live streaming dataset

Emotion label	Emotion	Number of images
0	Anger	4953
1	Happy	8989
2	Neutral	6198
3	Sad	6077
4	Surprise	4002

2.2 Proposed FER Model

A Convolution Neural Network (CNN) is used where we will feed batches of 48 × 48 × 1 Gray-scaled images. For the static image dataset, the old class labels are mapped to the new one; for example, the emotion Happy, which was previously labeled 3, is now designated 0. For the live streaming dataset, we have considered all the five emotion classes. After that, we will split the data into training and validation sets in both cases. As neural networks are very sensitive to non-normalized data, the picture arrays are normalized. We utilized the min-max normalization formula mentioned below with min = 0 and max = 255 for gray-scaled images.

$$x_{min-max} = \frac{x - min(X)}{max(X) - min(X)}$$

We validate the result of training using a testing dataset. We again rescale and zoom for validation. The more images the better training we can give. We shuffle the data because we can train with many data and it will not get confused. CNN with Max Pooling technique is used which takes more advanced features for recognition. For example, in a vehicle, it will take the wheel size and by the wheel size, it will predict the vehicle. Softmax is used here which can deal with more than two samples. ReLU is also a kind of activation function in neural networks [5] that we have used here. We make different blocks and keep increasing the number of pixels every time. This makes multiple convolutions.

Algorithm Steps for Emotion Detection

We have imported the essential libraries for mathematical calculations, plotting data, image processing, and building the CNN model for our facial emotion recognition project. Next, we have imported the dataset from the Kaggle website under the category - Facial Emotion Recognition challenge that comprises 35887 rows and 3 columns. A snapshot of the dataset is given below,

	emotion	pixels	Usage
0	0	70 80 82 72 58 58 60 63 54 58 60 48 89 115 121...	Training
1	0	151 150 147 155 148 133 111 140 170 174 182 15...	Training
2	2	231 212 156 164 174 138 161 173 182 200 106 38...	Training
3	4	24 32 36 30 32 23 19 20 30 41 21 22 32 34 21 1...	Training
4	6	4 0 0 0 0 0 0 0 0 0 0 3 15 23 28 48 50 58 84...	Training

1. A label text mapper has been created for the different emotions given by a single numeral. The number of data under each emotion is also given.

```
emotion_label_to_text = {0:'anger', 1:'disgust', 2:'fear', 3:'hap
piness', 4: 'sadness', 5: 'surprise', 6: 'neutral'}

3    8989
6    6198
4    6077
2    5121
0    4953
5    4002
1     547
Name: emotion, dtype: int64
```

2. Since the majority of data of static image dataset belong to three classes out of the seven, the CNN model will be trained on these three majority classes for better results.

3. Since the dataset contains images in the form of 48 * 48 pixel results, we use pyplot to plot the images of the dataset and the corresponding emotions in the form of greyscale images to get a clear idea. A snippet of the images created from the pixel values is given below (Fig. 2),

Fig. 2. A snippet of the images created from the pixel values

4. We then split our model into training and testing datasets and normalise the results since neural networks are quite insensitive to un-normalized data.

5. Then CNN with variable depths (batch normalization, dropout, and max-pooling layers) is applied to the datasets to identify the emotions.

6. For the live streaming dataset, we have used a similar approach with the same parameters settings to classify the emotions.

Then the accuracy results and loss results are plotted along with the confusion matrix to give us a clear idea of how our model performs. The charts have been provided in the results section. In addition, a few images have been checked on how the model performs. The workflow of the proposed model is highlighted in the following flowchart (Fig. 3).

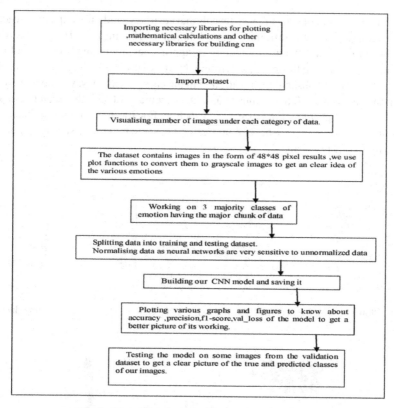

Fig. 3. Flowchart depicting FER model using CNN

3 Experimental Results

We have used three main classes of normal image datasets (in terms of majority values of data): 'Happy', 'Neutral', 'Sad' for our classification. Using the matplotlib and the seaborn libraries, we have plotted the accuracy and the value loss graphs, whose results are given below (Fig. 4),

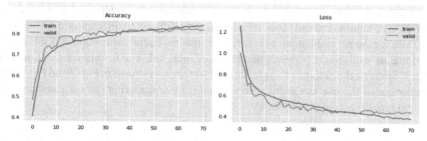

Fig. 4. Accuracy and loss calculation on normal image dataset

The epoch's result of static images reveals that accuracy gradually improves, reaching 82–83% accuracy on both the training and validation sets, but the model eventually begins to overfit training data. We used a variety of approaches, including dropout and batch normalization, to reduce the model overfitting. Next, we use the violin plot function from the seaborn library to observe the results and in the case of accuracy, we see that the plot concentrates in between 0.8–0.9 thus attaining an accuracy of slightly greater than 80%. The following graph plots have been given below. For the live streaming dataset, we have found less accuracy (52–53%) considering the same parameter settings, compared to static images (Figs. 5 and 6).

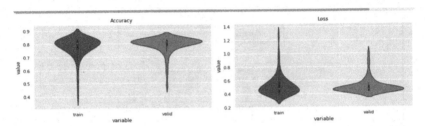

Fig. 5. Plots showing the accuracy and val_loss concentration in training and testing datasets

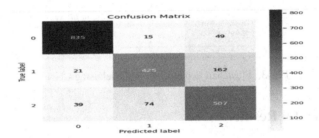

Fig. 6. The confusion matrix of the proposed FER using normal image dataset

It can be seen from the confusion matrix that for the happy class the performance of the model is good compared to the Sad and Neutral classes. An important explanation for the output can be that the Sad and Neutral classes have fewer data as compared to the happy class. Moreover, facial emotion expression varies from person to person, and in the case of neutral and sad class, it becomes very difficult to differentiate between the two (even for the normal human eye) for some images. Facial expression depends on the individual as well. Some people's neutral faces look sad. The results are mentioned in Table 3. Some of the outputs of our testing dataset are mentioned in Fig. 7 and Fig. 8. We have generated the live streaming testing dataset by considering our own images with different emotions (Fig. 8) (Table 4).

Table 3. Result of accuracies of the testing dataset for the FER model using normal image dataset

Total number of images	Algorithm used	Dataset class	Correct sample	Incorrect sample
2127	CNN	Happy	835	64
		Sad	425	183
		Neutral	507	113

Fig. 7. Sample output of the FER model showing the true and predicted classes of images

Fig. 8. Sample output of Facial Emotion Recognition (FER) of the testing dataset on Live Streaming dataset.

Table 4. Comparison of experimental results of the two datasets

Properties	Facial Emotion Recognition of testing dataset of normal images	Facial Emotion Recognition (FER) of testing dataset using Live Streaming dataset
Dataset used	Kaggle competitions	Own dataset
Emotions worked on	3	5
Model accuracy	0.8323	0.5699
Loss	0.4165	1.0916
Val_accuracy	0.8148	0.6707
Val_loss	0.4695	0.8509

4 Conclusion

In this paper, we present our first experimental campaign focused on the FER method using a CNN model, which successfully retrieves facial appearances. Our extensive experimental analysis shows that the proposed approach can increase the rate of facial expression detection. In complex backgrounds to a certain extent. Compared to normal images and live streaming models, in complex background situations, the model's accuracy of normal images is higher. We observe promising results, and we are planning to submit our predictions to the publicly available dataset, namely IRDatabase, Japanese female facial expression (JAFFE), etc. Aside from that, the suggested approach may be tested on other huge databases, which will assist us to ensure the model's resilience.

References

1. Mehendale, N.: Facial emotion recognition using convolutional neural networks (FERC). SN Appl. Sci. 2(3), 1–8 (2020). https://doi.org/10.1007/s42452-020-2234-1
2. https://www.kaggle.com/jonathanoheix/face-expression-recognition-dataset and https://github.com/amineHorseman/facial-expression-recognition-using-cnn
3. Orzechowski, W.: Object Shape Classification Utilizing Magnetic Field Disturbance and Supervised Machine Learning (Master's thesis, Universitat Politècnica de Catalunya) (2017)
4. Dalal, N., Triggs, B.: Histograms of oriented gradients for human detection. In: 2005 IEEE Computer Society Conference on Computer Vision and Pattern Recognition (CVPR 2005), vol. 1, pp. 886–893. IEEE (June 2005)
5. Coşkun, M., Uçar, A., Yildirim, Ö., Demir, Y.: Face recognition based on convolutional neural network. In: 2017 International Conference on Modern Electrical and Energy Systems (MEES), pp. 376–379. IEEE (November 2017)
6. Inthiyaz, S., Parvez, M.M., Kumar, M.S., saiSrija, J.S., Sai, M.T., Vardhan, V.A.: Facial expression recognition using KERAS. In: Journal of Physics: Conference Series, vol. 1804, no. 1, p. 012202. IOP Publishing (February 2021)
7. Sinha, A., Aneesh, R.P.: Real time facial emotion recognition using deep learning. Int. J. Innov. Implement. Eng. 1, 1–5 (2019)

8. Bhattacharyya, A., Chatterjee, S., Sen, S., Sinitca, A., Kaplun, D., Sarkar, R.: A deep learning model for classifying human facial expressions from infrared thermal images. Sci. Rep. **11**(1), 1–17 (2021)

9. Saha, S., et al.: Feature selection for facial emotion recognition using cosine similarity-based harmony search algorithm. Appl. Sci. **10**(8), 2816 (2020)

10. Ghosh, M., Kundu, T., Ghosh, D., Sarkar, R.: Feature selection for facial emotion recognition using late hill-climbing based memetic algorithm. Multimed. Tools Appl. **78**(18), 25753–25779 (2019). https://doi.org/10.1007/s11042-019-07811-x

11. Rodriguez, P., et al.: Deep pain: exploiting long short-term memory networks for facial expression classification. IEEE Trans. Cybern. **52**, 1–11 (2017)

12. Chakraborty, S., Mandal, S.B., Shaikh, S.H.: Quantum image processing: challenges and future research issues. Int. J. Inf. Technol. **14**, 475–489 (2018). https://doi.org/10.1007/s41870-018-0227-8

13. Littlewort, G., Bartlett, M., Fasel, I., Susskind, J., Movellan, J.: Dynamics of facial expression extracted automatically from video. Image Vis. Comput. **24**(6), 615–625 (2006)

14. Bartlett, M.S., Littlewort, G., Frank, M.G., Lainscsek, C., Fasel, I., Movellan, J.R.: Automatic recognition of facial actions in spontaneous expressions. J. Multimed. **1**, 22–35 (2006)

An UAV Assisted Need Assessment and Prediction System for COVID-19 Vaccination

Mrinmoy Sadhukhan[2]([✉]), Swaraj Chowdhury[1], Manish Biswas[1], Indrajit Bhattacharya[1], and Sudakshina Dasgupta[3]

[1] Kalyani Government Engineering College, Department of MCA, Kalyani, West Bengal, India
[2] School of Computer and Information Sciences, Indira Gandhi National Open University, Kolkata, West Bengal, India
mrinmoy.sadhukhan1996@gmail.com
[3] Government College of Engineering and Textile Technology, Department of Information Technology, Serampore, West Bengal, India

Abstract. Health monitoring by government in rural and Urban areas become very much challenging task as they require huge amount of technicians, doctors and funds to complete. In the time of COVID-19 pandemic, it is difficult to allow doctors to visit rural areas for monitoring the health of public, rather than allocate their duties in COVID-19 hospitals to save critical patients. But, it is also necessary to monitor health of public to vaccinate them priority wise in the scarcity of COVID-19 vaccines. In this paper we have proposed a novel UAV (Unmanned Aerial Vehicle) assisted health monitoring system which can be operated in any remote location to get required data about the health condition of the people. After collecting the desired data from the user, system saves them in memory. In the control room, UAV uploads the collected data to the server for analysis. From the analysed data the system can decide whom need to be vaccinated immediately. UAV system will analyse the data with respect to different parameters like age, co-morbidity, blood pressure and other attributes. From this analysed data using machine learning algorithm, system also predicts how many days might be taken to complete the whole vaccination process.

Keywords: UAV · Health monitoring · IOT · COVID-19 · SARIMA

1 Introduction

Embedded technologies of IOTs (Internet Of Things) has many aspects of applications like health monitoring, weather monitoring, smart applications etc. In the pandemic situation normal health monitoring system is not sufficient as they require huge amount of man power, whereas IOT based health monitoring system is sufficient to work with one or two technicians only. In the Proposed

S. Mukhopadhyay et al. (Eds.): CICBA 2022, CCIS 1579, pp. 298–310, 2022.
https://doi.org/10.1007/978-3-031-10766-5_24

System UAV can fly in any locality and activate its Wi-Fi hot-spot. People with the help of this hot-spot connect their smart phones and fill up a form with their personal information and some basic health related information like their body-temperature, symptoms, vaccinated or not etc. UAV system uploads collected data to a server coming back to the control room. After analyzing this data, system can conclude which people need to be vaccinated as a priority basis to fight against COVID-19. On the basis of this analyzed and pre-processed data system also predicts how long it might take to complete the vaccination process

1.1 Motivation

The motivation behind the work is to make a lightweight, GPS enabled UAV system to collect the health data from any specific area and make them available in server for further processing. The system predicts the rate of vaccination as well as the estimated time frame to complete the vaccination process for a specific area.

1.2 Contribution

The main contribution of this work are the following (1) design a GPS (Global Positioning System) enabled UAV system, which can fly over a specific geo-location, (2) design a light weight UAV, so that it can fly with longer time period and collect data using wifi hot-spot module, (3) use of machine learning model (Seasonal Auto Regressive Integrated Moving Average) for predicting the completion time of vaccination based on real time and historical dataset.

2 Objectives

This proposed system is built with some key objectives such as to help government in any disaster situation by collecting data for any kind of decision making step. Besides, in pandemic situation system can also help to survey a locality which is badly affected by COVID-19 and needs quick vaccination. In some critical situation where tragedy occurs by act of god and the whole internet facility goes down, our system can also help government by collecting proper requirement and needs of people. The main goal of the system is to collect data and then process them in terms of needs or requirements for decision makers. Those crucial data is shared with government sectors, to process those data and step forward for a better settlement. The system can help in collecting and communicating towards medical team to track overall health condition of a locality with respect to recent outbreak of second wave of covid in contact-less fashion and also help the decision makers to estimate the proportion of vaccination had already done and still need to be done. There are lots of possibilities with our system in medical field for collecting the data in lockdown time to access the needs for the medical facility and what type of facilities would be immediately required. On the basis of this collected data the authority can directly reach out to needy ones. In this work an UAV is used, that is enabled with Wi-Fi hot-spot facility. It will fly over a particular locality(specified latitude and longitude) and collect data from mobile smart phones available with the users using Wi-Fi hot-spot connectivity. After complete survey of that area, UAV returns back to home and retrieve those data. Later from those critical data, by pre-processing and fitting those to the machine learning model it can be predicted about the time frame when all people might be vaccinated. Here for prediction purposes classical machine learning algorithm SARIMA (Seasonal Auto Regressive Integrated Moving Average) [10] has been used.

3   Literature Survey

Mohammad et al. [1] proposed a crop health monitoring system using unmanned aerial vehicle (UAV) and wireless sensor networks. System collects data dynamically from fixed based station or mobile cluster. In this paper author also proposed a Bayesian classifier to select best cluster head at the time of data collection. S. Sankarasrinivasan et al. [2] proposed a novel approach to detect crack and assess surface degradation in time civil structure inspection with the help of UAV and image processing. UAV system paired with matlab via wireless network, is used in real time for image processing. Mohd Asim Sayeed et al. [3] proposed a efficient data transmission approach among wireless sensor networks by employing the UAV as a relay to reduce multi-hop characteristics. Author also introduced a multi-head clustering algorithm to avoid transmission choking of the designated cluster head. In the UAV data transmission is facilitate through ant colony optimization algorithm. Seyed Omid Sajedi et al. [4] proposed unique UAV based structural health monitoring system which uses Bayesian inference for deep vision where uncertainty can be quantified using the Monte Carlo dropout sampling. The system is used to investigate cracks, local damage identification, and bridge component detection. Milan Erdelj et al. [9] presented the some application of UAV where disaster occurs such as monitoring, forecast and early warning systems, disaster information fusion, situational awareness and logistics, damage assessment, standalone communication system, and search and rescue missions. Author also raises some key issues in UAV assisted disaster management such as Battery life time, flight time, flight height, communication protocol, UAV localization, Data fusion and handover issues. Tamal Mondal et al. [5] proposed practical swarm optimization technique for Resource Allocation Problem. RAP has been considered for designing such an allocation model for scarce resources like food, water, clothes, medical equipment, and rescue members. Authors provided the intended number of resources to all the affected sites using optimization technique, while preserving a pre-computed amount of resources in RP for utilizing in the future. H. Shakhatreh et al. [6] presented UAV civil applications and their challenges. They also discussed the current research trends and provide future insights for potential UAV uses. Authors highlighted the key challenges for UAV civil applications, including charging challenges, collision avoidance and swarming challenges, and networking and security-related challenges. In the paper author also presented high-level insights on how these challenges might be approached and overcome it. Sara Pérez Carabaza [7] proposed a MTS planner based ant colony optimization that includes communication and collision avoidance constraints. This algorithm ensures that the UAVs are able to complete the optimized search trajectories without risk of collision or loss of communication with the ground control station. It also helps UAV deployments without continuous communication to the ground control station. The proposed algorithm is compared against two state of the art techniques based on Cross Entropy Optimization and Genetic Algorithms. Norzailawati Mohd Noor [8] reviewed a development of UAV/Drone remote sensing applications in urban areas and its issues respectively. Classification, design methods and challenges are discussed appropriately. And the applications of UAV in urban areas is also proposed. N. Naren et al. [11] proposed a prototype of contact less COVID-19 screening and detection system named Covidrone. The system consists of bio medical sensors (SpO_2, body temperature measuring unit, voice recorder, camera, OCR(Optical Character Recognition)) with disinfectant module to collect data from user. A trained DNN module in the system can accurately detect COVID-19 based on this collected data. This system also suggests the people for further medication and preventive measures to follow. The test reports are saved in cloud for further accessing and analyzing by medical staff. Shengqiang et al. [12] proposed a DRS algorithm to solve Drone assisted Management problem. This algorithm energy efficiently reduce total time cost to service elderly chronic diseases. Authors further formulate the Charging driven Drone assisted Management (CDM) problem to maximize the service utility.

4 Proposed System

The Proposed structure of the system is depicted below in Fig. 1. UAV is flown over a desired location by setting up longitude and latitude and maintains a proper altitude to collect data with desired data rate. UAV activates its Wi-Fi to collect data from smartphones within its communication radius. It stores data in flash memory for temporary purposes. After that it returns back to control room, data is processed and uploaded to the server. These pre processed data is later used for prediction using machine learning algorithm. The proposed algorithm of the system is depicted in Algorithm 1. The design of the system is divided into two parts: UAV design and Android APP design. They are detailed in following subsections.

4.1 UAV Design

UAV is designed with NodeMCU[1] and MPU6050[2]. NodeMCU is an open source prototyping board. The name "NodeMCU" combines "node" and "MCU"

---

[1] NodeMCU: 'https://nodemcu.readthedocs.io/en/release/'.

[2] MPU6050: 'https://www.electronicwings.com/sensors-modules/mpu6050-gyroscope accelerometer-temperature-sensor-module'.

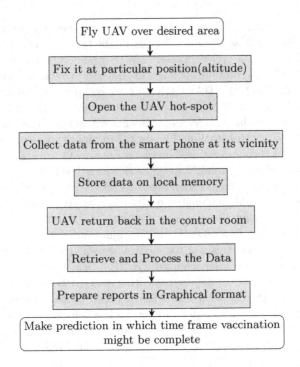

Fig. 1. Work flow of proposed architecture

(micro-controller unit). The term "NodeMCU" typically refers to the firmware rather than the associated development kits. The prototyping hardware typically used as a dual in-line package (DIP) which integrates a USB controller with a smaller surface mounted board containing the MCU and antenna. The design was initially based on the ESP-12 module of the ESP8266, which is a Wi-Fi SoC integrated with a Tensilica Xtensa LX106 core, widely used in IoT applications. The MPU6050 is a Micro Electro Mechanical Systems (MEMS) which consists of a 3-axis Accelerometer and 3-axis Gyroscope inside it. This helps us to measure acceleration, velocity, orientation, displacement and many other motion related parameter of a system or object. This module also has a (DMP) Digital Motion Processor inside it which is powerful enough to perform complex calculation and thus free up the work for Micro controller. It helps UAV to fly at designated longitude and latitude with a constant acceleration and maintains its speed from a certain altitude. The circuit diagram of UAV system is depicted in Fig. 2.

4.2   Android App Development

Android app is designed with the help of Android studio, CSS and JavaScript. Through the android app UAV collects data about people name, phone number, date of Birth, body temperature, gender, vaccination done or not. If yes, the vaccination date and if any symptoms are their or not.

Algorithm 1. Algo_health_monitoring

This algorithm collects data from a desired location, process them and produce report for need assessment.

1: Fly UAV over the desire area. The UAV is operated from its control room to a remote location(as specified by longitude and latitude). UAV is maintained at a particular position from where it can achieve its maximum data rate.
2: Open the hot-spot associated with the UAV. Collect data from the mobile nodes at its vicinity(with in communication range) using Wi-Fi hot-spot.
3: UAV return back to the control room and data is uploaded to the Server.
4: Server analyses the data and create reports in graphical format for need assessment.
5: From the analysed data system predicts when vaccination drive might be completed for people at any specified locality.

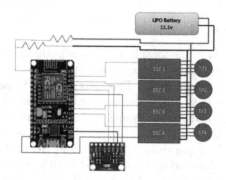

Fig. 2. The circuit diagram

4.3 Data Collection

Real time data set is collected from UAV system by flying to some specific area. Later these data-set is uploaded to server for further pre-processing. For training the machine learning model requires huge amount of historical data, which are collected from COWIN website[3] and COVID19INDIA website[4]. These website gives us day to day vaccination data for any specific location. We collected the vaccination data from starting date 16-jan-2021 to 11-june-2021. Data collected from UAV system consists of Name, Gender, Date-Of-Birth, Body-temperature, Date, Vaccinated or not and Symptoms. The Structure of Database in given below. From this data format we can easily segregate vaccinated or non-vaccinated people age group wise and may take necessary actions as per requirement.

---

[3] Cowin: 'https://dashboard.cowin.gov.in/'.
[4] Covid-19 Vaccination Data: 'https://github.com/covid19india/api'.

Vaccination_Data						
Name (string)	Gender (string)	Date-Of-Birth (date)	Body-temperature (float)	Date (date)	Vaccinated or not (boolean)	Symptoms (string)

4.4 Data Storage

In the time of data collection data is stored in internal storage memory and after returning back to control room data is uploaded to server. Data rate during data collection using UAV depends on various factors like wind speed, wind direction, atmospheric temperature and the altitude.

4.5 Data Analysis

Collected data is stored in the local heap storage in the ESP8266 (Wi-Fi module with 4 MB flash). After collecting data, the drone returns back to its base station and data is retrieved from the drone. This data needs to be parsed before uploading to the server. The data analysis is performed by the decision makers based on their needs. *Vaccination*: Analysing the data we might find the number of people vaccinated in the particular area, and also measure vaccination rate with respect to number of people resides in that area. *Second Wave*: Increase in covid cases might be observed now a days and in this situation going for regular checking. We can use the data to figure out the requirement of vaccination at an urgent basis. *Co-morbidity*: People who have a weak immune system are more susceptible to contract coronavirus. Studies have shown that people with pre-existing conditions face a higher mortality rate compared to people affected with no co-morbidity. Prominent forms of co-morbidity are high blood pressure, diabetes, cardiovascular diseases, arthritis, stroke, and cancerous conditions. If someone have one of the previously mentioned conditions, then they need to be vaccinated in priority basis. From this above conditions quick decisions might be taken regarding the vaccination process. *Awareness*: All the previous factors like the percentage of vaccination, various parameter of co-morbidity symptoms are collected and accumulated for the server and after analyzing all these parameter, the data is communicated to the health care unit and it might be helpful for government/health care unit to identify the possible locations with greater chances to spread the COVID-19 disease. Accordingly they can aware the people in that particular location for taking extra care of their health and hygiene. On the basis of this kind of data we can directly reach out to those needy people. Analyzed data for bally-bazar (West Bengal) areas and its near by locations is depicted using pie chart in Fig. 3. From the Fig. 3 for locality 1 it can be observed that there are total 1350 people among them 250 people with comorbitiy, 50 people with Breathing problem, 300 people with cough and 150 people have fever. Rest 615 people have all type of symptoms. From rest 615 people among them 600 people not vaccinated and rest 15 are vaccinated.

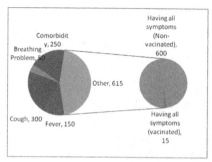
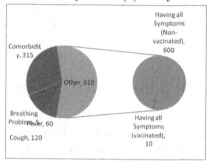
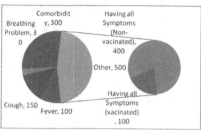

(a) Analysed Data For Locality 1   (b) Analysed Data For Locality 2

(c) Analysed Data For Locality 3

Fig. 3. Analysed data

4.6   Proposed Prediction System

Here for prediction purposes we have used classical machine learning algorithm SARIMA(Seasonal Auto Regressive Integrated Moving Average), which is mainly used for time series prediction with trends and seasonal components. In SARIMA method term AR is 'Auto Regressive', means it is a linear regression model that uses its own lags as predictors. It performs well when the predictors are correlated and dependent with each other. Here SARIMA method is applied to predict, in how many days total vaccination of any locality might be completed based on past historical vaccination data set. To feed the data in SARIMA method for training model, day to day vaccination data set is used. The data set is collected from cowin app for howrah municipality area. For testing purposes pre-processed data set is used. Which is collected by UAV system flying to bally bazar and it's nearby locality. In the Fig. 4, a graph on date vs number of total vaccinated people is plotted.

SARIMA method can produce best result depending upon the prefect tuning of different hyper parameters. In SARIMA method we have seven type of parameters, they are p,d,q,P,D,Q and m, where p is Autoregressive order, d is Differencing order, q is Moving average order Seasonal parameters, P is Seasonal auto-regressive order, D is Seasonal differencing order, Q is Seasonal moving

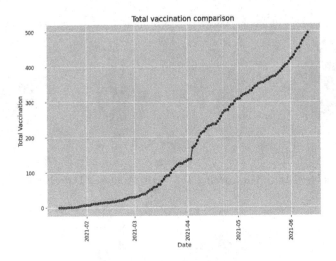

Fig. 4. Date vs Total number of vaccinated people

average order and m is Number of time steps for a single seasonal period. For prediction purpose we have chosen the parameter value for p = 3, d = 2, q = 1, P = 2, D = 2, Q = 1 and m = 12. Here p,d,q are non seasonal part and P,D,Q,m are seasonal part of the parameter. Here d and D value both are set to 2 to make the data set stationary. Here other parameter values is founded by applying grid search method. A widely known estimator Akaike Information Criterion (AIC) is used here to choose the set of parameters from Grid Search result having lowest AIC value. To determine the goodness of fit of the model, we use Box-Ljung residuals. In Fig. 5 we plot residuals from naive method and the histogram of residuals. From the Fig. 5, we can observe that the residuals seem to be normally distributed around 0 with a constant mean and variance and no significant correlation in the residuals series. This observation helps us to understand that the model is well fitted with historical data set and can be used for prediction purposes.

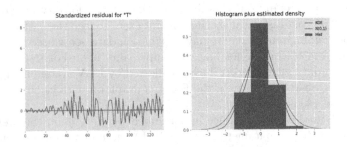

Fig. 5. Residuals of model.

To measure the performance of the model in Table 1 a comparison is given between state-of-the-art machine learning algorithms SARIMA [10], Prophet [10], Gluonts [10]. Here RMSE (Root mean square error) and MAE (Mean absolute error) method is used to calculate the error rate of the models. From Table 1, it can be observed that SARIMA method outperform other two algorithms with lower error rate as it can capture trend and seasonality properly. SARIMA algorithm with auto regressive, seasonality and moving average features can predict the future seasonal trend with more accurate than other algorithms. For this SARIMA model has been chosen in our prediction algorithm.

Table 1. Comparison of different machine learning model.

Model name	RMSE	MAE
SARIMA	2.725	2.526
Prophet	8.844	8.485
Gluonts	12.210	12.253

The final Predicted result of the model for bally bazar and its nearby locality is shown in Fig. 6. In the Fig. 6, blue color is used to show predicted output, how many number of people can be vaccinated in some given time frame and red color is used to show originally how many number of people has been vaccinated.

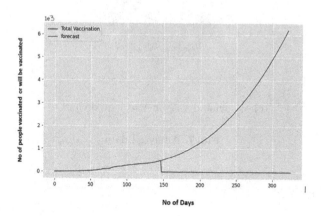

Fig. 6. Prediction result by SARIMA method. (Color figure online)

5   Result and Snapshot

Once UAV is positioned at a location it activates the hot-spot. User access the mobile app and filled the form. After collecting data from user, UAV saves its heap memory and return back to the control room. Data is upload on the server for analysis. The analysed data for Belurmath and nearby locality is depicted in Fig. 7. From the Fig. 7 we can found how many number people are vaccinated age group wise and how many number of people have different symptoms irrespective of different age group.

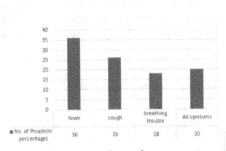

(a) No of vaccinated people vs symptom graph

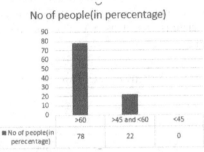

(b) No vaccinated people vs age group

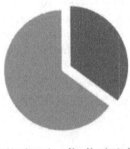

(c) Vaccinated vs Non-Vaccinated chart

Fig. 7. Analysed data

6   Conclusion

Data is very critical thing in this present situation. In this work our main goal is to collect data and then process them in terms of our needs or requirements to share those crucial data with decision making authority. So, they can process those data as there requirements and can step forward for a better settlement. In the time of building of UAV system many different challenges was encountered, which can be grouped into data transfer and data collection related problems. In data transfer related challenges we found that, data transfer rate varies in different location when UAV get obstructed by large trees and buildings. Some times due to heavy connection in Wi-Fi hot-spot bandwidth, data transfer rate might fall drastically. Also some times Wi-Fi unit refuses to connect due to huge pressure or suddenly stop working which later needs to be restarted. In data collection related challenges the data collected from UAV are of different format rather than data collected from COWIN AND COVID19INDIA websites. In future we have to built a common data format which helps train the model directly on collected data.

To predict, in how many days vaccination process might be completed based on this pre processed data, we have used machine learning based model SARIMA. In future we would like to use some different deep learning based recurrent neural network techniques to obtain more accurate results. We might conclude that, there are many possibilities to enhance the proposed system to address these challenges and deploy UAV system to serve in man-kind for better future.

References

1. Uddin, M.A., Mansour, A., Le Jeune, D., Ayaz, M., Aggoune, E.M.: UAV-assisted dynamic clustering of wireless sensor networks for crop health monitoring. In: MDPI, vol. 18, Issue 2 (2018)
2. Sankarasrinivasan, S., Balasubramanian, E., Karthik, K., Chandrasekar, U., Gupta, R.: Health monitoring of civil structures with integrated UAV and image processing system. In: Procedia Computer Science, vol. 54, pp. 508–515 (2015). https://doi.org/10.1016/j.procs.2015.06.058
3. Sayeed, M.A., Shree, R.: Optimizing unmanned aerial vehicle assisted data collection in cluster based wireless sensor network. In: ICIC Express Letters, vol. 13, pp. 37–374, May 2019
4. Sajedi, S.O., Liang, X.S.O.: Uncertainty-assisted deep vision structural health monitoring. In: Comput. Aided Civ. Inf. **36**, 126–142 (2021)
5. Mondal, T., Boral, N., Bhattacharya, I., Das, J., Pramanik, P.: Distribution of deficient resources in disaster response situation using particle swarm optimization. Int. J. Disas. Risk Reduction **41**, 101308 (2019)
6. Shakhatreh, H., et al.: Unmanned Aerial Vehicles (UAVs): a survey on civil applications and key research challenges. In: IEEE Access, vol. 7 (2019)
7. Pérez-Carabaza, S., Scherer, J., Rinner, B., López-Orozco, J.A., Besada-Portas, E.: UAV trajectory optimization for minimum time search with communication constraints and collision avoidance. In: Engineering Applications of Artificial Intelligence (2019), vol. 85, pp. 357–371. https://doi.org/10.1016/j.engappai.2019.06.002
8. Noor, N.M., Abdullah, A., Hashim, M.: Remote sensing UAV/drones and its applications for urban areas: a review. In: IOP Conference Series: Earth and Environmental Science, vol. 169 (2018)
9. Erdelj, M., Natalizio, E.: UAV-assisted disaster management: applications and open issues. In: 2016 International Conference on Computing, Networking and Communications (ICNC), pp. 1–5 (2016)
10. Papastefanopoulos, V., Linardatos, P., Kotsiantis, S.: COVID-19: a comparison of time series methods to forecast percentage of active cases per population. In: MDPI, 3 June 2020

11. Naren, N., et al.: IoMT and DNN-enabled drone-assisted Covid-19 screening and detection framework for rural areas. In: IEEE Internet of Things Magazine, vol. 4(2), pp. 4–9 (2021). https://doi.org/10.1109/IOTM.0011.2100053
12. Jiang, S., Jin, Y., Xia, K.: Drone assisted robust emergency service management for elderly chronic disease. In: Hindwai vol. 2021 (2021). https://doi.org/10.1155/2021/5552350

Video-Based Depression Detection Using Support Vector Machine (SVM)

Nishu Yadav, Astha Singh[✉], and Divya Kumar

Motilal Nehru National Institute of Technology Allahabad, Prayagraj, India
{nishu.2020sw10,astha,divyak}@mnnit.ac.in

Abstract. Depression is categorized as a mood disorder that causes a persistent feeling of irritability, sadness, and hopelessness in a person's daily life, which eventually leads to a mixed feeling of guilt and helplessness. Also known as a major depressive disorder or termed a clinical depression, it affects how one feels, thinks, and behaves throughout the day and may lead to various emotional and physical problems every day until appropriately treated. The stigma around mental health stops many people from seeking medical help when in need or even getting a quick diagnosis. Therefore, there is a need for a system where a person's mood is analyzed in hindsight and suggests a counselling session to them. In this study, we propose a depression detection system that can make an early prediction of a person dealing with depression by using video footage of that person as input which can be recorded anywhere in the workplace or any standalone centre. This video is eventually used to form a feature set by feature extraction and is then used to examine and identify depression symptoms.

Keywords: Image processing · Feature extraction · Depression detection · Machine learning

1 Introduction

Human beings are social species and need cooperation and communication with others to survive and thrive as a healthy society. They are guided by their instincts and emotions to communicate with others by mainly expressing these six happy, anger, sad, fear, surprise, and disgust. Most of the days, we go through the emotions of happiness, surprise, and fear, but some days are complex, and we experience sadness, fear, worry, disgust, and loneliness. The emotions on these hard days are a result of the natural and immediate response to a demand or threat situation where one may have experienced a failure they wanted success at, or from losing something/someone dear, struggles of life, or have their self-pride hurt.

The prolonged state of constant fear and sadness may leave one to be hopeless and be the reason the person starts withdrawing from its everyday active life and starts trying to avoid certain situations out of worry, where these withdrawals turn into some feeling of guilt and hopelessness, indicating depression.

© The Author(s), under exclusive license to Springer Nature Switzerland AG 2022
S. Mukhopadhyay et al. (Eds.): CICBA 2022, CCIS 1579, pp. 311–325, 2022.
https://doi.org/10.1007/978-3-031-10766-5_25

While feeling sad is normal and fleeting like all other emotions, generally triggered through some hurtful, disappointing, or challenging events, depression is an abnormal emotional state that affects our feelings, thinking, perceptions and behaviour chronically and is not necessarily be branched out from a challenging situation. The fundamental symptom includes a depressed mood or anhedonia and needs to be present in addition to 5 or more key symptoms for a continuous two-week period. The key symptom includes feelings of worthlessness or guilt, energy loss and fatigue, diminished sleep and weight where appetite is also affected in some manner, suicidal ideas, or there may be an attempt of it. Practically, the detection and diagnosis of depression are often very challenging to clinicians [17]. Many a time, the person is either unaware of or tries to hide it away, making the detection more difficult. So, a non-verbal communication method like reading the facial expression needs to be in place to detect depression early.

In this paper, we have demonstrated the depression presence via the study of features extracted from face images (the input video footage extracts images per frame). Various image processing methods like face detection, feature extraction and feature classification (for those extracted features to classify them into depression or non-depression trait) are applied in this paper. The work trains with the features of depression and the test images extracted from videos are tested with these features. An emotion prediction is made based on these results. Then built on the frequency of these emotions, the level of depression is deduced.

The coming sections will be carried out in a manner wherein Sect. 2 we will discuss the summary of previous works and try to establish the basis of this research work explaining the course of action we will take. Section 3 will define our proposed work and the results of the work we carried out with Sect. 4 concluding the paper and discussing the future scope of this work.

2   Recent Work

Recent researches have proved to be very effective in depression detection. The first basic step of this type of researches includes establishing a relation between facial expressions and depression, followed by the requirement to find the relevant data sets to work on, and the final step is to find the various feature extraction and classification techniques best suited for the work. To better understand this, we have divided the section into three parts and explained each part in detail as follow,

2.1   Facial Expressions in Depression

Many studies have been conducted to pick out the actual expressions of a face that are dominant to a depression event. In a study [9] for deducing the relationship between facial expression and depression detection, the manual and automatic FACS Coding (Facial Action Coding System) approaches were followed and studied for discovering the different AUs (Action Units) involved in different emotions displayed by patients of depression throughout their treatment course with various clinical interviews. The action unit AU12 for smile emotion had a meagre presence in highly depressed patients, whereas the action units involved in depressed patients at high presence were AU14, AU15 and AU10, where AU14 is related to contempt emotion, AU15 for sadness and AU10 being related to emotion disgust. Other potent AUs observed were AU (1, 4, 6, 10, 17, or 24). These clinical interviews were recorded in video form for depressed patients along with the non-depressed ones. The results obtained revealed that AU14 involved with contempt emotion is the most prominent feature for depression detection.

The study of features related to eye motions and head poses to comprehend the depressed patient's eye activities and head pose/motion has been made in one such study [2]. The feature classification from eye activity has proved to show better results in severe depression detection. The facial features used in 'Multi-Scale Entropy' (MSE) measurement on the recorded clinical interview video of patients can help in depression detection [12]. MSE finds out the measure of fluctuations that occurs over a single pixel over a time scale in the video. The entropy level of a non-depressed patient was very high, whereas it was deficient in a depressed patient. Depressed patients were even observed to be expressing significantly less of how they feel and their emotions.

2.2   Depression Data Set Analysis

The detection of depression from a machine learning model will require enough data to train the model with high accuracy. Some may form data sets on their own using a collection of videos or images produced. At the same time, the subjects are given a mental health questionnaire like Beck Depression Inventory (BDI) [1], Zung Self-Rating Depression Scale, Hamilton Rating Scale for Depression (HRSD), also known as the Hamilton Depression Rating Scale (HDRS) or abbreviated to HAM-D, and others. Researchers may also use the required databases, which are available over the internet and has been created specifically for the research purpose [3].

The datasets available on request over the internet for detection of depression include - BlackDog (Black Dog Institute depression dataset) [24], Audio/Visual Emotion Challenge depression dataset (AVEC) [18,21,26], University of Pittsburgh depression dataset (Pitt) [28], Distress Analysis Interview Corpus-Wizard of Oz (DAIC-WoZ) [7,10], et cetera. Each of these data set provide either audio or video or both data for research purpose only. In a study [2], there has been an analysis made on the combination as mentioned above of the first three data sets to detect depression by training them with an SVM classifier. This study finds that the best results were achieved when a wide variety of data sets were used for training.

The eye activity model shows better performance for both individual and combination datasets. Another study presented a method that used facial geometry analysis along with speech analysis for depression detection [23]. This work finds that the smaller duration videos have a low frequency of expressions that are involved with depression. So, longer duration videos have to be recorded for better results in depression detection. Data sets have been created by recording the patient videos while they are answering the questions asked by the clinician in the interviews. Interviews that were captured and stored were done for both the depressed and non-depressed patients. [9,12]. In another study, results have shown a meaningful relationship between features of faces and the vocal prosody of the depressed patient [6].

In some study [25], the patient's physical health, emotional behaviour, and social interaction were monitored via wearable devices to identify depression. Many times researchers collect their data set by playing some movie clips [8] to elicit the emotions in the subject and capture them while they watch it along with a separate depression questionnaire dataset and hence compare the results from both. In another way, a task of negative and positive emotion recognition in a series of the face image is noted for data set [22]. In another study [16], it was found that instead of frame by frame video analysis of depression detection, better results can be achieved when the video is reviewed as a whole. For this, the first step was manual initialization of the patient's face region, after which the face activities are tracked using the KLT (Kanade- Tomasi-Lucas) tracker throughout the video, which extracts the curvature information from the image extracted via the frame. The approach showed better results as it can pick out even the most minor movements within the face area.

2.3   Techniques for Feature Extraction of Depression

The paper [19] worked on Motion History Histogram(MHH), which was proposed originally in [20] for the recognition of human action. An MHH feature extracted from a video clip would be an image of M grayscale, which is the same size as the frame of the video where M is the video's motion level, where a high value denotes fast movements, and low value signifies slow movement. MHH is the movement patterns (pixel value change) on each pixel.

In another approach [13], Gabor Wavelet Technique is used for evaluating the individual face features. The work done here for face recognition is unaffected by the pose and orientation. Several Gabor filters are applied to extract facial features. Gabor filters have some specific basic properties for invariance, so they can be used for face recognition unaffected to face's orientation and pose. For the feature set, the mean and standard deviation of 40 Gabor filters is extracted [11] which are hence combined and passed through an SVM classifier to be classified. The central regions selected in the face are the eye, nose, and mouth, which can be extracted with the Haar feature-based Adaboost algorithm. In larger databases, this method has been proved to reduce the processing time of face recognition. Facial action units are detected, and the combination of a variety of these facial AUs can detect the complex emotions for the analysis of face expression [27].

3   Proposed Work and Experimentation

Using facial expressions for depression detection from images alone can be a challenging task. Therefore, a comprehensible, meaningful statement of a depressed face and the factors that differentiate it from other emotions is required. A depressed face is dissimilar from a sad one where a frown is involved, and a downward eye concludes a helpless, dejected mood. In many cases, a depressed person puts forward a blank face or sometimes a happy face to hide the depression.

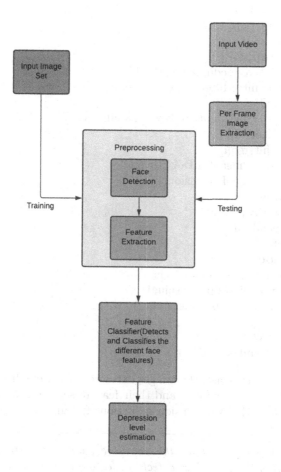

Fig. 1. A proposed system for depression detection

In this study, a system is proposed that works on the facial clues taken from recorded videos of people to detect the presence of depression in them. The whole process is divided into three phases, training, testing and classification, as shown in Fig. 1.

In the first phase, a model is trained, where we first extract the features of disgusted, happy, and contempt faces via an image database of 90 images and train an SVM classifier with those extracted feature sets.

Training Phase:

■Face Detection
1. Take an initial list of image set as img_set[], cropped[], gray[], face[]
2. **for i in img_set[]**
3. gray[i] = img_set[i].grayscale()
4. face[i] = face_cascade(gray[i])
5. cropped[i] = face[i]

■Feature Extraction
1. filtered=[]
2. **for i in cropped[]**
3. filtered[i] = cropped[i].resize(160,160)
4. filtered[i] = filter(filtered[i],gaborKernel)

■Feature Set Creation
1. dictionary=, keyCount=0, key=[], value=[]
2. **for i in filtered[]**
3. fImage = filtered[i]
4. (mean, std) = meanStdDev(fImage)
5. raw = fImage.oneDimension()
6. data = (raw-mean)/std
7. key.append(keyCount)
8. value.append(data)
9. keyCount++
10. exit **for loop**
11. value.append('add emotion class')
12. dictionary = dict(zip(key,value))
13. trainFeatureSet = pca(dictionary)

■ Model training
1. model = SVC(C=10)
2. model.fit(trainFeatureSet)

During the testing phase, the images extracted per frame from the video are passed through the Gabor filter, and their feature set is extracted, followed by their normalization (PCA dimension reduction) for all the images.

Testing phase:

A feature set is prepared for the extracted frames of testing video data set by following the same face detection, feature extraction and feature set creation process(as done in training phase) and name it as 'testFeatureSet'.

In the last phase, the test feature set is evaluated using an SVM classifier, and hence the frequency of all the three types of faces in the video(happy/contempt/disgust) is recorded. On the basis of these occurrences, their relative comparison gives a classification that evaluates the range of depression present and expected in the person.

■ Prediction Model
1. p = model.predict(testFeatureSet)
2. testFeatureSet['class'] = p
3. happyCount = contemptCount = disgustCount = 0
4. **for** i in **testFeatureSet['class']**
5. **if** testFeatureSet['class'] == 1 **then**
6. happyCount ++
7. **else if** testFeatureSet['class'] == 2 **then**
8. contemptCount ++
9. **else if** testFeatureSet['class'] == 3 **then**
10. disgustCount ++
11. exit **for loop**

In the instances where the frequency of contempt/disgust is high, we can conclude the person to be severely depressed. In the same manner, if contempt/disgust frequency is moderate, then a judgement of light depression is made, and the person is not depressed if it is negligible or very low.

3.1 Training Phase

Input Data Set: The underlying purpose here is to measure the record of negativity (discussed later) in the video data set. A depressed face has a lower count of smile features (AU 12); in case there is a presence of a smile, then it is accompanied with disgust(AU 10) and contempt (AU 14). A lower number of smiles count along with negative valence emotions [4] as disgust and contempt in the total frames of the video data set denotes the negative effects of depression. Therefore, we record and classify the presence of these facial features in the video feed. For this, a training data set is prepared first, from a group of 30 happy, contempt, and disgusted faces each. In this paper, we have taken a collection of 90 happy, contempt and disgusted faces from a combination of JAFFE [15] database and some pictures collected from the internet as shown in Fig. 2, 3 and 4.

Face Detection: Pre-processing of images in the dataset requires face detection as the initial stage. The face detector proposed in the Viola and Jones algorithm based on learning a sequence of Haar-like features and a boosting technique shows a real-time performance achievement. More than 160,000 Haar-like features are selected initially to create an integral image; then, it runs through an Adaboost trainer that extracts 2500 relevant features, then a cascading classifier takes these best features and discards non-faces, finally detecting a face. In our work, all the images in the dataset are first turned to black and white through grayscale conversion and then passed through a frontal face haar cascade that extracts the face region and all the non-face images are rejected in this stage. The face region of these images is then cropped and stored in a separate folder for further steps as feature extraction and such.

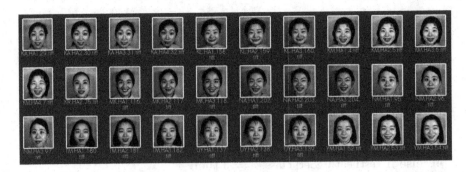

Fig. 2. Input happy faces.

Fig. 3. Input contempt faces

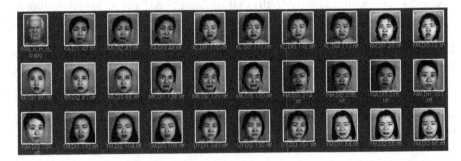

Fig. 4. Input disgust faces

Extracting Face Features: After face detection, the next step is extracting the feature set of the images. It is done by first passing the image through a filter and highlighting the facial features like a tug at the corner of lips, pulled up cheeks, et cetera. Here we have selected the Gabor filter for the work. *Gabor filter* is a convolution filter that generates features that represent the texture and edges of the image. This filter will highlight the dominant edges of the face involved in the 3 image classes (happy, contempt, and disgust) and form a feature set. Numerous digital filters are defined by varying the Gabor parameters and forming a filter bank. Through the Gabor filter bank, one can find the features that are relevant for their purpose.

$$g(a, b; \lambda, \theta, \psi, \sigma, \gamma) = exp(-(a'^2 + \gamma b'^2)/(2\sigma^2))exp(i(2\pi a'/\lambda + \psi)) \quad (1)$$

$$where a' = a\cos\theta + b\sin\theta; \quad (2)$$

$$b' = -a\sin\theta + b\cos\theta \quad (3)$$

In the given equation, a and b represents pixel's position;

λ being wavelength of the sine component;
θ is filter' orientation;
ψ as the offset of phase;
σ, gaussian envelope's standard deviation; and
γ being spatial aspect ratio.

Here, we have taken a set of 40 filter banks with varying orientations and scales as taken in the conducted study of facial expression analysis [9]. The 5 scales used in our work are 3.0, 3.1, 3.2, 3.3, 3.4 (refer to λ in Eq. 1) with 8 orientations as 0, 25, 45, 70, 90, 123, 146, 158 (refer to θ in Eq. 1).

We first downsize the images to $160 * 160$ (to reduce feature set) and then apply the filter on each image, which gives an output of 40 images of each input of happy, disgusted and contempt faces. Then we merge each of these 40 images into a single image and define the prominent features for extraction in later steps. This process repeats for all the 90 images in the dataset.

Feature Set Creation. For each of the outputs of the Gabor filter, we form a feature set for all the 90 images using its mean deviation and standard deviation. The mean of the entire image is calculated, and then subtraction is done with the flattened image followed by a division with the standard deviation of the entire image. This data forms the feature vector of each image and is stored in a CSV file. Then PCA is applied to reduce the dimensionality to $30 * 30$, and each emotion is given a class as happy $= 1$ (shown in Fig. 7), contempt $= 2$, disgust $= 3$ and a feature set is formed for each emotion and is then merged into a single CSV file, with a total of 3 emotion classes as shown in Fig. 10. We feed this merged feature set file to the SVM classifier and obtain a prediction model. The prediction for the "class" field of emotions takes place in the testing phase (Figs. 5, 6 and 8).

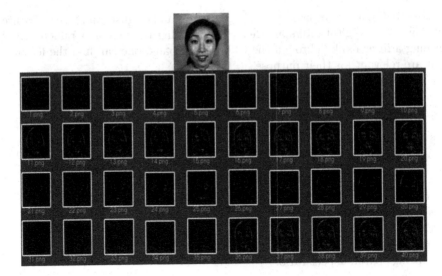

Fig. 5. Images formed for the happy image when different filters of Gabor Filter Bank is applied

Fig. 6. Facial features extracted using Gabor Filter Bank

25	26	27	28	29	class
)22556451	40.0486916115722	44.1689614503277	48.7711751926063	37.8448288412504	1
359972885	-15.407751793875	-19.8146289236673	-27.8398925972632	-27.0288324733833	1
)88615764	70.9725940709549	72.9584540326247	51.6136626328466	63.1810883545426	1
575456179	-35.1774100063266	-33.9763431831317	-15.0958161407789	-39.8094677114107	1
)49300873	15.2190903929441	16.5821133614537	13.5794268023204	17.8586171924613	1
?38326799	3.84271896861445	5.72206338028224	16.8324279823392	1.17383368845013	1
592959528	-3.5576797140497	-0.178133068469078	17.3259929705334	-9.38792746385323	1
)72908249	-7.50951281754317	-5.27522367671514	-17.5708852909287	-0.010734319131213	1
162333596	-9.88683861466827	-9.45713803959752	3.37136810667215	2.27562206271134	1
167500230	5 207506720000640	1 5002505556545	2 602527725200000	0 762006624454540	1

Fig. 7. Feature set of happy images with class as 1

333187853	14.3176180967153	-11.9147670051966	2.07946837377716	-4.2730841894276	1
653509331	4.22844727492068	-4.13731820621889	0.701561002252863	-0.369397122069651	1
396136251	-1.53134784019827	0.935779079272438	0.408547856124848	0.242038864569846	1
400109276	-0.534358050303233	1.29393153272274	-0.064193442186322	0.073214899697463	1
814713298	-0.029577630449594	0.2933605724480791	-0.269047975098891	-0.380579779883242	1
99283E-12	4.98536672013938E-12	5.12309118738674E-12	-2.17221900189468E-12	-6.2010179976979E-12	1
520677768	-31.6986027214904	-36.7837653805119	43.6202422322304	-39.2472937837079	2
533842446	-7.54883206104597	3.75848074929875	-34.5148197628025	-13.38976915904	2
015236932	-11.3364151895068	-19.5087536100729	-27.2687427407367	-13.6894045424421	2
142378784	-21.1843798822418	-5.39480183452843	56.7105963811431	-8.84938126051664	2
279683876	56.2597685431207	-49.0820603169264	-24.0819685518492	8.25323351833164	2

Fig. 8. A train feature set formed by merging all 3 feature set

3.2 Testing Phase

Video Feed: The test video set considered here is the interactive emotional dyadic motion capture database (IEMOCAP) [5]. This data set contains the recordings of ten actors in a dyadic manner by capturing two actors in a single video session (so, a total of 5 sessions that had two actors in each). These actors had to perform a total of 3 scripts that had distinct emotional content. Along with these scripts, they (actors) were asked to change the dialogues according to some theoretical scenarios to evoke specific emotions.

In this paper, we have first converted the dyadic session to a series of individual videos and images of a single actor are extracted per frame at a time and stored in a separate folder. For testing, we take the first 30 images as shown in Fig. 9.

Fig. 9. Image Frames extracted from the test input video

Frame Extraction and Feature Set Creation: A typical video shot at 30fps will generate 1800 frames (30 (frames in a second) * 60) in a minute. From the video database, we extract one frame for every second and use this for testing. The frames extracted this way is then processed using the Viola-Jones face detection algorithm, and the subject's face is cropped out and saved for further process. After this face detection stage, the facial feature is extracted and produced a feature set from Gabor filters.

Same as in the training phase, the training phase creates the feature set for the first 30 frame images as shown in Fig. 10, and based on this feature set, the 'class' field is predicted (shown in Fig. 11) by passing it through the SVM model trained previously in the testing phase.

3.3 Classifier Phase

The proposed model considered here uses an SVM classifier for the classification of facial features. SVM classifier technique works on the objective to find a hyperplane that can distinctly classify the data points by plotting variable data points to the n-dimensional space and finding the separator for them.

	0	1	2	3	4	5
0	-7.46244155312309	-73.3201690641775	93.4613821157174	15.8069850257741	-14.7248715783193	-18.3571466008428
1	-39.1968565505086	-70.895321950496	32.7656476082531	18.2091044573602	9.94218366497512	-2.47200630661994
2	-58.929501926167	75.3995249689723	-2.99585548716754	-26.875325372526	16.8689843512779	-19.900136477402
3	-8.10681778405111	-45.2318633185671	106.334294466328	5.33486904861196	-35.7913453739588	-21.7552713586977
4	1.96834761085719	-56.3907508670817	70.4535322988613	13.4149018756805	55.9994338481554	-21.762423451792
5	-8.64849107367567	-74.7775922761827	83.4200844109828	4.46097079802631	-38.2271102125181	-22.3246997565976
6	-10.6801373709438	-77.2044381657356	76.6755410262373	1.94048791228445	-35.2698247296908	-21.385511943556
7	39.829525754975	-28.6236155256955	41.7154777763616	-33.4179550736555	11.3668647454007	14.3457742705992
8	-59.9464055835142	-11.7981691140134	22.463321952048	9.81531996222673	-2.93457352483455	7.61684707059112
9	46.7502526786076	2.7199885008014	-27.5706942961451	-59.8109151370105	1.28034769121857	11.3873576003317

Fig. 10. A test feature set formed from the first 30 frame images extracted

27	28	29	class
)8156	-0.334906107656373	0.079392021148086	1
34769	1.23944956403874	0.983054039645158	1
L5163	0.628388008928058	2.09365034441399	1
31442	-0.119376052126128	-0.403053509795108	1
)2849	-0.802765021372566	-0.388835875641673	2
L1479	0.436782954367866	-0.003468392616078	1
)2076	-0.731321879071014	-0.442634840448364	1
73555	-0.027061184178363	-0.046609922624893	1
31154	-1.79781657015885	-0.593814226854436	1
)4468	-2.33133193290938	5.62604229589235	1
32293	-1.0938970431697	-2.62624689365854	1
?7871	6.14671003339422	-4.80475672711811	1
)7325	0.185492469518344	-0.092329259820701	2
30431	0.430019343367788	-0.563148145623319	2

Fig. 11. Prediction of the class set formed for the test images

Based on the frequency of emotional features predicted in the testing stage, it indicates the level of depression using Table 1. The low indicates that the overall presence is around 30 to ~33%, moderate lies between 33% to ~60% and a value ≥65% is considered high. The model we have trained uses the Viola-Jones algorithm for face detection and is based on the Jaffe database with a prediction score of 88% tested on the IEMOCAP database, in a different study [14] done on the same lines of the method using the KLT Algorithm for face detection, had been tested on a self-created dataset of students had prediction result of 62% on the well known validated depression dataset of BlackDog.

Table 1. Estimation of depression level

Happy feature	Disgust/contempt feature	Estimated depression
Low	Low	Sad/less expressive
High	High	Severe depression
Low	High	Severe depression
Moderate	Low	Sad
High	Low	Not depressed
Moderate	High	Mildly depressed

4   Conclusions

With the changes in technology, family, relationship dynamics, and economic hardship, there has been seen an increase in stress among adults in recent years. The detection of depression at an early stage is crucial for the mental health of a person, especially in these Covid times now.

A study is made on the facial expressions found in depressed patients and the methods that can be used to detect them. A data set is formed by taking happy, disgust and contempt images are taken from JAFFE [15] database and the internet. This data set is used to create a training data set. Face detection algorithm Viola-Jones is used for detecting faces, and a bank of 40 Gabor filters are applied to these data set to extract the varying features of the images. A feature set is created for training that is formed from the feature vector deduced from the filtered images. The trained model developed here has a prediction score of 88%. The same process is done for the testing phase, and the prediction is made.

Future work includes a collection of high variance data set for training and comparing the accuracy of the model by training the feature set with different classifiers. For further improvements, there can be some more feature inclusion like the head motion, eye activity or vocal prosody analysis coincident with video analysis to improve the accuracy of prediction.

References

1. Al Jazaery, M., Guo, G.: Video-based depression level analysis by encoding deep spatiotemporal features. IEEE Trans. Affect. Comput. **12**(1), 262–268 (2021). https://doi.org/10.1109/TAFFC.2018.2870884
2. Alghowinem, S., Goecke, R., Cohn, J.F., Wagner, M., Parker, G., Breakspear, M.: Cross-cultural detection of depression from nonverbal behaviour. In: 2015 11th IEEE International Conference and Workshops on Automatic Face and Gesture Recognition (FG), vol. 1, pp. 1–8. IEEE (2015)
3. Ashraf, A., Gunawan, T., Riza, B., Haryanto, E., Janin, Z.: On the review of image and video-based depression detection using machine learning. Indones. J. Electr. Eng. Comput. Sci. **19**, 1677 (2020). https://doi.org/10.11591/ijeecs.v19.i3.pp1677-1684
4. Association, H., et al.: HUMAINE emotion annotation and representation language (EARL): Proposal (2006)
5. Busso, C., et al.: IEMOCAP: interactive emotional dyadic motion capture database. Lang. Resour. Eval. **42**(4), 335–359 (2008). https://doi.org/10.1007/s10579-008-9076-6
6. Cohn, J.F., et al.: Detecting depression from facial actions and vocal prosody. In: 2009 3rd International Conference on Affective Computing and Intelligent Interaction and Workshops, pp. 1–7. IEEE (2009)
7. DeVault, D., et al.: Simsensei kiosk: a virtual human interviewer for healthcare decision support. In: Proceedings of the 2014 International Conference on Autonomous Agents and Multi-Agent Systems, AAMAS 2014, pp. 1061–1068. International Foundation for Autonomous Agents and Multiagent Systems, Richland, SC (2014)

8. Gavrilescu, M., Vizireanu, N.: Predicting depression, anxiety, and stress levels from videos using the facial action coding system. Sensors **19**(17), 3693 (2019)
9. Girard, J.M., Cohn, J.F., Mahoor, M.H., Mavadati, S., Rosenwald, D.P.: Social risk and depression: evidence from manual and automatic facial expression analysis. In: 2013 10th IEEE International Conference and Workshops on Automatic Face and Gesture Recognition (FG), pp. 1–8. IEEE (2013)
10. Gratch, J., et al.: The distress analysis interview corpus of human and computer interviews. In: Proceedings of the Ninth International Conference on Language Resources and Evaluation (LREC 2014), pp. 3123–3128 (2014)
11. Haghighat, M., Zonouz, S., Abdel-Mottaleb, M.: CloudID: trustworthy cloud-based and cross-enterprise biometric identification. Expert Syst. Appl. **42**(21), 7905–7916 (2015)
12. Harati, S., Crowell, A., Mayberg, H., Kong, J., Nemati, S.: Discriminating clinical phases of recovery from major depressive disorder using the dynamics of facial expression. In: 2016 38th Annual International Conference of the IEEE Engineering in Medicine and Biology Society (EMBC), pp. 2254–2257. IEEE (2016)
13. Karthika, R., Parameswaran, L.: Study of gabor wavelet for face recognition invariant to pose and orientation. In: Suresh, L.P., Panigrahi, B.K. (eds.) Proceedings of the International Conference on Soft Computing Systems. AISC, vol. 397, pp. 501–509. Springer, New Delhi (2016). https://doi.org/10.1007/978-81-322-2671-0_48
14. Kumar, S., Varshney, D., Dhawan, G., Jalutharia, H.: Analysing the effective psychological state of students using facial features. In: 2020 4th International Conference on Intelligent Computing and Control Systems (ICICCS), pp. 648–653 (2020). https://doi.org/10.1109/ICICCS48265.2020.9120909
15. Lyons, M.J., Kamachi, M., Gyoba, J.: Coding facial expressions with Gabor wavelets (IVC special issue). arXiv preprint arXiv:2009.05938 (2020)
16. Maddage, N.C., Senaratne, R., Low, L.S.A., Lech, M., Allen, N.: Video-based detection of the clinical depression in adolescents. In: 2009 Annual International Conference of the IEEE Engineering in Medicine and Biology Society, pp. 3723–3726. IEEE (2009)
17. Malhi, G.S., Mann, J.J.: Depression. Lancet **392**(10161), 2299–2312 (2018)
18. de Melo, W.C., Granger, E., Hadid, A.: Depression detection based on deep distribution learning. In: 2019 IEEE International Conference on Image Processing (ICIP), pp. 4544–4548 (2019). https://doi.org/10.1109/ICIP.2019.8803467
19. Meng, H., Huang, D., Wang, H., Yang, H., Ai-Shuraifi, M., Wang, Y.: Depression recognition based on dynamic facial and vocal expression features using partial least square regression. In: Proceedings of the 3rd ACM International Workshop on Audio/Visual Emotion Challenge, pp. 21–30 (2013)
20. Meng, H., Pears, N., Bailey, C.: A human action recognition system for embedded computer vision application. In: 2007 IEEE Conference on Computer Vision and Pattern Recognition, pp. 1–6. IEEE (2007)
21. Pampouchidou, A., et al.: Facial geometry and speech analysis for depression detection. In: 2017 39th Annual International Conference of the IEEE Engineering in Medicine and Biology Society (EMBC), pp. 1433–1436 (2017). https://doi.org/10.1109/EMBC.2017.8037103
22. Pampouchidou, A., Marias, K., Tsiknakis, M., Simos, P., Yang, F., Meriaudeau, F.: Designing a framework for assisting depression severity assessment from facial image analysis. In: 2015 IEEE International Conference on Signal and Image Processing Applications (ICSIPA), pp. 578–583. IEEE (2015)

23. Pampouchidou, A., et al.: Facial geometry and speech analysis for depression detection. In: 2017 39th Annual International Conference of the IEEE Engineering in Medicine and Biology Society (EMBC), pp. 1433–1436. IEEE (2017)

24. Sharifa, M., et al.: From joyous to clinically depressed: mood detection using spontaneous speech. In: Twenty-Fifth International FLAIRS Conference (2012)

25. Tasnim, M., Shahriyar, R., Nahar, N., Mahmud, H.: Intelligent depression detection and support system: statistical analysis, psychological review and design implication. In: 2016 IEEE 18th International Conference on e-Health Networking, Applications and Services (Healthcom), pp. 1–6. IEEE (2016)

26. Valstar, M., et al.: AVEC 2013: the continuous audio/visual emotion and depression recognition challenge. In: Proceedings of the 3rd ACM International Workshop on Audio/Visual Emotion Challenge, pp. 3–10 (2013)

27. Vikram, K., Padmavathi, S.: Facial parts detection using viola jones algorithm. In: 2017 4th International Conference on Advanced Computing and Communication Systems (ICACCS), pp. 1–4. IEEE (2017)

28. Yang, Y., Fairbairn, C., Cohn, J.F.: Detecting depression severity from vocal prosody. IEEE Trans. Affect. Comput. 4(2), 142–150 (2012)

Ontology-Based Healthcare Hierarchy Towards Chatbot

Prottay Kumar Adhikary[1], Riyanka Manna[2], Sahinur Rahman Laskar[1], and Partha Pakray[1(✉)]

[1] Department of Computer Science and Engineering,
National Institute of Technology Silchar, Silchar, India
{prottay_ug,sahinur_rs,partha}@cse.nits.ac.in
[2] Gandhi Institute of Technology and Management,
Hyderabad, Telengana, India
rmanna@gitam.edu

Abstract. Ontology refers to relationship-based hierarchical descriptions of concepts within a particular domain. Ontology, in the field of medicine, describes the concepts of medical terminologies and the relation between them, thus, enabling the sharing of medical knowledge. This paper aims to develop an ontology-based healthcare hierarchy and point out the research scope towards the chatbot application. The research scope includes the integration of the ontology-based healthcare hierarchy in the chatbot application by the establishment of relationships among individuals and real-world entities.

Keywords: Semantic web · Ontology · Healthcare · Chatbot

1 Introduction

The growth of Artificial Intelligence (AI) and Natural Language Processing (NLP) research in recent years suggests that the future will be mostly machine-dependent. The majority of information is now accessible via the Web. The human reader must understand the context, chronology, and usefulness of the information available online. The problem is that they are not machine-readable. Therefore, the term "Semantic web" appears to relate to this issue. To turn the existing Web into one massive personal information store, modification, and retrieval database, rather than a collection of interconnected but semantically separated data islands [8]. To cope up with this challenge, the concept of Ontology comes under the limelight.

Ontology is a set of concepts and categories in a topic area or domain that shows their properties and relationships. It is a system for representing knowledge in the form of concepts, nodes that map relationships between these concepts, and constraints. Through Semantic mapping, we can support the semantic analysis of such relationships to share the knowledge constructs. A semantic mapping is the product of this process. When we talk about semantics, we are

S. Mukhopadhyay et al. (Eds.): CICBA 2022, CCIS 1579, pp. 326–335, 2022.
https://doi.org/10.1007/978-3-031-10766-5_26

talking about the study of linguistic meaning. It can be used in full texts or just a few words. For example, "We should train the model using T5" and "The train has arrived", where the word 'Train' is theoretically the same or may mean the same thing, but if we examine them closely, we can see minor differences in meaning. The entire premise of the concept is that data must be represented in a way that enables the discovery of relationships. Ontology organizes data in a way that makes these connections obvious. As humans, we understand certain contexts and what things signify, and we may use this knowledge to answer specific questions by connecting the data we have. To offer a computer the same power, we must first provide it with the knowledge that is easily readable by machines. Instead of connecting documents on the web, we must connect data on the web to accomplish this.

In this paper, we have made an ontology in the form of the current health care system. We have created an ontology that will improve the storage and management of medical data. The suggested ontology will reflect the current healthcare system's structure. The need for an online-based healthcare system prompted the development of the ontology. Although ontology design is most commonly associated with Information Retrieval (IR), the hierarchy can be useful in other areas of NLP, such as semantic role labeling, which determines the roles of various parts of sentences based on the considered predicate, which can be a verb or a noun. The ontology can be applied to a variety of fields, including healthcare chat-bots, medicine administration, and more. The entities or classes that have been created in the project of ontology development are viewed with a mind on the re-usability of the overall design in other systems.

The rest of this paper is placed out as follows: Sect. 2 presents the related works. The ontology development for the healthcare domain and future scopes are discussed in Sect. 3 and 4. Finally, in Sect. 5, the paper is concluded with a discussion on future work.

2   Related Work

The term 'Ontology' has been used to describe a wide range of topics. The basic goal of an ontology is to make a system meaningful to the machines. A physical exercise ontology has been created, which comprises a hierarchical structure that follows the human body structure as well as numerous forms of motion constraints [4]. Another research in the cooking domain demonstrated how to create an ontology model that allows queries to be processed and exact answers to be created using the ontology knowledge base. It was designed to help the Question Answering (QA) process in the recipe suggestion process. We'll start with what's already out there because we're focusing on the healthcare domain and ontology-related work [9]. As our work concentrates on the healthcare domain and ontology-related work, we will start with what's already out there.

To make people's lives better and longer, researchers have been trying to explore and integrate new technologies into the existing healthcare system. By implementing the ontology, it is easier to track or trace the system entities, which might help the development furthermore. In the healthcare domain, many people have contributed with their precious work. The live conversational ontology-based method has been deployed to handle PrEP and PEP counseling dialogue, which automatically performed conversation between the machine and user [1]. Here, NLP methods have been used in conjunction with the agent's reasoning abilities to help the agent. A deterministic and planned strategy has been used to automate the counseling rather than a generative approach in order to cover certain essential topics to communicate to the drug user when designing the conversation system. A community-based ontology has been developed for COVID, where they began the development of CIDO[1], a community-driven open-source biomedical ontology in the field of coronavirus infectious illness. CIDO provides standardized annotation and depiction of diverse coronavirus infectious illnesses, including their etiology, transmission, epidemiology, pathogenesis, host-coronavirus interactions, diagnosis, prevention, and treatment, in a human-computer interpretable format [6]. The MOSES European Project [2] has created an ontology-based QA system for searching, creating, maintaining, and adapting semantically organized web content in accordance with the semantic vision. The project's test goal is to build an ontology-based knowledge management system and an ontology-based search engine for the websites of two European universities that accepts questions and generates natural language replies. The work's main contribution is the creation of a multilingual environment, which necessitates the ability to handle numerous languages as well as, more importantly, multiple conceptualizations.

As previously stated, ontology-based relationships can be used for information retrieval, information interrogation, digital libraries, question answering, etc. Our contribution can enhance the semantics of systems like HealFavor [7]. As part of this project, a chat-based application that can provide healthcare services remotely has been developed. The creation of an ontology and how that system could assist real-world applications will be described in the following sections.

3   Ontology Development: Healthcare Domain

The ontology development relies on the specific domain of interest and principles of modelling established [10]. The entities and the individuals show the semantic view of the considering domain, in our case, it is the healthcare domain. The relationships which are established between the individuals have been focused on the real world entities of the healthcare domain. To define the classes we have used the most available terms of a healthcare domain such as doctors, tests, medicines, prescription, and diseases. There are six classes on our developed ontology, which are shown below:

Class: Under the super-class 'owl: Thing', the other classes has been developed. The classes and the subclasses have been designed as follows:

---

[1] https://github.com/CIDO-ontology/cido.

- 'patient': It has 3 subclasses 'discharged', 'admitted' and 'emergency'. These denote the types of patients after coming to any kind of health-center.
- 'doctor': It contains the mostly visited types of doctors which are 'dermatologist', 'gynecologist, 'podiatrist', 'chiropractor', 'surgeon', 'orthopaedic', 'neurologist', 'ent', 'dentist', 'cardiologist'.
- 'tests': It contains 'physical_visual_examination', 'cellular_chemical_analysis', 'diagnostic_imaging'.
- 'diseases': It holds the types of diseases like 'allergies', 'degenerative', 'infectious' and 'non_infectious' disease. The last two type of diseases also contain subclasses. Out of which 'non_infectious' has 'copd', 'cancer', 'osteoporosis' and 'infectious' has types based in the infectious agents which are 'bacteria', 'viruses'. 'fungi', 'parasites'.
- 'medicine': It contains the types of medicines as classes, such as 'suppositories', 'capsule', 'drop', 'injection', 'tablet', 'syrup'.
- 'prescription': Basically, two types of prescription exist, 'handwritten' and 'typed'.

The hierarchy is shown in Fig. 1.

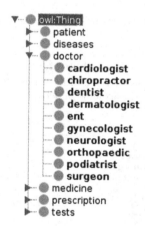

Fig. 1. Class-hierarchy of our ontology development

Relationship: The relationship represents the connectivity between two classes, here some classes are connected using object properties, which are as follows:

- 'gives': It connects two entity which is 'doctor' and 'medicine'. At urgent care, any doctor can give medicine to a patient such as an injection immediately to save someone's life.
- 'refers': It connects the entities named 'doctor' and 'tests'. Doctors refer to tests to determine the cause and nature of some diseases.
- 'writes': It connects 'doctor' and 'prescription'. An example might be 'Cardiologists writes prescription'.

The relationships are shown in Fig. 2.

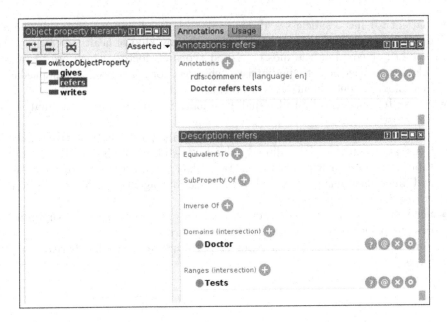

Fig. 2. Relationship between classes

Individuals: Individuals are the attributes for the classes that are being made such as, under the doctor class we have individuals like 'Dr._A', 'Dr._B', 'Dr._C', 'Dr._D'. The individuals has been visualized in Fig. 3.

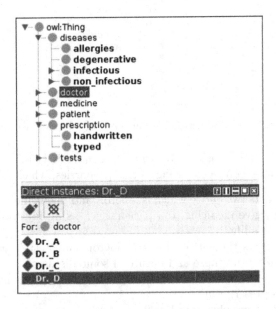

Fig. 3. Individual attributes under classes

The main concept behind making an ontology is to make it applicable for the semantic web and make it reusable so that it could be useful for the machines to understand and learn things. The developed classes are connected to each other, which has semantic meaning. As an example, 'doctor' is connected to the other class 'diseases', so if a machine wants to find the relationship it can read the relationship and take actions based on that. The ontology also has attributes under the classes, which can be used to store the individual data like patients' names, doctors' names, names of the diseases, medicine names, different types of tests, etc. Table 1 shows the metrics of the Developed ontology.

Table 1. Ontology metrics

Metrics	Count
Axiom	181
Logical axiom count	98
Declaration axioms count	77
Class count	54
Object property count	3
Data property count	3
Individual count	17
Sub class of	48
Annotation Assertion	6

To develop the ontology *Ontology Language (OWL)* has been used which represents the classes and relationships in a format appropriate for interaction with any semantic web. The software we have used to implement this is called Protégé[2] which is developed by Stanford Center for Biomedical Informatics Research (BMIR). They create cutting-edge ways to obtain, represent, and analyse information on human health at their Lab. Their work contributes to the Institute of Medicine's goal of a Learning Health System by converting biological data into decision-making insights. The software Protégé has a GUI that helps to create, edit and modify Ontologies. There are mainly two approaches available on this application. We have chosen the OWL-based approach to make our ontology. Using the OWL framework we can improve the ontology even further such as the application queries may be readily mapped to the ontology for the relevant domain knowledge. This OWL framework has classes, properties, instances, and reasoning to get started. For our ontology development, the healthcare domain has been considered as a thing, then we have considered the entities of the healthcare domain as the classes after that subclass represents the type of the entities or properties of the classes we had. Figure 4 the OWLViz of our ontology, which allows users to examine and incrementally browse class hierarchies in an OWL ontology, allowing comparison of the stated class hierarchy.

---

[2] https://protege.stanford.edu/.

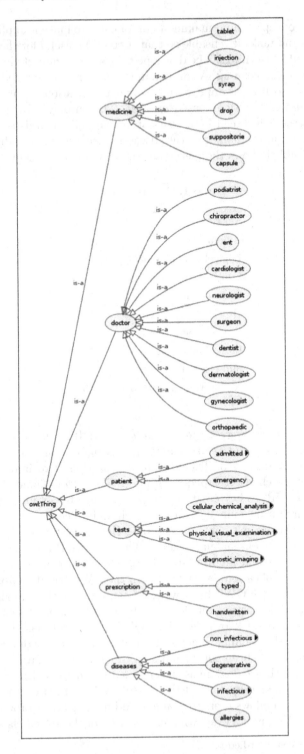

Fig. 4. OWLViz of the ontology

4   Towards Chatbot Application

Significant attention draws in healthcare-based AI research, which leads to improvement in automatic diagnosis by cutting costs in today's disparity between customer affordability and healthcare [5]. There is a need to improve patient-doctor communication since existing technology does not permit time-consuming exercise. The chatbot is an application of such technology that has the potential of responding to different situations based on experience. The goal of such technology is to revolutionize the healthcare domain by benefiting the patients and doctors but not replacing the conventional practice of visiting a doctor. Various prominent systems have been developed to enhance healthcare facilities. Such as DeepMind health AI technology [11] that allows quick diagnosis based on past patient information. For a faster prognosis, HealthTap[3], Molly[4] uses similar cases from the database and connects doctors with patients. In [7], the authors proposed a chatbot system, namely, HealFavor, as shown in Fig. 5. The objective of their system is to provide quick assistance for the patient via chatbot conversation. They used RASA [3] framework to implement the chatbot system with a curated dataset. In their system, Recurrent Embedding Dialogue Policy [12] is utilized by the motivation of Facebook AI Research's (FAIR) StarSpace algorithm [13]. Despite recent progress in the area, it is clear that suitable rules are almost non-existent. The drawback of HealFavor [7], which we have identified, is that there is a need for the establishment of relationships between real-world entities and individuals. Such that the user or patient gets the proper response from the dialogue management system. In this work, we have developed an ontology-based hierarchy that will be integrated into the healthcare chatbot application for further research. Moreover, there is a need for sophisticated evaluation metrics that can provide justification and satisfaction from the

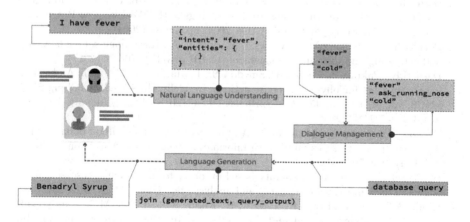

Fig. 5. System architecture of HealFavor [7]

---

[3] https://www.healthtap.com/.

[4] https://www.sensely.com/.

user's point of view. In [7], the authors performed a user experience survey to examine the performance of a healthcare chatbot application by considering a rating scale. Also, it requires medical expert's intervention for evaluation.

5 Conclusion and Future Work

This work presents an ontology-based hierarchy for the healthcare domain, where we have established the relationships between individuals and entities of the real world. Also, we have reviewed the related works of ontology concept and healthcare domain and discussed its future scope in the healthcare chatbot application that will be helpful in the real-time conversation for providing rapid assistance via one-to-one interaction. Our future research will focus on improving and fine-tuning the ontology with more specific information, as well as the semantic structure of the remaining entities, and integrate the developed ontology into the healthcare chatbot application.

Acknowledgment. We would like to thank Center for Natural Language Processing (CNLP) and Artificial Intelligence Lab, Department of Computer Science and Engineering at National Institute of Technology, Silchar, India for providing the requisite support and infrastructure to execute this work.

References

1. Amith, M.T., Cui, L., Roberts, K., Tao, C.: Towards an ontology-based medication conversational agent for prep and pep. In: Proceedings of the Conference. Association for Computational Linguistics. Meeting, pp. 31–40. NIH Public Access (2020)
2. Basili, R., Hansen, D.H., Paggio, P., Pazienza, M.T., Zanzotto, F.M.: Ontological resources and question answering. In: Proceedings of the Workshop on Pragmatics of Question Answering at HLT-NAACL 2004, pp. 78–84 (2004)
3. Bocklisch, T., Faulkner, J., Pawlowski, N., Nichol, A.: Rasa: open source language understanding and dialogue management. CoRR abs/1712.05181 (2017)
4. Dash, S.K., Pakray, P., Porzel, R., Smeddinck, J., Malaka, R., Gelbukh, A.: Designing an ontology for physical exercise actions. In: Gelbukh, A. (ed.) CICLing 2017. LNCS, vol. 10761, pp. 354–362. Springer, Cham (2018). https://doi.org/10.1007/978-3-319-77113-7_28
5. Dranove, D., Forman, C., Goldfarb, A., Greenstein, S.: The trillion dollar conundrum: complementarities and health information technology. Am. Econ. J. Econ. Pol. **6**(4), 239–70 (2014)
6. He, Y., et al.: CIDO, a community-based ontology for coronavirus disease knowledge and data integration, sharing, and analysis. Sci. Data **7**(1), 1–5 (2020)
7. Khilji, A.F.U.R., Laskar, S.R., Pakray, P., Kadir, R.A., Lydia, M.S., Bandyopadhyay, S.: HealFavor: dataset and a prototype system for healthcare chatbot. In: 2020 International Conference on Data Science, Artificial Intelligence, and Business Analytics (DATABIA), pp. 1–4. IEEE (2020)
8. Kuck, G.: Tim Berners-Lee's semantic web. South Afr. J. Inf. Manag. **6**, a297 (2004)

9. Manna, R., Pakray, P., Banerjee, S., Das, D., Gelbukh, A.: CookingQA: a question answering system based on cooking ontology. In: Sidorov, G., Herrera-Alcántara, O. (eds.) MICAI 2016. LNCS (LNAI), vol. 10061, pp. 67–78. Springer, Cham (2017). https://doi.org/10.1007/978-3-319-62434-1_6

10. Masolo, C., Borgo, S., Gangemi, A., Guarino, N., Oltramari, A., Schneider, L.: The wonderweb library of foundational ontologies (2002)

11. Powles, J., Hodson, H.: Google DeepMind and healthcare in an age of algorithms. Health Technol. **7**(4), 351–367 (2017). https://doi.org/10.1007/s12553-017-0179-1

12. Vlasov, V., Drissner-Schmid, A., Nichol, A.: Few-shot generalization across dialogue tasks. CoRR abs/1811.11707 (2018)

13. Wu, L.Y., Fisch, A., Chopra, S., Adams, K., Bordes, A., Weston, J.: StarSpace: embed all the things! In: Proceedings of the Thirty-Second AAAI Conference on Artificial Intelligence, (AAAI 2018), the 30th innovative Applications of Artificial Intelligence (IAAI-18), and the 8th AAAI Symposium on Educational Advances in Artificial Intelligence (EAAI 2018), New Orleans, Louisiana, USA, 2–7 February 2018, pp. 5569–5577. AAAI Press (2018)

Real-Time Piracy Detection Based on Thermogram Analysis and Machine Learning Techniques

B. Sanjana[✉], M. Sirisha, Pruthvi Dinesh, G. R. Sunil Kumar, and Surekha Borra

Department of ECE, K. S. Institute of Technology, Bangalore, Karnataka, India
sanjanabadarinath2000@gmail.com

Abstract. Movie Piracy is increasing these days, and it has a profound impact on the economic growth of film industries all over the world. Hence curbing piracy has become a critical step in avoiding massive losses to the film industry. This paper proposes a thermogram based anti-piracy system using Machine learning models. A local dataset is created by capturing the images in different scenarios by employing a thermal camera. AlexNet is used for extracting the features from captured images and the extracted features are trained with several Machine Learning models in MATLAB for their performance evaluation. The images captured in real-time are processed to extract the features and then directed to the classifier to predict the anomaly class. The alert message is sent to theatre officials regarding the presence of active recording device. An accuracy of 99.7% is achieved with Support Vector Machine (SVM) model on the local dataset.

Keywords: Camcorder · Movie piracy · Thermogram · AlexNet

1 Introduction

Cinema piracy is emerging as the biggest threat to the Film Industry in recent years. It has grown tremendously, making it easier than ever to access pirated movies on online platforms at one's fingertip. An increase in piracy has a severe impact on the economic growth of film industries all over the world. It is inferred from a survey that pirated videos receive over 230 billion views every year. As well, a study says that in the United Kingdom, about 30% of the population watch pirated movies, costing the industry £500 million every year. In India, piracy is considered as an offense, and pirates are prisoned for three years with a penalty of 10 lakh rupees as per the Cinematograph Act of 2019. Apart from this, filmmakers, producers, independent creators, and distributors lose interest in making sequels and remakes. Lower-class artists risk their job, welfare, and pensions.

The illegal copying of movie for the purpose of selling it at a lower market price is referred to as movie piracy. Some of the ways in which piracy can occur are Camera recording, DVD & VOD ripping, Telesync, Digital distribution copy, Telecine, and WEB-DL. Camcorder piracy can be classified into pre-release and post-release piracy. In pre-release piracy, the movie is pirated during exclusive screenings to sponsors, reviewers,

S. Mukhopadhyay et al. (Eds.): CICBA 2022, CCIS 1579, pp. 336–350, 2022.
https://doi.org/10.1007/978-3-031-10766-5_27

and VIPs. During this time, piracy may occur in two possible ways. In one of the ways, guests can record the movie and make the copy available for unauthorized dissemination. These copies are generally of low audio and video quality. This kind of piracy is known as cam. On the other hand, while the movie is being projected, theatre operators can record the film by employing camcorder mounted on the tripod at the theatre backend. A telesync system is used to derive sound from the audio system directly. In post-release piracy, both theatre operators and audiences can pirate the movie and sell it at a lower price or share the pirated videos freely on social media [1–3].

In this paper, an antipiracy system is developed using machine learning techniques by employing a thermal camera in a Theatre environment. The proposed approach focuses mainly on finding the presence of active camcorders held by pirates in the theatre, thereby reducing piracy in real time. Section 2 presents literature survey, Sect. 3 presents the proposed piracy detection approach, Sect. 4 presents the results, and Sect. 5 concludes the paper.

2 Literature Survey

Kumar et al. [4] presented a system with IR transmitters connected horizontally and vertically to the servomotors, causing them to rotate at +45 and −45°. This configuration of IR emitters will cover the entire screen. When the video is recorded, it is captured such that a matrix of transmitted rays emerges on the screen due to the movement of IR emitters. If the power supply to the IR emitters is interrupted, the risk of piracy is more. Hence to overcome this problem, the transmitter and the projector are interconnected so that the projector does not switch ON independently. This connection is established by integrating a password system using keypad. This ensures that the power supply to the IR transmitters, servomotors, and projector is denied until the user enters correct password. The transmitter ejects infrared rays when powered ON. Then a signal is received by the receiver which is fed as an input command to the Arduino Uno microcontroller which activates a relay. The relay interconnects the projector and power supply, acting as a switch. Hence it allows the projector to start the movie projection. The projector will not switch on if there is any obstruction between IR transmitter and receiver thereby preventing piracy. The model was tested with various recording devices to observe the disturbance in the recording by setting the frequency of IR transmission to 38 kHz. Installation of this model is easy and, it is also efficient for different distances and frequency ranges.

Chandana et al. [5] presented a system to prevent movie piracy with the help of automated IR emitter screen and steganographic method. In this system, RFID cards are employed to prevent unauthorized people from projecting the movie, and the captured video is degraded by use of IR LEDs behind the screen. Initially, when the Microcontroller is turned on through the relay, RFID reader pairs with the RFID card that carries a predefined unique code. This code is encrypted using the steganography method. Each film is assigned with one tag and the allocated RFID card is possessed by the theatre officials. When the card is scanned, it is checked for its validity. If the card is valid, the LCD displays the card number along with the message "movie can be played", else an alert message along with the GPS location is sent to the theatre owner, and the "Invalid access" message is displayed in the LCD. To degrade the recorded video quality, IR LEDs were installed behind the screen so that the camcorders are susceptible to IR light, making the captured video blurred. But there will be no disturbance to the audience while watching the movie.

Asborn et al. [6] presented a model where IR signals are used to prevent video recording in theatres. In this system, the projector and anti-piracy screening system operate in parallel. The microcontroller performs system authentication. When the microcontroller is turned on, the keypad is activated, allowing the password to be entered. If the password entered is correct, then the output of the microcontroller is sent to the relay module and subsequently to the driver. As the microcontroller's output is low, the driver amplifies the signal and activates the relay to operate the IR LEDS and the projector. If the connection between the IR LED screen and the projector is short-circuited or disconnected, the operator will be notified through the Buzzer or LED indication. As the IR wavelength is longer than the visible light, the audience can watch the movie without any disturbance in the movie. But camcorder being susceptible to IR rays, the recorded video gets degraded.

Sanath [7] proposed an anti-piracy system using IR LEDs to curb piracy. Initially, the IR LED is placed behind the theatre screen, and the IR receiver authentication is administered by the theatre officials. The IR receiver device validates the information on the smart card using the reference data stored in comparator. The digital output of the comparator is then supplied to the driver. When driver relay is driven, the microcontroller verification unit is activated. Once the microcontroller turns ON, keypad gets activated for entering the password. Then, the password will be verified. After password verification, output of the microcontroller is sent to the driver through a buffer. The amplified output from buffer drives the IR emitter circuit to transmit the IR rays towards the receiver circuit placed near the projector. These IR signals are sensitive to camcorders which degrades the quality of the recorded video.

Gouri Raut [8] presented an image processing technique to reduce theatre piracy. The system is divided into two parts: the camera positioning unit and the camera deactivation unit. The camera positioning unit consists of a webcam interfaced with PC. The code is written such that the webcam is constantly scanning for the camera. If the camera is found, a signal is sent to the Raspberry pi microcontroller. After locating the focal point and the position of the camera, a flag is passed to the Raspberry pi module. Later, the raspberry pi activates the IR transmitters connected to the servomotors emitting IR rays towards the camera focal point to decrease the quality of the recorded video.

Abhishek et al. [9] presented RFID-based anti-piracy screening system. This system is comprised of two objectives: the first one is to embed Infrared transmitters in the form of a pattern to reduce the quality of the captured video and the second one is to identify the pirate using RFID tags. The projector emits the frames which are embedded with some patterns that camcorders are sensitive to, decreasing the quality of the movie in the captured video. RFID system is used to identify the pirate. Each person who purchases a movie ticket receives an RFID tag. When the user punches the RFID tag, RFID reader scans the tag and sends an OTP to the respective user's phone. Then the user must enter the OTP using a keypad before entering the screening system. These users' information helps theatre administrators in tracking down the person attempting to pirate the movie.

Khan et al. [10] presented a model in which IR LED screen and watermarking techniques are used to prevent piracy in theatres. A watermark containing the logo of the producer and the theatre details is inserted into the movie file. Then the movie is encrypted to obtain a distorted video file using Arnold's scrambling algorithm. Later, the producer sends the encrypted movie to the theatre. The producer embeds his logo into the movie file, to extract it later as evidence of ownership. Once the system turns ON, a message is sent to the theatre owner. Then, the theatre owner communicates the OTP to be entered with the theatre operator. The key entered using a keypad can be seen on the LCD for confirmation. If the OTP entered by the operator matches with the OTP that is communicated by the owner, the movie begins to play. Along with this, IR LED system gets activated. If there is a mismatch in OTP or GPS location, the movie is not played, and a message will be sent to the owner notifying the unauthorized entry. Also, when pirates try to capture the film with camcorders, the image quality is degraded by the IR LEDs arranged in the form of a matrix behind the screen.

Chen et al. [11], presented piracy tracking method that uses temporal psychovisual modulation (TPVM). When the movie starts playing, the projector emits frames with predefined patterns inserted in real-time. By using the TPVM technology, the pirated copies get distorted. TPVM stacks hidden pattern on the theatre screen using the difference between image formation of the digital camera and human-eye perception. Human vision perceives the images as continuous blending of the light beams, whereas digital camera captures the images as discrete samples, including a "blackout" phase in every sample period. Depending on this difference, the movie will be divided into frames in the form of a specific pattern and projected at a faster rate so that the recorded video will be distorted. The pattern embedded in the movie file can be used to track the information of the pirate.

Shukla et al. [12] presented a novel watermarking method for digital cinema using discrete wavelet transform (DWT) and scene-change detector. A watermark is inserted into the frame where there will be a change of scenes in the movie. The scene changed frames in the movie file are identified using a statistical measure technique that uses correlation as a measure. Initially, the video is split into scenes based on the correlation measure between frames. These frames are filtered out by placing them in a bin and by specifying the cut-off value using the SESAME and HiBiSLI methods. The watermark is created as per Digital Cinema Initiatives specifications by incorporating projection information such as show time, date, and name of the theatre. The prepared watermark is a color image, which is then converted into a grayscale of size 256×256. Then the watermark is embedded into the scene-changed frame using the Daubechies wavelet. The host video frame is split into four sub-bands by applying DWT. The four sub-bands include LH, LL, HH, HL, and HH. Daubechies wavelet implants watermark within the LL sub-band. Copyright protection can be proved by extracting the watermark image from a particular frame of the pirated watermarked movie when a scene change occurs. The extracted image is recovered by resizing and converting it into the proper integer form. This extracted image is used to acquire pirate information.

Roopalakshmi [13] proposed a methodology for estimating pirate positions in theatres using multimodal aspects against cinema piracy. It includes three phases. In the first phase, the original movie and the recorded video clip are aligned to acquire exact frame mappings. The resulting frame pairs are aligned temporally as well as spatially. The two video clips are depicted concisely with the help of visual signatures and the most identical frames are selected and evaluated to acquire stable key point pairs from both the video clips. Later, geometric distortion model is estimated by the geometric parameters obtained from the key point pairs. Specifically, the Normalized DLT algorithm and the estimated point to point mappings are used to determine the homographic matrix of projective geometry. In the third phase, the camcorder viewing axis is computed by employing rotation and translation parameters derived from the homographic matrix. Later, the intersection of the theatre seating plane and viewing axis of camcorder is calculated to obtain the camcorder location, thereby estimating the pirate position. The proposed framework estimated the position of pirate with 38.25, 22.45, 11.11 cm as a mean absolute error.

Venkata Kishore Kumar [14] presented an anti-piracy system involving IR LED's and Image Processing techniques. A scanner containing a hidden camera is placed behind the theatre screen to scan the whole theatre. The images from the scanner are then processed using image processing algorithm to detect the presence of camcorders or any other recording devices. If any recording device is found, IR LED system is initiated to emit the IR rays. Since camcorders are sensitive to IR rays, the quality of the recorded video gets degraded. Along with the IR LED system, there is an alerting system that is operated using GSM. This alerting system sends a message to the theatre manager stating that there is an active recording device. Also, an alert message is sent if the IR LED system fails to turn-on even after the camcorder is found.

Akshatha [15] proposed a card based anti-piracy screening system having two levels of authentication. Initially, the smart card owned by the respective theatre manager has information that is compared with preloaded reference data stored in the comparator. The digital output of the comparator is given as input to the optocoupler. Optocoupler provides electrical isolation between the comparator and the driver, preventing the flow of back emf into the comparator. The signal from the comparator is transmitted to the driver, which is composed of pairs of Darlington transistors, where the signal is amplified and inverted. This driver is used to activate the microcontroller by driving the relays. This concludes the first level of authentication. The microcontroller provides the second level of authentication. When the microcontroller turns on, the keypad gets activated to enter the password. If the entered password is valid, the microcontroller output becomes low, the driver amplifies the signal and triggers the relay to control the IR LEDs. Signals generated by the IR LEDs mounted along the perimeter and behind the theatre screen are directed at the audience. As a result, the invisible IR light interferes with the acquisition function of the camera, thereby preventing piracy.

Praveen [16] proposed a technique to estimate the pirate position in theatres. This work employs zero padding and projective transformation techniques to determine the angle of tilt in the input image by comparing it with reference image. Reference images are ones that are captured without any tilt angle and kept as a base or reference and input images are those which are captured with different tilt angles. The input images are compared with the reference images and zero-padded to eliminate the tilt angle. Then the Projective transformation is applied for correcting the distortion in the zero padded image. Output image of the projective transform is referred to as response variable and has a black region at the corner. This area is often triangular and is generated due to zero padding. To determine the image's tilt angle, the black triangle is cropped and converted from RGB format to black and white image. Trace angle and horizontal beam are marked by selecting the starting and ending points in the black and white crop image. The cosine angle (tilt angle) between the two beams is calculated using these points and is useful in determining the position of the camera in theatre and helps in deterring piracy.

Nilesh Dubey [17] presented a Discrete wavelet transform based watermarking technique to combat piracy. The two key aspects of this approach are extraction of the watermark from the recorded video and estimating the pirate position in the theatre. A watermark consisting of information regarding the timestamp and place of piracy is generated to form a payload. The sequence of ordering in the payload is reference hour, pin code, and registration number of theatres. The generated payload will be converted to binary, then to a matrix, and subsequently to an image watermark. Later, Arnold transform is applied to the basic watermark image to obtain a scrambled watermark, so that no one can identify the watermark. After tilling the Arnold transformed basic watermark as per the host video frame size, the scrambled periodic watermark is generated. The movie is now split into frames, and these image frames are converted from RGB to YCbCr color format. The 'Y' component of the frame is then subjected to a three-level DWT for further processing. The host image is then embedded with the periodic watermark. Then, inverse DWT is applied to the host image and is converted back to the RGB format. Finally, by combining all the frames, the watermarked video of the movie is obtained. Illegal camcorder capture of cinema is prevented by extracting the watermark from the pirated movie using a blind extraction approach to locate the pirate position using the watermark message.

To curb piracy, many anti-piracy systems were proposed in the literature with a variety of approaches. In few of the approaches, watermarking techniques are used to build the systems. But watermarking technique involves complex procedures and might damage the movie content. While in other approaches [18–23] only IR LED screens are employed to degrade the recorded video quality, but there is no specific method to detect the piracy.

3 Methodology

In this section, machine learning based anti-piracy system is presented. The model mainly relies on Support Vector Machine as shown in the Fig. 1.

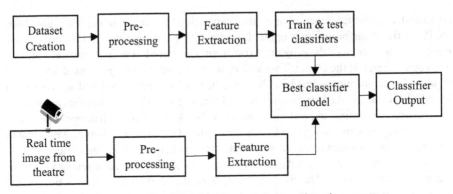

Fig. 1. Proposed machine learning based piracy detection system

The following are the basic steps involved:

1. Acquiring dataset images.
2. Training and testing several machine learning models for their performance and choosing the best model.
3. Testing the selected classifier model for real-time images.
4. Notify the theatre owner about the piracy by sending the alert message regarding piracy.

A thermal camera is employed to capture the images of theatres in different conditions to create the dataset. The dataset includes two classes of images, one of which is labelled as 'abnormal' and contains images with recording devices, while the other class is labelled as 'normal' and contains images with no recording devices. The acquired dataset consists of 4200 images in each class and 8400 images in total. The training images are resized to the dimension of 227×227 and fed to AlexNet for feature extraction. AlexNet extracts 1000 features from each of the resized images and these features are utilized for training multiple machine learning models in MATLAB. The best model that yields high accuracy is chosen for classification in real-time. Since Quadratic SVM yielded the highest accuracy, it is selected as a classifier. Later, the theatre images are acquired at regular intervals in real-time. Then these images are resized and fed to AlexNet for feature extraction. Extracted features are later directed to Quadratic SVM model to classify the images into normal and abnormal. If the predicted class is abnormal then an alert message is sent to the theatre official indicating the presence of recording device.

Quadratic SVM is a kernel optimization technique used to obtain the soft margin between the datapoints that are non-linearly separable. SVM being a binary classifier, can also perform multiclass classification by dividing the problem into several binary classifications. It employs one-versus-one approach for multiclass classification. The procedure followed in SVM for binary classification is described as follows:

Let m points are contained in a training dataset and is given by,

$$(x_1, y_1), \ldots \ldots, (x_m, y_m)$$

where y_i corresponds to the class which x_i belongs and y_i can take the values 1 or -1. Each x_i is a real vector of dimension p.

By dividing the cluster of points x_i, such that $y_i = 1$ and $y_i = -1$ lie on either side of the maximum margin hyperplane.

The hyperplane for the set of x points is represented by the equation

$$w^T x - a = 0 \tag{1}$$

while a refers to bias, w refers to the normal vector to hyperplane.

The parameter $\frac{a}{||w||}$ specifies the hyperplane offset along normal vector from the origin.

The hyperplane equations for the normalized dataset can be written as

$$w^T x - a = 1 \ for \ y_i = 1 \ and$$
$$w^T x - a = -1 \ for \ y_i = -1 \tag{2}$$

The two marginal hyperplanes are separated by a distance of $\frac{2}{||w||}$. This distance can be maximized by minimizing the parameter $||w||$.

The constraint i is introduced to restrict data points from falling into the margin.

$$w^T x - a \geq 1 \ for \ y_i = 1 \ or$$
$$w^T x - a \leq -1 \ for \ y_i = -1 \tag{3}$$

The generalized form of above equations is expressed as

$$y_i \left(w^T x_i - a \right) \geq 1, \ for \ 1 \leq i \leq m \tag{4}$$

Hinge loss function is employed to calculate the soft margin as the dataset is nonlinearly separable.

$$max \left(0, 1 - y_i \left(w^T x_i - a \right) \right)$$

When the constraint in Eq. (4) is satisfied, the above function becomes Zero, indicating that xi is on the appropriate side of the margin.

The purpose of optimization is to minimize

$$\left[\frac{1}{n} \sum_{i=1}^{m} max(0, 1 - yi(wT \ xi - a)) \right] + \lambda ||w||^2 \tag{5}$$

where the parameter λ leads to trade-off between increasing margin size and ensuring that the x_i point is on the correct side of the margin.

The kernel approach is used to generate optimal linear solutions by performing a nonlinear translation of data to a higher dimensional space. The converted data points are indicated as (x_i), and the kernel function is given as $\varphi(x_i)$

$$k \left(x_i, x_j \right) = \varphi(x_i) \cdot \varphi(x_j) \tag{6}$$

In the transformed space, the real vector w satisfies the below equation,

$$w = \sum_{i=1}^{m} c_i y_i \varphi(xi) \tag{7}$$

where c_i are obtained by solving the problem of optimization.
Maximize,

$$f(c_1 \ldots c_m) = \sum_{i=1}^{m} c_i - \frac{1}{2} \sum_{i=1}^{m} \sum_{j=1}^{m} y_i c_i (\varphi(x_i) \cdot \varphi(x_j)) y_j c_j \tag{8}$$

The pair wise inner product $(\varphi(x_i).\varphi(x_j))$ is replaced by the kernel function. Hence the above equation becomes,

$$f(c_1 \ldots c_m) = \sum_{i=1}^{m} c_i - \frac{1}{2} \sum_{i=1}^{m} \sum_{j=1}^{m} y_i c_i(x_i, x_j) y_j c_j \tag{9}$$

subject to $\sum_{i=1}^{m} c_i y_i = 0$, and $0 \leq c_i \leq \frac{1}{2n\lambda}$ for all i.
In general, the kernel function will be

$$k(x_i, x_j) = (x_i \cdot x_j + 1)^d \tag{10}$$

where d represents the degree of polynomial.
Therefore, the expression for quadratic kernel used in the proposed work becomes

$$k(x_i, x_j) = (x_i \cdot x_j + 1)^4 \tag{11}$$

4   Results

Results of comparison of 4 Machine Learning algorithms in terms of accuracies is listed in Table 1.

Table 1. Comparison with other classifier models

Classifier	SVM quadratic	SVM linear	KNN coarse	Tree coarse
Accuracy	99.7%	98.8%	97.3%	94.7%

The confusion matrix for all the 4 machine learning models is shown in Table 2. In the confusion matrix, the True positive (TP) refers to correct number of positive predictions. False positives (FP) refer to prediction counts that are wrongly predicted as true. True negatives (TN) refer to correct false predictions count. False negatives (FN) refer to prediction counts that are wrongly predicted as false.

Table 2. Confusion matrix

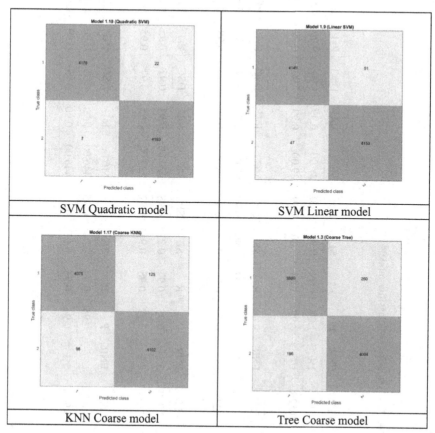

SVM Quadratic model	SVM Linear model
KNN Coarse model	Tree Coarse model

Considering the confusion matrix of Quadratic SVM, the values of TP, TN, FP and FN for class 1 (i.e., abnormal class: images with presence of active recording devices) are 4178, 4193, 7 and 22 respectively. For class 2 (i.e., normal class: images with no active recording devices) the values of TP, TN, FP and FN are 4193, 4178, 22 and 7 respectively. Similarly for all the models TP, TN, FP and FN values are obtained from the confusion matrix.

By using these values of the confusion matrix, further 13 parameters are evaluated to determine the algorithm that suits best for the dataset. The parameters evaluated for each of the classes are: True negative rate (TNR), True positive rate (TPR), False positive rate (FPR), False negative rate (FNR), sensitivity (SE), specificity (SP), Misclassification (MC), Precision (P), Recall (R), Intersection over Union (IoU), DICE similarity coefficient (DSC), Pixel Score (Pxl) and Boundary F-1 Score (BF score).

From the Table 3 it can be observed that Quadratic SVM has got more True positive values and correspondingly excel in all the parameters. Therefore, Quadratic SVM yields highest accuracy.

Table 3. Comparison of classifier models

SVM quadratic: accuracy = 99.7%

Class	TP	TN	FP	FN	TPR	TNR	FPR	FNR	P	R	SE	SP	MC	IoU	DSC	Pxl	BF
1	4178	4193	7	22	99%	99.83%	0.17%	1%	1.00	0.99	0.99	1.00	29.00	0.99	1.00	0.99	1.00
2	4193	4178	22	7	99%	99.48%	0.52%	1%	0.99	1.00	1.00	0.99	29.00	0.99	1.00	0.99	1.00

SVM linear: accuracy = 98.8%

Class	TP	TN	FP	FN	TPR	TNR	FPR	FNR	P	R	SE	SP	MC	IoU	DSC	Pxl	BF
1	4149	4153	47	51	99%	98.88%	1.12%	1%	0.99	0.99	0.99	0.99	98.00	0.98	0.99	0.98	0.99
2	4153	4149	51	47	99%	98.79%	1.21%	1%	0.99	0.99	0.99	0.99	98.00	0.98	0.99	0.98	0.99

KNN coarse: accuracy = 97.3%

Class	TP	TN	FP	FN	TPR	TNR	FPR	FNR	P	R	SE	SP	MC	IoU	DSC	Pxl	BF
1	4075	4102	98	125	97%	97.67%	2.33%	3%	0.98	0.97	0.97	0.98	223.00	0.95	0.97	0.95	0.97
2	4102	4075	125	98	98%	97.02%	2.98%	2%	0.97	0.98	0.98	0.97	223.00	0.95	0.97	0.95	0.97

Tree coarse: accuracy = 94.7%

Class	TP	TN	FP	FN	TPR	TNR	FPR	FNR	P	R	SE	SP	MC	IoU	DSC	Pxl	BF
1	3950	4004	196	250	94%	95.33%	4.67%	6%	0.95	0.94	0.94	0.95	446.00	0.90	0.95	0.90	0.95
2	4004	3950	250	196	95%	94.05%	5.95%	5%	0.94	0.95	0.95	0.94	446.00	0.90	0.95	0.90	0.95

The ROC curves shown in Table 4, depicts the performance of the classification models that are listed. ROC curve plots the values of False positive rate versus True positive rate at different classification thresholds. More positive predictions can be increased by lowering the classification threshold which further increases both False Positive and True Positive values. It can be noted from ROC curve of quadratic SVM that True positive rates (TPR) are relatively high which results in more accurate predictions of anomaly class.

Table 4. ROC curves

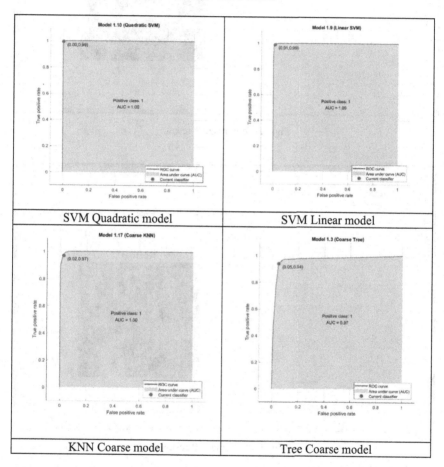

The real time images acquired are processed by the trained Quadratic SVM model and are predicted for their category. Sample results are shown in Fig. 2 and Fig. 3. The test image 1 is from anomaly class. As expected, the model has predicted the image as abnormal class and the result is displayed in MALAB command window as well as the figure window. The test image 2 belongs to normal class and it is correctly predicted by the model and the corresponding result is displayed.

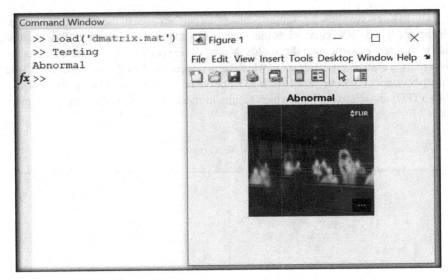

Fig. 2. Test image 1 results

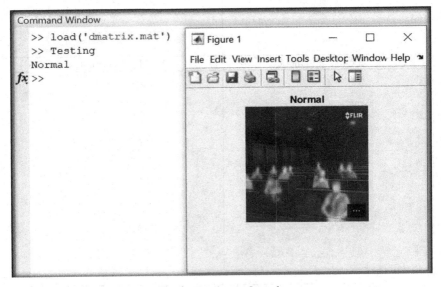

Fig. 3. Test image 2 results

5   Conclusion

The piracy of movie in theatres is a major issue in recent years. Hence, in many countries the situation has resulted in the demise of several filmmaking companies and industries. Our work focused on development of an anti-piracy system using Machine Learning Models and Thermogram Analysis. It can be observed that the quadratic SVM classifier yields higher accuracy for AlexNet based features. With the proposed model, identification of presence of camcorders in Thermal camera coverage area is successful. However, the whole theatre may be not covered. In future, the model can be enhanced by installing a greater number of cameras and increasing the number of images in the dataset.

Funding. This research work is funded (GRD-907) by the Karnataka Science and Technology Promotion Society, Department of Information Technology, Biotechnology and Science & Technology, Government of Karnataka, India under the category of Research Grant for Scientist/Faculty (RGS/F), Vision Group of Science and Technology (VGST) Scheme.

References

1. Quinn, D., Chen, L., Mulvenna, M.: Social network analysis: a survey. Int. J. Ambient Comput. Intell. (IJACI) **4**(3), 46–58 (2012)
2. Kaur, P., Gupta, S., Dhingra, S., Sharma, S., Arora, A.: Towards content-dependent social media platform preference analysis. Int. J. Ambient Comput. Intell. (IJACI) **11**(2), 30–47 (2020)
3. Angadi, S., Nandyal, S.: Human identification system based on spatial and temporal features in the video surveillance system. Int. J. Ambient Comput. Intell. (IJACI) **11**(3), 1–21 (2020)
4. Kumar, B.V.V.R., Vardhan, B.A., Gupta, C.H.R., Surekha, P.: Reduction of movie piracy using an automated anti-piracy screen recording system: anti-piracy screen recording system. In: 2019 4th International Conference on Information Systems and Computer Networks (ISCON), pp. 301–304, November 2019. https://doi.org/10.1109/ISCON47742.2019.9036271
5. Chandana, P.S., Rekha, D.M., Akshatha, H.M., Raghavendra, Y.M., Pallavi, S.: Movie piracy reduction using automated infrared transmitter screen system and steganography technique. Int. J. Eng. Res. Technol. **8**(13) (2020)
6. Asborn, T., Prem Kumar, L., Michael Jose, S., Santhosh Kumar, M.: Anti-piracy screening system. Int. J. Innov. Res. Technol. **6**(2) (2019)
7. Ankalage, S.S., Nagarathna N., Venu, L., Sandeep, N.: Anti-piracy screening system. Int. J. Eng. Res. Technol. **9**(05) (2020)
8. Raut, G., Bakade, K., Kulkarni, S.V.: IR based theatre piracy reduction by using image processing. Int. J. Adv. Res. Comput. Commun. Eng. **7**(3) (2018)
9. Abhishek, K.A., Chetan, G., Deepak, M.S., Akash, M., Rohith, M.N.: Camcorder piracy-RFID based anti-piracy screen. Int. J. Sci. Res. Dev. **6**(03) (2018)
10. Khan, J., Shenoy, A., Bhavana, K.M., Savalgi, M.S., Borra, S.: Secure anti-piracy system. In: Satapathy, S.C., Bhateja, V., Janakiramaiah, B., Chen, Y.-W. (eds.) Intelligent System Design. AISC, vol. 1171, pp. 827–835. Springer, Singapore (2021). https://doi.org/10.1007/978-981-15-5400-1_78
11. Chen, Y., et al.: Movie piracy tracking using temporal psychovisual modulation. In: 2017 IEEE International Symposium on Broadband Multimedia Systems and Broadcasting (BMSB), pp. 1–4 (2017)
12. Shukla, D., Sharma, M.: Digital movies tracking using scene-based watermarking system. Radioelectron. Commun. Syst. **62**(5), 202–213 (2019). https://doi.org/10.3103/S07352727 19050029
13. Roopalakshmi, R.: A brand new application of visual-audio fingerprints: estimating the position of the pirate in a theater - a case study. Image Vis. Comput. **76**, 48–63 (2018)
14. Rejeti, V.K.K., Gowtham, J., Hemanth, B.: Preventing movie piracy. Int. J. Adv. Res. Sci. Eng. Technol. **7** (2020)

15. Akshatha, S., Deepika Vishwanath, K., Neetha, C., Raksha, V.M., Manjula Devi, T.H.: Card based anti-piracy screening system. Trans. Electr. Electron. Eng. **4** (2016)

16. Thakur, P.S., Kumar, S.: Technique for estimation of the position of the pirate in-theater piracy. In: 2015 Second International Conference on Advances in Computing and Communication Engineering, pp. 515–518 (2015)

17. Dubey, N., Modi, H.: A robust discrete wavelet transform based adaptive watermarking scheme in YCbCr color space against camcorder recording in cinema/movie theatres. Eng. Sci. (2021)

18. Borra, S., Viswanadha Raju, S., Lakshmi, H.R.: Visual cryptography based lossless watermarking for sensitive images. In: Panigrahi, B.K., Suganthan, P.N., Das, S., Satapathy, S.C. (eds.) SEMCCO 2015. LNCS, vol. 9873, pp. 29–39. Springer, Cham (2016). https://doi.org/10.1007/978-3-319-48959-9_3

19. Borra, S., Dey, N., Ashour, A.S., Shi, F.: Digital image watermarking tools: state-of-the-art. In: ITITS, pp. 450–459, August 2017

20. Lakshmi, H.R., Borra, S.: Difference expansion based reversible watermarking algorithms for copyright protection of images: state-of-the-art and challenges. Int. J. Speech Technol. **24**(4), 823–852 (2021). https://doi.org/10.1007/s10772-021-09818-y

21. Borra, S., Thanki, R., Dey, N.: Digital Image Watermarking: Theoretical and Computational Advances. Series: Intelligent Signal Processing and Data Analysis. CRC Press, Taylor & Francis Group (2018). [ISBN 9781138390638]

22. Lakshmi, H.R., Borra, S.: Digital video watermarking tools an overview. Int. J. Inf. Comput. Secur. **16**(1,2), 1–19 (2021). [Indexed in Scopus, EI, ACM]. [ISSN 17441765]

23. Thanki, R., Borra, S.: A survey on prevention techniques for camcorder video piracy in movie theatres. Recent Pat. Eng. **15**(1) (2021)

A Comparative Study of Prediction of Gas Hold up Using ANN

Nirjhar Bar[1,2]([✉]) [ID], Asit Baran Biswas[2], and Sudip Kumar Das[2] [ID]

[1] St. James' School, 165, A. J. C. Bose Road, Kolkata 700014, West Bengal, India
nirjhar@hotmail.com
[2] Department of Chemical Engineering, University of Calcutta, 92, A. P. C. Road, Kolkata 700009, West Bengal, India

Abstract. The primary aim of this paper is to present a way by which the gas hold-up can be predicted for gas non-Newtonian liquid flow. The type of conduit used here are the helical coils of different diameter. The helical coils are vertically oriented. The data are collected from our previous experiment and its subsequent publications. A principle component analysis (PCA) based network performance is compared with the Levenberg-Marquardt (LM) algorithm based network. The closeness of the error parameters indicate that both training algorithm can predict both the hydrodynamic parameters with acceptable accuracy. The final analysis and the evaluation of the statistical parameters related to the errors prove the successful nature of the modelling using the PCA based network.

Keywords: Helical coil · Gas hold up · ANN · PCA

1 Introduction

The knowledge of hydrodynamic parameters of two-phase gas-liquid flow in coil geometry is essential for the design of oil pipeline system, nuclear reactor, in air crafts, heat exchangers, steam generators and other process equipment in chemical, food and drug industries. The complexity of flow through coil is much more compared to straight pipe. Observation from the literature survey reveals the existence of large number of research activity around the world related to the flow of liquid (single phase flow) through various conduits in relation to helical coils oriented horizontally or vertically [16,23]. The nature of two-phase (gas and liquid) flow system through the curved pipes is extremely complex. In gas-liquid flow, separation of flow can be observed when it flows through the coil and is due to the density differences of the two phases. Hence, it generates significant slip between the phases. This process is the continuous function of the coil geometry [17,22,23,26]. When the two-phase flow within helical coils are considered then it has not been investigated as much as it is expected. The literature survey in relation to the flow of gas-Newtonian liquid flowing through the helical coils have been reported earlier [13,22].

S. Mukhopadhyay et al. (Eds.): CICBA 2022, CCIS 1579, pp. 351–362, 2022.
https://doi.org/10.1007/978-3-031-10766-5_28

The research related to gas-non-Newtonian liquid flow has received some attention in the last few decades. This is due to the fact that many industries are now created where they use the system where the complex rheological behaviours of the liquid are exhibited. Literature review suggests that in the past few years, flow through helical coils have been studied mainly related to heat transfer, i.e., Single phase [27] and steam-water two-phase flow [15,19,28]. But the literature review has suggested that non-Newtonian liquid together with gas flow through the coils have limited study [2,25]. The Scientific endeavour to find and understand the mechanism associated with the gas-non-Newtonian liquid flow becomes extremely difficult when it is attempted with the mathematical approach. The physical description of the fluid flow most often don't match with the mathematical modelling. This is due to a number of factors, i.e., the friction with the wall, the shear that is present at the interface of the two phases, the change in the direction of the flow, etc. The phenomena related to the momentum transfer in between both the phases and the phase separation itself become very difficult for the purpose of mathematical modelling. This is the point where machine learning becomes extremely helpful and now is widely used by scientists and engineers all over the world.

The predictive ability and the usefulness of Artificial Neural Network is well known in many applications of science and engineering. This is the very reasons, the modelling of the multiphase flow process with the help of neural network is quiet appropriate. The positivity of using artificial neural network modelling is that no mathematical insight is necessary for the formulation of the modelling. So, the complexity of the different flow properties in relation with the two-phase flow, as mentioned in the previous paragraph are not required for the training algorithms to get the final result through prediction. The final result can be achieved by using the parameters that can be measured easily (e.g., liquid velocity, viscosity of liquid as well as gas, surface tension, gas velocity, diameter of the conduits etc.). The gas-hold up [3] has been successfully predicted using single layered Multilayer Perceptron with the use of four distinct transfer functions (TFs) trained with backpropagation algorithm for air and non-Newtonian (gas-liquid) flow passing through the helical coils having circular cross-section of different diameters oriented horizontally. The prediction related to gas-liquid (gas-non-Newtonian) flow passing through different conduits (globe valve, elbow, gate valve and orifice) have also been successfully predicted using the same Multilayer Perceptron having four distinct TFs with the use of only one hidden layer trained with backpropagation algorithm [1,4–7,20]. The prediction related to the gas hold up as well as the frictional pressure drop has also been successfully performed for gas-non-Newtonian fluid flow using pipes having circular cross section oriented vertically for various diameters [8].

In the present paper the authors presented the testing and development of modelling related to two (Principle component analysis and Levenberg-Marquardt) different ANN training algorithms to predict two-phase gas hold up. The data have been collected from the experiments performed earlier on gas-liquid (air and SCMC solutions with density of $0.2\,\text{kg/m}^3$) flow through helical coils (circular cross-section) having different diameters oriented vertically [11–13].

2   Materials and Methods

2.1   Experiment

The experimental apparatus consists of one air supply system, one liquid storage tank, few centrifugal pumps, one test section, controlling and measuring system for the flow rate, the pressure drop, and gas hold up along with other accessories. The detail of the experiment has been reported in the earlier publications [11–13].

Flexible, transparent and Thick walled PVC pipes having internal diameter ranging from 0.00933 to 0.01200 m have been used as coil pipe. The length of the coil tube that is used for this experiment is 15 m. These PVC pipes have been wound around a hard cylindrical PVC frame of certain diameter for the formation of the helical coils.

The test liquids, i.e., dilute solution of the SCMC, i.e., sodium salt of carboxymethyl cellulose (Loba Cheme Private Limited, Mumbai, India) have been prepared by dissolving and mixing tap water with necessary amount of SCMC. Then the solution has been stirred till the point where a homogeneous solution is obtained. Trace amount of formalin has been added to prevent the biological degradation. Then the required amount of SCMC solution has been allowed to flow through a T-section. Where it has been mixed with the necessary amount of air. Both the SCMC solution and the air are pressed through the T-junction by the use of different pumps. This mixture is then passed through the helical coils oriented vertically. The content of the tank has been kept at constant temperature. This process has been maintained by the circulation of water through a coil made up of copper. Then SCMC solution of certain concentration $(0.2\,\text{kg/m}^3)$ is mixed in water to be used as non-Newtonian liquids. The atmospheric air has been used as the second fluid. From the characteristics of SCMC solution it has been observed that it posses the properties of the time-independent pseudoplastic type of fluid. The Ostwald deWaele model of fluid or power-law model of fluid describes the rheological behavior of the SCMC solution.

2.2   Artificial Neural Network Architecture

In the field related to fluid dynamics when the solution is not easily tractable, the use of ANN has been proven to be an alternative. From Table 1 the representation as well as the description of the numerical values of the various parameters can be observed.

For this study the two of the most commonly used algorithms have been used. Two of the algorithms are of second order, i.e., Levenberg-Marquardt (LM)and

Principle component analysis (PCA) have been used. All of these algorithms are being used for the last 15 years in various applications in Chemical Engineering and other fields [10, 18, 21].

The Levenberg-Marquardt algorithm is a very popular backpropagation algorithm. It is a 2nd order learning algorithm. The value of the λ (combination coefficient) is kept as 0.01. For this algorithm λ is the only user dependent parameter, which is set at the starting point only. It is not necessary to modify this value of the combination coefficient any more throughout the duration of the training. When combination coefficient is large, this algorithm transform into steepest descent but when it is small then this algorithm transform into Gauss-Newton. So, the Levenberg-Marquardt algorithm combines all the best features related to this two algorithms while avoiding most of the limitations.

The PCA algorithm consists of two phases (i.e., both unsupervised and supervised). The first stage is when the principal components are chosen using a process of feature extraction. This choice of number of principal components can be chosen by the user or it is predefined in the software used. During the 2nd stage, i.e., the supervised stage is associated with the same Levenberg-Marquardt algorithm as discussed in this section.

Table 1. Range of the data

Measurement type	Range
Coil diameters	
Tube (m)	$0.00933 \leq D_t \leq 0.012$
Coil (m)	$0.133 \leq D_c \leq 0.2662$
Physical properties of SCMC solution	
Concentration (kg/m^3)	0.2
Physical properties related to air	
Viscosity of air (Ns/m^2)	0.00001846
Density (kg/m^3)	1.1614
Flow rate	
Liquid flow rate Q_l (m^3/s)	1.334×10^{-5} to 1.5×10^{-4}
Gas flow rate Q_g (m^3/s)	4.4×10^{-6} to 5.025×10^{-4}
Measuring parameter	
Gas hold up	$0.051 \leq \alpha_g \leq 0.864$
Total number of data for ANN analysis for frictional pressure drop as well as the hold up	280

The final evaluation of the prediction performance had been measured using AARE (average absolute relative error) and standard deviation (SD) apart from the correlation co-efficient (R) and MSE [3, 9].

2.3   Modelling of the Network

Data for the purpose of modelling have been collected from the experimental study performed earlier [11–13]. The parameters used in the network as inputs (observed from Table 1) have been the following:

- flow rate of SCMC solution - Q_l
- flow rate of air - Q_g
- diameter of tube - D_t
- diameter of coil - D_c

Air density, ρ_s as well as air viscosity, μ_s remains constant. The acceleration due to gravity, g is also constant. This is the reason they are ineffective when they are used as input parameter for training of the network. Hence they are never used during the analysis. Two-phase (air and SCMC solution) gas hold up i.e., α_g is the output parameters. The parameters of ANN analysis used for training using different algorithms are described in Table 2. The hidden layer is optimised by the variation related to the numbers of the processing elements (1 to 20). This very procedure has already been tested in our earlier papers related to other conduits [1,3–5,7,8,21]. The analysis for pressure drop and gas hold up is done separately. For this analysis the variables are applied without normalisation in accordance with our past experience [1,3–5,7,8,21].

During training the connection weights modify themselves to reduce the training error. The possibility of over-fitting or over-training [14,24] at training phase cannot guarantee best results. The cause is over-fitting or over-training. So cross-validation is also done during training. It is necessary to apply stopping criterion during training to reduce time consumption. It is dependent on the value of minimum MSE (mean squared error) as observed during cross-validation. The stopping criteria vary according to the need of the training algorithm.

After randomization the total data is divided into three parts. 70% data points out of the total data has been used for the purpose of training. Along with training 20% of the data are used for cross-validation. The rest of the 10% data are used for prediction.

A hyperbolic tangent ($\tanh \beta x = \frac{e^{\beta x} - e^{-\beta x}}{e^{\beta x} + e^{-\beta x}}$) transfer function in the hidden and output layer for LM and PCA network has been used. The variation of hidden layer processing elements are done ranging from 1 to 20.

For PCA network 100 unsupervised iterations had been used before the supervised state. The number of principal components are kept as 3. During the supervised state a maximum of 10^3 epochs have been used associated with a stopping criteria of 10^2 epochs.

3 Results and Performance

3.1 Optimisation of ANN

The variation of least value related to cross-validation error with respect to processing elements number within the hidden layer in the case of gas hold up is presented in Figs. 1 and 2 for LM and PCA respectively. The network is considered pruned when the cross-validation error is minimum. Figures 1 and 2 present these optimized points related to the processing elements and the least value related to cross-validation error reached while training the network. Once the network is optimized, it is used for final prediction.

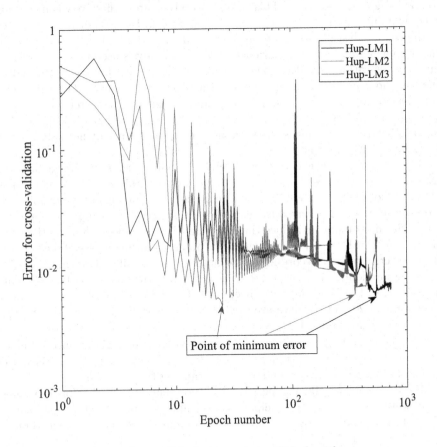

Fig. 1. Cross-validation curve using LM algorithm

3.2   Analysis of Final Prediction

Figures 3 and 4 are the depiction of the comparison in between the experimental and the output prediction for the LM and PCA algorithms in the hidden as well as output layer when tanh βx transfer function is present within the hidden layer related to the prediction of gas hold up. The visual observation of Figs. 3 and 4 reiterates the usefulness and the utility of ANN prediction again. The visual observation of Figs. 3 and 4 yields the fact that the points are closer to the diagonal for PCA based network (4) than the LM network (3). The observation of Table 2 also proves this fact. The comparative lower values of the error parameters for the relative error is evident from the Table 2. The observation of the mean squared error also makes it clear that for all the randomisations PCA

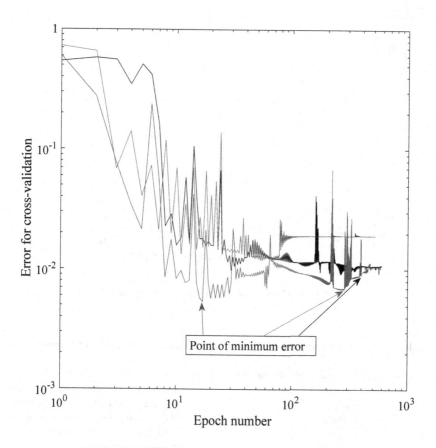

Fig. 2. Cross-validation curve using PCA algorithm

performed better than that of the normal LM algorithm. Finally, the value of R conclusively proves that the performance of the PCA based network is better than that of the prediction using the LM algorithm. The error values of Table 2, the visual observation of Figs. 3 and 4 gives the confirmation that a PCA based network has predicted the gas hold up better than the LM network.

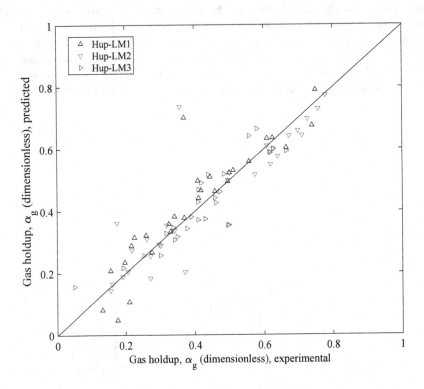

Fig. 3. Comparison plot for LM algorithm

Table 2. Final performance of LM and PCA algorithms related to the gas hold up

Algorithm type	Minimum error during cross-validation	AARE	SD	MSE	R
LM	0.00576	0.185325	0.224336	0.006777	0.906698
	0.005978	0.157098	0.374131	0.008697	0.896333
	0.00491	0.171496	0.378997	0.003656	0.897364
PCA	0.008967	0.100222	0.105173	0.002091	0.965157
	0.006833	0.136625	0.222172	0.005206	0.939013
	0.005371	1.166471	0.251043	0.004395	0.890546

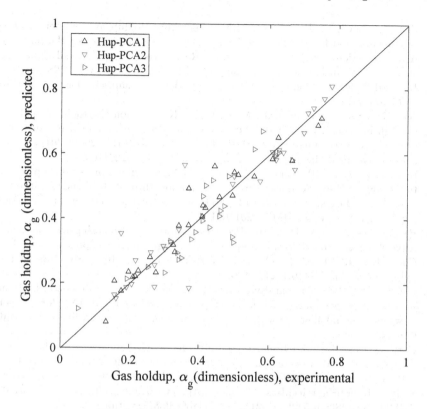

Fig. 4. Comparison plot for PCA algorithm

4   Conclusions

The LM and PCA network have been successfully modelled for the data related to the prediction of the gas hold up for gas-non-Newtonian liquid (air, SCMC solution) flowing through vertical helical coils. The results clearly depicts the successful nature of the modelling for both cases. The PCA based network was able to predict the gas hold up better than the network with LM training algorithm.

References

1. Bar, N., Bandyopadhyay, T.K., Biswas, M.N., Das, S.K.: Prediction of pressure drop using artificial neural network for non-Newtonian liquid flow through piping components. J. Petrol. Sci. Eng. **71**(3–4), 187–194 (2010). https://doi.org/10.1016/j.petrol.2010.02.001. http://linkinghub.elsevier.com/retrieve/pii/S0920410510000392

2. Bar, N., Biswas, A.B., Biswas, M.N., Das, S.K.: Holdup analysis for gas-non-newtonian liquid flow through horizontal helical coils-empirical correlation versus ANN prediction. In: Paruya, S., Kar, S., Roy, S. (eds.) International Conference on Modeling, Optimization and Computing, (ICMOC 2010), vol. 1298, pp. 104–109 (2010). https://doi.org/10.1063/1.3516284. http://aip.scitation.org/doi/abs/10.1063/1.3516284

3. Bar, N., Biswas, A.B., Biswas, M.N., Das, S.K.: Gas-non-Newtonian liquid flow through horizontally oriented helical coils - prediction of frictional pressure drop using ANN. Artif. Intell. Syst. Mach. Learn. **3**(7), 412–418 (2011). http://www.ciitresearch.org/dl/index.php/aiml/article/view/AIML072011002

4. Bar, N., Biswas, A.B., Das, S.K., Biswas, M.N.: Frictional pressure drop prediction using ANN for gas-non-Newtonian liquid flow through 45° bend. Artif. Intell. Syst. Mach. Learn. **3**(9), 608–613 (2011). http://www.ciitresearch.org/dl/index.php/aiml/article/view/AIML082011021

5. Bar, N., Biswas, M.N., Das, S.K.: Prediction of pressure drop using artificial neural network for gas non-Newtonian liquid flow through piping components. Ind. Eng. Chem. Res. **49**(19), 9423–9429 (2010). https://doi.org/10.1021/ie1007739. http://pubs.acs.org/doi/abs/10.1021/ie1007739

6. Bar, N., Das, S.K.: Comparative study of friction factor by prediction of frictional pressure drop per unit length using empirical correlation and ANN for gas-non-Newtonian liquid flow through 180° circular bend. Int. Rev. Chem. Eng. **3**(6), 628–643 (2011)

7. Bar, N., Das, S.K.: Frictional pressure drop for gas-non-Newtonian liquid flow through 90° and 135° circular bend: prediction using empirical correlation and ANN. Int. J. Fluid Mech. Res. **39**(5), 416–437 (2012). https://doi.org/10.1615/InterJFluidMechRes.v39.i5.40. http://www.dl.begellhouse.com/journals/71cb29ca5b40f8f8,1d542bee45211141,2e344b6e3fa8f553.html

8. Bar, N., Das, S.K.: Modeling of gas holdup and pressure drop using ANN for gas-non-Newtonian liquid flow in vertical pipe. Adv. Mater. Res. **917**, 244–256 (2014). https://doi.org/10.4028/www.scientific.net/AMR.917.244. http://www.scientific.net/AMR.917.244

9. Bar, N., Mitra, T., Das, S.K.: Biosorption of Cu(II) ions from industrial effluents by rice husk: experiment, statistical, and ANN modeling. J. Environ. Eng. Landscape Manag. **29**(4), 441–448 (2021). https://doi.org/10.3846/jeelm.2021.14386. https://journals.vgtu.lt/index.php/JEELM/article/view/14386

10. Basheer, I., Hajmeer, M.: Artificial neural networks: fundamentals, computing, design, and application. J. Microbiol. Methods **43**(1), 3–31 (2000). https://doi.org/10.1016/S0167-7012(00)00201-3. http://linkinghub.elsevier.com/retrieve/pii/S0167701200002013

11. Biswas, A.B., Das, S.K.: Holdup characteristics of gas-non-Newtonian liquid flow through helical coils in vertical orientation. Ind. Eng. Chem. Res. **45**(21), 7287–7292 (2006). https://doi.org/10.1021/ie060420i. http://pubs.acs.org/doi/abs/10.1021/ie060420i

12. Biswas, A., Das, S.: Two-phase frictional pressure drop of gas-non-Newtonian liquid flow through helical coils in vertical orientation. Chem. Eng. Process. Process Intensification **47**(5), 816–826 (2008). https://doi.org/10.1016/j.cep.2007.01.030. http://linkinghub.elsevier.com/retrieve/pii/S0255270107000438

13. Biswas, A.B.: Studies on two-phase gas-non-Newtonian liquid flow through helical coils. Ph.D. thesis, University of Calcutta (2007)

14. Chaudhuri, B.B., Bhattacharya, U.: Efficient training and improved performance of multilayer perceptron in pattern classification. Neurocomputing **34**(1–4), 11–27 (2000). https://doi.org/10.1016/S0925-2312(00)00305-2. http://linkinghub. elsevier.com/retrieve/pii/S0925231200003052

15. Colombo, M., Colombo, L.P., Cammi, A., Ricotti, M.E.: A scheme of correlation for frictional pressure drop in steam-water two-phase flow in helicoidal tubes. Chem. Eng. Sci. **123**, 460–473 (2015). https://doi.org/10.1016/j.ces.2014.11.032. https:// linkinghub.elsevier.com/retrieve/pii/S0009250914006848

16. Das, S.K.: Water flow through helical coils in turbulent condition. In: Cheremisinoff, N.P. (ed.) Advances in Engineering Fluid Mechanics: Multiphase Reactor and Polymerization System Hydrodynamics, vol. 71, chap. 13, pp. 379–403. Elsevier (1996). https://doi.org/10.1016/B978-088415497-6/50015-2. http:// linkinghub.elsevier.com/retrieve/pii/B9780884154976500152

17. Gourma, M., Verdin, P.: Two-phase slug flows in helical pipes: slug frequency alterations and helicity fluctuations. Int. J. Multiphase Flow **86**, 10–20 (2016). https://doi.org/10.1016/j.ijmultiphaseflow.2016.07.013. https:// linkinghub.elsevier.com/retrieve/pii/S0301932216301136

18. Himmelblau, D.M.: Applications of artificial neural networks in chemical engineering. Korean J. Chem. Eng. **17**(4), 373–392 (2000). https://doi.org/10.1007/ BF02706848. http://link.springer.com/10.1007/BF02706848

19. Li, Y.x., Wu, J.h., Wang, H., Kou, L.p., Tian, X.h.: Fluid flow and heat transfer characteristics in helical tubes cooperating with spiral corrugation. Energy Procedia **17**, 791–800 (2012). https://doi.org/10.1016/j.egypro.2012.02.172. https:// linkinghub.elsevier.com/retrieve/pii/S1876610212005085

20. Maiti, S.B., Bar, N., Das, S.K.: Terminal settling velocity of solids in the pseudoplastic non-Newtonian liquid system - experiment and ANN modeling. Chem. Eng. J. Adv. **7**, 100136 (2021). https://doi.org/10.1016/j.ceja.2021.100136. https:// linkinghub.elsevier.com/retrieve/pii/S2666821121000521

21. Maiti, S.B., Let, S., Bar, N., Das, S.K.: Non-spherical solid-non-Newtonian liquid fluidization and ANN modelling: minimum fluidization velocity. Chem. Eng. Sci. **176**, 233–241 (2018). https://doi.org/10.1016/j.ces.2017.10.050. http:// linkinghub.elsevier.com/retrieve/pii/S0009250917306668

22. Mandal, S.N., Das, S.K.: Gas-liquid flow through helical coils in vertical orientation. Ind. Eng. Chem. Res. **42**(14), 3487–3494 (2003). https://doi.org/10.1021/ ie0200656. http://pubs.acs.org/doi/abs/10.1021/ie0200656

23. Mandal, S.N., Das, S.K.: Gas-liquid flow through helical coils in horizontal orientation. Can. J. Chem. Eng. **80**(5), 979–983 (2008). https://doi.org/10.1002/cjce. 5450800522. http://doi.wiley.com/10.1002/cjce.5450800522

24. Reed, R.: Pruning algorithms—a survey. IEEE Trans. Neural Netw. **4**(5), 740–747 (1993). https://doi.org/10.1109/72.248452. http://ieeexplore.ieee.org/document/ 248452/

25. Thandlam, A.K., Majumder, S.K.: Dynamic interaction model to analyze hydrodynamics of gas-non-Newtonian-liquid flow in vertical helical coil pipe (VHCP). Int. J. Fluid Mech. Res. **43**(4), 281–307 (2016). https://doi.org/ 10.1615/InterJFluidMechRes.v43.i4.10. http://www.dl.begellhouse.com/journals/ 71cb29ca5b40f8f8,11d09f2f1b3d1a6b,172338230e99ccb2.html

26. Vashisth, S., Nigam, K.: Prediction of flow profiles and interfacial phenomena for two-phase flow in coiled tubes. Chem. Eng. Process. Process Intensification **48**(1), 452–463 (2009). https://doi.org/10.1016/j.cep.2008.06.006. https:// linkinghub.elsevier.com/retrieve/pii/S0255270108001438

27. Wang, M., et al.: Experimental studies on local and average heat transfer characteristics in helical pipes with single phase flow. Ann. Nuclear Energy **123**, 78–85 (2019). https://doi.org/10.1016/j.anucene.2018.09.017. https://linkinghub. elsevier.com/retrieve/pii/S0306454918304869

28. Xiao, Y., Hu, Z., Chen, S., Gu, H.: Experimental study of two-phase frictional pressure drop of steam-water in helically coiled tubes with small coil diameters at high pressure. Appl. Thermal Eng. **132**, 18–29 (2018). https://doi.org/10. 1016/j.applthermaleng.2017.12.074. https://linkinghub.elsevier.com/retrieve/pii/ S1359431117369041

Understanding the Voice of Customers Using Artificial Neural Networks: A Study of Food Aggregators in the Cachar District of Assam

Dhritiman Chanda[1]([✉]) [iD], Nilanjan Mazumder[2] [iD], D. Ghosh[3] [iD],
and Deepjyoti Dutta[4] [iD]

[1] Faculty of Commerce and Management, Vishwakarma University, Pune, India
operationsdchanda@gmail.com
[2] Department of Business Administration, University of Science and Technology, Meghalaya,
Baridua, India
[3] Department of Business Administration, Assam University, Silchar, Silchar, India
[4] CITI Bank, Chennai, India

Abstract. The evolution of online food delivery system started in India in the late 2000's and since then many Food Aggregators have come up with a variety of prospects for the customers. This process of Business to Customer services had found itself to be very popular especially in the last few years and after the COVID 19 attack the business had flourished to a large extent. People do not prefer to come out of their abodes and try to procure the eatables by maintaining proper social distancing. There have been a number of local Food Aggregators that have emerged in the Cachar District only recently and post 2020 especially in the lockdown phase they have accelerated their operations in the Valley by joining hands with a number of food outlets. These local entrepreneurial efforts are still in the growth phase and are trying to meet the customer demands to enhance their satisfaction level. Speaking of enhancing the satisfaction of the customers, there are many factors that work before meeting their overall satisfaction and these factors if are considered carefully would not only increase the customer loyalty towards the respective. Purposive Sampling was used in this study to get the responses from the online food buyers. It used Artificial Neural Networks to understand the pattern of the buying behavior of customers in this area and tried to create a model that would enhance the understanding of the Food Aggregators in regards to the buying frequency of the customers and take steps accordingly.

Keywords: Food Aggregators · COVID 19 · Cachar District · Customer Satisfaction · Entrepreneurial efforts · Purposive Sampling · Artificial Neural Networks

1 Introduction

A swift transformation and expansion are observed in the food delivery industry as, a fresh company pops up every now and then to grab hold of the market of the country. It was seen that an average Indian resident spends approximately 25% of their income over foodstuff and drinkables. For the material retail stops, it was revealed that the income is generated via food alone was about 50%. On a different perspective, superior foodstuffs are not ubiquitous. Enhancement of disposable income, trends in westernization and transformation in living styles of people are the major cause behind the vigorous expansion of online foodstuff delivery marketplace. Increase in the use of Internet and better cell phones has supported this whole transformation to make the progress of the entire market in a swift manner. Online food ordering can offer convenience and comfort to customers by allowing them to shop for food and order it online. It can also provide them with a variety of features and services that make it easier and more secure to shop for food. (Hansen 2008; Gupta 2019). Furthermore, Yeo et al. in 2017 showed the factors that influence online food purchases are extremely important to retailers. It was also found factors that determine the usefulness and easiness to use of online foodstuff ordering in Turkey were identified as perceived importance, trust in e-retailers, and innovativeness in technology (Alagoz and Hekimoglu 2012). In the present era of global businesses, the trends and patterns are becoming highly evolving and dynamic, tools used for statistics are going precise on prediction and forecasting. In the emerging scenario quantitative analysis has come to rescue ensuring precision in forecasting and prediction for businesses and marketing, particularly in buyer activities and in the buyer purchase decision making process what we also known as the consumer choice model, which is widely accepted in the business frontiers. To achieve the distinctiveness in targeting of products and services one has to get an insight over the customer buying decision processes and hence prediction plays an important role in the framework which eventually helps in generating market strategies while ensuring cost effectiveness by making precise prediction of consumer choices and preferences. There have been extensive use of tools such as discriminant analysis, regression models and widely accepted econometric models to predict and achieve correct prediction of the buyers choices but artificial neural network revolutionized the prediction capacity by bio mimicking with the help of immense data feeding and machine learning to analyze for decision making by organizations and is widely used business houses to develop market strategies (Gan et al. 2005).

2 Need of the Study

The world has been facing a serious challenge in terms of the Covid 19 virus and its variants. With the consequent waves coming it is a call of the situation that the civilians stay within their premises and maintain the norms of the pandemic to stop the chain of spread. Staying inside home won't promise the availability of daily food items and in order to do that many food aggregators have flourished in the country especially in the Southern part of Assam after the 2020 lockdown. There are several factors that attract a regular customer to avail the services of a food aggregator and these factors vary from one geographical location to another. Knowing the factors and the frequency of buying from the food aggregators based on these factors helps to build a model of the buying behavior of the customers of this region that would help the organizations to take their steps for future more accurately.

3 Literature Review

Authors	Key findings
Yeo et al. (2017)	Being user-friendly will allow customers to complete their transactions quickly. This is beneficial for both the customer and the merchant. Having a variety of promotions and discounts will also attract price-sensitive customers
Pigatto et al. (2017)	Dimension "content" was the one with the highest occurrence of turnout, followed by the aspect "functionality" and then the dimension "usability."
See-Kwong et al. (2017)	Three of the most important factors that business owners consider when it comes to choosing food delivery service is the increase in revenue, expanse in the customer reach
Kapoor and Vij (2018)	The attributes of a mobile app, such as visual design and navigation design, are critical to the conversion rate of an online food aggregator. The study revealed that visual design, navigation design, and information design are some of the factors that influence a food aggregator's conversion rate. A visually appealing interface always catches the eyes of the viewer
Das (2018)	Discovered that the following six factors have relatively high internal consistency, • Easiness to use • Effectiveness in cost • Accessibility at all times • Easiness in payment • Delivery on the doorstep • Variety and options of restaurant
Maimaiti et.al. (2018)	As the O2O meal delivery system provides a convenient dining experience, food availability and accessibility rise
Laddha (2019)	The popularity of online food ordering among millennials is due to a lack of time to prepare food, as well as variety and price. Consumer satisfaction could be improved by better understanding their expectations and giving more enticing options when purchasing meals online
Munshi (2019)	The Author opined that with emerging food joints and startups to meet the customer demands the focus on cleanability, flexibility in changeover and operator-safety will be the major issues in the coming times
Gupta (2019)	The author opines that dish name, image, specialty, and prices are some of the major factors to attract the attention of consumers on any food delivery over online service platform

(continued)

(continued)

Authors	Key findings
Chetan et al. (2019)	The study concludes that consumer satisfaction is highly related to the following in case of online food aggregator services, Namely: Convenience as time saver, Control over Technology, Information, Convenience in relation to customer intention
Thamaraiselvan et al. (2019)	The authors indicated those application interfaces, real-time information, availability of choices are among the major factors in the Indian context to attract consumers attention
Suhartanto et.al. (2019)	This research uncovers a significant conclusion regarding the relationship amongst e-service quality and quality of food, implying that service by the provider effects food quality. As a result, the authors argue that consumer loyalty is driven by food quality, E-Service quality, and perceived value
Ghosh (2020)	Quality, Customer service, Price, Delivery, and Time were discovered by the author in the study, with Quality being the most important in terms of customer satisfaction
Keeble et al. (2020)	The male subjects who responded with young age had a higher degree, had offsprings below the age of 18, or recognized with an ethnicity had a higher likelihood on utilising an meal service delivered over online order on a platform across countries, according to the poll
Senthil et al. (2020)	The study revealed that Convenience, Discounts and offers are the major factors that drive the millennials to use mobile phone apps of online food delivery aggregators
Annaraud and Berezina (2020)	Customer happiness in OFD services is influenced by food quality, control, customer service, and service fulfilment, according to this study, and customer satisfaction influences behavioural intentions. Food quality is directly linked to satisfaction, whereas control, convenience, customer service, and fulfilment as a whole are all linked to it

(continued)

(*continued*)

Authors	Key findings
Gupta and Duggal (2020)	As per the findings, consumers' attitudes and continuance intention are heavily influenced by perceived benefits. The following are indeed the contexts that are included: Benefit of convenience, The software has a user-friendly UI. Food ordering options were virtually endless. Ordering from any location is simple. Food is available all the time throughout the week, with a variety of online payment choices, as well as a value benefit with food goods that are worth the money. Better discounts, Better cashbacks and perks
Li et al. (2020)	This study has detailed a variety of FD platforms consequences that are affecting a variety of stakeholders in various ways. While attempts have been made to classify the effects as "good" or "bad," there is a case to be made that each influence should be classed separately. Even during Covid-19 period, for example, online FD had a affirmative effect in that it enabled people to buy foodstuff without moving out of their homes (i.e., an affirmative impact on customers), but it also exposed delivery employees more. The future of online restaurants is exciting, and we need to begin thinking about what's happening on and asking if things could be done better in order to ensure that the sector progresses in a healthy way that fulfils the interests of all stakeholders involved
Amaraboina and Niranjan (2020)	Numerous aspects on consumer purchasing behaviour in online food delivery platforms was taken into concern, as well as the best strategy for increasing value added. To infer management implications from the responses, descriptive analysis such as t-test and factor analysis were undertaken. In the report, the full results of the analysis are revealed
Goyal and Goyal (2021)	It was discovered that there are substantial relationships flanked by apparent buyer efficacy and trust on green brands, which influence green consumption intentions. The relationship between green brand trust and green consumption intention is partially mediated by social image. The correlations discovered between the variables have both practical and theoretical ramifications

(*continued*)

(continued)

Authors	Key findings
Spivakovskyy et al. (2021)	Practical advice for picking the most appropriate mobile marketing tools have been established based on the research findings, and these recommendations take into account the interests of both customers and firms employing marketing tools. The key selection criteria have been discovered to include enterprise internal business procedures, marketing objectives, and customer attitudes. The guidelines established in this study give firms the tools they need to deploy marketing expenditures rationally
Chauhan et al. (2021, April)	Customer dissatisfaction led to service breakdown as a result of the service provider's insufficient follow-up. Delayed delivery times were one of the factors that led to app switching. Customers were also found to be fairly eager to demand cash on delivery for food. Insecurity about website usage and meal delivery delays were the leading causes of negative emotions among users. Customers' happy emotions were fuelled by cash back offers, which made them happy and excited for their next purchase. The majority of aggregator users were identified in metro cities, with many more towns yet to be discovered. Good internet speed is a very crucial factor nowadays for customers surfing online food items
Pinto et al. (2021)	Aggregator appeal is a critical component in online food delivery services and can have a substantial impact on the buyer's propensity to return. Because of the enhanced convenience afforded by app platforms, consumers continue to favour online meal ordering
Srivastava and Srivastava (2021)	Age and educational qualification of the customers have association with the preference of online food aggregators. The research also proves a large part of the consumer base who are ordering food consider food aggregators and convenience, comfortable payment options, good delivery service, availability of Ratings and Reviews, and ample food choice are some of the reasons behind the success of their success
Niu et al. (2021)	According to the research, the web - based "food & transportation" price under two logistics solutions have contrasting associations with the charges, and the restaurant's offline foodstuff cost may grow and then decrease in the online order rate. Consequently, when a restaurant's online marketplace prospects are limited, platform logistics is recommended

Source: Collected by the authors for the study.

4 Research Gap

There have studies done in this regard in the other parts of the country but the Cachar District of Assam is yet to explore the main factors that are responsible for imparting a better impression on the customers of the region. Also, after the pandemic attacked this part of the country many food aggregators have come up in this region and considering the above reasons the study finds itself well placed.

4.1 Research Questions

1. What are the main factors playing the main role in deciding the satisfaction factors for a Food Aggregator?
2. What does the Voice of the Customer of the Cachar District of Assam say about their inclination towards buying from the food aggregators?

5 Objectives

1. To identify and indicate the factors that have a significant impact in deciding Customer Satisfaction towards Food Aggregators.
2. To predict if the customers will be inclined towards procuring the service from the Food Aggregators

6 Scope of the Study

Field of study: Factors behind Customer Satisfaction
Business demarcation: Food aggregators
Geographical demarcation: Cachar District in the Southern Part of Assam

7 Methods and Data

The methods implemented in this study and the data analysis tools and procedures runs as below (Table 1).

Table 1. Methods and data

Study type	Descriptive
Population	Cachar District of Assam
Population count	1906364 (Directorate of Census Operations Assam 2011)
Sample size	385
Sampling type	Purposive sampling

(*continued*)

Table 1. (*continued*)

Study type	Descriptive
Data type	Primary data
Demographic variants	Age, Income

Table 2. Likert's 5 pointer scale

Least important	Less important	Neutral	Important	Highly important
1	2	3	4	5

Customer feedback Likert's scale (Table 2)

Calculation of Sample Size

For calculation of the Sample Size, the parameters that were considered for the study are

Population of Cachar District: 1906364 (Directorate of Census Operations Assam 2011)

Margin of error: 5% (standard error margin)

Confidence level: 95%

$$N = NX / [(N - 1)E^2 + X]$$

$$X = Z(c/100)^2 r(100 - r)$$

$$E = Sqrt \left[\frac{(N - n)X}{n(N - 1\}} \right]$$

Here,

n - Sample size,

N - Population size

r - Fraction of responses

Z(c/100) - Critical value,

c - Confidence level

The sample size for the given population above comes out to be 385

Source- Raosoft, Inc (2004), http://www.raosoft.com/samplesize.html.

Demographic distribution of respondents (Table 3)

Table 3. Sample distribution

Serial number	Demographic Profile	Number of respondents (385)	Percentage (%)
1	Age		
	16–26	101	26.23376623
	26–36	127	32.98701299
	36–46	79	20.51948052
	46–56	67	17.4025974
	56 and above	11	2.857142857
2	Income		
	0–20000	173	44.93506494
	20000–40000	103	26.75324675
	40000–60000	67	17.4025974
	60000–80000	27	7.012987013
	80000 and above	15	3.896103896

One of the most used internal consistency testings for reliability is the Cronbach Alpha Coefficient especially when the Likert's scaling system is implemented. Having a .70 or more than that value as a Reliability coefficient is considered good the study under consideration (Table 4).

Table 4. Reliability analysis

Reliability statistics	
Cronbach's Alpha	N of items
.850	11

8 Analysis and Findings

The antecedents that play a major role in deciding Customer Satisfaction towards Food Aggregators can be listed as below (Table 5).

Table 5. Factors, and their references.

Factors	Reference/Authors
Hygiene	(Jaafar et al. 2011)
Delivery time	(Hansen 2008; Gupta 2019)
Payment option	(Hansen 2008; Gupta 2019)
Service support/delivery tracking	(Hansen 2008; Gupta 2019)
Food outlets available	(Lan et al. 2016), (Vinaik et al. 2019)
Appealing food images	(Ballantine 2005)
Privacy and security	(Jones and Vijayasarathy 1998) (Mukherjee and Nath 2007)
Delivery person etiquette	(Chandrasekhar et al. 2019)
Value for price	(Nagle et al. 2010, Darke et al. 1995)
Responsiveness	(Hu et al. 2009)
Application interface	(Hansen 2008; Gupta 2019)

The respondents/customers were forwarded a structured questionnaire and their frequency of buying was noted based on their demographic factors. 80% of the response was fed to the system to build a process of understanding their buying behavior based on their responses and the rest 20% was then fed to the system to find out the accuracy of the study. A step-by-step representation of the process is shown below (Fig. 1).

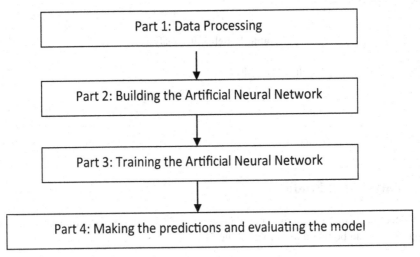

Fig. 1. Step-by-step representation of the process

Part 1: Data Processing
The data collected is fed to the system
   Importing the dataset:

```
dataset =pd.read_excel('Data_Set.xlsx', 'Sheet1')
X =dataset.iloc[:, :-1].values
y =dataset.iloc[:, -1].values
```

Splitting the dataset into the Training set and Test set. The training set takes 80% of the data and the testing set takes 20% of the data to analyze the inputs and outputs.

```
fromsklearn.model_selectionimporttrain_test_split
```

```
X_train,X_test,y_train,y_test=
train_test_split(X,y,test_size= 0.2,random_state= 0).
```
Feature Scaling
It is used to standardize the data in order to feed the data set into the machine learning algorithm

```
fromsklearn.preprocessingimportStandardScaler
sc=StandardScaler()
X_train=sc.fit_transform(X_train)
X_test=sc.transform(X_test)
```

Part 2: Building the Artificial Neural Network
A neural network is a collection of interrelated nodes also addressed as neurons structured into a multi-layer structural design, capable of processing information and mimic the biological neural networks. Neural Networks are estimated functions that are usually unknown and can only be achieved with considerable data feeding as inputs. ANN is adaptive and to a large extent capable of machine learning and recognitions of patterns by assessing the behavior of the data fed, and imperatively with adequate training process (Bogatinov et al. 2016). After a network structure is determined, it should be trained. The initial phase of the weights are assigned in the form of numbers subsequently the weights gets adjusted as per the training so as to ensure minimization of error within the predicted and actual output.

Deliana and Rum (2017) indicated that Neural network analysis is a very effective in understanding and to recognize the preferences of the consumers, in the present study the authors made an attempt understand the patterns and behavior of the buying choices with while predicting for predicting their future choices. Ćirić and Predić (2021) identified that Long Short term memory that are recurrent neural networks come as very convenient in predicting in case of the understanding the trends and prediction of future purchases in case of online stores. The results of such studies can be well utilized by business houses to device market strategies. In case of a neural network the output is subjected to an activation function, which determines whether or not this neuron is involved in the final decision, Relu is an activation method and the Sigmoid function value lies in between 0 to 1.

Initializing the ANN

```
ann=tf.keras.models.Sequential()
```

Adding the input layer and the first hidden layer

```
ann.add(tf.keras.layers.Dense(units=6,activation='relu'))
```

Adding the second hidden layer

```
ann.add(tf.keras.layers.Dense(units=6,activation='relu'))
```

Adding the output layer

```
ann.add(tf.keras.layers.Dense(units=1,activation='sigmoid'))
```

Part 3 - Training the ANN

Adam Optimizer takes the best parts of the two viz. Momentum and Root Mean Square propagation and improves on them to produce a more efficient gradient design. Binary Cross Entropy compares Each of the projected probabilities to the actual class output, which can be either 0 or 1. The score is then calculated, penalizing the probabilities depending on their deviation from the predicted value. This refers to how close or far the value is to the actual value. The Accuracy matrix is simplest way to calculate the accuracy of any classification machine learning model is to divide the total number of points in the test data by the number of correctly categorized points in the test data. The Confusion Matrix is a matrix that represents this accuracy.

Compiling the ANN

```
ann.compile(optimizer='adam',loss='binary_crossentropy',
metrics=['accuracy'])
```

Training the ANN on the Training set

```
ann.fit(X_train,y_train,batch_size=32,epochs=100)
```

Part 4 - Making the predictions and evaluating the model

The final step after the training part is used to see the accuracy score and the output of the testing. Predicting the Test set results

```
y_pred=ann.predict(X_test)
y_pred=(y_pred>0.5)
print(np.concatenate((y_pred.reshape(len(y_pred),1),
y_test.reshape(len(y_test),1)),1))
```

Making the Confusion Matrix

```
fromsklearn.metricsimportconfusion_matrix,accuracy_score
cm=confusion_matrix(y_test,y_pred)
print(cm)
accuracy_score(y_test,y_pred)
[[6 2]
[5 2]]
0.5333333333333333
```

Prediction on a New Dataset

```
pred_dataset=pd.read_excel('Data_Set.xlsx','Sheet2')
pred_dataset=sc.transform(pred_dataset)
y_pred=ann.predict(pred_dataset)
y_pred=(y_pred>0.5)
print(y_pred)
A sample output of prediction:
print(ann.predict(sc.transform([[3,2,4,4,4,4,5,3,2,4,
2,2,4]]))>0.5)[[False]]
```

That signifies the customer won't be interested in procuring the services in the future.

Although the output information showed relatively lower accuracy at the initial phase but accordingly with larger data feeding the accuracy level improved. It was observed that data of the customer making smaller purchases had significant impact on the output. Suchacka, G., and Stemplewski, S. (2017) in their study on Application of neural network to predict purchases in online store used only eleven samples to propose a neural network which turned out to be very promising as the emphasis was on accuracy of learning aspect by the model. However, it was also suggested by the authors that to develop precision on the prediction further experiments with larger dataset.

9 Conclusion

The study concentrated upon mainly the factors that played a role of satisfaction over the Age and Income levels of the people of Cachar District of Assam. It retrieved information from the locals of this region using a structured questionnaire and depending on their feedback it tried to find out whether in the future the potential customers would be interested in procuring the services provided by them. It can be considered as a model which would help any organization to know about the inclinations of the customers towards buying their product based on the demographic factors and the factors affecting their service in their day-to-day operations.

10 Limitations of the Study and Future Scope

Due to financial constraints, the study has found itself within the Geographical Proximity of only the Cachar District of the Southern Part of Assam. It is limited with factors found from the Literature Review and the responses from the respondents hailing specifically from this valley. were contacted strictly on an online basis and face to face communication was not preferred. The ongoing pandemic has resulted some limitations in various aspects of the study as the respondents. The more responses that will be fed in to system the better output it is expected to be received, so with the passage of time the model will become more robust with more inputs.

References

Alagoz, S.M., Hekimoglu, H.: A study on TAM: analysis of customer attitudes in online food ordering system. Proc. Soc. Behav. Sci. **62**, 1138–1143 (2012)

Amaraboina, S., Niranjan, S.K.: Study of consumer behavior towards product bundling in online food delivery and its impact on stakeholders (2020)

Annaraud, K., Berezina, K.: Predicting satisfaction and intentions to use online food delivery: what really makes a difference? J. Foodserv. Bus. Res. **23**(4), 305–323 (2020)

Ballantine, P.W.: Effects of interactivity and product information on consumer satisfaction in an online retail setting. Int. J. Retail Distrib. Manag. (2005)

Bogatinov, D.S., Bogdanoski, M., Angelevski, S.: AI-based cyber defense for more secure cyberspace. In: Handbook of Research on Civil Society and National Security in the Era of Cyber Warfare, pp. 220–237. IGI Global (2016)

Chauhan, S., Upadhyay, Y., Singh, S.K.: Innovative service recovery of customers by food aggregators using sentiment analysis. In: IOP Conference Series: Materials Science and Engineering, vol. 1116, no. 1, p. 012199. IOP Publishing, April 2021

Chetan Panse, D.S.R., Sharma, A., Dorji, N.: Understanding consumer behaviour towards utilization of online food delivery platforms. J. Theoret. Appl. Inf. Technol. **97**(16) (2019)

Ćirić, M., Predić, B.: Pseudo-multivariate LSTM neural network approach for purchase day prediction in B2b. Facta Universitatis Ser.: Autom. Control Robot. **19**(3), 151–162 (2021)

Das, J.: Consumer perception towards "online food ordering and delivery services": an empirical study. J. Manag. (JOM) **5**(5), 155–163 (2018)

Deliana, Y., Rum, I.A.: Understanding consumer loyalty using neural network. Polish J. Manag. Stud. **16** (2017)

Directorate of Census Operations Assam: District Census Handbook. Government of India, January 2011. Https://Censusindia.Gov.In/2011census/Dchb/1817_Part_B_Dchb_Cachar.Pdf

Gan, C., Limsombunchao, V., Clemes, M.D., Weng, Y.Y.: Consumer choice prediction: Artificial neural networks versus logistic models (2005)

Ghosh, D.: Customer satisfaction towards fast food through online food delivery (OFD) services: an exploratory study. Int. J. Manag. (IJM) **11**(10) (2020)

Goyal, M., Goyal, R.K.: Confirming antecedents of green consumption intention: a sustainable model for food aggregators. IETE J. Res. 1–12 (2021)

Gupta, M.: A study on impact of online food delivery app on restaurant business special reference to Zomato and Swiggy. Int. J. Res. Anal. Rev. **6**(1), 889–893 (2019)

Gupta, V., Duggal, S.: How the consumer's attitude and behavioural intentions are influenced: a case of online food delivery applications in India. Int. J. Cult. Tour. Hosp. Res. (2020)

Hansen, T.: Consumer values, the theory of planned behaviour and online grocery shopping. Int. J. Consum. Stud. **32**(2), 128–137 (2008)

Jones, J.M., Vijayasarathy, L.R.: Internet consumer catalog shopping: findings from an exploratory study and directions for future research. Internet Res. (1998)

Kapoor, A.P., Vij, M.: Technology at the dinner table: ordering food online through mobile apps. J. Retail. Consum. Serv. **43**, 342–351 (2018)

Keeble, M., et al.: Use of online food delivery services to order food prepared away-from-home and associated socio-demographic characteristics: a cross-sectional, multi-country analysis. Int. J. Environ. Res. Public Health **17**(14), 5190 (2020)

Laddha, D.: Impact of consumer demographics on usage of online food services. IUJ J. Manag. (2019)

Li, C., Mirosa, M., Bremer, P.: Review of online food delivery platforms and their impacts on sustainability. Sustainability **12**(14), 5528 (2020)

Maimaiti, M., Zhao, X., Jia, M., Ru, Y., Zhu, S.: How we eat determines what we become: opportunities and challenges brought by food delivery industry in a changing world in China. Eur. J. Clin. Nutr. **72**(9), 1282–1286 (2018)

Mukherjee, A., Nath, P.: Role of electronic trust in online retailing: a re-examination of the commitment-trust theory. Eur. J. Mark. (2007)

Munshi, A.: Assessment of competitiveness of food-tech start-ups in India. Indian J. Public Adm. **65**(1), 201–224 (2019)

Niu, B., Li, Q., Mu, Z., Chen, L., Ji, P.: Platform logistics or self-logistics? Restaurants' cooperation with online food-delivery platform considering profitability and sustainability. Int. J. Prod. Econ. **234**, 108064 (2021)

Pigatto, G., Machado, J.G.D.C.F., dos Santos Negreti, A., Machado, L.M.: Have you chosen your request? Analysis of online food delivery companies in Brazil. Br. Food J. (2017)

Pinto, P., Hawaldar, I.T., Pinto, S.: Antecedents of behavioral intention to use online food delivery services: an empirical investigation (2021)

See-Kwong, G., Soo-Ryue, N. G., Shiun-Yi, W., Lily, C.: Outsourcing to online food delivery services: perspective of F&B business owners. J. Internet Bank. Commer. **22**(2) (2017)

Senthil, M., Gayathri, N., Chandrasekar, K.S.: Changing paradigms of Indian foodtech landscape-impact of online food delivery aggregators. Int. J. Food Syst. Dyn. **11**(2), 139–152 (2020)

Spivakovskyy, S., Spivakovska, T., Bazherina, K.: Mobile marketing tools in the market of restaurant food delivery services in Ukraine. Transnatl. Mark. J. **9**(1), 129–149 (2021)

Srivastava, M.K., Srivastava, M.A.K.: Online Food Delivery: Study with Special Reference to Food Aggregators

Suchacka, G., Stemplewski, S.: Application of neural network to predict purchases in online store. In: Wilimowska, Z., Borzemski, L., Grzech, A., Świątek, J. (eds.) Information Systems Architecture and Technology: Proceedings of 37th International Conference on Information Systems Architecture and Technology—ISAT 2016—Part IV. AISC, vol. 524, pp. 221–231. Springer, Cham (2017). https://doi.org/10.1007/978-3-319-46592-0_19

Suhartanto, D., Helmi Ali, M., Tan, K.H., Sjahroeddin, F., Kusdibyo, L.: Loyalty toward online food delivery service: the role of e-service quality and food quality. J. Foodserv. Bus. Res. **22**(1), 81–97 (2019)

Thamaraiselvan, N., Jayadevan, G.R., Chandrasekar, K.S.: Digital food delivery apps revolutionizing food products marketing in India. Int. J. Recent Technol. Eng. **8**, 662–665 (2019)

Yeo, V.C.S., Goh, S.K., Rezaei, S.: Consumer experiences, attitude and behavioral intention toward online food delivery (OFD) services. J. Retail. Consum. Serv. **35**, 150–162 (2017)

Personalized Healthcare Chatbot: Dataset and Prototype System

Prateek Mishra, Pankaj Dadure, K. V. N. Pranav, Medisetti SriHarsha, Devi Prasad Upadhyay, Nirmita Biswas, and Partha Pakray[✉]

National Institute of Technology Silchar, Assam, India
justwriteprateek@gmail.com, krdadure@gmail.com, kvnp179@gmail.com, medisettisriharsha1729@gmail.com, devip17072000@gmail.com, nirmita_ug@cse.nits.ac.in, parthapakray@gmail.com

Abstract. Intelligent chatbot systems are popular applications in the fields of robotic and natural language processing. Nowadays, the strain on medical advisors encourages the use of healthcare chatbots to provide meditations and suggestions. In this paper, we have presented a dataset and a healthcare chatbot developed on the RASA framework that uses the NLP methods for disease detection and provides medical advice. The designed dataset has been verified and refined with the help of medical experts. The proficiency of the designed healthcare chatbot has been tested on the collected data using RASA test methods and validation. The model scored an F1-score of 77.3% and accuracy of 78.7%. Moreover, human evaluation achieves an accuracy of 56.50%. The dataset is publicly available at https://github.com/Medic-Bot-India/rasaModel.

Keywords: Chatbot · Intelligent chatbot system · RASA framework · Transformer Embedding Dialogue

1 Introduction

The rise of big data in the healthcare industry is setting the stage for natural language processing (NLP) and other artificial intelligence (AI) tools to improve the delivery of care [6]. In the medical field, AI-powered chatbots can be used to evaluate patients and direct them to the right help [7]. When people are attempting to figure out what's triggering their symptoms, chatbots are seen to be a more trustworthy and efficient alternative to web searches. Chatbots, according to healthcare specialists, could assist people who are unsure where to seek treatment. Many patients are unsure when their symptoms necessitate a trip to the doctor and when they can just contact their doctors via telemedicine [3]. Clinical teams can benefit from AI chatbots by reducing their everyday workloads. After analyzing the patient data, bots can propose an online talk with a physician rather than a visit to their actual office. In general, chatbot technology deployed in medical settings promises to relieve medical practitioners' workload. This is especially true in the current circumstance, where the spread of COVID-19 is putting a tremendous

S. Mukhopadhyay et al. (Eds.): CICBA 2022, CCIS 1579, pp. 378–388, 2022.
https://doi.org/10.1007/978-3-031-10766-5_30

strain on healthcare providers [16]. Medical centers might substantially reduce the strain on their systems with the help of this technology. Furthermore, the healthcare chatbots also make more consistent and accurate diagnoses and also lead to serving a more number of patients in less time.

Chatbots can also help with specific problems. Recently Northwell Health[1] deployed a chatbot to reduce the amount of no-shows for diagnostic testing, which are crucial for diagnosing colorectal cancer. Patients are encouraged by the personalized chatbot, which addresses their fears or misunderstandings regarding the treatment and provides information in a responsive and conversational manner. Researchers can track patient satisfaction, cancellations, no-shows, and successfully completed exams using the app. User privacy is one of the major challenges with AI chatbots in healthcare. Users of such software solutions may be wary of disclosing personal information to bots. Business owners that construct healthcare platforms work hard to ensure that data security procedures are in place to keep their platforms safe from cyber-attacks [13]. User privacy is essential when it comes to any type of AI deployment, and sharing information about one's medical issues with a chatbot appears to be less trustworthy than sharing the same information with a human doctor.

In this paper, we have contributed a dataset and an healthcare chatbot developed on the RASA framework that uses the NLP methods for diagnosis and provides medical advice. The designed dataset has been verified and refined with the help of a medical expert. Moreover, the proficiency of the designed healthcare chatbot has been tested on the collected data, and it achieved the remarkable human evaluated accuracy. The paper is structured as follows: Sect. 2 describe the background knowledge of the intelligent chatbot system. Section 3 gives a detailed account of the dataset. Section 4 provides detailed description about the system architecture. Section 5 describes the experimental setup and results. Section 6 concludes with summary and directions of further research and developments.

2   Background

Natural and intuitive interaction system is a primary research field of the human-computer interaction domain. The interactive system can interact with users using natural language are being researched vigorously at present. In the recent times, healthcare domain has become the more popular and commercially successful sector for AI-NLP based applications such as healthcare chatbot. In this pandemic situation, the healthcare chatbot play an important role. According to a report from Accenture[2], over 40% of healthcare executives consider AI the technology and have the greatest impact on their organizations within the next three years. Healthcare providers are already using various types of artificial

---

[1] https://www.healthcareitnews.com/news/northwell-health-deploys-chatbot-reduce-colonoscopy-no-shows.

[2] https://www.accenture.com/.

intelligence [15], such as predictive analytics or machine learning to achieved their designed objective.

The mental health analysis chatbot [8] has provided psychiatric advice through dialogue. This bot utilized various methods to recognize the user's emotions: multi-modal based emotion awareness from the conversation, tone, facial expression, intelligent correspondence such as psychiatric cases-based reasoning, long-term monitoring, and ethical judgment. This technique allows to monitor the sensitive emotional changes of the users. The counseling of employee's mental health at working place has become more important in recent years. A self-mental chatbot health instructor [4] which usually uses a mobile device as a communication platform. In this investigation, the LINE, popularly used in Japan, and help to develop the chatbot-based self-care application. This research aims to create an autonomous psychiatric device that can be used by a large number of employees with different degrees of self-care motivation. The Disha [11] is a machine learning based language dependant chatbot which communicate in Bangla and help the users to diagnose and confers about the diseases based on the symptoms given by users, provides the daily health recommendation, and inform about the health infection. The Disha system has been analysed with six different supervised machine learning techniques [5] (Decision Tree, Random Forest, Multinomial NB, SVM, AdaBoost, and kNN) where SVM shows the best results.

A recognizable health assistant, 'Aapka Chikitsak' [1] includes a multi-language Speech Software for primary education and guidance to patients with chronic conditions and women in need of precautions. It transforms the user speech into text that was processed and understood with the help of natural language processing and output that was then transformed into speech and returned to the user. This chatbot deals with women's health care, particularly the most common illnesses in rural India. It provides a physician with preventive steps, home remedies, medical tips, symptoms, and dietary recommendations based on location. It was a beneficial application and provided an efficient and immediate solution. The Google machine learning developed the medical consulting system called "MedBot" [12] in which the conversational knowledge includes 16 symptoms. MedBot suggested in some ways that the user must meet the doctor in certain harmless symptoms. The decision tree based healthcare chatbot 'K-Bot' [10] trained on a dataset that contains the various symptoms and their respective prognosis. The K-bot has shown that simple classification approach have ability to bifurcate the symptoms by considering them as a feature and leads to specific decision. However, this tree based approach is a kind of rule based classification based on the features and have the frailty in some cases. The text-based healthcare chatbot [2] is part of the open source behavioral intervention platform (Mobile Coach) which provides a modular architecture and rule engine for the design of fully-automated digital health interventions.

3   Dataset Collection and Annotation

3.1   Sources

We have used Princeton University's website[3] for acquiring credible data on symptoms of diseases. In addition to this, to map the diseases with their prescribed medicine, we have used Drugs.com website[4]. To understand the symptoms of patients and the difference between diseases with common symptoms, we have consulted with medical experts to gain an internal insight into commonly occurring symptoms like stomach pain or abdominal pain. At the time of dataset creation, the experts briefed some important conflicts which mostly occurred in the symptoms of the diseases such as cold and cough, fever etc. This expert consultation is used to define intents carefully so that the designed chatbot can identify intents with greater probability and correctness.

3.2   Corpus Creation

Intents. The corpus data involves intents about the diseases and their corresponding responses which mainly includes symptoms of the disease, symptoms-related queries, questions related to patients' information. Many diseases have common symptoms which have been carefully taken care of with help of healthcare experts [17]. The symptoms of each disease are represented as an intent that can be used by the designed chatbot to identify the diseases. The designed dataset contains symptoms of the following diseases: Headache, Cough, Cold, Nasal blockage, Fever, Conjunctivitis, Gerd, Diabetes, Allergy rhinitis, Fungal infection, Chickenpox, Typhoid, Psoriasis, Obesity, Insomnia, Psychosis, Depression, Pneumonia, Bronchial asthma, Coronavirus, Low blood pressure, High blood pressure, Ringworm, Toothache, Migraine, Arthritis, Stomach Pain, Period cramps, Vitamin-D deficiency/rickets, Anaemia, Weakness, Eye problem, Ear pain, Night blindness, Mild heart disease/heart attack. Moreover, different combinations of user sentences have been taken into the consideration to describe the symptoms and their compilation. The sample of the designed training data with different sentence possibilities and defined intent is given below:

Responses. Responses are messages that our model sends to the user. The corpus for responses was created using data from drugs.com and consulting health care professionals. The dataset contains medication and advice for all diseases. Our dataset includes defined responses for every identified intent.

Stories. Stories are the representation of dialogue flow between the user and the model. These stories are a type of training data used to train the assistant's dialogue management model. In our dataset stories consists of intents (data for identifying diseases) and actions (response for the symptoms identified). Based on the

---

[3] https://uhs.princeton.edu/health-resources.
[4] https://drugs.com/.

Intent	Possible user sentences
Headache	– I am having headache
	– My head is spinning
	– I am having constant pain in head
	– Both side of my head is hammering
	– Unbearable pain in forehead
	– Constant dull ache on both sides of head
	– I got severe head pain

intents and entities from our dataset the model would learn to predict the next action.

4   System Architecture

4.1   RASA NLU

The two primary components of the Rasa Open Source architecture are natural language understanding (NLU) and dialogue management [9]. The prime task of NLU is to handle the intent classification, entity extraction, and response retrieval. Basically, it processes user responses which is generated by using the trained pipeline. On the other side, the dialogue management component decides the next action in a conversation based on the context.

4.2   NLU Pipeline

See Fig. 1.

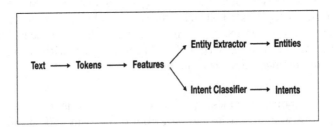

Fig. 1. NLU pipeline

The NLU pipeline[5] defines the processing steps that convert unstructured user messages into intents and entities. The pictorial representation of the NLU pipeline is shown in Fig. 2. The key purpose of a pipeline is to streamline the process in data analysis. The following points describe each components in the pipelines used to train the model.

---

[5] https://rasa.com/docs/rasa/tuning-your-model/.

WhitespaceTokenizer: This tokenizer uses the white-spaces as a separator to convert the raw text data into the tokens. It splits text and creates a token for every white-space separated word sequence.

RegexFeaturizer: It provides features for entity extraction and intent classification by creating vector representation of users message using regular expression. During training the RegexFeaturizer creates a list of regular expressions defined in the training data format. For each regex, a feature will be set marking whether this expression was found in the user message or not.

LexicalSyntacticFeaturizer: It's used to create lexical and syntactic features of a user message to aid entity extraction.

CountVectorsFeaturizer: It creates the features for intent classification and response selection by creating bag-of-words representation of user messages, intents, and responses based on the open source scikit-learn library.

DIETClassifier: This is the Dual Intent Entity Transformer (DIET) used for intent classification and entity extraction, and to provide entities, intent ranking as output.

EntitySynonymMapper: This is used to mapped the synonymous entity values of the disease symptoms. For example, pain in head or headache considered as a same entity.

ResponseSelector: Response Selector component can be used to build a response retrieval model to directly predict a bot response from a set of candidate responses. The prediction of this model is used by the dialogue manager to utter the predicted responses. It embeds user inputs and response labels into the same space and follows the exact same neural network architecture and optimization as the DIETClassifier.

FallbackClassifier: This is used to classify a user message with the intent nlu_fallback in case the previous intent classifier not able to classify an intent. Fallback actions are used to ensure low confidence messages should be handled gracefully.

4.3   Policies

The designed chatbot uses policies to decide which action needs to be performed at each step in a conversation. The designed chatbot has used the following policies for dialogue flow between the user and the bot:

Memoization Policy: The memoization policy remembers the stories of the training data. It matches the current conversation stories in stories.yml file. If so, it will predict the next action from the matching stories of training data with a confidence of 1.0. If no matching conversation is found, the policy predicts None with confidence 0.0[6].

TED Policy: The Transformer Embedding Dialogue (TED) Policy is a multi-task architecture for next action prediction and entity recognition. The architecture consists of several transformer encoders which are shared for both

---

[6] https://rasa.com/docs/rasa/policies#memoization-policy.

tasks. A sequence of entity labels is predicted through a Conditional Random Field (CRF) tagging layer on top of the user sequence transformer encoder output corresponding to the input sequence of tokens. For the next action prediction the dialogue transformer encoder output and system action labels are embedded into a single semantic vector space[7].

4.4 Actions

After each user message, RASA Core will predict an action that the assistant should perform next. An action[8] can be a simple response, i.e. sending a message to the user, or it can be a custom function to execute. When an action is executed, it is passed a tracker instance, and so can make use of any relevant information collected over the history of the dialogue: slots, previous responses, and the results of previous actions.

5 Designed Prototype

We have designed the front-end interface for our designed chatbot using PHP and bootstrap. The connection between the front-end and the AI model is established using javascript and socket.io. Figure 2 shows the chatbot interface of our prototype and a snippet of interaction between a user and chatbot.

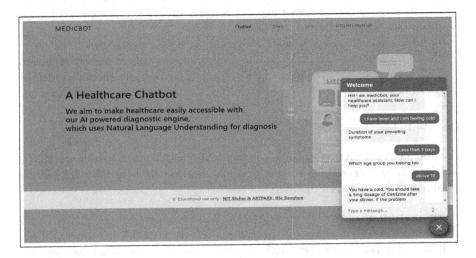

Fig. 2. Medicbot interface

---

[7] https://rasa.com/docs/rasa/policies#ted-policy.
[8] https://rasa.com/docs/rasa/actions.

6   Results

Data validation was carried out to ensure that no errors or major inconsistencies have occurred in our domain, NLU data, or story data. If data validation fails, model training can also fail or result in poor performance. In addition, we also tested the natural language understanding model separately. Whenever the designed chatbot may receive messages that were not seen in the training data, fallback actions are used, so these low-confidence messages are handled gracefully.

6.1   Analysis of Intent Recognition

RASA test commands were used to evaluate the model in test data. We evaluated the intent classification by F1-score, accuracy and precision using cross-validation [14]. The F1 score is a measure of model's accuracy over the dataset used. It is generally the harmonic mean of the model's precision and recall/sensitivity. It is significantly useful when considering the uneven class distribution in the classification model compared to the measured accuracy, which only considers the correctly categorized results. Evaluation results of this metrices f1 score, accuracy, and precision are presented in Table 1.

Table 1. Values of evaluation results

Metric	Train score	Test score
F1 score	0.982	0.773
Accuracy	0.982	0.787
Precision	0.983	0.798

6.2   Human Evaluation

To evaluate the performance of our proposed healthcare assistant, we have conducted the manual evaluation on a large scale of questionnaires. Each of the defined disease in the corpus have been tested using the 4–5 queries with different phrasing style and keywords. Each evaluator has asked the question and based on that the healthcare assistant suggests the medicines and precautions. Moreover, the obtained bot response has been ranked on the scale of 1, 2, and 3, where 1 indicate that the bot response is out of domain and invalid, 2 indicate that the bot response is partially satisfying the evaluator question and 3 indicate that the bot response is completely satisfying the evaluator question. Maximum possible marks were calculated by 3 * total no. of questions which in our case results to 3 * 187 = 561. And for the net score gained by the session was summation of all the scores got which in our case resulted in 317. Thus we get accuracy = 317/561 * 100 = 56.50%. Therefore, the final accuracy of our health assistant is = 56.50%.

- As concerned to information expressed in natural language, we infer that the proposed model can also account for the order of the keywords/words, apart from its ability to understand the long-term alignment of the words.
- At the time of corpus generation, we have found that some of the diseases have the same symptoms, which creates the obstacle to predicting medicine and medication for patients. To resolve this, we have interacted with the medical expert to achieve state-of-the-art performance.
- Diseases having similar symptoms have been differentiated using additional symptoms received from the patient. The contextual analysis of Rasa comes in handy in these cases.
- The designed chatbot accounts for the patients age and other essential factors to differentiate the medication for adults and children.
- After deployment, the conversations with the patients stored into the database that has been further used to train the model, which increases the training data and the accuracy of our chatbot.
- To test the proficiency of the designed chatbot, human evaluation has been performed, which reduces the risk of machine error which may remain after testing and validation of the model.
- Fallback actions ensure the system is capable of handling out-of-scope queries that chatbots often encounter.
- A dialogue flow between chatbot and a patient is represented in Table 2, where the chatbot assists the patient with medication.

Table 2. Dialogue flow representation

Patient	Bot
Hii	
	Hii! I am medicbot, your healthcare assistant. How can I help you?
I have circular rashes on my skin and I am feeling itchy	
	Duration of your prevailing symptoms
Less than 3 days	
	Which age range you fall into?
Above 18	
	You have ringworm. You should apply lotrimin ointment on the infected area, do visit a doctor
	Wash the infected area regularly. Don't use wet clothes
	Is there anything else I can help you with?
No	
	Have a good day

7 Conclusion

The primary aim of this work is the creation of a healthcare dataset that covers almost 35 diseases. In addition to this, we have implemented the healthcare chatbot, which relies on the RASA framework. The designed chatbot detects the disease based on the symptoms, test stories, and policies of the dialogue flow, and based on that, it suggests the medication and advice for further prevention. Moreover, human evaluation has also been carried out to find out the accuracy of chatbots in real-world scenarios. In the future, this system will be expanded with a dataset of more diseases and entity extraction for more complicated sentences and entities.

Acknowledgement. We would like to thank the Department of Computer Science and Engineering and the Center for Natural Language Processing (CNLP) at the National Institute of Technology Silchar for providing the requisite support and infrastructure to execute this work. The work presented here falls under the Student Innovation Grant Program of ARTPARK, a joint initiative of IISc Bangalore and AIfoundry, seed-funded by the Department of Science and Technology (DST) and the Government of Karnataka.

References

1. Bharti, U., Bajaj, D., Batra, H., Lalit, S., Lalit, S., Gangwani, A.: Medbot: conversational artificial intelligence powered chatbot for delivering tele-health after Covid-19. In: 2020 5th International Conference on Communication and Electronics Systems (ICCES), pp. 870–875. IEEE (2020)
2. Haug, S., Paz Castro, R., Kowatsch, T., Filler, A., Dey, M., Schaub, M.P.: Efficacy of a web-and text messaging-based intervention to reduce problem drinking in adolescents: results of a cluster-randomized controlled trial. J. Consult. Clin. Psychol. **85**(2), 147 (2017)
3. Hjelm, N.: Benefits and drawbacks of telemedicine. J. Telemed. Telecare **11**(2), 60–70 (2005)
4. Kamita, T., Ito, T., Matsumoto, A., Munakata, T., Inoue, T.: A chatbot system for mental healthcare based on sat counseling method. Mob. Inf. Syst. **2019**, 1–11 (2019)
5. Kotsiantis, S.B., Zaharakis, I., Pintelas, P., et al.: Supervised machine learning: a review of classification techniques. Emerg. Artif. Intell. Appl. Comput. Eng. **160**(1), 3–24 (2007)
6. Kumar, S., Singh, M.: Big data analytics for healthcare industry: impact, applications, and tools. Big Data Min. Anal. **2**(1), 48–57 (2018)
7. Nadarzynski, T., Miles, O., Cowie, A., Ridge, D.: Acceptability of artificial intelligence (AI)-led chatbot services in healthcare: a mixed-methods study. Digit. Health **5**, 2055207619871808 (2019)
8. Oh, K.J., Lee, D., Ko, B., Choi, H.J.: A chatbot for psychiatric counseling in mental healthcare service based on emotional dialogue analysis and sentence generation. In: 2017 18th IEEE International Conference on Mobile Data Management (MDM), pp. 371–375. IEEE (2017)
9. Ong, Y.F., Madhavi, M., Chan, K.: OpenNLU: open-source web-interface NLU toolkit for development of conversational agent. In: 2020 Asia-Pacific Signal and

Information Processing Association Annual Summit and Conference (APSIPA ASC), pp. 381–385. IEEE (2020)

10. Pradhan, R., Shukla, J., Bansal, M.: 'k-Bot' knowledge enabled personalized healthcare chatbot. IOP Conf. Ser. Mater. Sci. Eng. **1116**, 012185 (2021)

11. Rahman, M.M., Amin, R., Liton, M.N.K., Hossain, N.: Disha: an implementation of machine learning based Bangla healthcare chatbot. In: 2019 22nd International Conference on Computer and Information Technology (ICCIT), pp. 1–6. IEEE (2019)

12. Rosruen, N., Samanchuen, T.: Chatbot utilization for medical consultant system. In: 2018 3rd Technology Innovation Management and Engineering Science International Conference (TIMES-iCON), pp. 1–5. IEEE (2018)

13. Verma, A., Chandra, P., Joshi, A.: AI chatbots, it's feasibility and reliability in modern world. Int. Res. J. Eng. Technol. (IRJET) **08**(7), 735–739 (2021)

14. Yacouby, R., Axman, D.: Probabilistic extension of precision, recall, and f1 score for more thorough evaluation of classification models. In: Proceedings of the First Workshop on Evaluation and Comparison of NLP Systems, pp. 79–91 (2020)

15. Yu, K.H., Beam, A.L., Kohane, I.S.: Artificial intelligence in healthcare. Nat. Biomed. Eng. **2**(10), 719–731 (2018)

16. Yuki, K., Fujiogi, M., Koutsogiannaki, S.: Covid-19 pathophysiology: a review. Clin. Immunol. **215**, 108427 (2020)

17. Zhou, X., Menche, J., Barabási, A.L., Sharma, A.: Human symptoms-disease network. Nature Commun. **5**(1), 1–10 (2014)

Telegram Bot for Emotion Recognition Using Acoustic Cues and Prosody

Ishita Nag[1]([✉]) [ID], Salman Azeez Syed[2] [ID], Shreya Basu[1] [ID], Suvra Shaw[3] [ID], and Barnali Gupta Banik[4] [ID]

[1] Department of Computer Science and Engineering, Institute of Engineering and Management, Kolkata, India
ishitanag04@gmail.com
[2] Department of Information Technology, Netaji Subhas University of Technology, New Delhi, India
[3] Department of Computer Science and Engineering, University of Engineering and Management, Kolkata, India
[4] C. R. Rao Advanced Institute of Mathematics, Statistics and Computer Science (AIMSCS), University of Hyderabad Campus, Hyderabad, Telangana 500 046, India

Abstract. In recent times, voice emotional recognition has been established as a significant field in Human Computer Interaction (HCI). Human emotions are intrinsically expressed by linguistic (verbal content) information and paralinguistic information such as tone, emotional state, expressions and gestures which form the relevant basis for emotional analysis. Accounting the user's affective state in HCI systems is essential to detect subtle user behaviour changes through which the computer can initiate interactions instead of simply responding to user commands. This paper aims to tackle existing problems in speech emotion recognition (SER) by taking into account the acoustic cues and prosodic parameters to detect user emotion. Here, the work will be mainly on the Ryerson Audio-Visual Database (RAVDESS) to extract Mel Frequency Cepstral Coefficients (MFCC) from signals to recognise emotion. The librosa library will be used for processing and extracting audio files before testing and classification is carried out using 4 different classifiers for a comparative study. This SER model is then integrated into a Telegram Bot to develop an intuitive, user-friendly interface as an application for psychological therapy.

Keywords: Speech Emotion Recognition (SER) · Multi-Level Perceptron (MLP) · Telegram bot

1 Introduction

1.1 Motivation

The introduction of the first modern computer system with a graphical user interface (GUI) in 1964 by Douglas Engelbert made the computer more accessible to the general public since it moved away from complex binary codes for operation, with this being

S. Mukhopadhyay et al. (Eds.): CICBA 2022, CCIS 1579, pp. 389–402, 2022.
https://doi.org/10.1007/978-3-031-10766-5_31

the first advancement towards human computer interaction (HCI). HCI later went on to become a significant research field in the 1980s. In HCI, the aim to improve the quality of communication between humans and computers is made much simpler and naturalistic through this GUI. Since then, there has been a paradigm shift towards multi-modal approaches where even voice interfaces are clubbed with GUI to develop adaptive, active and intelligent interfaces over passive and command-based ones which are much harder to operate. Such voice interfaces not only introduce speech recognition as in identification of words but also bring the possibility of understanding human emotions through various expressions. This gave rise to speech emotion recognition (SER).

Although there exist multiple social media platforms, Telegram, launched by brothers Nikolai and Pavel Durov, has around 400 million monthly active users with nearly 1.5 million new users joining each day making it one of the most popular messaging apps. A Telegram chatbot is an automated third-party application that runs within Telegram and can interact with users by sending messages. Telegram offers an API for developing bots for social interactions, CRM integration, ticketing systems, and other purposes. Other social messaging platforms, such as Facebook Messenger and WhatsApp, have strict chatbot rules, such as a 24-h window. However, there are no such rules in place with Telegram, which is a huge advantage. Also, unlike Facebook Messenger and WhatsApp, Telegram allows one to use chatbots in groups.

1.2 Aims and Objectives

This paper mainly focuses on machine learning techniques using these acoustic cues and its related parameters to drive emotion recognition through prosody and vocal bursts. SER is carried out over a large RAVDESS dataset, used to extract a broad range of 5 different features using 4 individual classifiers. A comparative analysis helps pick out the best result in accordance with accuracy, precision, weighted average, recall and f1-score. The second aim of this paper is to integrate the SER model into a Telegram bot. The Botfather bot and the python-telegram-bot library are the primary components required for our model's Telegram bot integration. BotFather is the default Telegram bot that assists in creating new bots and modifying existing ones. It generates the Telegram bot's Access Token, which is used during programming to interact with our functions. python-telegram-bot is an open-source wrapper python library for the Telegram Bot API which aids the development of various functionalities, primarily via the telegram.ext package. Joseph Weizenbaum developed the first NLP computer algorithm, ELIZA, in 1964. It was one of the first bot programs developed with the intention of simulating a psychotherapist. The first swell of AI technological innovation took the shape of chatbots. Voice-activated dialogic agents such as Siri, Google Now, Cortana, and Samsung S Voice are not classified as chatbots. Bots have progressed to serve a multitude of roles. Social media platforms enable developers to create a chatbot for their brand or service, allowing customers to carry out some of their daily activities from inside their texting platform. Telegram bots are relatively new in the chatbot space, but they have made a name for themselves.

2 Background & Literature Review

2.1 MFCC Extraction

Among the many SER approaches mentioned, most of these mainly target classification of MFCC features using a few different classifiers and their various combinations. There has been increasing focus over deep learning techniques due to their enhanced accuracy since they are able to learn complex acoustic and emotional cues and their ability to even capture low level features such as raw waveforms or spectrograms which simple classifiers cannot handle. The authors of [1] used such a deep learning method to learn emotion-related aspects domestically and globally from speech and log-mel spectrograms, using CNN-LSTM in both 1D and 2D. For speaker-dependent studies, the 2D CNN-LSTM achieved a precision of 95.33% on Berlin EmoDB and 89.16% on IEMOCAP. 3-stage support vector machine (SVM) has been utilized in [2] over Berlin EmoDB to classify 7 different emotions by extracting MFCC features to obtain accuracy of 68% whereas authors in [5] have implemented the KNN algorithm as classifier on Berlin EmoDB to extract MFCC feature to obtain 50% accuracy. Nalini et al. in [11] use AANN to extract spectral features such as MFCC and residual phase whose performance is evaluated using FAR, FRR and accuracy. Proves to show that combination of residual phase with MFCC can improve accuracy of SER.

2.2 Hybrid Classifier Models

Several papers also discuss newer hybrid methods in quest for increased accuracy and dataset versatility. Authors in [3] have employed HMM and SVM classifiers for the extracted MFCC and LFCC features from the SAVEE database. Four emotional areas are considered for emotion detection from speech, yielding a precision of 61.25% for MFCC and 46.88% for LFCC using the OAO approach of SVM on the gaussian kernel, which yielded the best results as compared to OAA and polynomial kernels. From this the authors has reached the conclusion that better emotional trends in speech data are observed using MFCC rather than LFCC and HMM classifier is better than SVM. Deep belief networks (DBN) have been employed in [6] instead of GMM to represent complicated and non-linear high-level associations between low-level features utilizing the HMM classifier. The hidden markov toolset (HTK) was used to extract MFCC from the benchmark FAU Aibo emotion dataset, resulting in a best UAR of 45.08% on 1-state HMM, compared to 44.1% and 43.5% on 3-state and 5-state HMM, respectively. Models that combine different HMMs have also been found to better represent emotion fluctuation, resulting in a UAR of 45.60%. Furthermore, in real-life circumstances, speaker nominalization provided the best UAR of 46.36%. Different noise models have also been employed in some articles to improve the quality of the speech at three SNR levels: 15 dB, 10 dB, and 5 dB. Because the database was collected in automobile settings, the roughly matched training and testing environment for LISA-AVDB could explain the good identification accuracy of loud speech at higher SNR. On EMO-DB, a combination of GMM as well as HMM based classifiers yield a recognition accuracy of 83.8%. Thus, it has been deduced that emotion identification in speech signals is strongly dependent on the acoustic environment [7].

2.3 Other Papers

Qiron Mao et al. in [10] focus on finding salient affect-related features on which the accuracy of SER depends. They use CNN for unsupervised, automatic feature learning from a few labelled samples and SVM classifier. SER accuracy is tested on 4 different public emotional databases to obtain robust performance in changing scenarios. Authors in [4] have extracted LPFC to represent signals and applied the HMM classifier for classification of 6 emotions and have achieved average and best accuracies of 78% and 96% respectively over a specifically designed emotion corpus.

Some papers have also shown the works done on gender and age classification. Hierarchical classification models were used for SER. Different feature sets were investigated based on the task of determining the speaker's age, gender, and emotion. The eGeMAPS dataset was critical in completing this assignment. Models were created using MLP neural networks. The findings revealed that having a distinct classifier for each gender and age group outperforms having a single model for both genders and ages [8].

3   Methodology

In this section, the proposed technique for the SER model has been discussed in detail along with each individual component involved such as the dataset used, classifiers applied and the features extracted.

3.1   Classifiers

For a more comprehensive comparative analysis, we use the same dataset over 4 different classifiers namely Multi-layer Perceptron (MLP), Support Vector Machine (SVM), Decision Tree (DT) and Random Forest (RF) classifiers. Each classifier differs in some aspects and when applied to different datasets, their performance also varies. Different classifiers also behave differently on the same dataset and since these classifiers or machine learning models are built based on certain assumptions on the characteristics of the dataset, that classifier performs the best whose assumptions are most in-line with the datasets. In the end, selection of any classifier depends on the use case. This is where a large dataset is useful to truly compare performances of varying classifiers.

3.1.1   Multi-Level Perceptron (MLP)

MLP is a kind of fully linked feedforward Artificial Neural Network (ANN), with only one hidden layer in the most basic version. MLPs have been proven to be capable of approximating an XOR operator as well as a variety of other non-linear functions. In supervised learning, MLP are frequently used and it uses backpropagation for training and stochastic gradient descent to optimize the log-loss function and as a result it trains iteratively as the loss function parameters are constantly updated. They learn to represent the correlation between inputs and outputs by training on a set of input-output pairings. The network can thus be seen simply as an input-output model, with the weights and biases serving as the model's free parameters [15]. The number of hidden layers and the number of units in these layers are important considerations in MLP architecture. Its non-linear activation and multiple layers allow it to distinguish non-linearly separable data which is very useful for our SER analysis. We use the ReLU activation function which can be defined as:

$$f(x) = x + = \max(0, x)$$

where x denotes input to a neuron in the AAN. This activation function performs better gradient propagation to enable efficient computing in supervised learning models. The parameters that have been considered in the paper for building the MLP classifier are: alpha (value = 0.001), batch_size (value = 250), solver (taken as adam), epsilon (value = 1e−08), hidden_layer_sizes (value = (500,)), learning_rate (taken as adaptive), max_iter (value = 500).

3.1.2 Support Vector Machine (SVM)

SVM is a supervised learning model based on statistical learning frameworks following the structural risk minimization principle. Classification is done by constructing an N-dimensional hyperplane and using an efficient hyperplane searching technique which suitably separates input data to categories. Such searching helps reduce processing time by minimizing the training area. Training is done using this linear kernel function. Since it involves no assumptions on data type, it is able to circumvent overfitting. The parameters involved here are: kernel (taken as linear) and C, which is a regularization parameter (value = 1). SVMs identify the support vectors vj, weights wfj, and bias b to categorize the input information. For classification of the data, the following expression is used:

$$sk(v, vj) = \left(\rho v^e vj + k\right)^z$$

In the equation mentioned above, k is a constant value, and b represents the degree of the polynomial. For a polynomial $\rho > $ zero:

$$v = \left(_{i=0}\Sigma^n w_{fj} sk(vj, v) + b\right)$$

In the equation mentioned above, sk represents the kernel function, v is the input, vj is the support vector, wfj is the weight, and b is the bias [16].

3.1.3 Decision Tree (DT)

These are non-parameterized supervised learning models which are given certain simple decision rules. Its' job is to use these decision rules to predict the values of target variables. This classifier can perform multi-class classification on datasets, which makes it ideal for SER utilizing a white box model. It also solves multi-output problems by building N independent models, one for each output given N inputs. The Decision Tree model's tree structure incorporates the concept of multi-level classification, which can significantly reduce the level of confusion. However, this model is prone to overfitting which needs careful pruning or setting depth of tree are essential to avoid this. The parameter that has been considered while constructing the decision tree is max_depth which denotes the maximum depth of the tree and is set to 6. Overfitting is caused by a larger maximum depth value, whereas underfitting is caused by a lower maximum depth value.

3.1.4 Random Forest (RF)

Random Forest is a supervised learning algorithm that selects the best prediction from numerous individual decision trees using ensemble learning. So, this multitude of uncorrelated decision trees work individually on various sub-samples of the dataset to perform a prediction and the best of which can outperform any individual constituent model through better predictive performance. These individual predictions are averaged to improve prediction and control over-fitting. The Random Forest classifier is mainly used for large datasets, and since RAVDESS dataset is also quite large, this classifier has been used. The parameters that have been considered for the random forest classifier are: n_estimators (default value = 100), random_state (value = 0).

A decision tree is generated on a whole dataset, using all of the relevant features/variables, whereas a random forest selects observations/rows and certain features/variables at random to build numerous decision trees from, then averages the results. So, both the classifiers have been used in this study to provide a better comparison.

The confusion matrices for the Decision Tree, Random Forest, Support Vector Machine, and Multi-Layer Perceptron techniques show that the anger emotion had the highest precision, implying that it was convenient to recognise. Neutral feelings, on the other hand, was the most challenging for all of the schemes to detect. Unlike our other classifiers, the MLP method relies on an artificial neural network (ANN) for classifying, and it delivered the highest precision in recognising emotions when likened to others [18].

3.2 Dataset

The most important element in carrying out SER is selection of an appropriate dataset which provides reliable and valid emotional expressions. The focus is mainly on speech, so the need is to look for datasets having more variations in the said speech performed by multiple actors. In this paper, RAVDESS (Ryerson Audio-Visual Database of Emotional speech and song) has been used as the dataset which consists of 24 professional actors (12 male, 12 female) from Canada, in a neutral North American accent, vocalizing two lexically-related utterances. This dataset has been rated by 319 raters from the same region for testing the reliability and validation. The model has been evaluated for 4 different emotions: calm, happy, angry and disgust where calm and neutral are selected as threshold conditions. There are two levels of emotional intensity in each expression: normal and intense. Such intensity variations help in clear and unambiguous results due to facial and vocal expressions being able to be more accurately identified [12]. This allows emotion detection for identifying both intensive expressions and subtle changes. Each recording of an actor is available in three modality formats: Audio-only (16 bit, 48 kHz.wav), Audio-Video (720p H.264, AAC 48 kHz, .mp4), and Video-only (no sound). In this work, the audio recording with 60 wav files for each of the 24 actors for a total of 1440 files studied over all 4 classifiers have been used. The selection of this database is supported by the fact that it provides a large data set for training and testing making it particularly suitable for emotion classifiers using supervised learning algorithms such as all the ones used here including MLP, SVM, Random Forest and Decision Tree.

Some datasets, such as the Surrey Audio-Visual Expressed Emotion (SAVEE) Database, use performers that have had extensive training and are asked to demonstrate various human emotions; this type of dataset is regarded as an Actor-based dataset. Another type is the elicited dataset, which involves exposing a set of people to a range of emotional cases and recording their responses, such as the eNTERFACE' 05 Audio-Visual Emotion Database. The final type of dataset is spoken datasets, that are gathered from real-life situations in order to elicit genuine emotions, such as capturing callers to a customer call centre. In this work, it was required to find a suitable set of data that was readily available and contained the primary feelings; the dataset was also required to include a large number of actors instead of relying on one or two performers. As a result, the RAVDESS dataset was chosen. The RAVDESS dataset includes visual and audio data for 24 actors who were asked to sing and talk two lines ("Kids are talking by the door," "Dogs are sitting by the door") while displaying various human emotions [17].

3.3 Feature Selection and Extraction

Feature selection is the task of automatically or manually selecting the features that provide the maximum to the target variable or output that one is interested in. To reduce the computational cost of modelling and, in some cases, to improve the model's performance, the number of input variables should be reduced. Feature extraction is the process in which the input dataset is measured quantitatively to draw differences between different emotional states and classes. These features are extracted from the speech signals we have given as input. In this paper, 5 features have been extracted: MFCC, Mel Spectrogram, Chroma, Contrast and Tonnetz.

i)   MFCC- The Mel-Frequency Cepstral Coefficients (MFCC) feature extraction technique is popular for extracting speech features, and current research strives to improve its performance. For security purposes, MFCC is used in speech recognition systems and so on. The Mel scale is a scale that is used to compare the perceived frequency of a tone to the frequency that can be measured. It modulates the frequency to more closely match what the human ear can hear.

ii) Mel Spectrogram- A mel spectrogram is a spectrogram where the frequencies are converted to the mel scale. This belongs to the librosa package.

iii) Chroma- The chroma feature is a condensed descriptor that reflects a musical audio source's tonal component. This is part of the librosa package as well.

iv) Contrast- A current technique of proposing a contrast sensitive mechanism in auditory neural processing is to suggest an auditory contrast spectrum extraction algorithm, which is a relative representation of auditory temporal and frequency spectrum.

v)   Tonnetz- This also belongs to the librosa package. Calculates the features of the tonal centroid (tonnetz) The perfect fifth, minor third, and major third are all represented as two-dimensional coordinates in this form, which uses the method of 1 to project chroma characteristics onto a 6-dimensional basis.

MFCC has been chosen as it is a simulation of the human hearing system that aims to artificially recreate the ear's operating principle, assuming the human ear is a reliable speaker recognition system. MFCC features found in the observed difference in the human ear's important bandwidths were used to keep the phonetically crucial aspects of the speech signal using frequency filters separated linearly at low frequencies and logarithmically at high frequencies [13].

3.4 Experimental Procedure

The RAVDESS dataset has been taken in this process. The necessary libraries such as the librosa (package which provides the necessary building blocks for music and audio analysis), soundfile, pickle (for serializing and de-serializing a Python object structure), NumPy (is a library that contains multidimensional array objects as well as a set of routines for processing them), and sklearn (includes a number of useful machine learning and statistical modelling techniques, such as classification, regression, and clustering) have been imported. After that, some of the emotions have been chosen for observation which are:'calm','happy','angry','disgust' out of the total eight available emotions in the dataset. Feature extraction has been executed to extract the features such as mfcc, chroma, mel and so on. The entire dataset has been divided into two parts: training set and testing set (20%).

Using the training and testing dataset, different classifiers have been applied in order to compare which model gives the best accuracy.

After this, the Telegram bot has been set up to integrate with the SER model. All the commands for this Telegram bot, named Ascertus, are displayed in the bot menu. The/start command is used to launch our application. It shows a brief description of our project. The /emo command retrieves a voice sample and displays its predicted emotion. Voice samples from telegram are typically saved as.ogg audio files. This is then fed into the MLP classifier (the classifier with the highest training accuracy) to determine the emotion. Finally, the /exit command is used to terminate the application.

The motive of the updater class of the telegram.ext package is to receive updates from Telegram and deliver those to the dispatcher. The dispatcher supports handlers for various types of data: Telegram updates, basic text commands, and even arbitrary types Handler classes such as CommandHandler and MessageHandler handle telegram commands and user input. The Python pickle module is required to use our classifiers in our Telegram bot application. Pickling is a method for converting a Python object (list, dictionary, etc.) into a character stream. The idea is that this character stream contains all of the information required to reconstruct the object in a subsequent Python script. Along with creating the pickle files, we begin writing the app.py script. It is the main Python file that will be used to run and manage the Telegraph bot's functionalities. It is preferable to set the Telegram API access token within the host environment rather than in the project's source code.

The bot menu displays all of the commands for this Telegram bot, Ascertus. Our application is launched using the /start command. As soon as the bot is launched, it displays a brief description of the project that has been developed in this paper. The /emo command retrieves a voice sample and displays the emotion predicted by the sample. Telegram voice samples are typically saved as OPUS audio files. An Ogg Opus file is an audio file in the.ogg format, which is a lossy audio format designed for Internet streaming. This is then fed into the MLP classifier (the classifier with the highest training accuracy) to determine the emotion. Finally, the /exit command is used to terminate the application with a thank you message. A telegram.Message object has been used in each step to display the instructions to the user via the reply text function. Also, an error handler function is used in case there are any problems with the program flow.

A modest telegram chatbot has been developed here, using machine learning algorithms to assist the user in their emotion analysis. Some previous research articles have implemented speech emotion recognition models into chatbots, but one dedicated to a Telegram bot is uncommon. Because of Telegram's rapid growth, we are able to reach the widest possible audience for our initiative.

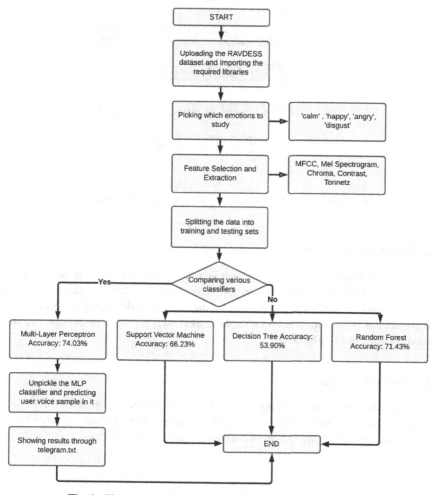

Fig. 1. Flowchart showing the workflow of the complete model.

The entire experimental procedure has been represented in a flowchart given below in Fig. 1.

4   Results

4.1   Accuracy

After carrying out the comparison of the different classifiers on the RAVDESS dataset for speech emotion recognition, a maximum accuracy of 74.03% has been achieved with the MLP classifier as shown in Fig. 2.

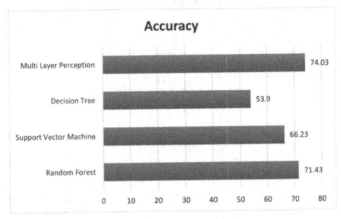

Fig. 2. Graph showing the accuracy obtained by various classifiers.

4.2   Classification Report

In machine learning, a classification report is a performance evaluation indicator. The precision, recall, F1, and support scores for the model are displayed in the classification report visualizer. The classification report for the various models that have been used in this project has been summarized in **Table 1.** as shown below. A graph has also been plotted for the same in **Fig. 3.**

4.3   Weighted Average

The weighted average shown in Fig. 4 takes into account how many of each class were used in the computation, having less of one class means that its precision/recall/F1 score has a smaller impact on the weighted average for each of those factors.

Table 1. Table showing the maximum value obtained for each observed emotion using all the four classifiers described in the paper.

	Maximum value of precision	Maximum value of recall	Maximum value of f1-score
Angry	Random Forest - 0.69	Multi-Layer Perceptron - 0.81	Random Forest - 0.70
Calm	Random Forest - 0.93	Multi-Layer Perceptron - 0.88	Random Forest - 0.90
Disgust	Multi-Layer Perceptron - 0.71	Random Forest, Support Vector Machine - 0.73,	Multi-Layer Perceptron - 0.64
Happy	Multi-Layer Perceptron - 0.81	Multi-Layer Perceptron - 0.64	Multi-Layer Perceptron - 0.71

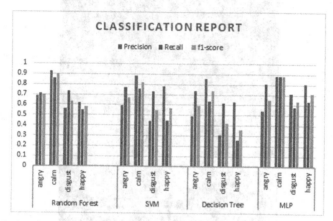

Fig. 3. Graph showing the comparison of various classification reports of all the classifiers used in the model.

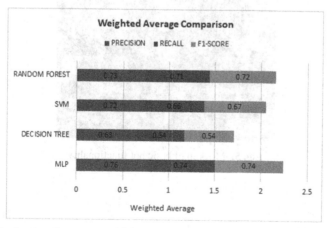

Fig. 4. Graph showing the average weighted comparison for the values of precision, recall and f1-score for the different classifiers.

4.4 Telegram Bot Integration

The integration of complex Machine Learning models into user-friendly applications like a chatbot requires effort in fine-tuning the model and adjusting it accordingly. The following image shown in Fig. 5 provides a glimpse of bot functionality performing basic emotion recognition. One can later build upon these produced results to draw inferences on more detailed data and perform diagnosis.

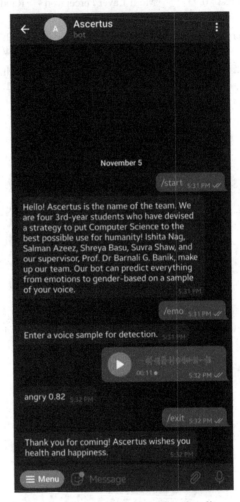

Fig. 5. Mockup of basic bot functionality

5 Discussions and Conclusions

Several methods have been researched in SER ranging from simple supervised models, deep learning models to even complex models with stacked classifiers. However, all these methods provide a specific and well-defined emotion detection algorithm by suitably modifying the parameter selection and fine-tuning the model for higher accuracies in particular scenarios. This paper aims for a more generalized model by providing comparative analysis of the most relevant yet simple classifiers over a wide range of selection features and incorporating it within a user-friendly chatbot. This telegram chatbot provides a more congenial environment which takes a step away from the enigmatic complex emotion recognition models. The idea for development of a chatbot comes from the fact that, unfortunately, mental conditions are not easily recognized or are frowned upon by the society. As a consequence, a mentally affected individual may not be aware of his condition, deducing it as stress or peer pressure. Even the aware may be conscience-stricken so as to not make it public. This mortification or false contrition can be justified as the world sees it so. Through this application of SER, the aim is to provide exposure to such situations, provide a user-friendly interface to realize, cope with their state of affairs and help improve the status quo. This accurate identification is also crucial for a person to be more self-aware, confident and have far better metacognition [14]. Although this paper highlights the foundations of this interactive psychotherapy python bot, work is still being conducted to include finer details as mentioned in the future works towards the end of this paper.

6 Future Work

This paper deals with simplistic yet reliable SER incorporated in a user-friendly telegram chatbot. However, when dealing with real-life situations, it calls for more robust algorithms that have close to none chances of providing inaccurate readings. Since only SER has been tackled, there is room for more multi-modal mechanisms through video and text inputs to deal with scored values. In addition to emotion, the next objective is to incorporate gender detection for even better fine-grained recognition and diagnosis. This allows for specialized and distinctive classification and therapy. As one can imagine, the application is far from complete and will require several iterations adding finer details in each step to reach somewhere close to completion. Hence, this paper marks the first step towards greater intelligence in psychological therapy.

References

1. Zhao, J., Mao, X., Chen, L.: Speech emotion recognition using DEEP 1d 2D CNN LSTM networks. Biomed. Signal Process. Control **47**, 312–323 (2019)
2. Milton, A., Sharmy Roy, S., Tamil Selvi, S.: SVM scheme for Speech emotion recognition USING MFCC feature. Int. J. Comput. Appl. **69**(9), 34–39 (2013)
3. Chenchah, F., Lachiri, Z.: Acoustic emotion recognition using linear and nonlinear cepstral coefficients. Int. J. Adv. Comput. Sci. Appl. **6**(11) (2015)
4. Nwe, T.L., Foo, S.W., De Silva, L.C.: Speech emotion recognition using hidden Markov models. Speech Commun. **41**(4), 603–623 (2003)

5. Demircan, S., Kahramanlı, H.: Feature extraction from speech data for emotion recognition. J. Adv. Comput. Networks 2(1), 28–30 (2014)

6. Le, D., Provost, E.M.: Emotion recognition from spontaneous speech using Hidden Markov models with deep belief networks. In: 2013 IEEE Workshop on Automatic Speech Recognition and Understanding (2013)

7. Tawari, A., Trivedi, M.: Speech emotion analysis in noisy real-world environment. In: 2010 International Conference on Pattern Recognition

8. Shaqra, F.A., Duwairi, R., Al-Ayyoub, M.: Recognizing emotion from speech based on age and gender using hierarchical models. In: The 10th International Conference on Ambient Systems, Networks and Technologies (ANT), 29 April–2 May 2019, Leuven, Belgium (2019)

9. Nediyanchath, A., Paramasivam, P., Yenigalla, P.: Multi-head attention for speech emotion recognition with auxiliary learning of gender recognition. In: 2020 IEEE International Conference on Acoustics, Speech and Signal Processing (ICASSP)

10. Mao, Q., Dong, M., Huang, Z., Zhan, Y.: Learning salient features for Speech Emotion Recognition using convolutional Neural Networks. IEEE Trans. Multimedia 16(8), 2203–2213 (2014)

11. Nalini, N.J., Palanivel, S., Balasubramanian, M.: Speech emotion recognition using residual phase and MFCC features. Int. J. Eng. Technol. 5(6), 4515–4527 (2013)

12. Livingstone, S.R., Russo, F.A.: The ryerson audio-visual database of emotional speech and song (RAVDESS): a dynamic, multimodal set of facial and vocal expressions in North American English. PLoS ONE 13(5), e0196391 (2018)

13. Alim, S.A., Alang Rashid, N.K.: Some Commonly Used Speech Feature Extraction Algorithms. Pub: 12th Dec, 2018

14. Lausen, A., Hammerschmidt, K.: Emotion recognition and confidence ratings predicted by vocal stimulus type and prosodic parameters. Humanities and Social Sciences Communications, vol. 7, no. 1 (2020)

15. Sanjita, B.R., Nipunika, A.: Speech Emotion Recognition using MLP Classifier. IJESC, vol. 10, no. 5, May 2020

16. Amjad, A., Khan, L.: Effect on speech emotion classification of a feature selection approach using a convolutional neural network. Peer J. Comput. Sci., 7, Pub: 3rd Nov, 2021

17. Martin, O., Kotsia, I., Macq, B.: The eNTERFACE' 05 audio-visual emotion database. In: 22nd International Conference on Data Engineering Workshops (ICDEW'06); Pub: 24th Apr, 2006

18. Madhavi, A., Priya Valentina, A., Mounika, K., Rohit, B., Nagma, S.: Comparative analysis of different classifiers for speech emotion recognition. In: Kiran Mai, C., Kiranmayee, B.V., Favorskaya, M.N., Chandra Satapathy, S., Raju, K.S. (eds.) Proceedings of International Conference on Advances in Computer Engineering and Communication Systems. LAIS, vol. 20, pp. 523–538. Springer, Singapore (2021). https://doi.org/10.1007/978-981-15-9293-5_48

An Efficient CoD Management Using Semaphore in Online Retail System

Samiran Gupta[1] and Babul P. Tewari[2]([⊠]) [iD]

[1] Department of Computer Science and Engineering, Asansol Engineering College,
Asansol 713301, India
[2] Department of Computer Science and Engineering,
Indian Institute of Information Technology, Bhagalpur 813210, India
bptewari.cse@iiitbh.ac.in

Abstract. Electronic commerce (E-commerce) along with online shopping is rapidly increasing now-a-days specially in current scenario of COVID 19 pandemic. Such immensely expanding online marketing creates a plethora of opportunities for the companies to trade wider on the globe as well as enabling the customers to avail better products at their increased convenience. In this paper, we have addressed the affects of financial loss related to the return and replacement policy of online shopping particularly in Cash-on-Delivery (CoD) payment method. We have proposed a software solution using semaphore programming tool for the efficient management of CoD payment method. Analysing the customer's previous transaction records, the proposed method determines suitable policy for the return and replacement option of the concerned customer. The objective is to minimize the financial loss for an unnecessary cancellation and replacement policy without hampering customers' interest. Hence we have proposed an algorithm for efficient CoD management. The proposed algorithm uses counting semaphore to implement a customer reputation variable which will help the companies to keep track of each customer for each transaction precisely and determine a suitable penalty policy for the return and replacement option of the said customer. The working principle is demonstrated through a flow chart. We have performed extensive simulations in python to establish the novelty of the proposed approach.

Keywords: E-commerce · Counting semaphore · Return · Replacement · Cash on delivery

1 Introduction

Marketing through digital media using Internet communication is significantly uprising everywhere [1]. The ease of communication with the digital media using the Internet makes online marketing as the most viable option for a large number of population. This is efficiently integrated with wireless network and its several variants such as ad-hoc network, sensor network, vehicular network, etc.

In the last few years, there is an exponential growth in the number of user population, equipped with the use of modern pervasive devices for online marketing using the Internet. This makes the electronic commerce (e-commerce) business as one of the largest increasing sectors [5]. This also encouraging the first generation entrepreneurs and vast range being industrialized by small and medium enterprises (SMEs) [6].

Such increasing number of users using e-commerce in recent years has consistently been seen in the performance of electronic-retail (e-retail) business. Online shopping facilitates the customers to compare their product with similar items and to review the feedback. In addition to these, online shopping allows the customers to fulfill their purposes with minimum physical contacts. This makes it an essential reason for the inclination of a large number of user population towards the e-commerce based online shopping. Apart from e-commerce, mobile commerce or m-commerce has also registered itself as one of the widely accepted means of shopping. The explosive growth in the market of online shopping is mostly caused by:

- Ease of Internet usage to a handsome number of people.
- Safe in pandemic situation like Covid19.
- Increasing trust/preference towards online merchant.
- Widespread advancement in the mobile handheld devices.

However such online shopping requires a suitable payment option to run the business process smoothly.

Cash on delivery (CoD) is one of the popular payment methods during online shopping. In CoD payment option, the customers need to pay the requited amount once the ordered item is delivered at the residence or in the given addresses. This causes more satisfaction to the customers as it is based on releasing the money upon getting the ordered item delivered [4]. Very often CoD option introduces a delivery charge that is mostly paid by the customers. However, if the customer denies to receive the ordered item or cancels the said item then in both cases the overhead of dispatching the item as well as the intermediate transport cost is wasted. It is therefore raises the need for an efficient CoD technique in online shopping which is the major concern of this paper.

In this paper, we have addressed an efficient CoD management for online shopping. We first demonstrated the need for suitable CoD management and then argue for a semaphore based software solution of the same. In this context we have developed a suitable algorithm that uses the semaphore tool to implement the appropriate CoD management technique. The working principle has also been demonstrated with suitable flow chart. We performed extensive simulations to establish the novelty of the proposed approach in terms of profit and loss.

We organize the rest of the papers as follows. Section 2 describes some existing works. The main motivation behind this work is described in Sect. 3. In Sect. 4, we describe the proposed semaphore based software solution. The proposed algorithm is described in Sect. 5. The simulation results are described in Sect. 6. Finally, we conclude the paper in Sect. 7.

2   Related Works

In last few years, a considerable research took place to solve the problems of e-commerce based online retails systems. CoD management in online marketing has drawn a significant attention [2,3]. Erin Torkelson [7] proposed a method for handling debt transfer and cash transfer in South African paradigm. The cash transfer technique is bundled with financial inclusion method in global scenario. It helps to reduce the contradiction among several cash transfer systems and provides the growth with respect to financial systems. Li et al. [8] proposed an optimal pricing technique for online marketing management. The main aim of this method is to optimize demand, back-ordering, size and price of the product. This method is used to control inventory management systems by handling cash on delivery scheme. Finally, it helps to maximize the profit of the company with respect to all proposed situations. Rudkowski et al. [9] describe today and tomorrow mapping and modelling of retail customer journey. Basically, this description helps to analyse two basic aims with respect to pop-ups like brand-based and marketplace-based system. It helps to identify similarities and differences of both the brands and presented a view as a three-step-process: (i) pre-purchase, (ii) purchase, and (iii) post-purchase from the market. Verstraete et al. [10] proposed a data driven technique for predicting natural phenomena (viz. weather) with respect to online product retail system. It handles low margin with high volume purchase system. It also analyses two parameters i.e. delivery time and financial system of the country, based on the sales. Rita et al. [11] proposed details analysis of e-services based on certain parameters such as behavior of the customers, satisfaction of the customers, and quality of the e-services. Finally, it highlights the behavior of the customer trust including the following parameters: number of sites visited, choice number of the customer, and repurchase choice of the customers. Xu and Jackson [12] analyze several influence parameters of the retail system. In this system, retailing system is omni-channel method. Finally, we compared two strategies, such as (i) external that includes policy return flexibility, and (ii) internal that includes familiarity, patience, and tolerance of ambiguity. Constantinos-Vasilios Priporas [13] shared detailson the expectation of customers based on smart retailing system. This also highlights frequently developing technologies and shopping experience. In a nutshell, this highlights recommendation, expectation, and perception of the customers based on behaviors. Finally, we compare both the systems i.e. practical and theoretical implications. Wiese et al. Grewal et al. [14] proposed a review article for different offline and online strategy and related agendas. It infers that various retailers use multiple channels like online system, catalogs, brick with mortar for strategy management. This article efficiently reflects past researches for off-line and on-line frameworks. In [15], there are several impacts for e-retailing methods as described with respect to customer behaviors. It includes complete information from initial stage i.e. product ordering to delivery stage including delivery mode also. Wilcox and Gurau [16] proposed a modeling system for business with the help of customer relationship management for online retailing system. It helps in orientation of the customer, implementation of the strategy, modelling and planning of the relationship of customers. In last few years, fuzzy logic also got popularized in the area of e-commerce with several businesses such as combination of customer and business. In [17], fuzzy based technique is proposed for evaluating trust of the customers with respect to business to consumer in online marketing system in e-commerce.

This paper uses semaphore programming tool to arrive at an efficient CoD management for the e-retail system. Unlike the works explained in the literature, our work focuses on how to arrive an efficient CoD management technique so that the business retailer has less suffering and that too without hampering the customer interest.

3   Background and Motivation

Nowadays, online shopping has an increasing trend specially in the period of Covid19. The major reason behind this is that, the customers can enjoy a contact less delivery of their product. Moreover, online shopping facilitates the customers to satisfy their needs irrespective of the time and location. This not only reduces the overhead involved in marketing but also saves the time to a significant extent. In addition to this, several flexible payment options has made this e-commerce platform suitable for the business retailer as well as the customers. Following are the major concern areas:

- **Expediency:** Customers prefer online shopping in comparison to the conventional stores because online shopping is available beyond the working hour of conventional store. It allows to buy the desired products with the minimum or no physical contacts. This makes online shopping to be most feasible option during pandemic.
- **Improved networking media:** Advancement of the pervasive devices and ease of using the Internet communication has made the online shopping much popular. The improved multimedia applications along with cloud computing technology makes the online retailing business much effective. Here, customers can buy their product with a wide variety of price comparisons from different selling vendors without any physical overhead. Improved communication media also provides an up-to-date information regarding all products customer desires.
- **Wide variety of payment option:** There is a wide variety of payment options make the online shopping safe and popular. This includes, credit and debit card, Internet banking, CoD etc.

Despite the fact of significant popularity, there are several issues that have considerable influence on the success e-commerce based online shopping right from the security aspects, manpower and time management and in the payment procedure mutually agreed by the customers and the sellers. Among many such payment options, CoD is one of the popular payment methods where the customer has to pay the price upon receiving the ordered product. However, the overhead related to the transportation of the product becomes wasted if the concerned customer either refuses to accept the item or even cancels the same. So how to repay or minimizing the chances of such incident is the major focus of the study.

3.1 Cash on Delivery (CoD) Mode

CoD is a mode of payment that enables the buyers to pay for the product once they receive it on their doorsteps. There is a considerable study which establish that, CoD is being popular payment option in a country like India and others. A significant percentage of the e-retail activities involving the online customers prefer buying items through CoD payment method. Thus, CoD has become a generic mode of payment because the customers find it more reliable and easier. Moreover, these days with the trend of Cashless payment services like credit and debit card, GPay, Paytm, PhonePe and Net banking have come into the limelight, attracting a large scale of customers, but nevertheless, CoD is still very popular due to the following major advantages:

- Easy and safe payment option that the customers always look for.
- There are number of people who are not comfortable to use the online cashless payment options. CoD is a very good choice for them because of least technical overhead.
- Conventionally, CoD is a suitable option having less involvement of network security issue and thus becomes an useful payment option for those customers who are less confident in using online payment gateway.

3.2 Need for an Efficient CoD Management

In this section, we establish the need for an efficient CoD management in online shopping. Refund and replacement of the ordered item are two important aspects of online shopping that the customers enjoy. These two features increase the customer satisfaction while making the online business more reliable. However, it is also an admitted fact that the company may require to face a financial loss due to this policy because of the intermediate transportation overhead of the ordered item. Therefore, there is a need to incorporate a suitable policy that can minimize this financial loss without affecting the customer's interest. The major concern in this context are as follows:

- **Return:** If the customers willingly refuse to accept the product or even cancel the same, it causes an wastage of cost due to the intermediate transportation overhead. This is unlike the prepaid delivery of the ordered item where the customers mostly accept the product because the payment has been made before the scheduled arrival of the item.
- **Replacement:** This feature allows the customers to look for an alternative item if the delivered item does not meet their requirement. Although such policy enhances the customers satisfaction but at the cost of reduced profit margin of the company. The reason behind this is that of the multiple shipments of the ordered item.

It is evident that both return and replacement policy may cause a financial loss for the company and thus raises the need for an efficient CoD management for online shopping.

4   Proposed Semaphore Based Software Solution

We propose a semaphore based software solution that controls the cost overhead due to the return and replacement policy of online shopping. The objective is to improve the performance of the online business platform which reduces the cost overhead of the vendor with minimum affect to the customer's interest. The idea is to make an attempt for identifying the customer's valid reason for cancelling or replacing the ordered item. We address a software solution based on counting semaphore that can restrain the tendency for such activity on the customer side. This is done by keeping track of the customer's previous transaction. Once the unnecessary cancellation or replacement of the ordered item is made the cost overhead can be reduced to a significant extent.

The proposed software solution consists of a positive integer used for counting and helps to coordinate the access mechanism of the resources, where the initial semaphore count is equal to the number of free resources. Threads then increase or decrease the count with the increase or decrease in free resources respectively. The semaphore count tending to zero indicates that no more resources are present and the threads try to decrease the semaphore block, wait until count becomes greater than zero. Since semaphores need not be acquired and released by the same thread, they can be used for asynchronous event notification as well (here we have customer reputation count). Also, semaphores are stateful, hence can be used asynchronously without acquiring a mutex lock by the condition variables, i.e. setting a lock before using a shared resource and release after using it to make that particular part of code inaccessible to the threads.

5   The Proposed Algorithm

The objective of the proposed algorithm is to track the customer's previous transaction and to control the unnecessary cancellation or return policy when the ordered item is already in transit. Based on the concept of counting semaphores, we declare a variable to count the customer reputation (on a scale of 0-10), where 10 is the highest reputation and 0 is the lowest one. Whenever, a transaction is made, the rating counter is triggered and according to the success or failure of the transaction, customer reputation will be manipulated. The maximum default rating of a customer is 10 which decreases by 1 for every failed transaction. We define failed transaction by means of return or replacement policy and can be recovered by 1 for every successful transaction. Rating 10 means the customer can use CoD feature without any extra effort. However, customers with ratings between 5 and 9 opting for CoD will be taken to a survey page (i.e. may contain ads to generate revenue to the company, recovering some loss on the previous failed transactions) and go through a survey (i.e. depending on their respective rating) helping the company to identify the cause for transaction failure. If x be the customer rating, rev be the review level, then rev can be expressed in Eq. (1).

$$rev = \frac{ceil(x-4)}{2}. \tag{1}$$

Here, we use ceiling function to obtain an integral value. This formula returns only three values for all the ratings, 1, 2 and 3. These three may be designed as hierarchical review levels (i.e., level 1, level 2 and level 3) based on the kind or amount of details, we want from the customer or if we want to serve ads. Further, if a customer has reached a rating less than 5, then in order to regain CoD access, an online payment of 10% of the actual amount of the product needs to be made as a security deposit which will later be compensated at the time of delivery (i.e., the customer pays on 90% amount in cash at the time of delivery).

The algorithm first walks through the customer details, retrieving the rating at that point of time along with the transaction details. The customer is not allowed to avail CoD transaction if the customer rating is 0, i.e., the lowest. Such customers may increase their rating through online payments. The customers with a non-zero rating will have access to CoD as per their rating. In case, if a customer refuses to accept the product at the time of delivery or somehow misses to receive the delivery, 100% money will be refunded. If the customer has already paid 10% of the price online in order to unblock the CoD facility (blocked previously due to return/replacement), in this case the customer gets a money refund of Rupees 30 if product maximum retail price (MRP) is greater than 999, else refund of Rupees 20 will be made. This return will also take down one rating point from the customer's pocket. Now, if a customer returns the product within the replacement period, the customer gets 100% refund, only at the loss of one rating point. Finally, the algorithm awards the customer with one rating point on one successful transaction (i.e. no return/replacement). The customer rating is updated in the database for the next order and the execution stops here. While the working principle of the proposed software solution is depicted through a flow chart shown in Fig. 1 and the formal description of the algorithm is presented in Algorithm 1. Note that, description of several notations used in the algorithm and flow chart are mentioned in Table 1. The flow of execution of the proposed method is described in Fig. 1

Algorithm 1: Efficient CoD management using semaphore

Input: $cust_id, x$, $MRP1$, $MRP2$, OP, rev

1 Initialize counting semaphore as 10, $x = 10$;

2 **if** *Semaphore variable(x)=10 or Order received in Cash Online* **then**

3   collect the $MRP1$ in online payment (op);

4   Check for successful delivery;

5   **if** $x < 10$ **then**

6   set x:=x+1;

7   **if** *delivery failed* **then**

8   return $MRP1$;

9   update x=:x-1;

10 **else**

11   check the customer status(semaphore);

12   **if** *status=open* **then**

13   check the delivery;

14   **if** *not delivered* **then**

15   check OP status;

16   **if** $OP = true$ and $MRP1 > 999$ **then**

17   return (op-30);

18   **else**

19   return (op-20);

20   set x=x-1;

21   **else**

22   check OP;

23   collect $MRP2$;

24 **if** *status!=open* **then**

25   check the value of x;

26   **if** $x < 5$ **then**

27   collect 10 percent of MRP as OP;

28   Set *status* $= open$;

29   set remaining price as $MRP2$;

30   **else**

31   **if** $x \geq 5$ **then**

32   execute review and feedback to enhance semaphore value to make the status open;

33 check whether customer initiate the return or not;

34 set $x := x - 1$;

35 initiate the return;

36 check the value of x;

37 set $x := x + 1$ if less than 10;

38 . Return

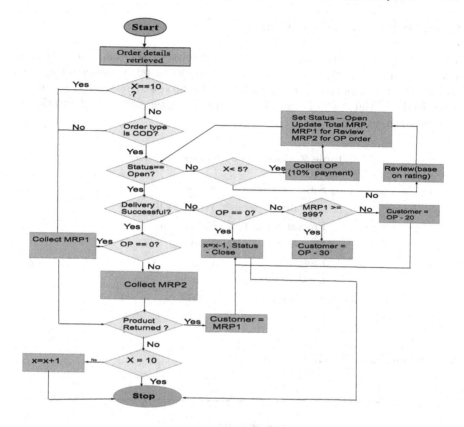

Fig. 1. Flow of steps

Table 1. Description of notations

Notation	Description
Cust-id	Customer identification in company database
x	Customer Rating
MRP1	Actual price of the ordered product
MRP2	90% price of the product
OP	10% price of the product paid online
status()	Determine CoD unblock strategy for the customer
rev	120 Review level to unblock CoD
Check-return	Check if a return or replacement is made
Check-status	Determine if CoD is allowed for the customer

6   Results and Discussion

We evaluate the performance of the proposed software solution through extensive computer simulation. While simulating, we focus on customer rating, loss and profit and demonstrated accordingly. The proposed method is simulated using Pythons Matplotlib libraryvia with the computer system configuration as mantioned in Table 2.

Table 2. Computer system specifications

Software/Hardware	Specifications
Operating System	Windows 10
Programming Tool	Python 3.7
Matpotlib	1.2.0
Processor	Intel core i5
RAM	8 GB
Hard Disk	1 TB

6.1   Simulation Results

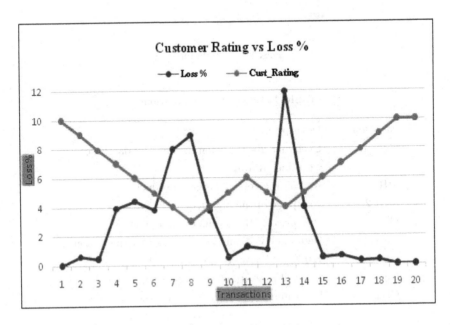

Fig. 2. Customer rating and loss

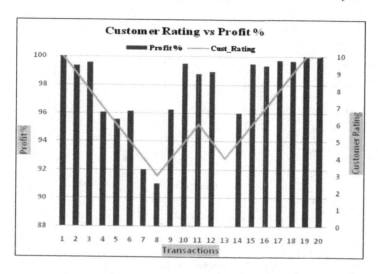

Fig. 3. Customer rating and profit

In Fig. 2, we demonstrate the customer rating percentage of loss against several transactions. As shown, we have considered 20 transactions plotted in x-axis and such transactions are considered based on a realistic online transaction scenario. The loss incurred on each of those is shown through blue lines. Y-axis has customer rating from 0-10, plotted against the loss percentage on those transactions. It is observed that as the customer rating decreases, loss percentage rises up and vice-versa.

The profit percentage and customer rating variations are demonstrated in Fig. 3. It is evident that profit percentage increases with the increase in customer rating against the different transactions. Here too, we have considered 20 different transactions and noted that profit percentage directly varies with the customer rating as demonstrated in Fig. 3.

In Fig. 4 we demonstrate the loss density where, we plot the percentage of loss in X-axis and Y-axis shows customer rating. Evidently, the percentage of loss increases with the decrease in customer rating. This results infer that our earlier observation is proved to be true.

Figure 5 demonstrates the profit histogram. In this figure, we plot customer rating in Y-axis and percentage of profit is plotted on X-axis. It is noted that as the customer rating varies from 0–10, we observe that the profit percentage also follows the same. This confirms our inference and we conclude that using this mechanism, we can minimize the loss subjected on return and replacement scenarios through CoD by maintaining good customer rating.

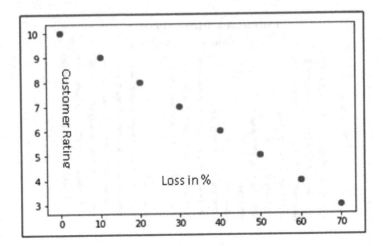

Fig. 4. Customer rating and loss

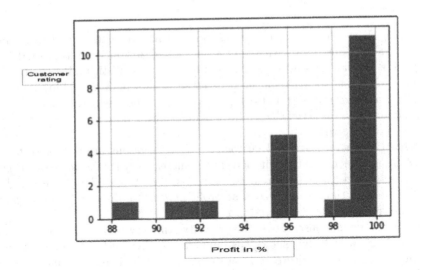

Fig. 5. Profit histogram

7   Conclusion

E-commerce and Online markets through digital platform have become more popular these days which has also become effective during Covid19 pandemic situation. There is a continuous growth in the popularity of customer friendly shopping window. In a competitive scenario, all the vendors are trying to provide their customers a better shopping experience, hence all sorts of money-waiver schemes and coupons have come into fashion. However, the e-retailers also need to look for a provision to minimize their loss that they would face due to the return and replacement policy. In this paper, we have addressed a software based solution using semaphore programming tool for this problem. Considering the record of transaction there is a restriction that can be imposed as a financial penalty for unnecessary return and replacement procedure particularly in CoD payment method. Through this paper, the effects of customer behaviours have been analysed against the overall profit and loss caused to the vendors and it is evident that a large number of return and replacements means more loss to the companies and vice versa. We have proposed an algorithmic solution that can minimize the affect of financial loss of the online vendors. The novelty of the proposed approach is established through appropriate solution.

References

1. Elia, G., Margherita, A., Passiante, G.: Digital entrepreneurship ecosystem: how digital technologies and collective intelligence are reshaping the entrepreneurial process. Technol. Forecast. Soc. Chang. **150**, 119791 (2020)
2. Ha, X.S., Le, T.H., Phan, T.T., Nguyen, H.H.D., Vo, H.K., Duong-Trung, N.: Scrutinizing trust and transparency in cash on delivery systems. In: Wang, G., Chen, B., Li, W., Di Pietro, R., Yan, X., Han, H. (eds.) SpaCCS 2020. LNCS, vol. 12382, pp. 214–227. Springer, Cham (2021). https://doi.org/10.1007/978-3-030-68851-6_15
3. Ha, X.S., Le, H.T., Metoui, N., Duong-Trung, N.: DeM-CoD: novel access-control-based cash on delivery mechanism for decentralized marketplace. In: IEEE 19th International Conference on Trust, Security and Privacy in Computing and Communications (TrustCom), pp. 71–78(2020)
4. Le et al.: Assuring non-fraudulent transactions in cash on delivery by introducing double smart contracts. Int. J. Adv. Comput. Sci. Appl. **10**(5), 677–684 (2019)
5. Das, S.K., Kumar, A., Das, B., Burnwal, A.P.: Ethics of e-commerce in information and communications technologies. Int. J. Adv. Comput. Res. **3**(1), 122–124 (2013)
6. Trianni, A., Cagno, E., Neri, A., Howard, M.: Measuring industrial sustainability performance: empirical evidence from Italian and German manufacturing small and medium enterprises. J. Clean. Prod. **229**, 1355–1376 (2019)
7. Torkelson, E.: Collateral damages: cash transfer and debt transfer in South Africa. World Dev. **126**(104711), 1–11 (2020)
8. Li, R., Liu, Y., Teng, J.T., Tsao, Y.C.: Optimal pricing, lot-sizing and backordering decisions when a seller demands an advance-cash-credit payment scheme. Eur. J. Oper. Res. **278**(1), 283–295 (2019)
9. Rudkowski, J., Heney, C., Yu, H., Sedlezky, S., Gunn, F.: Here today, gone tomorrow? mapping and modelling the pop-up retail customer journey. J. Retail. Consum. Serv. **54**(101698), 1–25 (2019)
10. Verstraete, G., Aghezzaf, E.H., Desmet, B.: A data-driven framework for predicting weather impact on high-volume low-margin retail products. J. Retail. Consum. Serv. **48**, 169–177 (2019)
11. Rita, P., Oliveira, T., Farisa, A.: The impact of e-service quality and customer satisfaction on customer behavior in online shopping. Heliyon **5**(10), 1–15 (2019)
12. Xu, X., Jackson, J.E.: Investigating the influential factors of return channel loyalty in omni-channel retailing. Int. J. Prod. Econ. **216**, 118–132 (2019)

13. Priporas, C.V., Stylos, N., Fotiadis, A.K.: Generation Z consumers' expectations of interactions in smart retailing: a future agenda. Comput. Hum. Behav. **77**, 374–381 (2017)
14. Grewal, D., et al.: Strategic online and offline retail pricing: a review and research agenda. J. Interact. Mark. **24**(2), 138–154 (2010)
15. Agarwal, A., Yadav, V.K.: Impact of technology in E-retailing operations: a consumer perspective. Procedia Soc. Behav. Sci. **189**, 252–258 (2015)
16. Wilcox, P.A., Gurău, C.: Business modelling with UML: the implementation of CRM systems for online retailing. J. Retail. Consum. Serv. **10**(3), 181–191 (2003)
17. Kaur, B., Madan, S.: A fuzzy expert system to evaluate customer's trust in B2C E-Commerce websites. In: International Conference on Computing for Sustainable Global Development (INDIACom), pp. 394–399(2014)

Real-Time Price Discovery Solution
for Agri-Commodities at e-Marketplaces:
A Hybrid Approach

Joyanta Basu[1]([⊠]) [iD], Shashank Sharma[2], Rupam Mukhopadhyay[1], Amitava Akuli[1],
Mrinal Pandey[3], Nabarun Bhattacharyya[1], and B. K. Murthy[4]

[1] CDAC Kolkata, Sector - V, Salt Lake, Kolkata 700091, West Bengal, India
`{joyanta.basu,rupam.mukhopadhyay,amitava.akuli,`
`nabarun.bhattacharya}@cdac.in`
[2] CDAC Pune, Panchavati, Pashan, Pune 411 008, Maharashtra, India
`shashank.sharma@cdac.in`
[3] North Cap University, Sector 23A, Gurugram 122017, Haryana, India
`mrinalpandey@ncuindia.edu`
[4] IIT Bhilai Innovation and Technology Foundation, Sejbahar, Raipur 492015, Chhattisgarh,
India
`ceoibitf@iitbhilai.ac.in`

Abstract. In this paper, the authors present the price discovery system of agricultural commodities like Bengal gram, Groundnut, and Maize in local agri-markets of Telangana state of India. The price discovery process determines the price of the commodity in the marketplace through the interactions of buyers and sellers. In this paper, the authors evaluated the price information collected from the local marketplaces and analyzed 42415 records to build the price discovery model. The authors proposed a hybrid model by fusion of time series analysis and regression model in the current paper. The proposed developed hybrid model provided encouraging results for predicting three agri-commodities prices of Telangana state of India.

Keywords: Price discovery · Hybrid model · Time series analysis · Regression

1 Introduction

Price discovery is an integral part of commodity trading. Agricultural commodity prices are often random and fluctuating. They are influenced mainly by eventualities and are highly unpredictable in natural calamities like droughts, floods, and attacks by pests and diseases [1]. These lead to considerable risk and uncertainty in the process of price modeling and forecasting. Agricultural commodity prices play a vital role in consumers' access to food. They directly influence their actual earnings, especially among the lower class, who spend a significant wealth of their income on food. Since food price is an essential component of our daily lives, policymakers need reliable forecasts of food prices to manage food security. Before liberalization and globalization, food price forecasting was a low value-added activity. Domestic and international market forces presently determine the food prices. It leads to increased price variability and accords importance to reliable price forecasting techniques. The price forecasts are essential for farmers also as they base their production and marketing decisions on the expected prices that may have financial repercussions many months later. Information asymmetry leads to market distortions even in e-Marketplaces. The asymmetry could be due to lack of proper information dissemination (e.g., prevalent prices), lack of awareness of benchmarks (e.g., quality norms), variations in quality assessment (arbitrariness), lack of standardized methodology (certifications), etc. The price discovery mechanisms in vogue are arbitrary and opaque, leaving the seller and buyer with very few options. Distress sale is a common phenomenon. One way to reduce this stress on the system is by allowing access to marketable produce to a larger population of buyers.

Accurately predicting the agricultural commodity price is required to evade market risk, increase agricultural income, and accomplish government macroeconomic regulation. Because of economic and financial issues, last few years, commodity prices have undergone strong fluctuations that have reshaped the global economic equilibrium. The study of the dynamics of futures and spot prices for agricultural commodities assumes particular importance, especially within the framework of the recent global food balances crisis, where concerns were raised about the possible role of futures and speculation in increasing the price of some agricultural commodities.

The significant problems of price discovery lie in identifying variables following their relevant influence on price discovery and developing a machine learning model for online price prediction. After exploration of field data of commodity price and data cleansing & wrangling, authors are applied different state-of-the-art models and finally proposed a hybrid model combined with time series and regression model to address the price discovery problem. It is the significant contribution of the authors in this paper.

The rest of the article is organized as follows. Section 2 includes a literature survey of agricultural commodities price discovery system followed by Sect. 3, describing the methodology and proposed flow diagram, data collection, data statistics, data pre-processing, and data normalization. Section 3 also explains feature selection, hybrid model building for price discovery, and model development experimentally studied in the following sections. Section 4 presents the findings and discussions on experimental analysis of the price discovery model of agri-commodities. Finally, in Sect. 5, conclusions and future works are summarized.

2 Literature Survey

Numerous studies have been explored to ascertain whether the price information is reflected in the spot market or its underlying futures market under various intervals since the introduction of futures in the Indian commodity market [2]. Derivatives trading in the commodity market has been a topic of enthusiasm of research in the field of finance. There have been contrary views on the impact of derivatives trading. Several studies have been done to study the impact of the introduction of futures trading in commodity markets on price volatility. There have been two sets of findings. One states that introducing derivatives in the stock market has increased volatility and market performance. The other says that the introduction of derivatives has reduced the volatility in the stock market, thereby increasing its stability.

Some interesting studies have already analyzed the role of "financialization" of commodities futures and spot markets; however many authors [1] have highlighted the need to deepen empirical evidence to better identify the relationship between spot and futures prices utilizing appropriate methodological instruments.

Since the 1990s, feature-based model selection has been applied for a time series forecasting problem. In [3] paper, authors explained a decision tree-based model to forecast stationary time series. Similarly, the authors of the paper [4] proposed rule induction based on a decision tree to calculate the optimal model from time-series features. Feature reduction is one of the important tasks before classification. In [5], the authors worked on selecting features on a historical database and finally verified the efficiency of feature reduction.

Adya et al. [6] used an expert system for model selection to forecast complex time series, which helps decision-making. They applied the features reduction method before classification to reduce features' redundancy. Ali, *et al.* [7] used Random Forest-based feature reduction technique. He also explored three classifiers: decision tree, feed-forward neural network, and support vector machine for performance comparison. J. H. Zhang et al. [8] exploit a time series prediction model based on a wavelet neural network for the prediction of Tomato prices. L. Zhemin et al. [9] studied potato price prediction based on a dynamic, chaotic neural network. P. F. He et al. [10] showed the predicting Chinese soybean price based on APSO-SVR. Y. T. Zhou et al. [11] studied short-term wheat price prediction using QBR neural network. D. Zhang [12] applied QR-RBF neural network model to predict soybean price in China. We may conclude from above that different mathematical models are popularly used to forecast various agricultural commodities. The 'no free lunch' theory [12] reveals no single model applicable for all the commodities. Finding the optimal model for predicting the price of a specific commodity is no easy task for scientists. Very few studies have been carried out on agricultural commodities price prediction for the Indian scenario. The authors of the paper [13] worked on price forecasting & anomaly detection for two agricultural commodities, namely onion, and potato in India. Recent studies [14] of authors show the forecasting of spot prices of five agricultural commodities (castor seed, cottonseed, soybean seed, rape mustard seed, and guar seed) of National Commodity and Derivatives Exchange in India using deep-learning models. The authors stated that the long short-term memory (LSTM) network performed better than the time-delay neural network (TDNN) and other linear models. Similarly, in paper [14], authors worked on short-Term forecasting of six years of sunflower seed data and five years of soybean seed data of Andhra Pradesh and Maharashtra in India, respectively. The authors observed that the artificial neural network model performed a better forecasting model than the autoregressive integrated moving average (ARIMA) model on selected data. In the present paper, the authors are working with four years of field data of three commodities: Bengal gram, Groundnut, and Maize of Telangana state of India. Within this data, three years of data have been used to build the model, and another one-year data is used to evaluate the system. Here authors have proposed a hybrid model to predict the commodity prices of three agri-commodities. The methodology of the present work has been described in the next section in detail.

3 Methodology

This paper aims to identify variables in accordance with their relevant influence on price discovery for selected agri-commodities, followed by developing a Machine Learning Model for price discovery [15]. A block diagram of the real-time price discovery for e-Marketplace is shown in Fig. 1. The diagram comprises two main blocks – training and testing. Different crop features are used as input to the model, and output is short term predicted price of the crop.

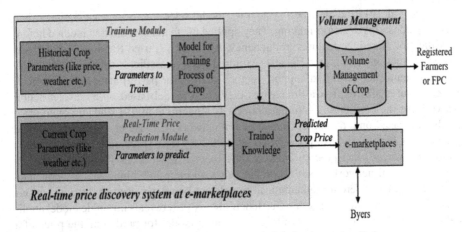

Fig. 1. Block diagram of the proposed solution for time price discovery

3.1 Proposed Flow Diagram

Figure 2 refers to a generalized flow chart of the price discovery solution for selected agri-commodities. For analysis purposes, we have used google colab notebooks. Collaboratory, or "Colab" for short, allows us to write and execute Python in our browser.

3.2 Data Collection

Data set was collected from Agriculture Marketing Department, Govt. of Telangana. The data set comprises the price trends across various marketplaces for three commodities, i.e., Bengal Gram, Maize, and Groundnut.

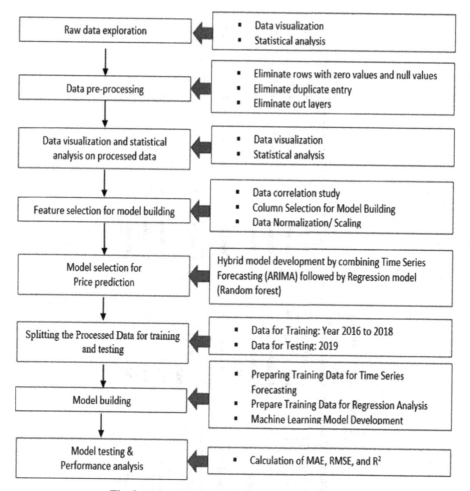

Fig. 2. Generalized flow diagram for model building

Parameters of Data. From the collected dataset, it has been observed that there are thirteen numbers of fields in the dataset for analysis. Table 1 shows the sample data set for price data prediction. The data indicates that the date, market, and yard-wise price of Bengal Gram, Groundnut, and Maize are presented. There are different varieties of commodities available within the dataset. Table 2 shows the information of all dataset parameters in detail. After careful observations, we have observed that input parameters are DDate, AmcCode, AmcName, YardCode, YardName, CommCode, CommName, VarityCode, VarityName, and Arrivals. In addition, output parameters are the Minimum, Maximum, and Model price of the commodities.

Table 1. Sample data set

Date	AMCCode	AMCName	YardCode	YardName	CommCode	CommName	VarityCode	VarityName	Arrivals	Minimum	Maximum	Model
1/2/2016	309	Narayanpet	1342	Narayanpet	14	Bengal Gram	14	Common	2	4569	4569	4569
1/4/2016	284	Jogipet	1208	Jogipet	14	Bengal Gram	14	Common	1	4600	4600	4600
1/13/2016	309	Narayanpet	1342	Narayanpet	14	Bengal Gram	14	Common	2	4629	4629	4629
4/23/2016	278	Suryapet	1091	Suryapet	30	Groundnut pods	30	Common	4	5050	5050	5050
4/25/2016	246	Warangal	886	Warangal	30	Groundnut pods	30	Common	10	5000	5400	5250
4/26/2016	246	Warangal	886	Warangal	30	Groundnut pods	30	Common	10	4500	5300	5300
2/16/2019	300	Badepally	1327	Badepally	5	Maize	5	Common	46	1801	1875	1875
2/18/2019	219	Jagtial	1125	Jagtial	5	Maize	5	Common	46	1718	1857	1818
2/22/2019	238	Jangoan	1169	Jangaon	5	Maize	5	Common	13	2000	2000	2000

Table 2. Different fields of the dataset

Variable name	Data type	Description	Format/units	Example
DDate	Date	Date	dd-mm-yy	1/12/2016
AmcCode	Number	Code of AMC	–	323
AmcName	Text	Name of AMC	–	Banswada
YardCode	Number	Code of Yard	–	1123
YardName	Text	Name of Yard	–	suryapet
CommCode	Number	Code of the commodity	–	30
CommName	Text	Name of the commodity	–	Groundnut
VarityCode	Number	Code of variety	–	229
VarityName	Text	Name of the variety	–	local
Arrivals	Number	Quantity of arrivals	Quintals	224
Minimum	Number	Minimum price	INR	3651
Maximum	Number	Maximum price	INR	4461
Model	Number	Predicted price	INR	4391

3.3 Data Statistics

After data loading three commodities, i.e., Bengal Gram, Groundnut, and Maize, we have analyzed all data. Total 42415 records with 13 columns are found in the file. The statistical distribution is shown in Table 3.

Table 3. Statistical characteristics of the raw data files.

	AmcCode	YardCode	CommCode	VarityCode	Arrivals	Minimum	Maximum	Model
count	42415.000000	42415.000000	42415.000000	42415.000000	42415.000000	4.241500e+04	42415.000000	42415.000000
mean	263.698385	996.266109	13.748556	31.110173	207.207809	1.499202e+03	1280.775433	1207.413250
std	44.301170	484.020298	11.203884	58.181481	736.643144	8.984378e+04	1790.448024	1672.015115
min	186.000000	3.000000	5.000000	5.000000	0.000000	0.000000e+00	0.000000	0.000000
25%	222.000000	1080.000000	5.000000	5.000000	0.000000	0.000000e+00	0.000000	0.000000
50%	268.000000	1138.000000	5.000000	5.000000	0.000000	0.000000e+00	0.000000	0.000000
75%	304.000000	1327.000000	30.000000	30.000000	73.000000	1.526000e+03	1600.000000	1569.500000
max	368.000000	1629.000000	30.000000	243.000000	19196.000000	1.850193e+07	58469.000000	54656.000000

3.4 Data Pre-processing

This section has checked and removed null values and outliers present in the raw data. We have also observed a considerable number of rows with zero values. We also dropped the rows containing zero values. We could have approximated the zero values with mean, mode, etc. Though, there could be a chance that the model would learn the approximation policy itself. This may create an adverse effect on the final price prediction. The data distribution before and after pre-processing is shown in Table 4.

Table 4. Data visualization before and after pre-processing.

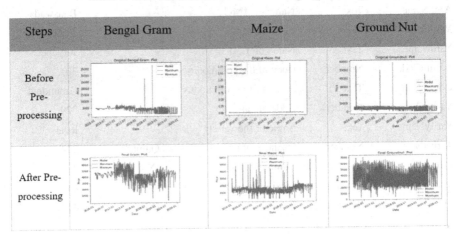

3.5 Feature Selection

Every data is possessed with information, and data analysis is the process of unlocking that information. However, data needs to be prepared and formatted before putting it through any analytics pipeline. The correlation matrix helps select those independent features, which highly depend on the price prediction. After pre-processing, data is summarized column-wise to find correlations. The correlation matrix for price prediction is shown in Fig. 3

After looking at the correlation matrix, it has been observed that there is a strong correlation among max price, min price, and model price. Since they are output variables and we want to predict model price only, we can drop the minimum price and maximum price column and other categorical data columns. Based on the correlations, merging or removing several columns may require optimization. Since all the categorical data has one related numeric column, we are considering only numeric column for such column pairs, i.e. AmcName <-> AmcCode, YardName <-> YardCode, CommName <-> CommCode, VarityName <-> VarityCode.

3.6 Data Normalization/Scaling

Data scaling helps to normalize the data within a particular range. The goal of normalization is to change the values of numeric columns in the dataset to use a standard scale without distorting differences in the ranges of values or losing information. The range of

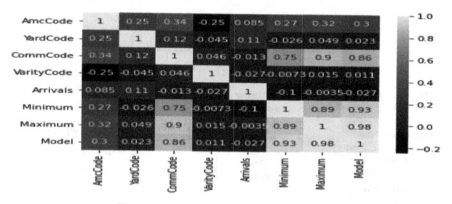

Fig. 3. Correlation matrix for price prediction

all column data (features) should be normalized so that each feature contributes approximately proportionately during model building. We are using min-max scaling for all input variable columns.

3.7 Hybrid Model Building for Price Discovery

After the pre-processing steps, it was evident that crop-specific time-series analysis is not possible due to the lack of available data points. To overcome this problem, we have considered the following two sets of data for model building:

SET 1: Day-wise average price of crops (time series data).

SET 2: Different crop prices across the AMCs (considering the specific crop type, variety, etc.) from the day-wise average price.

Now, we feed the SET 1 data to train a sequential model, which will give us a price prediction irrespective of AMC, crop type, variety, etc. We called it **Global Price** (G). Crop prices may vary due to various reasons, such as inflation, high or low yield, weather conditions, etc. To identify such influencing factors, we required a considerable amount of data absent in the present scenario. To tackle such conditions, we introduce the concept of **Global Price**.

On the other hand, SET 2 data is fed to a regression model, which will give us the variation of crop price from the **Global Price** across the different AMCs (considering the specific crop type, variety, etc.) within the state. This model's output indicates the fluctuation of prices from the Global average prices among the AMCs. We call this predicted value **Local Price Deviation (L)**.

Figure 4 shows the schematic diagram of the proposed hybrid algorithm step-by-step with input and output parameters. By combining the outputs from the said two models, we can predict the final crop price. Thus, our final prediction results from combining the output from the sequential model and the regressor. So, we termed our model as a hybrid model for price prediction.

Predicted Price = Global Price (Sequential model output) + Local Variation (Regression Model Output).

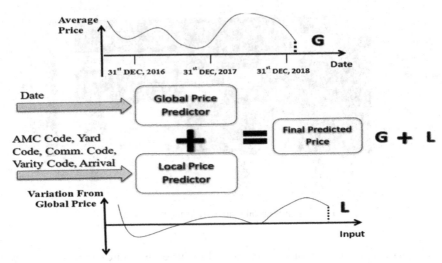

Fig. 4. Schematic diagram of the proposed hybrid model

3.8 Final Pre-processed Data for Model Building

We have split the given data into train and test-data set for time series analysis based on date parameters. A total of 18,676 data are available from 2016 to 2019. The splitting of data for building the model (training) and performance analysis (testing) is described in Table 5.

Table 5. Final dataset and distribution

Total data points	Train data	Test data
18,676 (From 2016–2019)	16,217 (From 2016–2018)	2,459 (2019 data only)

We are considering the date-wise average of model price for time series forecasting. This model's training & test data will have only two columns, i.e., Date and Model price average for a given date. For regression analysis, we consider all input variables (except date) and deviation of model price from average model price. The identified features are AmcCode, YardCode, CommCode, VarityCode, Arrivals, and Model_Diff (Variation in model price from average price).

3.9 Model Development

Time series forecasting is a significant part of data science and machine learning technologies that involve fitting statistical/machine learning models to make predictions. These tools are as simple as extrapolating historical trends into the future to sophisticated stochastic autoregressive models such as ARIMA. Deep learning models such as

Long Short-term Memory (LSTM), Gated GRU are increasingly adding sophistication to forecasting practices. Several tools have been explored to fit the price data and forecast crop prices. In the present scope of the paper, a comparison of different models is not presented. Based on the performance of the various models, finally, two models have been identified for proposed hybrid model building, i.e., ARIMA (Autoregressive Integrated Moving Average) and XGBoost regression model building.

ARIMA (Autoregressive Integrated Moving Average). The ARIMA model, is fitted to the time series data for analyzing the data or predicting future data points on a time scale. The most significant advantage of this model is that it can be applied in cases where the data shows evidence of non-stationarity. The auto-regressive means that the evolving variable of interest is regressed on its prior value. Moving average indicates that the regression error is a linear combination of error terms whose values occurred contemporaneously and at various times in the past. The significance of integration in the ARIMA model is that the data values have been replaced with the difference between their values and the previous values. ARIMA yields better results in forecasting the short term, whereas LSTM yields better results for long-term modeling.

We are using the ARIMA model with the following parameters:

$p = 5$: The number of lag observations included in the model, also called the lag order.

$d = 1$: The number of times the raw observations are differenced, also called the degree of difference.

$q = 0$: The size of the moving average window, also called the order of moving average.

After several experiments on the available dataset, parameter values of the ARIMA model have been finalized for this present work.

3.10 XGBoost Regression Model Building

XGBoost is a scalable and accurate implementation of gradient boosting machines, and it has proven to push the limits of computing power for boosted trees algorithms. It is a decision tree-based ensemble algorithm.

4 Results and Discussions

The following parameters are considered for analyzing the performance of the developed price prediction model.

- Root Mean Square Error (RMSE): It is a typical way to measure the error of a model in predicting quantitative data. Formally it is defined as follows:

$$RMSE = \sqrt{\sum_{i=1}^{n} \frac{\left(\hat{y}_i - y_i\right)^2}{n}}$$

$\hat{y}_1, \hat{y}_2, \ldots \hat{y}_n$ are predicted values, $y_1, y_2, \ldots y_n$ are actual/observed values, and n is the number of observations.

- Mean Absolute Error (MAE): It is defined as the mean of all absolute errors, i.e., the difference of predicted and actual values. This is written as follows:

$$MAE = \frac{\sum_{i=1}^{n} |\hat{y}_i - y|}{n}$$

- R^2 (R-squared): It denotes the proportion of variance of the target variable that the model can explain. So, for better model always achieves more proportion of variance. If this value is close to 1, that corresponds to a good model, and if this value is close to 0 corresponds to a bad model.

Figure 5 shows the actual and predicted price data plot using the ARIMA time series model. On the other hand, Fig. 6 shows the plot of actual and predicted price data using the XGBoost regression model. Where blue lines indicate the actual or observed data and orange means the predicted data of the model.

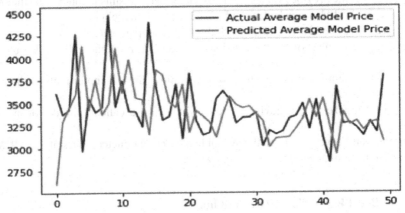

Fig. 5. The plot of actual and predicted price data using time series model

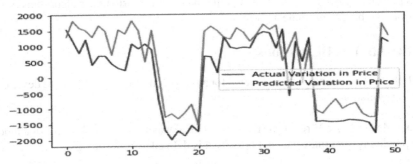

Fig. 6. The plot of actual and predicted price data using the regression model

Figure 7 plot shows actual and predicted price data using proposed hybrid model. It has been observed from the figure that predicted data is more or less following the actual data of the commodity price.

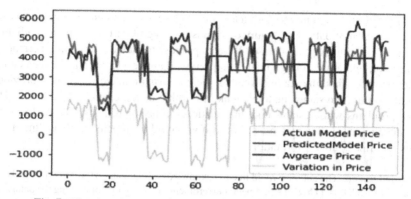

Fig. 7. The plot of actual and predicted price data using the hybrid model

The performance analysis results with the developed algorithm are shown in Table 6 which shows that the R-squared values are encouraging as it is close to 1. We can interpret that 77% of the data fit the proposed hybrid model. And this value of r-squared indicates a better fit for the model though there are opportunities to improve the performance.

Table 6. Result of performance analysis

RMSE	MAE	R^2
609.86	453.73	0.77

5 Conclusion

For predicting crop price, continuous time series data over a more significant period is the utmost requirement for identifying trends and seasonality affecting the price variations. However, the supplied data is not continuous regarding both crop and markets. Also, data has been provided for a short period.

Considering the above constraints, we proposed a hybrid model to predict price by combining time series and regression analysis. During performance analysis, we found that the R^2 value is 0.77, which is encouraging with the available dataset. Quality of crop is also an integral part of the price prediction, which is missing in the given dataset. We propose including crop-specific quality parameters like discolor, immature, foreign matter, admixture, damage, etc., within the data collection framework. Though data like weather, yield information, etc., have been provided, we could not use the same due to a chunk of missing data present in the data set. This creates problems while establishing the relationship between fields. The performance of the developed solution could be improved if we could overcome the above limitations and incorporate quality information.

To improve the system's performance, we propose to collect the systematic and scientific collection of data. The quality of crop is an integral part of the price prediction, which is missing in the given dataset. We also propose to include the quality parameters like discolor, immature, foreign matter, admixture, damage, etc., within the data collection framework. Though data like weather, yield information, etc., have been provided, we could not use the same due to a chunk of missing data present in the data set. This creates problems while establishing the relationship between fields. The performance of the developed solution may be improved if we could overcome the above limitations and incorporate quality information.

Acknowledgment. The authors would like to acknowledge Telangana AI Mission (T-AIM) (ET wing and NASSCOM), ITE&C Department, Government of Telangana for proving the dataset for experiments during 'Telangana AI Mission's Agri AI Grand Challenge, 2021'. We are thankful to all collaborating institutions for motivating and constant support to carry out research activities in this area.

References

1. Headey, D., Fan, S.: Anatomy of a crisis: the causes and consequences of surging food prices. Agric. Econ. **39**, 375–391 (2008). https://doi.org/10.1111/j.1574-0862.2008.00345.x
2. Zhang, D., Chen, S., Liwen, L., Xia, Q.: Forecasting agricultural commodity prices using model selection framework with time series features and forecast horizons. IEEE Access **8**, 28197–28209 (2020). https://doi.org/10.1109/ACCESS.2020.2971591
3. Prudêncio, R.B.C., Ludermir, T.B.: Meta-learning approaches to selecting time series models. Neurocomputing **61**, 121–137 (2004). https://doi.org/10.1016/j.neucom.2004.03.008
4. Wang, X., Smith-Miles, K., Hyndman, R.: Rule induction for forecasting method selection: Meta-learning the characteristics of univariate time series. Neurocomputing **72**(10–12), 2581–2594 (2009). https://doi.org/10.1016/j.neucom.2008.10.017
5. Widodo, A., Budi, I.: Feature enhancement for model selection in time series forecasting. In: 2013 International Conference on Advanced Computer Science and Information Systems (ICACSIS), pp. 367–373, September 2013. https://doi.org/10.1109/ICACSIS.2013.6761603
6. Adya, M., Lusk, E.J.: Development and validation of a rule-based time series complexity scoring technique to support design of adaptive forecasting DSS. Decis. Support Syst. **83**, 70–82 (2016). https://doi.org/10.1016/j.dss.2015.12.009
7. Ali, A.R., Gabrys, B., Budka, M.: Cross-domain Meta-learning for Time-series Forecasting. Procedia Comput. Sci. **126**, 9–18 (2018). https://doi.org/10.1016/j.procs.2018.07.204
8. Zhang, J.H., Kong, F.T., Wu, J.Z., Zhu, M.S., Xu, K., Liu, J.J.: Tomato prices time series prediction model based on wavelet neural network. Appl. Mech. Mater. **644–650**, 2636–2640 (2014). https://doi.org/10.4028/www.scientific.net/AMM.644-650.2636
9. Zhe-min, L., Shi-wei, X., Li-guo, C., Jian-hua, Z.: Prediction study based on dynamic chaotic neural network-Taking potato time-series prices as an example. Syst. Eng. Theory Pract. **35**(8), 2083–2091 (2015). https://doi.org/10.12011/1000-6788(2015)8-2083
10. He, P.F., Li, J., Zhang, D.Q.: Predicting Chinese soybean price based on APSO-SVR. Soybean Sci. **36**(9), 632–638 (2017)
11. Zhou, Y.T., Jia, F.W., Wen, K.: Study on short-term wheat price prediction in China. Price, Theory Pr. **3**, 107–110 (2018)
12. Wolpert, D.H., Macready, W.G.: No free lunch theorems for optimization. IEEE Trans. Evol. Comput. **1**(1), 67–82 (1997). https://doi.org/10.1109/4235.585893

13. Madaan, L., Sharma, A., Khandelwal, P., Goel, S., Singla, P., Seth, A.: Price forecasting & anomaly detection for agricultural commodities in India. In: Proceedings of the Conference on Computing & Sustainable Societies - COMPASS 19 2019, pp. 52–64. https://doi.org/10.1145/3314344.3332488

14. Mahto, A.K., Alam, M.A., Biswas, R., Ahmed, J., Alam, S.I.: Short-term forecasting of agriculture commodities in context of indian market for sustainable agriculture by using the artificial neural network. J. Food Qual. **2021**, 1–13 (2021). https://doi.org/10.1155/2021/9939906

15. Minghua, W., Qiaolin, Z., Zhijian, Y., Jingui, Z.: Prediction model of agricultural product's price based on the improved BP neural network. In: 2012 7th International Conference on Computer Science & Education (ICCSE), pp. 613–617, July 2012. https://doi.org/10.1109/ICCSE.2012.6295150

PriHealth: A Fingerprint-Based Mobile Primary Healthcare Management System

Jide Kehinde Adeniyi[1], Tunde Taiwo Adeniyi[2], Roseline Oluwaseun Ogundokun[1],
Sanjay Misra[3], Akshat Agrawal[4(✉)], and Ravin Ahuja[5]

[1] Department of Computer Science, Landmark University, Omu Aran, Nigeria
{adeniyi.jide,ogundokun.roseline}@lmu.edu.ng
[2] Department of Computer Science, University of Ilorin, Ilorin, Nigeria
[3] Department of Computer Science and Communication, Ostfold University College,
Halden, Norway
[4] Amity University, Gurgaon, Hariyana, India
akshatag20@gmail.com
[5] Shri Vishwakarma Skill University, Haryana, India

Abstract. Primary health institution as the main health care institution that addresses the health challenges of individuals in rural areas and those with limited financial capacity in Nigeria houses quality information. However, this information is not properly managed and is not easily available for patients and health personnel. This is because the traditional filing system is still prevalently used and in cases where databases are used, access to a computer system is still limited. With the popularity of mobile devices, an avenue for easy and quick access to medical records presents itself. However, this also gives rise to record security issues. Taking advantage of the fingerprint scanner on most of these devices, this paper presents the development of a mobile primary health care system - PriHealth. The system uses fingerprint authentication to secure access to the back-end of the system which is the database that holds medical records. The accuracy of the approach showed an encouraging result of 97%.

Keywords: Primary health care institution · Biometrics · Hospital management system · Biometric identification · Fingerprint

1 Introduction

A primary health institution refers to health institutions that give essential health care using quality and socially acceptable technology and methods. Information is a valuable asset in health institutions (hospitals), hence the need for a method to manage health information [1]. The traditional method used to require the creation of a physical file to hold individual information. However, this method is slow for information retrieval and also insecure. The improvement in technology led to the introduction of health management systems. In a hospital setting, the need to improve medical treatment, services,

---

The original version of this chapter was revised: Affiliation of the Author Roseline Oluwaseun Ogundokun has been changed to "Department of Computer Science, Landmark University, Omu Aran, Nigeria"; affiliation of the Author Sanjay Misra has been changed to "Department of Computer Science and Communication, Ostfold University College, Halden, Norway". The correction to this chapter is available at https://doi.org/10.1007/978-3-031-10766-5_35

© The Author(s), under exclusive license to Springer Nature Switzerland AG 2022, corrected publication 2022
S. Mukhopadhyay et al. (Eds.): CICBA 2022, CCIS 1579, pp. 432–445, 2022.
https://doi.org/10.1007/978-3-031-10766-5_34

and patient data storage is crucial [2]. The ultimate purpose of a health-management system is to generate relevant data that can be used to make transparent, evidence-based decisions about healthcare interventions [3]. The Health Management System (HMS) is created to reduce hospital paperwork and alleviate the scarcity of healthcare workers [4].

In recent years, the use of information and communication technology (ICT) to improve health care services has gained widespread recognition [5, 6]. As a result, the importance of information and communication technology (ICT) in providing effective online healthcare services cannot be overstated [7, 34], although it comes with its challenges. Some of the issues include patient privacy and the usage of easily guessed passwords, which might facilitate unwanted access. Even though most computer networks are subject to intrusion attacks, privacy in the health sector is increasing these days [4]. Furthermore, the capacity to remotely monitor a patient's health is critical [8, 9]. The advent of biometrics opened a promising future for HMS security challenges. The electronic identification and verification of an individual based on their physiological or behavioral features are known as biometrics. Signature dynamics, skin patterns, body odor, ear shape, voice verification, fingerprints, iris scans, hand geometry, facial feature recognition, and many other biometrical identification procedures are used today [9, 10].

One of the most widely utilized biometrics for authentication is fingerprint technology. This is due to its low cost and high accuracy. This is even more pronounced on mobile devices where a fingerprint sensor is attached to the back or front of the device. The study aims at developing an enhanced mobile application hospital information system using Finger Recognition Biometrics Technology for Primary health care institutions. This will increase the confidentiality and availability of patient information to the patients and the medical professionals.

The remaining part of the paper is arranged as thus: Sect. 2 presents the literature review on health care information security and related researches were discussed as well. Material and methods adopted in the study are discussed in Sect. 3. Section 4 presented the result gotten from the proposed system implementation and the discussion is presented as well. The paper is concluded in Sect. 5.

2 Literature Review

Some authors have examined health care information security, some of which are examined in this section. In Shakil et al. [11], the authors examined the security of cloud-based health care information. They developed a framework for the cloud-based health care information system. Furthermore, biometrics was proposed as a solution to the traditional method of securing health information systems (using a PIN, Password, and so on). Their paper proposed the use of signature using the Backpropagation Neural Network. Their system gave an EER of 0.12.

Zhao et al. [12] presented a paper that entails the development of a primary health care system. They examined the application of the developed primary health care system in primary medical units. The Electronic Health Record (EHR), Virtual Private Network (VPN), and real-time data backup were used to develop the system. The result after observing the system in operation for 12 months showed that the developed system has good management qualities.

In Chung and Park [13], the authors proposed a peer-to-peer-based cloud system for the management of medicines. The system was designed to speed up data processing and alleviate delays in wireless body area networks (WBANs), which are common challenges in cloud health services. This should increase the response time of the cloud-based system. The proposed system was in the form of a chatbot. The architecture of an urban health information system is proposed in Chen et al. [14]. The architecture focused on the application portal, the application platform, the business system, and the support platform. The proposed architecture was presented for the urban parts of China. The paper also introduced an algorithm for regional health information data conversion from heterogeneous databases to XML documents. Omar et al. [15] proposed a patient-targeted data management system. The system leveraged on data privacy challenge by using blockchain technology. A Cryptographic method was used to protect patients' data.

3   Material and Methods

In this section, we propose a Health Management System that resides on a server. The proposed Health Management system has two parts: the front-end and the back-end. The architectural design depicted in Fig. 1 shows the system's entities.

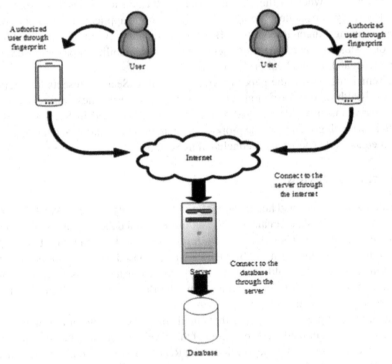

Fig. 1. Proposed system architecture

3.1 Authenticating User Access/Front End

To log in to the system on the mobile platform, the user's fingerprint is used. The fingerprint was selected because most smartphones come with a fingerprint scanner at the back (or sometimes front) of the devices. For a user to be authenticated by the mobile device, the individual must have registered their fingerprint. Registered fingerprints are saved on the server. A typical enrolment and authentication process of a palmprint follows the same steps. The steps are acquisition, preprocessing, features extraction, and matching or saving as a template. The last stage depends on whether it is an enrolment or an authentication process. During an enrolment, features are saved as a template. However, during an authentication process, features extracted are compared with those in the template (this is termed matching). The detailed step followed by the system is:

Start:

    Step 1: Acquisition of fingerprint image.

    Step 2: Conversion of the image into greyscale form.

    Step 3: Conversion of the greyscale image into binary form.

    Step 4: Apply thinning process on the binary image.

    Step 5: Unsharp Masking of the binarized image for sharpening of the edges.

    Step 6: Feature (minutiae) extraction (Find total numbers of ridges-end points and bifurcation points).

    Step 7: feature selection using Genetic Algorithm (GA)

    Step 8: Verify both minutiae points; if the total number of minutiae points in two fingerprint photos is the same, it means that both fingers are the same or matched; otherwise, they are not the same and belong to two different people.

End.

Fingerprint Acquisition

The fingerprint acquisition stage captures fingerprints for the system. In the presented system, the fingerprints were obtained through the fingerprint scanner built with the mobile devices. The user is required to place any convenient (usually the leading finger) finger-tip on the scanner at the back of the device. A total of 300 individuals were enrolled in the system to test it. Most of the recipients used android phones, hence the system was developed on the android platform. Samsung, Tecno, infinix, and Xiaomi products were used to capture the user's fingerprint. The acquired fingerprint is 48px by 67px. This size is maintained throughout the preprocessing steps.

Preprocessing

After the fingerprint image is gotten, the next is the processing of the image to prepare it for the extraction of features. The processes undergone are collectively referred to as preprocessing. The fingerprint from the android scanner usually contains unevenly distributed grey values; hence the acquired finger image is subjected to preprocessing.

The preprocessing stage involved include binarization and thinning. Binarization was used in altering the grayscale images to black and white images (binary images).

Binarization

A value of one indicates that the pixel is white, whereas a value of zero indicates that the pixel is black in binarization (0 = white, 1 = black). This conversion of a grayscale image to a binary image is accomplished by applying a threshold. When a threshold is applied to a picture, the input threshold is examined for each pixel value. Pixel values that are less than the threshold value is set to zero, while those that are larger than the threshold value is set to one. Each pixel value within the image is either zero or one at the end of this procedure, and the image has been converted to binary form. The ridges in the fingerprint are highlighted in black after this conversion, while the valleys are highlighted in white [16, 17].

Thinning

After binarization of the fingerprint images was done, then thinning was done. Image thinning is the process of decreasing the thickness of all ridgelines into single pixel width. Thinning process converts the original x, y location and angle of direction of the minutiae points of the image, which assures the true calculation of minutiae points [18]. Thinning was also used to reduce the extra pixel of ridges till the ridges are just one pixel broad [19, 20]. Holt thinning algorithm was used for thinning the fingerprint image. Holt thinning algorithm approaches skeletonization with two iterations written in a logical expression. It also made use of the eight neighboring pixels [21].

NO	N	NE
O	M	L
SO	S	SE

Fig. 2. The surrounding pixels of a center pixel M

The concept is to make the two rules below a single logical expression. The iteration or rules are as depicted in (1) and (2) [22]:

$$v(M) \wedge (\sim edge(M) \vee (v(L) \wedge v(S) \wedge (v(N) \vee v(O)))) \tag{1}$$

$$v(M) \wedge (\sim edge(M) \vee (v(O) \wedge v(N) \wedge (v(S) \vee v(L)))) \tag{2}$$

is the value of the point, such that a black means it's true and a white implies it is false. confirms if the point is located at the edge of the image. are the pixels around point M as shown in Fig. 2. The algorithm executes the first iteration, followed by the second [22].

Features Extraction

For features extraction, a minutiae-based approach and textural approach were used. The minutiae-based approach entails extracting the minutiae and the Genetic Algorithm was used for this. The textural approach used a circular Local Binary Pattern for the extraction of features. The details are explained below.

Minutiae-Based Feature Extraction Using Genetic Algorithm

These points were passed to the Genetic Algorithm for the selection of the key features. A genetic algorithm is an algorithm that is based on biological evolution. It is a stochastic global optimization algorithm [23, 24]. The algorithm is stated below [25, 26].

Input: the preprocessed fingerprint image
Output: An output image

Start:

    Step 1: Create a random population of fingerprints to start the genetic process by defining the population size.

    Step 2: Set the iteration counter to zero.

    Step 3: For each fingerprint:

    Step 4: Convert a bit string to obtain the value of a variable, v1.

    Step 5: Calculate each fingerprint's fitness, f1, using Manhattan distance.

    Step 6: Choose the person in the population who has the most fitness and preserve it as an antibody.

    Step 7: Calculate the relative and cumulative fitness, as well as the average fitness, fa.

    Step 8: Make a roulette wheel option.

    Step 9: Variable crossover is used to perform crossover operations on the population.

    Step 10: Variable is used to perform mutation operations on the population.

    Step 11: Step 5 should be repeated for each fingerprint, and the individual with the highest fitness in the population should be saved as the current antibody. If this antibody's fitness is higher than the prior antibody, it should be replaced.

    Step 12: Replace the existing population with this new one (by elitism: old generation taken over by the better fitter new generation)

    Step 13: Return to Step 1 if the number of iterations is less than the maximum iteration number (the stopover condition); otherwise, deliver the variable's ideal values.

End

Crossing Number

Finally, by the pixel-by-pixel computation of Crossing Number, a basic picture scan may find pixels that correspond to minutiae (CN). The CN of ridge ending and a bifurcation is 1 and 3 respectively. The CN is expressed in (3) [27, 28].

$$CN = \frac{1}{2} \sum\nolimits_{i=1}^{8} |L_i - L_{i-1}| \tag{3}$$

where L_i is the neighboring pixels around the current pixel being considered.

Textural Features Extraction

The circular Local Binary Pattern (CLBP) was used to extract the textural features of the fingerprint. The CLBP is an effective textural feature extraction method. The CLBP is theoretically given as: Given the location of a pixel (x_a, y_a) and neighborhood (O, S), the location of the sampling point (x_b, y_b) can be given in (4) [29, 30].

$$(x_b, y_b) = \left(x_a + S\cos\left(\frac{2\pi b}{O}\right), y_a - S\sin\left(\frac{2\pi b}{O}\right) \right)$$ (4)

The sampling point's intensity value is given as/with $k \in \{0, 1, \ldots, O-1\}$. The LBP is then given in (5).

$$LBP_{OS}(x_b, y_b) = \sum_{b=0}^{O-1} S(v_b - v_a)2^b$$ (5)

where v_a and v_b are the intensity values of the pixel at the center and the kth neighborhood pixel in the circular neighborhood (O, S). The thresholding function $S(u)$ is given in Eq. (6).

$$S(u) = \begin{cases} 1, u \geq 0 \\ 0, u < 0 \end{cases}$$ (6)

Fusion and Matching

After the minutiae features are extracted and the textural features are extracted, both feature sets are matched separately using the Manhattan distance. The matching score is fused using the sum rule. The fused score is then compared with an obtained threshold. The Equal Error Rate (EER) graph is used to obtain this threshold. The Manhattan distance and the sum rule are given in Eqs. (7) and (8) [31–33].

$$d(a, b) = \sum_{i=1}^{s} |a_i - y_i|$$ (7)

where $a = (a_1, a_2 \ldots, a_s)$ and $b = (b_1, b_2, \ldots, b_s)$ are two points in s-dimensional space.

$$S_B = \sum_{j=1}^{n} S_j$$ (8)

where S_B is the sum of the biometric scores, n is the number of biometric traits, and S_j is the score of biometric trait j.

4   Results and Discussion

From the architectural design of the proposed system, users access records on the android app through the android enabled computer devices (phones, tabs, android emulators on PC, etc.). Access to the database on the server can be from the website or the mobile phone. Access on the mobile phone requires authentication using the fingerprint. For a user to be granted access, the user must have been enrolled. This part deals with the security of the database user. The database itself resides on a server. A use-case diagram illustrating the interaction between the user and the system is depicted in Fig. 3. From the use-case diagram in Fig. 3, it can be observed that patients can only view records of their medical history after they log in. Any modification privilege was not granted to the patients. The application admin can create a new record for a new patient, edit the existing record, and delete records. However, the administrator cannot enter any medical

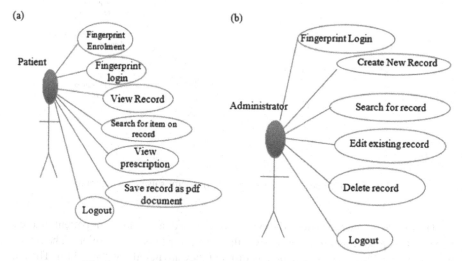

(a)

(b)

Fig. 3. (a) Patient's use-case diagram (b) App Admin use case

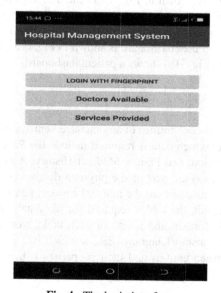

Fig. 4. The login interface.

detail. In order words, the administrator can only perform administrative duties as they do in traditional management scenarios.

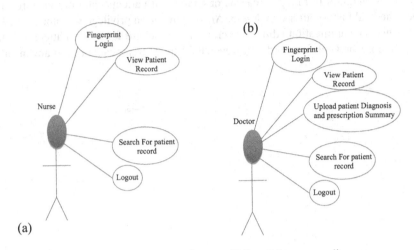

Fig. 5. (a) Nurse's use case diagram (b) Doctor's use-case diagram

The doctor is however allowed to view, edit, upload, and search for patient medical records. This gives them full control over the medical details of the patient. The nurses are also allowed to view the patient's record, but they are not allowed to edit it. The use case diagram for the doctors and the nurses is shown in Fig. 5. The interfaces for the login on the application are shown in Fig. 4. As the user logs in with the fingerprint, the identity of the user is detected (patient, doctor, administrator, or nurse). This in turn affects the privilege given to the individual. A typical registration interface is shown in Fig. 6(a). A typical Admin user dashboard is shown in Fig. 6(b). A doctor's dashboard is shown in Fig. 7(a) and Fig. 7(b) shows a patient dashboard.

4.1 Database Design

The database as one of the core entities of any management system was designed peculiarly. The entities about which data is required include the Patient, Patient Diagnosis History, Doctor Prescription, and Patient Medical History. A number of the required attributes (data dictionaries) are part of the physical database design. This procedure began with the analysis phase, where the relevant entities, relationships, and attributes were identified. As a result, the tables required for the database, as well as the corresponding field names, format, and length of each table, were determined. Figure 8 depicts the Entity-Relationship Diagram (ERD), which is a graphical representation of the relationship between entities and their properties within the system's planned database.

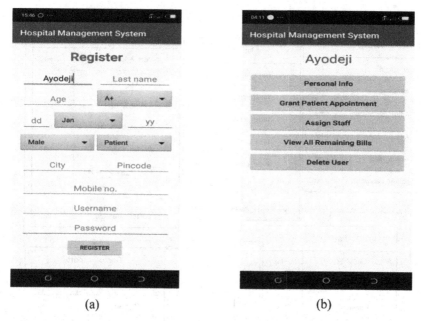

Fig. 6. (a) a typical registration interface (b) The Admin user dashboard

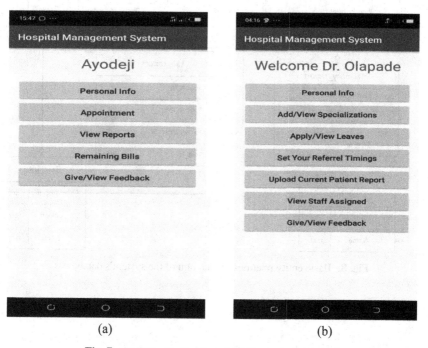

Fig. 7. (a) Patient's dashboard (b) Doctor's dashboard

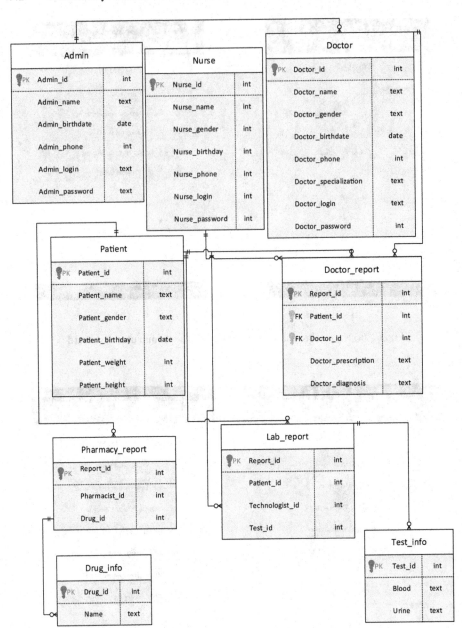

Fig. 8. Basic entity relationship diagram of the system's database

4.2 Result

To test the system, users of a primary health care hospital were registered on the system. Table 1 shows the result obtained from the designed system. The accuracy of the system is 0.97. The False Acceptance Ratio (FAR) and the False Rejectance Ratio (FRR) are 0.6667 and 0.01333 respectively. They produced precision and recall of 0.95 and 0.96.

Table 1. Confusion matrix of the biometric authentication of the design system

Actual	Predicted		
		NO	YES	
	NO	147	3	150
	YES	2	144	150
		149	151	300

Where,

$$Accuracy = \frac{TP + TN}{Total}$$

$$FAR = FPR = \frac{FP}{(FP + TN)}$$

$$FRR = FNR = \frac{FN}{(TP + FN)}$$

$$Precision = \frac{TP}{TP + FP}$$

$$Recall = \frac{TP}{TP + FN}$$

5 Conclusion

This study presented the design and development of a biometric-authenticated mobile hospital management system. The system made use of the fingerprint sensor on the device for the authentication of users. The designed mobile authentication system achieved an accuracy of 0.97, with a FAR of 0.6667 and an FRR of 0.01333. The result obtained after testing the system proved encouraging. The system is currently being used at a local primary health care system and the feedback has been great. The system is designed to provide secure access to medical records for both the patient and the medical personnel. However, the designed application has been limited to primary health only, based on the challenge identified. Expanding the system to a larger medical institution with other sections (such as the pharmaceutical department etc.) could be an area to examine in the future.

References

1. World Health Organization (WHO), Primary Health Care. https://www.who.int/news-room/fact-sheets/detail/primary-health-care. Accessed 2 July 2021
2. Awotunde, J.B., Ogundokun, R.O., Misra, S.: Cloud and IoMT-based big data analytics system during COVID-19 pandemic. Internet Things **2021**, 181–201 (2021)
3. Wendl, U., Wyczisk, H.: Time Management System for Medical Applications, particularly in a Hospital Setting (2011). https://patents.google.com/patent/US8046239. Accessed 11 May 2020
4. Mogli, G.D.: Role of Biometrics in healthcare privacy and security management system. Sri Lanka J. Bio-Med. Inform. **2**(4), 156–165 (2011)
5. Mesmoudi, S., Feham, M.: Bsk-wbsn: biometric symmetric keys to secure wireless body sensors networks. Int. J. Network Secur. Appl. (IJNSA) **3**(5), 155–166 (2011)
6. Adeniyi, E.A., Ogundokun, R.O., Awotunde, J.B.: IoMT-based wearable body sensors network healthcare monitoring system. Studies in Computational Intelligence **2021**(933), 103–121 (2021)
7. Ikhu-Omoregbe, N.A., Azeta, A.A.: A voice-based mobile prescription application for healthcare services (VBMOPA). Int. J. Electr. Comput. Sci. IJECS-IJENS **10**(02), 73–78 (2010)
8. Abayomi-Alli, A., Ikuomola, A., Aliyu, O., Abayomi-Alli, O.: Development of a Mobile Remote Health Monitoring system–MRHMS. African J. Comput. ICT, 14–22 (2014)
9. Azeta, A.A., et al.: Preserving patient records with biometrics identification in e-Health systems. In Data, Engineering and Applications, pp. 181–191. Springer, Singapore (2019)
10. Jhaveri, H., Sanghavi, D.: Biometric security system and its applications in healthcare. International Journal of Technology (2014
11. Shakil, K., Zareen, F., Alam, M., Jabin, S.: BAMHealthCloud: a biometric authentication and data management system for healthcare data in cloud. J. King Saud Univ. Comput. Inf. Sci. **32** (2017). https://doi.org/10.1016/j.jksuci.2017.07.001
12. Zhao, Y., Liu, L., Qi, Y., Lou, F., Zhang, J., Ma, W.: Evaluation and design of public health information management system for primary health care units based on medical and health information. J. Infect. Public Health (2019). https://doi.org/10.1016/j.jiph.2019.11.004
13. Chung, K., Park, R.C.: P2P-based open health cloud for medicine management. Peer-to-Peer Networking Appl. **13**(2), 610–622 (2019). https://doi.org/10.1007/s12083-019-00791-7
14. Chen, J., Zhang, L., Ackah-Arthur, H., Omari, M., Xi, J.: An architecture of urban regional health information system and its data conversion algorithm. SpaCCS Workshops **2017**, 339–349 (2017)
15. Al Omar, A., Rahman, M.S., Basu, A., Kiyomoto, S.: MediBchain: a blockchain based privacy preserving platform for healthcare data. In: Wang, G., Atiquzzaman, M., Yan, Z., Choo, K.-K. (eds.) SpaCCS 2017. LNCS, vol. 10658, pp. 534–543. Springer, Cham (2017). https://doi.org/10.1007/978-3-319-72395-2_49
16. Hoang, N.: Detection of surface crack in building structures using image processing technique with an improved otsu method for image thresholding. Advances in Civil Engineering (2018). Doi: https://doi.org/10.1155/2018/3924120
17. Kang, S., Iwana, B.K., Uchida, S.: Cascading modular U-Nets for document image binarization. In: 2019 International Conference on Document Analysis and Recognition (ICDAR), pp. 675–680 (2019). doi:https://doi.org/10.1109/ICDAR.2019.00113
18. Suthar, S.B., Goradia, R.S., Dalwadi, B.N., Patel, S.M., Patel, S.: Performance scrutiny of thinning algorithms on printed gujarati characters and handwritten numerals. In: Mishra, D., Nayak, M., Joshi, A. (eds.) Information and Communication Technology for Sustainable Development. Lecture Notes in Networks and Systems. 9. Springer, Singapore (2018). https://doi.org/10.1007/978-981-10-3932-4_27

19. Bolelli, F., Grana, C.: Improving the performance of thinning algorithms with directed rooted acyclic graphs. In: Ricci, E., Rota Bulò, S., Snoek, C., Lanz, O., Messelodi, S., Sebe, N. (eds.) ICIAP 2019. LNCS, vol. 11752, pp. 148–158. Springer, Cham (2019). https://doi.org/10.1007/978-3-030-30645-8_14

20. Bai, X., Ye, L., Zhu, J., Zhu, L., Komura, T.: Skeleton filter: a self-symmetric filter for skeletonization in noisy text images. IEEE Trans. Image Process. **29**(1815–1826), 2020 (2020). https://doi.org/10.1109/TIP.2019.2944560

21. Gramblička, M., Vasky, J.: Comparison of Thinning Algorithms for Vectorization of Engineering Drawings. Journal of Theoretical and Applied Information Technology, 94(2) (2016)

22. Patil, T., Nandusekar, S.: Different techniques used in the process of feature extraction from fingerprint. Int. J. Innov. Eng. Res. Technol. (IJIERT) **6**(9) 2019

23. Zhi, H., Liu, S.: Face recognition based on genetic algorithm. J. Vis. Commun. Image R. **58**, 495–502 (2019). https://doi.org/10.1016/j.jvcir.2018.12.012

24. Mirjalili, S., Song Dong, J., Sadiq, A.S., Faris, H.: Genetic algorithm: theory, literature review, and application in image reconstruction. In: Mirjalili, S., Song Dong, J., Lewis, A. (eds.) Nature-Inspired Optimizers. SCI, vol. 811, pp. 69–85. Springer, Cham (2020). https://doi.org/10.1007/978-3-030-12127-3_5

25. Ahmed, B.T., Abdulhameed, O.Y.: Fingerprint recognition based on shark smell optimization and genetic algorithm. Int. J. Adv. Intell. Inform. **6**(2), 123–134 (2020). https://doi.org/10.26555/ijain.v6i2.502

26. Singh, R.K., Panchal, V.K., Singh, B.K.: A review on genetic algorithm and its applications. In: 2018 Second International Conference on Green Computing and Internet of Things (ICGCIoT), 2018, p. 376–380 (2018). https://doi.org/10.1109/ICGCIoT.2018.8753030

27. Sagayam, G.M., Ponraj, D.N., Winston, J., Yaspy, J.C., Jeba, D.E., Clara, A.: Authentication of biometric system using fingerprint recognition with euclidean distance and neural network classifier. Int. J. Innov. Technol. Explor. Eng. (IJITEE) **8**(4) (2019)

28. Virdaus, I.K., Mallak, A., Lee, S.-W., Ha, G., Kang, M.: Fingerprint Verification with Crossing Number Extraction and Orientation-Based Matching, Research Gate (2017)

29. Toudjeu, I.T., Tapamo, J.-R.: Circular Derivative Local Binary Pattern Feature Description for Facial Expression Recognition, Advances in Electrical and Computer Engineering, 19(1) (2019)

30. Wang, J., Fan, Y., Li, N.: Dominant color and texture feature extraction for banknote discrimination. J. Electron. Imaging **26**(4) (2017). doi: 10.1117/1. JEI.2 6.4.043011

31. Nishom, M.: Perbandingan Akurasi Euclidean Distance, Minkowski Distance, dan Manhattan Distance pada Algoritma K-Means Clustering berbasis Chi-Square, Jurnal Informatika: Jurnal Pengembangan IT (JPIT) 4(01) (2019). https://doi.org/10.30591/jpit.v4i1.1253

32. Religia, Y., Sunge, A.S.: Comparison of distance methods in K-Means algorithm for determining village status in Bekasi District. In: 2019 International Conference of Artificial Intelligence and Information Technology (ICAIIT), pp. 270–276 (2019). https://doi.org/10.1109/ICAIIT.2019.8834604

33. Ismail, Z.H., Chun, A.K.K., Razak, M.I.S.: Efficient herd – outlier detection in livestock monitoring system based on density – based spatial clustering. In: IEEE Access, vol. 7, pp. 175062–175070 (2019). https://doi.org/10.1109/ACCESS.2019.2952912

34. Ogundokun, R.O., Awotunde, J.B., Misra, S., Umoru, D.O.: Drug verification system using quick response code. Commun. Comput. Inf. Sci. **1350**, 535–545 (2020)

Correction to: PriHealth: A Fingerprint-Based Mobile Primary Healthcare Management System

Jide Kehinde Adeniyi, Tunde Taiwo Adeniyi,
Roseline Oluwaseun Ogundokun, Sanjay Misra, Akshat Agrawal,
and Ravin Ahuja

Correction to:
Chapter "PriHealth: A Fingerprint-Based Mobile Primary Healthcare Management System" in: S. Mukhopadhyay et al. (Eds.): *Computational Intelligence in Communications and Business Analytics*, **CCIS 1579, https://doi.org/10.1007/978-3-031-10766-5_34**

In the originally published version of chapter 34 the affiliations of two Authors were indicated incorrectly. This has been corrected as follows: affiliation of the Author Roseline Oluwaseun Ogundokun has been changed to "Department of Computer Science, Landmark University, Omu Aran, Nigeria"; affiliation of the Author Sanjay Misra has been changed to "Department of Computer Science and Communication, Ostfold University College, Halden, Norway".

The updated original version of this chapter can be found at
https://doi.org/10.1007/978-3-031-10766-5_34

Author Index

Printed in the United States
by Baker & Taylor Publisher Services